BUSINESS PROGRAMMING USING dBASE IV

A Structured Approach to Systems Development

Sudesh M. Duggal

Northern Kentucky University

Macmillan Publishing Company
New York

Maxwell Macmillan Canada
Toronto

Maxwell Macmillan International
New York   Oxford   Singapore   Sydney

Editor: Vernon R. Anthony
Production Editor: Constantina Geldis
Cover Designer: Russ Maselli
Production Buyer: Pamela D. Bennett

This book was set in Aster by Clarinda Company and was printed and bound by Semline, Inc., a Quebecor America Book Group Company. The cover was printed by Phoenix Color Corp.

Copyright © 1992 by Macmillan Publishing Company,
a division of Macmillan, Inc.

Printed in the United States of America

All rights reserved. No part of this book may be reproduced or transmitted in any form or by any means, electronic or mechanical, including photocopy, recording, or any information storage and retrieval system, without permission in writing from the Publisher.

Macmillan Publishing Company
866 Third Avenue
New York, New York 10022

Macmillan Publishing Company is part of the
Maxwell Communication Group of Companies.

Maxwell Macmillan Canada, Inc.
1200 Eglington Avenue East, Suite 200
Don Mills, Ontario M3C 3N1

dBASE IV® is copyright © Ashton-Tate. All rights reserved. dBASE IV is a registered trademark. Used with permission.

Library of Congress Cataloging-in-Publication Data
Duggal, Sudesh.
    Business programming using dBase IV / Sudesh Duggal.
        p.   cm.
    Includes index.
    ISBN 0-02-330588-6
    1. dBase IV (Computer program) 2. Business—Computer programs.
    3. Data base management—Computer programs. 4. Microcomputers—
Programming.   I. Title.
    HF5568.4.D243D84 1992
    650'.0285'57565—dc20   90-24074
                                                                               CIP

Printing: 1 2 3 4 5 6 7 8 9   Year: 1 2 3 4

*To my parents,
Mehar Chand and Teka Devi Duggal,
whose encouragement shaped my life*

PREFACE

Unlike other books on dBASE IV, *Business Programming Using dBASE IV* focuses on dBASE programming using the structured approach to system development. The concepts of dBASE IV, the program development process using structured programming fundamentals, and the structured approach to system development are integrated within this single, comprehensive volume.

The book is designed for one-semester introductory Business Programming, Programming Logic, or Program Design and Implementation courses, but it can be used in several other ways, such as

- A general course covering the fundamental concepts of dBASE IV (by not covering the programming part) in a College of Business or in a computer science department
- An introductory course in programming using structure design tools and techniques for the computer information systems major or computer science major
- A supplement to a Database Management or Data Modeling and Implementation course for information systems or computer science majors
- A supplement to an Accounting Information Systems course for accounting majors

The main objective of this book is to explore the different features of dBASE IV programming which lead to the design of complex business application software using a structured approach to system development. No prior knowledge of dBASE IV or structured programming is required. The book uses a problem-oriented approach, introducing the concepts of structured programming and structured design by developing a series of business application programs which lead to the design of a complete system. The dBASE concepts needed in the solution of the programming problems are introduced in a building-block approach; as you progress through the chapters, the programs become more complex, introducing additional techniques and tools of structured design.

Some of the outstanding features of the book are listed below:

- A section on directories and disk files in Chapter 1 provides an understanding of the use of the disk directories for organizing files on hard disk.
- Tutorials on the basic concepts of dBASE IV provide practical experience with the software in the first three chapters.
- Extensive use of illustrations throughout the book helps you to understand the concepts easily.
- Early introduction to dBASE programming in Chapter 3 provides opportunity to learn about the programming feature of dBASE IV at an early stage.

- A complete chapter (Chapter 4) introduces the program development process using structured programming design tools and techniques needed in the design of dBASE programs.
- A complete chapter (Chapter 9) introduces a structured approach to system development and structured system implementation using the program development process.
- Development of batch programs in Chapters 4–7, menu programs in Chapters 8–9, and interactive programs in Chapters 10–13 illustrates the concepts of the structured approach to system development and leads to the design of an invoice generating system, a business application system.
- The review questions at the end of each chapter provide an opportunity to apply the concepts covered in that chapter.
- The hands-on assignments at the end of Chapters 4–13 provide an opportunity to apply the concepts learned in these chapters. These assignments consist of a series of application programs which, when developed by students, will lead to the development of a business application system—such as an accounts receivable system and payroll system—used in the real world.
- Chapters on label and report generation provide the ability to generate labels and reports without writing programs, using the label and report generator utility, the user-friendly and most powerful feature of dBASE IV.
- A chapter on foreign files provides a method of converting dBASE files to ASCII files which can be used with other software packages and other programming languages, and vice versa.
- Appendices A–C provide valuable information on the basic concepts of DOS, installation of dBASE IV, and customizing the dBASE environment. All the dBASE commands and functions used in the book are summarized in Appendix D.
- The instructor's manual, including chapter outlines, answers to all review questions, 15–20 multiple choice questions per chapter, and solutions to hands-on assignments in the text, provides help to instructors using this book.

After studying the material covered in this book, you will have a good understanding of structured design, structured programming, and dBASE programming and, of course, you will have acquired a working knowledge of dBASE IV.

I am grateful to many individuals who contributed to the development of this book. The following reviewers provided helpful comments and suggestions: Troy Abshire, Sowela Technical Institute; James Aman, Wilmington College; Don Barker, Gonzaga University; Paul Bell, Central Oklahoma Area Vocational-Technical; Charles Biondi, Cumberland County College; Michael Elias, Pennsylvania State University, Wilkes-Barre; Brenda Erz, Lamar Salter Vocational-Technical School; David Hale, Texas Technical University; Professor Clarence J. Hartman, Jr., Phillips Junior College; Gene R. Taylor, Central Oregon Community College; Jane Varner, Montgomery College; and Ken Wichart, Wayne Community College. My thanks go to my editor, Vernon Anthony, for his support and patience during the two years this book was in progress. I also appreciate the help I received from everyone at Macmillan Publishing Company who worked on this book. Finally, my special thanks to all the friends and family members (Raj, Rajat, and Sandeep Duggal) for their patience and forbearance during the time in which I was busy writing and reviewing this book.

CONTENTS

PART 1 BASIC TOPICS—dBASE IV 1

Chapter 1 Introduction to dBASE IV 3

    Learning Objectives 3
1.1 Overview 4
1.2 Introduction to dBASE IV Terminology 4
    1.2.1 What Is a Database? 4
    1.2.2 What Is a Database Management System? 5
    1.2.3 What Is a Relational Database Management System? 6
    1.2.4 What Is dBASE IV? 6
    1.2.5 Components of Database Files 6
    1.2.6 Different Types of dBASE IV Files 9
    1.2.7 Database Terminology 9
    1.2.8 dBASE IV Capacity Constraints 9
1.3. Getting Ready for dBASE IV 11
    1.3.1 Directories and Disk Files 12
    1.3.2 Creating a Directory 14
    1.3.3 Changing the Directory 15
    1.3.4 Creating a Subdirectory 18
    1.3.5 Logging on to a Subdirectory 19
    1.3.6 Displaying a Directory 19
    1.3.7 Deleting a Directory 22
1.4 Your First Encounter with dBASE IV 26
    1.4.1 Installing dBASE IV 27
    1.4.2 Copying the Tutorial Disk 27
    1.4.3 Loading dBASE IV 35
    1.4.4 Different Operating Modes of dBASE IV 39
    1.4.5 Basics of Dot Prompt 40
    1.4.6 Exiting dBASE IV 42
1.5 Summary 42
    Key Concepts 43
    Review Questions 44

Chapter 2 Creating and Accessing Database Files 45

    Learning Objectives 45
2.1 Overview 46
2.2 Creating a Database File 46
    2.2.1 Creating a Database File Structure 48
    2.2.2 Adding Data to the Database File 65
    2.2.3 Closing the Database File 71
2.3 Accessing Database Files 73
    2.3.1 Opening a Database File 74
    2.3.2 The DISPLAY Command 74
    2.3.3 The LIST Command 79
    2.3.4 Printing the Database 81
2.4 A Few Shortcuts 84
    2.4.1 Use of the Function Keys 85
    2.4.2 Use of the History Buffer 87

x   Contents

2.5	Justification for Loading dBASE IV from the APPLICATION Directory	88
2.6	Summary	89
	Key Concepts	90
	dBASE Commands and Functions	90
	Review Questions	90

PART 2   PROGRAM DEVELOPMENT USING dBASE IV   93

Chapter 3   Introduction to dBASE IV Programming   95

	Learning Objectives	95
3.1	Overview	96
3.2	dBASE IV Programming	96
	3.2.1 Creating a dBASE Program	97
	3.2.2 Saving the dBASE Program	99
	3.2.3 Executing the dBASE Program	100
	3.2.4 Modification of a dBASE Program	101
	3.2.5 Documenting a Program	104
	3.2.6 The DO WHILE-ENDDO Command	105
	3.2.7 Adding Headings to a Report	112
	3.2.8 The IF-ELSE-ENDIF Command	114
	3.2.9 Listing of the dBASE Program	116
3.3	Using an External Text Editor	117
	3.3.1 The SET DEVELOPMENT ON/OFF Command	117
3.4	Summary	122
	Key Concepts	122
	dBASE Commands and Functions	123
	Review Questions	123

Chapter 4   Design of dBASE Programs   124

	Learning Objectives	124
4.1	Overview	125
4.2	The Program Development Process	125
	4.2.1 The Analysis Phase	125
	4.2.2 The Design Phase	126
	4.2.3 The Detailed Design Phase	126
	4.2.4 The Coding Phase	126
	4.2.5 The Testing and Debugging Phase	126
4.3	Types of Programs	127
	4.3.1 Batch Programs	127
	4.3.2 Menu Programs	127
	4.3.3 Interactive Programs	127
4.4	An Illustrative Example: Case Study 1	127
	4.4.1 The Analysis Phase	129
	4.4.2 The Design Phase	134
	4.4.3 The Detailed Design Phase	143
	4.4.4 The Coding Phase	147
	4.4.5 The Testing and Debugging Phase	163
4.5	Summary	164
	Key Concepts	166
	dBASE Commands and Functions	167

	Review Questions	167
	Hands-on Assignment	167

Chapter 5 Arithmetic Operations in dBASE — 171

	Learning Objectives	171
5.1	Overview	172
5.2	The CALCULATOR Command	172
5.3	The INT () Function	173
5.4	Memory Variables	174
	5.4.1 Creating Memory Variables	174
	5.4.2 Displaying Memory Variables	177
	5.4.3 Memory Variables Limitations	178
	5.4.4 Saving Memory Variables	178
	5.4.5 Deleting Memory Variables	179
	5.4.6 Restoring Memory Variables	180
5.5	dBASE Summary Statistics	182
	5.5.1 The COUNT Command	182
	5.5.2 The SUM Command	182
	5.5.3 The AVERAGE Command	187
5.6	An Illustrative Example: Case Study 2	191
	5.6.1 The Analysis Phase	193
	5.6.2 The Design Phase	199
	5.6.3 The Detailed Design Phase	199
	5.6.4 The Coding Phase	201
	5.6.5 The Testing and Debugging Phase	209
5.7	Modification of Case Study 2	209
5.8	Summary	220
	Key Concepts	221
	dBASE Commands and Functions	221
	Review Questions	221
	Hands-on Assignment	222

Chapter 6 Data Editing and Modifying a Database — 225

	Learning Objectives	225
6.1	Overview	225
6.2	Moving Around in a Database File	226
	6.2.1 The SKIP Command	226
	6.2.2 The GOTO Command	228
6.3	Editing Data in a Database File	229
	6.3.1 The EDIT Command	230
6.4	Modifying the Database File Structure	233
	6.4.1 The MODIFY STRUCTURE Command	233
6.5	An Illustrative Example: Case Study 3	240
	6.5.1 The Analysis Phase	243
	6.5.2 The Design Phase	247
	6.5.3 The Detailed Design Phase	247
	6.5.4 The Coding Phase	247
	6.5.5 The Testing and Debugging Phase	255
6.6	Modified Version of Case Study 3	255

6.7	Summary	260
	Key Concepts	260
	dBASE Commands and Functions	260
	Review Questions	260
	Hands-on Assignment	261

Chapter 7 Sorting and Control Breaks 264

	Learning Objectives	264
7.1	Overview	265
7.2	Sorting the Database File	265
	7.2.1 The SORT Command	266
7.3	The COPY Command	275
	7.3.1 The COPY FILE TO Command	275
	7.3.2 The COPY TO Command	276
	7.3.3 The COPY STRUCTURE TO Command	284
7.4	Control Breaks	287
7.5	An Illustrative Example: Case Study 4	289
	7.5.1 The Analysis Phase	293
	7.5.2 The Design Phase	299
	7.5.3 The Detailed Design Phase	301
	7.5.4 The Coding Phase	301
	7.5.5 The Testing and Debugging Phase	301
7.6	Summary	308
	Key Concepts	309
	dBASE Commands and Functions	309
	Review Questions	309
	Hands-on Assignment	310

Chapter 8 Case Structure and Menu Driven Program 317

	Learning Objectives	317
8.1	Overview	317
8.2	The IF-ELSE-ENDIF Command Revisited	318
	8.2.1 The IF-ENDIF Command	319
	8.2.2 The IF-ELSE-ENDIF Command	320
	8.2.3 The Nested IF-ELSE-ENDIF Command	323
	8.2.4 The Case Control Structure	327
8.3	An Illustrative Example: Case Study 5	329
	8.3.1 The Analysis Phase	331
	8.3.2 The Design Phase	332
	8.3.3 The Detailed Design Phase	334
	8.3.4 The Coding Phase	334
	8.3.5 The Testing and Debugging Phase	339
8.4	Summary	339
	Key Concepts	340
	dBASE Commands and Functions	340
	Review Questions	340
	Hands-on Assignment	341

Contents   xiii

PART 3 SYSTEM DEVELOPMENT USING dBASE IV PROGRAMMING 343

Chapter 9 System Development   345

    Learning Objectives   345
9.1 Overview   346
9.2 What Is a System?   346
9.3 The Structured Approach to System Development   347
9.4 The Invoice Generating System   347
9.5 An Illustrative Example: Case Study 6   352
    9.5.1 The Analysis Phase   354
    9.5.2 The Design Phase   355
    9.5.3 The Detailed Design Phase   355
    9.5.4 The Coding Phase   358
    9.5.5 The Testing and Debugging Phase   358
9.6 Development of Other Programs of the System   363
    9.6.1 Subprogram INV1.PRG   363
    9.6.2 Subprogram INV2.PRG   365
    9.6.3 Subprogram INV3.PRG   369
9.7 Summary   379
    Key Concepts   379
    Review Questions   380
    Hands-on Assignment   380

Chapter 10 File Maintenance: Deleting a Record   391

    Learning Objectives   391
10.1 Overview   392
10.2 Deleting Records from the Database Files   392
    10.2.1 Deleting Records Within the Edit Mode   392
    10.2.2 Deleting Records with the DELETE Command   394
10.3 Listing Including or Excluding the Deleted Records   396
    10.3.1 The DELETED () Function   397
    10.3.2 The SET DELETED ON/OFF Command   397
10.4 Recalling Deleted Records   398
    10.4.1 The RECALL Command   399
    10.4.2 The RECALL FOR Command   401
10.5 Purging Deleted Records   402
    10.5.1 The PACK Command   402
    10.5.2 The SET DELETED ON and COPY Commands   404
10.6 An Illustrative Example: Case Study 7   405
    10.6.1 The Analysis Phase   406
    10.6.2 The Design Phase   407
    10.6.3 The Detailed Design Phase   410
    10.6.4 The Coding Phase   413
    10.6.5 The Testing and Debugging Phase   414
10.7 Summary   417
    Key Concepts   418
    dBASE Commands and Functions   418
    Review Questions   419
    Hands-on Assignment   419

Chapter 11 File Maintenance: Adding a Record — 423

	Learning Objectives	423
11.1	Overview	424
11.2	Indexing the Database File	424
	11.2.1 Creating the Single Field Index Tags	427
	11.2.2 Creating Multiple Index Files	434
	11.2.3 Using Index Tags	435
	11.2.4 Creating the Multiple Field Index Tags	440
	11.2.5 Converting Index Files to Index Tags	442
11.3	Searching the Indexed Database Files	445
	11.3.1 The FIND Command	445
	11.3.2 The SEEK Command	446
11.4	Searching the Nonindexed Database Files	448
	11.4.1 The LOCATE and CONTINUE Commands	448
11.5	An Illustrative Example: Case Study 8	451
	11.5.1 The Analysis Phase	452
	11.5.2 The Design Phase	453
	11.5.3 The Detailed Design Phase	453
	11.5.4 The Coding Phase	456
	11.5.5 The Testing and Debugging Phase	459
11.6	Summary	459
	Key Concepts	461
	dBASE Commands and Functions	461
	Review Questions	461
	Hands-on Assignment	462

Chapter 12 File Maintenance: Updating a Record — 466

	Learning Objectives	466
12.1	Overview	467
12.2	Data Editing Revisited	467
	12.2.1 The EDIT Command	467
	12.2.2 The BROWSE Command	468
12.3	Conditional Editing	475
	12.3.1 The EDIT FOR Format	476
	12.3.2 The LOCATE and EDIT Commands	476
	12.3.3 The LOCATE and EDIT WHILE Commands	479
12.4	Global Editing	480
	12.4.1 The REPLACE Command	481
	12.4.2 The LOCATE and CONTINUE Commands	483
12.5	An Illustrative Example: Case Study 9	484
	12.5.1 The Analysis Phase	485
	12.5.2 The Design Phase	488
	12.5.3 The Detailed Design Phase	488
	12.5.4 The Coding Phase	489
	12.5.5 The Testing and Debugging Phase	491
12.6	Update Procedure for Case Study 9	491
12.7	Summary	494
	Key Concepts	495
	dBASE Commands and Functions	495
	Review Questions	495
	Hands-on Assignment	496

Chapter 13   Multiple Files — 500

Learning Objectives — 500
13.1 Overview — 501
13.2 Accessing Multiple Database Files — 501
   13.2.1 Opening Multiple Database Files — 501
   13.2.2 Defining the Relationship Among Database Files — 507
13.3 An Illustrative Example: Case Study 10 — 508
   13.3.1 The Analysis Phase — 511
   13.3.2 The Design Phase — 514
   13.3.3 The Detailed Design Phase — 514
   13.3.4 The Coding Phase — 516
   13.3.5 The Testing and Debugging Phase — 519
13.4 Orders Procedure for Case Study 10 — 519
   13.4.1 The Analysis Phase — 520
   13.4.2 The Design Phase — 521
   13.4.3 The Detailed Design Phase — 521
   13.4.4 The Coding Phase — 523
   13.4.5 The Testing and Debugging Phase — 524
13.5 Invoice Procedure for Case Study 10 — 527
   13.5.1 The Analysis Phase — 528
   13.5.2 The Design Phase — 529
   13.5.3 The Detailed Design Phase — 529
   13.5.4 The Coding Phase — 529
   13.5.5 The Testing and Debugging Phase — 530
13.6 Summary — 536
Key Concepts — 536
dBASE Commands and Functions — 537
Review Questions — 537
Hands-on Assignment — 537

PART 4   dBASE IV UTILITIES — 543

Chapter 14   Creating Labels — 545

Learning Objectives — 545
14.1 Overview — 546
14.2 Label Generation — 546
   14.2.1 Designing a Label Format — 547
   14.2.2 Producing the Labels — 554
   14.2.3 Producing Selective Labels — 555
   14.2.4 Producing Printed Labels — 557
   14.2.5 Producing Text File for Labels — 558
14.3 Summary — 558
dBASE Commands and Functions — 558
Review Questions — 559

Chapter 15   Creating Reports — 560

Learning Objectives — 560
15.1 Overview — 561
15.2 Report Generation — 561
   15.2.1 Creating a Report Format — 561
   15.2.2 Producing the Report — 568

15.2.3 Producing a Conditional Report — 569
15.2.4 Producing a Printed Report — 570
15.2.5 Producing a Text File for Reports — 570
15.3 Control Break Reports — 571
15.3.1 Designing the Control Break Report Format — 572
15.4 Summary Reports — 577
15.4.1 Designing the Summary Report Format — 578
15.5 Summary — 579
dBASE Commands and Functions — 580
Review Questions — 580

Chapter 16 Foreign Files — 582

Learning Objectives — 582
16.1 Overview — 583
16.2 Exporting dBASE File Data to Foreign Files — 583
16.2.1 Converting dBASE Files to SDF Files — 583
16.2.2 Converting dBASE Files to Delimited Files — 587
16.3 Importing Data from Foreign Files into dBASE Files — 590
16.3.1 Importing Data from SDF Files into dBASE Files — 590
16.3.2 Importing Data from the Delimited Files into the dBASE Files — 593
16.4 Summary — 595
Key Concepts — 596
dBASE Commands and Functions — 596
Review Questions — 596

Appendix A Introduction to Microcomputers and DOS — 597

A.1 Overview — 598
A.2 Introduction to Microcomputers — 598
    A.2.1 Main Unit — 598
    A.2.2 Keyboard — 600
    A.2.3 Video Monitor — 607
    A.2.4 Printer — 607
A.3 Introduction to DOS — 607
    A.3.1 Loading DOS — 608
    A.3.2 DOS Commands — 609

Appendix B dBASE IV Installation — 620

B.1 Overview — 621
B.2 Hardware and Software Requirements — 622
    B.2.1 The CHKDSK Command — 622
B.3 Installing dBASE IV — 623
    B.3.1 Software Registration — 623
    B.3.2 Hardware Configuration — 624
    B.3.3 Installing System Files — 627
    B.3.4 Copying Other Files — 628
B.4 Uninstalling dBASE IV — 629
B.5 Modifying the Hardware Configuration — 631

Appendix C	**Customizing the dBASE IV Environment**	**635**
	C.1 Overview	636
	C.2 Explanation of CONFIG.DB File Commands	636
	C.3 Configuring dBASE IV for Special Needs	637
	C.3.1 Color Setting	637
	C.3.2 Loading dBASE IV Directly to the Dot Prompt Mode	638
	C.3.3 Automatic Start of a Program	638
	C.3.4 Changing the Monitor Setting	638
	C.3.5 Changing the Default Drive	639
	C.3.6 Removing the Status Bar	639
	C.3.7 Changing the Dot Prompt Symbol	639
	C.3.8 Programming of the Function Keys	639
	C.3.9 Setting the Path for Directories	639
	C.3.10 Use of the External Text Editor for Program Files	639
	C.3.11 Use of the External Text Editor for Memo Fields	640
	C.3.12 Changing Printer(s) Settings	640
Appendix D	**dBASE IV Commands and Functions**	**641**
	D.1 Introduction	642
	D.1.1 Conventions in This Book	642
	D.1.2 Syntax of dBASE IV Commands	642
	D.1.3 Rules for Using dBASE Commands	643
	D.2 dBASE Commands	643
	D.3 dBASE Functions	681
Index		**683**

PART 1

BASIC TOPICS—dBASE IV

Before you can start learning about programming in dBASE IV, you need to understand its basic concepts. Part 1 presents the minimum background you will need to learn programming in dBASE IV. It consists of two chapters.

Chapter 1 starts by introducing the basic terms and concepts used in database management systems. Then it explains the components of the database file and the different data types used in it. The use of disk directories to organize files on a hard disk is described next. Procedures for creating subdirectories, changing the current working directory, deleting directories, and using the path to access files from other directories are also introduced. Finally, the steps of loading dBASE IV and terminating your session with it are presented.

Chapter 2 introduces two basic functions of dBASE IV. The first is how to create and populate (add data to) a database file. Use of the CREATE command to create a database file and the APPEND and BROWSE commands to add data to it is introduced. The second function is how to access data from the database file. Using the USE command to open or activate a database file and the DISPLAY and LIST commands to access data from it is introduced. The justification of loading dBASE from the application directory as suggested in this text is also presented in this chapter.

Chapter 1

Introduction to dBASE IV

LEARNING OBJECTIVES

Upon successfully completing this chapter, you will be able to:

1. Describe the basic concepts used in database management systems.
2. Describe the components of a database file.
3. Distinguish between the different data types.
4. Describe the functions of the different types of files used in dBASE IV.
5. Describe different directory structures used in organization of the hard disk.
6. Organize the hard disk using hierarchical directory structure.
7. Describe how to create and delete subdirectories.
8. Describe how to log on to a subdirectory.
9. Describe how to obtain a directory listing of a subdirectory from another directory on the same or a different path.
10. Install dBASE IV to conform to the hardware configuration of your computer.
11. Load dBASE IV into the internal memory of your microcomputer.
12. Distinguish between loading and installing application software.
13. Distinguish between the three different modes of dBASE IV.
14. Change dBASE IV from control center mode to dot prompt mode.
15. Follow the conventions used in this book.

16. Understand the conventions used with dBASE IV commands.
17. Follow instructions and work with dBASE IV.
18. Terminate the dBASE IV session.

1.1 Overview

In the information-oriented business environment of the 1990s, data and information (processed data) are two of the most important commodities or assets of any organization. In fact, they are regarded as a resource, and the proper management of this resource is the major concern of every organization. The purpose of this chapter is to introduce you to dBASE IV—the most popular, effective, and powerful data management software package available for personal computers.

Chapter 1 is divided into three parts:

1. Introduction to dBASE IV terminology
2. Getting ready for dBASE IV
3. Your first encounter with dBASE IV

1.2 Introduction to dBASE IV Terminology

This section begins with a discussion of the terms and concepts used in database management systems by business and industry. These terms describe the basic concepts, the components of a database file, and the different types of files used in dBASE IV.

1.2.1 What Is a Database?

A **database** is an organized collection of related information designed to meet the various needs of an organization. You probably have seen and used a number of databases. A telephone directory, a library card catalog, a dictionary, and an encyclopedia are a few examples of databases.

A simple example of a database is an inventory card file, shown in Figure 1.1. This file is used by a small business to keep track of all the products it carries. All the necessary information for each product is

Figure 1.1 Inventory card file

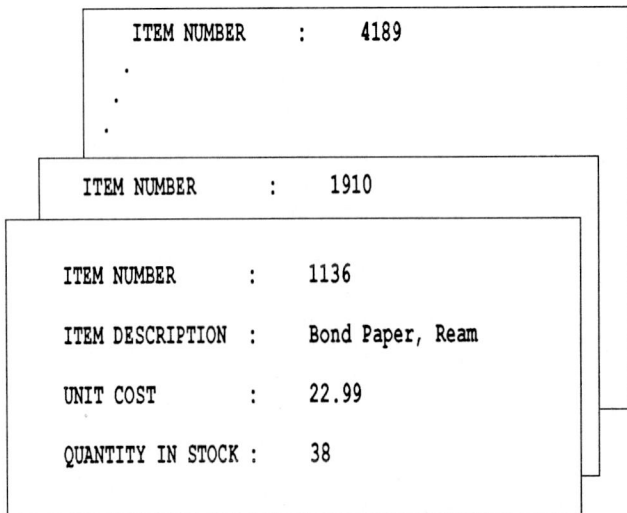

written on a single card (called a **record**). Each card contains four different units (called **fields**) of information. These units are the item number, the description, the unit cost, and the quantity in stock. The collection of all these cards forms a card file, which is called a **database file.**

Field

A **field** is the smallest unit of information present in a record. In the example, item number, item description, unit cost, and quantity in stock are four individual fields in each record of the inventory card database file.

Record

A record is a collection of related fields. In this example, item number, item description, unit cost, and quantity in stock are related fields because they pertain to one product. As such, these fields form a record.

Database File

A database file is a collection of related records. In our example, all records (cards) in the inventory card file are related because they pertain to one application, that is, inventory control. As such, these records form a database file.

The information in the inventory card file is organized in such a way that one card contains information about one product, and the whole card file contains the information for all the products in the store. Thus, the inventory card file consists of an organized collection of related information. As such, it forms a database. The inventory card database is very simple, consisting of only one database file.

Rarely are databases so simple. Usually several database files are contained in a single database. For example, in a larger business, some other database files will also be maintained—such as lists of suppliers, salespersons, and customers. These collectively form a database. The information in all the database files of this database will be related and will meet the information needs and requirements of this business.

In summary, a database is an organized collection of related information arranged to meet the needs of an organization or individual. It may consist of one or more database files.

1.2.2 What Is a Database Management System?

A package of computer programs and its documentation used to create, maintain, organize, and retrieve information from a database is called a **database management system (DBMS).** In other words, a DBMS is a software package that helps organizations manage their data resources. The following are some of the important functions of a DBMS:

1. Create and populate a database.
2. Retrieve data from the database.
3. Generate reports from the database.
4. Update information in the database.
5. Organize the data of the database.
6. Maintain integrity and consistency of the data.
7. Provide shareability of data to users.

1.2.3 What Is a Relational Database Management System?

There are three main types of DBMSs available: hierarchical, network, and **relational database management systems.** The type of DBMS depends on the organizational method used by the DBMS to create its databases. Because this book deals only with a relational DBMS, we will restrict our discussion to the method of organization used by the relational DBMS to create its databases.

In a relational DBMS, a database file is organized as a two-dimensional table consisting of a number of rows and columns. Each row represents a record in the database file, and each column represents a field in the record of the database file.

For example, the inventory card file discussed earlier will be organized as a table, as shown in Figure 1.2. This table contains nine rows, each representing a record of the inventory card database file. Each row contains four columns, each representing a field of the record of the inventory card database file. Therefore, a DBMS that represents its database file in the form of a table is called a relational DBMS.

1.2.4 What Is dBASE IV?

A relational DBMS, **dBASE IV** is the most popular and powerful DBMS available for personal computers. It organizes data in the database files in the form of tables.

dBASE IV provides two different methods of processing data stored in its database files: **interactive processing method** and **batch processing method.**

In the interactive processing method, two options are available: control center mode and dot prompt mode. In the control center mode, commands are supplied to dBASE by the selection of options available in the menu provided by the control center. In the dot prompt mode, they are supplied by the user typing the commands from the keyboard. In each case, the commands are interpreted by dBASE IV immediately and executed to produce results.

In the batch processing method, the commands are stored in the form of a program and are executed in a group mode. This method is also called **programming language mode.**

All three operating modes of dBASE IV are discussed in detail later in this chapter.

1.2.5 Components of Database Files

dBASE IV, as a relational DBMS, organizes its files in the form of tables. A table consists of two components—**database file structure** and **database file data.**

Figure 1.2 Inventory card file in tabular form

ITEM NUMBER	ITEM DESCRIPTION	UNIT COST	QUANTITY
1136	Bond Paper, Ream	22.99	38
1910	Ditto Paper, Ream	19.99	35
4012	King Kong Modem 1200	105.99	10
4045	Monochrome Monitor Z-1105	99.99	15
4072	Panasonic Printer KX-P108	269.99	8
3372	Printer Ribbon 10-Box	35.99	19
3375	Typewriter Ribbons 10-Box	23.79	67
1488	Xerographic Paper	19.99	45
4189	Zenith Microcomputer Z-158	829.99	5

Figure 1.3 Structure of the inventory card database file

FIELD NUMBER	FIELD NAME	FIELD TYPE	FIELD WIDTH	DECIMAL PLACES
1	ITEM_NUM	Character	4 Characters	
2	ITEM_DESC	Character	26 Characters	
3	UNIT_COST	Numeric	6 Characters	2 decimals
4	QUANTITY	Numeric	3 Characters	

Database File Structure

The structure of the database file describes each field in the database record, indicating its position in the record (**field number**), **field name**, **field type**, **field width** in characters, and the number of decimals present in the field. For example, the structure of the inventory card database file is given in Figure 1.3.

Field Number Field number refers to the position of the particular field with respect to the other fields within the database. For example, in Figure 1.3, the field number of the UNIT_COST field is three because of its position in the record of the database file as the third item.

Field Name Field name in the database file refers to the unique label or name that will identify a particular field in the record. A *label* or *name* is said to be unique if no two fields within a single database file have the same name. Field names conform to the following rules:

1. They can be up to ten characters long.
2. They must begin with a letter and may include letters, numbers, and an underline (_).
3. No other punctuation mark (except the underline) or blank spaces are allowed in the field name.
4. They should not be the same name as any dBASE command. A list of dBASE commands is given in Appendix D.

Field names should describe the information they are representing. Use of the underscore to improve readability is highly recommended. A few examples of valid and invalid field names are listed in Table 1.1.

Table 1.1 Valid and invalid field names

Valid Field Names	Invalid Field Names	Reason for Invalidness
UNIT_COST	AMOUNT DUE	Contains a blank space
MARK_UP	CUST:NAME	Contains a colon
RET_PRICE	50YEARSOLD	Starts with a number
SOC_SC_NUM	SOC_SEC_NUM	Contains more than 10 characters
DUE_OVER30		

Field Type Field type tells the database the type of information that will be stored in any field. dBASE IV offers six options of field or data types:

1. Character. Any text data or numeric data that are not to be used in computations are considered **character data type.** The maximum length of character data type is 254 characters. It is left justified.

   Examples: ITEM_NUM (2487)
   ITEM_DESC (Xerographic Paper)
   PHONE   (578-2542)

2. Numeric. Any numeric data on which computations are performed are considered **numeric data type.** This data type is most often used for business applications. The maximum length of numeric data is 20 characters. Numeric data usually have a fixed number of decimal places and are right justified.

   Examples: QUANTITY (107)
   UNIT_COST (17.25)
   TAX_DUE   (−237.45)

   Only digits, a decimal symbol ("."), and a positive or negative sign symbol ("+" or "−") are allowed in numeric data types.

3. Float. The **float data type** is basically the same as numeric data except the data values are extremely large or small and have no fixed number of decimal places. This data type is most often used for scientific applications.

   Examples: DISTANCE (234,962,785,000)
   MOLECULE (0.000000000015)

4. Logical. If the field represents a single character data type (Yes or No or True or False), then it is used as a **logical data type.**

   Examples: SCOREGT90 (T or F)
   ACCPASTDUE (Y or N)

5. Date. The **date data type** is used to store the date in mm/dd/yy format.

   Examples: BIRTH_DATE 10/31/89
   DUE_DATE   1/5/90

6. Memo. A field should be selected as a **memo data type** if it contains a very large amount of text data. Memo fields, used for long passages of text, work like a word processor; you can enter as long a "memo" as you wish, up to 5000 characters.

   Examples: Abstract of articles or messages

Field Width The field width for character, numeric, and float fields must be specified. You should select the minimum width that can store the largest value to be contained in the field. The character field can have up to 254 characters, and the numeric and float data fields can be up to 20 characters long including the decimal and a sign symbol. The other three fields have a fixed width. That is, a logical field has a width of 1 character, the width of the date field is 8 characters, and the memo field width is 10 characters.

Decimal Places For the fields defined as numeric or float data type, you need to specify the number of **decimal places** required. When the decimal places are included with numeric data, don't forget to count the decimal in the width. Decimal places are optional and are not needed for integer data.

Database File Data

The database file data are represented in the form of a table, as shown in Figure 1.2. Observe that each row represents a record. Each row (record) is made up of four columns. Each column represents a field. The characteristics of the field have already been described.

1.2.6 Different Types of dBASE IV Files

In addition to the database file, dBASE IV has several other kinds of files. The name of each consists of two parts—a primary file name and an extension. The **primary file name** can be any valid DOS file name; that is, it should conform to the following rules:

1. It can be up to eight characters long.
2. It can consist only of letters, numbers, and the underscore (_).
3. No other punctuation mark (except the underline) or blank spaces are allowed in a file name.
4. It should not be the same name as any dBASE command. A list of dBASE commands is given in Appendix D.

Single letter file names A through J should never be used because dBASE will confuse them with work area names (described in Chapter 13). For example, A.DBF is an invalid file name.

The **file extension** is a three-letter abbreviation preceded by a period after the file name. The extension represents the file type. dBASE IV uses 15 different extensions in defining files. These extensions, with their file types and a short description of each, are given in Table 1.2. You don't need to spend too much time trying to understand their functions now. When a particular type of file is introduced in the text, I'll provide a detailed explanation of it. The files are listed in Table 1.2 for future reference.

1.2.7 Database Terminology

In database literature, as in many other areas of computing, there is no standard terminology. The terms **table**, *column*, and *row* used here may be replaced by **relation, attribute,** and **tuple,** respectively, in other textbooks. Table 1.3 summarizes all these terms.

1.2.8 dBASE IV Capacity Constraints

Every software package has some capacity constraints, and users should be aware of these. The constraints of dBASE IV have been grouped for easy reference and are given in Table 1.4.

Table 1.2 dBASE IV file types

File Type	Extension	Short Description
Catalog Files	.CAT	These are used to maintain a catalog of related files for a specific application.
Database Files	.DBF	Database files are used to store data. These files contain the file structure as well as data records.
Database Text Files	.DBT	Database text files are used to store data for memo fields.
Format Files	.FMT	Format files are custom designed data-entry forms.
Form Files	.FRM	Report generator form files. These files are used by the report generator to create reports.
Label Forms	.LBL	Label form files are used by dBASE IV to print mailing labels.
Memory Variable Files	.MEM	Memory variable files are used to store memory variable data temporarily.
Index Files	.NDX	Index files are used with the database (DBF) files and are created by the index command. They allow very rapid searches for specific records in the database.
Master Index Files	.MDX	Master index files are introduced in dBASE IV to store all index tags.
Program Files	.PRG	Program files or command files are ASCII files containing a sequence of statements that perform desired functions. They can be created by any word processor or editor that produces ASCII text files.
Compiled Database Files	.DBO	Compiled database files are generated when program files are compiled.
Query Files	.QRY	Query files control a filter condition that can be used to examine files based on a condition.
Screen Files	.SCR	Screen files can be created with the CREATE SCREEN command to contain information about the screen layout of a custom designed data-entry form.
Text Files	.TXT	Text files can be created using the SET ALTERNATE switch to record a copy of all screen output onto a disk file.
View Files	.VUE	View files contain the information generated by a query operation.

Table 1.3 Summary of database terminology

English	Data Processing	Relational Theory	What Is Represented
Table	Flat File	Relation	Set of objects (e.g., people, places, transactions—not necessarily tangible)
Column	Field	Attribute	Facts about objects (e.g., name, shoe size, date, time, price)
Row	Record	Tuple	Individual object (e.g., a person, a place, a transaction)

Table 1.4 dBASE IV capacity constraints

Maximum records/file	1 billion
Maximum fields/record	128
Maximum database (.DBF) files open	10
Maximum index tags open/database	47
Maximum record size	4000 bytes 512,000 in memo fields
Maximum memory variables	256
Maximum memory for variables	6000 bytes (can be raised to 31K using CONFIG; 6K is default)
Number of data types	6
Variable types available	character, numeric, float date, logical, memo
Maximum character field size	254 bytes
Maximum numeric field size	19 bytes
Maximum float field size	19 bytes
Logic field size	1 byte
Date field size	8 bytes
Memo field size (in .DBF)	10 bytes
Maximum size of MEMO field	5000 bytes
Numeric accuracy	15–16 digits (not including decimal point)

1.3 Getting Ready for dBASE IV

The DOS version of dBASE IV is designed for the IBM personal computer or any other 100 percent compatible system. dBASE IV runs with the IBM personal computer DOS (PC-DOS) or the Microsoft DOS (MS-DOS) version 2.0 or higher. To be an effective user of dBASE IV, you'll need a reasonable working knowledge of personal computers and of DOS. If you are not familiar with PCs and DOS, read Appendix A before proceeding.

Because of the size of the dBASE IV program files, they require a minimum of 640K of RAM storage and a hard disk drive. A single hard disk can store many thousands of files, so it will become difficult to organize them when the number of applications, and in turn the number of files needed for each application, increases. For this reason, you should understand the use of disk directories for the organization of the files on a hard disk.

1.3.1 Directories and Disk Files

To organize the files on a hard disk drive, personal computers generally use two types of directory structures—flat and hierarchical. The **flat directory structure** stores all files in a single work area. The **hierarchical (tree) directory structure** allows you to divide the disk storage space into several work areas, each called a **directory.** Each work area (or directory) might hold files pertaining to a particular application. For example, all word processing data files and the word processing software package can be stored in a directory called MMATE. The spreadsheet software package and its related data files can be stored in another directory, named LOTUS.

To keep track of each work area (or directory), you should assign a name to it. The *directory name* can be up to eight characters long, and it must consist of only letters, numbers, and the underscore (_).

Initially, the hard disk drive has a single directory, called the *root directory* and represented by a backslash (\). The root directory can be divided into several subdirectories.

Suppose the directory listing of the disk drive C: (the hard disk) of your system is as shown in Figure 1.4. The first line of the listing indicates that the volume label name of the hard disk is ABC Company. The second line indicates that this is a directory listing of the root directory (as indicated by a backslash "\") of the hard disk on drive C:. The listing part tells us that there are five subdirectories within the root directory (\), namely, DOS, MMATE, LOTUS, BATCH, and SIDEKICK. It is important to note that an individual directory has been created for each application software package. Keeping them in their individual application software directories helps organize the files. The concept of the root directory and its five directories (each also called a **subdirectory**) can be represented in

Figure 1.4 Directory of the disk drive C:

```
C>DIR

Volume in drive C: is ABC COMPANY
Directory of C:\

COMMAND  COM    23258   12-18-85  1:11p
CONFIG   SYS       48   1-27-89   5:42p
AUTOEXEC BAT      123   1-24-89   9:08p
DOS          <DIR>      12-20-85 10:25a
MMATE        <DIR>      12-20-85 10:26a
LOTUS        <DIR>      12-20-85 10:27a
BATCH        <DIR>       2-15-86  2:33p
SIDEKICK     <DIR>       2-15-86  2:34p
       8 File(s)   8245280 bytes free
```

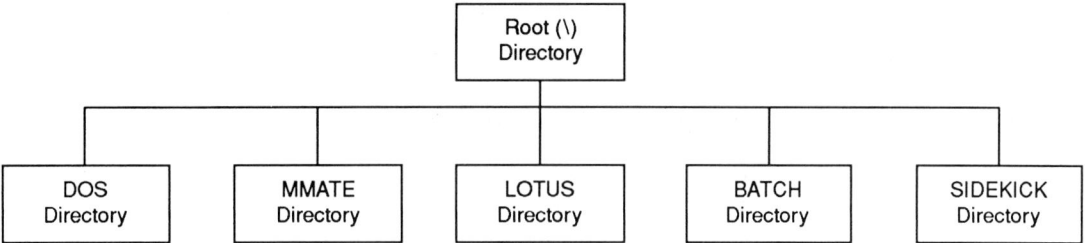

Figure 1.5 Hierarchical directory structure

a hierarchical directory structure, as shown in Figure 1.5. In this example, DOS, MMATE, LOTUS, BATCH, and SIDEKICK are called the subdirectories (child directories) of the root directory. The root directory is called the parent directory.

Multilevel Directories

A child directory can be further subdivided into many subdirectories. For example, Jane, John, Dave, and Mary are the four users of the MMATE application software package; and they want to keep their files separate. To accommodate their request, the MMATE directory can be divided into four subdirectories, such as MMATE\JANE, MMATE\JOHN, MMATE\DAVE, and MMATE\MARY. Now each subdirectory is reserved for a particular person. The hierarchical directory structure of this example is shown in Figure 1.6.

In Figure 1.6, MMATE\JANE, MMATE\JOHN, MMATE\DAVE, and MMATE\MARY are the child directories; and MMATE is their parent directory. Recall that in Figure 1.5, MMATE was itself a child directory of the root directory. Thus, the terms *parent directory* and *subdirectory (child directory)* are interchangeable, depending on what relationship is being emphasized, because one directory may be a subdirectory of another.

Figure 1.6 shows three levels of directories. The root directory is called the first-level directory. The DOS, MMATE, LOTUS, BATCH, and SIDEKICK directories are the second-level directories. MMATE\JANE, MMATE\JOHN, MMATE\DAVE, and MMATE\MARY are the third-level directories.

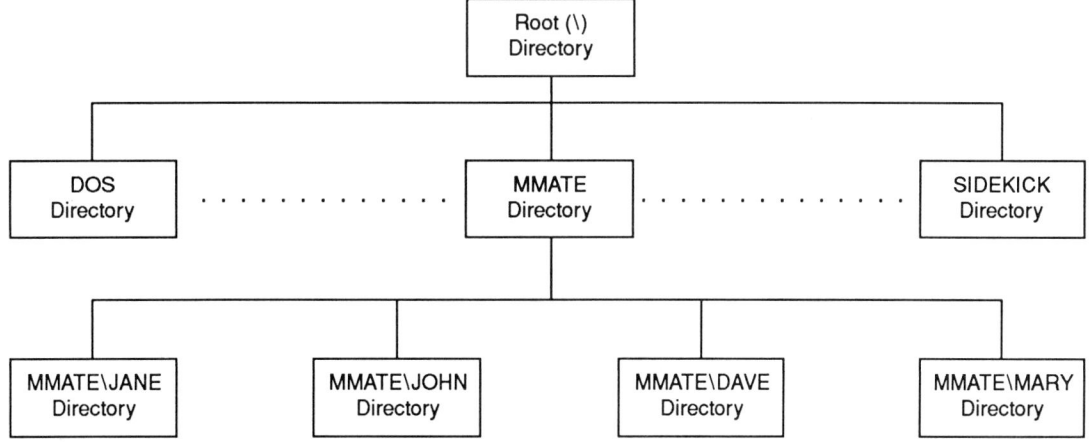

Figure 1.6 Hierarchical subdirectory structure

1.3.2 Creating a Directory

Suppose you have purchased a new software package called ENABLE, and you want to install it in a separate directory. To do so, you will need to create a new subdirectory named ENABLE from the root directory. This subdirectory can be created by using the MD command.

The MD Command

The MD (Make Directory) command is used to create a new directory. A directory can be created either from its parent directory or from the root directory. If you would like to create a new subdirectory named ENABLE from the root directory of drive C:, type the following command:

```
C>MD\ENABLE     <Return>
```

Note that in this command, the directory name is preceded by a backslash (\), which indicates that you want to create a subdirectory named ENABLE from the root directory. (Recall that "\" stands for root directory.)

After the execution of this command, the root directory will have a new subdirectory named ENABLE. If you would like to make sure that the ENABLE directory has been created, you should use the DIR command to get the directory listing of the default drive C:. The directory listing should be similar to that shown in Figure 1.7. The presence of the extra line, "ENABLE <DIR> 1-28-89 4:28p", in this listing (it is absent from the listing of Figure 1.4) proves that the ENABLE subdirectory has been created.

Now the question is how to look at the contents of this newly created directory. The directory listing of a subdirectory can be obtained by adding the directory specifications to the DIR command. If you want to obtain the directory listing of the ENABLE directory, type the following command:

```
C>DIR\ENABLE    <Return>
```

After the execution of this command, the screen will appear as shown in Figure 1.8. Figure 1.8 indicates that it is a listing of the ENABLE directory.

Figure 1.7 Directory of the disk drive C: with the ENABLE subdirectory

```
C>DIR

    Volume in drive C: is ABC COMPANY
    Directory of C:\

    COMMAND  COM      23258  12-18-85  1:11p
    CONFIG   SYS         48   1-27-89  5:42p
    AUTOEXEC BAT        123   1-24-89  9:08p
    DOS           <DIR>       12-20-85 10:25a
    MMATE         <DIR>       12-20-85 10:26a
    LOTUS         <DIR>       12-20-85 10:27a
    BATCH         <DIR>        2-15-86  2:33p
    SIDEKICK      <DIR>        2-15-86  2:34p
    ENABLE        <DIR>        1-28-89  4:28p
           9 File(s)    8245280 bytes free
```

Figure 1.8 Directory listing of the ENABLE directory

```
C>DIR \ENABLE

 Volume in drive C is ABC COMPANY
 Directory of C:\ENABLE

 .            <DIR>      12-20-88  11:25a
 ..           <DIR>      12-20-88  11:25a
      2 File(s)      8244256 bytes free
```

In the listing, "." stands for the current working directory. The **current working directory** is the directory in which you are currently logged on. At present, the working directory is the root directory, and ".." stands for the parent directory of your current working directory. These two lines are always present in any directory or subdirectory listing.

1.3.3 Changing the Directory

There is another method to list the contents of the ENABLE directory. It involves two steps. First log on or change to the ENABLE directory; then get its directory listing with the DIR command. To log on to the ENABLE directory, you need to change the current working directory from the root directory to the ENABLE subdirectory, which you can do by using the CD command.

The CD Command

The CD (change directory) command is used to change the current working directory to another directory. If you want to change the current working directory from the root directory to the ENABLE subdirectory, type the following command:

    C>**CD\ENABLE**   <Return>

After this command has been executed, the system will return with the system prompt C>, but you will be logged on to the ENABLE directory. There is, however, nothing on the screen to indicate that you are logged on to the ENABLE directory. There is a way to keep track of your current working directory by displaying its name with the system default prompt. This display can be achieved by the PROMPT PG command. To see how it works, type this command at the system prompt as shown:

    C>**PROMPT PG**   <Return>

The system will respond by displaying C:\ENABLE> as the system prompt, indicating that your current working directory is now the ENABLE directory. It is a good idea to include this command in the AUTOEXEC.BAT file, so every time the system is booted, it will execute this command. Now the system will always show the current working directory name in the system prompt. The procedure for adding this command to your AUTOEXEC.BAT file is given in Chapter 3. It is important to learn how to use the text editor first. Until you do, type this command at the start of each session with the computer or each time you reboot the computer.

Now if you would like to obtain the directory listing of the ENABLE directory, simply type DIR, and the screen should look as shown in Figure 1.8.

Let us review both methods discussed to obtain the directory listing of the ENABLE directory. In the first, a single DIR\ENABLE command was used. This command has two components: the DIR command component and the specifications (\ENABLE) component of the ENABLE directory. The second method used the following two commands:

```
C>CD\ENABLE      <Return>
C:\ENABLE>DIR    <Return>
```

The first command was used to change the current working directory from the root directory to the ENABLE directory. The second command was used to obtain the directory listing of the current working directory.

Because typing more commands increases the risk of errors, using a single command is always better than using two or more to achieve the same result. You should learn how to handle the files in different directories from the root directory or the current directory you are logged on to.

Let's have a little break here and get some practical experience with the information you have been reading.

TUTORIAL 1

Create a subdirectory named ENABLE from the root directory. Then obtain its listing using both of the methods explained in sections 1.3.2 and 1.3.3. (Don't forget to use the PROMPT PG at the start of your session with the computer, if it is needed.)

Solution

To complete Tutorial 1, follow these steps:

Step 1: Boot up your system. If the system prompt is C>, proceed with step 2. If the prompt is C:\>, skip step 2, and proceed to step 3.

Step 2: Type the PROMPT PG command as shown. (Recall that this command helps reflect the current working directory in your prompt.)

```
C>PROMPT $P$G    <Return>
```

The system will respond by displaying the modified DOS prompt C:\>.

Step 3: Obtain the listing of the current working directory (the root directory) by typing the DIR command at the C:\> prompt as shown:

```
C:\>DIR    <Return>
```

A listing of the root directory will be displayed on the screen. Obtain the printed copy of this listing by pressing <Shift-PrtSc>. Keep this listing for future use.

1.3 Getting Ready for dBASE IV

Step 4: Now type the MD\ENABLE command at the C:\> prompt as shown:

`C:\>`**`MD\ENABLE`**`     <Return>`

Step 5: When the system prompt returns, get the listing of the current working directory again by using the instructions in step 3. Compare this result with the printed listing obtained in step 3. The listing on the screen should have an extra line as shown:

`ENABLE     <DIR>     1-28-89  4:28p`

The presence of this line in the new listing indicates that the ENABLE directory has been created. You're a winner; you've completed the first part of the tutorial! Obtain the printed copy of the screen listing as indicated in step 3.

Now move on to the second part of this tutorial (obtaining the directory listing of this newly created EN-ABLE directory).

Step 6: To obtain the listing of the ENABLE directory from the root directory (the current working directory), type the DIR\ENABLE command at the C:\> prompt as shown:

`C:\>`**`DIR\ENABLE`**`     <Return>`

The system should return with a listing similar to Figure 1.8. If so, hurrah! Once again you're a winner. If not, check the command line, and reenter the correct command to get the right listing.

To obtain the listing of the ENABLE directory using the second method discussed in section 1.3.3, follow steps 7 and 8.

Step 7: First change the current working directory to the ENABLE directory by typing the CD\ENABLE command at the C:\> prompt as shown:

`C:\>`**`CD\ENABLE`**`     <Return>`

The system will return with the C:\ENABLE> prompt, indicating that your current working directory now is the ENABLE directory.

Step 8: To obtain the listing of the current working directory (the ENABLE directory), type the DIR command at the C:\ENABLE> prompt as shown:

`C:\ENABLE>`**`DIR`**`     <Return>`

The system should once again return a listing similar to Figure 1.8.

Step 9: Now change the current working directory to the root directory by typing the CD\ command at the C:\ENABLE> prompt as shown:

`C:\ENABLE>`**`CD\`**`     <Return>`

The system will respond by displaying the DOS prompt C:\>. Congratulations! You have successfully completed the first tutorial.

1.3.4 Creating a Subdirectory

Suppose you are enrolled in a course, such as IFS 100: Introduction to Information Systems, where the ENABLE package will be used, and you will have to do certain problems for that class. You would like to store all those problems in one subdirectory named ENABLE\SMITH (your last name). There are two ways to create a subdirectory, depending on your current working directory.

First Method: From the Root Directory

To create a new subdirectory (named ENABLE\SMITH) of the ENABLE directory when the current working directory is the root directory, you will need the following command:

```
C:\>MD\ENABLE\SMITH     <Return>
```

This command indicates that you want to create a subdirectory named ENABLE\SMITH of the ENABLE directory. Remember that the ENABLE directory is also a subdirectory of the root directory.

When the system prompt returns, obtain the listing of the ENABLE directory as discussed in sections 1.3.2 and 1.3.3. The listing should be as shown in Figure 1.9. The extra line in the listing, "SMITH <DIR> 1-25-89 10:05p," indicates that the ENABLE\SMITH directory has been created.

Second Method: From Its Parent Directory

If you are already logged on to the ENABLE directory and the default prompt is C:\ENABLE>, the following command will create a subdirectory named ENABLE\SMITH of the ENABLE directory:

```
C:\ENABLE>MD SMITH     <Return>
```

When the system prompt returns once again, obtain the listing of the ENABLE directory as discussed in sections 1.3.2 and 1.3.3. The listing should be as shown in Figure 1.9.

Recall that while creating the SMITH subdirectory from its parent (ENABLE) directory, you used the following command:

```
C:\ENABLE>MD SMITH     <Return>
```

This command told the system to create a subdirectory called SMITH of

Figure 1.9 Directory listing of the ENABLE directory after creating the ENABLE\SMITH directory

```
C>DIR \ENABLE

    Volume in drive C is ABC COMPANY
    Directory of C:\ENABLE

    .           <DIR>     12-20-88  11:25a
    ..          <DIR>     12-20-88  11:25a
    SMITH       <DIR>      1-25-89  10:05p
         3 File(s)    8244256 bytes free
```

the current working directory, that is, the ENABLE directory. But if you had typed the following command:

    `C:\ENABLE>`**`MD\SMITH`**   `<Return>`

with a backslash (\) after MD, the computer would have created a subdirectory SMITH of the root directory, as indicated by the backslash (not the subdirectory SMITH of the ENABLE directory). That is not what you wanted. You do not include a backslash (\) in the MD SMITH command because you do not want SMITH at the root directory.

1.3.5 Logging on to a Subdirectory

There are two ways to log on to a subdirectory, depending on your current working directory.

First Method: From the Root Directory

To log on to the newly created directory named ENABLE\SMITH from the root directory, you will have to type the following command:

    `C:\>`**`CD\ENABLE\SMITH`**   `<Return>`

When you do so, the system will return with the following prompt:

    `C:\ENABLE\SMITH>`

This new prompt indicates that you are now logged on to the ENABLE\SMITH subdirectory of the ENABLE directory.

Second Method: From Its Parent Directory

To log on to this new directory named ENABLE\SMITH from its parent directory ENABLE, you will have to type the following command:

    `C:\ENABLE>`**`CD SMITH`**   `<Return>`

When you do so, the system will return with the following prompt:

    `C:\ENABLE\SMITH>`

This prompt indicates that you are now logged on to the ENABLE\SMITH subdirectory of the ENABLE directory.

    Once again note that no backslash was used between CD and SMITH in the previous command because in the CD SMITH command, SMITH is not at the root directory. From this, we conclude that if you are at the root directory, you always need a backslash between the dBASE command and the directory name. But if you are not at the root directory, you do not need the backslash.

1.3.6 Displaying a Directory

A few examples of obtaining the directory listing of a subdirectory from different working directories are given in this section.

First Method: From the Root Directory

EXAMPLE 1: When logged on to the root directory, you can obtain its listing simply by typing the DIR command at the DOS prompt C:\> as shown:

    `C:\>DIR      <Return>`

This simple DIR command will display the listing of the files in the current working directory (root directory, in this case), as shown in Figure 1.4.

EXAMPLE 2: You can obtain the listing of any other directory from the root directory by adding the directory specifications to the DIR command. For example, to obtain the listing of the ENABLE directory from the root directory, you used the DIR\ENABLE command in section 1.3.2; and you obtained the listing shown in Figure 1.8.

EXAMPLE 3: To obtain the listing of the ENABLE\SMITH directory from the root directory, you will need the following command:

    `C:\>DIR\ENABLE\SMITH     <Return>`

When you enter this command, the system will display the listing of the ENABLE\SMITH directory as shown in Figure 1.10.

In the last two examples, the directory specifications, called paths, were added to the DIR command. A **path** is simply a collection of directory and subdirectory names connected by a backslash (\) to lead from the root directory to the subdirectory whose listing is required or from the current working directory to the subdirectory whose listing is required. For example, \ENABLE and \ENABLE\SMITH are the two paths to lead from the root directory to the target directory used in the last two examples.

Now let us obtain the listing of a directory other than the root directory.

Second Method: From a Directory on the Same Path

EXAMPLE 4: If your current working directory is ENABLE\SMITH, to produce a list of all the files stored in the ENABLE directory (parent directory of the ENABLE\SMITH directory), you will need to enter the following command:

    `C:\ENABLE\SMITH>DIR ..    <Return>`

Figure 1.10 Directory listing of the ENABLE\SMITH subdirectory

```
C>DIR \ENABLE\SMITH

   Volume in drive C is ABC COMPANY
   Directory of C:\ENABLE\SMITH

           .        <DIR>     12-20-88  11:25a
           ..       <DIR>     12-20-88  11:25a
            2 File(s)    8244256 bytes free
```

1.3 Getting Ready for dBASE IV

After the execution of this command, a listing of the ENABLE directory as shown in Figure 1.9 will be produced. Recall from the previous discussion that ".." stands for the parent directory.

EXAMPLE 5: If your current working directory is ENABLE\SMITH, you will need the following command to produce the listing of all the files of the root directory:

```
C:\ENABLE\SMITH>DIR\     <Return>
```

DIR\ will produce the listing of the root directory. Recall that the backslash (\) stands for the root directory.

Third Method: From a Directory on a Different Path

To produce a listing of a directory from another directory on a different path, you will need to include the path name in the directory command.

For example, imagine you have another subdirectory named ENABLE\JOHN of the ENABLE directory, as shown in Figure 1.11. You are logged on to the ENABLE\SMITH directory. To obtain a listing of the ENABLE\JOHN subdirectory, you can use two different paths. One starts from the root directory, proceeds to the ENABLE subdirectory, and finally goes to the ENABLE\JOHN subdirectory. The other path starts from the ENABLE\SMITH subdirectory, goes to its parent directory (that is, the ENABLE directory), and then goes to the ENABLE\JOHN subdirectory. These path options are illustrated in the following example.

EXAMPLE 6: To obtain a listing of the ENABLE\JOHN subdirectory using the path starting from the root directory to the ENABLE subdirectory and finally to the ENABLE\JOHN subdirectory, you will need the following command:

```
C:\ENABLE\SMITH>DIR\ENABLE\JOHN     <RETURN>
```

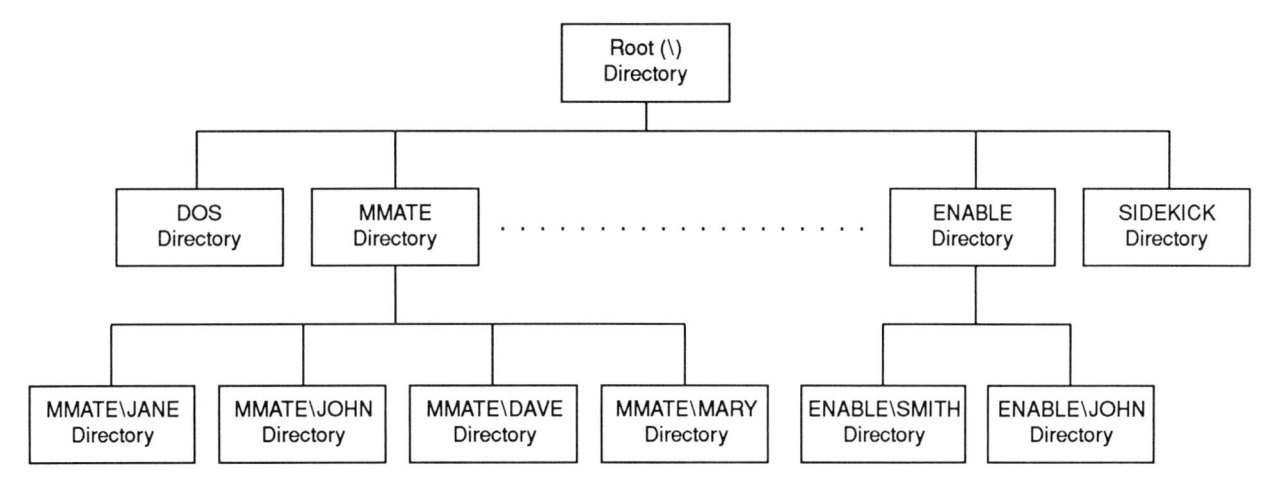

Figure 1.11 Hierarchical directory structure showing the ENABLE directory

Figure 1.12 Directory listing of the ENABLE\JOHN directory

```
Volume in drive C is ABC COMPANY
Directory of C:\ENABLE\JOHN

.            <DIR>       12-20-88  11:25a
..           <DIR>       12-20-88  11:25a
     2 File(s)    8244256 bytes free
```

EXAMPLE 7: To obtain the listing of the ENABLE\JOHN subdirectory using the path starting from the ENABLE\SMITH subdirectory and going to its parent directory (that is, the ENABLE directory and then to the ENABLE\JOHN subdirectory), you will need the following command:

```
C:\ENABLE\SMITH>DIR ..\JOHN     <Return>
```

Both commands used in examples 6 and 7 will have the same effect; that is, they will obtain a listing of the ENABLE\JOHN directory from the current working directory ENABLE\SMITH. However, they use different paths. The listing will be as shown in Figure 1.12.

1.3.7 Deleting a Directory

You have learned how to create a directory, how to log on to a directory, and how to produce a listing of a directory while logged on to another directory. Now let us go one step further and see how a directory can be deleted.

The RD Command

The RD (remove directory) command is used to delete a directory from its parent directory or from the root directory. A directory can be deleted only if it is empty (that is, after all the files contained in it except the entries "." and ".." have been deleted).

Suppose you want to delete the ENABLE directory created in section 1.3.2. Before you can delete this from the root directory, you should first remove the ENABLE\SMITH and ENABLE\JOHN directories from it.

First Method: From the Root Directory

To remove these two directories when positioned at the root directory, you will need the following commands:

```
C:\>RD\ENABLE\SMITH     <Return>
C:\>RD\ENABLE\JOHN      <Return>
```

When the system responds with the system prompt, the ENABLE\SMITH and the ENABLE\JOHN directories will be deleted from the ENABLE directory.

Second Method: From Its Parent Directory

To remove these directories from the ENABLE directory, you will need the following commands:

1.3 Getting Ready for dBASE IV

```
C:\ENABLE>RD SMITH    <Return>
C:\ENABLE>RD JOHN     <Return>
```

When the system responds with the system prompt, the ENABLE\SMITH and the ENABLE\JOHN directories will be deleted from the ENABLE directory.

After removing the ENABLE\SMITH and the ENABLE\JOHN directories from the ENABLE directory, you can remove the ENABLE directory from the root directory using the following command:

```
C:\>RD\ENABLE    <Return>
```

When you do so, the system will respond with the system prompt C:\>. Now if you get the directory listing of the default drive, you will notice that the listing contains only the five directories you initially started with, as shown in Figure 1.4. The listing will not contain the ENABLE directory because it has been removed.

TUTORIAL 2

a. Create the ENABLE\SMITH directory from the root directory.
b. Obtain the directory listing of the ENABLE directory from the root directory.
c. Create the ENABLE\JOHN directory from the ENABLE directory.
d. Obtain the directory listing of the ENABLE directory from the ENABLE directory, and get a printed copy.
e. Obtain the directory listing of the ENABLE\SMITH directory from the ENABLE\JOHN directory.
f. Delete the ENABLE directory. (Hint: Remember to remove the ENABLE\SMITH and ENABLE\JOHN directories first.)

Solution

a. To create the ENABLE\SMITH directory from the root directory, follow these steps:

   Step 1: Boot up your system. If the system prompt is C>, proceed with step 2. If the prompt is C:\>, skip step 2, and proceed to step 3.

   Step 2: Type the following command:

   ```
   C>PROMPT $P$G    <Return>
   ```

   The system will respond by displaying the modified prompt C:\>.

   Step 3: Now type the following command:

   ```
   C:\>MD\ENABLE\SMITH    <Return>
   ```

   When the system prompt returns, the ENABLE\SMITH directory has been created.

b. To obtain the listing of the ENABLE directory from the root directory, follow the instructions of step 4:

 Step 4: To obtain the listing of the ENABLE directory from the root directory (the current working directory), type the following command:

 C:\>**DIR\ENABLE**   <Return>

 The system should return with a listing as shown in Figure 1.9 (see page 18). If so, hurrah! Once again you're a winner. If not, check the command line, and reenter the correct command to obtain the right listing.

c. To create the ENABLE\JOHN directory from the ENABLE directory, follow steps 5 and 6.

 Step 5: Follow steps 1 and 2. Then log on to the ENABLE directory by typing the following command:

 C:\>**CD\ENABLE**   <Return>

 The system will return with the C:\ENABLE> prompt.

 Step 6: Now type the following command:

 C:\ENABLE>**MD JOHN**   <Return>

 When the system prompt returns, the ENABLE\JOHN directory has been created.

d. To obtain the listing of the ENABLE directory from the ENABLE directory, follow step 7.

 Step 7: To obtain the listing of the ENABLE directory from the current working directory (the ENABLE directory), type the following command:

 C:\ENABLE>**DIR**   <Return>

 The system should return with a listing as shown in Figure 1.13. If the listing is different, check the command, and reenter the correct command to obtain the right listing.

e. To obtain the listing of the ENABLE\SMITH directory from the ENABLE\JOHN directory, follow steps 8 and 9.

 Step 8: First log on to the ENABLE\JOHN directory.

Figure 1.13 Directory listing of the ENABLE directory after creating the ENABLE\SMITH directory

```
C:\ENABLE>DIR

    Volume in drive C is ABC COMPANY
    Directory of C:\ENABLE

        .           <DIR>     12-20-88  11:25a
        ..          <DIR>     12-20-88  11:25a
    SMITH           <DIR>      1-25-89  10:05p
    JOHN            <DIR>      1-25-89  10:05p
            4 File(s)    8244256 bytes free
```

Figure 1.14 Directory listing of the ENABLE\SMITH subdirectory

```
Volume in drive C is ABC COMPANY
Directory of C:\ENABLE\SMITH

   .          <DIR>       2-20-89  10:25a
   ..         <DIR>       2-20-89  10:25a
   2 File(s)     8244256 bytes free
```

If you are logged on to the root directory, type the following command:

C:\>**CD\ENABLE\JOHN**   <Return>

But if you are logged on to the ENABLE directory, type the following command:

C:\ENABLE>**CD JOHN**   <Return>

Either of the two methods explained previously will log you on to the ENABLE\JOHN directory. The system prompt will be C:\ENABLE\JOHN>.

Step 9: To obtain the listing of the ENABLE\SMITH directory, type either of the following commands:

C:\ENABLE\JOHN>**DIR\ENABLE\SMITH**   <Return>

C:\ENABLE\JOHN>**DIR ..\SMITH**   <Return>

The system should return with a listing as shown in Figure 1.14.

f. To delete the ENABLE directory, follow steps 10–12.

Step 10: Before you can delete the ENABLE directory, you need to delete all the files or subdirectories present in it. As indicated in Figure 1.13, the ENABLE directory contains two subdirectories, SMITH and JOHN. To delete these, use either step (a) or step (b).

(a): If you are logged on to the ENABLE\JOHN directory, switch to the root directory by typing the following command:

C:\ENABLE\JOHN>**CD**   <Return>

The system will respond by displaying the C:\> prompt. Now you are logged on to the root directory. To delete the ENABLE\SMITH and ENABLE\JOHN directories, type the following commands:

C:\>**RD\ENABLE\SMITH**   <Return>
C:\>**RD\ENABLE\JOHN**   <Return>

When the system prompt returns, get the listing of the ENABLE directory by typing the following command:

C:\>**DIR\ENABLE**   <Return>

(b): If you are logged on to the ENABLE\JOHN directory,

switch to the ENABLE directory by typing the following command:

`C:\ENABLE\JOHN>`**`CD ENABLE`**   `<Return>`

The system will respond by displaying the C:\ENABLE> prompt. Now you are logged on to the ENABLE directory. To delete the ENABLE\SMITH and ENABLE\JOHN directories, type the following commands:

`C:\ENABLE>`**`RD SMITH`**   `<Return>`
`C:\ENABLE>`**`RD JOHN`**   `<Return>`

When the system prompt returns, get the listing of the ENABLE directory by typing the following command:

`C:\ENABLE>`**`DIR`**   `<Return>`

Step 11: The listing should be as shown in Figure 1.8. If you are logged on to the root directory, proceed to step 12. If you are logged on to the ENABLE directory, switch to the root directory by typing the following command:

`C:\ENABLE>`**`CD\`**   `<Return>`

Step 12: To delete the ENABLE directory from the root directory, type the following command:

`C:\>`**`RD\ENABLE`**   `<Return>`

When the system prompt returns, get the listing of the root directory by typing the following command:

`C:\>`**`DIR`**   `<Return>`

The system should return with a listing as shown in Figure 1.4.

This completes Tutorial 2.

1.4 Your First Encounter with dBASE IV

In this section, you will have your first encounter with dBASE IV. After its installation, you will create an application directory called IN-VOICE, which will be a subdirectory of the DBASE directory in which dBASE IV is installed. (Please note that DBASE is a subdirectory of the root directory in which the software dBASE IV is stored. Don't confuse these two terms—DBASE and dBASE—and understand the difference between them. DBASE is the name of the directory; dBASE refers to the dBASE IV software.) Next you will copy all the files from the floppy disk you got with this textbook to the newly created directory. Then you will learn how to load dBASE IV into the computer's memory from the DBASE\INVOICE application directory with a path set to the DBASE directory. Next you will learn about the different operating modes of dBASE IV. Finally, you will learn how to terminate a session with dBASE IV.

1.4.1 Installing dBASE IV

Before you can use any application program package, you must install it on your computer. **Installation,** which customizes the application program to the hardware configuration of the computer system, needs to be performed only once.

You can install dBASE IV on your system by using the instructions provided in Appendix B and/or by using the *Getting Started with dBASE IV* manual that you received with your dBASE IV package.

The installation process, as explained in Appendix B, creates the DBASE directory in which the dBASE IV system files are copied. It also modifies the AUTOEXEC.BAT file so that dBASE IV can be started automatically from any directory. If dBASE IV is already installed on your system, read Appendix B so you understand the functions performed by the installation process.

1.4.2 Copying the Tutorial Disk

All the database, program, index, and other files used in this book belong to the invoice generating system. All these files are contained on the tutorial disk that came with this book. Because you will be working with these files to practice with the illustrative examples discussed in this book, you should copy all the files contained in the tutorial disk and keep the original disk for backup purposes. Therefore, before you proceed with loading dBASE IV on to the computer memory, make a copy of all the files stored on the tutorial disk.

Copy the tutorial disk on to the current working directory (or drive) of dBASE—the directory (or drive) used by dBASE IV to store and retrieve database, program, and other files. Which directory (or drive) you select as the current working directory (or drive) of dBASE depends on the environment in which you will be working, a laboratory or nonlaboratory environment.

Because of the size limitations of the external disk in the laboratory environment, where several students will be sharing the computer system with you, it is not possible to create an application subdirectory for each individual user. The students working in this environment will be storing their files on their own floppy disks. Therefore, the appropriate current working drive (or directory) in the laboratory environment should be the floppy disk drive.

Because dBASE IV will be used to develop several different application systems, each system will require several files. The database, program, index, and many more types of files will be used in each application. You can organize these files by storing those pertaining to different applications on different floppy disks.

But when you will be working individually on a computer system at home or in the office in a nonlaboratory environment, you will be storing all the files used by dBASE IV on the hard disk. These files may belong to several different application systems and should be properly organized. The best way to organize them, as already discussed in section 1.3, is by creating an individual subdirectory of the DBASE directory for each application system and storing its related files in that subdirectory. For example, if you want to develop four different systems named accounts payable, accounts receivable, inventory control, and payroll, you can create four subdirectories—ACC_PAY, ACC_REC, INV_CON, and PAYROLL—of the DBASE directory, as shown in Figure 1.15.

```
                    ┌──────────────┐
                    │   Root (\)   │
                    │  Directory   │
                    └──────────────┘
          ┌────────────┬─────────────┬─────────────┐
    ┌─────────┐  ┌──────────┐  ┌──────────┐  ┌──────────┐
    │   DOS   │..│  DBASE   │..│  ENABLE  │  │ SIDEKICK │
    │Directory│  │Directory │  │Directory │  │Directory │
    └─────────┘  └──────────┘  └──────────┘  └──────────┘
```

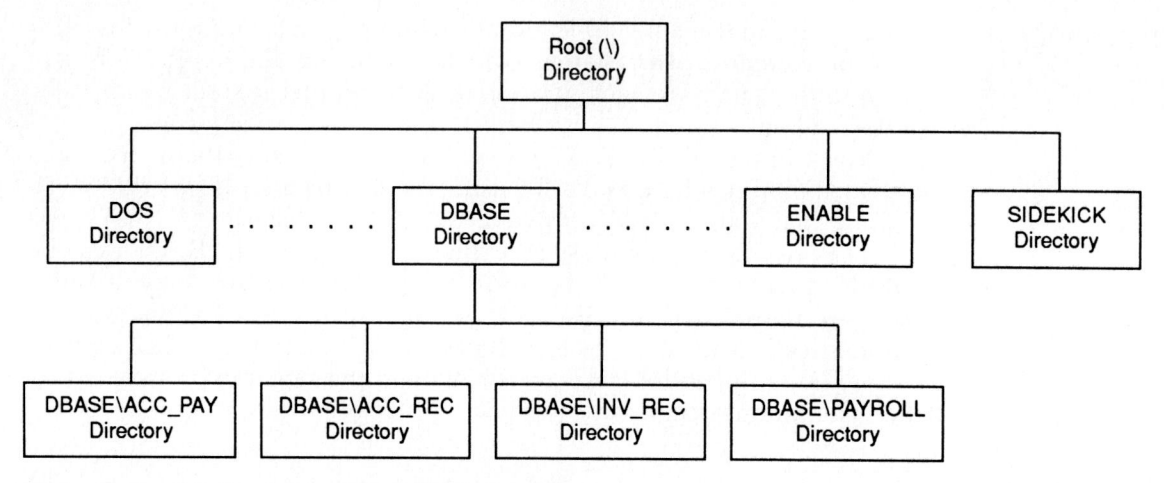

Figure 1.15 Subdirectories of the DBASE directory

Therefore, the most appropriate current working directory (or drive) in the nonlaboratory environment should be the application subdirectory of the DBASE directory.

Depending on the environment in which you will be working, proceed to copy the tutorial disk as described on the following pages. If you will be working in the laboratory environment, go to the next section, "Copying the Tutorial Disk to Another Floppy Disk"; but if you will be working in a nonlaboratory (individual) environment, skip the next section, and proceed to "Creating and Copying the Tutorial Disk to an Application Subdirectory."

Copying the Tutorial Disk to Another Floppy Disk

To learn how to copy the tutorial disk to another floppy disk, follow the steps of Tutorial 3 or 3A, depending on the number of floppy disk drives on your computer system. If your computer system contains two floppy disk drives, use Tutorial 3; if it contains only one floppy disk drive, proceed to Tutorial 3A.

TUTORIAL 3

Copy the tutorial disk that came with this textbook to another, already formatted, floppy disk using a computer system with two floppy disk drives.

Solution

To complete this tutorial, follow these steps:

Step 1: Boot up your system. The system will respond by displaying the system prompt C> or C:\>.

Step 2: Insert the tutorial disk in drive A: and the formatted floppy disk in drive B:. To copy all the files from the tutorial disk in

Figure 1.16 Directory of the floppy disk in drive B:

```
C>DIR B:

Volume in drive B is DUGGAL
Directory of B:

INV      DBF     2560   12-18-88 11:35p
INV1     PRG     3997   12-27-88  7:02p
INV1     BAK     3923   12-24-88  3:38p
  .        .      .        .        .
  .        .      .        .        .
INV42    BAK     2367   12-21-88 10:42a
INV42    PRG     2368   12-21-88 10:59a
        51 File(s)    245780 bytes free
```

drive A: onto the floppy disk in drive B:, type the following command:

C>`COPY A:*.* B:`   <Return>

The system will start copying the files from the tutorial disk in drive A: to the floppy disk in drive B:, copying one file at a time. The name of the individual file being copied will be displayed on the screen. When the system has copied all the files, the following message will be displayed on the screen: 51 files copied.

Step 3: When the system prompt appears again, obtain the listing of the floppy disk in drive B: by typing the following command:

C>`DIR B:`   <Return>

The system will display the listing as shown in Figure 1.16.

This completes Tutorial 3.

TUTORIAL 3A

Copy the tutorial disk that came with this textbook to another, already formatted, floppy disk using a computer system with one floppy disk drive.

Solution

To copy a floppy disk to another floppy disk on a computer system with a single disk drive, follow these steps:

a. Create a temporary directory.
b. Copy all the files from the tutorial disk to this temporary directory.
c. Now copy all these copied files from this temporary directory to another formatted floppy disk.

d. Delete all the files from the temporary directory, and then delete the temporary directory.

To complete this tutorial, follow these steps:

Step 1: Boot up your system. The system will respond by displaying the system prompt C> or C:\>. If the system prompt is C>, proceed with step 2. If the prompt is C:\>, skip step 2, and proceed to step 3.

Step 2: Type the PROMPT PG command as shown:

C>**PROMPT PG** <Return>

The system will return with the C:\> prompt.

Step 3: To create a subdirectory named TEMP of the root directory of drive C:, type the following command:

C:\>**MD\TEMP** <Return>

To make sure that the subdirectory has been created, get the new listing of the root directory by typing the DIR command at the system prompt C:\>. The new directory listing will look like that shown in Figure 1.17. Notice that the TEMP directory has been added to the listing.

Step 4: Now copy all the files from the tutorial disk to this new TEMP directory. To do this, insert the tutorial disk in drive A:, and type the following command:

C:\>**COPY A:*.* \TEMP** <Return>

The system will start copying the files from the tutorial disk in drive A: to the TEMP subdirectory, copying one at a time. The name of the individual file being copied will be displayed on the screen. When the system has copied all the files, the following message will be displayed on the screen: 51 files copied.

Figure 1.17 Directory listing of the disk drive C:

```
C:\>DIR

Volume in drive C is ABC COMPANY
Directory of C:\

COMMAND  COM     23258  12-18-85  1:11p
CONFIG   SYS        48   1-27-89  5:42p
AUTOEXEC BAT       123   1-24-89  9:08p
DOS          <DIR>        12-20-85 10:25a
MMATE        <DIR>        12-20-85 10:26a
LOTUS        <DIR>        12-20-85 10:27a
BATCH        <DIR>         2-15-86  2:33p
SIDEKICK     <DIR>         2-15-86  2:34p
TEMP         <DIR>         4-17-90 10:45a
        9 File(s)    234280 bytes free
```

Figure 1.18 Directory of the TEMP subdirectory

```
C:\>DIR \TEMP

Volume in drive C is ABC COMPANY
Directory of C:\TEMP

INV     DBF    2560   12-18-88  11:35p
INV1    PRG    3997   12-27-88   7:02p
INV1    BAK    3923   12-24-88   3:38p
 .       .      .        .        .
 .       .      .        .        .
 .       .      .        .        .
INV42   BAK    2367   12-21-88  10:42a
INV42   PRG    2368   12-21-88  10:59a
        51 File(s)   8078780 bytes free
```

Step 5: When the system prompt appears again, obtain the listing of the TEMP directory by typing the following command:

C:\>**DIR\TEMP**   <Return>

The system will display the listing of the TEMP subdirectory as shown in Figure 1.18.

Step 6: Now take out the tutorial disk from drive A: and insert the formatted floppy disk. To copy all the files from the TEMP subdirectories to this formatted floppy disk, type the following command:

C:\>**COPY\TEMP*.* A:**   <Return>

The system will start copying the files from the TEMP subdirectory to the floppy disk in drive A:, copying one at a time. When the system has copied all the files, the following message will be displayed on the screen:
51 files copied.

Step 7: When the system prompt appears again, obtain the listing of the floppy disk in drive A: by typing the following command:

C:\>**DIR A:**   <Return>

The system will display the listing as shown in Figure 1.19 (see page 32).

Step 8: This completes the process of copying the tutorial disk to another formatted floppy disk. Now delete all the files from the TEMP directory by typing the following command:

C:\>**DEL\TEMP*.***   <Return>

The system will respond by displaying the prompt:
Are you sure (Y/N)?
To complete the deletion process, respond by pressing the "Y" key. The system will respond by displaying the C:\> prompt.

Step 9: After deleting all the files from the TEMP subdirectory,

Figure 1.19 Directory of the floppy disk in drive A:

```
C:\>DIR A:

Volume in drive B is DUGGAL
Directory of B:

INV      DBF     2560   12-18-88  11:35p
INV1     PRG     3997   12-27-88   7:02p
INV1     BAK     3923   12-24-88   3:38p
 .        .       .       .         .
 .        .       .       .         .
 .        .       .       .         .
INV42    BAK     2367   12-21-88  10:42a
INV42    PRG     2368   12-21-88  10:59a
       51 File(s)    245780 bytes free
```

remove this subdirectory from the root directory C by typing the following command:

`C:\>RD\TEMP     <Return>`

The system will return with the C:\> prompt. To make sure that the subdirectory has been deleted, get the new listing of the root directory by typing the DIR command at the system prompt C:\>. The new directory listing will look like the one shown in Figure 1.20. Notice that the TEMP directory has been deleted from the listing.

This completes Tutorial 3A.

Creating and Copying the Tutorial Disk to an Application Subdirectory

In this section, you will learn how to create an application subdirectory of the DBASE directory and copy the tutorial disk to it. To do this, follow the steps of Tutorial 3B.

Figure 1.20 Directory listing of the disk drive C:

```
C> DIR

Volume in drive C is ABC COMPANY
Directory of C:\

COMMAND  COM    23258   12-18-85   1:11p
CONFIG   SYS       48    1-27-89   5:42p
AUTOEXEC BAT      123    1-24-89   9:08p
DOS          <DIR>       12-20-85  10:25a
MMATE        <DIR>       12-20-85  10:26a
LOTUS        <DIR>       12-20-85  10:27a
BATCH        <DIR>        2-15-86   2:33p
SIDEKICK     <DIR>        2-15-86   2:34p
        8 File(s)    234280 bytes free
```

1.4 Your First Encounter with dBASE IV

TUTORIAL 3B

Create an application subdirectory named INVOICE of the DBASE directory, and copy the tutorial disk to this newly created directory.

Solution

To complete this tutorial, follow these steps:

Step 1: Boot up your system. If the system prompt is C>, proceed with step 2. If the prompt is C:\>, skip step 2, and proceed to step 3.

Step 2: Type the PROMPT PG command as shown:

C>**PROMPT PG**   <Return>

The system will return with the C:\> prompt.

Step 3: Obtain a listing of the DBASE directory by typing the following command:

C:\>**DIR\DBASE**   <Return>

The screen will look as shown in Figure 1.21. Notice that there are three subdirectories of the DBASE directory: DBASE\SQLHOME, DBASE\SAMPLES, and DBASE\DBTUTOR.

Step 4: Now create a subdirectory named INVOICE of the DBASE directory. To do this, type the following command:

C:\>**MD\DBASE\INVOICE**   <Return>

To make sure that the subdirectory has been created, get the new listing of the DBASE directory. The new directory listing will look like that in Figure 1.22 (see page 34). Notice that the DBASE\INVOICE directory has been added to the listing.

Figure 1.21 Listing of the DBASE directory

```
C:\> DIR \DBASE

    Volume in drive C is ABC COMPANY
    Directory of C:\DBASE

    .            <DIR>     12-21-88   6:07p
    ..           <DIR>     12-21-88   6:07p
    SQLHOME      <DIR>     12-21-88   6:07p
    CONFIG  DB      532    12-21-88   6:07p
      .       .     .        .         .
      .       .     .        .         .
      .       .     .        .         .
    SAMPLES      <DIR>     12-21-88   6:07p
    DBTUTOR      <DIR>     12-21-88   6:07p
      .       .     .        .         .
      .       .     .        .         .
         43 File(s)    8245280 bytes free
```

Figure 1.22 New listing of the DBASE directory

```
C:\> DIR \DBASE

Volume in drive C is ABC COMPANY
Directory of C:\DBASE

.             <DIR>      12-21-88   6:07p
..            <DIR>      12-21-88   6:07p
SQLHOME       <DIR>      12-21-88   6:07p
CONFIG   DB     532      12-21-88   6:07p
   .       .     .          .         .
   .       .     .          .         .
   .       .     .          .         .
SAMPLES       <DIR>      12-21-88   6:07p
DBTUTOR       <DIR>      12-21-88   6:07p
INVOICE       <DIR>      12-16-88  10:44a
   .       .     .          .         .
   .       .     .          .         .
      44 File(s)    8244256 bytes free
```

Step 5: Now copy all the files from the tutorial disk to this new DBASE\INVOICE directory. To do this, insert the tutorial disk in drive A:, and type the following command:

C:\>**COPY A:*.* \DBASE\INVOICE**   <Return>

The system will copy all the files from the floppy disk in drive A: to the DBASE\INVOICE directory.

Step 6: When the system prompt appears again, obtain the listing of the DBASE\INVOICE directory by typing the following command:

C:\>**DIR\DBASE\INVOICE**   <Return>

The system will display the listing of the DBASE\INVOICE subdirectory as shown in Figure 1.23.

This completes Tutorial 3B.

Figure 1.23 Directory of the DBASE\INVOICE subdirectory

```
C:\>DIR \DBASE\INVOICE

Volume in drive C is ABC COMPANY
Directory of C:\DBASE\INVOICE

INV      DBF    2560    12-18-88  11:35p
INV1     PRG    3997    12-27-88   7:02p
INV1     BAK    3923    12-24-88   3:38p
  .       .      .          .         .
  .       .      .          .         .
  .       .      .          .         .
INV42    BAK    2367    12-21-88  10:42a
INV42    PRG    2368    12-21-88  10:59a
      51 File(s)    8078780 bytes free
```

1.4.3 Loading dBASE IV

The step after installing dBASE IV is to **load** it into the internal memory of your computer system, where it will be executed. dBASE IV (in fact, any application program) is installed only once, but it is loaded into computer memory every time it is used.

Once again, the selection of the directory from which dBASE IV should be loaded depends on the environment in which you will be working, laboratory or nonlaboratory.

Loading dBASE IV in the Laboratory Environment

In the laboratory environment, the directory from which dBASE IV should be loaded is the DBASE directory. Because in this environment the current working directory, the directory used by dBASE IV to store and retrieve the database, program, and other files, will be the floppy disk drive, the floppy disk drive should be set as a default drive after dBASE IV has been loaded. The procedure for loading dBASE IV from the DBASE directory and setting the floppy disk drive A: as the default drive is given in Tutorial 4. (If you are working in a nonlaboratory environment, skip this tutorial.)

TUTORIAL 4

Load dBASE IV from the DBASE directory, change the control from the **control center mode** to the **dot prompt mode,** and set the default drive to drive A:.

Solution

To complete this tutorial, follow these steps:

Step 1: Boot up your system. If the system prompt is C>, proceed with step 2. If the prompt is C:\>, skip step 2, and proceed to step 3.

Step 2: Type the PROMPT PG command as shown:

```
C>PROMPT $P$G    <Return>
```

The system will respond by displaying the modified DOS prompt C:\>.

Step 3: When the prompt reappears, type DBASE to start the execution of dBASE IV.

```
C:\>DBASE    <Return>
```

After a few seconds, you will see a copyright notice. Then at the bottom of the screen, you will see the following message: "Press <Return> to assent to the Licence Agreement and begin dBASE IV."

Step 4: Now simply press the <Return> key. The copyright notice will disappear from the screen, and the dBASE IV control center as shown in Figure 1.24 will be displayed.

```
┌─────────────────────────────────────────────────────────────────────┐
│                                                                     │
│   Catalog    Tools    Exit                          ▌9:32:45▐       │
│                      dBASE IV CONTROL CENTER                        │
│                                                                     │
│                  CATALOG: C:\ DBASE\UNTITLED.CAT                    │
│                                                                     │
│      Data     Queries     Forms     Reports    Labels   Applications│
│   ┌─────────┬─────────┬─────────┬─────────┬─────────┬─────────┐     │
│   │▌<create>▐│<create> │<create> │<create> │<create> │<create> │     │
│   ├─────────┼─────────┼─────────┼─────────┼─────────┼─────────┤     │
│   │         │         │         │         │         │         │     │
│   │         │         │         │         │         │         │     │
│   │         │         │         │         │         │         │     │
│   │         │         │         │         │         │         │     │
│   └─────────┴─────────┴─────────┴─────────┴─────────┴─────────┘     │
│                                                                     │
│   File:                                                             │
│   Description: Press ENTER or <create> to create a new file         │
│                                                                     │
│   Help:F1  Use:◄┘ Data:F2  Design:Shift-F2  Quick Report:Shift-F9  Menus:F10 │
│                                                                     │
└─────────────────────────────────────────────────────────────────────┘
```

Figure 1.24 Control center

Note: If you do not press the <Return> key after ten seconds, the copyright notice will automatically disappear from the screen, and the dBASE IV control center will be displayed.

dBASE IV has been loaded, and the program is now waiting for your instructions.

Step 5: To change dBASE IV from the control center mode to the dot prompt mode, follow these steps:

(a): Press <F10>, and select the Exit option from the menu bar at the top of the screen by using the <Right Arrow> key or the <Left Arrow> key and pressing <Return>.

OR

Select the Exit option from the menu bar by pressing <ALT-E>; that is, hold down the "Alt" key, and press the "E" key.

(b): Now select the Exit to dot prompt option from the Pull-down Menu using the <Up Arrow> key or the <Down Arrow> key and pressing <Return>.

At the bottom of the screen, in the left-hand corner, you will see a period (dot) along with the status bar as shown in Figure 1.25. This period, the dBASE command prompt, is referred to as "dot prompt" in this book.

Figure 1.25 Status bar

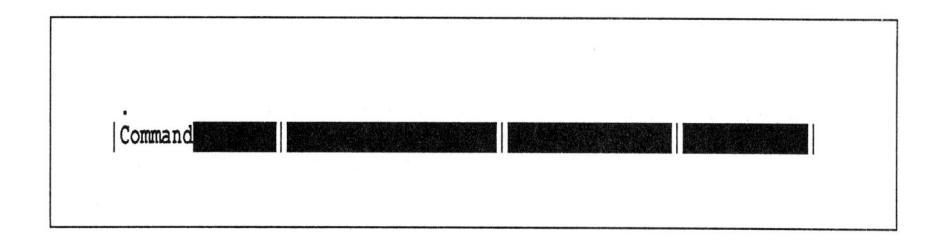

```
|Command|
```

Step 6: To set the default drive to drive A:, type the following command:

. **SET DEFAULT TO A:**   <Return>

When the dBASE returns by displaying the dot prompt, the disk drive A: will be designated as the default drive; that is, all dBASE commands will refer to the files stored in this drive.

This completes Tutorial 4. If you are working in the laboratory environment, skip the next section, and proceed to section 1.4.4.

Loading dBASE IV in the Nonlaboratory Environment

In the nonlaboratory environment, there are two possible directories from which dBASE IV can be loaded: the DBASE directory, where dBASE IV is loaded, and the application subdirectory of the DBASE directory. Now the question is which of these two options is more appropriate. Because your knowledge about dBASE IV may be limited at this point, it is not possible to go into a detailed discussion of these options in this chapter. This is postponed until the end of Chapter 2.

You will see in Chapter 2 that the latter option is more appropriate than the former. For this reason, we will always use this option; that is, we will always load dBASE IV from the application subdirectory of the DBASE directory. But because all the dBASE IV programs are stored in the DBASE directory, a path should be set to it. The procedure for loading dBASE IV from the DBASE\INVOICE directory with a path set to the DBASE directory is given in Tutorial 4A.

T U T O R I A L   4A

Load dBASE IV from the DBASE\INVOICE directory with a path set to the DBASE directory. Also change the control from the control center mode to the dot prompt mode.

Solution

To complete this tutorial, follow these steps:

Step 1: Boot up your system. If the system prompt is C>, proceed with step 2. If the prompt is C:\>, skip step 2, and proceed to step 3.

Step 2: Type the PROMPT PG command as shown:

C>**PROMPT PG**   <Return>

The system will respond by displaying the modified DOS prompt C:\>.

Step 3: Next log on to the DBASE\INVOICE directory by typing the following command:

C:\>**CD\DBASE\INVOICE**   <Return>

The system will display the C:\DBASE\INVOICE> prompt.

Step 4: Now set the path to the DBASE directory so that the system can access all the necessary programs of dBASE IV. To do this, type the following command:

C:\DBASE\INVOICE>**PATH=\DBASE**   <Return>

Step 5: When the prompt reappears, type DBASE to start the execution of dBASE IV.

C:\DBASE\INVOICE>**DBASE**   <Return>

After a few seconds, you will see a copyright notice. Then at the bottom of the screen, you will see the following message: "Press <Return> to assent to the Licence Agreement and begin dBASE IV."

Step 6: Now simply press the <Return> key. The copyright notice will disappear from the screen, and the dBASE IV control center as shown in Figure 1.24 will be displayed.

Note: If you do not press the <Return> key after ten seconds, the copyright notice will automatically disappear from the screen, and the dBASE IV control center will be displayed.

dBASE IV has been loaded, and the program is now waiting for your instructions.

Step 7: To change dBASE IV from the control center mode to the dot prompt mode, follow these steps:

a. Press <F10>, and select the Exit option from the menu bar at the top of the screen by using the <Right Arrow> key or the <Left Arrow> key and pressing <Return>.

OR

Select the Exit option from the menu bar by pressing <ALT-E>; that is, hold down the "Alt" key and press the "E" key.

b. Now select the Exit to dot prompt option from the Pull-down Menu using the <Up Arrow> key or the <Down Arrow> key and pressing <Return>.

At the bottom of the screen, in the left-hand corner, you will see a period (dot) along with the status bar as shown in Figure 1.25. This period, the dBASE command prompt, is referred to as "dot prompt" in this book.

This completes Tutorial 4A.

1.4.4 Different Operating Modes of dBASE IV

dBASE IV offers three different modes of operation: the dot prompt mode, the programming language mode, and the control center mode.

Dot Prompt Mode

The **dot prompt mode** was the only one available in all previous versions of dBASE. At it, you can enter any **dBASE command** (an instruction to dBASE to perform a particular function). As soon as the dBASE command is entered at the dot prompt mode, dBASE interprets and executes it. In other words, it allows you to interact with dBASE IV one command at a time. As such, it is also called the interactive mode.

The dot prompt mode, the basis for dBASE programming, helps you create procedures, design screen and report formats, and perform other tasks needed to develop large, complex business applications by taking advantage of advanced features of dBASE IV.

The main disadvantage of the dot prompt mode is that the user has to learn the dBASE commands and their syntax. Also, the commands have to be typed by the user. These disadvantages will be a handicap for the novice user or the unskilled typist.

Programming Language Mode

The most advanced and powerful feature of dBASE IV is its **programming language mode,** which puts dBASE IV ahead of almost all other DBMSs for microcomputers.

In the dot prompt mode, you interact with dBASE IV one command at a time. In other words, you enter a command and let dBASE execute it to perform the required function. Some tasks may require a series of commands. To perform these, the user must type the commands both correctly and in a specific sequence. If such a task is to be performed several times in a day, the set of commands will have to be retyped for each repetition. This situation will not only waste the user's time; it will also increase the chance for making mistakes in typing, which can lead to frustration for novice users.

The solution to this problem lies with the programming language mode, in which you can store the set of commands for performing any task in the computer's storage as a command file and give it a name. When the task is to be performed, you can retrieve and execute this command file by typing a single command. This process will increase users' efficiency and confidence. In this mode, the commands are processed in a group or batch mode. For this reason, this mode is also called the batch processing mode.

More complex tasks consisting of several dBASE commands can be designed by programmers and easily used by novices without detailed knowledge of dBASE programming. In other words, the programming language mode is better than the dot prompt mode for novice users because they do not have to remember most of the dBASE commands and their syntax. They have to remember only the few commands needed to execute the command files.

But we need the help of experienced programmers to design application software to be used by novice users. In other words, our aim is to prepare you as dBASE IV programmers who should be able to take advantage of the power and flexibility of dBASE programming and be able to design fully customized software systems to meet any business needs.

The main function of this book is to explore the different features of dBASE IV programming leading to the design of complex business application software using a structured approach to system development.

Control Center Mode

The **control center mode,** an alternative to the programming language mode, is a new user-friendly feature that has been added to dBASE IV. It provides an interactive mode of processing with the use of the Control Center Menu. The novice will find it easy to use. Users do not have to remember the commands and syntax or type the commands. dBASE executes the commands behind the scenes. Users can easily perform dBASE operations by simply selecting the options from menus presented by the control center, shown in Figure 1.24.

The only problem with the control center is that it provides access to only the most essential features of dBASE IV, which are enough for most purposes. But to develop complex application software requiring advanced features of dBASE IV, you must use the programming language mode. Because the purpose of this book is to explore only the programming feature of dBASE IV, we will use the control center mode only for those functions not available in the dot prompt mode.

For now, we do not need the control center, so I will not explain it further here.

1.4.5 Basics of Dot Prompt

This section introduces the interactive use of the dBASE IV commands at the dot prompt mode. To get the most out of this textbook, load dBASE IV as explained in Tutorial 4 or Tutorial 4A, and try the commands and examples as they are introduced. Alternately, you can work on all the tutorials and at least one assignment from the end of each chapter starting with Chapter 4.

All the database files used and programs developed in this book are on the tutorial disk supplied with it. If you have not copied the contents of this tutorial disk, do it now as explained in Tutorial 3, 3A, or 3B, depending on the environment in which you will be working with dBASE IV.

Conventions in This Book

The examples in this book follow these conventions:

- The word *press* is used for the keys you should press. The word *type* is used for information you must type in.
- The term *press <Ctrl-W>* means to hold down the "Ctrl" key, then press the "W" key once, and then release both the keys.
- The term *press <Ctrl,Alt-DEL>* means to hold down the "Ctrl" and "Alt" keys simultaneously, then press the "Del" key once, and then release all the keys.
- The function keys (F1 . . . F10) are followed with their assigned function, as shown in the following example: F1 Help.
- The instructions to be typed appear as shown:

    ```
    C:\>DIR\ENABLE     <Return>
    ```

The first part is the system prompt. You type only the boldface part of the instruction, that is, the DIR\ENABLE command, and press the <Return> key. Don't type the <Return> part with the instruction; it is present in the instruction to indicate that the <Return> key should be pressed after you are done typing the instruction.

Syntax of dBASE IV Commands

dBASE IV dot prompt commands follow a common syntax as shown:

```
VERB [<scope>] [<field/expression list>]
    [FOR<condition>][WHILE<condition>][TO
    PRINT/FILE<file name>]
```

The following is a description of the components of a dBASE command:

Verb: Represents a dot prompt command (for example, CREATE, USE, DISPLAY, LIST).

Scope: An optional qualifier that specifies what records of the database file the command applies to, depending on the current record order (for example, ALL, RECORD 5, NEXT 6, REST). The absence of the scope in the command defaults to the current record or to all the records of the database file.

Field List: A list of data field names separated by commas (for example, LAST_NAME, FIRST_NAME, AREA_CODE).

Expression List: A list of expressions separated by commas, where an expression is a formula consisting of fields, memory variables (defined later), constants, and operators (for example, UNIT_PRICE*QUANTITY, UNIT_PRICE*MARK_UP).

Condition: An expression that limits the records of the database file affected by the command (for example, FOR LAST_NAME = 'Smith' or WHILE UNIT_COST > 100). More than one condition can be used in a dBASE command. You can also combine conditions with a scope qualifier.

The scope, field list, expression list, and conditions are not required by most of the dBASE commands. These options are used to refine or restrict the effect of the dBASE commands.

Rules for Using dBASE IV Commands

When a dBASE command is introduced in this book, only the part of it needed in the context will be introduced. If you need the general format of the command, please refer to Appendix D.

Each of the dBASE commands must follow these rules:

1. The words in all capital letters represent valid dBASE command names. These commands must be entered exactly as shown, except that uppercase is *not* required.
2. The information contained in the angle brackets (<>) is to be supplied by the user. When supplying this information, the user need not type the angle brackets.
3. The information contained in the square brackets ([ ]) is optional. When supplying this information, the user does not type the square brackets.
4. An ellipsis (. . .) indicates repetition.
5. The items separated by a slash (/) are mutually exclusive; that is, *only* one of the items should be used.
6. All punctuation should be entered as shown in the model format.

1.4.6 Exiting dBASE IV

When you want to finish the dBASE IV session, always exit to the operating system prompt before you turn off your computer. To do so, just type QUIT at the dot prompt, and press the <Return> key. The system will display the message "*** END RUN dBASE IV ***" as shown and respond by displaying the C:\DBASE\INVOICE> prompt.

```
. QUIT
*** END RUN dBASE IV ***
C:\DBASE\INVOICE>
```

Now change the current working directory to the root directory by typing the CD\ command at the C:\DBASE\INVOICE> prompt as shown:

```
C:\DBASE\INVOICE>CD\     <Return>
```

The system will respond by displaying the DOS prompt C:\>. To terminate your session with the system, turn it off. If you want to continue your session with the system, you need to run the AUTOEXEC.BAT file. The setting of the path from the INVOICE application subdirectory to DBASE directory while loading dBASE IV has changed the path defined by the AUTOEXEC.BAT file, when the system was initially booted. Therefore, to reset the initial path, you need to run the AUTOEXEC.BAT file at this point. To do so, type the following command:

```
C:\>AUTOEXEC     <Return>
```

The system will respond by displaying the date and time. Respond by pressing the <Return> key. Finally, the system will respond by displaying the C:\> prompt. The system is now ready, and the initial path has been reset. Now you can continue your session with the computer system.

1.5 Summary

The chapter starts with an introduction to dBASE IV terminology, presenting basic terms and concepts used in database management

1.5 Summary

systems. Terms such as field, record, database file, database, database management systems, and relational database management systems are defined.

The components of the database file are described next, with a detailed description of the elements of the database file structure. Six different data types used in dBASE IV are explained. A list of the most commonly used types of dBASE IV files is summarized in a table along with a short description of the file type.

Terms not used in this text, or used infrequently, but that are used in database literature, are summarized in tables for future reference. The capacity constraints of dBASE IV are also described in this chapter.

The use of disk directories for the organization of the files on a hard disk is discussed in detail. The procedures for creating subdirectories, changing the current working directory, and deleting directories are explained. The concept of using the path to access files from other directories is also introduced.

Tutorials are added to provide hands-on experience with the computer and better understanding of the topics discussed in the text.

Section 1.4 provides your first encounter with dBASE IV. After the installation of dBASE IV, you actually create and use an application directory. Then you load dBASE IV from this newly created application directory with a path set to the DBASE directory. Next, you are introduced to the three different modes of operation available with dBASE IV. Advantages and disadvantages of each are discussed. Finally, you learn how to terminate your session with dBASE IV.

KEY CONCEPTS

attribute	field width
batch processing method	file extension
character data type	flat directory structure
control center mode	float data type
current working directory	hierarchical (tree) directory structure
database	installation
database file	interactive processing method
database file data	load
database file structure	logical data type
database management system (DBMS)	memo data type
date data type	numeric data type
dBASE command	path
dBASE IV	primary file name
decimal places	programming language mode
directory	record
dot prompt mode	relation
field	relational database management systems
field name	subdirectory
field number	table
field type	tuple

REVIEW QUESTIONS

1. Define each of the following terms:
   a. Field
   b. Record
   c. Database file
   d. Database
2. What is a database management system?
3. List seven important functions of a DBMS.
4. What is a relational database management system?
5. What is dBASE IV?
6. List different components of a database file. What is the purpose of the database file structure?
7. List different components of the database file structure.
8. List the rules for forming field names used in dBASE IV.
9. List six different field types used in dBASE IV.
10. List the rules for forming file names used in dBASE IV.
11. List the five most commonly used types of dBASE IV files.
12. List different directory structures used in the organization of a hard disk. What is the purpose of the hierarchical directory structure?
13. Define each of the following:
    a. Flat directory structure
    b. Hierarchical directory structure
    c. Root directory
    d. Subdirectory
    e. Parent directory
    f. Path
14. Explain how to create a subdirectory of the root directory.
15. Explain how to create a subdirectory of another directory from the root directory and from its parent directory.
16. Explain how to log on to a subdirectory.
17. Explain with an example how to obtain a directory listing of a directory from its parent directory.
18. Explain with an example how to obtain a directory listing of the root directory from its second- and third-level directory.
19. Explain with an example how to obtain a directory listing of a directory on a different path.
20. Explain how to delete a directory.
21. What is the difference between installing and loading a software program?
22. List the steps of copying the tutorial disk to another floppy disk using a computer system with two floppy disk drives.
23. List the steps of copying the tutorial disk to another floppy disk using a computer system with one floppy disk drive.
24. List the steps of creating an application subdirectory and copying the tutorial disk to this newly created directory.
25. List the steps of loading dBASE IV from the DBASE directory and setting the drive A: as the default drive.
26. List the steps of loading dBASE IV from an application subdirectory.
27. List the steps of changing dBASE IV from control center mode to dot prompt mode.
28. List and describe the three different operating modes of dBASE IV.
29. Explain what is meant by the term *press <Ctrl-W> keys*.
30. Explain what is meant by the term *press <Ctrl, Alt-W> keys*.
31. Explain the different components present in the following instruction:
    C:\>DIR\ENABLE\SMITH   <Return>
    What component(s) of this instruction should be typed by the user? What is the function of the <Return> component?
32. What is the function of the following in the use of dBASE commands?
    a. Angle bracket (<>)
    b. Square bracket ([])
    c. Ellipsis (. . .)
    d. Slash (/)

Chapter 2

Creating and Accessing Database Files

LEARNING OBJECTIVES

Upon successfully completing this chapter, you will be able to:

1. Use the database design screen to create the database file structure.
2. Add data to the database file using the APPEND and/or BROWSE commands.
3. Open a database file to access data from it.
4. Close an open database file.
5. Display the records contained in a database file using the DISPLAY and/or the LIST commands.
6. Display selected records from a database file.
7. Display records of a database file with selected fields.
8. Use the **TO PRINT** option or the **SET PRINT ON** command to obtain printed reports.
9. Create the screen listing and/or a printed copy of the databse file structure.

2.1 Overview

After your first success with dBASE IV following the directions in Chapter 1, you are now ready for another session in this chapter. Here you will learn how dBASE IV can be used:

1. To create a database file
2. To access data from the database file

2.2 Creating a Database File

In this section, you will start building your first database file. As already explained in Chapter 1, a database file consists of two components: a database file structure and database file data. The **database file structure** is the list of fields that indicates the kinds of information stored in the file. **Database file data** consist of records of data. The structure is present in the database file as a first record, followed by the records of data. Thus, to create a database file, follow three steps:

1. Create a database file structure.
2. Add data to the database file.
3. Close the database file.

Look again at the inventory card file of Chapter 1. The data of this file are shown in Figure 2.1. Note that these data are in tabular form consisting of rows and columns. The rows represent the records in the file, and the columns represent the fields of the records of the inventory card file.

The structure of this file is shown in Figure 2.2. It consists of field number, field name, field type, field width, and decimal places.

Before creating the structure of this file, you will need to load dBASE IV into the computer's memory. Recall the steps for loading dBASE IV as discussed in Tutorial 4 (if you are working in the laboratory environment) or Tutorial 4A (if you are working in the nonlaboratory environment). These steps are summarized in Table 2.1 (for loading dBASE IV in the laboratory environment) and Table 2.2 (for loading dBASE IV in the nonlaboratory environment) for your convenience and future reference.

Figure 2.1 Data of inventory card file

ITEM NUMBER	ITEM DESCRIPTION	UNIT COST	QUANTITY
1136	Bond Paper, Ream	22.99	38
1910	Ditto Paper, Ream	19.99	35
4012	King Kong Modem 1200	105.99	10
4045	Monochrome Monitor Z-1105	99.99	15
4072	Panasonic Printer KX-P108	269.99	8
3372	Printer Ribbon 10-Box	35.99	19
3375	Typewriter Ribbons 10-Box	23.79	67
1488	Xerographic Paper	19.99	45
4189	Zenith Microcomputer Z-158	829.99	5

Figure 2.2 Structure of inventory card file

FIELD NUMBER	FIELD NAME	FIELD TYPE	FIELD WIDTH	DECIMAL PLACES
1	ITEM_NUM	Character	4 Characters	
2	ITEM_DESC	Character	26 Characters	
3	UNIT_COST	Numeric	6 Characters	2 decimals
4	QUANTITY	Numeric	3 Characters	

Table 2.1 Steps for loading dBASE IV from the DBASE directory of drive C: and setting drive A: as the default drive

1. Boot up your system. If the system prompt is C>, proceed with step 2. If the prompt is C:\>, skip step 2, and proceed to step 3.

2. Type the PROMPT PG command as shown:

    C> **PROMPT PG**   <Return>

    The system will respond by displaying the modified DOS prompt C:\>.

3. When the prompt reappears, type DBASE to start the execution of dBASE IV.

    C:\> **DBASE**   <Return>

    After a few seconds, you will see a copyright notice. Then at the bottom of the screen, you will see the following message:

    "Press <Return> to assent to the Licence Agreement and begin dBASE IV."

4. Now simply press the <Return> key. The copyright notice will disappear from the screen, and the dBASE IV *control center* will be displayed. dBASE IV has been loaded, and the program is now waiting for your instructions.

5. To change dBASE IV from the control center mode to the dot prompt mode, follow these steps:

    a. Press <F10>, and select the Exit option from the menu bar at the top of the screen by using the <Right Arrow> key or the <Left Arrow> key and pressing <Return>.

    OR

    Select the Exit option from the menu bar by pressing <ALT-E>.

    b. Now select the Exit to dot prompt option by using the <Up Arrow> key or the <Down Arrow> key and pressing <Return>.

    At the bottom of the screen, in the left-hand corner, you will see a period (dot) along with the **status bar.** This period, the dBASE command prompt, is referred to as the "dot prompt" in this book.

6. To set the default drive to A:, type the following command:

    . **SET DEFAULT TO A:**   <Return>

    When the dBASE returns by displaying the dot prompt, the disk drive A: will be designated as the default drive; that is, all dBASE commands will refer to the files stored in this drive.

Table 2.2 Steps for loading dBASE IV from DBASE\INVOICE directory

1. Boot up your system. If the system prompt is C>, proceed with step 2. If the prompt is C:\>, skip step 2, and proceed to step 3.
2. Type the PROMPT PG command as shown:

   `C> PROMPT $P$G      <Return>`

   The system will respond by displaying the modified DOS prompt C:\>.
3. Next log on to the DBASE\INVOICE directory by typing the following command:

   `C:\>  CD\DBASE\INVOICE    <Return>`

   The system will display the C:\DBASE\INVOICE> prompt.
4. Now set the path to the DBASE directory so that the system can access all the necessary programs of dBASE IV by typing the following command:

   `C:\DBASE\INVOICE>  PATH=\DBASE    <Return>`

5. When the prompt reappears, type DBASE to start the execution of dBASE IV.

   `C:\DBASE\INVOICE>  DBASE    <Return>`

   After a few seconds, you will see a copyright notice. Then at the bottom of the screen, you will see the following message:

   "Press <Return> to assent to the Licence Agreement and begin dBASE IV."
6. Now simply press the <Return> key. The copyright notice will disappear from the screen, and the dBASE IV *control center* will be displayed. dBASE IV has been loaded, and the program is now waiting for your instructions.
7. To change dBASE IV from control center mode to the dot prompt mode, follow these steps:

   a. Press <F10>, and select the Exit option from the menu bar at the top of the screen by using the <Right Arrow> key or the <Left Arrow> key and pressing <Return>.

   OR

   Select the Exit option from the menu bar by pressing <ALT-E>.

   b. Now select the Exit to dot prompt option by using the <Up Arrow> key or the <Down Arrow> key and pressing <Return>.

   At the bottom of the screen, in the left-hand corner, you will see a period (dot) along with the *status bar*. This period, the dBASE command prompt, is referred to as the "dot prompt" in this book.

2.2.1 Creating a Database File Structure

The first step in creating a database file is to create the *structure*. The structure describes the attributes of the database file data, including the field name, field type, field width, and decimal places. In dBASE IV, the structure also specifies the field(s) to be used for the organization of the data.

2.2 Creating a Database File

The CREATE Command

The CREATE command allows you to define the structure of a new database file. The general form of this command is

```
CREATE <file name>
```

where <file name> is the name of the new database file to be created. Each database file name consists of a primary name and an extension separated by a period. For example:

```
INVNTORY.DBF
CUSTOMER.DBF
```

The user normally assigns only the primary name. You should always try to select primary file names that remind you of the contents of the database. The extension .DBF is automatically added by dBASE IV to the file name. You can also specify your own extension, in which case the extension specified by the user overrides the one assigned by dBASE.

The primary file name of a database can be any valid DOS file name. This file name should adhere to the rules described in section 1.2.6.

The file name can also contain special characters; however, the use of special characters in the file name can cause problems if system utilities are used. Therefore, avoid using special characters in file names.

The new file is created on the currently logged directory (also called the current working directory) unless otherwise specified by the user. Recall that you are logged on to DBASE\INVOICE directory on drive C:.

To create the structure of a database file, follow these steps:

1. Type CREATE with the new file name to create a new database file structure.
2. Enter the name, type, and width of each field needed in the database file.
3. Press <Ctrl-End> to terminate the process of creating the structure of the database file. This step will save the structure of the newly created database file and return the control to the dot prompt.

Now let's create the structure of the inventory card database file, whose data and structure are shown in Figures 2.1 and 2.2, respectively. This file will be named FILE1. To create FILE1, type the following command at the dot prompt:

```
CREATE FILE1    <Return>
```

This command indicates that the new file named FILE1 should be created on default drive C: and in the current working directory named DBASE\INVOICE, which is a subdirectory of the DBASE directory. When this command is executed, dBASE will display the **database design screen** as shown in Figure 2.3.

Error Message Box When you make an error while typing a command and you notice it before you have pressed <Return>, you can correct it by

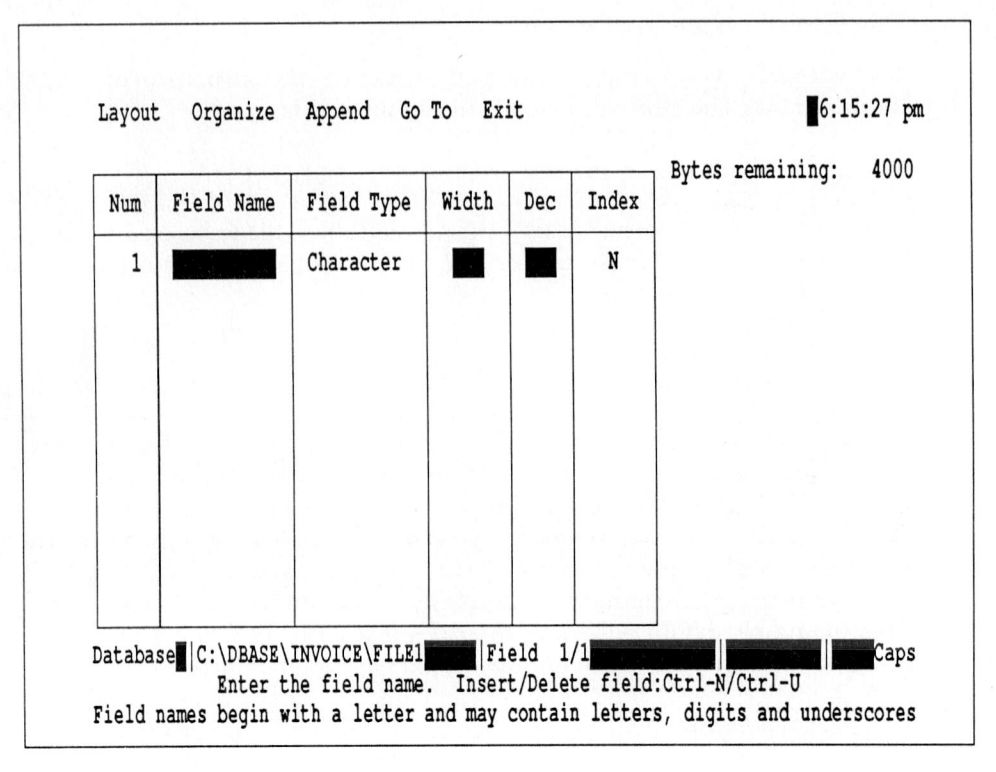

50 Chapter 2 / Creating and Accessing Database Files

```
 Layout   Organize   Append   Go To   Exit              6:15:27 pm

                                              Bytes remaining:   4000
┌─────┬────────────┬────────────┬───────┬─────┬───────┐
│ Num │ Field Name │ Field Type │ Width │ Dec │ Index │
├─────┼────────────┼────────────┼───────┼─────┼───────┤
│  1  │            │ Character  │       │     │   N   │
│     │            │            │       │     │       │
└─────┴────────────┴────────────┴───────┴─────┴───────┘

 Database C:\DBASE\INVOICE\FILE1      Field 1/1                Caps
        Enter the field name.  Insert/Delete field:Ctrl-N/Ctrl-U
   Field names begin with a letter and may contain letters, digits and underscores
```

Figure 2.3 Database design screen

                pressing <Backspace> as many times as needed to delete the wrong part of the command. Then retype the command. Or you can use the <Left Arrow> or <Right Arrow> key to move over to the misspelled letter and overwrite it with the correct one. When the command is correct, press <Return> to execute it.

                But if you have already pressed <Return> before you noticed a typing error, dBASE will not recognize the misspelled command; and it will respond with the error message box displaying the error name and offering three choices to correct it. For example, if you typed "CRAETE FILE1" instead of "CREATE FILE1," dBASE will display the error message box as shown in Figure 2.4. The error message box contains the error message and offers three choices for correcting the problem:

    Cancel: It terminates the execution of the current operation and returns to the dot prompt by displaying the clear dot prompt ready for entering a new command.

    Edit: It displays the misspelled command and allows you to edit this command. After making corrections, you can execute the corrected command by pressing <Return>.

    Help: It provides the dBASE IV help screen with additional information about the currently used command.

                When the error message box appears, you can select one of the choices by moving the cursor using the <Right Arrow> or <Left Arrow> key and pressing <Return> or by simply pressing the first letter of your choice.

2.2 Creating a Database File   51

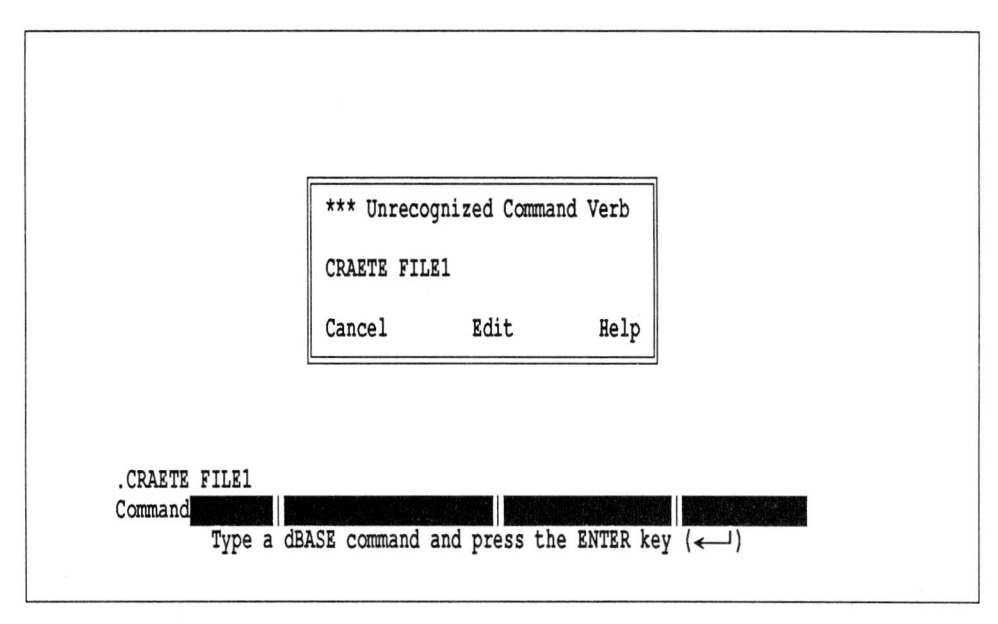

```
              *** Unrecognized Command Verb

              CRAETE FILE1

              Cancel        Edit        Help


.CRAETE FILE1
Command
         Type a dBASE command and press the ENTER key (←┘)
```

Figure 2.4 Dot prompt with error message box

Database Design Screen

The database design screen is used to create and modify database structures. It consists of several different parts, which I discuss in the following sections.

Menu Bar The top line of the database design screen represents the **menu bar,** as shown in Figure 2.5 (see page 52). This bar consists of five options: Layout, Organize, Append, Go to, and Exit.

Layout option:	This option is used for saving and printing the database structure of the database files.
Organize option:	This option is used for organizing the data in the database files in a meaningful sequence.
Append option:	The Append option is used to add or copy data to the database file.
Go to option:	This option is used to move the cursor to a specific field on the database design screen.
Exit option:	The Exit option is used to leave the database design screen.

The menu bar can be accessed in two different ways:

1. Using the F10 key: Pressing the F10 Menu key once will move the cursor to either the first option on the menu bar or the last

```
   Layout    Organize    Append    Go To    Exit
```

Figure 2.5 Menu bar

selection made from this menu during the current session with dBASE IV. A different option can be selected by moving the cursor along the menu bar using the <Right Arrow> or the <Left Arrow> key.

2. Using the Alt key: Pressing the Alt key in combination with the first letter of the option to be selected on the menu bar will move the cursor to the desired option.

For example, to select the Append option, you can either press the F10 Menu key and then use the <Right Arrow> or the <Left Arrow> key to highlight the Append option or simply press <Alt-A>, which will highlight the Append option.

Recall that you have used the menu bar earlier in Chapter 1, as well as in this chapter, when switching from the control center mode to the dot prompt mode. Refer to step 5 of Table 2.1 or step 7 of Table 2.2.

Each option of the menu bar has a **Pull-down Menu** associated with it. When an option of the menu bar is selected, the associated Pull-down Menu appears in a window on the screen just below the Menu bar option. Each menu consists of a series of choices arranged in a column with one of the menu choices highlighted. A message explaining the function performed by the highlighted choice appears at the bottom of the screen. The Pull-down Menu of the Layout option is shown in Figure 2.6, and the Pull-down Menus of the other four options are shown in Figure 2.7. Shaded choices are not available for the current function.

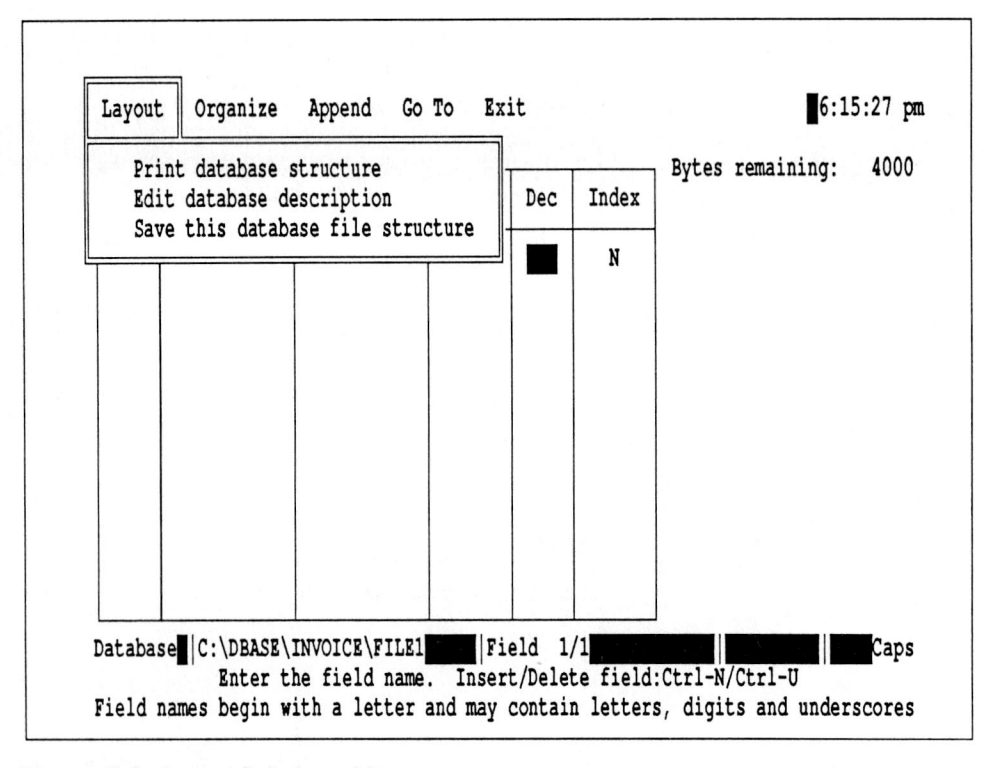

Figure 2.6 Layout Pull-down Menu

2.2 Creating a Database File 53

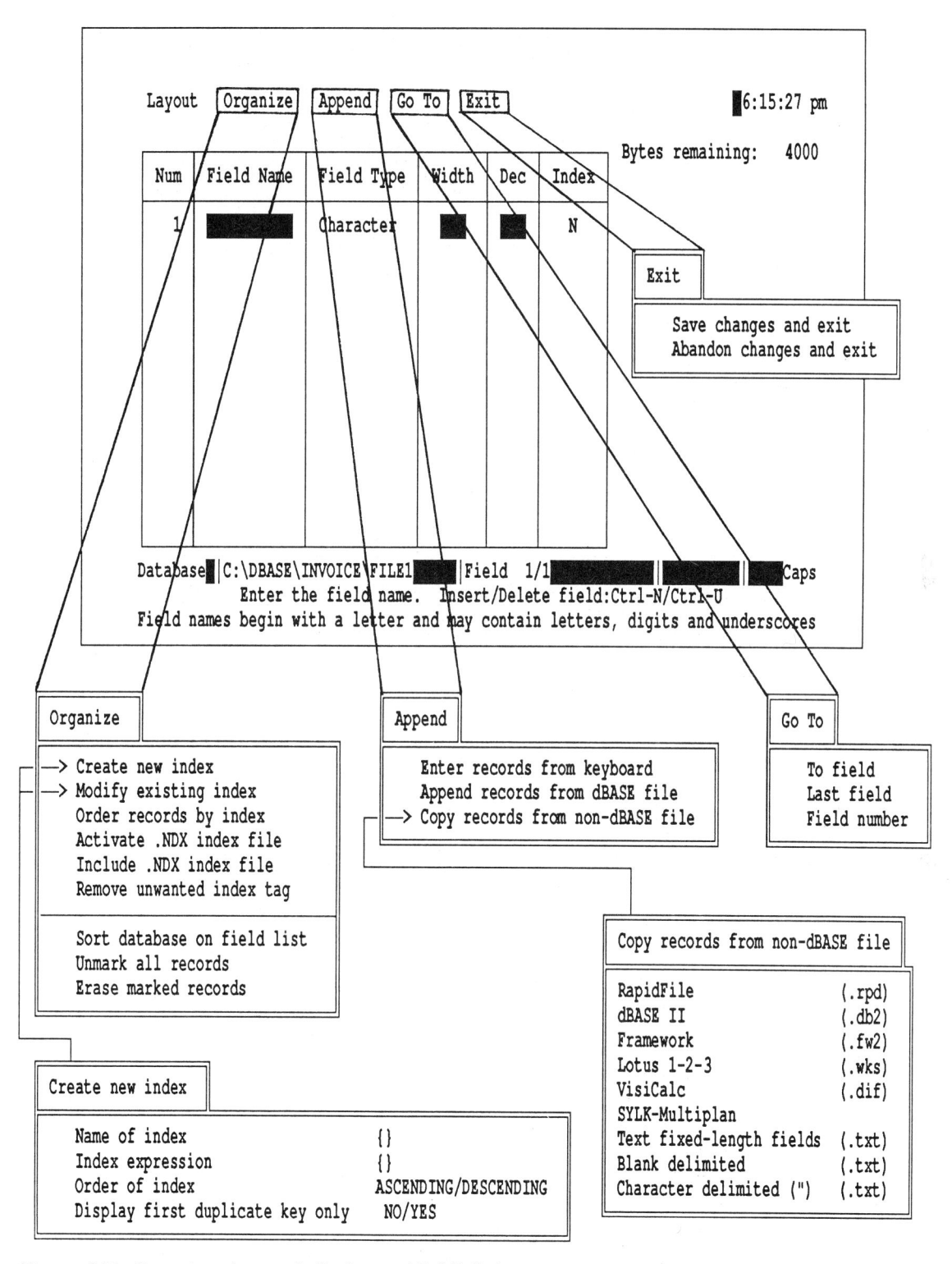

```
       Layout  Organize  Append  Go To  Exit              6:15:27 pm

                                            Bytes remaining:   4000
       Num  Field Name  Field Type  Width  Dec  Index

        1               Character                N
                                                        Exit

                                                        Save changes and exit
                                                        Abandon changes and exit











       Database  C:\DBASE\INVOICE\FILE1    Field 1/1                Caps
              Enter the field name.  Insert/Delete field:Ctrl-N/Ctrl-U
           Field names begin with a letter and may contain letters, digits and underscores
```

Organize	Append	Go To
→ Create new index → Modify existing index Order records by index Activate .NDX index file Include .NDX index file Remove unwanted index tag Sort database on field list Unmark all records Erase marked records	Enter records from keyboard Append records from dBASE file → Copy records from non-dBASE file	To field Last field Field number

Copy records from non-dBASE file

RapidFile	(.rpd)
dBASE II	(.db2)
Framework	(.fw2)
Lotus 1-2-3	(.wks)
VisiCalc	(.dif)
SYLK-Multiplan	
Text fixed-length fields	(.txt)
Blank delimited	(.txt)
Character delimited (")	(.txt)

Create new index

Name of index	{ }
Index expression	{ }
Order of index	ASCENDING/DESCENDING
Display first duplicate key only	NO/YES

Figure 2.7 Organize, Append, Go to, and Exit Pull-down menus

There are two ways to select a choice from the Pull-down Menus.

1. Move the cursor to highlight a choice by using the <Up Arrow> or <Down Arrow> key. Then press <Return> to actually select the option.
2. Press the first letter of the choice from the Pull-down Menu.

The first method has an advantage over the second. In the first method, before you actually select a choice, you highlight it by moving the cursor to it. A message appears on the bottom of the screen describing the function performed by the highlighted choice. This message can be used in making a selection.

There is a ">" sign before certain choices. The presence of this sign indicates that the choice has a Pull-down Submenu. When a choice with a ">" sign before it is selected (either by highlighting the choice and pressing <Return> or by pressing the first letter key of the choice), a Pull-down Submenu is displayed in a window on the screen just below the Pull-down Menu choice, with one of the submenu choices highlighted. A message explaining the function performed by the highlighted choice appears at the bottom of the screen. The Pull-down Submenus of the Organize and Append options are shown in Figure 2.7.

You can leave the Pull-down Submenu, Pull-down Menu, or menu bar at any time just by pressing <Esc>. If you are in a Pull-down Submenu and press <Esc> once, the cursor will move to the Pull-down Menu. Pressing <Esc> once again will move the cursor to the menu bar, and using <Esc> one more time will move the cursor to the work surface area

Table 2.3 Most commonly used menu navigation keys

Key	Function
F10 Menus	To activate the menu bar
<Alt-First letter of choice>	To make a selection from the menu bar
→	To move cursor highlight to the option on the right
←	To move cursor highlight to the option on the left
↑	To move cursor highlight up to the previous available menu option on the current Pull-down Menu
↓	To move cursor highlight down to the next available menu option on the current Pull-down Menu
↵	To select the current highlighted option
First letter of the choice	To select the option using its first letter
Esc	To back out to the previous menu or the database design screen
PgDn or End	To move cursor highlight to the last available option on the Pull-down Menu
PgUp or Home	To move cursor highlight to the first available option on the Pull-down Menu

of the database design screen. The most commonly used keys to navigate through the menus are summarized for future use in Table 2.3 along with a short description of their functions.

In the upper right-hand corner is the clock, which shows the current time. Immediately below this clock, the system indicates how many bytes are available for defining the database design form. A total of 4000 bytes is available to define this form, and the number of free bytes changes as you progress through the definition of the database design form.

Database Design Form In the middle section of the screen is a **database design form.** It is in tabular form containing six columns labeled num, field name, field type, width, dec, and index. You must fill in this table to create a database structure. Notice that dBASE is asking for information about each field in the record. Each field in your database file needs to be defined in this table. For each field, dBASE needs to know the field name, field type, field length, number of decimal places, and whether the field is used as an index or not.

Status Bar The status bar appears at the bottom of the screen. It displays the current operation or command, drive name, file currently in use, and other information, depending on the particular command. The status bar is shown in Figure 2.8.

The status bar provides important information about where you are in dBASE IV. It is made up of five sections that include the following information:

1. The first section displays the screen of dBASE IV you are using. In the previous example, the entry on the status bar is "database." It indicates that the screen used to define fields in the creation of a database file structure is currently in use.

2. The second section displays the location and name of the database file currently in use. This information consists of the disk drive name, the path, and the file name. In the previous example, this entry is "C:\DBASE\INVOICE\FILE1." This entry indicates that the database file named FILE1 is being created and will be stored in the DBASE\INVOICE directory, which is the current working directory.

    If you are working in the laboratory environment, the status bar will be as shown in Figure 2.9. Note that the second entry in this environment is simply "A:\FILE1." This entry indicates that the database file named FILE1 is being created and will be stored in the A: drive, which is the current working drive. All the figures in this book pertain to the nonlaboratory environment, so the

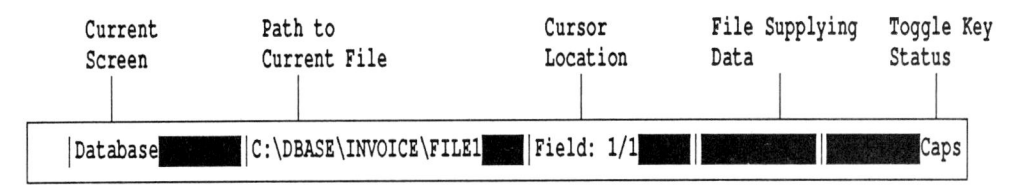

```
Current          Path to              Cursor          File Supplying    Toggle Key
Screen           Current File         Location        Data              Status
  |                  |                   |                |                |
|Database     |C:\DBASE\INVOICE\FILE1    |Field: 1/1     |                |Caps
```

Figure 2.8 Status bar using DBASE\INVOICE as the current working directory

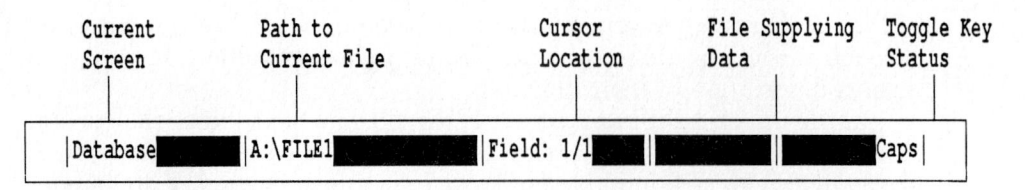

```
   Current         Path to              Cursor        File Supplying    Toggle Key
   Screen          Current File         Location      Data              Status
      |               |                    |             |                 |
  |Database|     |A:\FILE1|           |Field: 1/1|                      |Caps|
```

Figure 2.9 Status bar using the floppy disk drive as the current working directory

second entry in the status bar will be disk drive C: and a path for the application subdirectory INVOICE, which is used as the current working directory, as shown in Figure 2.8. If you are working in the laboratory environment, the corresponding entry in the status bar will be simply the floppy disk drive A:, which is used as the current working drive, as shown in Figure 2.9.

3. The third section displays cursor location. The information in this section depends on the work surface in use. The entries can be "Field:n/m," "Rec:n/m," or "Line:nCol:m."

    Field:n/m displays the information about the record of the database file. The value "m" indicates the total number of fields in the database record, and the value "n" indicates the field number being defined or edited.

    Rec:n/m displays the information about the whole database file. The value "m" indicates the total number of records in the database file, and the value "n" indicates the record number being displayed, viewed, or edited. You will encounter this entry again later in this chapter.

    Line:nCol:m is used for setting up a report. The value "n" indicates the line number, and the value "m" indicates the column number of the position of the cursor on the screen. The specific use of this entry will be discussed in Chapter 3.

    In Figure 2.8, the entry "Field: 1/1" on the status bar indicates that the cursor is on the first field and that the total number of fields defined for the database record is equal to one.

4. The fourth section displays the source of the data currently on the screen. For example, when creating a report form based on the contents of the customer database file, the entry shown in this section will be "File:CUSTOMER." In the example given in Figure 2.8, there is no entry in this section. The creation of the report form is discussed in Chapter 15.

5. The fifth section displays the settings of various toggle keys. For example, "Num" will appear in this section when the <NumLock> key is ON. If "Caps" appears, it means that the <Caps Lock> key is ON. When "Ins" appears, it indicates that the insert mode is ON, as compared to the overwrite mode, which is in effect when "Ins" does not appear. In the insert mode, anything typed from the keyboard will be inserted at the position of the cursor; and in the overwrite mode, anything typed from the keyboard replaces the character at the position of the cursor. Simply pressing these keys once changes their setting from ON to OFF and vice versa.

```
┌─────────────────────────────────────────────────────────────────────┐
│         Enter the field name.  Insert/Delete field:Ctrl-N/Ctrl-U    │
│    Field names begin with a letter and may contain letters, digits and underscores │
└─────────────────────────────────────────────────────────────────────┘
```

Figure 2.10 Navigation and message lines

If you are in the edit or browse mode, the presence of the entry "Del" in this section of the status bar indicates that the current record has been marked for deletion. This marking is discussed in Chapter 10.

In figure 2.8, the entry "Caps" on the status bar indicates that the keyboard is in the capital letter mode (upper case mode).

Navigation and Message Lines At the bottom of the screen are two lines that provide some help with and instructions for completing the database design form. These are shown in Figure 2.10.

The first line is called the **navigation line.** It provides instructions for completing this form. For example, the first part of the instructions in the navigation line in Figure 2.10 indicates that dBASE is asking you to enter the field name. The second half of this line explains the functions of two keys. The Ctrl-N key (while holding down the Ctrl key, press the N key once) is used to insert a blank field between two existing fields, and the Ctrl-U key is used to delete the current field.

The second line is called the **message line.** For example, the message line in Figure 2.10 reminds you that field names begin with a letter and may contain letters, digits, and underscores (_).

Defining the Database Form

The database design form, shown in Figure 2.3, consists of six columns labeled "Num," "Field Name," "Field Type," "Width," "Dec," and "Index." This form is used to define the structure of the database record. Each line will define a field present in the database record, and to do this, you need to furnish the information in each column of this form. Because the field number column already contains the value "1," you do not need to enter anything there. How to define the rest of the columns is explained in the next two sections.

Entering Field Names To define the database design form, follow the instructions of the navigation line. The instruction is "enter the field name." dBASE is asking you to enter the name of the first field you want to define. Recall that a field name can contain up to ten characters, and it must begin with a letter. The remaining characters can be letters, numbers, or the underline (_). As with database file names, no other punctuation mark or blank spaces are allowed. Field names should describe the information they are representing, and the use of the underscore (_) to improve readability is highly recommended.

The sample database we want to create will contain the following field names: ITEM_NUM, ITEM_DESC, UNIT_COST, and QUANTITY. When the cursor is in the field name column, enter the field name ITEM_NUM, and press <Return>. The cursor will jump to the field type column, where you will select the data type for the ITEM_NUM field.

Chapter 2 / Creating and Accessing Database Files

Table 2.4 Summary of dBASE IV data types

Data Type	Description	Examples
Character	Any text data or numeric data that are not to be used in computations. Maximum length of character data type is 254 characters. It is left justified.	ITEM_NUM (2487) ITEM_DESC (Xerographic Paper) Phone (578-2542)
Numeric	Any numeric data on which computations are performed. Maximum length of the numeric data type is 20 characters. It usually has a fixed number of decimal places. It is right justified. Only digits, decimal symbol ("."), and sign symbol ("+" or "−") are allowed in the numeric data type.	QUANTITY (107) UNIT_COST (17.25) TAX_DUE (−237.45)
Float	Float is basically the same as numeric data except the data values are very large or small with no fixed number of decimal places. This data type is best for scientific applications. Maximum length of the float data type is 20.	DISTANCE (234,962,785,000) MOLECULE (0.000000000015)
Logical	The field represents single character (Yes or No or True or False) data.	SCOREGT90 (T or F) ACCPASTDUE (Y or N)
Date	This data type is used to store a date in mm/dd/yy format. It has a fixed length of 8 characters supplied by dBASE IV.	10/31/88 1/5/89
Memo	This field is used to represent very large text data. Memo fields are used for long passages of text. It works like a word processor. It has a fixed length of 10 characters. The field in the record displays only the word *Memo*. You can enter as long a memo as you wish up to 5000 characters.	Abstract of articles or messages or comments

2.2 Creating a Database File

Note that after entering the field name, you had to press <Return>. You do so only if the field name length is fewer than ten characters long. If the field name is longer than ten characters, a bell will ring; and the cursor will automatically jump to the next column.

Selecting Data Type The next item dBASE wants to know is what type of data is being stored in the field. You can select one of the data types, that is, character, numeric, float, date, logical, or memo. A summary of all the data types, with a short description and a few examples, is given in Table 2.4.

Notice that the two lines at the bottom of the screen have changed and now read as shown in Figure 2.11. The navigation line indicates how to change the field type. The message line also gives a brief description of the character data type, which is the present selection of the field type.

You can scroll through the various data types by simply pressing the space bar. Each time you do so, a different data type will appear in the field type column, and the corresponding brief description of the data type will appear in the message line of the screen. When the desired data type appears in the field type column, press <Return> to make the selection.

In this case, you need to select the data type for the ITEM_NUM field, which is a character field. Press <Return> when the "Character" entry appears in the field type field. The cursor will jump to the width column, where you will assign the width to the ITEM_NUM field.

Recall that to define the data type, you first had to make a selection by using the space bar and then pressing <Return>. If the data type you want to define is not the character type, it will take extra time to search for the data type. You could save time in defining the field type by simply pressing the first character of the six data types available in dBASE IV, namely, C for character, N for numeric, F for float, D for date, L for logical, and M for memo fields, when the cursor is in the field type column.

Specifying Field Width

The next step in creating a database structure is to specify a maximum width for the field, that is, to indicate to dBASE IV the maximum number of characters or digits a field will hold. You need to specify the width for only three field types, namely, character, numeric, and float. The width of the other three field types (date, logical, and memo fields) will be specified by dBASE itself.

Observe that the two lines at the bottom of the screen have changed and now read as shown in Figure 2.12 (see page 60). The navigation line is instructing you to enter the field width, and the message line gives the limitations on the width of the field type you are defining. The limitations on the width of all the field types are summarized in Table 2.4.

```
                    Change field type: Space bar
    Character fields contain character information of a specified width
```

Figure 2.11 Navigation and message lines

```
          Enter the field width
  Character fields are 1 to 254 positions wide
```

Figure 2.12 Navigation and message lines

To assign a length of four characters to the ITEM_NUM field, enter 4, and then press <Return>. The cursor will skip the dec column (because character data do not need any decimal places) and jump to the index column. Here you will indicate whether the field ITEM_NUM is to be indexed or not.

Indexing the Field In this step of creating the database structure, you need to indicate to dBASE IV whether you want to use the field in question as an indexed field or not. Indexing a field of the database arranges the database file in ascending or descending order on the indexed field. You will learn about indexing in Chapter 11. The instructions at the bottom of the screen will change as shown in Figure 2.13.

There are only two options for indexing a field—Y or N. The default option is N, which is supplied by dBASE IV and is already displayed in that column. To change the option, simply press the space bar as indicated by the instruction in the navigation line. In our present example, we do not want to index the ITEM_NUM field, so make the selection "N" by pressing <Return>. The database design screen will look as shown in Figure 2.14.

Now repeat the same process, and define the rest of the fields ITEM_DESC, UNIT_COST, and QUANTITY. The only difference between defining ITEM_NUM and the rest of the fields will be in the definitions of the UNIT_COST and QUANTITY fields. The cursor will not skip the dec column because these fields are numeric. After you assign the width, the cursor will go to the dec column, where you will assign the number of decimal places to these fields.

Specifying Decimal Places In this section, you must specify the number of decimal places required by the field. The decimal places are required for only two types of fields—numeric and float—and must be at least two places (to be used for the decimal "." and the negative sign "−") less than the defined width of the field.

The instruction lines at the bottom of the screen will read as shown in Figure 2.15. The navigation line tells you to enter the number of decimal places, and the message line provides the rule for selecting the number of decimal places.

Enter a width of 2 for the UNIT_COST field and 0 (you do not have to enter 0, simply press <Return>) for the QUANTITY field, and press <Return>.

```
  Change option to index on this field: Space bar
```

Figure 2.13 Changed instruction line

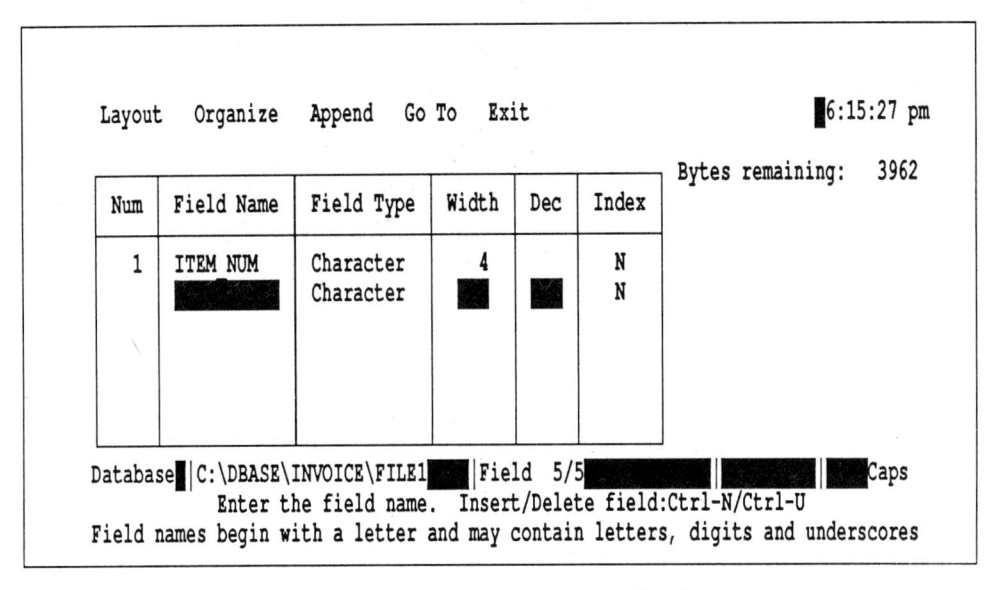

```
      Layout    Organize   Append   Go To   Exit              6:15:27 pm

                                                     Bytes remaining:    3962
  ┌─────┬────────────┬────────────┬───────┬──────┬───────┐
  │ Num │ Field Name │ Field Type │ Width │ Dec  │ Index │
  ├─────┼────────────┼────────────┼───────┼──────┼───────┤
  │  1  │ ITEM NUM   │ Character  │   4   │      │   N   │
  │     │            │ Character  │       │      │   N   │
  │     │            │            │       │      │       │
  │     │            │            │       │      │       │
  └─────┴────────────┴────────────┴───────┴──────┴───────┘

  Database│C:\DBASE\INVOICE\FILE1  │Field 5/5│              │Caps
           Enter the field name.   Insert/Delete field:Ctrl-N/Ctrl-U
    Field names begin with a letter and may contain letters, digits and underscores
```

Figure 2.14 Database design screen with one field defined

Making Changes and Corrections If you make a mistake while creating the database structure, such as entering a field name it cannot understand, dBASE will sound a tone, display a brief message below the status bar describing the nature of the error, and return the cursor to the point at which the error occurred. You can use the arrow keys on the numeric keypad to position the cursor for making changes, correct the error, and proceed with the process of creating the database. After you have finished defining the structure form, examine the form to make sure you have not made any errors.

To make any changes or corrections, use the following guidelines:

1. To move the cursor within a field, use the <Right Arrow> (→) or <Left Arrow> (←) key.
2. To move the cursor from one field to another field, use the <Down Arrow> (↓) or <Up Arrow> (↑) key.
3. To move the cursor one column to the right, use the <Tab> key. To move the cursor one column to the left, use the <Shift-Tab> keys.
4. To move the cursor one space back and erase the previous character, use the <Backspace> key.
5. To insert a blank field between two existing fields, use the <Ctrl-N> keys. To delete the current field, use the <Ctrl-U> keys.
6. To complete an entry and move to the next column, press <Enter>.

These guidelines are summarized in Table 2.5.

```
            Enter the number of decimal places
   Decimal width is 0 to 18 and must be at least 2 less than the field width
```

Figure 2.15 Changed instruction lines

Table 2.5 Most commonly used control keys with CREATE command

Key	Function
↑	To move cursor up one row
↓	To move cursor down one row
→	To move cursor one character to right
←	To move cursor one character to left
Tab	To move cursor one column to right
Shift-Tab	To move cursor one column to left
Backspace	To move cursor one space back and erase the previous character
Ctrl-N	To insert a blank field between two existing fields
Ctrl-U	To delete the current field
Enter or (Return)	To complete an entry and move to the next column

After all four fields have been defined, the database design screen will look as shown in Figure 2.16.

Saving the Database File Structure

When you have finished defining the database file structure, you can save it by either of the two methods described in the next two sections.

First Method After defining the last field, press <Return> when an empty field appears. dBASE will display the following message at the bottom of the screen, as shown in Figure 2.17: "Press ENTER to confirm. Press any other key to resume."

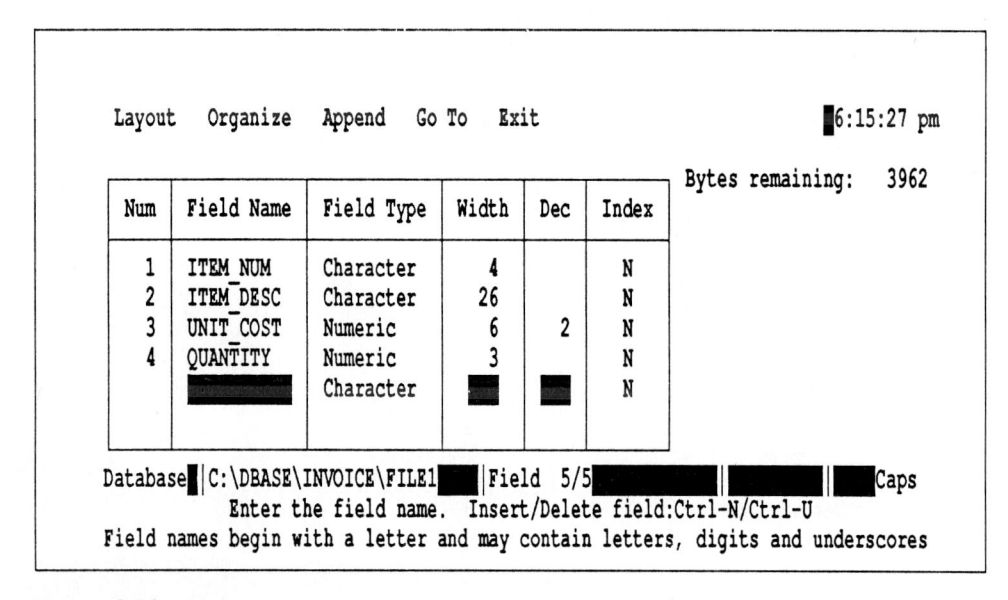

```
 Layout   Organize   Append   Go To   Exit                    6:15:27 pm

                                                    Bytes remaining:   3962
   ┌─────┬────────────┬────────────┬───────┬─────┬───────┐
   │ Num │ Field Name │ Field Type │ Width │ Dec │ Index │
   ├─────┼────────────┼────────────┼───────┼─────┼───────┤
   │  1  │ ITEM_NUM   │ Character  │   4   │     │   N   │
   │  2  │ ITEM_DESC  │ Character  │  26   │     │   N   │
   │  3  │ UNIT_COST  │ Numeric    │   6   │  2  │   N   │
   │  4  │ QUANTITY   │ Numeric    │   3   │     │   N   │
   │     │            │ Character  │       │     │   N   │
   └─────┴────────────┴────────────┴───────┴─────┴───────┘
 Database |C:\DBASE\INVOICE\FILE1    |Field 5/5              |     |Caps
            Enter the field name.  Insert/Delete field:Ctrl-N/Ctrl-U
   Field names begin with a letter and may contain letters, digits and underscores
```

Figure 2.16 Completed database design screen

2.2 Creating a Database File

```
  Layout    Organize   Append    Go To    Exit              6:15:27 pm

                                                   Bytes remaining:   3962
  ┌─────┬────────────┬────────────┬───────┬─────┬───────┐
  │ Num │ Field Name │ Field Type │ Width │ Dec │ Index │
  ├─────┼────────────┼────────────┼───────┼─────┼───────┤
  │  1  │ ITEM_NUM   │ Character  │   4   │     │   N   │
  │  2  │ ITEM_DESC  │ Character  │  26   │     │   N   │
  │  3  │ UNIT_COST  │ Numeric    │   6   │  2  │   N   │
  │  4  │ QUANTITY   │ Numeric    │   3   │     │   N   │
  │     │            │ Character  │       │     │   N   │
  └─────┴────────────┴────────────┴───────┴─────┴───────┘

  Database │C:\DBASE\INVOICE\FILE1    │Field 5/5                    │Caps
            Press ENTER to confirm. Press any other key to resume.
```

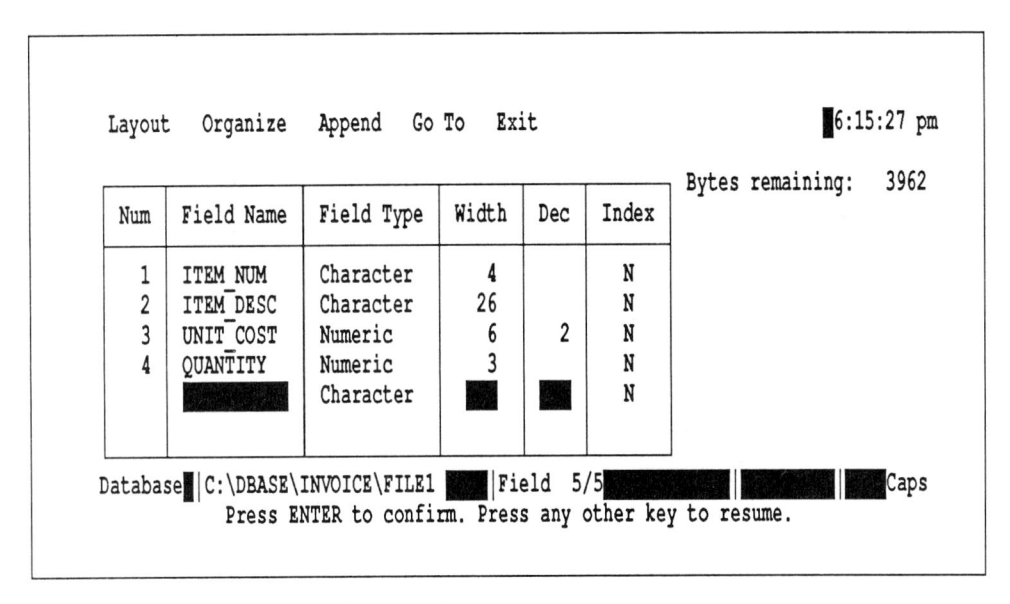

Figure 2.17 Completed database design screen

Press <Enter>. This will complete defining and saving the database structure. On the screen, you will see that the computer is asking if you want to enter the data in the database now or later. The "Input data records now? (Y/N)" message will be displayed, as shown in Figure 2.18.

If you want to enter the data right now, answer Y. If not, answer N. In this case, you will enter the data later, so type N and press <Return>. dBASE will return to the dot prompt. The structure of the database file FILE1 has been saved.

Second Method You can also save the database file structure by using the menu bar. Press <Alt-E> to highlight the Exit option of the menu bar.

```
  Layout    Organize   Append    Go To    Exit              6:15:27 pm

                                                   Bytes remaining:   3962
  ┌─────┬────────────┬────────────┬───────┬─────┬───────┐
  │ Num │ Field Name │ Field Type │ Width │ Dec │ Index │
  ├─────┼────────────┼────────────┼───────┼─────┼───────┤
  │  1  │ ITEM_NUM   │ Character  │   4   │     │   N   │
  │  2  │ ITEM_DESC  │ Character  │  26   │     │   N   │
  │  3  │ UNIT_COST  │ Numeric    │   6   │  2  │   N   │
  │  4  │ QUANTITY   │ Numeric    │   3   │     │   N   │
  │     │            │ Character  │       │     │   N   │
  └─────┴────────────┴────────────┴───────┴─────┴───────┘

  Database │C:\DBASE\INVOICE\FILE1    │Field 5/5                    │Caps
                     Input data records now?(Y/N)
```

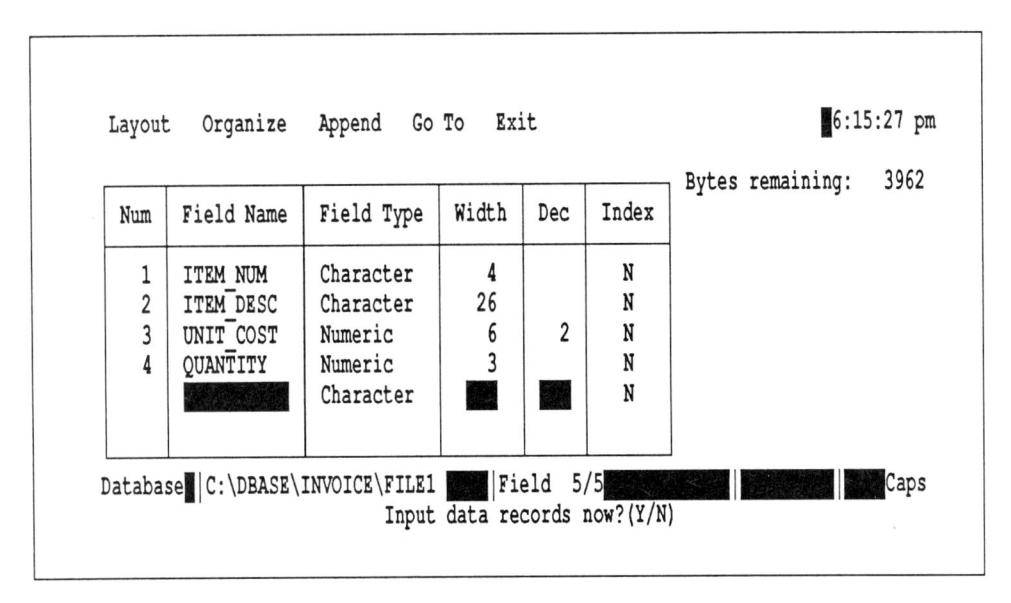

Figure 2.18 Completed database design screen

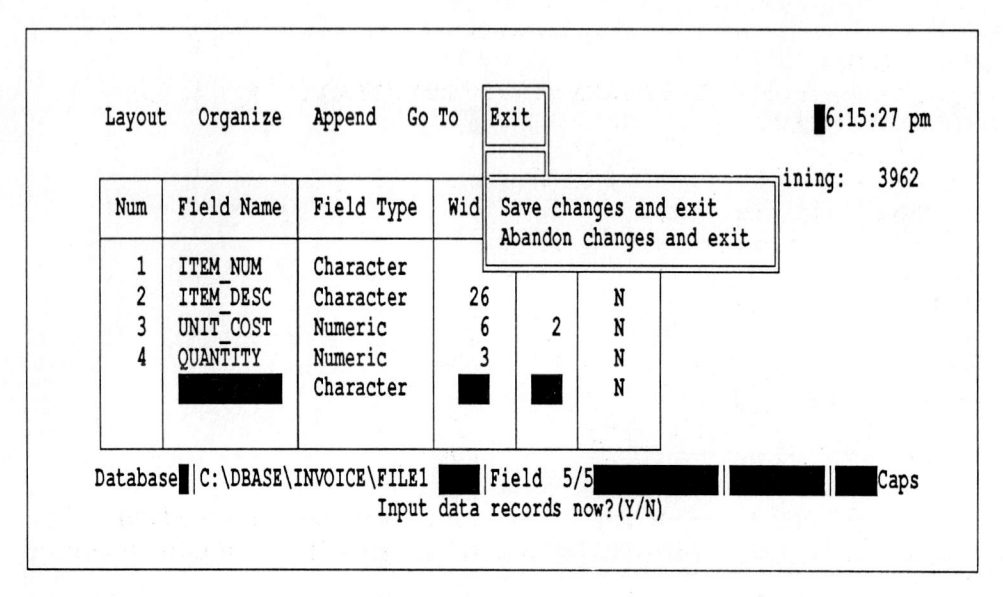

64 Chapter 2 / Creating and Accessing Database Files

```
 Layout   Organize   Append   Go To   Exit                    6:15:27 pm
                                     ┌────────────────────────┐
                                     │ Save changes and exit  │ining:   3962
 ┌───┬────────────┬────────────┬─────┤ Abandon changes and exit│
 │Num│ Field Name │ Field Type │ Wid └────────────────────────┘
 ├───┼────────────┼────────────┼─────────────────────────────────
 │ 1 │ ITEM_NUM   │ Character  │                              N
 │ 2 │ ITEM_DESC  │ Character  │  26                          N
 │ 3 │ UNIT_COST  │ Numeric    │   6          2               N
 │ 4 │ QUANTITY   │ Numeric    │   3                          N
 │   │            │ Character  │                              N
 └───┴────────────┴────────────┴─────────────────────────────────

 Database  C:\DBASE\INVOICE\FILE1      Field 5/5                  Caps
                 Input data records now?(Y/N)
```

Figure 2.19 Completed database design screen with Exit option highlighted

The Pull-down Menu for the Exit option will be displayed in a window on the screen, as shown in Figure 2.19.

Use the <Up Arrow> or <Down Arrow> key to move the cursor through the Pull-down Menu choices. Highlight the "Save changes and exit" choice, and then select it by pressing <Return>. The system will display the following message at the bottom of the screen, as shown in Figure 2.17: "Press ENTER to confirm. Press any other key to resume."

Press <Enter>. This will complete defining and saving the database structure. dBASE will return to the dot prompt. The structure of the database file FILE1 has been saved.

Displaying the Database File Structure

Now that the file has been created, you can display its structure (the way the database is organized) at any time. The DISPLAY STRUCTURE command displays the structure of the current open database file.

The DISPLAY STRUCTURE Command

The general format of this command is

    DISPLAY STRUCTURE

This command displays the structure of the currently selected database file in the currently logged directory.

Because you are logged on to the DBASE\INVOICE directory and the database file FILE1 created in the last section is still open, you type the following command to display the structure of this file:

    .DISPLAY STRUCTURE   <Return>

dBASE will display the structure of the database file FILE1, as shown in Figure 2.20. It contains the name, size (number of records in the file), and

```
.DISPLAY STRUCTURE
Structure for database : C:\DBASE\INVOICE\FILE1.DBF
Number of data records :       0
Date of last update    : 1/12/89
Field  Field name  Type         Width    Dec    Index
    1  ITEM_NUM    Character       4              N
    2  ITEM_DESC   Character      26              N
    3  UNIT_COST   Numeric         6     2        N
    4  QUANTITY    Numeric         3              N
** TOTAL **                       40
```

Figure 2.20 Structure of the database file FILE1

date of the last update together with the attributes of all the fields of the database file. The last line indicates the length of the record in number of bytes.

Note that the total number of bytes in the record length is one more than the length of the record. The sum of the field width is 39 bytes, whereas the total record length is 40 bytes. The extra byte is used to mark the deleted records, which will be explained in Chapter 10.

2.2.2 Adding Data to the Database File

The second step in creating a database file is adding data to the database file structure you have created. Three commands are available in dBASE IV for this task: APPEND, INSERT, and BROWSE. The APPEND or BROWSE commands are used to add data at the end of the database file. The INSERT command is used to add data between the current records of the database file. You will use both the APPEND and BROWSE commands in this section to add data to the database file FILE1.

The APPEND command displays 1 record at a time on the screen; the BROWSE command displays up to 17 records and as many fields as can fit on the screen. The BROWSE command can be used to add data to the database file only if records already exist in that file.

Because this database has no data records present in it, we can't use the BROWSE command to add data to the previously created database file FILE1. Therefore, we will use the APPEND command to add the first record and then use the BROWSE command to add the rest of the records of the inventory card file to this database file.

The APPEND Command

The general format of this command is

    APPEND

The APPEND command adds a new blank record to the end of the database currently in use and allows data entry into this new blank record. To add data to a newly created database file, use the following steps:

1. Open the database file, if it is not already open, by using the USE command (explained in section 2.3.1).

2. Type APPEND, and press <Return> or F9 Append (discussed in section 2.4.1). A new blank record appears on the screen. This is called the append mode.
3. Enter the data for each field in the area provided in the blank record. When the record is filled, a new blank record will be made available.
4. Repeat step 3 to enter the rest of the records in the database file.
5. Press <Ctrl-End> to terminate the process of adding data to the database file, and return the control to the dot prompt.
6. Close the open database file by typing USE (discussed in section 2.2.3) and pressing <Return>.

The database file FILE1 is currently in use. We have not closed this database after its creation. Therefore, to add data to it, type the following command:

```
.APPEND      <Return>
```

Because the APPEND command provides full-screen editing, dBASE will respond by displaying the edit screen for the database file FILE1, as shown in Figure 2.21. The edit screen consists of the menu bar, work surface area, and status bar.

The work surface area contains a single blank record, displaying each field on a separate line. Note that the fields appear in the same order as they were defined in the database structure. The field name appears on the left, followed by an area to enter the data, which appears in color (or reverse video on a monochrome monitor).

Initially, the cursor will be in the leftmost position of the first field, that is, the ITEM_NUM field. You can start entering the data provided in Figure 2.1. To do so, follow these steps:

1. Enter the first item number "1136." You will hear a beep sound after you type the last digit. The cursor will skip to the ITEM_DESC field.
2. Now enter the item description of the first record (that is, "Bond Paper, Ream"), and press <Return>. The cursor will move to the UNIT_COST field.
3. Next enter the unit cost for the first record ("22.99"). To do this, first enter "22," then enter the decimal point ("."), and finally

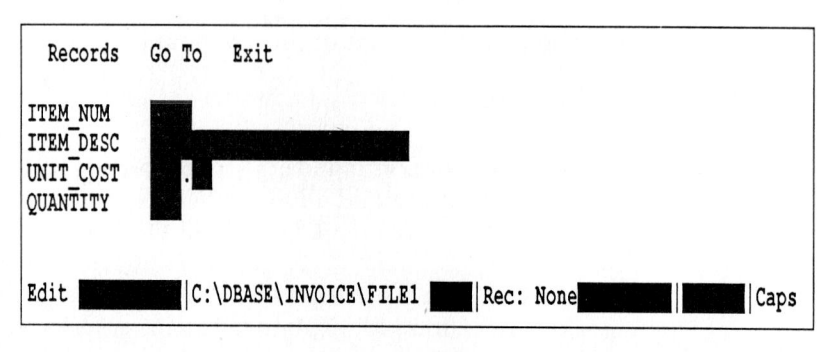

Figure 2.21 Edit screen for FILE1 database

```
Records   Go To   Exit

ITEM_NUM
ITEM_DESC
UNIT_COST
QUANTITY




Edit            |C:\DBASE\INVOICE\FILE1   |Rec: None        |Caps
```

Figure 2.22 Edit screen for FILE1 database with first record

```
Records    Go To    Exit

ITEM_NUM    1136
ITEM_DESC   Bond Paper, Ream
UNIT_COST   22.99
QUANTITY    38


Edit          |C:\DBASE\INVOICE\FILE1    |Rec: None          |Caps
```

enter "99." Again you will hear a beep, and the cursor will skip to the QUANTITY field.

4. Enter the quantity value from the first record of the database (that is, "38").

The edit screen will appear as shown in Figure 2.22.

After entering the data for the first record, verify the information visually to see if any changes or corrections are needed. To make the changes or corrections, use the guidelines listed in Table 2.6.

Table 2.6 Most commonly used control keys with APPEND command

Key	Function
↑	To move cursor up one row
↓	To move cursor down one row
→	To move cursor one character to right
←	To move cursor one character to left
Tab	To move cursor one column to right
Shift-Tab	To move cursor one column to left
Backspace	To move cursor one space back and erase the previous character
Ctrl-N	To insert a blank field between two existing fields
Ctrl-U	To delete the current field
Enter or (Return)	To complete an entry and move to the next column
Del	To delete one character over the cursor
Ins	To switch keyboard between Insert and Overwrite Mode
Ctrl-Y	To delete all characters to the right of cursor
Escape	To leave the current record without saving changes
PgUp	To move to the preceding record
PgDn	To move to the next record
Ctrl-PgUp	To enter the editor for adding memo field
Ctrl-PgDn	To exit the editor after adding memo field and returning back to the edit screen

If no corrections are needed, press <Return> or <PgDn>. The record will be stored, and another blank record will be displayed.

Before repeating this process for the rest of the records of the inventory card file of Figure 2.1, read the next paragraph. After adding the last record, when the new blank record is displayed, simply press <Return> when the cursor is in the first position of the field. dBASE will return to the dot prompt. This will terminate the process of adding data to the database file FILE1. When you have entered all the data of the database file FILE1, you could also terminate the process of adding data to the database file and return the control to the dot prompt by pressing <Ctrl-End>.

Instead of adding the rest of the records to the database in the append mode, we will use the browse screen mode to complete this process. To do this, we will use the BROWSE command. This procedure will give you some experience with the browse mode for data entry.

The BROWSE Command

The simple format of this command is

```
BROWSE
```

The BROWSE command is used for editing data and displaying 17 records at a time, with as many fields as will fit across the screen. Editing is discussed in Chapter 6. You can also use the BROWSE command to add records to a database file with existing records.

To add, edit, or view data in an existing database file, use the following steps. Note that the BROWSE command can be used to add data to a database file only if the file already has some data in it.

1. Open the database file. If the file is not already open, use the USE command, which is explained in section 2.3.1.
2. Type BROWSE and press <Return>. The screen will appear, displaying up to 17 records at a time, with as many fields as will fit across the screen. This is called the browse mode.
3. Add, edit, or view the data in the database file.
4. Press <Ctrl-End> to terminate the browse mode and return the control to the dot prompt. You can also terminate the browse mode by selecting the Exit option from the menu bar by pressing <Alt-E> (or by pressing F10 Menus and then selecting the Exit option from the Pull-down Menu) and pressing <Return>.
5. Close the open database file by typing USE (discussed in section 2.2.3) and pressing <Return>.

Now let us add the rest of the records of the inventory card file to the database file FILE1 using the browse screen. To switch from the edit screen to the browse screen, simply press the F2 key. The browse screen as shown in Figure 2.23 will be displayed on the screen. It consists of the menu bar, work surface area, status bar, navigation line, and message line. The work surface area contains the data of the first record, and the cursor is in the first field of this record.

2.2 Creating a Database File

Figure 2.23 Browse screen for FILE1 database with first record

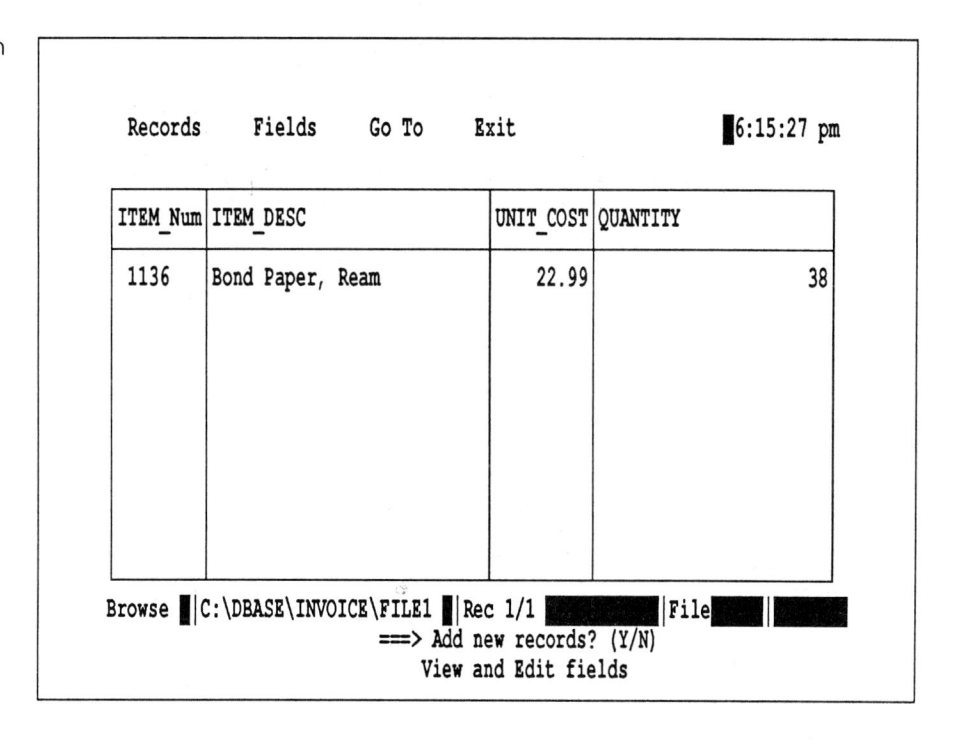

```
Records     Fields     Go To     Exit                    6:15:27 pm

| ITEM_Num | ITEM_DESC        | UNIT_COST | QUANTITY |
|   1136   | Bond Paper, Ream |   22.99   |    38    |

Browse   C:\DBASE\INVOICE\FILE1   Rec 1/1        File
         ===> Add new records? (Y/N)
              View and Edit fields
```

To add new records at the end of this file, just press the <Down Arrow> (↓) key to move down to the blank row. Because there is currently no record there, dBASE will display the following prompt, as shown in Figure 2.24:

```
===> Add new records? (Y/N).
```

Figure 2.24 Browse screen for FILE1 database with "Add new records?" prompt

```
Records     Fields     Go To     Exit                    6:15:27 pm

| ITEM_Num | ITEM_DESC        | UNIT_COST | QUANTITY |
|   1136   | Bond Paper, Ream |   22.99   |    38    |

Browse   C:\DBASE\INVOICE\FILE1   Rec 1/1        File
         ===> Add new records? (Y/N)
              View and Edit fields
```

Figure 2.25 Browse screen for FILE1 database after adding all the records

```
 Records    Fields    Go To    Exit                 6:15:27 pm

 ITEM_Num | ITEM_DESC                | UNIT_COST | QUANTITY
 ---------|--------------------------|-----------|----------
 1136     | Bond Paper, Ream         |   22.99   |    38
 1910     | Ditto Paper, Ream        |   19.99   |    35
 4012     | King Kong Modem 1200     |  105.99   |    10
 4045     | Monochrome Monitor Z-1105|   99.99   |    15
 4072     | Panasonic Ribbon 10-Box  |  269.99   |     8
 3372     | Printer Ribbons 10-Box   |   35.99   |    19
 3375     | Typewriter Ribbons 10-Box|   23.79   |    67
 1488     | Xerographic Paper        |   19.99   |    45
 4189     | Zenith Microcomputer Z-158|  829.99  |     5

 Browse  |C:\DBASE\INVOICE\FILE1 |Rec EOF/9        |File
           ===> Add new records? (Y/N)
               View and Edit fields
```

Answer "Y," and add the rest of the records of the inventory card file of Figure 2.1. After all the records have been added, the screen will look as shown in Figure 2.25.

To terminate the process of adding records to the database file and save them, follow these steps:

1. Select the Exit option of the menu bar in one of the following methods.
    a. Press F10 Menus and use the <Right Arrow> or <Left Arrow> key to select the Exit option.
    b. Press <Alt-E>.
2. After you select the Exit option of the menu bar, the Pull-down Menu for the Exit option will appear on the screen, as shown in Figure 2.26. Select the Exit option from the Pull-down Menu by using the <Up Arrow> or <Down Arrow> key, and then press <Return>. dBASE will return the dot prompt. This step will terminate the process of adding data to the database file FILE1.

If the database file includes a memo field, you will need to take an extra step to load the memo field. After entering the data for the other fields, place the cursor on the memo field, and press <Ctrl-PgDn>. This will activate the dBASE editor, which you can use to enter the memo field data and which is explained in Chapter 3. After you finish entering the memo field, press the <Ctrl-PgUp> to return to the normal screen.

When you are adding data using the APPEND or BROWSE commands, as each new record is displayed, all the fields will be blank. You will have to enter information in each field, which will waste a lot of time when entering records with duplicate information. For example, in a database file, the entry in the field EMP_CITY may be the same for several

Figure 2.26 Browse screen for database file FILE1 with first record

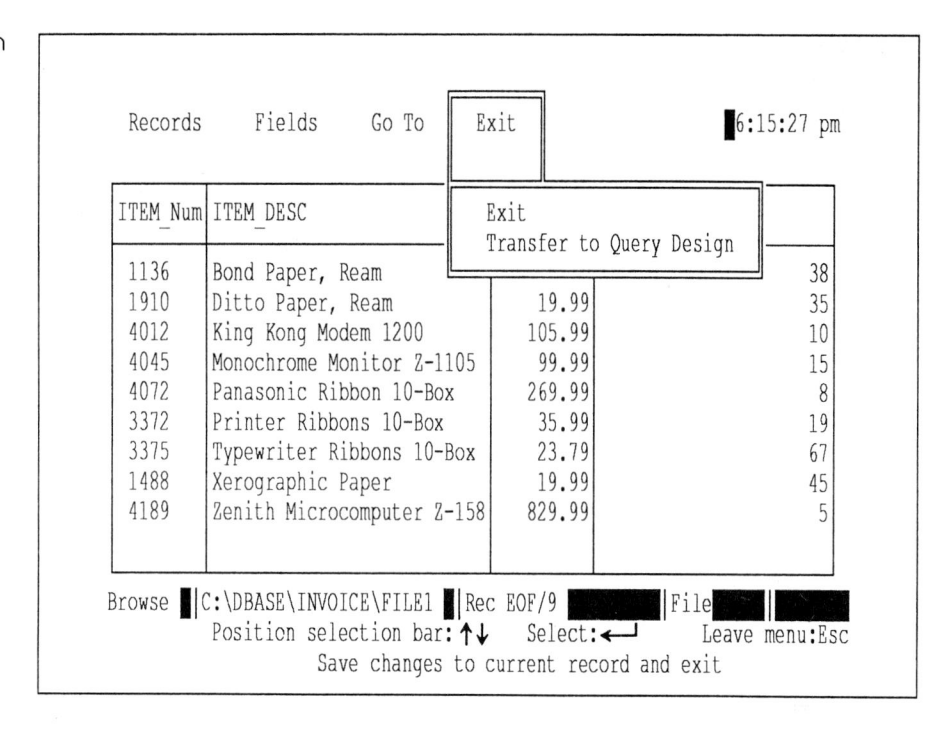

```
  Records      Fields      Go To     Exit                   6:15:27 pm

 ┌─────────┬──────────────────────┬─────────┬────────────────────────┐
 │ITEM_Num │ITEM_DESC             │  Exit                            │
 │         │                      │  Transfer to Query Design        │
 │  1136   │Bond Paper, Ream      │                              38  │
 │  1910   │Ditto Paper, Ream     │    19.99                     35  │
 │  4012   │King Kong Modem 1200  │   105.99                     10  │
 │  4045   │Monochrome Monitor Z-1105│ 99.99                     15  │
 │  4072   │Panasonic Ribbon 10-Box │ 269.99                      8  │
 │  3372   │Printer Ribbons 10-Box │   35.99                     19  │
 │  3375   │Typewriter Ribbons 10-Box│ 23.79                     67  │
 │  1488   │Xerographic Paper     │    19.99                     45  │
 │  4189   │Zenith Microcomputer Z-158│829.99                     5  │

  Browse   C:\DBASE\INVOICE\FILE1   Rec EOF/9           File
             Position selection bar: ↑↓   Select:↵    Leave menu:Esc
                    Save changes to current record and exit
```

records. To avoid duplication of data entry, you can use the SET CARRY ON command *before* using the APPEND or BROWSE command. The CARRY option is OFF by default. The SET CARRY ON command will change the default to ON. In the ON position, it will duplicate the data from the previous record into the current record. This step is very useful and will save you time when entering records with duplicate information. To enter the information in the new record, you can leave the duplicate fields unchanged and add the new values to the other fields. Unfortunately, you cannot select fields to be carried over; either all or none of the information is carried over.

There is an alternative method if you don't want the whole record to be carried over. When the CARRY option is OFF and you want to copy the information in a field from the previous record to the corresponding field, simply press <Shift-F8>. This step will also help save data-entry time for duplicate fields.

Using the APPEND command to add data is useful for small databases that must be built and will need very little editing during productive work. You should use the APPEND command only for creating and controlling data files that are created once and that you do not intend to maintain. The BROWSE command can be used to create large databases or databases that require a lot of editing.

When adding a large number of records, you should exit and save the database periodically and reenter the browse mode to continue adding records to the database. This will prevent the loss of the data entered but not saved in case of power failure.

2.2.3 Closing the Database File

There are several ways to close an active (open) database file. The simplest is with the USE command. Other methods will be discussed in Chapter 11.

The USE Command

The simplest form of the USE command is

```
USE
```

The USE command, without any file name specified with it, closes the active database file in the currently logged directory. To close the active database file FILE1, type the following command:

```
. USE    <Return>
```

When the dot prompt returns, the database file FILE1 will be closed.

TUTORIAL 5

Create and populate the database file FILE1 with the data given in Figure 2.1. Use the APPEND command to add the first record and then the BROWSE command to add the remainder of the records.

Solution

To complete this tutorial, follow these steps:

- Step 1: Boot up your system. If the system prompt is C>, proceed with step 2. If the prompt is C:\>, skip step 2, and proceed to step 3.
- Step 2: Type the PROMPT PG command as shown. Recall that this command helps monitor the current working directory.

    ```
    C>PROMPT $P$G    <Return>
    ```

    The system will return with the C:\> prompt.
- Step 3: Load dBASE IV, and change the control from the control center mode to the dot prompt mode. To complete this step, follow the instructions given in Table 2.1 or Table 2.2, depending on the environment in which you are working.
- Step 4: Type the following command at the dot prompt:

    ```
    . CREATE FILE1    <Return>
    ```

    dBASE will display Figure 2.3.
- Step 5: Use Figure 2.2 to define the database design form following the instructions of "Defining the Database Form" in section 2.2.1. The form should look as shown in Figure 2.16.
- Step 6: Now save the database file structure by pressing the <Alt-E> key to highlight the Exit option of the menu bar. Choose Save changes and exit from the Pull-down Menu, and press <Return> to select it. Again press <Return> at the prompt request. dBASE will return to the dot prompt.

The database file FILE1 structure has been created and saved. Verify this by displaying the structure of this file. To do so, type:

. **DISPLAY STRUCTURE**   <Return>

dBASE will return with a display similar to that of Figure 2.20.

Step 7: Now let's add data to this database file. To do this, type:

. **APPEND**   <Return>

dBASE will display Figure 2.21. Use Figure 2.1 to add the first record of data. The screen should look as shown in Figure 2.22.

Now press the F2 key. The browse screen as shown in Figure 2.23 will be displayed. The cursor will be on the first record. To add the rest of the records, move the cursor to the blank row below the first record by using the <Down Arrow> key. The prompt "Add new records? (Y/N)" will appear at the bottom of the screen. Answer "Y." Add the rest of the records, and the screen should appear as in Figure 2.25.

Step 8: Next, terminate the process of adding records to the database file FILE1. Press <Alt-E> to select the Exit option of the menu bar, then choose the Exit option from the Pull-down Menu using the <Down Arrow> key, and finally press <Return>. dBASE will return with the dot prompt, indicating the completion of the process.

Step 9: Close the database file FILE1 by typing the following command:

. **USE**   <Return>

This will close the database file and complete Tutorial 5.

2.3 Accessing Database Files

Having learned to create a database file, you will now learn to display its contents on the screen. The most commonly used commands to accomplish this are DISPLAY, LIST, and BROWSE. The BROWSE command was introduced in section 2.2, where it was used to add data to the database file FILE1. Recall that when you used this command, the data of the database file were displayed on the screen as shown in Figure 2.25. You can also use this command for viewing (or displaying) data. But it is primarily used for data editing, which is described in Chapter 12, where I provide a detailed discussion of this command. In this section, I introduce the other two commands for accessing database files: DISPLAY and LIST.

First we need to load dBASE IV from the DBASE\INVOICE directory. Recall that the database file FILE1 that you created in the previous section was stored in that directory. Load dBASE IV from that directory after setting a path to the DBASE directory. (If you need any help, refer to Table 2.1 or Table 2.2, depending on the environment in which you are working.) When the control center appears, change to the dot prompt as explained at the beginning of this chapter.

2.3.1 Opening a Database File

Before you can access the data from any database file, you must open it. Most dBASE commands (dot prompt commands) will not have any effect on a database file until it is open. The USE command opens an existing database file.

The USE Command

The simple format of the USE command is

```
USE [<file name>]
```

where <file name> is the name of an existing database file. Because only a database (.DBF) file can be accessed with the USE command, you do not need to specify the extension with the file name.

The USE <file name> form of the command is used to open an existing database file whose name is mentioned in the command. For sexample, to open the database file FILE1.DBF, created and populated in section 2.2, you will need to type the following:

```
.USE FILE1    <Return>
```

After the command has been executed, the contents of the database file FILE1 are copied to the computer's internal memory (RAM) and are available for access. We say that the database file FILE1 is now *active* or *open*. When the USE command is used to open a database file, it will close any previously open database file.

Recall that the items enclosed in square brackets ([]) are optional. So if we use the USE command without the file name, it will not open any database file because no database file name is mentioned with it. However, it will close any previously open database file. We used this simple form of the USE command in section 2.2.2 to close the active database file FILE1.

The Current Record

dBASE IV assigns a unique record number to each record in your database file in the sequence the records are added to the database file, starting with one and increasing the record number by one for every record added.

When working with the database files, dBASE IV keeps track of the record currently being accessed by means of a record pointer. When a database file is opened, dBASE sets the pointer to the first record of the database file. The record to which the record pointer is pointing is called the **current record.**

Now let us proceed with our main goal of displaying or viewing the contents of the database file FILE1. dBASE IV provides several options for doing this. You can display one, all, or selected records from the database file. You may also display the selected fields with these options. Let us proceed with the first dBASE IV command for displaying the contents of the database file.

2.3.2 The DISPLAY Command

The general format of the DISPLAY command is

```
DISPLAY [<Scope>] [<field/expression>]
        [WHILE <condition>] [FOR <condition>] [OFF]
        [TO PRINT]
```

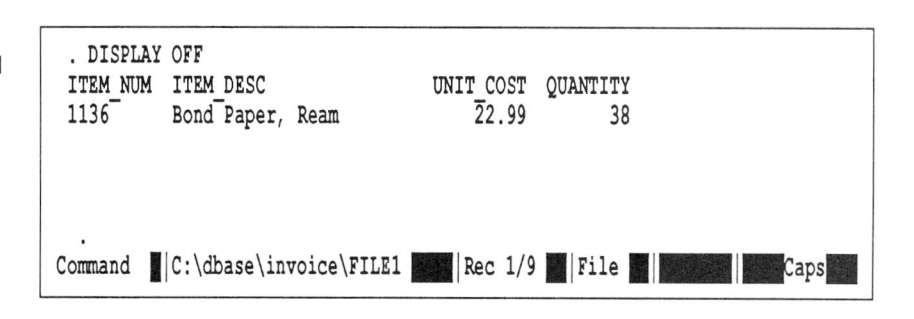

Figure 2.27 The report of the DISPLAY command

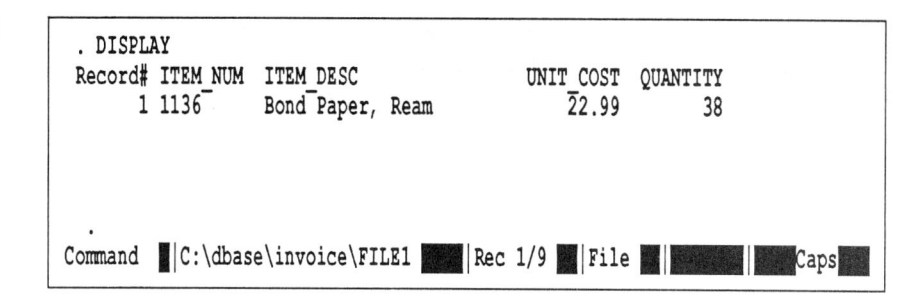

```
. DISPLAY
Record#  ITEM_NUM  ITEM_DESC              UNIT_COST  QUANTITY
      1  1136      Bond Paper, Ream           22.99        38
.
Command   C:\dbase\invoice\FILE1    Rec 1/9   File              Caps
```

where <Scope> specifies which parts of the database file are to be affected by the command, <field/expressions> is a list of field names and/or expressions, separated by commas, that restrict the display of fields and expressions that appear in the report, and <condition> is a valid search condition that selects the record from the database file to be displayed. The DISPLAY command has several different options available, depending on the parameters used.

DISPLAY

The DISPLAY command without any parameters displays the current record in the database file. Recall that you opened the database file FILE1 following the instructions in the previous paragraph. The record pointer will be pointing to the first record in the database file. To display the first record, type:

. **DISPLAY**   <Return>

dBASE will respond by displaying Figure 2.27. All fields of the first record are displayed in tabular form. The display also includes the record number.

DISPLAY OFF

This command will display the current record on the screen without displaying the record number. The OFF option suppresses the display of the record number. To see its effect, type:

. **DISPLAY OFF**   <Return>

The output will be as shown in Figure 2.28.

You can specify the records and fields to be displayed by including a scope, field list, or condition with the DISPLAY command. Scope options

Figure 2.28 The report of the DISPLAY OFF command

```
. DISPLAY OFF
ITEM_NUM  ITEM_DESC              UNIT_COST  QUANTITY
1136      Bond Paper, Ream           22.99        38
.
Command   C:\dbase\invoice\FILE1    Rec 1/9   File              Caps
```

Figure 2.29 The report of the DISPLAY NEXT 4 command

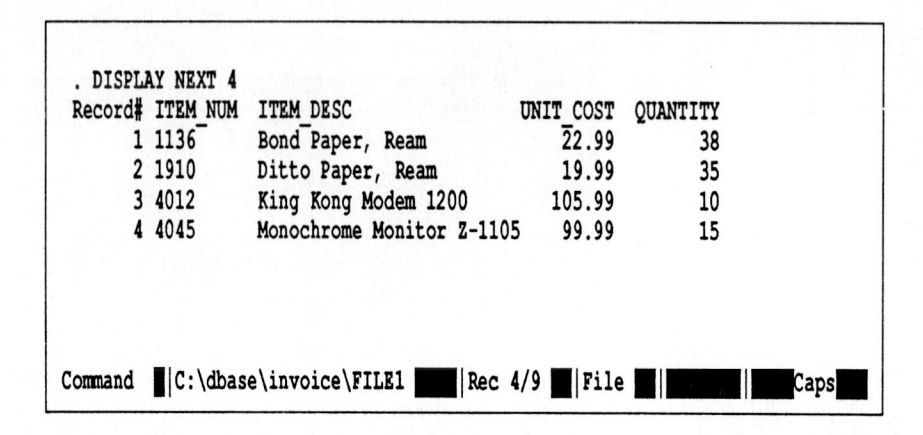

```
. DISPLAY NEXT 4
Record#  ITEM_NUM  ITEM_DESC              UNIT_COST  QUANTITY
     1   1136      Bond Paper, Ream           22.99       38
     2   1910      Ditto Paper, Ream          19.99       35
     3   4012      King Kong Modem 1200      105.99       10
     4   4045      Monochrome Monitor Z-1105  99.99       15


Command   ▌C:\dbase\invoice\FILE1    |Rec 4/9 ▌|File ▌|       |  Caps▌
```

such as NEXT, ALL, and REST can be included in the DISPLAY command to display several records. Some examples of the DISPLAY command with scope options NEXT and ALL are given in the following sections.

DISPLAY NEXT n

This command displays the current record and the (n−1) succeeding records; that is, it will display a total of n records starting from the current one. Note that n indicates the total number of records to be displayed.

To display the next four records, type:

    . DISPLAY NEXT 4   <Return>

dBASE will respond by displaying the report shown in Figure 2.29.

DISPLAY ALL

The DISPLAY ALL command will display all the records present in the database. It will display 20 records at a time and pause. Pressing any key will display the next 20 records, and this process will continue until the end of the database file is reached.

To display all the records of the database file FILE1, type:

    . DISPLAY ALL   <Return>

dBASE will respond as shown in Figure 2.30.

You can restrict the display of certain selected fields by adding the <fields> option to the DISPLAY command. The next example demonstrates the result of exercising this option.

DISPLAY ALL <field>

This command will display all the records in the database with only the selected fields mentioned after the DISPLAY ALL command. For example, type the following command:

    . DISPLAY ALL ITEM_NUM, ITEM_DESC, UNIT_COST
    <Return>

Figure 2.30 The report of the DISPLAY ALL command

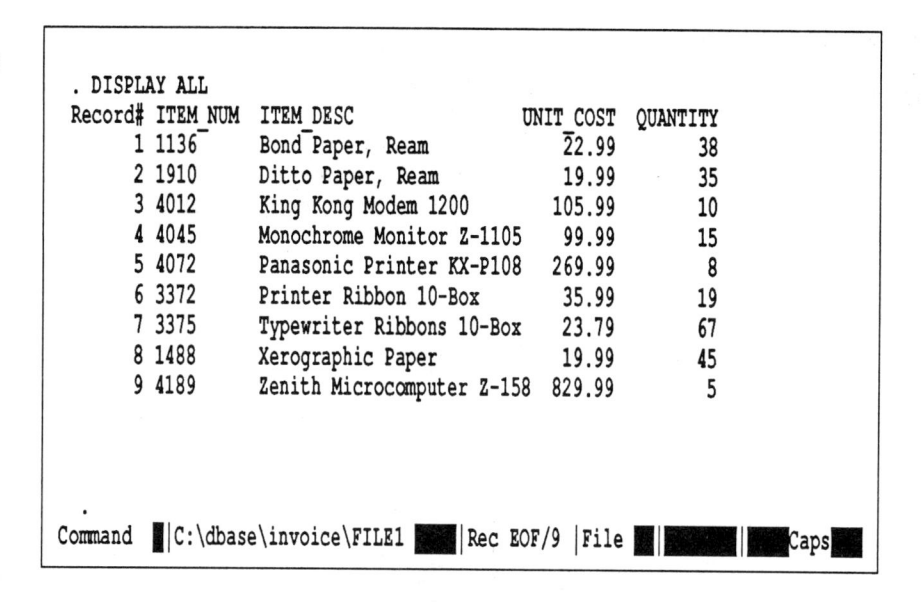

```
. DISPLAY ALL
Record#  ITEM_NUM  ITEM_DESC              UNIT_COST  QUANTITY
     1   1136      Bond Paper, Ream           22.99        38
     2   1910      Ditto Paper, Ream          19.99        35
     3   4012      King Kong Modem 1200      105.99        10
     4   4045      Monochrome Monitor Z-1105  99.99        15
     5   4072      Panasonic Printer KX-P108 269.99         8
     6   3372      Printer Ribbon 10-Box      35.99        19
     7   3375      Typewriter Ribbons 10-Box  23.79        67
     8   1488      Xerographic Paper          19.99        45
     9   4189      Zenith Microcomputer Z-158 829.99        5
.
Command  C:\dbase\invoice\FILE1  Rec EOF/9  File         Caps
```

Note that the fields are separated by commas. dBASE will respond by displaying the report as shown in Figure 2.31. Observe that this report contains only those fields present after the DISPLAY ALL (or LIST) command, that is, the ITEM_NUM, ITEM_DESC, and UNIT_COST fields. The LIST command will be discussed in section 2.3.3.

DISPLAY <field> FOR <condition>

The search condition is used to display from the database file a selective set of records that satisfy the condition. For example, the command

```
. DISPLAY ALL ITEM_NUM, ITEM_DESC, UNIT_COST FOR
UNIT_COST > 100       <Return>
```

Figure 2.31 The report of the DISPLAY ALL <fields> command

```
. DISPLAY ALL ITEM_NUM, ITEM_DESC, UNIT_COST
Record#  ITEM_NUM  ITEM_DESC              UNIT_COST
     1   1136      Bond Paper, Ream           22.99
     2   1910      Ditto Paper, Ream          19.99
     3   4012      King Kong Modem 1200      105.99
     4   4045      Monochrome Monitor Z-1105  99.99
     5   4072      Panasonic Printer KX-P108 269.99
     6   3372      Printer Ribbon 10-Box      35.99
     7   3375      Typewriter Ribbons 10-Box  23.79
     8   1488      Xerographic Paper          19.99
     9   4189      Zenith Microcomputer Z-158 829.99
.
Command  C:\dbase\invoice\FILE1  Rec EOF/9  File         Caps
```

Figure 2.32 The report of the DISPLAY ALL <field> <condition> command

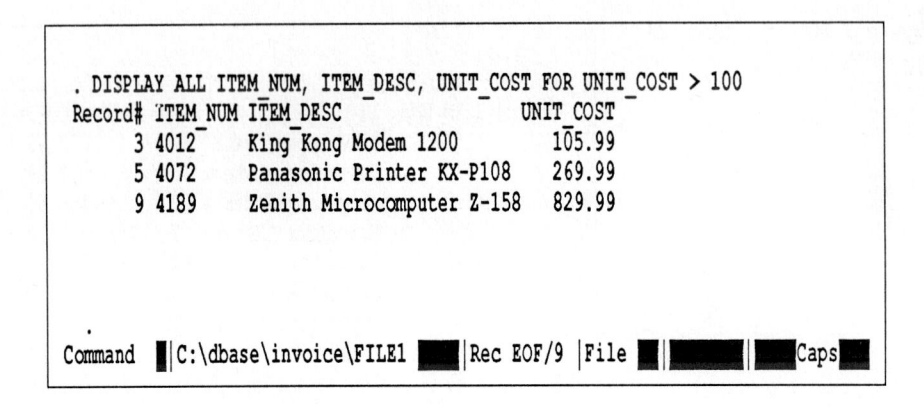

```
. DISPLAY ALL ITEM_NUM, ITEM_DESC, UNIT_COST FOR UNIT_COST > 100
Record#  ITEM_NUM  ITEM_DESC              UNIT_COST
      3  4012      King Kong Modem 1200      105.99
      5  4072      Panasonic Printer KX-P108 269.99
      9  4189      Zenith Microcomputer Z-158 829.99



Command   ┃C:\dbase\invoice\FILE1   ┃Rec EOF/9 ┃File ┃     ┃Caps┃
```

will respond by displaying the report shown in Figure 2.32. (dBASE IV accepts 1,024 characters per line. Due to text limitations here and throughout this book, commands may be represented on more than one line.)

This report consists of only those records of FILE1 that have a UNIT_COST value of more than $100 and contains only the ITEM_NUM, ITEM_DESC, and UNIT_COST fields.

DISPLAY HISTORY

This command displays the history of the commands entered at the dot prompt. dBASE can store up to 20 commands entered at the dot prompt in the history buffer. To display all the commands of this session, type the following command:

    .DISPLAY HISTORY   \<Return>

dBASE will respond by displaying the list of all the commands issued during this session, as shown in Figure 2.33.

You can restrict the number of dBASE history commands by adding the scope parameter to this command. For example, the command **DISPLAY HISTORY LAST 10** will display up to the last ten commands of the current session.

Figure 2.33 The report of the DISPLAY HISTORY command

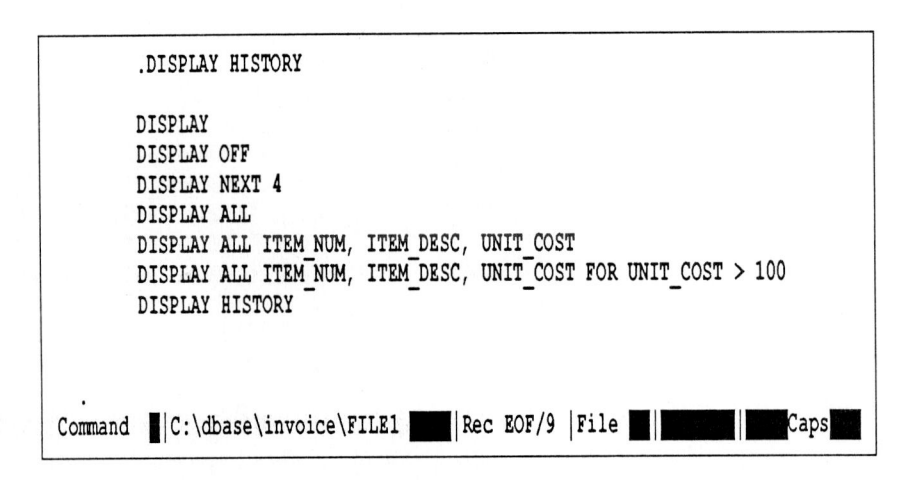

```
.DISPLAY HISTORY

DISPLAY
DISPLAY OFF
DISPLAY NEXT 4
DISPLAY ALL
DISPLAY ALL ITEM_NUM, ITEM_DESC, UNIT_COST
DISPLAY ALL ITEM_NUM, ITEM_DESC, UNIT_COST FOR UNIT_COST > 100
DISPLAY HISTORY



Command   ┃C:\dbase\invoice\FILE1   ┃Rec EOF/9 ┃File ┃     ┃Caps┃
```

2.3 Accessing Database Files

The default value for storing the number of dBASE IV commands in the computer's memory is 20. This number can be changed temporarily by using the *SET HISTORY TO* <n> command. It will change the number to the new value of "n." Using this command at the start of a session will change the default value to the new value specified for the period of the session. To change this value permanently, add this command to the CONFIG.DB file. You will learn how to do this in Chapter 3.

2.3.3 The LIST Command

The general format of the LIST command is

```
LIST [<Scope>] [<field/expression>]
     [WHILE <condition>] [FOR <condition>] [OFF]
     [TO PRINT]
```

where <Scope> specifies which parts of the database file are to be affected by the command, <field/expressions> is a list of field names and/or expressions, separated by commas, that restrict the listing of certain selected fields and expressions appearing in the report, and <condition> is a valid search condition that selects the record from the database file for listing. The LIST command also has several different options available, depending on the parameters used with it.

LIST

The LIST command works similarly to the DISPLAY ALL command; that is, it will display all the records in the database, but it will not pause every 20 records. It is a very useful command for a quick check of database contents. To pause anytime midlist, simply press <Ctrl-S>; to continue the listing, press any key.

To display (or list) all the records of the database file FILE1, type:

```
. LIST      <Return>
```

dBASE will respond by displaying the report shown in Figure 2.30.

LIST OFF

This command will list the entire database without displaying the record number along with the records. To see its effect, type:

```
. LIST OFF    <Return>
```

The output will be as shown in Figure 2.34 (see page 80).

LIST NEXT n

This command will list the next n number of records starting from the current record. To display the first six records, type:

```
. GOTO 1       <Return>
. LIST NEXT 6  <Return>
```

dBASE will respond by displaying the report as shown in Figure 2.35 (see page 80).

Figure 2.34 The report of the LIST OFF command

```
. LIST OFF
ITEM_NUM  ITEM_DESC              UNIT_COST  QUANTITY
1136      Bond Paper, Ream          22.99        38
1910      Ditto Paper, Ream         19.99        35
4012      King Kong Modem 1200     105.99        10
4045      Monochrome Monitor Z-1105 99.99        15
4072      Panasonic Printer KX-P108 269.99        8
3372      Printer Ribbon 10-Box     35.99        19
3375      Typewriter Ribbons 10-Box 23.79        67
1488      Xerographic Paper         19.99        45
4189      Zenith Microcomputer Z-158 829.99       5
.
Command   C:\dbase\invoice\FILE1   Rec EOF/9  File           Caps
```

The first command will move the record pointer to record number one, and the second command will list the next six records, starting from the position of the record pointer (the first record, in this case). You can restrict the display of certain selected fields by adding the <fields> option to the LIST command. The next example demonstrates this restriction.

LIST <field>

This command will list all the records in the database, but it will display only the fields mentioned after the LIST command. For example, type the following command:

```
. LIST ITEM_NUM, ITEM_DESC, UNIT_COST       <Return>
```

dBASE will produce the report as shown in Figure 2.31.

Figure 2.35 The report of the LIST NEXT 6 command

```
. LIST NEXT 6
Record#  ITEM_NUM  ITEM_DESC              UNIT_COST  QUANTITY
      1  1136      Bond Paper, Ream          22.99        38
      2  1910      Ditto Paper, Ream         19.99        35
      3  4012      King Kong Modem 1200     105.99        10
      4  4045      Monochrome Monitor Z-1105 99.99        15
      5  4072      Panasonic Printer KX-P108 269.99        8
      6  3372      Printer Ribbon 10-Box     35.99        19
.
Command   C:\dbase\invoice\FILE1   Rec 6/9    File           Caps
```

2.3 Accessing Database Files

LIST <field> FOR <condition>

This command will list all those records from the database file that meet all the conditions specified in the condition statement. For example, the command

```
. LIST ITEM_NUM, ITEM_DESC, UNIT_COST FOR
UNIT_COST > 100      <Return>
```

will produce the report shown in Figure 2.32.

The report lists all the records of the database file FILE1 whose UNIT_COST field value is greater than $100. Each record contains the ITEM_NUM, ITEM_DESC, and UNIT_COST fields.

2.3.4 Printing the Database

There are two ways to obtain a printed copy of any report displayed on the screen:

1. Through the use of the TO PRINT option
2. Through the use of the SET PRINT ON option

TO PRINT option

The TO PRINT option is used with the LIST or DISPLAY command to obtain a printed copy of the report instead of listing (or displaying) it only on the screen. The command

```
. LIST TO PRINT      <Return>
```

will produce the report on the screen as shown in Figure 2.36, as well as printing this report on the printer.

Figure 2.36 The report of the LIST TO PRINT command

```
. LIST TO PRINT
Record# ITEM_NUM  ITEM_DESC                 UNIT_COST  QUANTITY
      1 1136      Bond Paper, Ream              22.99        38
      2 1910      Ditto Paper, Ream             19.99        35
      3 4012      King Kong Modem 1200         105.99        10
      4 4045      Monochrome Monitor Z-1105     99.99        15
      5 4072      Panasonic Printer KX-P108    269.99         8
      6 3372      Printer Ribbon 10-Box         35.99        19
      7 3375      Typewriter Ribbons 10-Box     23.79        67
      8 1488      Xerographic Paper             19.99        45
      9 4189      Zenith Microcomputer Z-158   829.99         5


Command   ||C:\dbase\invoice\FILE1   |Rec EOF/9 |File              Caps
```

DISPLAY STRUCTURE TO PRINT

The TO PRINT option can also be used to create printed copies of any information to be kept as documentation for later use. The structure of the database file is one such item of information. To create a printed copy of the structure of the database file FILE1, type the following command:

```
. DISPLAY STRUCTURE TO PRINT     <Return>
```

It will produce a printed report as shown in Figure 2.20.

SET PRINT ON Option

If the SET PRINT ON command is used *before* the LIST command, the data will be displayed on the screen as well as printed on the printer. To see its effect, type:

```
. SET PRINT ON    <Return>
. LIST            <Return>
```

dBASE will respond by displaying the report on the screen as well as printing it on the printer, as shown in Figure 2.37.

dBASE has several default options. One of them is SET PRINT OFF, which means that the printer is set to OFF. In other words, everything entered on the keyboard, reports produced by dBASE commands, or programs will be displayed only on the screen.

But after the SET PRINT ON command, anything entered through the keyboard is displayed on the screen as well as on the printer. The reports produced by the dBASE command or programs will only be directed to the printer. After the need for the SET PRINT ON command is over, you should reset it back to OFF by entering the SET PRINT OFF command at the dot prompt.

Any time a dBASE default option is changed, it should be reset back to its default option after its use is completed.

Figure 2.37 Printed listing of the FILE1 database file

```
. SET PRINT ON
. LIST TO PRINT
Record#  ITEM_NUM  ITEM_DESC                UNIT_COST  QUANTITY
      1  1136      Bond Paper, Ream             22.99        38
      2  1910      Ditto Paper, Ream            19.99        35
      3  4012      King Kong Modem 1200        105.99        10
      4  4045      Monochrome Monitor Z-1105    99.99        15
      5  4072      Panasonic Printer KX-P108   269.99         8
      6  3372      Printer Ribbon 10-Box        35.99        19
      7  3375      Typewriter Ribbons 10-Box    23.79        67
      8  1488      Xerographic Paper            19.99        45
      9  4189      Zenith Microcomputer Z-158  829.99         5
```

2.3 Accessing Database Files 83

T U T O R I A L   6

Practice all the examples of the DISPLAY and LIST commands of sections 2.3.2, 2.3.3, and 2.3.4. Compare your results with the ones given in the book.

Solution

To complete this tutorial, follow these steps:

- **Step 1:** Boot up your system. If the system prompt is C>, proceed with step 2. If the prompt is C:\>, skip step 2, and proceed to step 3.
- **Step 2:** Type the PROMPT PG command as shown:

    `C>PROMPT $P$G     <Return>`

    The system will return with the C:\> prompt.
- **Step 3:** Load dBASE IV, and change the control from the control center mode to the dot prompt mode. To complete this step, follow the instructions given in Table 2.1 or Table 2.2, depending on the environment in which you are working.
- **Step 4:** Open the database file FILE1 by typing the following command:

    `USE FILE1     <Return>`

    dBASE will return by displaying the dot prompt. Recall that when a file is opened, the record pointer points to the first record of the database file FILE1.
- **Step 5:** a. To display the first record of the database file FILE1, type:

    `. DISPLAY     <Return>`

    dBASE will respond by displaying the results as shown in Figure 2.27.

    b. To display the first record of the database file FILE1 without the record number, type:

    `. DISPLAY OFF     <Return>`

    dBASE will respond by displaying the results as shown in Figure 2.28.

    c. To display the first four records of the database file FILE1, type:

    `. DISPLAY NEXT 4     <Return>`

    dBASE will respond by displaying the results as shown in Figure 2.29.

    d. To display all the records of the database file FILE1, type:

    `. DISPLAY ALL     <Return>`

dBASE will respond by displaying the results as shown in Figure 2.30.

e. To display all the records of the database file FILE1 containing only the ITEM_NUM, ITEM_DESC, and UNIT_COST fields, type:

```
. DISPLAY ALL ITEM_NUM, ITEM_DESC,
UNIT_COST     <Return>
```

dBASE will respond by displaying the results as shown in Figure 2.31.

f. To display all the records of the database file FILE1 whose UNIT_COST is greater than $100 and containing only the ITEM_NUM, ITEM_DESC, and UNIT_COST fields, type:

```
. DISPLAY ALL ITEM_NUM, ITEM_DESC,
UNIT_COST FOR UNIT_COST > 100    <Return>
```

dBASE will respond by displaying the results as shown in Figure 2.32.

g. To display the history of the commands entered at the dot prompt mode, type:

```
. DISPLAY HISTORY    <Return>
```

dBASE will respond by displaying the results as shown in Figure 2.33.

Step 6: Follow the instructions of section 2.3.3 to practice the following LIST command examples:

LIST

LIST OFF

LIST NEXT <n>

LIST <field>

LIST <field> FOR <condition>

The results should be as shown in Figures 2.30, 2.34, 2.35, 2.31, and 2.32, respectively.

Step 7: Follow the instructions of Section 2.3.4 to practice the following examples of the TO PRINT option and SET PRINT ON/OFF command:

LIST TO PRINT

DISPLAY STRUCTURE

LIST (with SET PRINT ON)

Compare your results with the output shown in Figures 2.36, 2.20, and 2.37, respectively.

This completes Tutorial 6.

2.4 A Few Shortcuts

You have learned several different dBASE commands in this chapter and had hands-on experience with them. While working on the tutorials of this chapter, you might have noticed that you had to do a lot of typing to enter those commands at the dot prompt. You might also have noticed that some of the commands were very close to their previously entered forms. In this section, you will learn how to save time in entering these commands by using some dBASE features.

2.4.1 Use of the Function Keys

The 10 function keys (marked F1, F2, . . . , F10) are represented in two columns on the left side of the keyboard. (There are 12 function keys along the top of the newer keyboards.) These are used to activate the special processing functions within the particular application software package.

In the dBASE IV environment, these keys have preassigned functions, which are listed and briefly described in Table 2.7 (see page 86). The listing of these keys along with their preassigned functions can be obtained by pressing the F6 Function key.

Try to use these function keys whenever possible. They save typing time and the frustration of typing errors. A few examples of the use of the function keys follow.

EXAMPLE 1: In Tutorial 5, step 6, the second paragraph can be modified as follows:

The database file FILE1 structure has been created and saved. Verify this by displaying the structure of this file. To do so, either press the F5 Display Structure key or type:

```
. DISPLAY STRUCTURE      <Return>
```

dBASE will return with a display similar to that of Figure 2.20.

EXAMPLE 2: In Tutorial 5, step 7 can be modified as follows:

Now let's add data to this database file. To do this, either press the F9 Append key or type:

```
. APPEND     <Return>
```

dBASE will display Figure 2.21.

EXAMPLE 3: In Tutorial 6, step 5(a) can be modified as follows:

To display the first record of the database file FILE1, either press the F8 Display key or type:

```
. DISPLAY    <Return>
```

dBASE will respond by displaying the results as shown in Figure 2.27.

EXAMPLE 4: In Tutorial 6, step 6, the listing of all the records of the database file FILE1 can be obtained either by pressing the F3 List key or by typing:

```
. LIST     <Return>
```

dBASE will respond by displaying the results as shown in Figure 2.30.

Table 2.7 Function key assignments and their functions

Function Key	Command	Explanation
F1	HELP	Places you in the help mode, where you can view a series of help screens. To end help, press the Esc key, and you will return to the dBASE dot prompt mode.
F2	ASSIST	Places you in the control center mode of dBASE IV.
F3	LIST	Invokes the LIST command, displaying information from the currently selected database file. If no database file has been selected, you will be prompted to enter the name of the database file.
F4	DIR	Invokes the DIR command within dBASE. This DIR command operates differently from the DOS DIR command—only .DBF (database) files are listed. If the listing of the other file types is desired, you can use wild cards with different file extensions. For example, Dir *.PRG or DIR *.NDX will list the program or index files instead of the database (.DBF) files.
F5	DISPLAY STRUCTURE	Invokes the DISPLAY STRUCTURE command. This command will list the structure of the currently selected database file.
F6	DISPLAY STATUS	Invokes the DISPLAY STATUS command. Displays the status of dBASE IV and the list of function key assignments.
F7	DISPLAY MEMORY	Invokes the DISPLAY MEMORY command. Displays the contents and specifications of the currently active memory variables.
F8	DISPLAY	Invokes the DISPLAY command. This command displays the current record of the open or active database file.
F9	APPEND	Invokes the APPEND command. The full screen edit mode is invoked, which allows the addition of new records to the currently selected open database file.
F10	EDIT	Invokes the EDIT command. The full screen edit mode is invoked, which allows changes to the existing records in the database file.

2.4 A Few Shortcuts

Table 2.8 Function key assignment

Function Key	Assignment
F1	Help
F2	Assist
F3	List
F4	Dir
F5	Display Structure
F6	Display Status
F7	Display Memory
F8	Display
F9	Append
F10	Edit

A Useful Suggestion

Obtain the listing of the function keys assignment by pressing the F6 Display Status key, and then get the printed copy of the screen by pressing <Shift-PrtSc>. Cut out the part of function key assignment as shown in Table 2.8, paste it on a 3" x 5" index card, and carry it with you. Use it whenever you work with dBASE IV; it will save you time and frustration. It will also help you become an expert in the use of dBASE IV.

2.4.2 Use of the History Buffer

In section 2.3.2, you learned that dBASE IV stores the previously typed commmands at the dot prompt in a history buffer. These commands can be recalled and used as they are, or they can be used after modifications, instead of retyping them. Modifying the commands in the buffer will save time and avoid the frustration of retyping errors. The <Up Arrow> or <Down Arrow> keys can be used to display and scroll through the list of previously used commands. When you find the desired command, you can execute it or make modifications employing the standard edit keys, then execute the command by pressing <Return>.

For example, in Tutorial 6, step 6, to obtain the listing of all the records of the database file FILE1 containing only the ITEM_NUM, ITEM_DESC, and UNIT_COST fields, you should not type the command LIST ITEM_NUM, ITEM_DESC, UNIT_COST. Instead obtain its equivalent DISPLAY command, make the required modifications, and then execute it. Use the <Up Arrow> or <Down Arrow> key, and scroll through the list of previously entered commands until you find the DISPLAY ALL ITEM_NUM, ITEM_DESC, UNIT_COST command. Now delete DISPLAY ALL by using either the <Backspace> key or the <Del> key, and type LIST in its place while the keyboard is in the Insert Mode. Now execute this command by pressing <Return>.

Use the history buffer to save retyping time and avoid the frustration of retyping errors.

2.5 Justification for Loading dBASE IV from the APPLICATION Directory

As stated in section 1.4.3, there are two possible ways to select the directory from which to load dBASE IV:

1. From the DBASE directory where dBASE IV is loaded
2. From the APPLICATION subdirectory of the DBASE directory

To determine which of these is more appropriate, assume you have decided to store all the programs and the database files used in this book in the DBASE\INVOICE directory. This discussion is restricted to the functions or commands presented in this chapter (creating the database file structure, displaying the structure, adding records to the database file, displaying the current record of the active database file, and listing all the records of the currently active file). These functions can be grouped into two categories: (1) searching the directory to store the newly created file and (2) searching the directory to open a database file to retrieve the data. We'll study the two options for these two categories of functions.

Option 1 is to load dBASE IV from the DBASE directory. When you want to create the database file FILE1 and store it in the DBASE\INVOICE directory, you will need one of the following commands:

```
. CREATE \DBASE\INVOICE\FILE1      <Return>
. CREATE .\INVOICE\FILE1           <Return>
```

Here you will have to include the path \DBASE\INVOICE or .\INVOICE to the directory where the file has to be stored.

To open the database file to retrieve the data, either mention the path in the USE command or set a path to this directory at the start of the session using the SET PATH TO\DBASE\INVOICE command or SET PATH TO.\INVOICE\FILE1, thus avoiding use of the path in the USE command. For example, to open a file FILE1 stored in the DBASE\INVOICE directory, you'll need the following command if the path is not set to this directory.

```
. USE \DBASE\INVOICE\FILE1    <Return>
```

But if the path command is used at the start of the session, you will need this command:

```
. USE FILE1    <Return>
```

As you have seen, to create and open the database file FILE1 from the DBASE\INVOICE directory, you need the two commands as shown in Figure 2.38(a) if no path is set to this directory.

But if the path is set to this directory at the start of the session by either of these commands

```
. SET PATH TO \DBASE\INVOICE    <Return>
. SET PATH TO .\INVOICE         <Return>
```

these two commands will change as shown in Figure 2.38(b).

```
    . CREATE \DBASE\INVOICE\FILE1           <Return>
OR  . CREATE .\INVOICE\FILE1                <Return>
    . USE \DBASE\INVOICE\FILE1              <Return>
OR  . USE .\INVOICE\FILE1                   <Return>
```
(a)

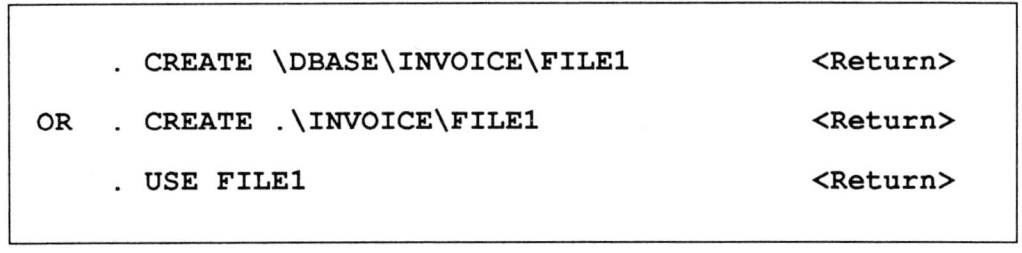

```
    . CREATE \DBASE\INVOICE\FILE1           <Return>
OR  . CREATE .\INVOICE\FILE1                <Return>
    . USE FILE1                             <Return>
```
(b)

Figure 2.38 CREATE and USE commands from the DBASE directory (a) without setting the path and (b) after setting the path

Even after setting the path to the target directory, you still have to mention the path in the CREATE command. However, the path is not needed in the USE command.

Option 2 is to load dBASE IV from the DBASE\INVOICE directory with the path set to the DBASE directory. To create and open the database file FILE1 to be stored in the \DBASE\INVOICE directory, you'll need the commands as shown in Figure 2.39. There will be no need to set any path.

If we use option 2 (load dBASE IV from the application directory—\DBASE\INVOICE), we do not need to include the path in the CREATE and USE commands. The commands are simple, short, and easy to type. Therefore, it takes less typing time and is the best option for loading dBASE IV. For this reason, this approach of loading dBASE IV from the application directory has been used and advocated in this book.

2.6 Summary

This chapter introduces two very important functions of dBASE IV: how to create and populate a database file and how to access data from it.

```
    . CREATE FILE1                          <Return>
    . USE FILE1                             <Return>
```

Figure 2.39 CREATE and USE commands from the DBASE\INVOICE directory

dBASE databases can be created using the CREATE command. The data field names, types, lengths, and indexes can be specified.

Once a database is created, its layout, or structure, can be displayed using the DISPLAY STRUCTURE command.

All databases that are activated or created within dBASE should be closed before exiting dBASE.

Records can be added to a database using the APPEND or BROWSE commands.

Information in the database can be displayed using the DISPLAY or LIST command. Both have various options that control their operation. DISPLAY has OFF, NEXT, ALL, <fields>, FOR <condition>, and TO PRINT options. LIST has OFF, NEXT, <fields>, FOR <condition>, and TO PRINT options.

Data in the databases can also be sent to the printer using the TO PRINT option of the DISPLAY and LIST commands. Additionally, the SET PRINT ON command allows the user to direct output to the printer.

KEY CONCEPTS

current record
database design form
database design screen
database file data
database file structure

menu bar
message line
navigation line
Pull-down Menu
status bar

dBASE COMMANDS AND FUNCTIONS

APPEND command
BROWSE command
CREATE command
DISPLAY command
DISPLAY ALL command
DISPLAY ALL <field> command
DISPLAY ALL <field> FOR <condition> command
DISPLAY HISTORY command
DISPLAY NEXT <n> command
DISPLAY OFF command
DISPLAY STRUCTURE command
LIST command

LIST <field> command
LIST <field> FOR <condition> command
LIST NEXT <n> command
LIST OFF command
SET CARRY ON command
SET HISTORY TO command
SET PRINT ON command
TO PRINT command
USE command
USE <file name> command

REVIEW QUESTIONS

1. List three steps in creating a database file.
2. Why can't a single letter name be assigned to database files?
3. List the different parts of the database design screen.
4. Explain how to select an option from the menu bar.
5. Explain how to select an option from the Pull-down Menu.
6. List the five different sections of the status bar. Give a brief description of each.

7. What is the purpose of a navigation line?
8. List the six columns of the database design form.
9. List two methods of selecting a data type, and explain each briefly.
10. What is the purpose of indexing a field in the record of the database file?
11. While defining the database form,
    a. what key(s) are used for moving the cursor within a field?
    b. what key(s) are used for moving the cursor from one field to another field?
    c. what key(s) are used for moving the cursor from one column to another column to the right?
    d. what key(s) are used for moving the cursor from one column to another column to the left?
12. While defining the database form, what key combination is used
    a. to insert a blank field between two existing fields?
    b. to delete the current field?
13. What is the function of the DISPLAY STRUCTURE command? Why should a printed copy of the database file structure be kept with the documentation?
14. What dBASE commands can be used to add data to the database file?
15. What is the main drawback of the BROWSE command over the APPEND command for adding data to the database file?
16. List the steps for adding data to the memo field.
17. While adding data to the database file, how can data be carried over from one record to the next? List two options available for carrying over data, and describe them briefly.
18. List and briefly explain the two different uses of the USE command.
19. List all the possible and/or different options available with the DISPLAY command.
20. List all the possible and/or different options available with the LIST command.
21. What is the purpose of the DISPLAY HISTORY command? How is it used to save time in entering commands at the dot prompt mode?
22. What is the purpose of the TO PRINT option? How is it different from the SET PRINT ON command?

PART 2

**PROGRAM DEVELOPMENT
USING dBASE IV**

The dBASE IV commands used in the creation, modification, and execution of dBASE programs are introduced in Chapter 3. The program development process used in the design of a dBASE program and the functions performed by each of its five phases are introduced in Chapter 4. Different control structures used to design the solution of the program (sequence control structure, selection control structure, and iteration control structure) are also introduced in this chapter.

The dBASE commands used to create, save, delete, and load the memory variables into RAM are presented next in Chapter 5, followed by the most commonly used dBASE summary statistical commands. Editing the contents of the database file or its structure is explained in Chapter 6. The SORT command (used to organize the data by physically rearranging the records of the database file and creating a new database file), the COPY command, and the concept of the control break are introduced in Chapter 7. A simple report listing batch program is developed at the end of Chapters 4–7 using the program development process and the dBASE concepts discussed in these chapters.

The case control structure, which is an extension of the selection control structure and the dBASE command DO CASE-ENDCASE used with it, are introduced in Chapter 8. These are used to develop the menu program. A simple menu program using the program development process is also designed in this chapter.

Chapter 3

Introduction to dBASE IV Programming

LEARNING OBJECTIVES

Upon successfully completing this chapter, you will be able to:

1. Write a simple dBASE program to create a report.
2. Create program files using the dBASE text editor.
3. Modify an existing program file using the dBASE text editor.
4. Execute a program file.
5. Change the default features of dBASE IV using the SET command.
6. Use an external text editor to create and modify a program file.
7. Modify the AUTOEXEC.BAT file.
8. Modify the CONFIG.DB file.

3.1 Overview

In Chapter 2, you learned how to create a database file and access the data from it. You had experience working with several dBASE IV commands. After working with the dot prompt mode of dBASE IV, you are now about to move on to the most powerful feature of dBASE IV, the programming mode.

The dot prompt mode, where you interact with dBASE IV using one command at a time, is the basis for the programming mode, in which you can store a set of commands in a computer file called a command file (also called a program file). You can access the program file later to execute the commands contained in it as a group (or in a batch). As described in Chapter 1, the programming mode has the following advantages over the dot prompt mode:

1. Increased speed of execution
2. Elimination of typing errors
3. Availability of ready-made applications for novice users

In this chapter, you will be introduced to the programming mode and get acquainted with the basic principles used in structured programming. You will also learn how to create, edit, save, and execute simple dBASE IV programs.

3.2 dBASE IV Programming

A program is a collection of instructions or commands to perform a particular task. When the instructions are written in dBASE, it is called a **command file** or a **dBASE program file.** I refer to it as a "program file" or simply a "program" in the rest of this book. To perform a particular task, we need a sequence of instructions or commands. Recall that to display all the records of the database file FILE1, you needed the following commands:

```
. USE FILE1      <Return>
. DISPLAY ALL    <Return>
```

Note: The previous discussion assumed that the database file in question (FILE1) is stored on the floppy disk in disk drive A: (if you are working in the laboratory environment) or in the DBASE\INVOICE directory (if you are working in the nonlaboratory environment). It also assumed that you have loaded dBASE IV from the DBASE directory and set the disk drive A: as the default drive following the steps listed in Table 2.1 or from the DBASE\INVOICE directory with a path set to the DBASE directory following the steps listed in Table 2.2, depending on the environment in which you are working. I make the same assumption for all the files used with dBASE IV in the rest of the book.

Whenever you want to perform this task, you must enter these commands. But it is troublesome to enter them over and over again, particularly for the novice user. It is easy to make typing mistakes. To avoid this, you can store these instructions in the computer's auxiliary storage and retrieve and execute them whenever the need arises. Such files, called command files or dBASE program files, are stored with a .PRG extension. The next section explains how you can create dBASE program files using the dBASE text editor.

3.2.1 Creating a dBASE Program

dBASE IV has a built-in text editor for developing dBASE programs. The **dBASE text editor** is a word processor whose primary function is creating and editing dBASE IV program files. The dBASE program files created using the dBASE built-in text editor are in standard ASCII text file format. To create and edit dBASE programs, the text editor is invoked by the MODIFY COMMAND command.

The MODIFY COMMAND Command

The format of the MODIFY COMMAND is

```
MODIFY COMMAND <program file name>
```

where <program file name> is the name of the program file to be created or edited. The PRG extension is automatically added to the program by dBASE if the program is created using the dBASE text editor.

MODIFY COMMAND is used to invoke the dBASE IV text editor for creating and modifying dBASE programs. When the MODIFY COMMAND command is given to dBASE IV, it searches for the specified file in the current working directory or the directory specified in the path with the program file name. If the file already exists, the dBASE text editor brings it to the screen for editing. If the file does not exist, the dBASE text editor creates it.

Now let us create a small program file named PROG1 and save it in the current working directory. It should contain the two commands discussed in section 3.2. To create this dBASE program file, you'll need the following command:

```
. MODIFY COMMAND PROG1      <Return>
```

This will invoke the dBASE text editor, and a blank screen, as shown in Figure 3.1, will be presented (see page 98).

The dBASE IV text editor screen consists of the menu bar, ruler, work surface area, and the status bar. Within the ruler, a "v" stands for tab stops, which are used for indenting the dBASE commands within the program to improve readability. The work surface area is used for entering and displaying the commands.

The commands, typed from the keyboard, are displayed on the work surface area. dBASE is not case sensitive; that is, the commands can be entered in mixed lower and uppercase letters. But for clarity and readability, use only one case, either upper or lower. All commands in this book are in uppercase.

Each command must be terminated with a <Return>. The length of a command cannot exceed 1024 characters. If the command is longer than the width of the screen, it will keep moving to the left of the screen to provide space for the rest of the command to be entered. When you obtain

Figure 3.1 dBASE text editor screen

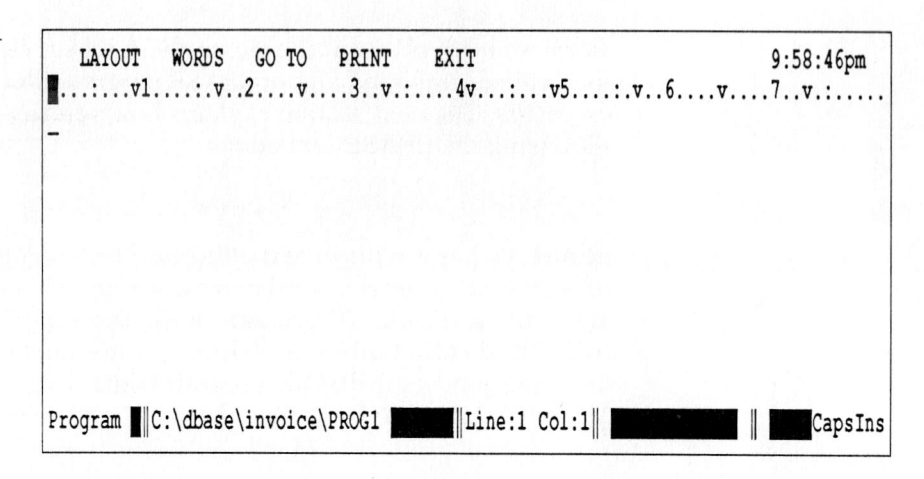

```
 LAYOUT   WORDS   GO TO   PRINT   EXIT                    9:58:46pm
 ...:...v1....:.v..2....v....3..v.:....4v...:..v5....:.v..6....v....7..v.:....




















 Program  C:\dbase\invoice\PROG1     Line:1 Col:1              CapsIns
```

the listing of the program file, the command lines longer than the width of the screen will automatically be wrapped around to the next line. The wrapped text will not look neat, but wrapping does not affect command content. The dBASE IV text editor can create and edit program files containing as many as 32,000 lines of code.

As in Figure 3.1, dBASE is now in the program edit mode, and there is no dot prompt. The following two commands can be typed, but do not type a dot (.) with them.

```
USE FILE1      <Return>
DISPLAY ALL    <Return>
```

Use the following guidelines to create or edit the program files.

1. Use the arrow keys to move the cursor on the screen.
2. Use the <PgUp> and <PgDn> keys to scroll the cursor up and down the screen.
3. Use the <Ins>, <Del>, and <Backspace> keys to make corrections.
4. Use <Ctrl-N> to insert a line at the cursor location and <Ctrl-Y> to delete a line at the cursor location.
5. Use the <Esc> key to leave the text editor without saving the changes in the program file.
6. Use <Ctrl-W> (or <Ctrl-End>) to save the program file and exit the text editor.
7. Use <Ctrl-KW> to save the program file to another file name.
8. Use <Ctrl-KR> to read another program file into the current program file at the cursor location.

These guidelines are listed and summarized in Table 3.1 for future reference.

After the commands have been entered, the work surface area will be similar to Figure 3.2.

3.2 dBASE IV Programming

Table 3.1 Frequently used keys for the MODIFY COMMAND command

Key	Function
↑	To move cursor up one line
↓	To move cursor down one line
→	To move cursor one character to right
←	To move cursor one character to left
PgUp	To scroll screen up one page
PgDn	To scroll screen down one page
Ins	To change the overwrite mode to the insert mode and vice versa
Del	To delete the character over the cursor
Backspace	To move the cursor one space back and erase the previous character
Ctrl-N	To insert a blank line at the cursor location
Ctrl-Y	To delete the entire line over the cursor
Esc or Ctrl-Q	To abort the editing of the program file without saving changes
Ctrl-W or Ctrl-End	To save the program file with all changes
Ctrl-KW	To save the program file to another file name
Ctrl-KR	To read another program file into the current program file at the cursor location
Enter or (Return)	To terminate a command (This will insert a new line if the insert mode is ON.)

3.2.2 Saving the dBASE Program

To exit from the text editor and save this program, press <Ctrl-W> or <Ctrl-End>. The program file will be saved under the PROG1.PRG name and stored in the current working directory. The extension .PRG will be added by dBASE. When the program is saved, dBASE will return with the dot prompt.

Figure 3.2 dBASE text editor with PROG1

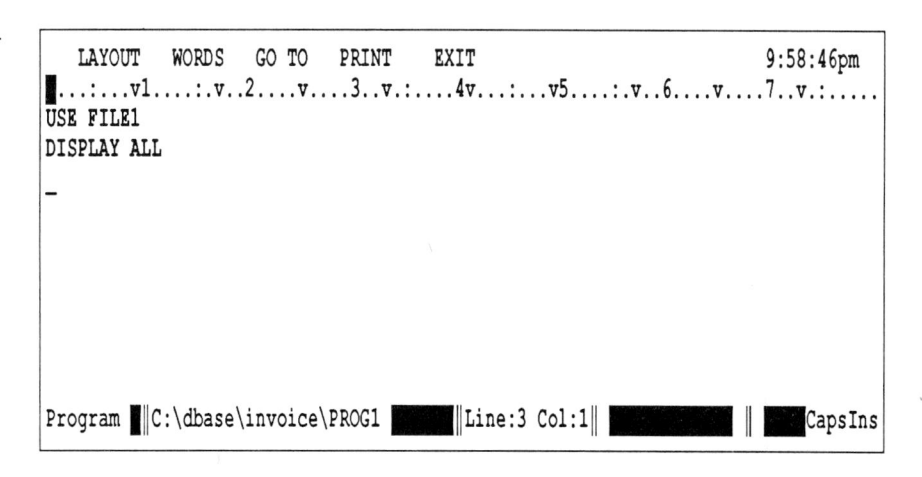

```
   LAYOUT   WORDS   GO TO   PRINT    EXIT                        9:58:46pm
█..:...v1....:.v..2....v....3..v.:....4v...:...v5....:.v..6....v....7..v.:....
USE FILE1
DISPLAY ALL
─




                                                                                
 Program ▌▌C:\dbase\invoice\PROG1    ▌▌Line:3 Col:1▌▌          ▌▌    ▌CapsIns
```

3.2.3 Executing the dBASE Program

To execute the program files, use the DO command.

The DO Command

The format of the DO command is

```
DO <program file name>
```

where <program file name> must be the name of a program file (.PRG).

The DO command executes the program specified in the program file name; that is, it instructs dBASE IV to execute the commands included in the program file and perform the operations specified by those commands. Because only program files can be specified with the DO command, there is no need to include the .PRG extension with the program file name. But if the program file has a different extension from .PRG, include that extension with the file name.

The program file PROG1 created in the previous section can be executed by typing the following command:

```
. DO PROG1     <Return>
```

dBASE will compile and then execute PROG1 and respond by displaying the result as shown in Figure 3.3.

Unlike dBASE III and its predecessors, dBASE IV has its own compiler. All the previous versions of dBASE used the interpreter, which means that every time a program was executed, each line was checked for syntax errors by the dBASE interpreter and then translated into machine language before execution. Therefore, the execution of the programs was not efficient with previous versions of dBASE.

dBASE IV has its own built-in compiler. When the program is executed for the first time, dBASE IV compiles the program file (.PRG) into an object file with the same program file name but with the .DBO extension. The compiling process checks each command line for syntax

Figure 3.3 The output produced by PROG1

```
. DO PROG1
Compiling line     2
Record# ITEM_NUM  ITEM_DESC               UNIT_COST  QUANTITY
     1  1136      Bond Paper, Ream           22.99        38
     2  1910      Ditto Paper, Ream          19.99        35
     3  4012      King Kong Modem 1200      105.99        10
     4  4045      Monochrome Monitor Z-1105  99.99        15
     5  4072      Panasonic Printer KX-P108 269.99         8
     6  3372      Printer Ribbon 10-Box      35.99        19
     7  3375      Typewriter Ribbons 10-Box  23.79        67
     8  1488      Xerographic Paper          19.99        45
     9  4189      Zenith Microcomputer Z-158 829.99        5
.
Command   C:\DBASE\INVOICE\FILE1    Rec EOF/9    FILE    Caps
```

3.2 dBASE IV Programming

errors and then translates the commands into machine language. Then dBASE IV executes this (.DBO) program to produce the desired results. dBASE does not have to go through the compilation process for every future program execution. It simply executes the already compiled program, which accounts for the increased efficiency and speed of dBASE IV.

3.2.4 Modification of a dBASE Program

Now we will modify the program file created in the previous section (PROG1) so it will display the whole database file as before but limit the fields to ITEM_NUM, ITEM_DESC, and UNIT_COST. To do this, we must edit the existing program file, PROG1.PRG. Invoke the dBASE text editor by typing the following command:

. **MODIFY COMMAND PROG1**   <Return>

dBASE will respond by displaying the information as shown in Figure 3.2.

To start with, the cursor will be positioned at the first position in the first row. The program file can be edited by using the <Ins>, <Del>, <Backspace>, and arrow keys. Move the cursor to the position one space after the word *all*, and press the <Ins> key once. This will put the editor in the insert mode, which is indicated by the entry "Ins" on the right-hand corner of the status bar. Now complete the command by entering ITEM_NUM, ITEM_DESC, and UNIT_COST. The modified program file should look like that in Figure 3.4.

To save this modified version of the program, press <Ctrl-W> or <Ctrl-End>. The screen will clear, and the control will return to the dot prompt. When programs are edited and saved, the dBASE text editor also keeps the unedited program file, saving it under the same program name but with a .BAK extension.

To verify this, get a directory listing of the current working directory by typing the following command:

. **DIR PROG1.***   <Return>

This command is asking for a listing of all the files named PROG1 in the current working directory. The system will respond by displaying the listing as shown in Figure 3.5 (see page 102).

Figure 3.4 dBASE text editor with modified PROG1

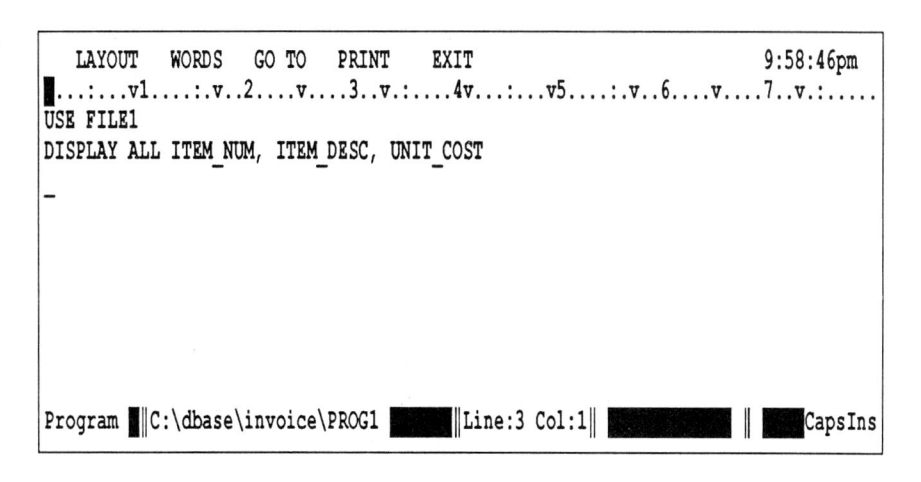

```
  LAYOUT    WORDS    GO TO    PRINT    EXIT                      9:58:46pm
■...:...v1....:.v..2....v....3..v.:....4v...:...v5....:.v..6....v....7..v.:.....
USE FILE1
DISPLAY ALL ITEM_NUM, ITEM_DESC, UNIT_COST
_




   Program   C:\dbase\invoice\PROG1      Line:3 Col:1              CapsIns
```

Figure 3.5 Directory of the DBASE\INVOICE subdirectory

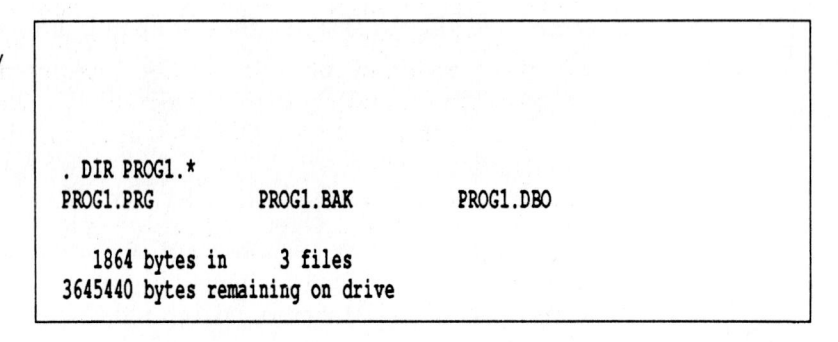

```
. DIR PROG1.*
PROG1.PRG          PROG1.BAK          PROG1.DBO

   1864 bytes in     3 files
3645440 bytes remaining on drive
```

The DIR (dBASE) command works like the DIR (DOS) command except that when the DIR (dBASE) command is used without any parameters, it lists only the database (.DBF) files and not all the files, as with the DIR (DOS) command. The other types of files can be displayed by adding the extension or using a wild card character in the place of the extension.

Note that the listing in Figure 3.5 contains three entries named PROG1. The first is PROG1.PRG, which is the modified version of the program file. The second is the old version of the program file stored under the new name, PROG1.BAK, and the third is the compiled version of the PROG1 stored as PROG1.DBO.

To execute the modified version of the program file PROG1.PRG, type the following command:

```
. DO PROG1     <Return>
```

dBASE will respond by displaying a slightly different report than before, as shown in Figure 3.6. When the modified version of the program PROG1 is executed, it differs from the original version, so dBASE IV will first compile and then execute it.

How does dBASE know about the changes in a program file? When a program is compiled, its compiled version (.DBO) keeps the date/time

Figure 3.6 The output produced by a modified PROG1

```
. DO PROG1
Compiling line     2
Record#  ITEM_NUM  ITEM_DESC                  UNIT_COST
      1  1136      Bond Paper, Ream               22.99
      2  1910      Ditto Paper, Ream              19.99
      3  4012      King Kong Modem 1200          105.99
      4  4045      Monochrome Monitor Z-1105      99.99
      5  4072      Panasonic Printer KX-P108     269.99
      6  3372      Printer Ribbon 10-Box          35.99
      7  3375      Typewriter Ribbons 10-Box      23.79
      8  1488      Xerographic Paper              19.99
      9  4189      Zenith Microcomputer Z-158    829.99
.
Command  C:\dbase\invoice\FILE1     Rec EOF/9    FILE       Caps
```

3.2 dBASE IV Programming

stamp from the original program file. When the original version of the program is changed and saved, its date/time stamp changes. When this modified version of the program file is executed, the compiler compares the date/time stamps of this program file with that of the previous compiled program file. If they match, no compiling is needed, and only the execution is performed. If they don't match, dBASE will compile the program file and create a new object code with a new date/time stamp and then execute this newly created object code.

Clearing the Screen

If you carefully observe the output displayed in Figures 3.3 and 3.6, you will notice there are two extra lines (".DO PROG1" and "Compiling line 2") at the top of the reports. To produce a report without any extra information on the screen, clear the screen before displaying the program output by using the CLEAR command.

The CLEAR Command

The format of the CLEAR command is

```
CLEAR
```

The function of this command is to clear the screen. To modify program file PROG1.PRG, invoke the dBASE text editor once again by typing this command:

```
. MODIFY COMMAND PROG1      <Return>
```

dBASE will respond by displaying the information as given in Figure 3.4.

Now add the CLEAR command between the two existing commands in the program. To do this, move the cursor to the "D" (the first letter of the DISPLAY command), and press <Ctrl-N>. This will introduce a blank line between the two commands, as shown in Figure 3.7.

Now move the cursor to the blank line, and type the CLEAR command. The screen will look as shown in Figure 3.8 (see page 104).

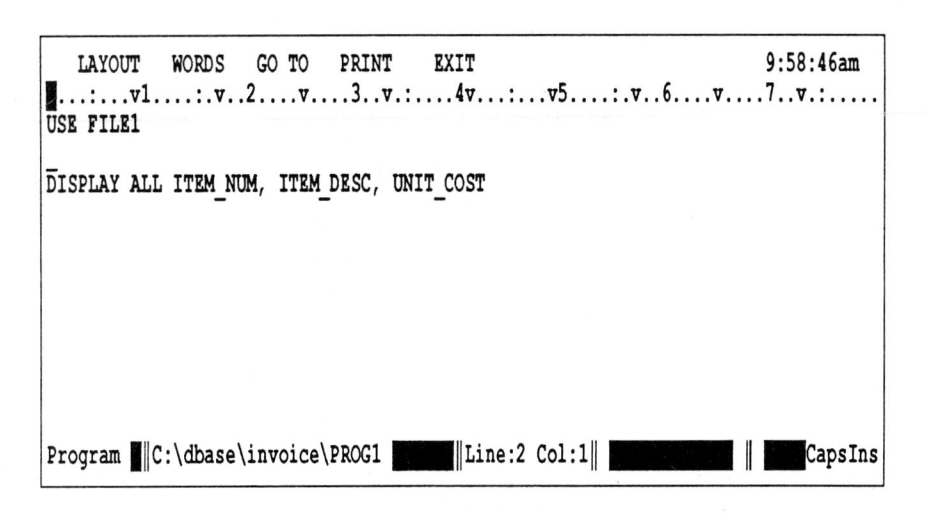

Figure 3.7 Unedited version of PROG1

```
   LAYOUT    WORDS    GO TO    PRINT    EXIT                    9:58:46am
█...:...v1....:.v..2....v....3..v.:....4v...:...v5....:.v..6....v....7..v.:.....
USE FILE1

DISPLAY ALL ITEM_NUM, ITEM_DESC, UNIT_COST





 
 



Program  ║C:\dbase\invoice\PROG1    ║Line:2 Col:1║           ║   CapsIns
```

Figure 3.8 Edited version of PROG1

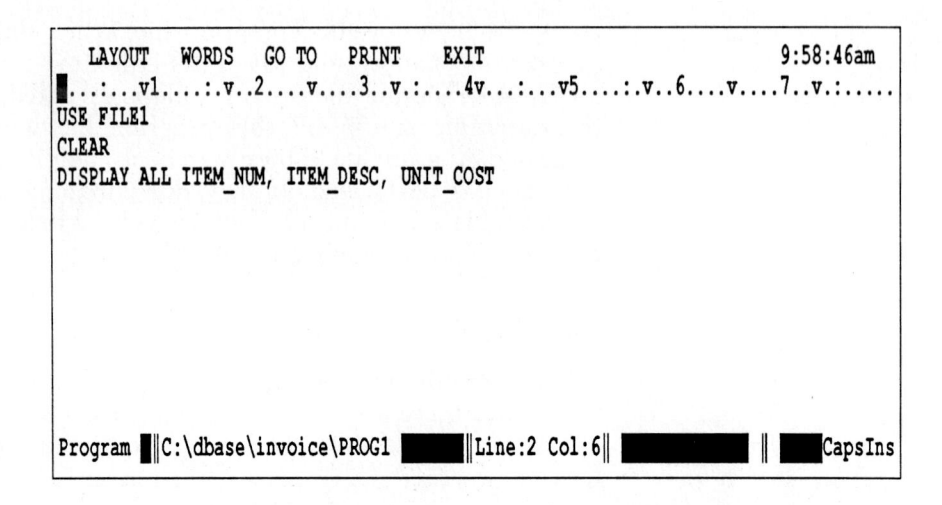

```
   LAYOUT   WORDS    GO TO    PRINT    EXIT                    9:58:46am
▌...:...v1....:.v..2....v....3..v.:....4v...:..v5....:.v..6....v....7..v.:....
USE FILE1
CLEAR
DISPLAY ALL ITEM_NUM, ITEM_DESC, UNIT_COST




Program ▌C:\dbase\invoice\PROG1   ▌Line:2 Col:6▌            ▌ ▌CapsIns
```

Any database files opened in the program should be closed at the end of each program by adding the USE command. Move the cursor to the blank line below the DISPLAY ALL command, and type USE. The modified version of the program will be as shown in Figure 3.9.

Now save this final edited version of the program by pressing <Ctrl-W> or <Ctrl-End>. The screen will clear, and the control will return to the dot prompt.

This final edited version of the program PROG1 can be executed by typing the following command:

. **DO PROG1**   <Return>

When this command is executed, dBASE will produce the report shown in Figure 3.10. The report appears as expected with no extra lines at the top.

3.2.5 Documenting a Program

Documentation is an important part of the program. **Program documentation** refers to those explanatory notes included in the program to enhance its neatness and readability. In dBASE IV, these notes can be included by placing an asterisk at the start of a line with any comments

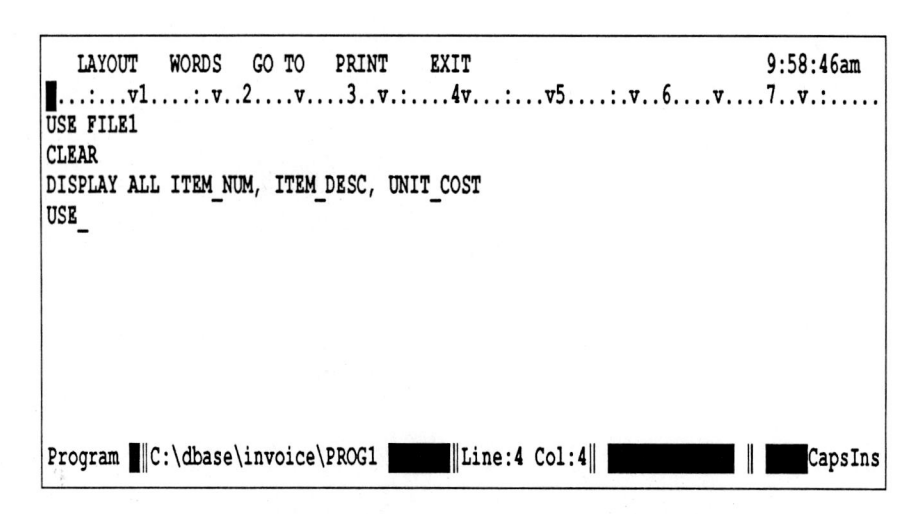

Figure 3.9 Final edited version of PROG1

```
   LAYOUT   WORDS    GO TO    PRINT    EXIT                    9:58:46am
▌...:...v1....:.v..2....v....3..v.:....4v...:..v5....:.v..6....v....7..v.:....
USE FILE1
CLEAR
DISPLAY ALL ITEM_NUM, ITEM_DESC, UNIT_COST
USE_




Program ▌C:\dbase\invoice\PROG1   ▌Line:4 Col:4▌            ▌ ▌CapsIns
```

Figure 3.10 The output produced by the final modified version of PROG1

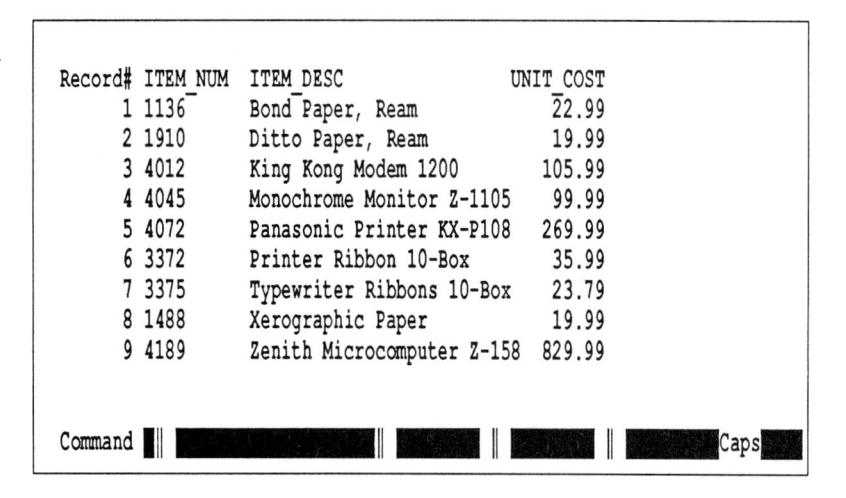

```
Record# ITEM_NUM  ITEM_DESC              UNIT_COST
     1  1136      Bond Paper, Ream           22.99
     2  1910      Ditto Paper, Ream          19.99
     3  4012      King Kong Modem 1200      105.99
     4  4045      Monochrome Monitor Z-1105  99.99
     5  4072      Panasonic Printer KX-P108 269.99
     6  3372      Printer Ribbon 10-Box      35.99
     7  3375      Typewriter Ribbons 10-Box  23.79
     8  1488      Xerographic Paper          19.99
     9  4189      Zenith Microcomputer Z-158 829.99
```

following the asterisk. Comments may include the description of the program, its logical structure, and the functions performed by each module. Because dBASE ignores program lines starting with an asterisk, they can be placed anywhere in the program.

Once again invoke the dBASE text editor, and add the documentation shown in Figure 3.11. After all the documentation is complete, save this documented version of the program PROG1.

3.2.6 The DO WHILE-ENDDO Command

In the previous section, you were shown how to create, save, execute, and modify a small program. This section introduces the DO WHILE-ENDDO commands, which are used to perform controlled repetitive tasks.

The DO WHILE-ENDDO commands are used to construct the repetitive process (also called a *loop*) in a program. The loop is initiated by the DO WHILE command. The commands placed between the DO WHILE and ENDDO commands are repeated until the condition specified in the DO WHILE command is false. The ENDDO command is required and marks the end of the repetitive process.

Figure 3.11 Documented version of PROG1

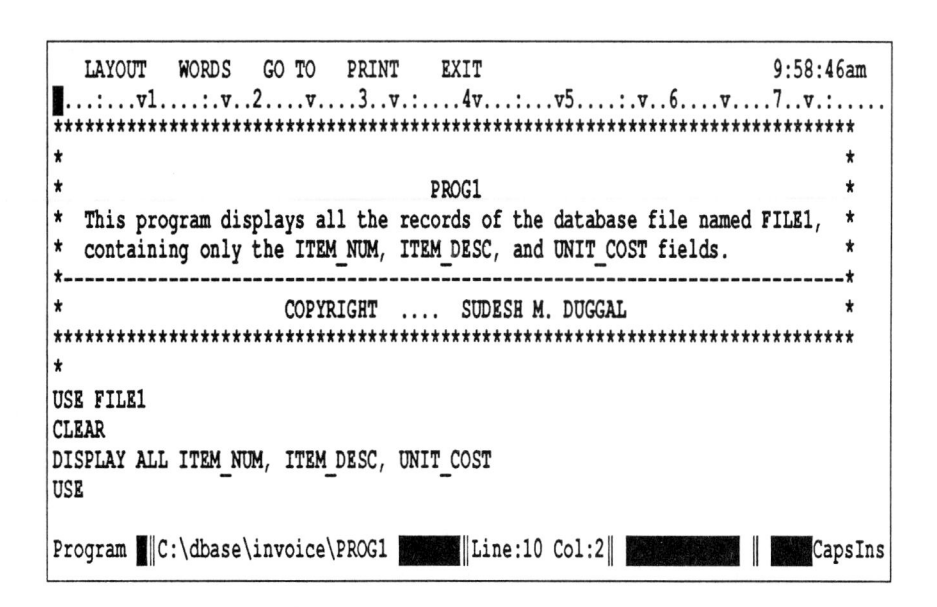

```
  LAYOUT    WORDS    GO TO    PRINT    EXIT              9:58:46am
...:....v1....:.v..2....v....3..v.:....4v...:...v5....:.v..6....v....7..v.:.....
*******************************************************************************
*                                                                             *
*                           PROG1                                             *
* This program displays all the records of the database file named FILE1,     *
* containing only the ITEM_NUM, ITEM_DESC, and UNIT_COST fields.              *
*-----------------------------------------------------------------------------*
*                  COPYRIGHT  ....  SUDESH M. DUGGAL                          *
*******************************************************************************
*
USE FILE1
CLEAR
DISPLAY ALL ITEM_NUM, ITEM_DESC, UNIT_COST
USE
```

The format of this command is as follows:

```
DO WHILE <condition>
   <commands>
ENDDO
```

where <condition> is a logical conditional statement used to determine the condition under which the commands should continue to be repeated, and <commands> are the valid dBASE commands that are repeated.

Now you will modify the program PROG1 of the previous section by introducing the DO WHILE-ENDDO command. First invoke the text editor. Then change the program as shown in Figure 3.12. Remember that blank lines can be inserted by pressing the <Ctrl-N>.

Three new concepts are introduced in this program. The first is the DO WHILE-ENDDO command itself, which consists of two separate commands. The DO WHILE command starts the loop process, and the commands

```
DISPLAY ITEM_NUM, ITEM_DESC, UNIT_COST
SKIP
```

placed between the DO WHILE and ENDDO commands are executed repeatedly as long as the conditions stated in the DO WHILE command are met. The ENDDO command terminates the loop process.

The second concept is the function EOF (), which is a logical test condition used with the DO WHILE command.

The EOF () Function

The format of the EOF () function is

```
EOF ( )
```

where EOF stands for end of file.

The EOF () is a dBASE function used as a logical condition to control loop repetition in a DO WHILE command to process every record in the database file. When the record pointer points to the end of file marker, the function returns the logical true (.T.) value; otherwise, it returns the logical false (.F.) value.

The third new concept introduced in this program is the use of the SKIP command. The format of this command is

```
SKIP [<number>]
```

where <number> is the number of records the pointer should move. It can be a positive or negative number or an expression whose calculated value is a number.

The SKIP command moves the record pointer forward or backward in a database file by a specified number of records from its current location. If no number is specified, the cursor is advanced to the next record. A detailed discussion of the SKIP command will be given in Chapter 6.

Figure 3.12 PROG1 with DO WHILE-ENDDO commands

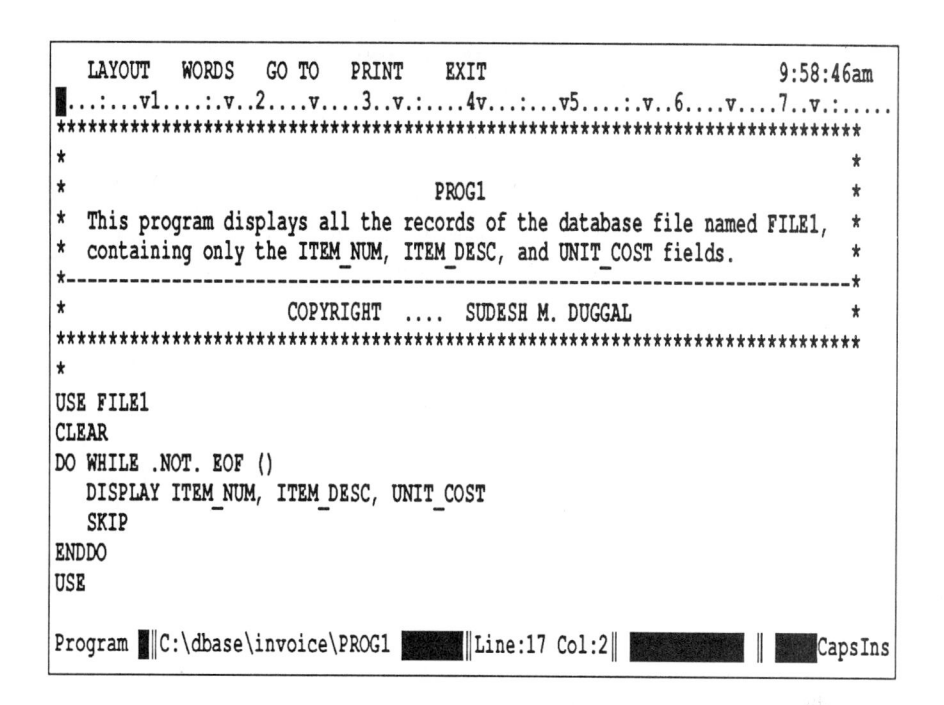

```
  LAYOUT   WORDS   GO TO   PRINT    EXIT                        9:58:46am
 ...:....v1....:.v..2....v....3..v.:....4v...:...v5....:.v..6....v....7..v.:....
 ***********************************************************************
 *                                                                     *
 *                            PROG1                                    *
 * This program displays all the records of the database file named FILE1, *
 * containing only the ITEM_NUM, ITEM_DESC, and UNIT_COST fields.      *
 *---------------------------------------------------------------------*
 *                   COPYRIGHT  ....  SUDESH M. DUGGAL                 *
 ***********************************************************************
 *
 USE FILE1
 CLEAR
 DO WHILE .NOT. EOF ()
    DISPLAY ITEM_NUM, ITEM_DESC, UNIT_COST
    SKIP
 ENDDO
 USE

 Program  C:\dbase\invoice\PROG1    Line:17 Col:2              CapsIns
```

In this example, the DO WHILE command will start the loop process. The commands

```
DISPLAY ITEM_NUM, ITEM_DESC, UNIT_COST
SKIP
```

placed between the DO WHILE and ENDDO commands will be executed repeatedly as long as the conditions stated in the DO WHILE commands are met. In other words, the condition ".NOT. EOF()" will be true if the end of the file has not been reached. This means that the DISPLAY command will display the contents of the first record, and the SKIP command will move the pointer to the next record. The DO WHILE command will repeat the process, the next record will be displayed, and the record pointer will move to the subsequent record. This process will continue until the end of the file is reached.

When the conditions of the DO WHILE command are met, that is, when EOF is reached and ".NOT. EOF ()" returns the logical (.F.) value, the loop will be terminated. Program control will jump to the command following the ENDDO command.

Now save the program and execute it by typing the following command:

```
. DO PROG1     <Return>
```

dBASE will respond by displaying the results as shown in Figure 3.13 (see page 108).

A close examination of the report indicates that there are a few extra lines in it. The line "Record no. x" is repeated several times. After the first record is displayed, the effect of the SKIP command is displayed as "Record no. 2," which indicates that the record pointer is now pointing to record number 2 in the database file. This message is repeated with a new

Figure 3.13 Result of PROG1 using the DO WHILE-ENDDO command

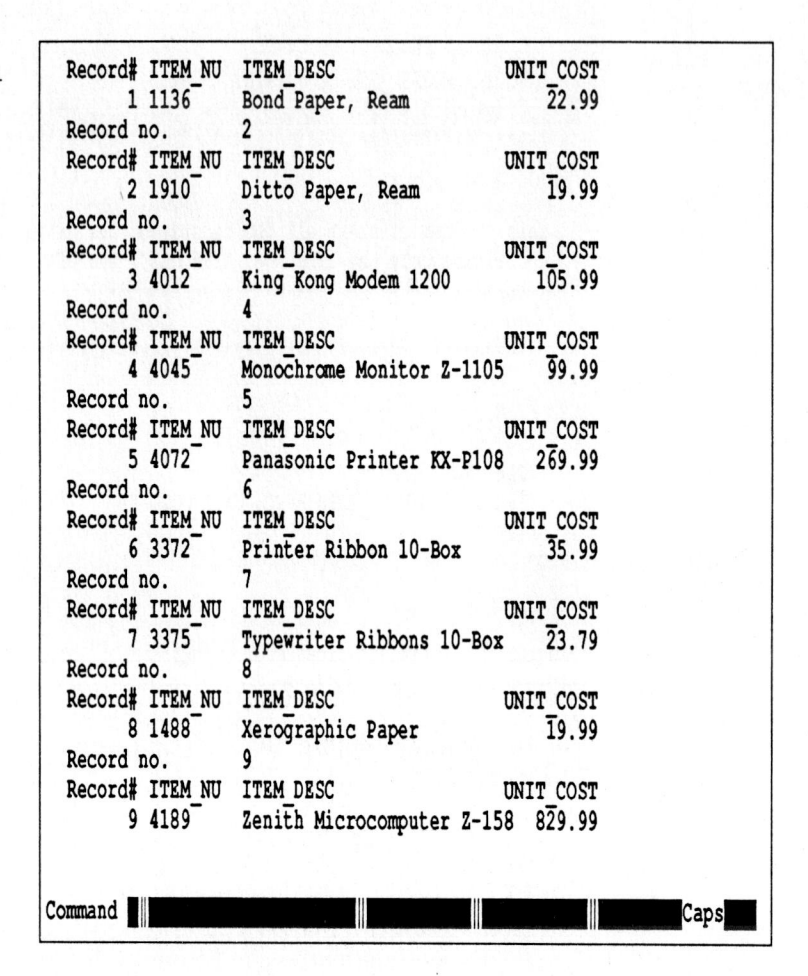

```
Record#  ITEM_NU  ITEM_DESC               UNIT_COST
      1  1136     Bond Paper, Ream            22.99
Record no.    2
Record#  ITEM_NU  ITEM_DESC               UNIT_COST
      2  1910     Ditto Paper, Ream           19.99
Record no.    3
Record#  ITEM_NU  ITEM_DESC               UNIT_COST
      3  4012     King Kong Modem 1200       105.99
Record no.    4
Record#  ITEM_NU  ITEM_DESC               UNIT_COST
      4  4045     Monochrome Monitor Z-1105   99.99
Record no.    5
Record#  ITEM_NU  ITEM_DESC               UNIT_COST
      5  4072     Panasonic Printer KX-P108  269.99
Record no.    6
Record#  ITEM_NU  ITEM_DESC               UNIT_COST
      6  3372     Printer Ribbon 10-Box       35.99
Record no.    7
Record#  ITEM_NU  ITEM_DESC               UNIT_COST
      7  3375     Typewriter Ribbons 10-Box   23.79
Record no.    8
Record#  ITEM_NU  ITEM_DESC               UNIT_COST
      8  1488     Xerographic Paper           19.99
Record no.    9
Record#  ITEM_NU  ITEM_DESC               UNIT_COST
      9  4189     Zenith Microcomputer Z-158 829.99

Command                                            Caps
```

record number every time the SKIP command is executed. To stop the printing of this message, you can use the SET TALK OFF command.

The SET TALK ON/OFF Command

The TALK option is ON by default in dBASE IV. In the On mode, it displays all the interactive messages on the screen during processing of the commands from the dot prompt, keeping you informed about the results of commands and calculations. For example, in the previous example, it kept you informed about the position of the record pointer by displaying the message after executing the SKIP command.

The ON option is very helpful in the dot prompt mode because it keeps you informed about the status of dBASE IV at the end of the execution of each command. However, the interactive messages displayed by the ON option are not only distracting during program file execution; they also clutter the screen with unwanted information. The SET TALK OFF command can be used to suppress these interactive messages, thus eliminating the distraction and cluttering of the screen at the start of each program file. Set it back to ON before the end of the program to provide information feedback during the dot prompt mode.

Because the ON option displays the results of commands and calculations during program execution, it can be used for debugging the program. After debugging, you can set it back to the OFF option. Program debugging will be discussed in Chapter 4.

Also, the heading is printed before each line. As discussed in Chapter 2, when the DISPLAY command is used, it will first print the heading and then display the data record. The SET HEADING OFF command can be used to take care of this problem.

The SET HEADING ON/OFF Command

The HEADING option is ON by default in dBASE IV. In the on mode, it displays the field names as column titles for each displayed field, memory variable, or expression with the DISPLAY, LIST, SUM, and AVERAGE commands. The SET HEADING OFF command is used to suppress display of the column titles. Once the command is issued, it will remain in effect until you exit dBASE IV or reset it by using the SET HEADING ON command.

If you use this command before the DO WHILE loop, the DISPLAY command will display all the records without any headings. But because you do need the headings to appear at least once before the very first record, include the SET HEADING OFF command after the DISPLAY command inside the DO WHILE loop.

You may not have noticed that the status bar is always being displayed at the bottom of the screen in every report produced by the execution of the dBASE program files. You can also eliminate this display by using the SET STATUS OFF command.

The SET STATUS ON/OFF Command

The STATUS option is ON by default in dBASE IV. In the on mode, dBASE displays the current working environment by displaying the status bar on row 22 of the screen.

The ON option is very helpful when you are working in the dot prompt mode because it keeps you informed about the current working environment, such as the current command, drive name, current database in use, current record number, keyboard case mode, insert/overwrite mode, and NumLock status. But the presence of the status bar in the output report is unattractive. You can use the SET STATUS OFF command to suppress its appearance in the output reports. You should use the SET STATUS OFF command at the start of each program file to eliminate the status bar from the output reports displayed on the screen. Use SET TALK ON before the end of the program to provide information feedback during the dot prompt mode.

When the status bar is off, the toggle key indicators (also called *scoreboard information*) appear on row 0 at the top of the screen.

The revised version of the program PROG1 is given in Figure 3.14 (see page 310). When this program is executed, using the SET TALK OFF and SET STATUS OFF commands before the DO WHILE command will suppress the printing of the interactive messages and the display of the status bar in the report on the screen. And when the DO WHILE loop is executed for the first time, the DISPLAY command will display the first data record with the heading before it. Next, execute the SET HEADING OFF command, which will turn off the effect of writing the heading before displaying the next data record. So when the DISPLAY command is

Figure 3.14 PROG1 with SET HEADING OFF inside the DO WHILE-ENDDO loop

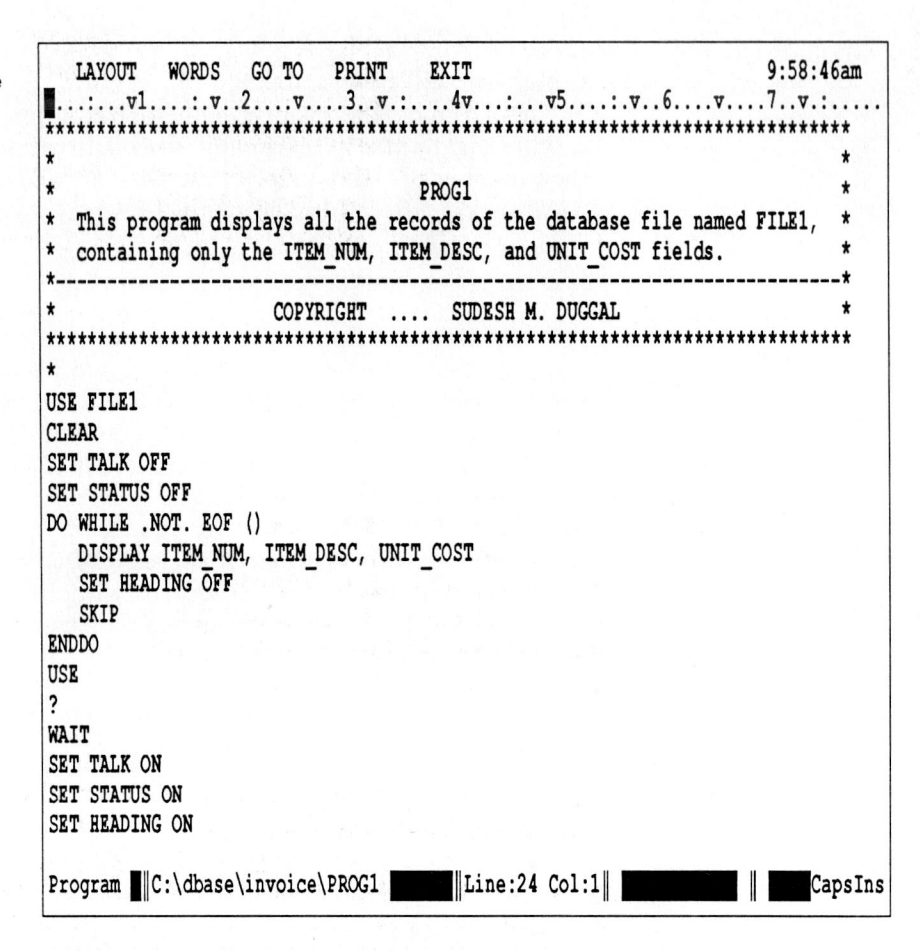

```
 LAYOUT   WORDS   GO TO   PRINT    EXIT                    9:58:46am
...:...v1...:..v..2....v....3..v.:....4v...:...v5....:.v..6....v....7.v.:.....
***************************************************************************
*                                                                         *
*                              PROG1                                      *
* This program displays all the records of the database file named FILE1, *
* containing only the ITEM_NUM, ITEM_DESC, and UNIT_COST fields.          *
*-------------------------------------------------------------------------*
*                    COPYRIGHT  ....  SUDESH M. DUGGAL                    *
***************************************************************************
*
USE FILE1
CLEAR
SET TALK OFF
SET STATUS OFF
DO WHILE .NOT. EOF ()
    DISPLAY ITEM_NUM, ITEM_DESC, UNIT_COST
    SET HEADING OFF
    SKIP
ENDDO
USE
?
WAIT
SET TALK ON
SET STATUS ON
SET HEADING ON

Program   C:\dbase\invoice\PROG1      Line:24 Col:1               CapsIns
```

executed for the second time or in successive turns, only the corresponding data record will be displayed. This process will continue until you reach the end of the file.

It seems that these program changes will take care of the problems of interactive messages, display of the status bar, and repeated headings in the output report produced by the execution of PROG1. To check it out, execute this program by typing the following command:

. **DO PROG1**   \<Return\>

dBASE will respond by displaying the report as shown in Figure 3.15.

A careful examination of the report indicates that the ITEM_DESC and UNIT_COST fields in the first record are not aligned with their corresponding fields in the rest of the records. This misalignment is caused by the built-in feature of dBASE IV used with the DISPLAY, LIST, SUM, and AVERAGE commands. The system assigns to each field to be printed in the report a width equal to the larger field size or the field name width plus one space between the two fields for separating the columns.

Thus, in this example, when the first record was displayed, the HEADING option was ON, so the ITEM_NUM field was assigned a width of eight characters (the larger of the length of the field name of ITEM_NUM field width, which is eight characters, and its field width, which is four characters, as defined in the definition of the structure of the database file). But on subsequent displays, because the HEADING OFF

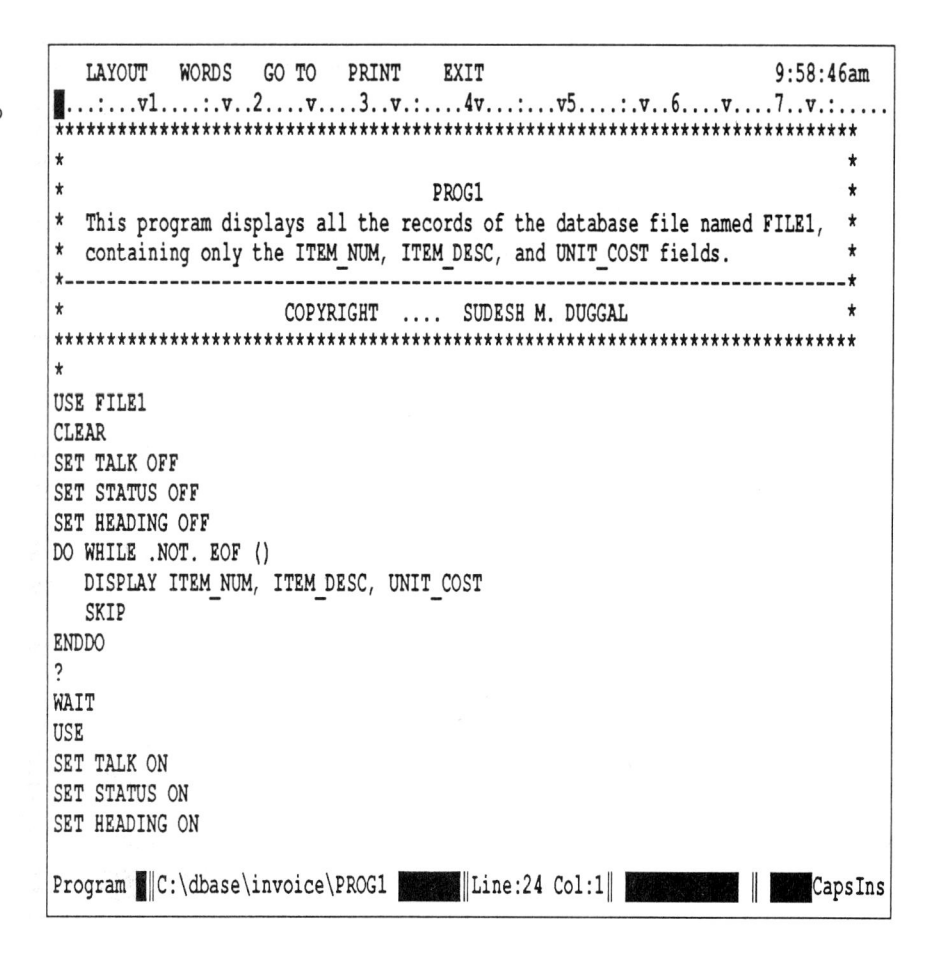

Figure 3.15 Report of PROG1 using SET HEADING OFF inside the DO WHILE-ENDDO loop

```
Record# ITEM_NUM  ITEM_DESC                UNIT_COST
      1 1136 Bond Paper, Ream                  22.99
      2 1910 Ditto Paper, Ream                 19.99
      3 4012 King Kong Modem 1200             105.99
      4 4045 Monochrome Monitor Z-1105         99.99
      5 4072 Panasonic Printer KX-P108        269.99
      6 3372 Printer Ribbon 10-Box             35.99
      7 3375 Typewriter Ribbons 10-Box         23.79
      8 1488 Xerographic Paper                 19.99
      9 4189 Zenith Microcomputer Z-158       829.99

Press any key to continue..._
```

option was in effect and the heading was not to be printed, this field was assigned a width of only four characters, which is equal to the width of the field, causing the alignment problem in the report.

The previous discussion indicates that we cannot place the SET HEADING OFF command inside the DO WHILE loop. So put this command outside the DO WHILE loop. After you make these modifications, the revised version of the program PROG1 will be as shown in Figure 3.16.

Figure 3.16 PROG1 with SET HEADING OFF outside the DO WHILE-ENDDO loop

```
   LAYOUT   WORDS   GO TO   PRINT    EXIT                   9:58:46am
▌...:...v1....:..v..2....v....3..v.:....4v...:..v5....:.v..6....v....7..v.:.....
********************************************************************************
*                                                                              *
*                             PROG1                                            *
* This program displays all the records of the database file named FILE1,      *
* containing only the ITEM_NUM, ITEM_DESC, and UNIT_COST fields.               *
*------------------------------------------------------------------------------*
*                  COPYRIGHT .... SUDESH M. DUGGAL                             *
********************************************************************************
*
USE FILE1
CLEAR
SET TALK OFF
SET STATUS OFF
SET HEADING OFF
DO WHILE .NOT. EOF ()
   DISPLAY ITEM_NUM, ITEM_DESC, UNIT_COST
   SKIP
ENDDO
?
WAIT
USE
SET TALK ON
SET STATUS ON
SET HEADING ON

Program  ▐C:\dbase\invoice\PROG1 ▌▐Line:24 Col:1▐      ▐ ▐CapsIns
```

Figure 3.17 Report of PROG1 using SET HEADING OFF outside the DO WHILE-ENDDO loop

```
1 1136 Bond Paper, Ream                  22.99
2 1910 Ditto Paper, Ream                 19.99
3 4012 King Kong Modem 1200             105.99
4 4045 Monochrome Monitor Z-1105         99.99
5 4072 Panasonic Printer KX-P108        269.99
6 3372 Printer Ribbon 10-Box             35.99
7 3375 Typewriter Ribbons 10-Box         23.79
8 1488 Xerographic Paper                 19.99
9 4189 Zenith Microcomputer Z-158       829.99

Press any key to continue..._
```

Recall that you can delete any line by positioning the cursor on the line and pressing <Ctrl-Y>. You can add a blank line by positioning the cursor at the first position of the line before which a blank line is to be added and then pressing <Ctrl-N>.

If this program is executed, it will not have any headings. The report produced by this program will be as shown in Figure 3.17.

Notice in Figure 3.16 that three other commands—SET TALK ON, SET STATUS ON, and SET HEADING ON—have also been added at the end of the program. Remember that at the top of the program, we set these three commands to OFF. Even after program execution, the effect of these three commands will remain as long as the current dBASE IV session is not terminated. To cancel their effect, set these instructions back ON by adding these three instructions to the end of the program. Follow this rule:

Whenever a SET command is used to set on or set off a particular function in a program, reverse its effect before ending the program.

3.2.7 Adding Headings to a Report

The report produced by the instructions in the previous section is difficult to use without the headings. It needs to be made more readable, which you can accomplish by identifying the fields by appropriate headings. You can use the @ ... SAY command to add headings to the report. Not only does this dBASE IV command allow you to position the output on the screen, but it also helps format the output to be sent to the printer.

The @ ... SAY Command

The general format of the command is

```
@ <row>,<column> SAY [<message>]
```

where <row> is the row number, and <column> is the column number for the screen or printer. The optional <message> can be a character string, memory variable, field, or expression.

The @ ... SAY command consists of two components: @ <row>, <column> and SAY [<message>]. The first component positions the cursor or print head to the row and column positions specified by <row> and <column>. You can use a number, memory variable, field, or expression whose evaluated value is an integer for either <row> or

Figure 3.18 PROG1 with @ ... SAY command

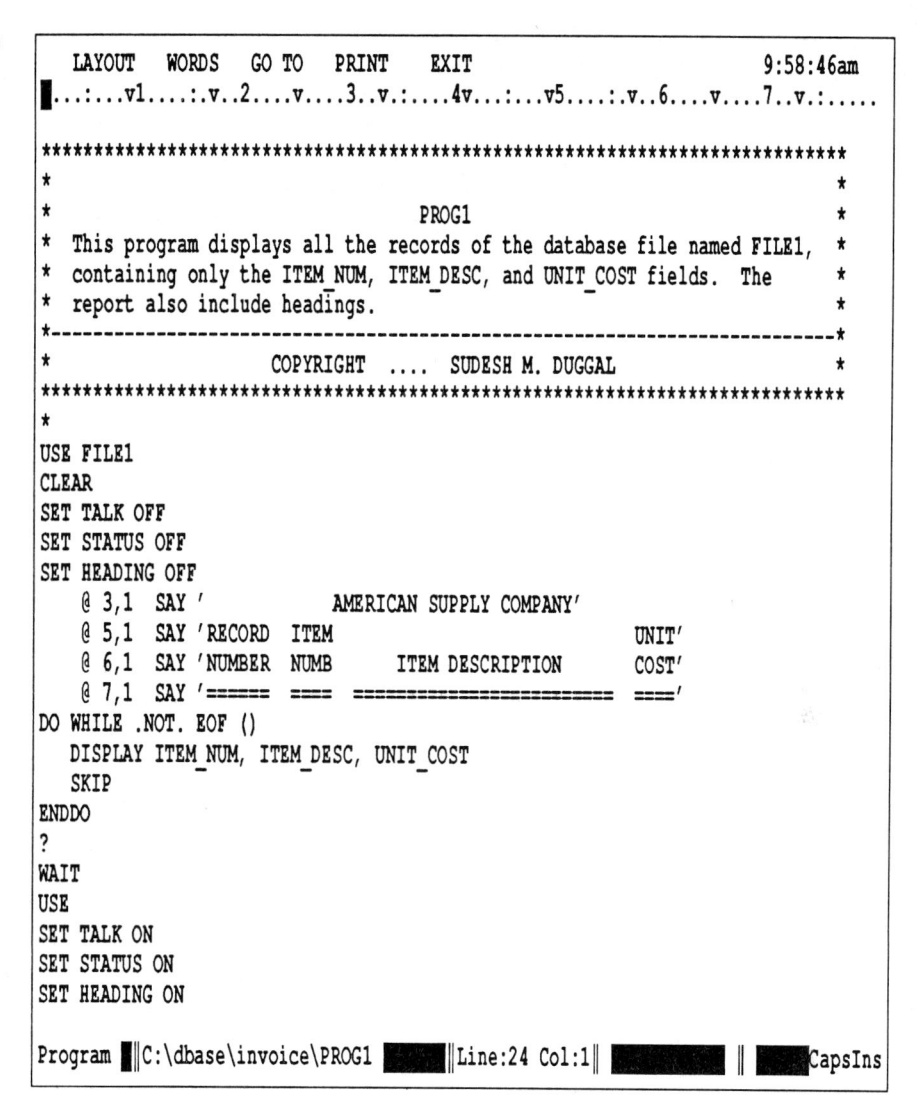

```
  LAYOUT    WORDS    GO TO    PRINT    EXIT                      9:58:46am
...:...v1....:.v..2....v....3..v.:....4v...:..v5....:.v..6....v....7..v.:.....

************************************************************************
*                                                                      *
*                            PROG1                                     *
* This program displays all the records of the database file named FILE1, *
* containing only the ITEM_NUM, ITEM_DESC, and UNIT_COST fields. The    *
* report also include headings.                                        *
*----------------------------------------------------------------------*
*                   COPYRIGHT  ....  SUDESH M. DUGGAL                  *
************************************************************************
*
USE FILE1
CLEAR
SET TALK OFF
SET STATUS OFF
SET HEADING OFF
    @ 3,1  SAY '            AMERICAN SUPPLY COMPANY'
    @ 5,1  SAY 'RECORD   ITEM                                UNIT'
    @ 6,1  SAY 'NUMBER   NUMB      ITEM DESCRIPTION          COST'
    @ 7,1  SAY '======   ====   ========================   ===='
DO WHILE .NOT. EOF ()
    DISPLAY ITEM_NUM, ITEM_DESC, UNIT_COST
    SKIP
ENDDO
?
WAIT
USE
SET TALK ON
SET STATUS ON
SET HEADING ON

Program  ▌▌C:\dbase\invoice\PROG1  ▌▌Line:24 Col:1▌▌                ▌▌CapsIns
```

<column>. The second component—SAY [<message>]—is optional. It displays or prints any user-defined expression at the location specified by the first component of this command.

The standard monitor screen is made up of 25 rows (numbered 0 to 24) and 80 columns (0 to 79). The address of the upper left corner is 0,0; the address of the bottom right corner is 24,79. Line 0 is normally used to display messages and should be avoided.

We can use this command to add headings to the report produced by instructions in section 3.2.6 and shown in Figure 3.17. The modified version of our original program PROG1 after including the instructions for headings is given in Figure 3.18.

The first @ ... SAY command prints the main heading "AMERICAN SUPPLY COMPANY" on row 3 of the screen. The next two commands print column headings, and the following command produces an underline of the column headings on rows 5, 6, and 7, respectively, on the screen. When this program is executed, dBASE will produce the report as shown in Figure 3.19 (see page 114).

Figure 3.19 Report of PROG1 using @ ... SAY command

```
            AMERICAN SUPPLY COMPANY

RECORD  ITEM                              UNIT
NUMBER  NUMB    ITEM DESCRIPTION          COST
======  ====    =======================   ====

    1   1136  Bond Paper, Ream             22.99
    2   1910  Ditto Paper, Ream            19.99
    3   4012  King Kong Modem 1200        105.99
    4   4045  Monochrome Monitor Z-1105    99.99
    5   4072  Panasonic Printer KX-P108   269.99
    6   3372  Printer Ribbon 10-Box        35.99
    7   3375  Typewriter Ribbons 10-Box    23.79
    8   1488  Xerographic Paper            19.99
    9   4189  Zenith Microcomputer Z-158  829.99

Press any key to continue..._
```

3.2.8 IF-ELSE-ENDIF Command

In this section, you will be introduced to the decision-making command IF-ELSE-ENDIF, which provides a means for selecting one of two choices. The general format of this command is

```
IF <condition>
   <commands set I>
[ELSE
   <commands set II>]
ENDIF
```

where <condition> is a dBASE logical expression, <commands set I> and <commands set II> are a set of any number of dBASE IV commands, ELSE is an optional part of the command, and ENDIF is the required command to end the IF command structure.

If the <condition> portion of the command is true, then the <commands set I> is executed; if the <condition> is false, <commands set II> is executed. If there are no commands in the <commands set II>, then the ELSE part of the command can be omitted; and the format of the command will reduce to:

```
IF <condition>
   <commands>
ENDIF
```

This section introduces this simple IF-ENDIF format. The full form of this command, IF-ELSE-ENDIF, will be introduced in Chapter 8. The final modified version of the program PROG1 in which the IF-ENDIF command has been included is shown in Figure 3.20.

The command IF UNIT_COST > 100 will test if the record at which the pointer is pointing has a value of the UNIT_COST field greater than $100. If it does, the DISPLAY command will display the ITEM_NUM, ITEM_DESC, and UNIT_COST fields of that record. If the value of the UNIT_COST field is not greater than $100, the DISPLAY command will

Figure 3.20 PROG1 with IF-ENDIF command

```
   LAYOUT   WORDS   GO TO   PRINT    EXIT                        9:58:46am
 ...:....v1....:.v..2....v....3..v.:....4v...:..v5....:.v..6....v....7..v.:....

 **************************************************************************
 *                                                                        *
 *                            PROG1                                       *
 * This program displays all the records of the database file named FILE1, *
 * containing only the ITEM_NUM, ITEM_DESC, and UNIT_COST fields. The      *
 * report also include headings.                                           *
 *------------------------------------------------------------------------*
 *                  COPYRIGHT  ....  SUDESH M. DUGGAL                     *
 **************************************************************************
 *
 USE FILE1
 CLEAR
 SET TALK OFF
 SET STATUS OFF
 SET HEADING OFF
     @ 3,1  SAY '           AMERICAN SUPPLY COMPANY'
     @ 5,1  SAY '          ITEMS COSTING MORE THAN $100.00'
     @ 7,1  SAY 'RECORD   ITEM                                UNIT'
     @ 8,1  SAY 'NUMBER   NUMB     ITEM DESCRIPTION           COST'
     @ 9,1  SAY '======   ====    ======================      ===='
 DO WHILE .NOT. EOF ()
    IF UNIT_COST > 100
        DISPLAY ITEM_NUM, ITEM_DESC, UNIT_COST
    ENDIF
    SKIP
 ENDDO
 ?
 ? '          *** --- END OF REPORT --- ***'
 ?
 WAIT
 USE
 SET TALK ON
 SET STATUS ON
 SET HEADING ON

 Program  C:\DBASE\INVOICE\PROG1      Line:1 Col:1                     Ins
```

skip that record. The next ENDIF command will terminate the effect of the IF command. The SKIP command will skip the pointer to the next record in the database file.

Because the IF-ENDIF and SKIP commands are placed between the DO WHILE and ENDDO commands, the process of selecting the record with a value of the UNIT_COST field more than $100 and skipping to the next record will be repeated as long as the condition of the DO WHILE command is in effect, that is, until the end of the file is reached. Thus, this program will read all the records of the database file FILE1 and display only those having a value of the UNIT_COST field more than $100. Note that in this case, the ELSE clause is not used. The other commands in this version of the program PROG1 have already been used in the previous version; therefore, they need no explanation.

Figure 3.21 Records of database file FILE1 whose UNIT_COST > $100

```
           AMERICAN SUPPLY COMPANY

        ITEMS COSTING MORE THAN $100.00

RECORD  ITEM                              UNIT
NUMBER  NUMB    ITEM DESCRIPTION          COST
======  ====    ========================  =====

  3     4012    King Kong Modem 1200      105.99
  5     4072    Panasonic Printer KX-P108 269.99
  9     4189    Zenith Microcomputer Z-158 829.99

              *** --- END OF REPORT --- ***

Press any key to continue..._
```

When this program is executed, the report shown in Figure 3.21 will be produced. The report contains three records. The message "*** --- END OF REPORT --- ***" indicates the end of the report.

3.2.9 Listing of the dBASE Program

In the last several sections, you have used the MODIFY COMMAND command to display as well as edit the contents of the dBASE program file. But to simply display the contents of the dBASE program file, you can use the dBASE IV TYPE command.

The TYPE Command

The general format of the command is

```
TYPE <program file name>
     [TO PRINT/TO FILE <text file name>]
```

where <program file name> is the name of the program file whose contents are to be displayed, TO PRINT and TO FILE are optional parameters to be used to print or to send the program file contents to another text file, and <text file name> is the name of the target text file.

The TYPE command is used to display, print, or send the contents of an ASCII text or program file to another text file. When you use this command, provide the extension with the program or text file name.

To display the contents of the program file PROG1, type the following command:

```
. TYPE PROG1.PRG    <Return>
```

dBASE will respond by displaying the result as shown in Figure 3.20. To obtain the printed copy of the contents of the program file PROG1, add the TO PRINT option to the previous command. The command will become:

```
. TYPE PROG1.PRG TO PRINT    <Return>
```

If this command is typed and the printer is ON, dBASE will produce a printed copy of the program file PROG1 similar to the listing shown in Figure 3.20. The printed copy of the program file can be used for documentation purposes.

3.3 Using an External Text Editor

So far we have used the dBASE IV built-in text editor. Because most of your time will be spent working with the text editor, you can use one of your own choice as long as it is capable of producing standard ASCII text files.

If you opt to use an **external text editor,** inform dBASE IV. When the MODIFY COMMAND command is issued, instead of invoking the dBASE IV text editor, dBASE should invoke your selected text editor. When you exit from your text editor after creating or editing a program file, the control should then return to the dBASE IV dot prompt.

This effect can be achieved by adding the necessary dot prompt command in your CONFIG.DB file, as explained in section C.2 of Appendix C. For example, if you decide to use the WordStar text editor instead of the dBASE IV text editor, you will need to add the TEDIT = WS command to your CONFIG.DB file. If you are using another selected text editor, read Appendix C before proceeding.

When you use the external editor for creating and editing program files, always add the extension to the file name. It is only the dBASE text editor that adds the .PRG extension, not the external editor.

There is another problem with using an external text editor. When you use the dBASE IV text editor to edit an existing program file (.PRG), the program object file (.DBO) is deleted and recreated automatically. This procedure is not performed when you use an external text editor. However, this procedure can be achieved by using the SET DEVELOPMENT ON command.

3.3.1 The SET DEVELOPMENT ON/OFF Command

The DEVELOPMENT option is ON by default in dBASE IV. In the on mode, when you ask dBASE IV to execute a program file, the date of the program source file and object file created with an external text editor are compared. If the source file is newer, dBASE IV will recompile the source program file to create a matching object file before executing it.

So whenever you are using an external editor, it is strongly recommended that you use the SET DEVELOPMENT ON command, either by including this command in your CONFIG.DB file or by entering it at the start of the session.

TUTORIAL 7

In this tutorial, you will modify the AUTOEXEC.BAT file so that when the system is booted, it will always display the directory path in the system prompt.

Solution

Recall that we have been using the PROMPT PG command at the start of every session to attain the same result. If we include this command in the AUTOEXEC.BAT file, every time the system is booted, it will consult the AUTOEXEC.BAT file. The presence of the PROMPT PG command will instruct the system to display the directory path in the system prompt. This will eliminate the need to use the command at the start of every session.

To add this command to the AUTOEXEC.BAT file, follow these steps:

Step 1: Boot up your system. The prompt C> should be displayed by the system.

Step 2: Load dBASE IV using the steps of Table 2.1 or Table 2.2, depending on the environment.

Step 3: At the dot prompt, type the following command:

```
. MODIFY COMMAND C:\AUTOEXEC.BAT       <Return>
```

This command will invoke the dBASE IV text editor, access the AUTOEXEC.BAT file from the root directory of drive C:, and display it on the screen as shown in Figure 3.22.

Step 4: Move the cursor to the first letter D of the word DATE in line 3, and press <Ctrl-N>. This will add a blank line between the second and third lines.

Step 5: Move the cursor to the blank line, and type the following command:

```
PROMPT $P$G      <Return>
```

Now the screen should be as shown in Figure 3.23.

Step 6: Press <Ctrl-W> to save the modified version of the AUTOEXEC.BAT file.

Step 7: Now type "QUIT" to terminate the dBASE IV session.

The AUTOEXEC.BAT file has been modified. Reboot your system by pressing <Ctrl,Alt-Del>. The system prompt C:\> should be displayed by

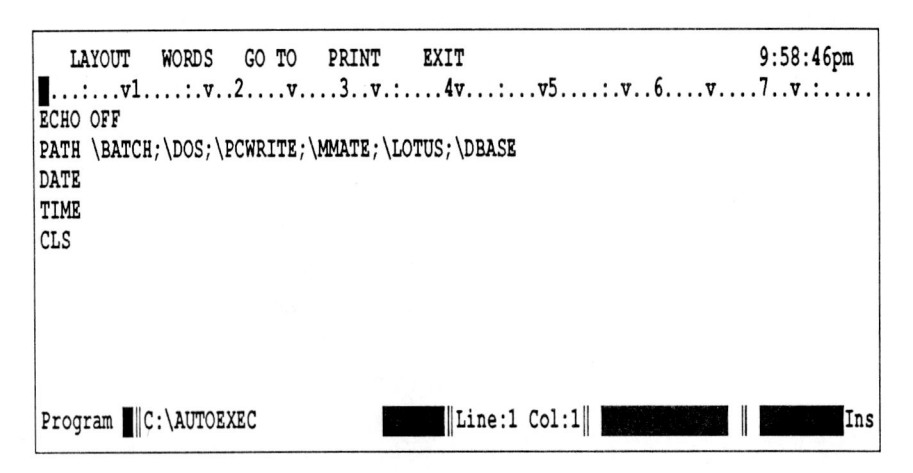

Figure 3.22 Listing of AUTOEXEC.BAT file

```
   LAYOUT    WORDS    GO TO    PRINT    EXIT                        9:58:46pm
▌...:...v1....:..v..2....v....3..v.:.....4v...:...v5....:.v..6....v....7..v.:.....
ECHO OFF
PATH \BATCH;\DOS;\PCWRITE;\MMATE;\LOTUS;\DBASE
DATE
TIME
CLS




Program  ▌C:\AUTOEXEC            ▌Line:1 Col:1▐           ▐            Ins
```

Figure 3.23 Listing of modified AUTOEXEC.BAT file

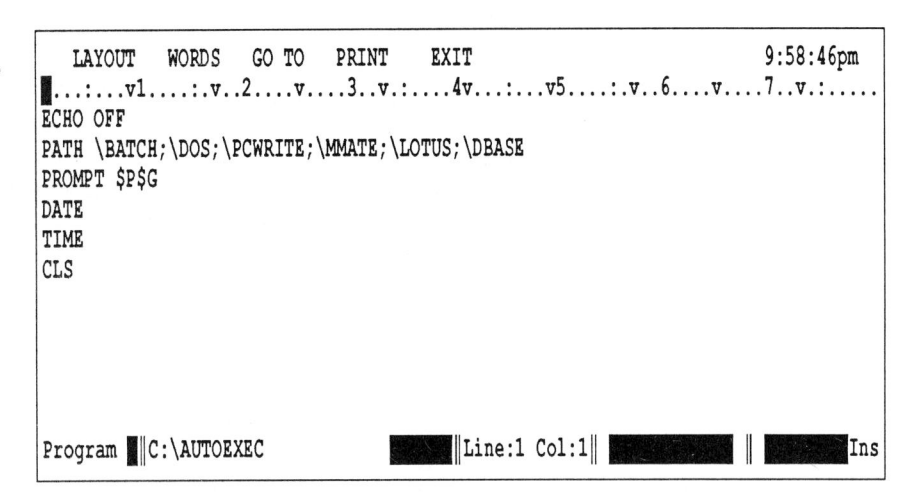

```
   LAYOUT   WORDS   GO TO   PRINT   EXIT                    9:58:46pm
▌...:...v1....:.v..2....v....3..v.:....4v...:...v5....:.v..6....v....7..v.:....
ECHO OFF
PATH \BATCH;\DOS;\PCWRITE;\MMATE;\LOTUS;\DBASE
PROMPT $P$G
DATE
TIME
CLS




Program  ▌C:\AUTOEXEC              ▌Line:1 Col:1▌            ▌        ▌Ins
```

the system. If it is, congratulations! You have successfully completed Tutorial 7.

TUTORIAL 8

In this tutorial, you will modify the CONFIG.DB file so that when dBASE IV is loaded, it will bypass the control center mode and go directly to the dot prompt mode. Also, instead of displaying the dot prompt ".", it should display the "dBASE:>" prompt.

Solution

Recall that every time you have loaded dBASE IV using steps 1–5 of Table 2.1 or steps 1–6 of Table 2.2, it displayed the control center. To change it to the dot prompt, you had to follow step 6 or step 7, depending on the method used for loading dBASE IV. You can eliminate this step by simply deleting the COMMAND=ASSIST command from the CONFIG.DB file. (Refer to Appendix C, section C.2.2.)

Also, when dBASE IV is in the dot prompt mode, it displays the dot or "." as its prompt. You need to modify this prompt to "dBASE:>", referred to as the "dBASE prompt" in subsequent references in this book. This change can be achieved by adding the PROMPT = dBASE:> command to the CONFIG.DB file. (Refer to Appendix C, section C.2.7.)

To make these modifications in the CONFIG.DB file, follow these steps:

- Step 1: Boot up your system. The prompt C:\> should be displayed by the system. (Notice the effect of Tutorial 7.)
- Step 2: Load dBASE IV using the steps of Table 2.1 or Table 2.2, depending on the environment.
- Step 3: At the dot prompt, type the following command:

    . **MODIFY COMMAND C:\DBASE\CONFIG.DB**
    <Return>

Figure 3.24 Listing of CONFIG.DB file

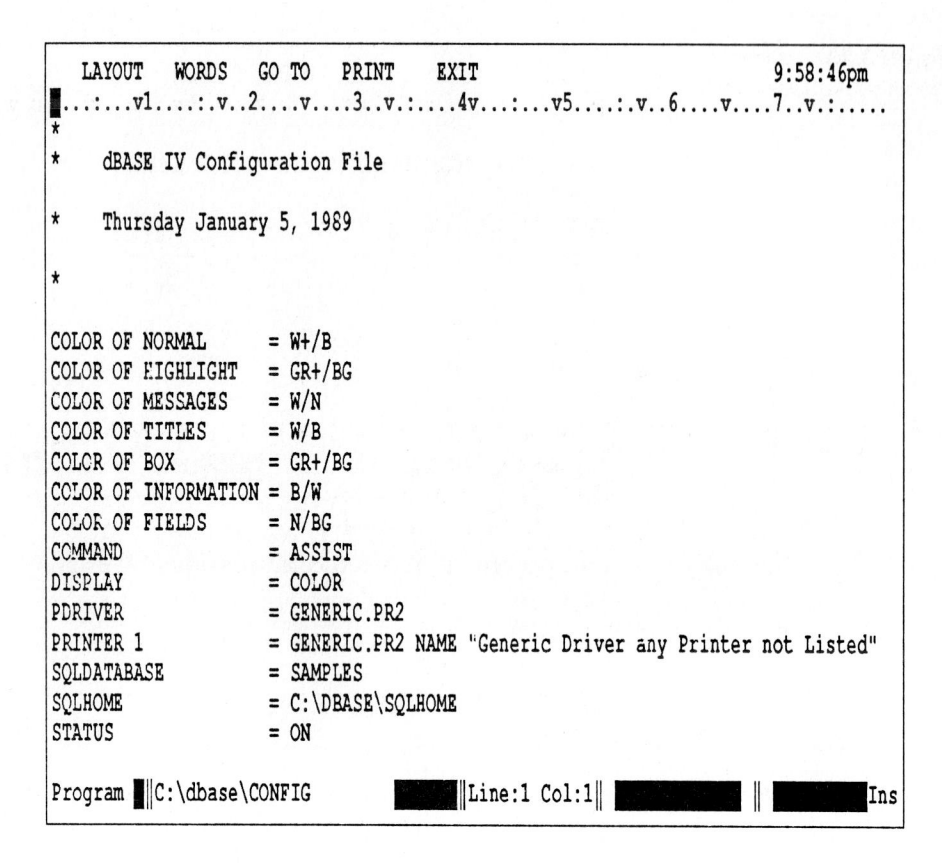

```
  LAYOUT   WORDS   GO TO   PRINT    EXIT                        9:58:46pm
...:...v1....:.v..2....v....3..v.:....4v...:...v5....:.v..6....v....7..v.:....
*
*    dBASE IV Configuration File
*
*    Thursday January 5, 1989
*
*
COLOR OF NORMAL     = W+/B
COLOR OF HIGHLIGHT  = GR+/BG
COLOR OF MESSAGES   = W/N
COLOR OF TITLES     = W/B
COLOR OF BOX        = GR+/BG
COLOR OF INFORMATION = B/W
COLOR OF FIELDS     = N/BG
COMMAND             = ASSIST
DISPLAY             = COLOR
PDRIVER             = GENERIC.PR2
PRINTER 1           = GENERIC.PR2 NAME "Generic Driver any Printer not Listed"
SQLDATABASE         = SAMPLES
SQLHOME             = C:\DBASE\SQLHOME
STATUS              = ON

Program  ||C:\dbase\CONFIG            ||Line:1 Col:1||         ||          Ins
```

This command will invoke the dBASE IV text editor, and the CONFIG.DB file from the DBASE directory will be displayed on the screen as shown in Figure 3.24. Note that in the previous command, you had to add the path for the CONFIG.DB file so that the dBASE text editor could get the file from the DBASE directory.

Step 4: Move the cursor to the first letter C in line 8, put the keyboard in the overwrite mode, and type the following command:

PROMPT   = dBASE:>   <Return>

This change will delete the

COMMAND   = ASSIST

line from the CONFIG.DB file and add the

PROMPT   = dBASE:>

line to it. The screen should now look like that shown in Figure 3.25.

Step 5: Press <Ctrl-W> to save the modified version of the CONFIG.DB file.

Step 6: Type **"QUIT"** to terminate the dBASE IV session.

The CONFIG.DB file has been modified. Now load dBASE IV once again using steps 1–5 of Table 2.1 or steps 1–6 of Table 2.2. The system should

Figure 3.25 Listing of modified CONFIG.DB file

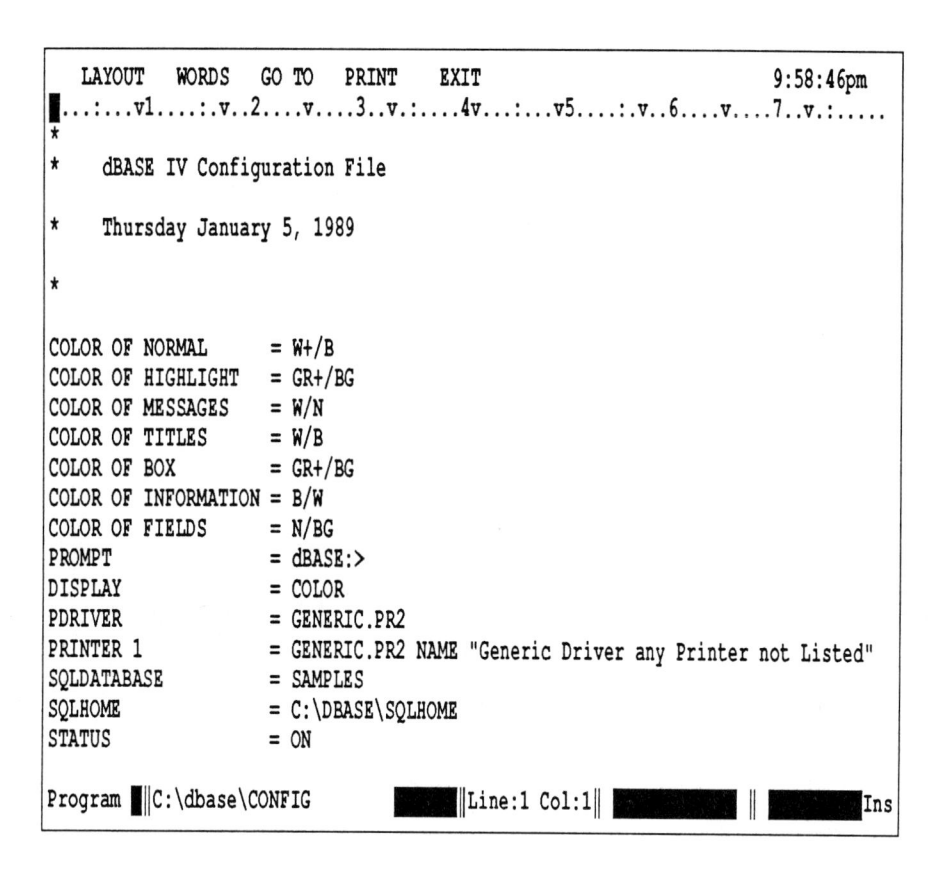

```
   LAYOUT   WORDS   GO TO   PRINT   EXIT                   9:58:46pm
■...:...v1....:.v..2....v....3..v.:....4v...:...v5....:.v..6....v....7..v.:.....
*
*    dBASE IV Configuration File

*    Thursday January 5, 1989

*

COLOR OF NORMAL      = W+/B
COLOR OF HIGHLIGHT   = GR+/BG
COLOR OF MESSAGES    = W/N
COLOR OF TITLES      = W/B
COLOR OF BOX         = GR+/BG
COLOR OF INFORMATION = B/W
COLOR OF FIELDS      = N/BG
PROMPT               = dBASE:>
DISPLAY              = COLOR
PDRIVER              = GENERIC.PR2
PRINTER 1            = GENERIC.PR2 NAME "Generic Driver any Printer not Listed"
SQLDATABASE          = SAMPLES
SQLHOME              = C:\DBASE\SQLHOME
STATUS               = ON


Program ▌║C:\dbase\CONFIG      ▌║Line:1 Col:1║  ▌   ║    ▌Ins
```

bypass the control center mode and go directly to the dot prompt mode (called dBASE prompt), and the screen should look like that shown in Figure 3.26.

If the system skips the control center mode and your screen looks like Figure 3.26, congratulations! You have successfully completed Tutorial 8. You can finish your dBASE session by typing "QUIT" now.

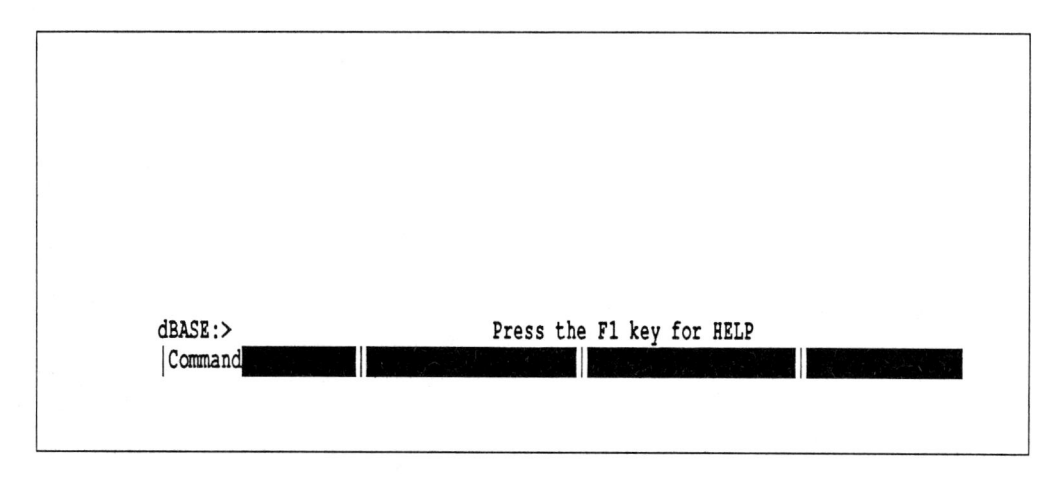

```
dBASE:>              Press the F1 key for HELP
|Command
```

Figure 3.26 dBASE prompt

TUTORIAL 9

In this tutorial, create every version of the PROG1 program file discussed in this chapter, and then execute it. Your output should match that shown in the examples in the chapter.

The detailed steps of this tutorial are not given here because they have been explained in the chapter. This is an exercise for you to complete. Follow the instructions given throughout this chapter, and complete this tutorial.

3.4 Summary

dBASE programs consist of a set of dBASE commands grouped to accomplish a specific task. These programs can be created and modified using the MODIFY COMMAND command.

dBASE programs are executed by typing the DO command followed by the program name.

The CLEAR command is used to clear the screen so that a report can be displayed without anything else on the screen.

The USE command is used to close the database files at the end of the program.

The COMMENT command (an * in the first column of the statement) is used for the internal documentation of the program.

A group of statements can be executed repetitively by placing them between the DO WHILE and ENDDO commands.

The decision-making command IF-ELSE-ENDIF can be used to select from the database file records that satisfy a particular condition.

The EOF () function can be used as a logical condition with the DO WHILE-ENDDO command to process all the records of a file.

The SKIP command is used to move the pointer to the next record, which helps access all the records of a database file.

Headings can be added to the report using the @ ... SAY command.

To change the default options of dBASE, SET TALK ON/OFF, SET HEADING ON/OFF, SET STATUS ON/OFF, and SET DEVELOPMENT ON/OFF can be used.

All these features are used to create a program that selects certain records from a file and displays them. This chapter introduced the basic structures used in structured programming. You should create and test all versions of program file PROG1 given in this chapter before you go on to the next chapter.

KEY CONCEPTS

command file
dBASE program file
dBASE text editor

external text editor
program documentation

dBASE COMMANDS AND FUNCTIONS

@ ... SAY command
CLEAR command
COMMENT (*) command
DIR command
DO command
DO WHILE-ENDDO command
EOF () command

IF-ELSE-ENDIF command
MODIFY COMMAND command
SET DEVELOPMENT ON/OFF command
SET HEADING ON/OFF command
SET STATUS ON/OFF command
SET TALK ON/OFF command
SKIP command

REVIEW QUESTIONS

1. What are the advantages of the programming mode over the dot prompt mode?
2. Define the term *command file* or *dBASE program file*.
3. List the steps in creating program files.
4. Explain the function of the following dBASE commands:
   a. MODIFY COMMAND
   b. DO
   c. DO WHILE-ENDDO
   d. IF-ELSE-ENDIF
   e. SKIP
   f. EOF ()
   g. @ ... SAY
5. While using the dBASE text editor, what keys should be pressed to
   a. add a blank line?
   b. delete a line?
   c. exit the text editor and save the changes?
   d. exit the text editor without saving the changes?
   e. save the program file to another file name?
   f. read another program file into the current program file at the point of the cursor?
6. How does dBASE know when to compile a program file and when to use the old compiled version?
7. Explain the following SET commands:
   a. SET TALK ON/OFF
   b. SET HEADING ON/OFF
   c. SET STATUS ON/OFF
   d. SET DEVELOPMENT ON/OFF
8. List the differences between the dBASE text editor and the external text editor.
9. List the steps used to modify the AUTOEXEC.BAT file.
10. List the steps used to modify the CONFIG.DB file.

Chapter 4

Design of dBASE Programs

LEARNING OBJECTIVES

Upon successfully completing this chapter, you will be able to:

1. Explain the different phases of the program development process.
2. Explain the different steps of the analysis phase.
3. Understand the differences between batch, menu, and interactive programs.
4. Explain the different logical control structures used in program design.
5. Explain the function of the initiate processing step and list all the possible activities used in developing a batch program.
6. Explain the function of the main processing step and list all the possible activities used in developing a batch program.
7. Explain the function of the terminate processing step and list all the possible activities used in developing a batch program.
8. Design a structure chart for a simple batch business program.
9. List the rules to be followed to create a structure chart.
10. Write pseudocode for a simple batch business program.
11. Code a simple batch business program in dBASE IV programming language.
12. List the coding conventions to be followed to create a well-documented program.
13. Explain the importance of program design before writing its coding.

14. Explain what is meant by testing and debugging.
15. Explain the difference between syntax errors and logical errors.
16. Analyze, design, and code a simple report listing program in dBASE programming language.

4.1 Overview

This chapter presents design, coding, testing, and debugging guidelines for a simple, complete report listing of a batch program containing headings and detail lines. It starts with the program development process, explaining the function of the five phases. Different types of programs needed to develop business application software are introduced next. Then the five phases of the program development process are applied to a batch case study program. These steps permit you to develop a complete solution for this sample case study containing screen layout form, structure chart, pseudocode, and the coded program. All the dBASE commands used in the development of the case study program are explained. Finally, the procedures for testing and debugging are explained. The program that is developed will be tested for accuracy and debugged, if needed, to make it error free.

4.2 The Program Development Process

You developed a simple program in Chapter 3. Its final version produced an inventory report listing containing only those records of the INV database file whose UNIT_COST field value is greater than $100. As you recall, we had to make several modifications to that program to obtain an acceptable output. This program was very simple and short, but what if it had been much more complex and larger? We couldn't use such a trial and error method because it would require a great deal of time and several modification attempts to produce acceptable results.

Programs are not usually developed as presented in Chapter 3. In fact, program development should be accomplished in a systematic and disciplined manner using certain rules to produce programs that are logically correct, easily understood, and easily maintained. The program development process is used to develop programs in a systematic manner following a series of orderly steps leading to known and predictable results. The program development process consists of five phases: (1) analysis, (2) design, (3) detailed design, (4) coding, and (5) testing and debugging. These phases are described in the following sections.

4.2.1 The Analysis Phase

The first step in program development is the **analysis phase,** in which program specifications to be developed are reviewed and analyzed. These provide a detailed description of the processing steps needed in the program, in the structure of the input database file(s), and in the format of the output report required as a result of program processing.

Understanding the various aspects of the problem in question, such as the output to be produced, the input data available to be processed, and the processing steps needed to produce the output from the given input data, is vital to the program development process. A complete knowledge of the database file(s) to be used by the program is also required. The main function of the analysis phase is to produce a clear understanding of the problem, its components (such as the input database file[s] and the output to be produced), and the processing tasks needed to solve the problem. The end result is the identification of the processing tasks needed to solve the problem.

4.2.2 The Design Phase

The next step in the program development process is the **design phase,** in which the processing tasks identified during the problem analysis phase are defined in order to perform program functions. These program functions are further organized into a program structure to create an overall program solution. The end product of this step is the solution of the problem representing only the main processing steps in the form of a structure chart.

4.2.3 The Detailed Design Phase

After the design phase has been completed, the next step is the **detailed design phase,** in which the actual computer operations required for each program function as defined in the design phase are identified. The final product of this step is a detailed solution of the problem in English, which is called **pseudocode.**

4.2.4 The Coding Phase

The fourth step in the program development process is the **coding phase,** in which pseudocode instructions are translated into a programming language. When this process, called *coding,* is completed, the end result is a coded program consisting of a set of commands that directs the computer to carry out the processing functions needed to solve the problem.

After the coding is completed, the coded program is entered into the computer system, creating a program file using either dBASE or any external text editor. This program file is called the *source program.*

4.2.5 The Testing and Debugging Phase

The last step is the **testing and debugging phase,** in which the source program is tested to see if any errors exist in it. An error in the program is called a **bug,** and the process of locating and correcting these errors is called **debugging.**

There are two possible types of programming errors: (1) syntactical and (2) logical. **Syntactical errors** occur when the rules of grammar for the programming language are violated. Computers cannot process commands with grammatical errors. These errors can be located with the help of the diagnostic messages generated by the compiler. **Logical errors** are those in the logic of the problem solution. Computers will be able to process these commands but will fail to produce the expected results. Logical errors are located by program testing, which involves executing the program using test data. The end product of this phase is a computer program free of syntactical and logical errors.

Before designing dBASE programs, we need to know how many different types of programs are used in the development of business application software because each type of program requires different processing steps to develop the application program.

4.3 Types of Programs

There are three different types of programs used in the development of business application software: batch programs, menu programs, and interactive programs.

4.3.1 Batch Programs

Batch programs are those in which data are used as input either by defining them in the program itself or by obtaining them from the database or memory files (discussed in Chapter 5). No data are supplied by the user interactively during program execution. In other words, in batch programs, no data from any external source(s) are used. The development of batch programs is discussed in Chapters 4–7.

4.3.2 Menu Programs

Menu programs are those in which several different processing options are presented to the user, who selects one. Depending on the user's selection, the menu program performs the associated processing. No data from any database or memory file(s) in the menu program are used. The development of menu programs is discussed in Chapters 8 and 9.

4.3.3 Interactive Programs

Interactive programs are those in which data are used as input by defining them in the program itself, by obtaining them from the database or memory file(s), or by the user supplying them interactively during program execution. The development of interactive programs is discussed in Chapters 10–13.

The program development process used to design the programs in a systematic manner is the same for all types of programs. That is, each program goes through the five development phases of the program development process explained in the previous section. But the processing steps required in the solution of the program differ, depending on program type.

4.4 An Illustrative Example: Case Study 1

Program Description

Write a program to produce an inventory report listing for American Supply Company consisting of only those records from the INV database file whose UNIT_COST field value is more than $10. The report should also include headings.

Input File(s)

The INV database file whose structure is shown in Figure 4.1 is used as an input file.

Figure 4.1 Structure of the INV database file

```
Structure for database : C:\DBASE\INVOICE\INV.DBF
Number of data records :      30
Date of last update    : 12/25/87
Field  Field Name  Type       Width    Dec   Index
    1  ITEM_NUM    Character      4            N
    2  ITEM_DESC   Character     26            N
    3  UNIT_COST   Numeric        6      2     N
    4  QUANTITY    Numeric        3            N
    5  RET_PRICE   Numeric        7      2     N
    6  REOD_POINT  Numeric        3            N
    7  REOD_QTY    Numeric        3            N
    8  DEPT_NUM    Numeric        3            N
** Total **                      56
```

Output

Program output should be an inventory report listing. It is a single-screen report, as shown in Figure 4.2. The headings should be as shown, and the detail line should consist of the ITEM_NUM, ITEM_DESC, QUANTITY, and UNIT_COST fields only.

Processing Steps

Use the following steps to develop the solution of the program:

1. The headings should be printed as shown in the inventory report listing. The date and time should be included in the headings.

Figure 4.2 Inventory report listing: Case Study 1

```
                     AMERICAN SUPPLY COMPANY
08/20/89                INVENTORY REPORT                    02:29:25
                  ITEMS COSTING MORE THAN $10.00

       ITEM                                   QTY ON      UNIT
      NUMBER        ITEM DESCRIPTION           HAND       COST

       1136      Bond Paper, Ream               38       22.99
       1910      Ditto Paper, Ream              35       19.99
       4012      King Kong Modem 1200           10      105.99
       4045      Monochrome Monitor Z-1105      15       99.99
       4072      Panasonic Printer KX-P108       8      269.99
       3372      Printer Ribbon 10-Box          19       35.99
       3375      Typewriter Ribbons 10-Box      67       23.79
       1488      Xerographic Paper              45       19.99
       4189      Zenith Microcomputer Z-158      5      829.99


                  *** --- END OF REPORT --- ***


                  PRESS ANY KEY TO CONTINUE . . .
```

2. The column headings should be enclosed between the two lines, as shown in Figure 4.2.
3. Each record of the INV.DBF database file should be tested. If the value of the UNIT_COST field is greater than $10, it should be printed in the output report; otherwise, it should be skipped.
4. At the end of the output report, print the message "*** --- END OF REPORT --- ***" to indicate the end of the output, and then freeze the screen to allow the user to view the output.
5. The whole output should be enclosed in the box, as shown in Figure 4.2.

The five phases of the program development process for Case Study 1 follow.

4.4.1 The Analysis Phase

The analysis phase is the first step in the program development process. Review and analysis of the program specifications lead to the clear understanding of the output report to be produced, the input database file(s) used to produce it, and the steps needed to solve the problem.

Let us proceed with the program development process of Case Study 1. The first step consists of analyzing the output report to be produced, the input database file(s) used in the program to produce the required results, and the identification of the processing steps needed to solve the problem.

Analysis of the Output Report

The inventory report listing shown in Figure 4.2 represents the desired format of the output report of Case Study 1. Analysis of the listing reveals that the output consists of three main heading lines, including the current date and time of the day, followed by two column heading lines, which are enclosed between the two lines. The headings are followed by detail lines, which are single-spaced. The message "*** --- END OF REPORT ---***" appears one row below the last detail line to indicate the end of the output report. At the end of the report, the screen is frozen to allow the user to view the output. The message "PRESS ANY KEY TO CONTINUE . . . ■" is displayed on row 23 to instruct the user how to continue after viewing the output.

After analyzing the output report for the inventory report listing of Case Study 1, prepare the screen layout form as shown in Figure 4.3. It consists of the headings and column headings as suggested in Figure 4.2, together with the format of the detail line, as indicated by two format lines present on rows 9 and 10. The presence of the format lines on two consecutive rows suggests that there should be no blank line present between the detail lines of the output report. In other words, the report should be single-spaced. If a double-spaced report is required, this can be represented on the screen layout form by placing the two format lines on rows 9 and 11, that is, by leaving a line blank between the two format lines.

The symbol "x" present in the format of the detail line of the screen layout form means that a character (a letter or a special character) can be inserted in its place, and the symbol "9" indicates that a digit can be inserted in its place. The other symbols present in the screen layout form appear as they are.

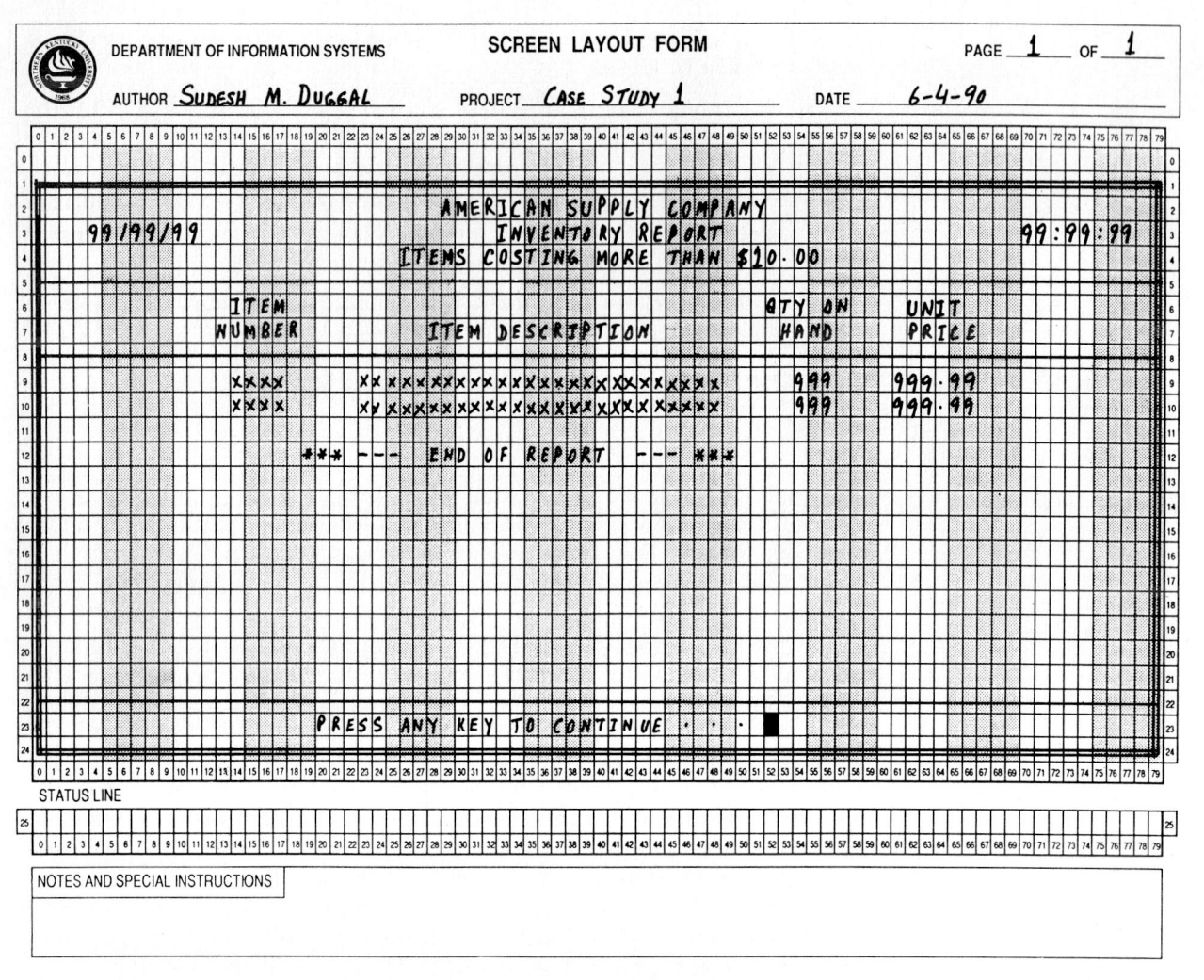

Figure 4.3 Screen layout form for Case Study 1

Analysis of the Input Database File(s)

A review of the structure of the INV database file shown in Figure 4.1 indicates that there are 30 records in the input database file; the output report will contain only 9 of these. Only those records of the INV database file whose UNIT_COST field value is greater than $10 are present in the report. Also observe that each record of the database file consists of eight fields (ITEM_NUM, ITEM_DESC, UNIT_COST, QUANTITY, RET_PRICE, REOD_POINT, REOD_QTY, and DEPT_NUM). However, the detail line in the output report contains only four fields (ITEM_NUM, ITEM_DESC, QUANTITY, and UNIT_COST). Therefore, we conclude that we do not need to include all the records of the database file in the output report and that all the fields present in the input database records do not have to be present in the output report.

Analysis of the Processing Steps

After analyzing the output report and the input database file(s), the next step in the analysis phase is analyzing the processing steps needed to solve the problem. The required processing steps are identified, and the problem is subdivided into smaller components. These components are independent modules, and the technique of breaking the program into them is termed *structured programming.*

The main objective of structured programming is to provide logically correct programs that are easy to understand and maintain, particularly by someone other than the original author. The other objectives of structured programming are to

1. Facilitate the design of a long and complex problem
2. Divide the components among people for independent development of the components
3. Create programs that are easy to maintain
4. Create programs that are easy to read and understand
5. Create programs that are efficient

A review of the program specifications and the output required as shown in Figure 4.2 reveals that the first step in the solution of the case study is to print the headings, which will include column headings. The next step is to open the INV.DBF database file and process its records.

Processing involves comparing the value of the UNIT_COST field of each record of the database file with $10. If the result of the comparison is "true," the record will be printed on the output report, as shown in the data flow analysis diagram in Figure 4.4. But if the result of the comparison is "false," the record will be skipped; that is, the record will not be printed on the report, as shown in the data flow analysis diagram in Figure 4.5. This process of comparing the UNIT_COST field value with $10 and printing the records is repeated for all the records of the INV database file.

After all the records of the INV database file have been processed, the message "*** --- END OF REPORT --- ***" should be printed to indicate the end of the report. Then the screen should be frozen to allow the users to view the output. Finally, the file should be closed.

The review of the program developed in Section 3.2.8 also reveals that a few other steps, such as clearing the screen, changing the default modes, and resetting the default modes, will also be needed in the solution of the problem.

Altogether, the following processing steps will be needed in the solution of Case Study 1:

1. Change default modes.
2. Print report headings, including clearing the screen.
3. Open the INV.DBF database file.
4. Process all the records of the INV database file; that is, repeat steps 5 and 6 for each record of the file. When all the records are processed, go to step 8.
5. Select the record whose UNIT_COST field value is greater than $10.
6. Print this selected record.
7. Skip to the next record.
8. Close the database file.
9. Print the end of the report message.
10. Freeze the screen.
11. Reset the default modes.

Figure 4.4 Data flow analysis of Case Study 1 (for a record with UNIT_COST field value > $10)

```
INV Database File

Record#  ITEM_NUM  ITEM_DESC                 UNIT_COST  QUANTITY  ...  DEPT_NUM
   1      1136     Bond Paper, Ream            22.99       38     ...    100
   2      5818     Calendar Refill              4.99       32     ...    500
   3      5960     Calendar Stands              5.69       14     ...    500
   4      3802     Correction Fluid 10-Box      3.39       65     ...    300
   5      3570     Correction Tape 10-Box       4.29       49     ...    300
   6      4005     Disks Data Case              5.99       18     ...    400
   7      1910     Ditto Paper, Ream           19.99       35     ...    100
          .        .                            .           .     ....    .
          .        .                            .           .     ....    .
          .        .                            .           .     ....    .
  28      3375     Typewriter Ribbons 10-Box   23.79       67     ...    300
  29      1488     Xerographic Paper           19.99       45     ...    100
  30      4189     Zenith Microcomputer Z-158 829.99        5     ...    400
```

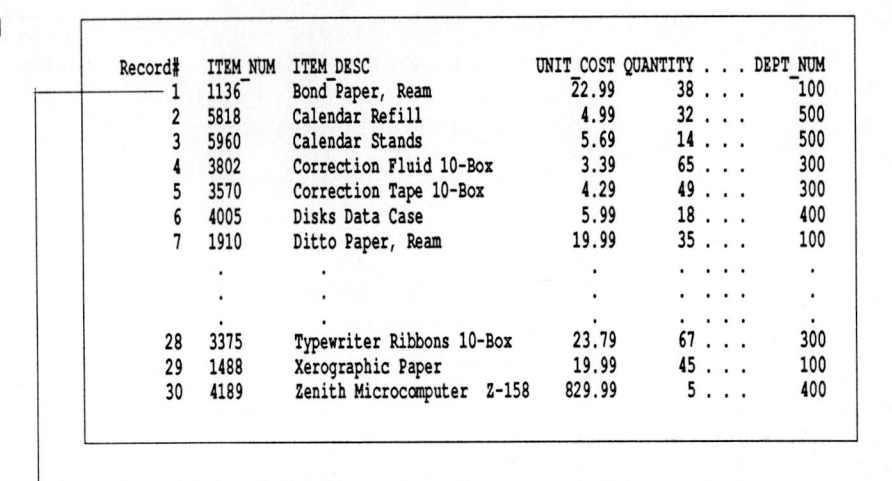

```
COMPUTER INTERNAL MEMORY

  ITEM_NUM        ITEM_DESC              UNIT_COST    QUANTITY
  
   1136        Bond Paper, Ream            22.99         38


  UNIT_COST field compared with $10.00    Result of comparison

         22.99 > 10.00                            T
```

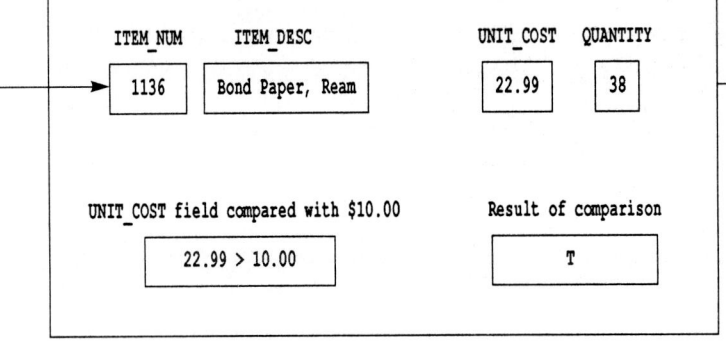

```
Output

                        AMERICAN SUPPLY COMPANY
  08/20/89                 INVENTORY REPORT                      02:29:25
                       ITEMS COSTING MORE THAN $10.00

               ITEM                              QTY ON    UNIT
              NUMBER     ITEM DESCRIPTION         HAND     COST

               1136      Bond Paper, Ream          38      22.99
```

Figure 4.5 Data flow analysis of Case Study 1 (for a record with UNIT_COST field value < or = $10)

```
INV Database File

Record#  ITEM_NUM  ITEM_DESC                UNIT_COST  QUANTITY ... DEPT_NUM
   1      1136     Bond Paper, Ream           22.99      38   ...   100
   2      5818     Calendar Refill             4.99      32   ...   500
   3      5960     Calendar Stands             5.69      14   ...   500
   4      3802     Correction Fluid 10-Box     3.39      65   ...   300
   5      3570     Correction Tape 10-Box      4.29      49   ...   300
   6      4005     Disks Data Case             5.99      18   ...   400
   7      1910     Ditto Paper, Ream          19.99      35   ...   100
   .        .           .                       .         .   ...    .
   .        .           .                       .         .   ...    .
   .        .           .                       .         .   ...    .
  28      3375     Typewriter Ribbons 10-Box  23.79      67   ...   300
  29      1488     Xerographic Paper          19.99      45   ...   100
  30      4189     Zenith Microcomputer Z-158 829.99      5   ...   400
```

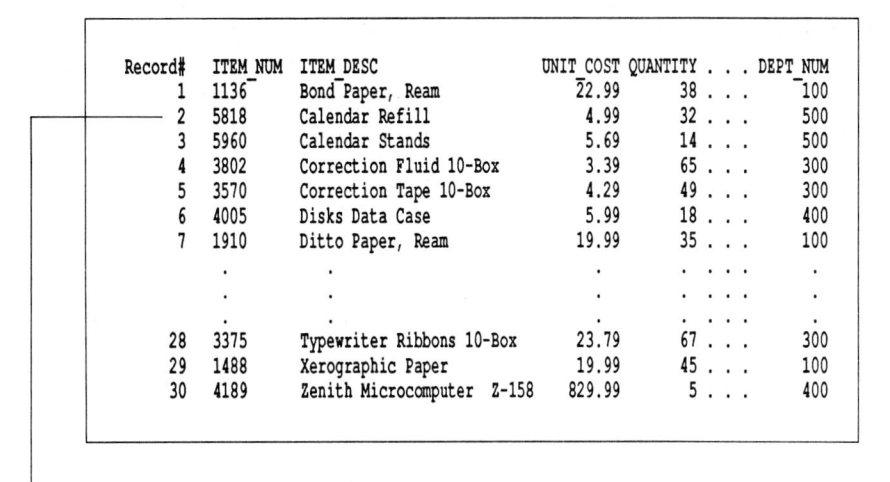

COMPUTER INTERNAL MEMORY

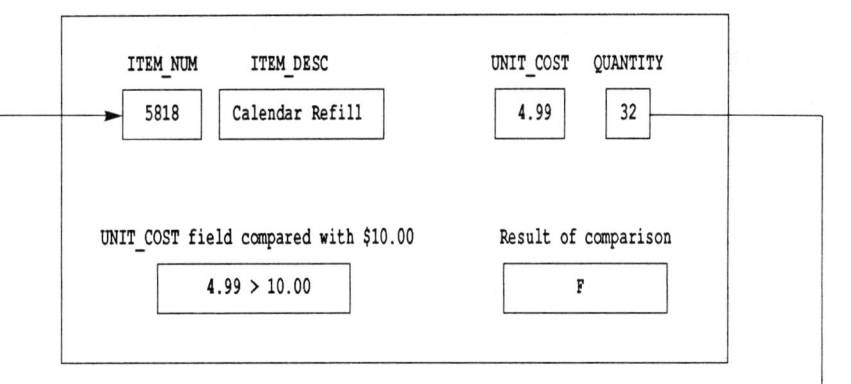

ITEM_NUM	ITEM_DESC	UNIT_COST	QUANTITY
5818	Calendar Refill	4.99	32

UNIT_COST field compared with $10.00

4.99 > 10.00

Result of comparison

F

Output

```
                        AMERICAN SUPPLY COMPANY
 08/20/89                    INVENTORY REPORT                    02:29:25
                        ITEMS COSTING MORE THAN $10.00

          ITEM                                  QTY ON    UNIT
         NUMBER      ITEM DESCRIPTION            HAND     COST

          1136      Bond Paper, Ream              38      22.99
```

The first step is to change default modes, and this step obviously should be performed at the start of the program. The next step should print the heading of the report. Because the output in this problem is a single-screen output, the heading will be printed only once. After printing the report headings, the records of the database file should be processed, which requires opening the INV database file. Thus, the first three steps—change default modes, print report headings, and open the INV database file—should be performed only once and at the start of the solution of the problem.

After opening the INV database file, the next step is to process the records of this database file, one at a time. This means that you should look at each record of the input database file and test it to see if it satisfies the condition, that is, if the UNIT_COST field value is greater than $10. If it is, only then will the record be printed on the output report. If it is not, it will not be printed. The record pointer then skips to the next record in the database file. This process continues with all the records of the database file; that is, steps 4–7 are repeated for each record of the INV.DBF database file.

When all the records of the database file have been processed, the program processing should proceed to step 8; that is, the database file should be closed. Next the processing should proceed to step 9, where the end of the report message should be printed, and then the screen should be frozen in step 10 to allow the users to view the report. Finally, the default modes should be reset in step 11. Completion of these steps terminates the solution of the problem.

This discussion indicates that the steps in the solution of this problem (in fact, any problem) can be broken down into three main categories.

1. The activities or the functions performed only once at the start of program processing
2. The activities or the functions repeated for each record of the database file
3. The activities or the functions performed only once but at the end of program processing

These three categories are discussed in detail in the next section.

4.4.2 The Design Phase

The function of this step is to take the result of the problem analysis, that is, the problem broken down into several smaller, manageable components, and transform it to a structure chart. A **structure chart** is a graphic representation of the problem's solution representing only the main steps of the problem solution. This chart is also referred to as a *hierarchy chart*.

The shell structure chart given in Figure 4.6 is the starting point for almost any batch program. The boxes represent program modules, which in turn represent a program function, that is, a specific processing task performed by the computer. A module contains the function name and the number representing its hierarchical relationship with other modules in the structure chart. The normal sequence of execution of structure chart modules is from top to bottom and from left to right unless specified otherwise.

4.4 An Illustrative Example: Case Study 1

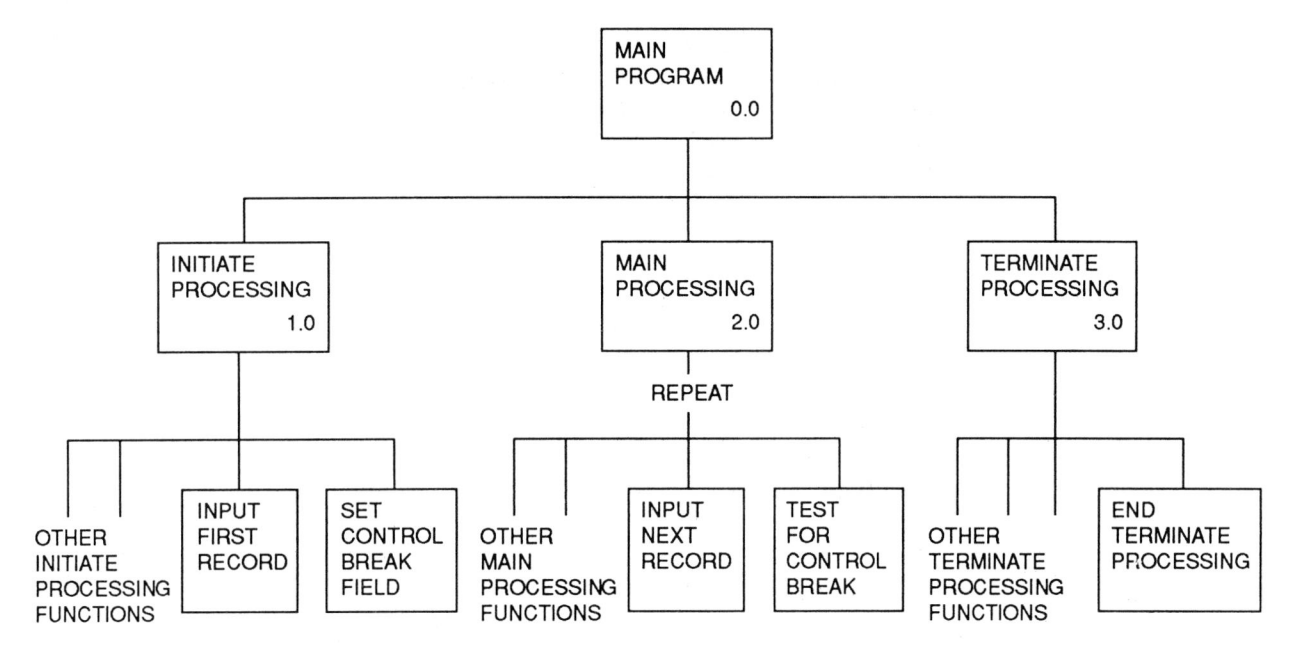

Figure 4.6 Shell structure chart for batch programs

Logical Control Structures

The logic in a structured program can be viewed as a set of basic building blocks put together in various combinations. There are three logical control structures (building blocks) used in the structure chart of any problem representing the order in which the processing functions should be executed:

1. Sequence control structure
2. Selection control structure (a decision)
3. Iteration control structure (a loop or repeat)

Sequence Control Structure The **sequence control structure** implies that the commands are executed sequentially, that is, in the order in which they appear in the problem solution. The sequence control structure is represented in the structure chart shown in Figure 4.7, where the modules are executed in sequential order, that is, from top to bottom and then from left to right. In other words, the 0.0 Main Program module is executed first, followed by the 1.0 Initiate Processing module, the 2.0 Main Processing module, and the 3.0 Terminate Processing module.

Selection Control Structure The **selection control structure** presents two options, but only one operation is to be carried out, depending on a particular condition, which is either true or false. This operation is represented in the structure chart shown in Figure 4.8. When the 2.1 Perform Calculations module is executed, either the 2.1.1 Perform Step A or the 2.1.2 Perform Step B module is performed, depending on the selection criteria.

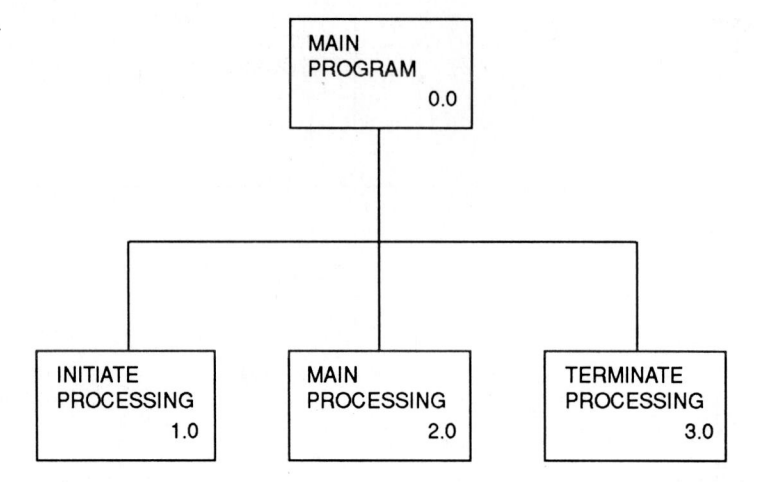

Figure 4.7 Sequence control structure

```
                    MAIN
                    PROGRAM
                              0.0
       ┌───────────────┼───────────────┐
   INITIATE          MAIN           TERMINATE
   PROCESSING        PROCESSING     PROCESSING
         1.0              2.0              3.0
```

Iteration (Repeat) Control Structure The **iteration control structure,** also known as a **loop** or *repetition control structure,* is used for the repeated execution of a module or a set of modules until some condition is satisfied. The iteration control structure is represented in the structure chart shown in Figure 4.9, where the 2.1 Perform Calculations, 2.2 Accumulate Totals, and 2.3 Print Detail Line modules are performed repeatedly for each record of the database file until all the records of the INV.DBF database file have been processed.

Major Processing Steps of a Batch Program

Now go back to the shell structure chart shown in Figure 4.7, which is the starting point for the solution of each batch program. This chart indicates that the solution of any problem can be divided into three major processing steps:

1. Initiate processing
2. Main processing
3. Terminate processing

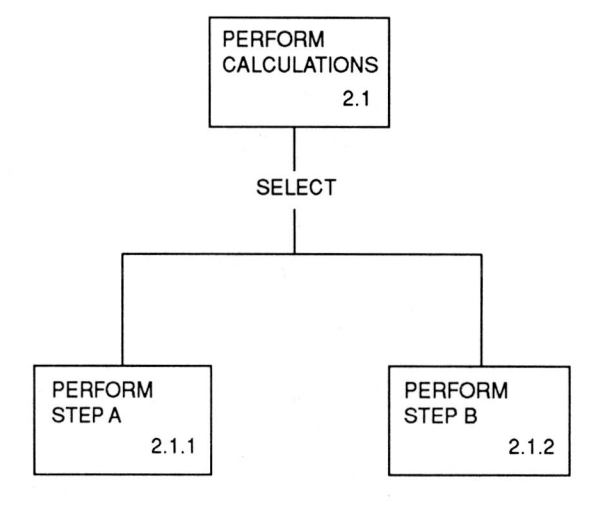

Figure 4.8 Selection control structure

```
              PERFORM
              CALCULATIONS
                          2.1
                   |
                SELECT
            ┌──────┴──────┐
        PERFORM         PERFORM
        STEP A          STEP B
              2.1.1           2.1.2
```

Figure 4.9 Iteration (repeat) control structure

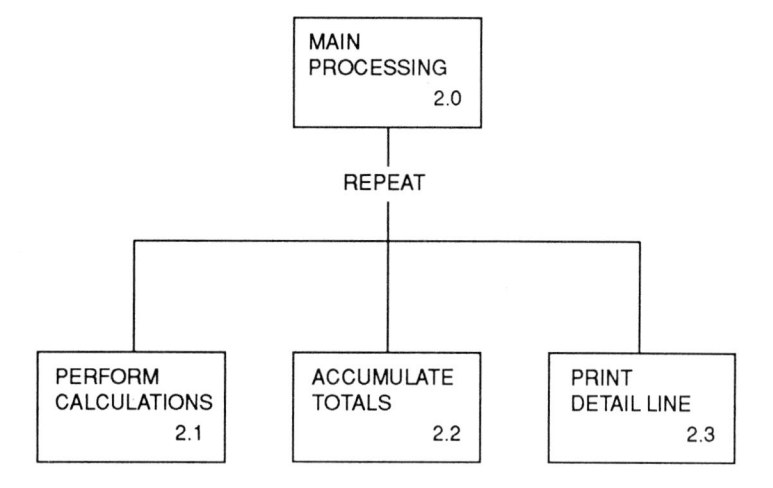

```
                    MAIN
                 PROCESSING
                       2.0
                        |
                     REPEAT
        _____|_____
        |               |                |
    PERFORM         ACCUMULATE        PRINT
   CALCULATIONS       TOTALS       DETAIL LINE
        2.1            2.2             2.3
```

Initiate Processing The activities included in the **initiate processing** part of the solution are the ones that occur only once, at the beginning of program processing, and are not needed anywhere else in the program. These include:

1. Housekeeping, including changing default modes and setting procedures
2. Define variables, including declaring variables, defining program constants, initializing variables and accumulators, defining control variables, and loading memory variables
3. Print report headings or process headings routine, including initializing the page counter, clearing the screen, printing the headings, and initializing the line counter
4. Open file(s), including sorting or indexing
5. Set control areas

The first three activities listed can occur in any sequence in the solution of the problem, but always before the last two activities. The last two activities should always occur in the sequence given; that is, the files should be opened before the control areas are defined.

Main Processing **Main processing** consists of activities that occur repeatedly, usually once for each record of the database file to be processed. The activities include:

1. Perform calculations.
2. Accumulate totals.
3. Print detail line, including incrementing the line counter.
4. Test screen full, including freezing the screen (or testing for the end of the page) and printing report headings.
5. Skip to the next record.

6. Test control breaks, including the control break processing consisting of the following steps:
   a. Print control total
   b. Reset control accumulator
   c. Reset compare area(s)
   d. Freeze screen
   e. Perform headings routine

The activities needed in the solution of any problem from this list should be present in the given sequence.

Terminate Processing The activities included in the **terminate processing** part of the problem solution are the ones that occur only once, at the end of the program processing, and are not needed anywhere else in the program. These activities are

1. Print total lines
2. Close data files, including creating backup file(s) and packing database file(s)
3. End of job, including printing the end of the report message, freezing the screen to allow users to view the report, resetting the default modes, resetting the procedures, and returning to the calling program

These activities should also occur in the same sequence as listed.

In the solution of any problem, all the activities from each of the processing categories listed may not be present. But if they are, they should follow the sequence listed.

The processing steps needed in the solution of a batch program are listed in Table 4.1 for future reference.

Creation of the Structure Chart

Creating the structure chart is the first step in designing the solution of the problem. It is very important that this design step be carefully developed. Here are a few rules you should follow to create a structure chart of good design:

1. The structure chart should contain as many highly cohesive modules as possible.
2. The structure chart should have loose coupling among its modules.
3. The span of control of a module in a structure chart should not be more than seven.

There are three new terms introduced in these rules. I'll explain them before proceeding with the design of the structure chart.

Cohesion **Cohesion** is the measurement of the strength of the relationship between the elements of a module; that is, it measures how closely the

4.4 An Illustrative Example: Case Study 1

Table 4.1 Processing steps needed in a batch program

Initiate Processing:	1.	Housekeeping, including changing default modes and setting procedures
	2.	Define variables, including declaring variables, defining program constants, initializing variables and accumulators, defining control variables, and loading memory variables
	3.	Print report headings or process headings routine, including initializing the page counter, clearing the screen, printing the headings, and initializing the line counter
	4.	Open file(s), including sorting or indexing
	5.	Set control areas
Main Processing:	1.	Perform calculations
	2.	Accumulate totals
	3.	Print detail line, including incrementing the line counter
	4.	Test screen full, including freezing the screen (or testing for the end of the page) and printing report headings
	5.	Skip to the next record
	6.	Test control breaks, including the control break processing consisting of the following steps: a. Print control total b. Reset control accumulator c. Reset compare area(s) d. Freeze screen e. Perform headings routine
Terminate Processing:	1.	Print total lines
	2.	Close data files, including creating backup file(s) and packing database file(s)
	3.	End of job, including printing the end of the report message, freezing the screen to allow users to view the report, resetting the default modes, resetting procedures, and returning to the calling program

commands in a module are related to each other. Ideally, all the modules of a structure chart should be highly cohesive. It is not possible to have an ideal design, that is, to design a structure chart in which all the modules are highly cohesive. However, the attempt should be made to create a structure chart that contains as many highly cohesive modules as possible, as stated in rule 1.

An example of a highly cohesive module is a functionally cohesive module, that is, a module in the structure chart that performs one, and only one, task, and each command in the module directly contributes to accomplishing that task. For example, the 1.2 Print Report Headings module shown in Figure 4.10 directly contributes to printing the report heading and is functionally cohesive.

Figure 4.10 Functionally cohesive module

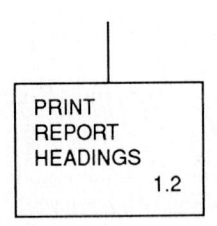

```
┌─────────┐
│ PRINT   │
│ REPORT  │
│ HEADINGS│
│      1.2│
└─────────┘
```

If the structure chart contains functionally cohesive modules, changes to be made in the program during its maintenance can be easily traced and will not affect other program modules. In other words, highly cohesive modules can be maintained in less time and without affecting the other modules in the structure chart. Thus, it will cost less to maintain them.

A module that is not functionally cohesive is called *coincidental cohesive*, that is, a module in which totally unrelated commands are grouped. For example, the 2.1 Perform Calculations & Print Detail Line module of Figure 4.11 is coincidental cohesive because no single task is accomplished in it. In the first part of this module, the calculations are performed; in the second part, the detail line is printed. Two different functions needed in the program are together by coincidence.

Coupling Coupling is a measurement of the relationship between the modules of the structure chart of a program. Ideally, a change in a module should have no impact on any other module of the structure chart, but this situation is not always feasible. All we can do is try to reduce this impact. So if we can produce a structure chart in which a change to any module has as little impact on another module as possible, the modules of this structure chart are said to be loosely coupled.

To have loose coupling between the modules in a structure chart, the connection between the modules should be such that:

1. Every module in the structure chart is entered at the top and exits at the bottom of the module.
2. A module is called only by a module directly above it in the hierarchical chart.
3. Two modules on the same level should never communicate with each other.

Recall that cohesion measures the strength of the relationship between the statements or commands within a module and coupling

Figure 4.11 Coincidental cohesive module

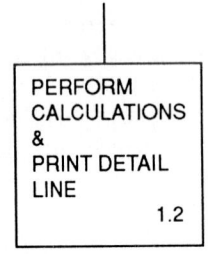

```
┌──────────────┐
│ PERFORM      │
│ CALCULATIONS │
│ &            │
│ PRINT DETAIL │
│ LINE         │
│           1.2│
└──────────────┘
```

measures the strength of the relationship between the modules within a program. Because the change of one module will affect another module, it is impossible to eliminate the coupling effect altogether. Our purpose in designing the solution of the problem is to reduce its effect as much as possible by creating loosely coupled modules. Take care in designing the solution of the problem for the following types of coupling.

Common coupling occurs when a constant defined as a memory variable (discussed in Chapter 5) is used in many modules of the same program. This type of coupling creates *tight coupling* and as such is not a desired type of coupling. Tight coupling should be avoided in designing the solution of any problem.

Control coupling occurs when one module passes a switch (also called a control or an indicator) to another module of the same program for the purpose of controlling the logic of the called module. Also referred to as tight coupling, this should be avoided.

Data coupling occurs when the data are passed from one program to another within a system, and the results are returned to the calling program. This type of coupling always exists and cannot be avoided. Data coupling is also termed loose coupling.

Span of Control The **span of control** of a module is the number of modules immediately subordinate to it. For example, in the repeat control structure shown in Figure 4.9, the span of control of the 2.1 Main Processing module is three because there are three modules immediately subordinate to this module: 2.1 Perform Calculations, 2.2 Accumulate Totals, and 2.3 Print Detail Line. For a well-designed structure chart, the maximum span of control as indicated in rule 3 should not exceed seven.

Now that you are equipped with all these tools and the 11 processing steps needed for the solution of Case Study 1 as listed in the analysis phase, let's complete the structure chart for this case study. The finished structure chart is shown in Figure 4.12.

In this structure chart, all the modules except 1.2 Print Report Headings and 2.1.1 Print Detail Line perform one function and are thus functionally cohesive. Module 1.2 Print Report Headings performs three functions (clear the screen, print the headings, and initialize the line counter). Because all three functions are always needed in this sequence whenever the headings are to be printed on a new screen, you should put these headings in one module. Breaking this module into three modules will simply make the structure chart more complex.

In the same way, the 2.1.1 Print Detail Line module performs two functions (print a detail line and increment the line counter). Every time a detail line is printed, the line counter needs to be incremented so that the next detail line can be printed on the next available line. These two functions will always occur together, so they have been combined in one module. All the modules in this structure chart are functionally or highly cohesive and loosely coupled.

The structure chart of Figure 4.12 satisfies the three rules for designing a good structure chart; it consists of highly cohesive, loosely coupled modules with the span of control of any module not more than three. So it is a well-designed solution of Case Study 1.

Now let's discuss a few things about this structure chart. Observe that all the activities of the initiate processing step have not been used in the

142 Chapter 4 / Design of dBASE Programs

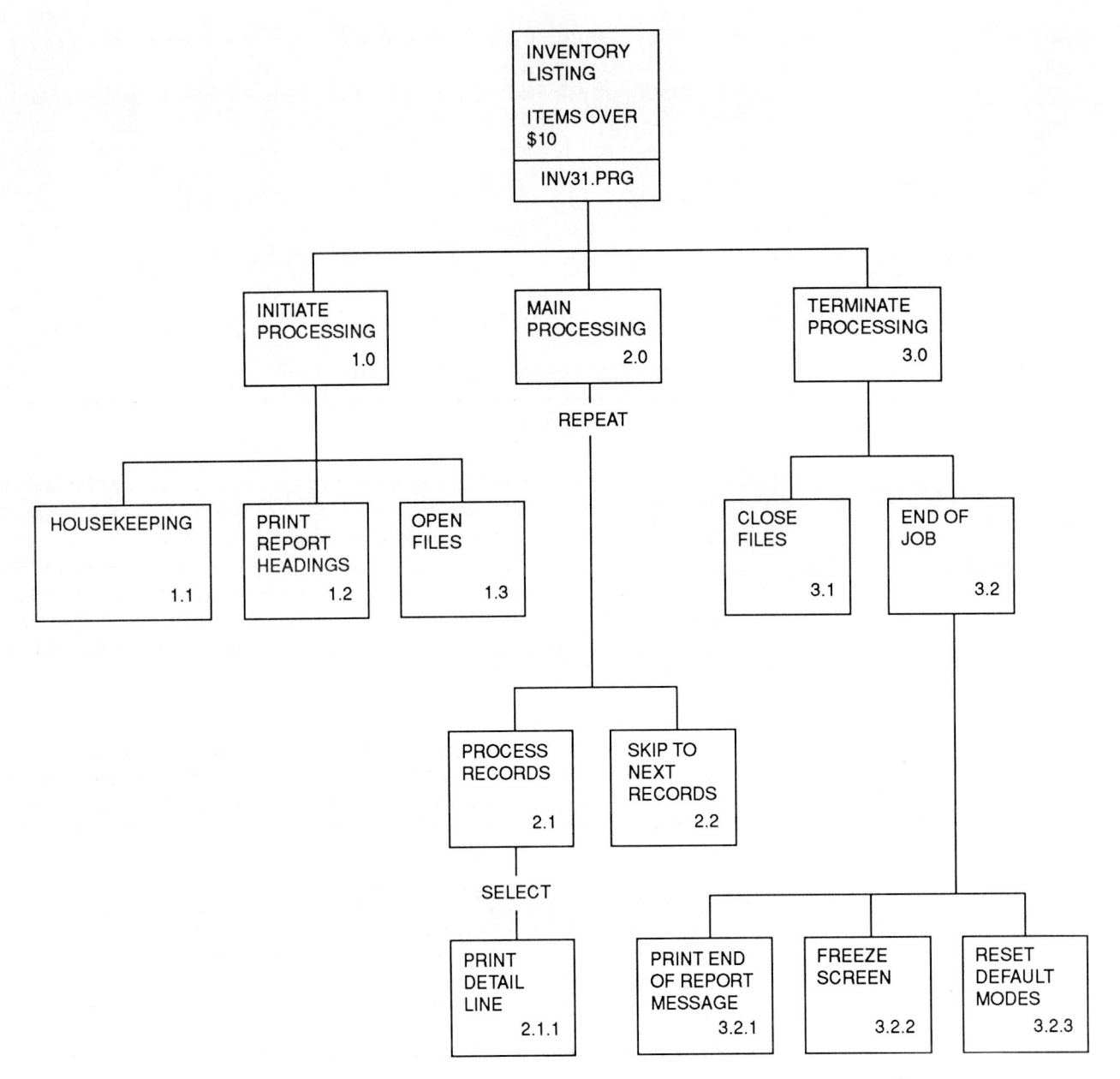

```
                    ┌─────────────────┐
                    │   INVENTORY     │
                    │   LISTING       │
                    │                 │
                    │   ITEMS OVER    │
                    │   $10           │
                    ├─────────────────┤
                    │   INV31.PRG     │
                    └────────┬────────┘
          ┌──────────────────┼──────────────────┐
          │                  │                  │
   ┌──────┴──────┐   ┌──────┴──────┐   ┌──────┴──────┐
   │  INITIATE   │   │    MAIN     │   │  TERMINATE  │
   │ PROCESSING  │   │ PROCESSING  │   │ PROCESSING  │
   │    1.0      │   │    2.0      │   │    3.0      │
   └──────┬──────┘   └──────┬──────┘   └──────┬──────┘
          │              REPEAT                │
   ┌──────┼──────┐         │          ┌───────┴───────┐
   │      │      │         │          │               │
┌──┴──┐┌──┴──┐┌──┴──┐      │      ┌───┴───┐      ┌────┴────┐
│HOUSE││PRINT││OPEN │      │      │ CLOSE │      │ END OF  │
│KEEP-││REPORT││FILES│     │      │ FILES │      │  JOB    │
│ING  ││HEAD-││     │      │      │       │      │         │
│     ││INGS ││     │      │      │  3.1  │      │  3.2    │
│ 1.1 ││ 1.2 ││ 1.3 │      │      └───────┘      └────┬────┘
└─────┘└─────┘└─────┘      │                          │
                    ┌──────┴──────┐                   │
                    │             │                   │
              ┌─────┴─────┐ ┌─────┴─────┐             │
              │  PROCESS  │ │  SKIP TO  │             │
              │  RECORDS  │ │   NEXT    │             │
              │           │ │  RECORDS  │             │
              │    2.1    │ │    2.2    │             │
              └─────┬─────┘ └───────────┘             │
                 SELECT                               │
              ┌─────┴─────┐             ┌─────────────┼─────────────┐
              │  PRINT    │             │             │             │
              │ DETAIL    │       ┌─────┴─────┐ ┌─────┴─────┐ ┌─────┴─────┐
              │  LINE     │       │ PRINT END │ │  FREEZE   │ │  RESET    │
              │           │       │ OF REPORT │ │  SCREEN   │ │ DEFAULT   │
              │  2.1.1    │       │  MESSAGE  │ │           │ │  MODES    │
              └───────────┘       │   3.2.1   │ │   3.2.2   │ │   3.2.3   │
                                  └───────────┘ └───────────┘ └───────────┘
```

Figure 4.12 Structure chart for Case Study 1

design of the solution of this problem. Only those needed for this problem are present in the structure chart.

Also, as discussed earlier, the select control structure selects one module out of two or more modules, depending on the selection condition. In the previous example of Figure 4.8, we have two modules under the select control structure. Depending on the select condition, either the 2.1.1 Perform Step A module or 2.1.2 Perform Step B module will be selected and processed. But sometimes there is only one module under the select control structure, as shown in Figure 4.13. In this situation, either module 2.1.1 Print Detail Line will be selected and processed, or it will not be selected and not processed, depending on the selection criteria.

Figure 4.13 Select control structure with only one option

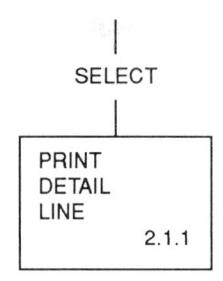

```
        |
      SELECT
        |
  ┌───────────┐
  │ PRINT     │
  │ DETAIL    │
  │ LINE      │
  │      2.1.1│
  └───────────┘
```

In Case Study 1, if the unit price for the record in question is greater than $10, it will be selected, and the selected record will be printed. Otherwise the record will not be selected, and the printing of the record that does not satisfy the condition of UNIT_COST greater than $10 will be skipped.

4.4.3 The Detailed Design Phase

The function of this step is to take the result of the design phase (that is, the structure chart), identify the actual computer operations required for each program function represented in it, and produce the detailed solution of the problem. Detailed design aids such as flowcharts, Nassi-Shneidermann forms, Warnier-Orr diagrams, or pseudocode are used to develop the detailed design. Pseudocode is the only detailed design tool used in this book, so the others will not be discussed here.

Pseudocode is a generic name for an English-like program documentation language. The structure chart of Figure 4.12 and the screen layout form of Figure 4.3 are used to develop the detailed solution of the problem in English-like form.

The process of converting the structure chart to the pseudocode is achieved in two stages. First, the translation of the three control structures to pseudocode, as shown in Figure 4.14, is used to convert the structure chart of Figure 4.12 to the partial pseudocode shown in Figure 4.15(a). Note that the name and number of each module of the structure chart is changed to the headings of the pseudocode paragraphs with the same names and numbers. This conversion requires four steps.

In the first step, the three main processing functions of the structure chart of Figure 4.12 are converted to their equivalent partial pseudocode, as shown in Figure 4.15(b), using the sequence control structure with pseudocode of Figure 4.14(a).

In the second step, the module 1.0 Initiate Processing of the structure chart of Figure 4.12 is translated to its equivalent partial pseudocode, as shown in Figure 4.15(c). Once again, the sequence control structure with pseudocode of Figure 4.14(a) is used for the conversion.

In the third step, the 2.0 Main Processing module is translated to its equivalent partial pseudocode, as shown in Figure 4.15(d). Here the repeat control structure with pseudocode of Figure 4.14(c) is used.

The 2.1 Process Records module is further translated using the selection control structure with pseudocode of Figure 4.14(b), giving the end result shown in Figure 4.15(e) (see page 146).

In the fourth step, the module 3.0 Terminate Processing is translated to its equivalent pseudocode, as shown in Figure 4.15(f) (see page 146). In this example, the sequence control structure with pseudocode of Figure 4.14(a) is once again used.

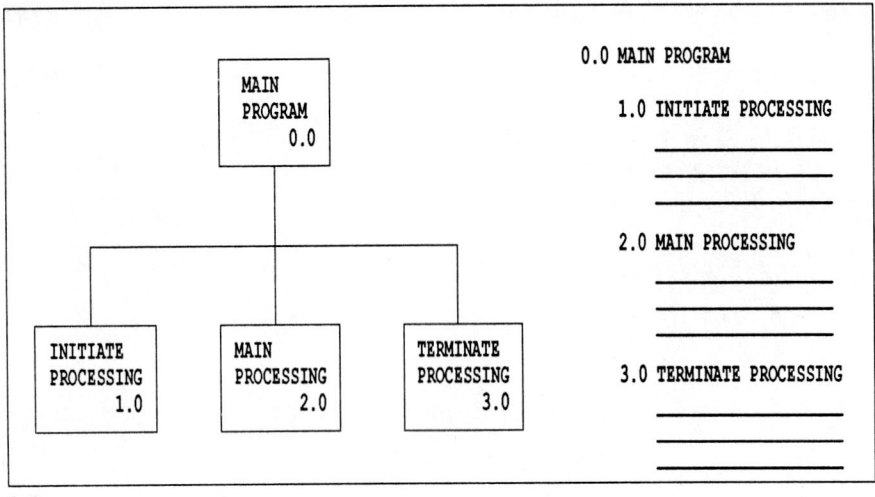

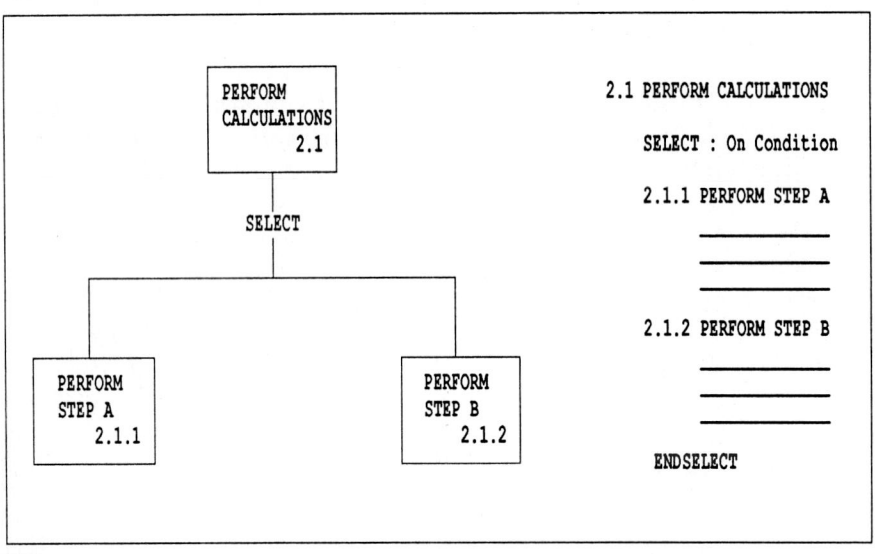

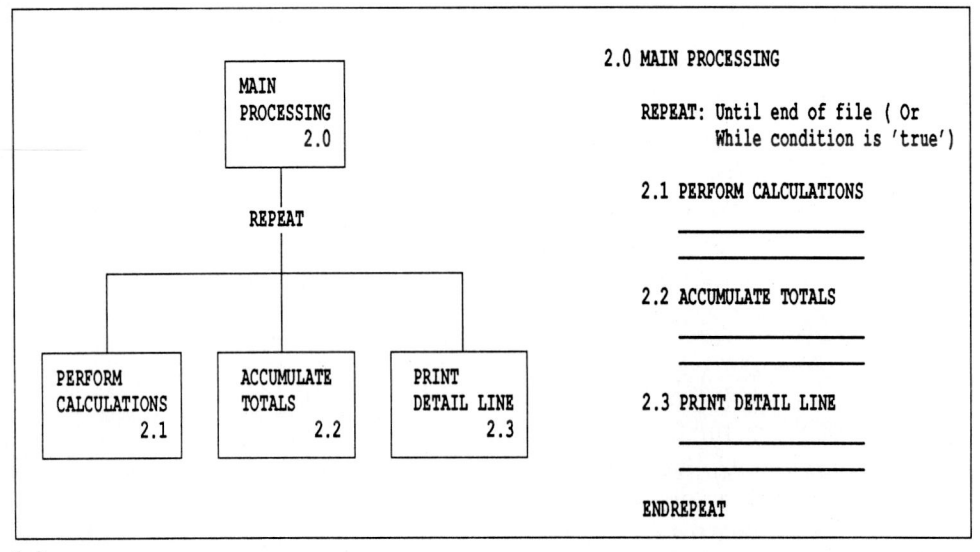

Figure 4.14 Translation of the three control structures to pseudocode. (a) Sequence control structure with pseudocode. (b) Selection control structure with pseudocode. (c) Repeat control structure with pseudocode

Figure 4.15(a) Partial pseudocode for Case Study 1

```
0.0 INVENTORY LISTING : INV31
    1.0 INITIATE PROCESSING
        1.1 HOUSEKEEPING
        1.2 PRINT REPORT HEADINGS
        1.3 OPEN FILE
    2.0 MAIN PROCESSING
        REPEAT: until end of file
            2.1 PROCESS RECORDS
                SELECT: Records with unit price more than $10.00
                    2.1.1 PRINT DETAIL LINE
                END SELECT
            2.2 SKIP TO NEXT RECORD
        END REPEAT
    3.0 TERMINATE PROCESSING
        3.1 CLOSE FILES
        3.2 END OF JOB
```

Figure 4.15(b) Partial pseudocode for Case Study 1

```
0.0 INVENTORY LISTING : INV31
    1.0 INITIATE PROCESSING
    2.0 MAIN PROCESSING
    3.0 TERMINATE PROCESSING
```

Figure 4.15(c) Partial pseudocode of 1.0 Initiate Processing module for Case Study 1

```
1.0 INITIATE PROCESSING
    1.1 HOUSEKEEPING
    1.2 PRINT REPORT HEADINGS
    1.3 OPEN FILE
```

Figure 4.15(d) Partial pseudocode of 2.0 Main Processing module for Case Study 1

```
2.0 MAIN PROCESSING
    REPEAT: until end of file
        2.1 PROCESS RECORDS
        2.2 SKIP TO NEXT RECORD
    END REPEAT
```

Figure 4.15(e) Partial pseudocode of 2.1 Process Records module for Case Study 1

```
2.0 MAIN PROCESSING
    REPEAT: until end of file
        2.1 PROCESS RECORDS
            SELECT: Records with unit price more than $10
                2.1.1 PRINT DETAIL LINE AND INCREMENT LINE COUNTER
                    2.1.1.1 INCREMENT LINE COUNTER
            END SELECT
        2.2 SKIP TO NEXT RECORD
    END REPEAT
```

Figure 4.15(f) Partial pseudocode of 3.0 Terminate Processing module for Case Study 1

```
3.0 TERMINATE PROCESSING
    3.1 CLOSE FILE
    3.2 END OF JOB
```

This section completes the discussion of the first stage of the conversion of the structure chart to the partial structure chart.

In the second stage, the logic of each module is expressed in detail for performing the function of that module. Each statement of the pseudocode closely resembles the commands that will be written in the programming language.

For example, the detailed solution of the print headings, a part of the 1.2 Print Report Headings module, is prepared using the screen layout form. In the screen layout form of Figure 4.3, there are three main heading lines followed by two column headings enclosed in two lines. Each line in the pseudocode pertains to a line to be printed in the heading of the report, as shown in Figure 4.16.

In the same way, each module has been developed to contain the detailed instructions for the logic of that module. The end product is the pseudocode shown in Figure 4.17.

At this point, the program design for Case Study 1 is complete. The program has been written except for coding it in dBASE programming language.

Pseudocode is not bound by any formal syntactical rules, but using the following conventions will make it easier to read:

1. Follow the indentation shown in Figure 4.17.

2. Use the name and number of each module of the structure chart as the name and number of the heading of the pseudocode paragraph.

3. Indicate the range of the elementary control structures, such as the select control structure, the case control structure (introduced in Chapter 8), and the repeat control structure, by using SELECT ... ENDSELECT, DOCASE ... ENDCASE, and REPEAT ... ENDREPEAT, respectively.

4.4 An Illustrative Example: Case Study 1   147

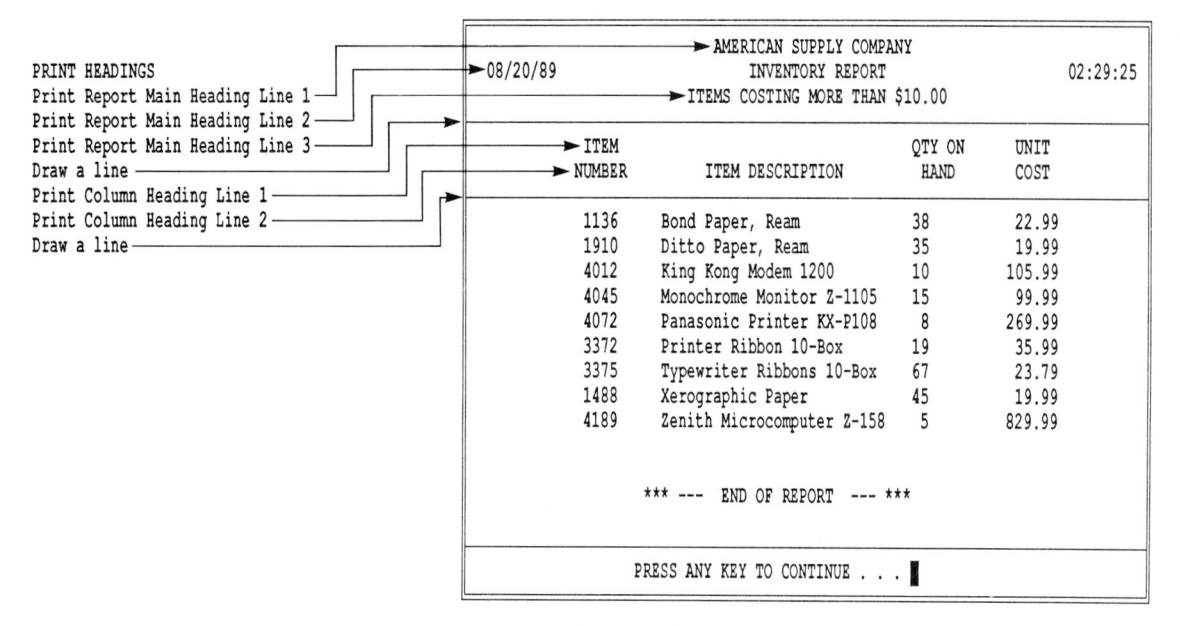

```
PRINT HEADINGS                                    ┌─► AMERICAN SUPPLY COMPANY
Print Report Main Heading Line 1 ─────┐   ┌─08/20/89           INVENTORY REPORT                02:29:25
Print Report Main Heading Line 2 ─────┤   │         ┌─► ITEMS COSTING MORE THAN $10.00
Print Report Main Heading Line 3 ─────┼───┤  ┌─► ITEM                              QTY ON    UNIT
Draw a line ──────────────────────────┤   │  ├─► NUMBER     ITEM DESCRIPTION        HAND     COST
Print Column Heading Line 1 ──────────┤      │
Print Column Heading Line 2 ──────────┘      │    1136    Bond Paper, Ream            38    22.99
Draw a line ─────────────────────────────────┘    1910    Ditto Paper, Ream           35    19.99
                                                  4012    King Kong Modem 1200        10   105.99
                                                  4045    Monochrome Monitor Z-1105   15    99.99
                                                  4072    Panasonic Printer KX-P108    8   269.99
                                                  3372    Printer Ribbon 10-Box       19    35.99
                                                  3375    Typewriter Ribbons 10-Box   67    23.79
                                                  1488    Xerographic Paper           45    19.99
                                                  4189    Zenith Microcomputer Z-158   5   829.99

                                                         *** --- END OF REPORT --- ***

                                                         PRESS ANY KEY TO CONTINUE . . .
```

Figure 4.16 Pseudocode of 1.2 Print Report Headings module for Case Study 1

4.4.4 The Coding Phase

The purpose of this phase in the program development process is to translate the pseudocode instructions of the program solution into programming language instructions. The pseudocode of Figure 4.17 is translated into dBASE commands, and the complete program for Case Study 1 is given in dBASE language in Figure 4.18.

Coding Conventions

A well-documented program is easy to understand. Thus, you should strive to write well-documented programs by following certain standards or conventions. Even though dBASE does not require any coding standards or conventions, their use makes the programs easy to understand, thus saving maintenance time and cost. The following coding conventions are useful in coding a program:

1. Each program should start with a program introduction containing the program name, its description, and the programmer's name:

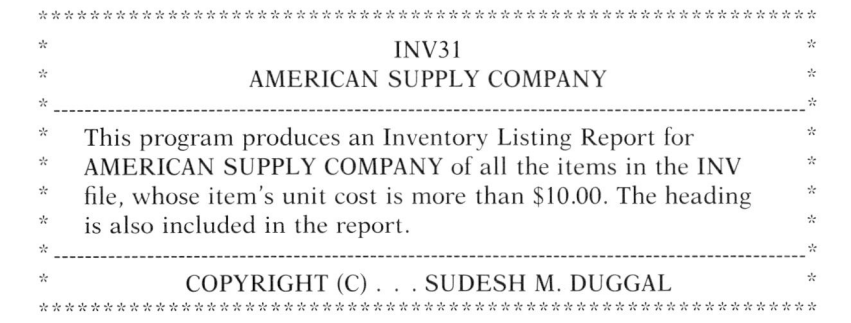

```
**************************************************************
*                          INV31                              *
*                 AMERICAN SUPPLY COMPANY                     *
*-------------------------------------------------------------*
*   This program produces an Inventory Listing Report for     *
*   AMERICAN SUPPLY COMPANY of all the items in the INV       *
*   file, whose item's unit cost is more than $10.00. The heading *
*   is also included in the report.                           *
*-------------------------------------------------------------*
*          COPYRIGHT (C) . . . SUDESH M. DUGGAL               *
**************************************************************
```

Figure 4.17 Pseudocode for Case Study 1

```
0.0 INVENTORY LISTING : INV31
    1.0 INITIATE PROCESSING
        1.1 HOUSEKEEPING
            CHANGE DEFAULT MODES
                Turn off the dBASE's heading feature
                Turn off the dBASE's user dialogue
                Turn off the dBASE's status bar
        1.2 PRINT REPORT HEADINGS
            CLEAR SCREEN
                Clear the screen
            PRINT HEADINGS
                Print Report Main Heading Line 1
                Print Report Main Heading Line 2
                Print Report Main Heading Line 3
                Draw a line
                Print Column Heading Line 1
                Print Column Heading Line 2
                Draw a line
            INITIALIZE LINE COUNTER
                Set line count = 9
        1.3 OPEN FILE
            Open INV database file
    2.0 MAIN PROCESSING
        REPEAT: until end of file
            2.1 PROCESS RECORDS
                SELECT: Records with unit price more than $10
                    2.1.1 PRINT DETAIL LINE
                        PRINT A LINE
                            Write Detail Line
                        INCREMENT LINE COUNTER
                            Add 1 to the Line Counter
                END SELECT
            2.2 SKIP TO NEXT RECORD
                Skip to next record of the database
        END REPEAT
    3.0 TERMINATE PROCESSING
        3.1 CLOSE FILE
            Close database file
        3.2 END OF JOB
            3.2.1 PRINT END OF REPORT MESSAGE
                Increment line counter by two
                Print End of the Report message
            3.2.2 FREEZE SCREEN
                Wait for response to continue processing
            3.2.3 RESET DEFAULT MODES
                Turn on the dBASE's heading feature
                Turn on the dBASE's user dialogue
                Turn on the dBASE's status bar
```

```
****************************************************************
*                         INV31                                 *
*                  AMERICAN SUPPLY COMPANY                      *
*---------------------------------------------------------------*
* This program produces an Inventory Listing Report for         *
* American Supply Company of all the items in the INV.DBF       *
* file, whose item's unit cost is more than $10. The            *
* heading is also included in the report.                       *
*---------------------------------------------------------------*
*            COPYRIGHT (C) . . . SUDESH M. DUGGAL               *
****************************************************************
*
**************************órbigo
* 1.0 INITIATE PROCESSING *
***************************
*
*** 1.1 HOUSEKEEPING ***
    *
    *** CHANGE DEFAULT MODES ***
        *
        SET HEADING OFF
        SET TALK OFF
        SET STATUS OFF
        *
*** 1.2 PRINT REPORT HEADING ***
    *
    *** CLEAR SCREEN ***
        *
        CLEAR
        *
    *** PRINT HEADINGS ***
        *
        @ 2,29 SAY 'AMERICAN SUPPLY COMPANY'
        @ 3,4  SAY DATE ()
        @ 3,33 SAY 'INVENTORY REPORT'
        @ 3,70 SAY TIME ()
        @ 4,26 SAY 'ITEMS COSTING MORE THAN $10.00'
        @ 5,0  TO  5,79
        @ 6,14 SAY 'ITEM'
        @ 6,52 SAY 'QTY ON'
        @ 6,62 SAY 'UNIT'
        @ 7,13 SAY 'NUMBER'
        @ 7,28 SAY 'ITEM DESCRIPTION'
        @ 7,53 SAY 'HAND'
        @ 7,62 SAY 'COST'
        @ 8,0  TO  8,79
        *
    *** INITIALIZE LINE COUNTER ***
        *
        LINECNT = 9
        *
*** 1.3 OPEN FILE ***
    *
    USE INV
```

Figure 4.18 Coding in dBASE for Case Study 1

```
*
***********************
* 2.0 MAIN PROCESSING *
***********************
*
DO WHILE .NOT. EOF ()
   *
   *** 2.1 PROCESS RECORDS ***
      *
      IF UNIT_COST > 10
         *
         *** 2.1.1 PRINT DETAIL LINE ***
            *
            *** PRINT A LINE ***
               *
               @ LINECNT,14 SAY ITEM_NUM
               @ LINECNT,23 SAY ITEM_DESC
               @ LINECNT,54 SAY QUANTITY
               @ LINECNT,61 SAY UNIT_COST
               *
            *** INCREMENT LINE COUNTER ***
               *
               LINECNT = LINECNT + 1
               *
      ENDIF    UNIT_COST > 10
      *
   *** 2.2 SKIP TO NEXT RECORD ***
      *
      SKIP
      *
ENDDO  .NOT. EOF ()
*
******************************
* 3.0 TERMINATE PROCESSING  *
******************************
*
*** 3.1 CLOSE FILE ***
   *
   USE
   *
*** 3.2 END OF JOB ***
   *
   *** 3.2.1 PRINT END OF REPORT MESSAGE ***
      *
      LINECNT = LINECNT + 2
      @ LINECNT,20 SAY '*** --- END OF REPORT --- ***'
      *
   *** 3.2.2 FREEZE SCREEN ***
      *
      @ 22,0  TO 22,79
      @  1,0  TO 24,79 DOUBLE
      STORE ' ' TO RESPONSE
```

Figure 4.18 Continued

```
        @ 23,20 SAY 'PRESS ANY KEY TO CONTINUE . . . ' GET RESPONSE
        READ
        *
*** 3.2.3 RESET DEFAULT MODES ***
        *
        SET TALK ON
        SET HEADING ON
        SET STATUS ON
```

Figure 4.18 Continued

2. The three major processing steps of the program, that is, 1.0 Initiate Processing, 2.0 Main Processing, and 3.0 Terminate Processing, should be clearly identified in the program:

   ```
   *****************************
   * 1.0 INITIATE PROCESSING *
   *****************************
   *
   *************************
   * 2.0 MAIN PROCESSING *
   *************************
   *
   **********************************
   * 3.0 TERMINATE PROCESSING *
   **********************************
   ```

3. Each function represented in the structure chart should be identified with the same heading and number in the program:

   ```
   *** 2.1 PROCESS RECORDS ***
       *
       IF UNIT_COST > 10
         *
         *** 2.1.1 PRINT DETAIL LINE ***
           *
   ```

   In this example, the functions 2.1 Process Records and 2.1.1 Print Detail Line are identified with the same heading and number as represented in the structure chart of Figure 4.12.

4. Blank lines should be used in the program to increase program clarity and readability. As in the previous example, a line with "*" in the first position represents a blank line.
   Note the first four rules are achieved by the use of the COMMENT command, explained in section 3.2.5.
   The statements in the dBASE program starting with an asterisk "*" are treated as COMMENT commands, which are nonexecutable and can be used for program documentation.

5. Indentation should be used as shown in Figure 4.18.
   a. All paragraphs within each major processing step should be indented consistently. For example, the paragraph Change Default Modes is indented three spaces:

```
*** 1.1 HOUSEKEEPING ***
*
   *** CHANGE DEFAULT MODES ***
   *
```

b. Each command within a paragraph should be indented in the same manner; that is, it should be indented consistently. For example, the commands SET HEADING OFF, SET TALK OFF, and SET STATUS OFF are indented three spaces:

```
*** CHANGE DEFAULT MODES ***
*
SET HEADING OFF
SET TALK OFF
SET STATUS OFF
*
```

6. The detail lines under DO WHILE, DO CASE, and IF commands should also be indented three spaces. Indentation helps show clearly the range associated with these commands:

```
DO WHILE .NOT. EOF ()
   *
   *** 2.1 PROCESS RECORDS ***
   *
   IF UNIT_COST > 10
      *
      *** 2.1.1 PRINT DETAIL LINE ***
         *
         *
      ENDIF   UNIT_COST > 10
   *
   *** 2.2 SKIP TO NEXT RECORD ***
   *
ENDDO .NOT. EOF ()
```

7. To establish the visual connection between the DO WHILE and its corresponding ENDDO command, the comments are used at the end of the ENDDO command. The comments are usually the conditions used in the DO WHILE command:

```
DO WHILE .NOT. EOF ()
   *
   .
   .
   .
   *
ENDDO .NOT. EOF ()
```

The comments placed after the ENDDO are ignored by dBASE and help establish a visual connection between DO WHILE and its corresponding ENDDO command.

8. To establish the visual connection between the IF and its corresponding ENDIF command, the comments are used at the end of the ENDIF command. The comments are usually the conditions used in the IF command:

IF UNIT_COST > 10
 *
 .
 .
 .
 *
ENDIF UNIT_COST > 10

The comments placed after the ENDIF command are ignored by dBASE and help establish a visual connection between IF and its corresponding ENDIF command.

9. A space should be used before and after the operational symbols. For example, a space is used before and after the ">" symbol in the IF UNIT_COST > 10 command.
10. The dBASE commands should be spelled out in full. dBASE allows the use of only the first four letters of the command, but this practice should be avoided.

These coding conventions are summarized in Table 4.2 for future reference.

Every program consists of three major processing steps (1.0 Initiate Processing, 2.0 Main Processing, and 3.0 Terminate Processing). The first of these consists of three activities that are performed only once, at the start of the program. These are 1.1 Housekeeping, 1.2 Print Report Headings, and 1.3 Open File. The first activity, 1.1. Housekeeping, as shown in Figure 4.19, consists of one subfunction, that is, change default modes. Its function is to change dBASE default modes. The dBASE commands used to perform this function are given in the next section.

The SET Command

dBASE has many default modes of operation that can be changed by using the SET command. Default modes indicate the way dBASE has been set to carry out the operation. For example, when we list records from a database file using either the DISPLAY or LIST command, the headings are always printed. This indicates that the default mode of heading operation is ON. To produce a list without a heading, we should set the heading mode OFF by using the SET HEADING OFF command. To produce customized reports, you do not want to use the dBASE heading feature; you want to set it OFF and add the heading as explained in section 3.2.7.

The SET TALK OFF command is also used to change the default mode (i.e., On Mode) of the talk operation. When some dBASE commands are executed, the dBASE's talk feature responds by displaying the messages on the screen. When we do not want these messages to be printed along with the report, the talk feature is set OFF.

Table 4.2 Coding conventions

1. Each program should start with a program introduction containing the program name, its description, and the programmer's name.
2. The three major processing steps of the program, that is, 1.0 Initiate Processing, 2.0 Main Processing, and 3.0 Terminate Processing, should be clearly identified in the program.
3. Each function represented in the structure chart should be identified with the same heading and number in the program.
4. Blank lines should be used in the program to increase program clarity and readability.
5. Indentation should be used as shown in Figure 4.18.
   a. All paragraphs within each major processing step should be indented consistently, for example, three spaces.
   b. Each command within a paragraph should also be indented consistently, for example, three spaces.
6. The detail lines under DO WHILE, DO CASE, and IF commands should also be indented three spaces. It helps show clearly the range associated with these commands.
7. To establish the visual connection between the DO WHILE and its corresponding ENDDO command, comments are used at the end of the ENDDO command. The comments are usually the conditions used in the DO WHILE command.
8. To establish the visual connection between the IF and its corresponding ENDIF command, the comments are used at the end of the ENDIF command. The comments are usually the conditions used in the IF command.
9. A space should be used before and after the operational symbols.
10. The dBASE commands should be spelled out in full. dBASE allows the use of only the first four letters of the command, but this practice should be avoided.

The next command, SET STATUS OFF, is used to eliminate the status bar displayed on the screen with the output report. Because all these commands have already been used and explained in Chapter 3, they are not explained here.

The second activity, 1.2 Print Report Heading, performs three functions (clear screen, print headings, and initialize line counter). These are shown in Figure 4.20. The first function, clear screen, consists of only one dBASE command, that is, the CLEAR command.

Figure 4.19 Housekeeping part of the initiate processing step of Case Study 1

```
*** 1.1 HOUSEKEEPING ***
   *
   *** CHANGE DEFAULT MODES ***
      *
      SET HEADING OFF
      SET TALK OFF
      SET STATUS OFF
         *
```

Figure 4.20 Print Report Heading of the initiate processing step of Case Study 1

```
*** 1.2 PRINT REPORT HEADING ***
   *
*** CLEAR SCREEN ***
   *
   CLEAR
   *
*** PRINT HEADINGS ***
   *
   @ 2,29 SAY 'AMERICAN SUPPLY COMPANY'
   @ 3, 4 SAY DATE ()
   @ 3,33 SAY 'INVENTORY REPORT'
   @ 3,70 SAY TIME ()
   @ 4,26 SAY 'ITEMS COSTING MORE THAN $10.00'
   @ 5, 0 TO  5,79
   @ 6,14 SAY 'ITEM'
   @ 6,52 SAY 'QTY ON'
   @ 6,62 SAY 'UNIT'
   @ 7,13 SAY 'NUMBER'
   @ 7,28 SAY 'ITEM DESCRIPTION'
   @ 7,53 SAY 'HAND'
   @ 7,62 SAY 'COST'
   @ 8,0 TO  8,79
   *
*** INITIALIZE LINE COUNTER ***
   *
   LINECNT = 9
   *
```

The CLEAR Command

As already explained in section 3.2.4, the CLEAR command is used to clear the screen (remove everything from the screen). This command is very useful when a report or a menu is to be displayed on the screen.

The second function consists of several @ ... SAY commands.

The @ ... SAY Command

The @ ... SAY command, discussed in section 3.2.7, is used for displaying the text and/or variable values on the screen. The commands shown in Figure 4.20 are used to create the customized heading for the listing report of this program.

The @ ... SAY command can be used to add the headings to the report. Not only does dBASE allow you to position the output on the screen, but it also helps format the output to be sent to the printer through the use of the @ ... SAY command. The general format of the command is

```
@ <row>,<column> SAY [<expression>]
```

This command writes an expression at the address represented by <row>,<column>. The expression may be a character string, a memory variable, or a field name.

```
@ 2,29 SAY 'AMERICAN SUPPLY COMPANY'
@ 3, 4 SAY DATE ()
@ 3,33 SAY 'INVENTORY REPORT'
@ 3,70 SAY TIME ()
@ 4,26 SAY 'ITEMS COSTING MORE THAN $10.00'
```

```
                                                   AMERICAN SUPPLY COMPANY
                         08/20/89                     INVENTORY REPORT                    02:29:25
                                                   ITEMS COSTING MORE THAN $10.00
```

Figure 4.21 Coding for main headings of Case Study 1

The standard monitor screen is made up of 25 rows and 80 columns. The rows are numbered 0 to 24, and the columns are numbered 0 to 79. The address of the upper left corner is 0,0; that of the bottom right corner is 24,79. Line 0 is normally used to display messages and should be avoided.

The function of each of the @ ... SAY commands in the print headings function is explained here. The first @ ... SAY command prints the first main heading line. The next three commands print the current date, the second main heading line, and the current time. The next @ ... SAY command prints the subheading line. These five commands and the headings they produce are given in Figure 4.21.

Two new function commands have been introduced in these five commands: DATE () and TIME ().

The DATE () Function

The format of the DATE () function is

```
DATE ()
```

The DATE () function returns the current system date in the default format of mm/dd/yy. For example, the command @ 3,4 SAY DATE () used previously displays the date "08/20/89," when the report was produced.

The TIME () Function

The format of the TIME () function is

```
TIME ()
```

The TIME () function returns the current system time in the default format of hh:mm:ss. For example, the command @ 3,70 SAY TIME () used previously displays the time "02:29:25," when the report was produced.

The command @ 5,0 TO 5,79 draws a single line from column 0 to column 79 on row 5 of the screen, which divides the title headings from the column headings. The next three @ ... SAY commands display the first column heading, and the next three commands display the second column headings, as shown in Figure 4.22. Finally, the command @ 8,0 TO 8,79 draws a single line from column 0 to column 79 on row 8 of the screen, which divides the column headings from the detail lines, which will be printed in the main processing step.

A new command @ ... TO has been introduced in the commands discussed previously.

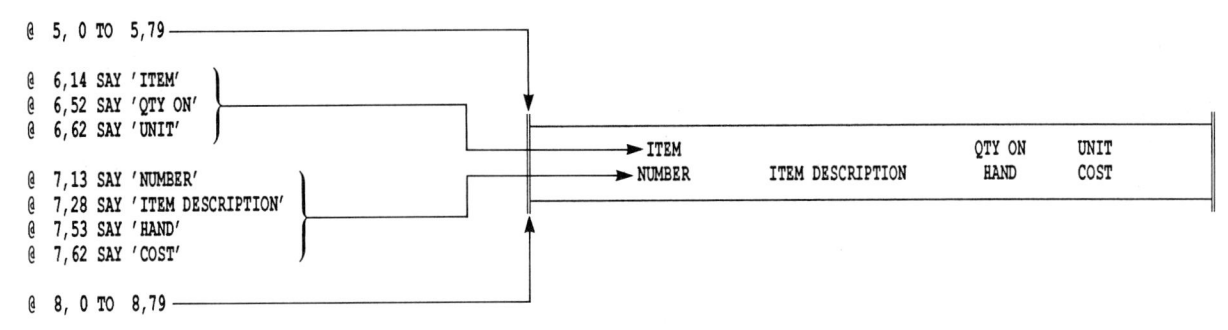

```
@ 5, 0 TO 5,79
@ 6,14 SAY 'ITEM'
@ 6,52 SAY 'QTY ON'
@ 6,62 SAY 'UNIT'

@ 7,13 SAY 'NUMBER'
@ 7,28 SAY 'ITEM DESCRIPTION'
@ 7,53 SAY 'HAND'
@ 7,62 SAY 'COST'

@ 8, 0 TO 8,79
```

```
                      ITEM                              QTY ON    UNIT
                      NUMBER    ITEM DESCRIPTION        HAND      COST
```

Figure 4.22 Coding for column headings of Case Study 1

The @ ... TO Command

The format of the @ ... TO command is

```
@ <row>,<column> TO <row>,<column> [DOUBLE]
```

where <row> is the row number, <column> is the column number for the screen or printer, and DOUBLE is the optional parameter.

This command is used to draw lines and/or boxes in the default mode of single-line drawing. If the optional double parameter is used, the lines or boxes will be drawn using the double-line mode. For example, the command @ 5,0 TO 5,79 draws a single line from column 0 to column 79 on row 5 of the screen, which divides the headings from the column headings. The end result of the print headings function is shown in Figure 4.23(a).

The third and last function of the 1.2 Print Report Headings module as shown in Figure 4.20 is initialize line counter. The command used in this function is LINECNT = 9. This command is an ASSIGNMENT command,

Figure 4.23(a) Coding for the Print Headings function of Case Study 1

```
                       AMERICAN SUPPLY COMPANY
        08/20/89         INVENTORY REPORT               02:29:25
                     ITEMS COSTING MORE THAN $10.00

                ITEM                             QTY ON    UNIT
                NUMBER    ITEM DESCRIPTION       HAND      COST
```

Figure 4.23(b) Housekeeping part of the initiate processing step of Case Study 1

```
*** 1.3 OPEN FILE ***
    *
    USE INV
    *
```

the function of which is to assign a value to a memory variable. Both the ASSIGNMENT command and the memory variables are discussed in detail in Chapter 5. The command LINECNT = 9 assigns a numeric value of 9 to the memory variable LINECNT. The memory variable LINECNT is used in this program to keep track of the line number of the screen in order to print the detail line.

The third and last activity of the 1.0 Initiate Processing module is 1.3 Open File, as shown in Figure 4.23(b). Its function is to open the INV database file. The dBASE command used to perform this function is the USE command.

The USE Command

As already explained in section 2.3.1, the function of the USE command is to open or close a database file. When the USE command is followed by a database file name, it opens that file. For example, the command USE INV in Figure 4.23(a) opens the INV database file.

This completes the discussion of the initiate processing step of program coding. Now let's proceed with the second major processing step of main processing, which is shown in Figure 4.18. This step consists of two activities that are performed over and over again for each record of the INV.DBF database file. The main function of this step is to process all the records of the INV.DBF database file by processing one record at a time. The two activities in this step are 2.1 Process Records and 2.2 Skip to Next Record. In the first activity, each record of the INV database file is tested to see if the value of the UNIT_COST field is greater than $10. If it is, the record is printed on the output report; otherwise it is not printed. In the second activity, the record pointer is moved to the next available record in the INV database file. These two functions are performed over and over until all the records of the INV.DBF database file have been processed. The repeated function is performed by the DO WHILE-ENDDO command, which is explained next.

The DO WHILE-ENDDO Command

As discussed in section 3.2.6, this command is used to perform a set of instructions repeatedly. The part of the DO WHILE-ENDDO command used in this program is given in Figure 4.24. Basically, the DO WHILE-ENDDO command consists of three components:

1. Initialization that performs the procedures necessary to begin execution of the DO WHILE-ENDDO loop.
2. Loop control that tests a stated condition and controls repeated execution of the DO WHILE-ENDDO loop.
3. The body of the loop, which consists of operations to be carried out within the loop. Within the body of the loop must be some element that will change, when appropriate, the test condition so that execution of the loop can be terminated.

All the instructions contained between the DO WHILE and the ENDDO commands are executed over and over until the condition of the DO WHILE command is not true.

Figure 4.24 The DO WHILE-ENDDO command

```
DO WHILE .NOT. EOF ()
    *
    Commands
    *
ENDDO  .NOT. EOF ()
```

The condition of the DO WHILE command in this case is .NOT. EOF (). This condition, a logical test, is true as long as the end of the file has not been reached. Thus, all the instructions contained in the DO WHILE and ENDDO commands will be reexecuted as long as the end of the file is not reached.

When the conditions of the DO WHILE command are met, program control jumps to the command following the ENDDO command. In our example, when the condition of the DO WHILE command is met, that is, the end of the file is reached, program control will be transferred to 3.0 Terminate Processing, which is the last major processing step of the program.

As mentioned earlier, the program should be well documented. To establish the visual connection between the DO WHILE and its corresponding ENDDO command, the comment .NOT. EOF () is used at the end of the ENDDO command. The comment is usually the condition used in the DO WHILE command, as shown in Figure 4.24. The comments placed after the ENDDO are ignored by dBASE but help establish a visual connection between DO WHILE and its corresponding ENDDO command.

The first activity of the 2.0 Main Processing step is 2.1 Process Records, shown in Figure 4.25. Its function is to test each record of the INV.DBF database file to see if the value of the UNIT_COST field is greater

Figure 4.25 Process Records module of main processing of Case Study 1

```
*** 2.1 PROCESS RECORDS ***
    *
    IF UNIT_COST > 10
        *
        *** 2.1.1 PRINT DETAIL LINE ***
            *
            *** PRINT A LINE ***
                *
                @ LINECNT,14 SAY ITEM_NUM
                @ LINECNT,23 SAY ITEM_DESC
                @ LINECNT,54 SAY QUANTITY
                @ LINECNT,61 SAY UNIT_COST
                *
            *** INCREMENT LINE COUNTER ***
                *
                LINECNT = LINECNT + 1
                *
    ENDIF   UNIT_COST > 10
    *
```

than $10. If it is, the record is included in the report; otherwise, it is not. The selection function is performed by the IF-ENDIF command, discussed next.

The IF-ENDIF Command

The IF-ENDIF command has already been introduced in section 3.2.8. This is a control command. If the condition of the IF command, that is, UNIT_COST > 10, is true, then the 2.1.1 Print Detail Line module contained in the IF and the ENDIF commands is processed. If the condition is not true, then this module is skipped.

There are two functions performed by the 2.1.1 Print Detail Line module. The first is print a line. Its function is to print the detail line. Print a line consists of four @ ... SAY commands that print the four fields of the detail line. These four commands will print the first record of the INV.DBF database file satisfying the UNIT_COST > 10 condition on row 9 of the screen. Recall that the value of 9 was assigned to the LINECNT memory variable in the 1.2 Print Report Headings module of the initiate processing step. These commands, along with the first printed record, are shown in Figure 4.26.

The second function is increment line counter, which increments the line counter by one so that the next detail line will be printed on the next line. The command used to increment the LINECNT memory variable is

```
LINECNT = LINECNT + 1
```

It is an assignment command. The right-hand side of the command LINECNT + 1 is evaluated, and the result is assigned to the memory variable on the left-hand side of the "=" sign, which in this case is the LINECNT memory variable itself. The initial value of the LINECNT is 9, as assigned in the initiate processing step. This value is increased by 1, and the new value of 10 (9 + 1) is assigned to the memory variable present on the left-hand side of the "=" sign, that is, to the LINECNT memory variable.

If the UNIT_COST of the item of the record in question is more than $10, the detail line for it will be printed; and the line counter will be increased by 1. But if the UNIT_COST is not more than $10, nothing will happen; that is, the detail line will not be printed, and the line counter will not be increased.

```
*** PRINT A LINE ***
*
  @ LINECNT,14 SAY ITEM_NUM
  @ LINECNT,23 SAY ITEM_DESC
  @ LINECNT,54 SAY QUANTITY
  @ LINECNT,61 SAY UNIT_COST
*
```

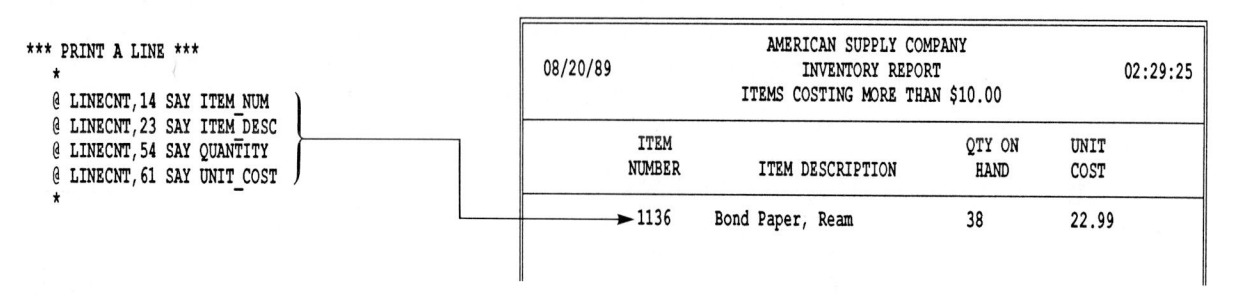

	AMERICAN SUPPLY COMPANY		
08/20/89	INVENTORY REPORT ITEMS COSTING MORE THAN $10.00		02:29:25
ITEM NUMBER	ITEM DESCRIPTION	QTY ON HAND	UNIT COST
1136	Bond Paper, Ream	38	22.99

Figure 4.26 Print a Line function of main processing of Case Study 1

4.4 An Illustrative Example: Case Study 1

To establish the visual connection between the IF and its corresponding ENDIF command, the comment UNIT_COST > 10 is used at the end of the ENDIF command. The comment is usually the condition used in the IF command, as shown:

```
IF UNIT_COST > 10
   .
   .
   .
ENDIF UNIT_COST > 10
```

The comments placed after the ENDIF are ignored by dBASE but help establish a visual connection between IF and its corresponding ENDIF command.

The second activity of the 2.0 Main Processing is 2.2 Skip to Next Record:

```
*** 2.2 SKIP TO NEXT RECORD ***
   *
   SKIP
   *
```

Its function is to move the record pointer to the next available record in the INV.DBF database file. The dBASE command used for this purpose is discussed next.

The SKIP Command

This command has already been discussed in section 3.2.6. Its function is to move the pointer to the next available record in the database file.

This completes the discussion of the 2.0 Main Processing step of the program coding. The last major processing step, 3.0 Terminate Processing, as shown in Figure 4.18, consists of two functions: 3.1 Close File and 3.2 End of Job.

The first function, 3.1 Close File, is shown in Figure 4.27. The purpose of this function is to close the open INV.DBF database file. Recall that employing the simple USE command closes the open database file, which was opened in the 1.0 Initiate Processing.

The second function, 3.2 End of Job, consists of three subfunctions (3.2.1 Print End of Report message, 3.2.2 Freeze Screen, and 3.2.3 Reset Default Modes). The first subfunction is given in Figure 4.28. Its purpose is to print a message at the end of the report to indicate the end of the report.

The first command increments the LINECNT memory variable by 2. The next command prints the message "*** --- END OF REPORT --- ***" two lines below the last detail line of the report.

Figure 4.27 Close File module of terminate processing of Case Study 1

```
*** 3.1 CLOSE FILE ***
   *
   USE
   *
```

Figure 4.28 End of Report message submodule of the terminate processing of Case Study 1

```
*** 3.2.1 PRINT END OF REPORT MESSAGE ***
   *
   LINECNT = LINECNT + 2
   @ LINECNT,20 SAY '*** ---  END OF REPORT  --- ***'
   *
```

The next subfunction, 3.2.2 Freeze Screen, is shown in Figure 4.29. Its purpose is to freeze the screen so that the user can review the report displayed on the screen and then continue the process, that is, scroll the screen by pressing any key.

The first command, @ 22,0 TO 22,79, draws a single line on row 22 of the screen from column 0 to column 79. The next command, @ 1,0 TO 24,79 DOUBLE, draws a double-line box between the (1,0) and (24,79) coordinates, as shown in Figure 4.3. The third command, STORE ' ' TO RESPONSE, is used to initialize a character memory variable named Response by storing a blank (b) value to it. The fourth command is a modified version of the @ ... SAY command.

The @ ... SAY ... GET Command

The general format of this command is

```
@ <row>,<column> SAY [<message>] [GET <variable>]
    [PICTURE <template>] [RANGE <low>,<high>]
    [CLEAR] [TO]
```

where <row> is the row number and <column> is the column number for the screen or printer. The optional <message> can be a character string, memory variable, field, or expression. The <variable> is the name of a database field or a memory variable. The <template> is a string of valid picture characters and other characters allowed in the template. The <low> and <high> are the values of the range allowed for the variable. These can be numbers or dates.

The function of the @ ... SAY command, already discussed in section 3.2.7, is to display or print any user-defined expression at the location specified by the <row>,<column> component of the command. The optional GET component of the command displays the contents of an

Figure 4.29 Freeze Screen submodule of the terminate processing of Case Study 1

```
*** 3.2.2 FREEZE SCREEN ***
   *
   @ 22,0  TO 22,79
   @  1,0  TO 24,79 DOUBLE
   STORE ' ' TO RESPONSE
   @ 23,20 SAY 'PRESS ANY KEY TO CONTINUE . . . ' GET RESPONSE
   READ
```

Figure 4.30 Reset Default Modes submodule of the terminate processing of Case Study 1

```
*** 3.2.3 RESET DEFAULT MODES ***
*
SET TALK ON
SET HEADING ON
SET STATUS ON
```

existing database field or a memory variable in a template matching the size and the data type of the database field or the memory variable. The Range option specifies the acceptable range for the variable displayed with the GET component. The Clear option is used for clearing the portion of the screen. The To option is used to draw the lines and/or the boxes.

Now let us return to the discussion of the fourth command used in the Freeze Screen submodule. The first part of the command, @ ... SAY, displays the following message on row 23 of the screen:

PRESS ANY KEY TO CONTINUE . . .

The second part, GET RESPONSE, displays the value of the Response memory variable immediately after the message. Recall that a blank (b̸) value was assigned by the previous command of this module. Thus, the complete function of the second command is to display the following line:

PRESS ANY KEY TO CONTINUE . . .■

and to freeze the screen. This step allows the user to review screen contents. When the user is ready to continue, he or she can do so by pressing any key, as noted in the message displayed. The READ command will assign this value to the Response memory variable, and the screen will start scrolling. Program control will move to the next function, that is, 3.2.3 Reset Default Modes, which is shown in Figure 4.30. In this function, the SET command is used to reset the Heading, Talk, and Status features to their default modes, that is, the On Mode.

This completes the discussion of the logic and the commands used in Case Study 1.

After completing the coding, the next step is to create the program file from this coded program. The MODIFY COMMAND command discussed in section 3.2.1 can be used to create the program file, called the *source program*.

4.4.5 The Testing and Debugging Phase

The last step in program development is the testing and debugging phase, in which the source program is compiled and tested for the accuracy of its logic; that is, it is translated into machine language to produce an *object program*. The object program is then executed to produce the output. When the program is executed for the first time, it is compiled by the language compiler before it is executed. The compiling process, as shown in Figure 4.31, consists of translating the source program into machine language and thus creating the object program.

Figure 4.31 Compilation of source program to object program

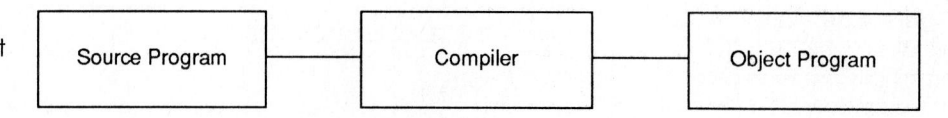

Source Program — Compiler — Object Program

The errors detected in the compiling process, usually referred to as syntactical errors, are listed by the compiler. Syntactical errors occur when programming language grammar rules are violated in the creation of the commands. Computers cannot process these incorrect commands. These errors are located with the help of messages generated by the compiler, which are referred to as *diagnostic messages*. These errors must be corrected, and the source program should be compiled again. When the compilation process does not indicate any syntactical errors, an object program is created.

After the creation of the object program, every time a command is given to execute this program, the compilation process is skipped; and the computer system uses the object program to produce the output. Completion of the compilation process and execution of the object program do not mean that the program is operating correctly and the results produced are correct. The function of the compiler is to check the program coding and make sure it is written in accordance with the syntactical requirements of the programming language. But the compiler has no way of knowing or checking the correctness of the program logic. In fact, it is the function of the testing process to ensure that the program is processing data in accordance with the programming specifications and producing the desired results.

Errors in logic of the problem solution are called logical errors. For example, if the logic of the problem requires a statement A + B and if it is entered in the program as A − B, we know that the program contains an error—a bug. A bug in the computer language means an error in program logic. The compiler cannot detect such errors, and the computers will be able to process these commands but will fail to produce the expected results. The logical errors are found by program testing, which involves executing the program using test data. The process of locating and correcting these errors is called debugging. The end product of the testing phase is an object program that when executed always produces correct and predictable results.

4.5 Summary

The program development process consists of the following five steps:

1. The analysis phase
2. The design phase
3. The detailed design phase
4. The coding phase
5. The testing and debugging phase

4.5 Summary

Analysis of the problem means reviewing and understanding program specifications and identifying the processing tasks needed in the solution of the problem.

The purpose of the design phase is to create the structure chart. The structure chart contains the major processing steps in the solution of the problem.

The major processing steps of the solution of the problem are written in the English language in the detailed design phase. This English version of the solution of the problem is called pseudocode.

In the coding phase, the pseudocode instructions are translated into dBASE commands, thus creating a source program.

The final phase of testing and debugging is used to trace and correct syntactical and logical errors. Syntactical errors are errors due to the violation of the rules of grammar of the programming language. Logical errors are errors in the logic of the solution to the problem.

The following are three types of programs:

1. Batch programs are those in which no data from any external source are used. That is, data not defined in the program itself or the files not opened in the program are not used.
2. Menu programs do not use any data. Their main function is to present different options to users and let them select one. Depending on the selection, the menu program will perform the processing step associated with the selection.
3. Interactive programs are ones in which data from internal as well as external sources (user supplied data) are used.

Three control structures used to design the solution of the problem are (1) sequence control structure, (2) selection control structure, and (3) iteration (repeat) control structure.

The modules in the sequence control structure are processed in sequential order, that is, from top to bottom and then from left to right.

In the selection control structure, only one module out of several presented is selected and processed, depending on the selection criteria.

The modules in the iteration (repeat) control structure are executed repeatedly until some condition is satisfied.

Major processing steps in the solution of any problem are (1) initiate processing, (2) main processing, and (3) terminate processing.

The functions performed in the initiate processing step are the ones that occur only once, at the start of program processing, and are not needed anywhere else in the program.

The functions performed in main processing are repeated for each record of the database file to be processed.

The functions performed in the terminate processing step occur only once, at the end of program processing, and are not needed anywhere else in the program.

The processing steps for a batch program in the initiate processing step are

1. Housekeeping
2. Define variables

3. Print report headings
4. Open file(s)
5. Set control areas

The processing steps for a batch program in the main processing step are

1. Perform calculations
2. Accumulate totals
3. Print detail line
4. Test screen full
5. Skip to next record
6. Test control breaks

The processing steps for a batch program in the terminate processing step are

1. Print total line
2. Close database files
3. End of job

Cohesion is the measure of the strength of the relationship between the elements of a module; that is, cohesion measures how closely the commands in a module are related to each other. Coupling is a measurement of the relationship between the modules of the structure chart of a program. The span of control of a module is the number of modules immediately subordinate to it.

KEY CONCEPTS

analysis phase
batch programs
bug
coding phase
cohesion
common coupling
control coupling
coupling
data coupling
debugging
design phase
detailed design phase
initiate processing
interactive programs

iteration control structure
logical errors
loop
main processing
menu programs
pseudocode
selection control structure
sequence control structure
span of control
structure chart
syntactical errors
terminate processing
testing and debugging phase

dBASE COMMANDS AND FUNCTIONS

@ ... SAY command
@ ... TO command
@ ... SAY ... GET command
ASSIGNMENT command
CLEAR command
DATE () function

DO WHILE-ENDDO command
IF-ENDIF command
SET command
SKIP command
TIME () function
USE command

REVIEW QUESTIONS

1. List the five phases of the program development process, and briefly explain each.
2. List the three steps of the analysis phase, and briefly explain each.
3. List the different types of programs used to develop business application software, and briefly explain each.
4. What is the purpose of the data flow diagram?
5. List the logical control structures used in designing the solution of a program.
6. List the three major processing steps in the solution of any program.
7. Explain the function of the initiate processing step, and list all possible activities of this step used to develop the batch program.
8. Explain the function of the main processing step, and list all possible activities of this step used in developing the batch program.
9. Explain the function of the terminate processing step, and list all possible activities of this step used to develop the batch program.
10. List the rules for designing a good structure chart.
11. What is meant by cohesion? What is meant by a functionally cohesive module?
12. Is it possible to create a structure chart in which all the modules are functionally cohesive?
13. What is meant by coupling? List the rules for designing a loosely coupled structure chart.
14. Explain the term "span of control."
15. What are the rules for creating a pseudocode?
16. List the rules to be used in the coding process.
17. What is the function of each of the following commands:
    a. @ ... SAY
    b. @ ... TO
    c. @ ... SAY ... GET
    d. ASSIGNMENT
    e. CLEAR
    f. DATE () function
    g. DO WHILE-ENDDO
    h. IF-ENDIF
    i. SET
    j. SET STATUS ON/OFF
    k. SKIP
    l. TIME () function
    m. USE
18. What is a syntactical error? How is it different from a logical error?
19. Explain the following terms:
    a. Bug
    b. Debugging
    c. Source program
    d. Object program
    e. Diagnostic message

HANDS-ON ASSIGNMENT

Programming Assignment 4A

Program Description Write a program ACR31.PRG to produce an accounts receivable report listing for American Supply Company. The listing should consist of only those receivables from the ACCREC database file for which payments have been received in April 1990. The report should also include headings.

Figure 4.32 Structure of the ACCREC database file

```
Structure for database : C:\DBASE\ACCREC\ACCREC.DBF
Number of data records :      30
Date of last update    : 05/18/90
Field  Field Name  Type        Width    Dec    Index
    1  CUS_NUM     Character      11                N
    2  PUR_DATE    Date            8                N
    3  PUR_REF     Numeric         4      0         N
    4  PUR_AMT     Numeric         8      2         N
    5  PAY_DATE    Date            8                N
    6  PAY_REF     Numeric         4      0         N
    7  PAY_AMT     Numeric         8      2         N
** Total **                       52
```

Input File(s) The ACCREC database file, whose structure is shown in Figure 4.32, is used as an input file.

Output Program output should be an accounts receivable report listing. It is a single-screen report, as shown in Figure 4.33. The headings should be as shown in the accounts receivable report listing, and the detail line should consist of the CUS_NUM, PUR_DATE, PUR_REF, PUR_AMT, PAY_DATE, PAY_REF, and PAY_AMT fields only.

Processing Steps The following steps should be used to develop the solution of the program:

1. The headings should be printed as shown in the accounts receivable report listing. The date and time should be included in the headings.
2. The column headings should be enclosed between the two lines, as shown in Figure 4.33.
3. Each record of the ACCREC database file should be tested. If the value of the PAY_DATE field is greater than or equal to 03/31/90, it should be

Figure 4.33 Accounts receivable report listing: Programming Assignment 4A

```
                    AMERICAN SUPPLY COMPANY
08/20/89             ACCOUNT RECEIVABLE REPORT              02:29:25
             RECEIVABLE WITH PAYMENT IN APRIL 1990

CUSTOMER  PURCHASE  PURCHASE   PURCHASE   PAYMENT   PAYMENT    PAYMENT
 NUMBER     DATE    REFERENCE   AMOUNT      DATE   REFERENCE    AMOUNT

xxxxxxxxxx 99/99/99   9999      9,999.99  99/99/99   9999      9,999.99
xxxxxxxxxx 99/99/99   9999      9,999.99  99/99/99   9999      9,999.99

              ***  ---  END OF REPORT  ---  ***




                    PRESS ANY KEY TO CONTINUE . . .
```

printed in the output report; otherwise, it should be skipped.

4. At the end of the output report, print the message "*** --- END OF REPORT --- ***" to indicate the end of the output report. Then freeze the screen to allow the user to view the output.

5. The whole output should be enclosed in the box, as shown in Figure 4.33.

Programming Assignment 4B

Program Description Write a program PAY31.PRG to produce a payroll report listing for American Supply Company. It should consist only of those employees from the EMPLOYEE database file whose OTIME_PAY field value for the current pay period is more than zero. The report should also include headings.

Input File(s) The EMPLOYEE database file, whose structure is shown in Figure 4.34, is used as an input file.

Output The output of the program should be a payroll report listing. It is a single-screen report, as shown in Figure 4.35. The headings should be as shown in the payroll report listing, and the detail line should consist of the SOC_SC_NUM, EMP_NAME, REG_PAY, and OTIME_PAY fields only.

Processing Steps The following steps should be used to develop the solution of the program:

1. The headings should be printed as shown in the payroll report listings. The date and time should be included in the headings.

2. The column headings should be enclosed between the two lines, as shown in Figure 4.35.

3. Each record of the EMPLOYEE database file should be tested. If the value of the OTIME_PAY field is greater than $0, it should be printed in the output report; otherwise, it should be skipped.

4. At the end of the output report, print the message "*** --- END OF REPORT --- ***" to indicate the end of the output report. Then freeze the screen to allow the user to view the output.

5. The whole output should be enclosed in the box, as shown in Figure 4.35.

Figure 4.34 Structure for EMPLOYEE database file

```
Structure for database: B:EMPLOYEE.DBF
Number of data records:      30
Date of last update     : 06/13/88
Field  Field Name  Type       Width    Dec
    1  SOC_SC_NUM  Character     11
    2  EMP_NAME    Character     25
    3  DEPT_CODE   Numeric        3
    4  PAY_CODE    Numeric        2
    5  M_STATUS    Numeric        1
    6  N_DEP       Numeric        2
    7  REG_PAY     Numeric        8      2
    8  OTIME_PAY   Numeric        8      2
    9  FED_TAX     Numeric        6      2
   10  ST_TAX      Numeric        6      2
   11  SC_TAX      Numeric        6      2
   12  L_TAX       Numeric        6      2
   13  YTD_GPAY    Numeric        9      2
   14  YTD_FTAX    Numeric        8      2
   15  YTD_STAX    Numeric        8      2
   16  YTD_CTAX    Numeric        8      2
   17  YTD_LTAX    Numeric        8      2
** Total **                     126
```

Figure 4.35 Payroll report listing: Programming Assignment 4B

```
                    AMERICAN SUPPLY COMPANY
 08/20/89                PAYROLL REPORT                  02:29:25
                   EMPLOYEES WHO WORKED OVERTIME

        SOC SEC                               REGULAR    OVERTIME
        NUMBER        EMPLOYEE NAME             PAY        PAY


       XXXXXXXXXX   XXXXXXXXXXXXXXXXXXXXXXX   9,999.99   9,999.99
       XXXXXXXXXX   XXXXXXXXXXXXXXXXXXXXXXX   9,999.99   9,999.99

                   *** --- END OF REPORT --- ***








                PRESS ANY KEY TO CONTINUE . . . ▮
```

Chapter 5

Arithmetic Operations in dBASE

LEARNING OBJECTIVES

Upon successfully completing this chapter, you will be able to:

1. Use the dBASE CALCULATOR command.
2. Use the dBASE INTEGER function.
3. Create memory variables (use the STORE command).
4. Save memory variables onto disk files (use the SAVE TO command).
5. Delete memory variables from the computer's memory (use the RELEASE and RELEASE ALL commands).
6. Load memory variables from disk files into computer memory (use the USE and RESTORE commands).
7. Use the dBASE summary statistics features (use the COUNT, SUM, and AVERAGE commands).
8. Analyze, design, and code a program in dBASE programming language in which calculations and accumulating features are used and produce multiscreen output.

5.1 Overview

The chapter starts by introducing the CALCULATOR command and the INTEGER function. The different commands needed to create, save, delete, and load the memory variables into RAM are presented next, followed by the most commonly used dBASE summary statistical commands. Finally, a simple program, including calculations and accumulating features, that produces multiscreen output is analyzed, designed, coded, tested, and debugged.

5.2 The CALCULATOR Command

dBASE IV provides a useful command called the CALCULATOR command. The format of the command is

```
? <expression>
```

where <expression> may be a field name, an existing memory variable, or an expression. The function of the ? command is to display the result of the expression at the start of a new line. If the ? command is used alone (with no expression), it prints a blank line.

As the name suggests, this command can be used as a calculator. For example, to obtain the product of 15 and 3.5, type:

```
. ? 15 * 3.5    <Return>
```

dBASE will respond by displaying the result as:

```
52.5
```

When the field name is used in place of an expression or in the expression, it should be the field name of the database file currently in use. To display the value of the ITEM_DESC field of the first record of the INV database file, type the following command:

```
. USE INV          <Return>
. ? ITEM_DESC      <Return>
```

dBASE will respond by displaying:

```
Bond Paper, Ream
```

where bond paper, ream is the content (or value) of the ITEM_DESC field of the first record of the INV database file.

If you want to display more than one field using the ? command, separate them by a comma and a space. For example, to display the contents of the ITEM_DESC and UNIT_COST fields of the first record of the INV database file, you should type:

```
. ? ITEM_DESC, UNIT_COST     <Return>
```

dBASE will respond by displaying:

```
Bond Paper, Ream    22.99
```

To calculate and display the retail price of a ream of bond paper using a 50 percent markup on its unit cost, type:

```
. ? UNIT_COST * 1.5    <Return>
```

dBASE IV will respond by displaying the retail price as:

```
34.49
```

But dBASE III or III PLUS will return the retail price as 34.485. dBASE IV rounds the result; dBASE III does not. Therefore, you will need to round this value. You can do so by using the INT () function, which is discussed in section 5.3. Remember that rounding will be needed only if you are using dBASE III.

5.3 The INT () Function

The most commonly used mathematical function in business applications is the INT () (INTEGER) function. Its general format is

```
INT <expression>
```

where <expression> may be a number, a numeric variable, or a numeric expression. The INT () function converts a numeric value to an integer by truncating its decimal portion. For example:

```
. ? INT (6.327)    will yield 6
. ? INT (-3.25)    will yield -3
```

The main use of the INT () function is for rounding the dollar amount. To round an expression to two decimal places, use the following formula:

INT (expression * 100 + 0.5) / 100

Let us use this formula to round $432.937 to two decimal places. Type the following command:

```
. ? INT (432.937 * 100 + 0.5) / 100    <Return>
```

dBASE will respond by yielding the result as:

```
432.94
```

Let us use this formula again to round $432.934 to two decimal places. Type the following command:

```
. ? INT (432.934 * 100 + 0.5) / 100    <Return>
```

dBASE will now respond by yielding the result as:

```
432.93
```

Now let us try this formula with the example discussed in the previous section. The command ? UNIT_COST * 1.5 yielded a result of 34.485. To round the result of this calculation to two decimal places, you should type:

```
. ? INT ( (UNIT_COST * 1.5) * 100 + 0.5) / 100
<Return>
```

This time dBASE will respond with the rounded value as 34.49 as compared with the previously displayed unrounded value of 34.485.

5.4 Memory Variables

So far you have stored data in database files on disk. When programming, you will need to store the intermediate results of calculations temporarily so you can use them in future processing. Random access memory (RAM) can be a temporary storage area to save the results as memory variables. A **memory variable** is a memory location set aside in RAM to store a data element. dBASE IV provides four types of memory variables: character, numeric, data, and logical.

Memory variable names follow the same rules as field names, conforming to the following rules:

1. They can each be up to ten characters long.
2. They must begin with a letter and may include letters, numbers, and an underline (_).
3. No other punctuation mark or blank spaces are allowed in the field name.
4. They should not be the same name as any dBASE command. A list of dBASE commands is given in Appendix D.

Memory variable names should describe the information they are representing, and the use of the underscore to improve readability is highly recommended.

5.4.1 Creating Memory Variables

Memory variables can be created in two different ways: using the STORE TO command and using the ASSIGNMENT command.

The STORE TO Command

The format of the STORE TO command is

```
STORE <expression> TO <memory variable list>
```

where <expression> is a literal, a variable name, a field name, or an expression and <memory variable list> is the list of memory variable(s) to be created and/or initialized.

5.4 Memory Variables

The function of the STORE TO command is to create and initialize by assigning the value of the expression to one or more memory variables or simply to initialize the existing memory variable by assigning the value of the expression.

To create a new memory variable named MARK_UP and assign the markup factor value of 1.5 to it, type the following command:

```
. STORE 1.5 TO MARK_UP      <Return>
```

dBASE will respond by displaying:

```
1.5
```

Now let us use this memory variable with the data of the INV database file. To calculate the retail price by multiplying the UNIT_COST field of the data record of the INV database file and the MARK_UP memory variable as previously defined, type the following command:

```
. ? UNIT_COST * MARK_UP      <Return>
```

dBASE will respond by displaying the result as:

```
34.49
```

Note that this result is the same as that obtained when the following command was used:

```
. ? UNIT_COST * 1.5     <Return>
```

To store a character string to a memory variable, you must enclose the string in double quotes (" "), single quotes (' '), or square brackets ([ ]). For example, if you type the following command:

```
. STORE 'Retail Price = ' TO RETAIL      <Return>
```

it will assign the string value 'Retail Price = ' to the retail memory variable. Now let us use this string memory variable in the following command:

```
. ? RETAIL, UNIT_COST * MARK_UP      <Return>
```

dBASE will respond by displaying:

```
Retail Price =    34.49
```

The STORE TO command can be used to create and/or assign a date value to the memory variable. To assign a date value to a memory variable, enclose the date in curly brackets called braces ({ }). For example, to assign the date 8/3/89 to the TODAY_DATE memory variable, type the following command:

```
. STORE {8/3/89} TO TODAY_DATE      <Return>
```

dBASE will respond by displaying:

```
08/03/89
```

The STORE TO command can also be used to create and/or assign a logical value to the memory variable. To do this, enclose the logical value by periods (.T. or .F.). For example, to assign the logical true value (.T.) to the TEST_TRUE memory variable, type the following command:

```
. STORE .T. TO TEST_TRUE     <Return>
```

dBASE will respond by displaying

```
T
```

All the examples discussed so far deal with assigning the value of the expression to a single variable. The STORE TO command can also be used to assign a single value to several memory variables using a single command. This procedure is very useful when several variables need to be initialized by the same value. For example, to initialize the four variables of TOTAL1, TOTAL2, TOTAL3, and TOTAL4 with an initial value of 0, you will need the following command:

```
. STORE 0 TO TOTAL1, TOTAL2, TOTAL3, TOTAL4
<Return>
```

The ASSIGNMENT Command

An alternative method to the STORE TO command is the ASSIGNMENT command. Its format is

```
<memory variable name> = <expression>
```

where <expression> and <memory variable name> have the same meaning as in the STORE TO command except that you cannot have a list of memory variable names on the left-hand side of the assignment operator.

The following commands used earlier in this section with the STORE TO command are valid using the assignment operator:

MARK_UP = 1.5
RETAIL = 'Retail Price = '
TODAY_DATE = {8/3/89}
TEST_TRUE = .T.

But to assign a value of 0 to the four memory variables of TOTAL1, TOTAL2, TOTAL3, and TOTAL4 using the assignment operator, you'll need these four commands:

TOTAL1 = 0
TOTAL2 = 0
TOTAL3 = 0
TOTAL4 = 0

There is no single command available for this purpose using the assignment operator. Therefore, the STORE TO command is more effective when the same value is to be assigned to several variables because it will require a single command, as compared to several commands using the assignment operator.

5.4.2 Displaying Memory Variables

After creating the memory variables, you can display detailed information such as the names, data types, sizes, and contents of all the currently active memory variables by using the DISPLAY MEMORY command.

The DISPLAY MEMORY Command

The format of the DISPLAY MEMORY command is

```
DISPLAY MEMORY [TO PRINT]
```

where the TO PRINT option, if used with the command, will direct the output to the printer. To display the contents of the RAM memory, type the following command:

```
. DISPLAY MEMORY    <Return>
```

or simply press the F7 Display Memory function key. dBASE will respond by displaying the information as shown in Figure 5.1.

Figure 5.1 shows only one screen of information. In fact, the information consists of several screens, but that on the rest of the screens is not needed at the present time, so I won't discuss it now. You can press any key repeatedly to scroll the rest of the screens, or you can press the <Esc> key once. When you have finished with this listing, dBASE returns with the dot prompt.

There are five columns in the listing of Figure 5.1. The first lists the names of the memory variables. The second lists the "pub" abbreviation, which indicates that the variable is a public variable. There are two types of variables: public or private. A **private variable** can be accessed only by the program in which it is defined; a **public variable** can be accessed by

Figure 5.1 Display of RAM with memory variables

```
. DISPLAY MEMORY
        User Memory Variables

TOTAL4       pub    N            0   (0.000000000000000000)
TOTAL3       pub    N            0   (0.000000000000000000)
TOTAL2       pub    N            0   (0.000000000000000000)
TOTAL1       pub    N            0   (0.000000000000000000)
TEST_TRUE    pub    L    .T.
TODAY_DATE   pub    D    08/03/89
RETAIL       pub    C    "Retail Price = "
MARK_UP      pub    N         1.50   (1.500000000000000000)

    8 out of 500 memvar defined (and 0 array elements)
```

any program. The third column lists the data type, representing N for numeric, C for character, D for date, and L for logical data types. The fourth lists the value assigned to these variables. The values of the numeric variables in this column are represented in the way the variables are displayed on the screen. The fifth column lists the values assigned to the numeric variables in the way these values are actually stored by dBASE.

Instead of displaying all the available memory variables, you can display one or more using the ? command, as shown:

```
. ? MARK_UP, TEST_TRUE    <Return>
```

dBASE will respond by displaying:

```
1.5 .T.
```

5.4.3 Memory Variables Limitations

dBASE IV allows you to define up to 500 memory variables. In Figure 5.1, only 8 of these have been defined, leaving 492 more memory variables.

5.4.4 Saving Memory Variables

Memory variables are temporarily stored in the computer's RAM storage until they are deleted from the computer's memory (discussed in section 5.4.5) or the computer is turned off. As soon as the computer is turned off, all memory variables are lost. To save the memory variables permanently in a data file for future use, use the SAVE TO command.

The SAVE TO Command

The format of the SAVE TO command is

```
SAVE TO <memory file name> [ALL LIKE/EXCEPT
    <skeleton>]
```

where <memory file name> is the name of the file in which the memory variables are stored, and <skeleton> refers to the "skeleton" of the memory variable name used with the ALL LIKE or ALL EXCEPT option to specify a group of memory variables.

The function of the SAVE TO command is to store all or part of the currently active memory variables to a disk file. To save all the currently active memory variables to a file named INV, you need to type the following command:

```
. SAVE TO INV    <Return>
```

This command will save all the current memory variables in the file named INV with an extension of .MEM. Because these memory variables are to be used with the INV database file, you should assign the memory variable file the *same* name as that of the database file. This will help you remember the names of the files. When we have too many data files and corresponding memory variable files, keeping track of them becomes too difficult if you use different names for the memory variable files.

5.4 Memory Variables

To save a part of the currently active memory variables, use the options ALL LIKE or ALL EXCEPT with the SAVE TO command. For example, to save all the active memory variables with names beginning with "TO" (TOTAL1, TOTAL2, TOTAL3, TOTAL4, and TODAY_DATE) in the file named TOINV.MEM, you can use the following command:

. SAVE ALL LIKE TO* TO TOINV   <Return>

The "*" wild card in this variable skeleton stands for any number of characters. Thus "TO*" stands for all the memory variables whose name starts with the letters "TO" followed by any number of characters. This command will save the five memory variables of TOTAL1, TOTAL2, TOTAL3, TOTAL4, and TODAY_DATE in the TOINV.MEM file.

To save all the active memory variables whose name consists of six characters of which the first five are "TOTAL" in the file named TOTAL.MEM, you can use the following command:

. SAVE ALL LIKE TOTAL? TO TOTAL   <Return>

The "?" wild card in this variable skeleton stands for one character in the sixth position of the name of the memory variable. Thus, TOTAL? stands for all the memory variables whose name consists of six characters, the first five characters are "TOTAL," and any single character is in the sixth position. This command will save four memory variables—TOTAL1, TOTAL2, TOTAL3, and TOTAL4—in the TOTAL.MEM file.

The ALL EXCEPT option can be used to exclude a part of active memory variables from being saved to a memory variable file. For example, to save only those memory variables from all the active memory variables whose name does not start with the letter "T" in the file named RETAIL.MEM, you can use the following command:

. SAVE ALL EXCEPT T* TO RETAIL   <Return>

This command will save all the memory variables whose name does not start with the letter "T"; that is, it will save only the RETAIL and MARK_UP memory variables.

5.4.5 Deleting Memory Variables

Saving memory variables does not delete them from RAM. To delete the memory variables from RAM, use the RELEASE command.

The RELEASE Command

The format of the RELEASE command is

```
RELEASE <memory variable list> / ALL
        [LIKE/EXCEPT <skeleton>]
```

where <memory variable list> is the name of the memory variable or the list of the memory variables to be released or deleted. When a list of memory variables is used, the variables are separated by a comma. The ALL option is used to delete all currently active memory variables. As in the SAVE TO command, the <skeleton> refers to the "skeleton" of a variable name used with the ALL LIKE or ALL EXCEPT options to define a group of memory variables.

The function of the RELEASE command is to delete all or a selected group of memory variables from RAM.

1. To delete an individual memory variable, such as MARK_UP, you need to type the command:

   `. RELEASE MARK_UP     <Return>`

2. To delete a group of memory variables from all the currently active memory variables, for example, all the memory variables with names starting with the letter "T," you will need to type the following command:

   `. RELEASE ALL LIKE T*    <Return>`

3. To delete all the memory variables whose name does not start with the letter "T," you will need to enter the following command:

   `. RELEASE ALL EXCEPT T*    <Return>`

4. To delete all the currently active memory variables, you will need the following command:

   `. RELEASE ALL     <Return>`

Now delete all the currently active memory variables from the computer's memory. To do this, type the following command:

`. RELEASE ALL     <Return>`

dBASE will respond by displaying the dot prompt. To verify the effect of this command, either press the F7 Display Memory function key or type the following command:

`. DISPLAY MEMORY    <Return>`

dBASE will respond by displaying the listing as shown in Figure 5.2, which indicates that all the memory variables have been deleted from the computer's memory.

5.4.6 Restoring Memory Variables

Memory variables saved in a memory variable disk file can be restored to the computer's memory by using the RESTORE FROM command.

Figure 5.2 Display of RAM without any memory variables

```
. DISPLAY MEMORY
        User Memory Variables

 0 out of 500 memvar defined (and 0 array elements)
```

The RESTORE FROM Command

The format of the RESTORE FROM command is

```
RESTORE FROM <memory file name> [ADDITIVE]
```

where <memory file name> is the name of the memory file from which the memory variables are to be retrieved.

The function of the RESTORE FROM command is to retrieve all the memory variables from the specified memory variable file and place them in RAM. If the ADDITIVE option is not specified with the RESTORE FROM command, then all the currently active memory variables are erased from RAM before the new memory variables are retrieved and placed there.

To add new memory variables to the currently active memory variables in RAM, use the ADDITIVE option with the RESTORE FROM command. If the two memory variables, one already in RAM and the other being retrieved, have the same name, the retrieved variable will overwrite the existing variable.

Now to load all the memory variables from the INV.MEM disk file back to the computer's memory, you will need to type the following command:

```
. RESTORE FROM INV     <Return>
```

To verify that the memory variables have been loaded into the computer memory, either press the F7 Display Memory function key or type the following command:

```
. DISPLAY MEMORY     <Return>
```

dBASE will respond by displaying the listing as shown in Figure 5.1, indicating that the memory variables have been loaded back to the computer's memory.

Now you can use these memory variables with the INV database file. If you type these commands:

```
. USE INV     <Return>
. DISPLAY ITEM_NUM, ITEM_DESC, UNIT_COST *
MARK_UP     <Return>
```

dBASE will respond by displaying the results as follows:

```
Record#  ITEM_NUM  ITEM_DESC           UNIT_COST * MARK_UP
     1   1136      Bond Paper, Ream                  34.49
```

Note: The command line length of 1024 characters is allowed by dBASE IV. But when a long command is typed in a program file and a printed copy of its contents is obtained, only the part of the command that can be accommodated on the paper width will be printed. To obtain the printing of the whole command, you can use the semicolon (;) to divide it into several lines as long as the total number of characters in the command does not exceed the 1024 character limit. When a command is too long and cannot fit on one line, it can be continued onto the next line. After typing ";" at the end of the partial command, press the <Return> key. Then type the rest of the command on the next line. The command typed on two lines connected with the semicolon will be considered as one command. This option is available only in the programming mode of dBASE IV.

5.5 dBASE Summary Statistics

dBASE IV provides seven summary statistics commands: COUNT, SUM, AVERAGE, MAX, MIN, STD, and VAR, which can compute summary statistics on all or a portion of the numeric fields in the database file. Of these, the first three (COUNT, SUM, and AVERAGE) are most commonly used in business applications. Therefore, I discuss only these three commands.

5.5.1 The COUNT Command

The DISPLAY STRUCTURE command discussed in section 2.2.1 displays the structure of the currently selected database file. Apart from other information, this structure contains the size, which is the number of records present in the database file. Thus, use of the DISPLAY STRUCTURE command helps us find the size. But if you want to find the number of records present in the database file that satisfy a particular condition, you need another command. dBASE provides the COUNT command for this purpose.

The format of the COUNT command is

```
COUNT [<scope>] [FOR <condition>]
      [TO <memory variables>] [WHILE <condition>]
```

where the <scope> specifies which parts of the database file are affected by the command. <Condition> is a valid search condition that selects the records from the database file to be counted, and <memory variables> are the names of the memory variables to which the results of this command are to be stored.

The COUNT command has several different options available, depending on the parameters used.

The COUNT Format

The simplest form of the COUNT command is

```
COUNT
```

The simple COUNT command without any parameters counts the number of records present in the active database file. To count the number of records present in the INV database file, you need to type the following commands:

```
. USE INV    <Return>
. COUNT      <Return>
```

5.5 dBASE Summary Statistics

dBASE will respond by displaying

```
30 records
```

indicating that the INV database file contains 30 records.

The COUNT FOR Format

The format for the COUNT FOR command is

```
COUNT [FOR <condition>]
```

This command will count the number of records contained in the database file for which the given condition is true. If you apply this command to the INV database file by typing the following commands:

```
. USE INV                     <Return>
. COUNT FOR UNIT_COST > 10    <Return>
```

dBASE will respond by displaying:

```
9 records
```

indicating that there are nine records in the INV database file for which the value of the UNIT_COST field is greater than ten. In other words, this command helps us find the number of records in the INV database file whose unit cost is greater than $10. The result indicates that there are nine such items.

The COUNT FOR TO Format

The format for the COUNT FOR TO command is

```
COUNT [FOR <condition>] TO [<memory variables>]
```

This command counts the number of records contained in the database file satisfying a given condition and stores the results in a specified memory variable. You may want to find the number of items in the INV database file whose retail price is greater than $50 and store this result in the memory variable named RET_OVER50. (Recall that the retail price is obtained by multiplying the unit cost by the markup.) To do this, type the following commands:

```
. USE INV     <Return>
. COUNT FOR UNIT_COST * MARK_UP > 50 TO
  RET_OVER50  <Return>
```

dBASE will respond by displaying:

```
5 records
```

indicating that there are five records in the INV database file for which the retail price is greater than $50. This value will be stored in the

Figure 5.3 Display of RAM with memory variables

```
. DISPLAY MEMORY
        User Memory Variables

RET_OVER50  pub  N         5    (5.000000000000000000)
TOTAL4      pub  N         0    (0.000000000000000000)
TOTAL3      pub  N         0    (0.000000000000000000)
TOTAL2      pub  N         0    (0.000000000000000000)
TOTAL1      pub  N         0    (0.000000000000000000)
TEST_TRUE   pub  L   .T.
TODAY_DATE  pub  D   08/03/89
RETAIL      pub  C   "Retail Price = "
MARK_UP     pub  N         1.50 (1.500000000000000000)

    9 out of 500 memvar defined (and 0 array elements)
```

RET_OVER50 memory variable. To verify this, either press the F7 Display Memory function key or type the following command:

```
. DISPLAY MEMORY    <Return>
```

dBASE will respond by displaying the listing shown in Figure 5.3. A new memory variable named RET_OVER50 has been added to the existing list of the memory variables in Figure 5.3. It is a numeric variable with a value of five assigned to it.

5.5.2 The SUM Command

The SUM command computes the totals of the numeric field or fields for all the records in the database file or for selected records in the database file that meet the given conditions. The general format of the SUM command is

```
SUM [<expression>] [For <condition>]
    [WHILE <condition>] [TO <memory variables>]
```

where <expression> is a list of field names or expressions consisting of numeric fields. <Condition> is a valid search condition that selects from the database file the records to be summed, and <memory variables> is the names of the memory variables to which the results of this command are to be stored. The SUM command has several different options available, depending on the parameters used.

The SUM Format

The format of the SUM command is

```
SUM [<expression>]
```

where the <expression> parameter is optional. There are two forms of this format.

5.5 dBASE Summary Statistics

The first form of the SUM command is

```
SUM
```

The simple SUM command without any parameters will total all the numeric fields present in the data record for all the records of the active database file. Let's use this command on the INV database file. To do this, type the following commands:

```
. USE INV    <Return>
. SUM        <Return>
```

dBASE will respond by displaying the following:

```
30 records summed
UNIT_COST    QUANTITY
  1525.20        1271
```

indicating that the sum of the UNIT_COST and QUANTITY fields for all the records in the INV database file is 1525.20 and 1271, respectively.

The second form of the SUM command is

```
SUM <expression>
```

This form of the SUM command will total only the listed fields or expressions of numeric fields for all the records of the active database file. The field names or expressions should be separated by a comma, and you can include up to five names or expressions in the SUM command.

Let us use this command to find the total quantity of the items in stock by finding the sum of the QUANTITY field. We can also find the total inventory value of the stock by finding the sum of the inventory value of each item, which is the product of the QUANTITY and the UNIT_COST fields. To do this, type the following command:

```
. SUM QUANTITY, QUANTITY * UNIT_COST    <Return>
```

dBASE will respond by displaying:

```
   30 records summed
QUANTITY       QUANTITY * UNIT_COST
    1271                    17784.37
```

indicating that there are 30 different items in stock. Each item represents one record. The total number of items in stock is 1271, and the total value of the inventory value is $17,784.37.

The SUM FOR Format

The format for the SUM FOR command is

```
SUM [<expression>] [FOR <condition>]
```

where the <expression> and the FOR parameters are optional. There are two forms of this format.

The first form of the SUM FOR command is

```
SUM FOR <condition>
```

This format totals all numeric fields, but only for those records in the active database file for which the given condition is true.

Let us use this command on the INV database file to find the totals of all the numeric fields in the INV database file for which the value of the UNIT_COST field is less than $10. To do this, type the following command:

```
. SUM FOR UNIT_COST < 10      <Return>
```

dBASE will display this result:

```
    21 records summed
UNIT_COST      QUANTITY
    96.49          1029
```

indicating that there are 21 records in the INV database file for which the value of the UNIT_COST field is less than $10. The sum of the UNIT_COST and QUANTITY fields for these 21 records is $96.49 and 1029, respectively.

The second form of the SUM FOR command is

```
SUM <expression> FOR <condition>
```

This form of the SUM FOR command will total only the listed fields or expressions of numeric fields for all the records of the active database file for which the given condition is true. The field names or expressions should be separated by a comma, and you can include up to five of the fields or expressions in the SUM FOR command.

Let us use this command to find the total number of items in stock (by finding the sum of the QUANTITY field) for which the value of the UNIT_COST field is greater than $100. To do this, type the following command:

```
. SUM QUANTITY FOR UNIT_COST > 100      <Return>
```

dBASE will respond by displaying:

```
    3 records summed
QUANTITY
      23
```

indicating that there are 3 different items in the stock whose unit cost is more than $100, and the total quantity of these items is 23.

The SUM FOR TO Format

The format of the SUM FOR TO command is

```
SUM <expression> FOR <condition>
    TO <memory variables>
```

5.5 dBASE Summary Statistics

This command totals the listed fields for only those records in the database file for which the condition is true and stores the result to a memory variable or variables. When the TO option of the command is used, there should be a memory variable present in the TO option for each field or expression for which the total (or sum) is required. The memory variables should be separated by commas.

Let us use this command to find the total quantity of items in stock by finding the sum of the QUANTITY field. We will also find the total inventory value of the stock by finding the sum of the inventory value of each item, which is the product of the QUANTITY and the UNIT_COST fields for all those records in the INV database file for which the ITEM_NUM is less than 2000. Finally, we will store the results in the TOT1_QTY and TOT1_INVAL memory variables. To do this, type the following command:

```
. SUM QUANTITY, QUANTITY * UNIT_COST FOR ITEM_NUM
  < '2000' TO TOT1_QTY, TOT1_INVAL    <Return>
```

dBASE will respond by displaying:

```
     8 records summed
  QUANTITY        QUANTITY
     437           3488.25
```

indicating that there are 8 such items in stock because each item represents one record. The total number of items in stock is 437, and the total inventory value for these items is $3488.25.

In addition, the results of the SUM command will be stored in the TOT1_QTY and TOT1_INVAL memory variables. These memory variables now can be used with any database file as long as they are not released. To make sure that these memory variables are still present in RAM, either press the F7 Display Memory function key or type the following command:

```
. DISPLAY MEMORY    <Return>
```

dBASE will respond by displaying the listing as shown in Figure 5.4. Two new memory variables, named TOT1_QTY and TOT1_INVAL, have been added to the existing list of memory variables in Figure 5.4.

5.5.3 The AVERAGE Command

The third command in this category is the AVERAGE command, which computes the arithmetic mean of a numeric field or fields for all records in the database file or only for selected records that meet a given condition. The general format of the AVERAGE command is

```
AVERAGE [<expression>] [FOR <condition>]
    [WHILE <condition>] [TO <memory variables>]
```

where <expression> is a list of field names or expressions consisting of numeric fields. <Condition> is a valid search condition that selects from the database file the records to be averaged, and <memory variables> are the names of the memory variables where the results of this command are

Figure 5.4 Display of RAM with memory variables

```
. DISPLAY MEMORY
           User Memory Variables

TOT1_INVAL   pub   N        3488.25  (3488.25000000000000000)
TOT1_QTY     pub   N             437  (437.00000000000000000)
RET_OVER50   pub   N               5  (5.00000000000000000)
TOTAL4       pub   N               0  (0.00000000000000000)
TOTAL3       pub   N               0  (0.00000000000000000)
TOTAL2       pub   N               0  (0.00000000000000000)
TOTAL1       pub   N               0  (0.00000000000000000)
TEST_TRUE    pub   L   .T.
TODAY_DATE   pub   D   08/03/89
RETAIL       pub   C   "Retail Price = "
MARK_UP      pub   N            1.50  (1.50000000000000000)

11 out of 500 memvar defined (and 0 array elements)
```

to be stored. The AVERAGE command has several different options available, depending on the parameters used.

The AVERAGE Format

The simplest format of the AVERAGE command is

```
AVERAGE [<expression>]
```

where the <expression> parameter is optional. There are two forms of this command.

The first form of the AVERAGE command is

```
AVERAGE
```

The simple AVERAGE command without any parameters will compute the arithmetic mean of all the numeric fields present in the data record for all the records of the active database file.

Let's use this command on the INV database file. To do this, type the following commands:

```
. USE INV     <Return>
. AVERAGE     <Return>
```

dBASE will respond by displaying the following:

```
    30 records summed
UNIT_COST      QUANTITY
    50.84         42.37
```

indicating that the average of the UNIT_COST and QUANTITY fields for all the records in the INV database file is $50.84 and 42.37, respectively.

The second form of the AVERAGE command is

```
AVERAGE <expression>
```

5.5 dBASE Summary Statistics

This form of the AVERAGE command will compute the arithmetic mean of only the listed fields or expressions of numeric fields for all the records of the active database file. The field names or expressions should be separated by a comma, and you can include up to five of the field names or expressions in the AVERAGE command.

Let us use this command to compute the average quantity and the average cost of each item present in the INV database file. To do this, type the following command:

```
. AVERAGE QUANTITY, UNIT_COST    <Return>
```

dBASE will respond by displaying:

```
30 records averaged
QUANTITY     UNIT_COST
   42.37        50.84
```

indicating that there are 30 different items in stock because each item represents one record. The average quantity in stock for each item is 42.37, and the average UNIT_COST for each item is $50.84.

The AVERAGE FOR Format

The format for the AVERAGE FOR command is

```
AVERAGE [<expression>] [FOR <condition>]
```

where the <expression> and the FOR parameters are optional. There are two forms of this format.

The first form of the AVERAGE FOR command is

```
AVERAGE FOR <condition>
```

This format computes the arithmetic mean of all the numeric fields, but only for those records in the active database file for which the given condition is true.

Let us use this command on the INV database file to compute the average or the arithmetic mean of the UNIT_COST and QUANTITY fields for all the items in stock of the INV database file costing more than $100. To do this, type the following command:

```
. AVERAGE FOR UNIT_COST > 100    <Return>
```

dBASE will display the result as given:

```
3 records averaged
UNIT_COST     QUANTITY
   401.99         7.67
```

The results indicate that there are only three such items in stock, and the average quantity for each is 7.67.

The second form of the AVERAGE FOR command is

```
AVERAGE <expression> FOR <condition>
```

This form of the AVERAGE FOR command computes the arithmetic mean of the listed fields or expressions of numeric fields for all the records of the active database file for which the given condition is true. The field names or expressions should be separated by a comma, and you can include up to five of the field names or expressions in the AVERAGE FOR command.

Let us use this command to find the average of the UNIT_COST field for all the records in stock of the INV database file for which the value of the ITEM_NUM field is less than 2000. To do this, type the following command:

```
. AVERAGE UNIT_COST FOR ITEM_NUM < '2000'
<Return>
```

dBASE will respond by displaying:

```
   8 records averaged
UNIT_COST
    9.86
```

indicating that there are eight such items in stock. The average cost of these items is $9.86.

The AVERAGE FOR TO Format

The format of the AVERAGE FOR TO command is

```
AVERAGE <expression> FOR <condition>
        TO <memory variable>
```

This command computes the arithmetic mean of the listed fields for only those records in the database file for which the condition is true and stores the result to a memory variable or variables. When the TO option of the command is exercised, there should be a memory variable present in the TO option for each field or expression for which the arithmetic mean (or average) is required. The memory variables should be separated by a comma.

Let us use this command to find the average of the UNIT_COST field for all the records in stock of the INV database file for which the value of the ITEM_NUM field is less than 2000 and to store the results in the AVG1_UCOST memory variable. To do this, type the following command:

```
. AVERAGE UNIT_COST FOR ITEM_NUM < '2000' TO
AVG1_UCOST    <Return>
```

dBASE will respond by displaying:

```
   8 records averaged
UNIT_COST
    9.86
```

indicating that there are eight different items in stock for which ITEM_NUM is less than 2000, and the average cost of these items is $9.86.

Figure 5.5 Display of RAM with memory variables

```
. DISPLAY MEMORY
        User Memory Variables

AVG1_UCOST  pub  N        9.86   (9.860000000000000000)
TOT1_INVAL  pub  N     3488.25   (3488.250000000000000)
TOT1_QTY    pub  N         437   (437.000000000000000)
RET_OVER50  pub  N           5   (5.000000000000000000)
TOTAL4      pub  N           0   (0.000000000000000000)
TOTAL3      pub  N           0   (0.000000000000000000)
TOTAL2      pub  N           0   (0.000000000000000000)
TOTAL1      pub  N           0   (0.000000000000000000)
TEST_TRUE   pub  L    .T.
TODAY_DATE  pub  D    08/03/89
RETAIL      pub  C    "Retail Price = "
MARK_UP     pub  N        1.50   (1.500000000000000000)

12 out of 500 memvar defined (and 0 array elements)
```

Also, the results of the AVERAGE command will be stored in the AVG1_UCOST memory variable. This memory variable now can be used with any database file as long as it is not released. To make sure that this memory variable is still present in RAM, either press the F7 Display Memory function key or type the following command:

. **DISPLAY MEMORY**   <Return>

dBASE will respond by displaying the listing as shown in Figure 5.5. The memory variable, named AVG1_UCOST, has been added to the existing list of memory variables.

5.6 An Illustrative Example: Case Study 2

Program Description

Write a program to produce an inventory report listing for American Supply Company. The report should contain all the records of the database file named INV. The program should calculate the inventory value (INV_VAL) for each item of the INV database file in stock. The inventory value can be calculated by multiplying the quantity on hand by the unit cost. Then, by accumulating this inventory value, you can obtain the total inventory value (TOTINV_VAL) for all the stock.

Input File(s)

The INV database file, whose structure is shown in Figure 5.6, is used as an input file.

Output

The output of the program should be an inventory report listing. It is a multiscreen report, as shown in Figure 5.7. The headings should be as

Figure 5.6 Structure of the INV database file

```
Structure for database : C:\DBASE\INVOICE\INV.DBF
Number of data records :      30
Date of last update    : 12/25/87
Field  Field Name  Type       Width    Dec    Index
    1  ITEM_NUM    Character      4             N
    2  ITEM_DESC   Character     26             N
    3  UNIT_COST   Numeric        6      2      N
    4  QUANTITY    Numeric        3             N
    5  RET_PRICE   Numeric        7      2      N
    6  REOD_POINT  Numeric        3             N
    7  REOD_QTY    Numeric        3             N
    8  DEPT_NUM    Numeric        3             N
** Total **                      56
```

shown in the inventory report listing, and the detail line should consist of the ITEM_NUM, ITEM_DESC, QUANTITY, UNIT_COST, and INV_VAL fields. The total line should appear in the last screen only.

Processing Steps

Use the following steps to develop the program solution:

1. The headings should be printed as shown in the inventory report listing. The date and time should be included in the headings.
2. The column headings should be enclosed between the two lines, as shown in Figure 5.7.

Figure 5.7 Inventory report listing: Case Study 2

```
                       AMERICAN SUPPLY COMPANY
 08/27/89                 INVENTORY REPORT                 14:09:48

  ITEM                                 QTY ON    UNIT    INVENTORY
  NUMBER      ITEM DESCRIPTION         HAND      PRICE   VALUE

   5370    Staple Remover                55      1.39       76.45
   5375    Stapler                       29      6.29      182.41
   1060    Steno Notebook 10-Pk          84      4.55      382.20
   3375    Typewriter Ribbons 10-Box     67     23.79    1,593.93
   1488    Xerographic Paper             45     19.99      899.55
   4189    Zenith Microcomputer Z-158     5    829.99    4,149.95

                     TOTAL VALUE OF STOCK  =    $17,784.37

                  *** --- END OF REPORT --- ***



                  PRESS ANY KEY TO CONTINUE . . .
```

3. The inventory value (INV_VAL) for each record in stock of the INV database file should be calculated by multiplying the UNIT_COST and QUANTITY fields.
4. The inventory value (INV_VAL) for all the records of the INV database file should be accumulated in the TOTINV_VAL field.
5. Detail lines should not be printed past row 20.
6. When the screen is full or the final totals have been printed on the final screen, freeze the screen to allow the user to view the output.
7. Print the accumulated inventory value, stored in the TOTINV_VAL field on the last screen, one row below the last detail line.
8. At the end of the output report, print the message "*** --- END OF REPORT --- ***" to indicate the end of the report.
9. The whole output should be enclosed in the box, as shown in Figure 5.7.

The five phases of the program development process for Case Study 2 follow.

5.6.1 The Analysis Phase

In the analysis phase, the first step in the program development process, review and analysis of program specifications lead to the clear understanding of the output report to be produced, the input database file(s) used to produce the output, and the steps needed to solve the problem.

The first step in the program development process of Case Study 2 consists of analyzing the output report to be produced, the input database file(s) used in the program to produce the required results, and the processing steps needed to solve the problem.

Analysis of the Output Report

The inventory report listing represents the desired format of the output report of Case Study 2. Analysis of the inventory report listing reveals that it is similar to the one produced for Case Study 1, except that it has two heading lines instead of three. Also, the report should be single spaced and should consist of multiple screens.

After analyzing the output report, prepare the screen layout form as shown in Figure 5.8. Because it is similar to the screen layout form of Case Study 1, no further explanation is needed for it.

Analysis of the Input Database File(s)

A review of the structure of the INV database file shown in Figure 5.6 indicates that there are 30 records in the input INV database file, each consisting of eight fields: ITEM_NUM, ITEM_DESC, UNIT_COST, QUANTITY, RET_PRICE, REOD_POINT, REOD_QTY, and DEPT_NUM. The detail line of the output report consists of five fields, four of which (ITEM_NUM, ITEM_DESC, QUANTITY, and UNIT_COST) are from the data record of the INV database file. The fifth field, INV_VAL, is evaluated by multiplying the UNIT_COST and QUANTITY fields. From this discussion, we conclude that we do not need to include all the fields present in the data record of the input database file. The report may also contain

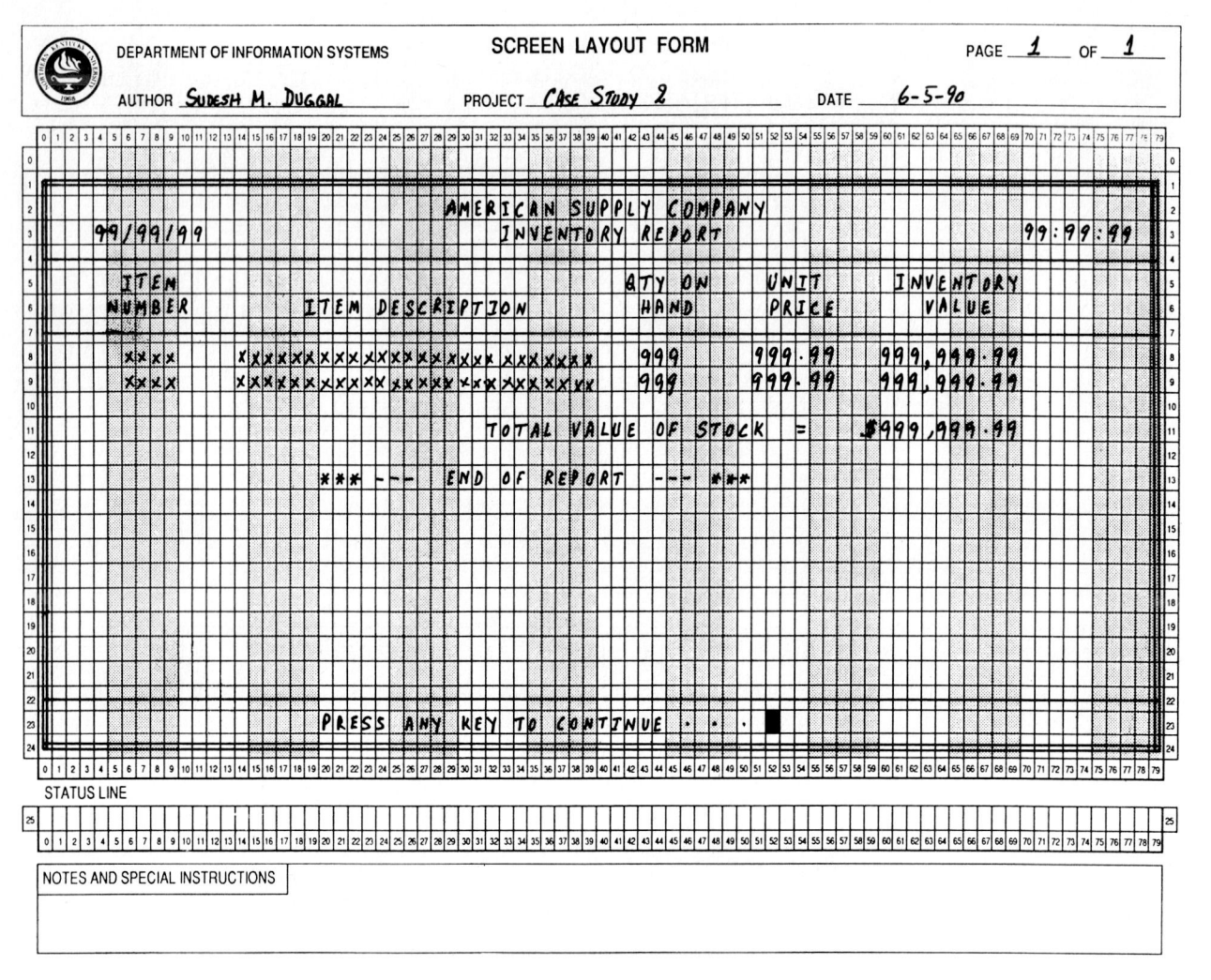

Figure 5.8 Screen layout for Case Study 2

some fields that can be obtained as a result of some calculations on the fields of the data record in the input database file.

Analysis of the Processing Steps

After analyzing the output report and the input database file(s), you must analyze the processing steps needed to solve the problem by identifying and subdividing the steps into smaller components. A review of the program specifications and the output required as shown in Figure 5.7 reveals that the first step in the solution of the case study is to print the headings, which, of course, includes printing column headings. The next step is to open the INV database file and process its records.

The processing of each record involves five steps. In the first, the inventory value of each record is calculated by multiplying the UNIT_COST and QUANTITY fields, and the result is stored in the INV_VAL memory variable. In the second step, the inventory value is accumulated in the TOTINV_VAL memory variable. The detail line is printed in the third step. These steps are shown in the data flow analysis diagram in Figure 5.9.

Figure 5.9 Data flow analysis of Case Study 2 (printing a detail record)

```
INV Database File

   Record#  ITEM_NUM  ITEM_DESC              UNIT_COST  QUANTITY ... DEPT_NUM
      1      1136     Bond Paper, Ream         22.99       38  ...    100
      2      5818     Calendar Refill           4.99       32  ...    500
      3      5960     Calendar Stands           5.69       14  ...    500
      4      3802     Correction Fluid 10-Box   3.39       65  ...    300
      5      3570     Correction Tape 10-Box    4.29       49  ...    300
      6      4005     Disks Data Case           5.99       18  ...    400
      7      1910     Ditto Paper, Ream        19.99       35  ...    100
             .         .                        .           .          .
             .         .                        .           .          .
             .         .                        .           .          .
     28      3375     Typewriter Ribbons 10-Box 23.79      67  ...    300
     29      1488     Xerographic Paper        19.99       45  ...    100
     30      4189     Zenith Microcomputer Z-158 829.99     5  ...    400
```

COMPUTER INTERNAL MEMORY

ITEM_NUM	ITEM_DESC	UNIT_COST	QUANTITY
1136	Bond Paper, Ream	22.99	38

22.99 x 38 = 873.62
INV_VAL
(= UNIT_COST * QUANTITY)

873.62 = 0 + 873.62
TOTINV_VAL
(= TOTINV_VAL + INV_VAL)

Output

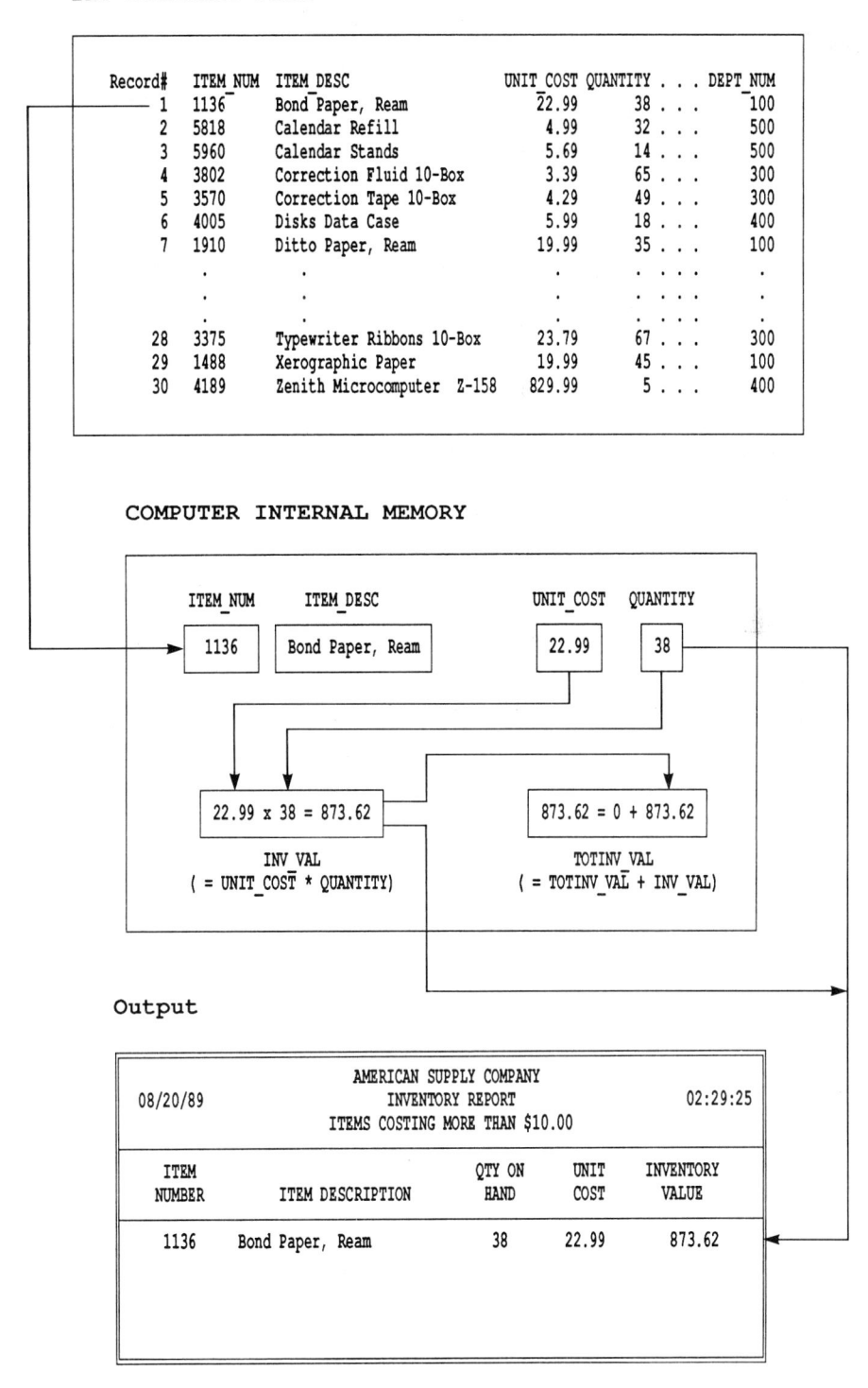

```
                     AMERICAN SUPPLY COMPANY
 08/20/89               INVENTORY REPORT                02:29:25
                   ITEMS COSTING MORE THAN $10.00

   ITEM                              QTY ON    UNIT    INVENTORY
  NUMBER    ITEM DESCRIPTION          HAND    COST      VALUE

   1136     Bond Paper, Ream           38    22.99     873.62
```

Because the output is a multiscreen report, you should test after printing each detail line to check whether the screen is full. If it is, perform two special functions. First, freeze the screen to allow the user to review the output along with a message indicating how to proceed with processing. Second, print the heading at the top of the next screen. Recall that the print report headings function as discussed in the initiate processing function performs three activities (clears the screen, prints the headings, and initializes the line counter).

In a multiscreen report, as in this program, the headings function is performed every time a new screen is needed for the output. This result indicates that the heading routine is performed first in the initiate processing and then repeatedly in the main processing functions for every screen needed in the output.

The two special steps just discussed—freezing the screen and printing the headings in the main processing—are needed only if the screen is full and more output is still to be displayed. If the screen is not yet full, the program will proceed with the next step, the fourth step of processing which is to skip the record pointer to the next available record in the database file.

All these steps—calculating the inventory value, accumulating its total, printing the detail line, testing for screen fullness, and skipping to the next record—are performed repeatedly for all the records of the INV database file.

After all the records of the INV database file have been processed, the total line showing the accumulated inventory value is printed. This step is shown in the data flow analysis diagram in Figure 5.10. The total line is printed, the INV database file is closed, the end of report message is printed, and the screen is frozen once again to allow the users to view the final screen. Finally, the default modes are reset.

To put all the functions discussed together, you will need the following processing steps in the solution of Case Study 2:

1. Housekeeping
2. Define variables
3. Print report headings
4. Open file(s)
5. Perform calculations
6. Accumulate totals
7. Print detail line
8. Test for screen full
9. If screen not full, proceed to step 11
10. Print report headings
11. Skip to next record
12. Print total line
13. Close file(s)
14. End of job
    a. Print end of report message
    b. Freeze screen
    c. Reset default modes

The first four steps should be performed only once, at the start of the program, and as such belong to initiate processing. The next seven steps should be performed again and again for each record of the INV database file. Therefore, these steps belong to main processing. The last three steps need to be performed after all the records of the INV database file have been processed. Therefore, these steps belong to terminate processing.

Figure 5.10 Data flow analysis of Case Study 2 (printing of the total line)

```
INV Database File

Record#  ITEM_NUM  ITEM_DESC              UNIT_COST  QUANTITY  ...  DEPT_NUM
   1     1136      Bond Paper, Ream          22.99      38     ...    100
   2     5818      Calendar Refill            4.99      32     ...    500
   3     5960      Calendar Stands            5.69      14     ...    500
   4     3802      Correction Fluid 10-Box    3.39      65     ...    300
   5     3570      Correction Tape 10-Box     4.29      49     ...    300
   6     4005      Disks Data Case            5.99      18     ...    400
   7     1910      Ditto Paper, Ream         19.99      35     ...    100
            .          .                        .        .             .
            .          .                        .        .             .
            .          .                        .        .             .
  28     3375      Typewriter Ribbons 10-Box 23.79      67     ...    300
  29     1488      Xerographic Paper         19.99      45     ...    100
  30     4189      Zenith Microcomputer Z-158 829.99     5     ...    400
```

```
COMPUTER INTERNAL MEMORY

    ITEM_NUM     ITEM_DESC            UNIT_COST    QUANTITY
     4189     Zenith Microcomputer      829.99        5


    829.99 x 5 = 4149.95        17784.37 = 13634.42 + 4149.95
         INV_VAL                        TOTINV_VAL
    ( = UNIT_COST * QUANTITY)      ( = TOTINV_VAL + INV_VAL)
```

```
Output

                        AMERICAN SUPPLY COMPANY
      08/27/89             INVENTORY REPORT              14:09:48

       ITEM                              QTY ON    UNIT    INVENTORY
      NUMBER     ITEM DESCRIPTION         HAND    PRICE     VALUE

       5370     Staple Remover             55     1.39      76.45
       5375     Stapler                    29     6.29     182.41
       1060     Steno Notebook 10-Pk       84     4.55     382.20
       3375     Typewriter Ribbons 10-Box  67    23.79   1,593.93
       1488     Xerographic Paper          45    19.99     899.55
       4189     Zenith Microcomputer Z-158  5   829.99   4,149.95

                          TOTAL VALUE OF STOCK  =   $17,784.37
```

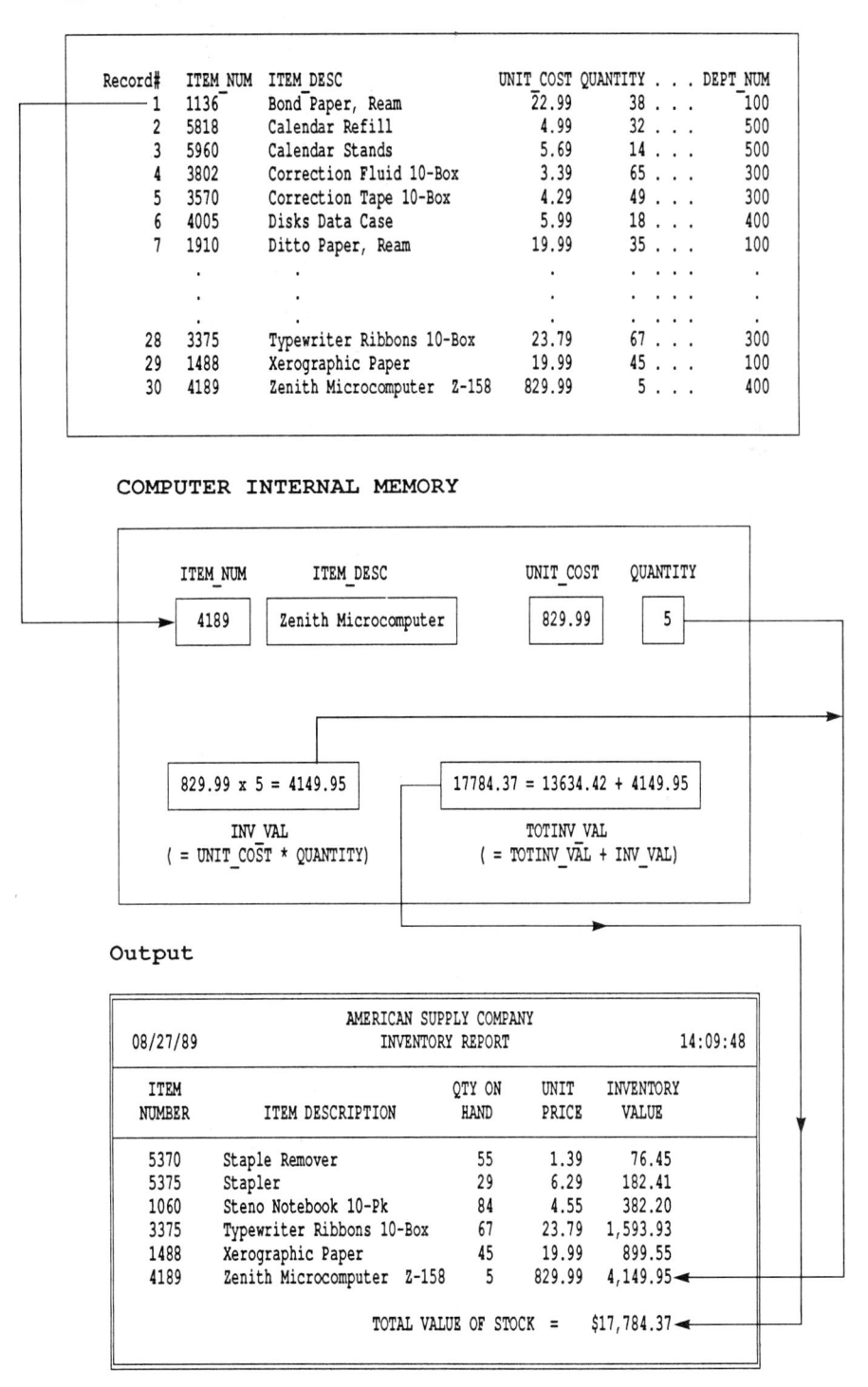

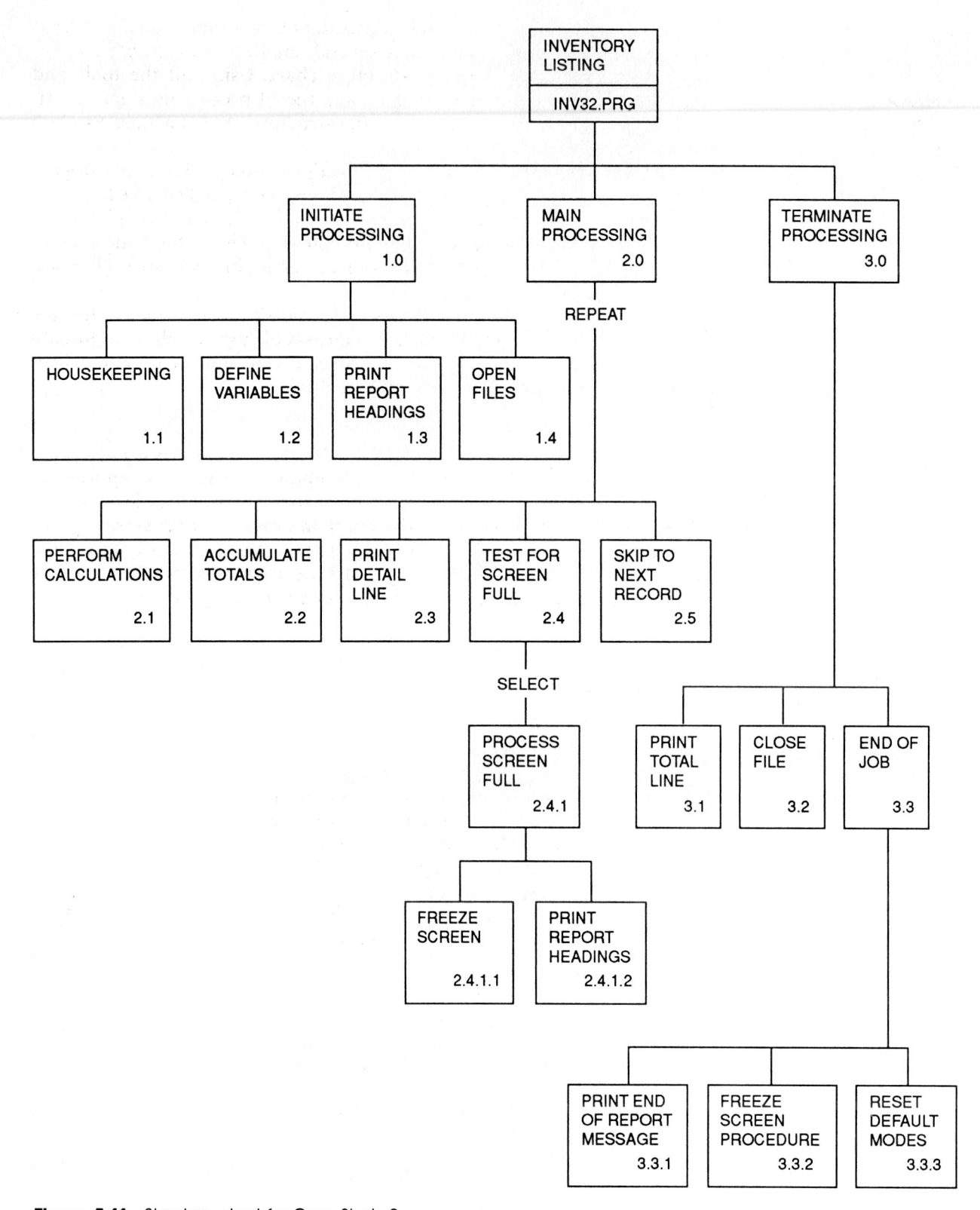

Figure 5.11 Structure chart for Case Study 2

5.6.2 The Design Phase

The function of this step is to take the result of the problem analysis, that is, the problem broken down into several smaller, manageable components, and transform it into a structure chart. Using all the tools and techniques discussed in Section 4.4.2 and the 14 processing steps identified in the analysis phase, complete the structure chart for Case Study 2 as shown in Figure 5.11.

In this structure chart, all the modules except 1.3 Print Report Headings (or 2.4.1.2 Print Report Headings) and 2.3 Print Detail Line perform one function. They are thus functionally cohesive. As explained in Chapter 4, these two modules are highly cohesive. Thus, all the modules in this structure chart are either functionally or highly cohesive. They are also loosely coupled.

The structure chart of Figure 5.11 satisfies the three rules for designing a good structure chart. It consists of highly cohesive, loosely coupled modules with the span of control of any module no more than five. So it is a well-designed solution of Case Study 2.

5.6.3 The Detailed Design Phase

The function of this step is to take the result of the design phase, that is, the structure chart, and identify the actual computer operations required for each program function represented in it, producing the detailed solution of the problem. Using the translation of the three control structures to pseudocode as given in Figure 4.14, the screen layout form of Figure 5.8, and the method described in section 4.4.3, we arrive at the structure chart of Figure 5.11 translated to pseudocode as given in Figure 5.12.

Figure 5.12 Pseudocode for Case Study 2

```
0.0 INVENTORY LISTING
    1.0 INITIATE PROCESSING
        1.1 HOUSEKEEPING
            CHANGE DEFAULT MODES
                Turn off the dBASE's heading feature
                Turn off the dBASE's user dialogue
                Turn off the dBASE's status bar
            1.2 DEFINE VARIABLES
                Set Inventory Value = 0
                Set Total Inventory Value = 0
            1.3 PRINT REPORT HEADINGS
                CLEAR SCREEN
                    Clear the screen
                PRINT HEADINGS
                    Print Report Main Heading Line 1
                    Print Report Main Heading Line 2
                    Draw a line
                    Print Column Heading Line 1
                    Print Column Heading Line 2
                    Draw a line
                INITIALIZE LINE COUNTER
                    Set line counter = 8
            1.4 OPEN FILES
                Open INV database file
```

Figure 5.12 Continued

> 2.0 MAIN PROCESSING
> REPEAT: until end of file
>> 2.1 PERFORM CALCULATIONS
>> Calculate Inventory Value by multiplying the quantity and unit cost fields
>> 2.2 ACCUMULATE TOTALS
>> Add inventory value to total inventory value
>> 2.3 PRINT DETAIL LINE
>>> PRINT A LINE
>>> Write Detail Line
>>> INCREMENT LINE COUNTER
>>> Add 1 to the Line Counter
>> 2.4 TEST FOR SCREEN FULL
>> SELECT: When screen is full
>>> 2.4.1 PROCESS SCREEN FULL
>>>> 2.4.1.1 FREEZE SCREEN
>>>> Wait for response to go to next page
>>>> 2.4.1.2 PRINT REPORT HEADINGS
>>>>> CLEAR SCREEN
>>>>> Clear the screen
>>>>> PRINT HEADINGS
>>>>> Print Report Main Heading Line 1
>>>>> Print Report Main Heading Line 2
>>>>> Draw a line
>>>>> Print Column Heading Line 1
>>>>> Print Column Heading Line 2
>>>>> Draw a line
>>>>> INITIALIZE LINE COUNTER
>>>>> Set line counter = 8
>> END SELECT
>> 2.5 SKIP TO NEXT RECORD
>> Skip to the next record of the database
> END REPEAT
> 3.0 TERMINATE PROCESSING
>> 3.1 PRINT TOTAL LINE
>> Increment line counter by one
>> Print Total line
>> 3.2 CLOSE FILE
>> Close database file
>> 3.3 END OF JOB
>>> 3.3.1 PRINT END OF REPORT MESSAGE
>>> Increment line counter by two
>>> Print End of the Report message
>>> 3.3.2 FREEZE SCREEN
>>> Wait for response to continue processing
>>> 3.3.3 RESET DEFAULT MODES
>>> Turn on the dBASE's heading feature
>>> Turn on the dBASE's user dialogue
>>> Turn on the dBASE's status bar

5.6.4 The Coding Phase

The purpose of this phase in the program development process is to translate the pseudocode instructions of the program solution into programming language instructions. The pseudocode of Figure 5.12 is translated into dBASE commands. The complete program for Case Study 2 in dBASE language is given in Figure 5.13.

```
*****************************************************************
*                         INV32                                  *
*                 AMERICAN SUPPLY COMPANY                        *
*----------------------------------------------------------------*
* This program produces an Inventory Listing Report for          *
* American Supply Company, containing all the items of           *
* the INV.DBF file. The program calculates the inventory         *
* value for each item by multiplying the quantity at hand        *
* by the unit cost. It also calculates the total inventory       *
* value for the whole stock. The heading is also included        *
* in the report.                                                 *
*----------------------------------------------------------------*
*           COPYRIGHT (C) . . . SUDESH M. DUGGAL                 *
*****************************************************************
*
***************************
* 1.0 INITIATE PROCESSING *
***************************
*
*** 1.1 HOUSEKEEPING ***
   *
   *** CHANGE DEFAULT MODES ***
      *
      SET HEADING OFF
      SET TALK OFF
      SET STATUS OFF
      *
*** 1.2 DEFINE VARIABLES ***
   *
   STORE 0 TO INV_VAL
   STORE 0 TO TOTINV_VAL
   *
*** 1.3 PRINT REPORT HEADINGS ***
   *
   *** CLEAR SCREEN ***
      *
      CLEAR
      *
   *** PRINT HEADINGS ***
      *
      @ 2,29 SAY 'AMERICAN SUPPLY COMPANY'
      @ 3,4  SAY DATE ()
      @ 3,33 SAY 'INVENTORY REPORT'
      @ 3,70 SAY TIME ()
      @ 4,0  TO  4,79
      @ 5,6  SAY 'ITEM'
      @ 5,42 SAY 'QTY ON'
```

Figure 5.13 Coding for Case Study 2

```
            @  5,52 SAY 'UNIT'
            @  5,60 SAY 'INVENTORY'
            @  6,5  SAY 'NUMBER'
            @  6,19 SAY 'ITEM DESCRIPTION'
            @  6,43 SAY 'HAND'
            @  6,52 SAY 'PRICE'
            @  6,62 SAY 'VALUE'
            @  7,0  TO  7,79
            *
        *** INITIALIZE LINE COUNTER ***
            *
            STORE 8 TO LINECNT
            *
    *** 1.4 OPEN FILES ***
        *
        USE INV
        *
    ***********************
    * 2.0 MAIN PROCESSING *
    ***********************
    *
    DO WHILE .NOT. EOF ()
        *
        *** 2.1 PERFORM CALCULATIONS ***
            *
            STORE (QUANTITY * UNIT_COST) TO INV_VAL
            *
        *** 2.2 ACCUMULATE TOTALS ***
            *
            TOTINV_VAL = TOTINV_VAL + INV_VAL
            *
        *** 2.3 PRINT DETAIL LINE ***
            *
            *** PRINT A LINE ***
                *
                @ LINECNT,6  SAY ITEM_NUM
                @ LINECNT,14 SAY ITEM_DESC
                @ LINECNT,44 SAY QUANTITY
                @ LINECNT,51 SAY UNIT_COST
                @ LINECNT,61 SAY INV_VAL PICTURE '999,999.99'
                *
            *** INCREMENT LINE COUNTER ***
                *
                LINECNT = LINECNT + 1
                *
        *** 2.4 TEST FOR SCREEN FULL ***
            *
            IF LINECNT = 20
                *
                *** 2.4.1 PROCESS SCREEN FULL ***
                    *
                    *** 2.4.1.1 FREEZE SCREEN ***
                        *
                        @ 22,0  TO 22,79
                        @  1,0  TO 24,79 DOUBLE
```

Figure 5.13 Continued

```
                    STORE ' ' TO RESPONSE
                    @ 23,20 SAY 'PRESS ANY KEY TO CONTINUE . . .'
                                GET RESPONSE
                    READ
                    *
              *** 2.4.1.2 PRINT REPORT HEADINGS ***
                    *
                *** CLEAR SCREEN ***
                    *
                    CLEAR
                    *
                *** PRINT HEADINGS ***
                    *
                    @ 2,29 SAY 'AMERICAN SUPPLY COMPANY'
                    @ 3,4  SAY DATE ()
                    @ 3,33 SAY 'INVENTORY REPORT'
                    @ 3,70 SAY TIME ()
                    @ 4,0  TO  4,79
                    @ 5,6  SAY 'ITEM'
                    @ 5,42 SAY 'QTY ON'
                    @ 5,52 SAY 'UNIT'
                    @ 5,60 SAY 'INVENTORY'
                    @ 6,5  SAY 'NUMBER'
                    @ 6,19 SAY 'ITEM DESCRIPTION'
                    @ 6,43 SAY 'HAND'
                    @ 6,52 SAY 'PRICE'
                    @ 6,62 SAY 'VALUE'
                    @ 7,0  TO  7.79
                    *
                *** INITIALIZE LINE COUNTER ***
                    *
                    STORE 8 TO LINECNT
                    *
          ENDIF   LINECNT = 20
              *
      *** 2.5 SKIP TO NEXT RECORD ***
              *
              SKIP
              *
ENDDO*.NOT. EOF ()
*
***************************
* 3.0 TERMINATE PROCESSING *
***************************
*
*** 3.1 PRINT TOTAL LINE ***
    *
    LINECNT = LINECNT + 1
    @ LINECNT,35 SAY 'TOTAL VALUE OF STOCK = '
    @ LINECNT,59 SAY TOTINV_VAL PICTURE '$999,999.99'
    *
*** 3.2 CLOSE FILE ***
    *
    USE
    *
```

Figure 5.13 Continued

```
*** 3.3 END OF JOB ***
    *
    *** 3.3.1 END OF REPORT MESSAGE ***
        *
        LINECNT = LINECNT + 2
        @ LINECNT,20 SAY '*** --- END OF REPORT --- ***'
        *
    *** 3.3.2 FREEZE SCREEN ***
        *
        @ 22,0 TO 22,79
        @  1,0 TO 24,79 DOUBLE
        STORE ' ' TO RESPONSE
        @ 23,20 SAY 'PRESS ANY KEY TO CONTINUE . . .' GET RESPONSE
        READ
        *
    *** 3.3.3 RESET DEFAULT MODES ***
        *
        SET TALK ON
        SET HEADING ON
        SET STATUS ON
```

Figure 5.13 Continued

The output of this program consists of three screens, as shown in Figures 5.14–5.16.

I'll now discuss the logic of the coding of the program represented in Figure 5.13. As with any program, it consists of three major processing steps—1.0 Initiate Processing, 2.0 Main Processing, and 3.0 Terminate Processing.

Figure 5.14 Inventory report listing for Case Study 2: screen 1

```
                         AMERICAN SUPPLY COMPANY
     08/27/89               INVENTORY REPORT              14:09:48

     ITEM                                QTY ON    UNIT    INVENTORY
     NUMBER     ITEM DESCRIPTION          HAND    PRICE      VALUE

      1136    Bond Paper, Ream             38     22.99      873.62
      5818    Calendar Refill              32      4.99      159.68
      5960    Calendar Stands              14      5.69       79.66
      3802    Correction Fluid 10-Box      65      3.39      220.35
      3570    Correction Tape 10-Box       49      4.29      210.21
      4005    Disks Data Case              18      5.99      107.82
      1910    Ditto Paper, Ream            35     19.99      699.65
      4141    Double Sided Disks 10-Pk     27      8.49      229.23
      2786    Highlighter Pen 10-Box       86      7.99      687.14
      4012    King Kong Modem 1200         10    105.99    1,059.90
      5130    Letter Opener                49      1.45       71.05
      1732    Message Pads  10-Pk          45      2.25      101.25


                   PRESS ANY KEY TO CONTINUE . . .
```

Figure 5.15 Inventory report listing for Case Study 2: screen 2

```
                    AMERICAN SUPPLY COMPANY
  08/27/89             INVENTORY REPORT                   14:09:48

   ITEM                                QTY ON    UNIT     INVENTORY
  NUMBER    ITEM DESCRIPTION            HAND    PRICE      VALUE

   4045    Monochrome Monitor Z-1105     15     99.99     1,499.85
   1975    Notebook Filler               65      1.79       116.35
   4072    Panasonic Printer KX-P108      8    269.99     2,159.92
   5890    Paper Puncher                 22      6.99       153.78
   2605    Pencil #2 Box                 54      6.29       339.66
   2818    Pencil Sharpener              17      7.99       135.83
   5000    Plastic Ruler                 87      0.89        77.43
   3372    Printer Ribbon 10-Box         19     35.99       683.81
   1359    Report Covers 10-Pk           87      2.79       242.73
   5225    Rubber Bands 10-Pk            72      3.45       248.40
   1536    Ruled Pads 8.5 X 11  10-Pk    38      4.55       172.90
   5250    Scissors                      34      4.99       169.66


              PRESS ANY KEY TO CONTINUE . . . ▮
```

The first major processing step (1.0 Initiate Processing) consists of four activities, which are performed only once at the start of the program. These are 1.1 Housekeeping, 1.2 Define Variables, 1.3 Print Report Headings, and 1.4 Open Files.

The first activity of housekeeping consists of one subfunction—change default modes, which changes the dBASE default modes, as already discussed in Chapter 4.

Figure 5.16 Inventory report listing for Case Study 2: screen 3

```
                    AMERICAN SUPPLY COMPANY
  08/27/89             INVENTORY REPORT                   14:09:48

   ITEM                                QTY ON    UNIT     INVENTORY
  NUMBER    ITEM DESCRIPTION            HAND    PRICE      VALUE

   5370    Staple Remover                55      1.39        76.45
   5375    Stapler                       29      6.29       182.41
   1060    Steno Notebook 10-Pk          84      4.55       382.20
   3375    Typewriter Ribbons 10-Box     67     23.79      1593.93
   1488    Xerographic Paper             45     19.99       899.55
   4189    Zenith Microcomputer  Z-158    5    829.99      4149.95

                 TOTAL VALUE OF STOCK =    $17,784.37

                  *** --- END OF REPORT --- ***




              PRESS ANY KEY TO CONTINUE . . . ▮
```

The second activity of define variables is new:

```
*** 1.2 DEFINE VARIABLES ***
*
   STORE 0 TO INV_VAL
   STORE 0 TO TOTINV_VAL
*
```

A new command is used here. It assigns a numeric value of zero (0) to the INV_VAL and TOTINV_VAL memory variables. Recall that a memory variable is a temporary location in the computer's memory used to store the intermediate results of calculations for future use. The first memory variable INV_VAL is used to store the inventory value of each record, which is obtained by multiplying the QUANTITY and UNIT_COST data field of each record of the INV database file. The second memory variable TOTINV_VAL is used to accumulate the inventory value of all the records of the database file. Both of these functions (calculation of the inventory value and its accumulation) are discussed in the main processing of this program.

The third activity, 1.3 Print Report Headings, performs three functions: clear screen, print headings, and initialize line counter. This activity has already been discussed in Chapter 4. The fourth and last activity of the 1.0 Initiate Processing is 1.4 Open Files, and it also has been discussed previously.

The second major processing step, 2.0 Main Processing, is shown in Figure 5.13. It consists of five activities, which are performed over and over again for each record of the INV database file. The main function of this step is to process all the records of the INV database file, one at a time. The five activities in this step are 2.1 Perform Calculations, 2.2 Accumulate Totals, 2.3 Print Detail Lines, 2.4 Test for Screen Full, and 2.5 Skip to Next Record.

The first activity of the main processing step is 2.1 Perform Calculations:

```
*** 2.1 PERFORM CALCULATIONS ***
*
   STORE (QUANTITY * UNIT_COST) TO INV_VAL
*
```

Its function is to multiply the two fields of the data record, QUANTITY and UNIT_COST, and store the result in the INV_VAL memory variable.

We could have achieved the same result by using the following ASSIGNMENT command:

```
   INV_VAL = QUANTITY * UNIT_COST
```

The expression QUANTITY * UNIT_COST on the right-hand side of the "=" sign will be evaluated, and the result will be assigned to the memory variable INV_VAL on the left-hand side of the "=" sign in the ASSIGNMENT command.

5.6 An Illustrative Example: Case Study 2

The second activity of the main processing step is 2.2 Accumulate Totals:

```
*** 2.2 ACCUMULATE TOTALS ***
   *
   TOTINV_VAL = TOTINV_VAL + INV_VAL
   *
```

This step consists of an ASSIGNMENT command. The expression TOTINV _VAL + INV_VAL on the right-hand side of the "=" sign is evaluated; that is, the inventory value stored in the INV_VAL is added to the TOTINV _VAL memory variable. Then the result is assigned to the memory variable TOTINV_VAL, the memory variable present on the left-hand side of the "=" sign in the ASSIGNMENT command.

We could have achieved the same result by using the following STORE TO command instead of the ASSIGNMENT command:

```
STORE (TOTINV_VAL + INV_VAL) TO TOTINV_VAL
```

Both commands can be used to perform the same function.

The third activity, 2.3 Print Detail Line, consists of two functions. The first is print a line, and its function is to print the detail line. The second function is increment line counter; its function is to increase the line counter memory variable LINECNT by one so that the next detail line is printed on the next line of the screen or printer. Both functions were discussed in Chapter 4.

The fourth activity, 2.4 Test for Screen Full, appears here for the first time. It is shown in Figure 5.17. When the output screen is a multiscreen report, the 2.4 Test for Screen Full module is used to test whether the screen is full or not. The limit on the screen is 24 lines, but the report is printed only up to line 20, leaving a few lines to display the message and

```
       ***  2.4 TEST FOR SCREEN FULL  ***
       *
       IF LINECNT = 20
           *
           *** 2.4.1 PROCESS SCREEN FULL ***
               *
               *** 2.4.1.1 FREEZE SCREEN ***
               *
               @ 22,0  TO  22,79
               @  1,0  TO  24,79 DOUBLE
               STORE ' ' TO RESPONSE
               @ 23,20 SAY 'PRESS ANY KEY TO CONTINUE . . .' GET RESPONSE
               READ
               *
               *** 2.4.1.2 PRINT REPORT HEADINGS ***
               *
       ENDIF LINECNT = 20
```

Figure 5.17 Test for Screen Full module of the main processing for Case Study 2

wait for a response to go to the next screen. If the screen is not full (that is, it can accommodate more detail lines), then no function is performed by this module. In other words, program control jumps to the next module. But if the screen is full (that is, it cannot accommodate more detail lines), then the submodule 2.4.1 Process Screen Full is processed.

The Process Screen Full submodule performs two functions. The first is 2.4.1.1 Freeze Screen, and its purpose is to freeze the screen and wait for the response from the user. This module allows the user to view the results displayed on the screen before proceeding to the next screen output. The second function is 2.4.1.2 Print Report Headings, and it performs three subfunctions: clear the screen, print the report headings, and initialize the line counter with a value where the next detail line should be printed. Both functions of the Test for Screen Full module have already been explained in Chapter 4.

The fifth and the last activity of the main processing step is 2.5 Skip to Next Record, whose function is to skip the record pointer to the next available record of the INV database file. This step has also been explained in Chapter 4.

When all the data records of the INV database file have been processed, program control will move to the last major processing step, 3.0 Terminate Processing, as shown in Figure 5.13. This step consists of three functions: 3.1 Print Total Line, 3.2 Close Files, and 3.3 End of Job.

The first function of print total line is shown in Figure 5.18. The first command of this module is to increase the line counter value by one. This will leave a blank line between the last detail line and the total line, which will be printed next. The next two @ ... SAY commands print the single line containing the message TOTAL VALUE OF STOCK = and the value of the TOTINV_VAL (total inventory value of the whole stock) memory variable.

Note that the PICTURE function has been used with the TOTINV_VAL memory variable. Its purpose is to specify the format in which the data field should be printed in the report. The symbols used with the numeric fields are given in Table 5.1, along with their functions.

The next module, 3.2 Close Files, will close the INV database file. This module has already been explained in Chapter 4. The last module, 3.3 End of Job, performs three functions: print end of report message, freeze screen, and reset default modes. All these functions have already been discussed in Chapter 4.

This completes the discussion of the logic and the commands used in the Case Study 2 program. The next step is to create the program file for this program. Use the MODIFY COMMAND command discussed in 3.2.1, and create the program file. Call this file INV32.PRG.

Figure 5.18 Print Total Line module

```
***   3.1 PRINT TOTAL LINE   ***
*
LINECNT = LINECNT + 1
@ LINECNT,35 SAY 'TOTAL VALUE OF STOCK = '
@ LINECNT,61 SAY TOTINV_VAL PICTURE '$99,999.99'
*
```

Table 5.1 Symbols used in output picture function

Symbol	Function
9	Used for digit and a sign
$	Used for inserting "$" symbol and replacing leading zeros by "$" symbol
,	Used for display of comma in the output
.	Used for display of decimal in the output
#	Used for digit, space, and sign
*	Used for replacing leading zeros by "*" symbol
L	Used for displaying the leading zeros in the output
Z	Used for suppressing the leading zeros in the output and replacing with a blank
C	Used to display CR after credit positive numeric value
X	Used to display DB after debt negative numeric value
(	Used to display negative numeric value in parenthesis

5.6.5 The Testing and Debugging Phase

The last step in program development is the testing and debugging phase, in which the source program is compiled and tested for the accuracy of its logic. The compiled program, called the object program, is then executed to produce the output. When the source program is executed for the first time, it is compiled by the language compiler before it is executed. Compiling consists of translating the source program into machine language and thus creating the object program.

The errors detected in the compiling process, usually referred to as syntactical errors, should be corrected, and the source program should be compiled again. When the compilation process does not indicate any syntactical errors, an object program is created.

Completion of the compilation process and execution of the object program do not mean that the program is operating correctly and the results produced are correct. The program still may contain logical errors, but the compiler cannot detect them. These are found by program testing, which involves executing the program using test data. Verify some of the records of the output to ensure its accuracy. If any discrepancies exist, make the needed corrections, and execute the program again. Repeat this step until the program produces correct and predictable results.

5.7 Modification of Case Study 2

A close look at the structure chart in Figure 5.11 reveals that the two modules 1.3 Print Report Headings and 2.4.1.2 Print Report Headings perform identical functions. A further analysis of the pseudocode and the coding for this structure chart reveals that both modules perform exactly the same three subfunctions—clear screen, print headings, and initialize line counter. The instructions in pseudocode and the coding of these modules are exactly the same, consisting of several lines and appearing in the program twice. These lines increase program size and complexity.

In a situation like this, when two or more modules perform exactly the same function and appear more than once in the program, they can be put once at the end of the program and be invoked by placing a single command where it is needed. In data processing terminology, this is called

```
****************************************************************
*                      PROCEDURE HEAD32                         *
*                     AMERICAN SUPPLY COMPANY                   *
* ------------------------------------------------------------- *
* The function of this procedure is to write headings at the    *
* top of each output screen for the INV32 program. It can be    *
* invoked from anywhere within the program to print the         *
* headings. After printing the headings the control will be     *
* returned to the next command in the program which invoked     *
* this procedure.                                               *
* ------------------------------------------------------------- *
*            COPYRIGHT (C) . . . SUDESH M. DUGGAL               *
****************************************************************
*
PROCEDURE HEAD32
   *
   *** CLEAR SCREEN ***
      *
      CLEAR
      *
   *** PRINT HEADINGS ***
      *
      @ 2,29 SAY 'AMERICAN SUPPLY COMPANY'
      @ 3,4  SAY DATE ()
      @ 3,33 SAY 'INVENTORY REPORT'
      @ 3,70 SAY TIME ()
      @ 4,0  TO  4,79
      @ 5,6  SAY 'ITEM'
      @ 5,42 SAY 'QTY ON'
      @ 5,52 SAY 'UNIT'
      @ 5,60 SAY 'INVENTORY'
      @ 6,5  SAY 'NUMBER'
      @ 6,19 SAY 'ITEM DESCRIPTION'
      @ 6,43 SAY 'HAND'
      @ 6,52 SAY 'PRICE'
      @ 6,62 SAY 'VALUE'
      @ 7,0  TO  7,79
      *
   *** INITIALIZE LINE COUNTER ***
      *
      STORE 8 TO LINECNT
      *
RETURN
```

Figure 5.19 Coding for procedure HEAD32 for Case Study 2

a subroutine; but in dBASE terminology, it is termed a **procedure**—a set of commands that performs a specific task and is needed more than once in the program. However, this set of commands can be placed at only one place in the program and can be invoked from any place in the program to perform the task.

A procedure is placed at the end of the program, and a program can contain several procedures. Each should have a unique name. Rules for forming a *procedure name* are the same as those for program files. The procedure should start with the PROCEDURE <procedure name> command and end with the RETURN command. The procedure can be invoked by the program with a DO <procedure name> command.

Let us include a procedure for the print report headings function at the end of the INV32 program and call it HEAD32. The procedure should start with the heading PROCEDURE HEAD32, with its major part as the contents of the 1.3 Print Report Headings module, and should end with the RETURN command. Its coding is shown in Figure 5.19.

Also note that another pair of modules, the 2.4.1.1 Freeze Screen module and the freeze screen submodule of the 3.3 End of Job module, performs the identical function (freeze the screen to allow the user to view the report displayed on the screen and continue the processing by pressing any key). This function will be used not only in this program more than once, but it will also be used by all the programs that create multiscreen output. This type of module is called a *utility module*.

Such a function should be developed as a procedure in a separate procedure file. A **procedure file** can consist of several procedures, each of

```
****************************************************************
*                      PROCEDURE FREEZE                         *
*                   AMERICAN SUPPLY COMPANY                     *
* ------------------------------------------------------------- *
* The function of this procedure is to freeze the screen to    *
* allow the user to view the report displayed on the screen    *
* and continue the processing by pressing any key. At the      *
* end the control will be returned to the next command in      *
* the Calling Program which invoked this procedure.            *
* ------------------------------------------------------------- *
*           COPYRIGHT (C) . . . SUDESH M. DUGGAL                *
****************************************************************
*
PROCEDURE FREEZE
    *
    @ 22,0  TO 22,79
    @  1,0  TO 24,79 DOUBLE
    STORE ' ' TO RESPONSE
    @ 23,20 SAY 'PRESS ANY KEY TO CONTINUE . . .' GET RESPONSE
    READ
    *
RETURN
```

Figure 5.20 Coding in dBASE for freeze procedure file

which should start with the PROCEDURE <procedure name> command and end with the RETURN command. A procedure file cannot be executed by itself, as a dBASE program file can, but it can be invoked by any program or other procedure file. The program file or the procedure file, which needs to use a procedure present in a procedure file, should first invoke the procedure file by using the SET PROCEDURE TO <procedure file name> command and then call the procedure by the DO <procedure name> command.

Let us develop a procedure file named UTILITY.PRG containing only one procedure, called FREEZE. The function performed by the freeze

```
****************************************************************
*                   PROCEDURE ENDOFJOB                          *
*                  AMERICAN SUPPLY COMPANY                      *
* ------------------------------------------------------------- *
* This procedure is invoked by any program, and its function    *
* is to print the End of Report message, Freeze Screen, and     *
* to Reset Default Modes. At the end of the procedure the       *
* control will be returned to the next command in the program   *
* which invoked this procedure.                                 *
* ------------------------------------------------------------- *
*              COPYRIGHT (C) . . . SUDESH M. DUGGAL             *
****************************************************************
*
PROCEDURE ENDOFJOB
*
*** 1.1 END OF JOB ***
   *
   *** 1.1.1 END OF REPORT MESSAGE ***
      *
      LINECNT = LINECNT + 2
      @ LINECNT,20 SAY '*** --- END OF REPORT --- ***'
      *
   *** 1.1.2 FREEZE SCREEN ***
      *
      @ 22,0  TO 22,79
      @  1,0  TO 24,79 DOUBLE
      STORE ' ' TO RESPONSE
      @ 23,20 SAY 'PRESS ANY KEY TO CONTINUE . . .' GET RESPONSE
      READ
      *
   *** 1.1.3 RESET DEFAULT MODES ***
      *
      SET TALK ON
      SET HEADING ON
      SET STATUS ON
      *
   *** 1.1.4 RESET PROCEDURES ***
      *
      SET PROCEDURE TO
      *
      RETURN
```

Figure 5.21 Coding for procedure endofjob for Case Study 2

5.7 Modification of Case Study 2

procedure is the same as that of either the submodule freeze screen of the 3.3 End of Job or 2.4.1.1 Freeze Screen module. Its coding is given in Figure 5.20 (see page 211).

A comparison of the coding of Case Study 1 and 2 indicates that the End of Job module is present in both. It performs three functions: print end of report message, freeze screen, and reset default modes. Because you'll need this module in future programs also, you should create a utility procedure for it and save the coding for future programs. Let us call it ENDOFJOB and store it in the UTILITY.PRG procedure file. Its coding is given in Figure 5.21.

A fourth function, reset procedures, has also been added to the endofjob utility. This function is commonly needed in the End of Job module. If it is not needed (that is, if there are no procedures to be reset), it will not have any effect. So its presence in this utility module will be useful.

Let us incorporate these changes in the solution of Case Study 2. After the modifications, the structure chart will change to that shown in Figure 5.22 (see page 215). Notice the change in the symbols. The symbol previously used for 1.3 Print Report Headings is as follows:

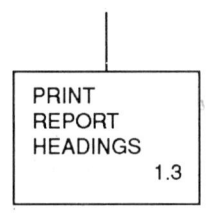

```
┌──────────────┐
│ PRINT        │
│ REPORT       │
│ HEADINGS     │
│          1.3 │
└──────────────┘
```

It represents a module that means the function performed by it is coded in the program itself. The new symbol in its place is now:

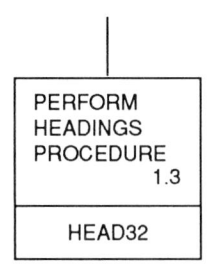

```
┌──────────────┐
│ PERFORM      │
│ HEADINGS     │
│ PROCEDURE    │
│          1.3 │
├──────────────┤
│   HEAD32     │
└──────────────┘
```

This symbol represents an internal procedure (that is, a subroutine, which means that the coding for it is at the end of the program as a procedure named HEAD32). The absence of the extension with the procedure name indicates it is an internal procedure.

Now look at the 2.4.1.1 Freeze Screen module. Its symbol in the structure chart of Figure 5.11 is

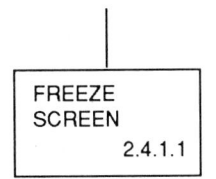

```
┌──────────────┐
│ FREEZE       │
│ SCREEN       │
│      2.4.1.1 │
└──────────────┘
```

It represents a module, which means its function is coded in the program itself. The new symbol in its place in the modified structure chart of Figure 5.22 is

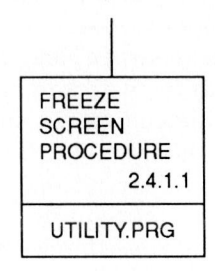

```
        |
 ┌─────────────┐
 │ FREEZE      │
 │ SCREEN      │
 │ PROCEDURE   │
 │      2.4.1.1│
 ├─────────────┤
 │ UTILITY.PRG │
 └─────────────┘
```

This symbol represents an external procedure, which means that its coding is in a separate program named UTILITY.PRG, which is called the procedure file.

The pseudocode for the modified structure chart of Figure 5.22 is given in Figure 5.23, and its coding is shown in Figure 5.24.

The presence of the SET PROCEDURE TO UTILITY in the 1.1 Housekeeping module invokes the procedure file named UTILITY. The command DO HEAD32 in the 1.3 Print Report Headings module calls the internal procedure HEAD32 to print the headings for the first screen. The command DO FREEZE in the 2.4.1.1 Freeze Screen Procedure module calls the external procedure freeze from the UTILITY.PRG procedure file to freeze the screen and allow the user to view the data when the screen is full. The command DO HEAD32 in the 2.4.1.2 Perform Heading Routine module calls the internal procedure HEAD32 to print the headings when the new screen of output is needed. Finally, the command DO ENDOFJOB in the 3.2 End of Job module calls the external procedure ENDOFJOB from the UTILITY.PRG procedure file. This procedure prints the end of report message, then calls the freeze utility, which freezes the screen and finally resets the default modes.

Whenever the command in the main program calls for an internal or external procedure to perform a task, program control is transferred to that procedure. After the execution of that procedure, the control returns to the command next to the command that invoked it. When an external procedure is used, the program that calls another program or procedure file is called the *calling program*. The program or the procedure file invoked is called the *called program*.

5.7 Modification of Case Study 2

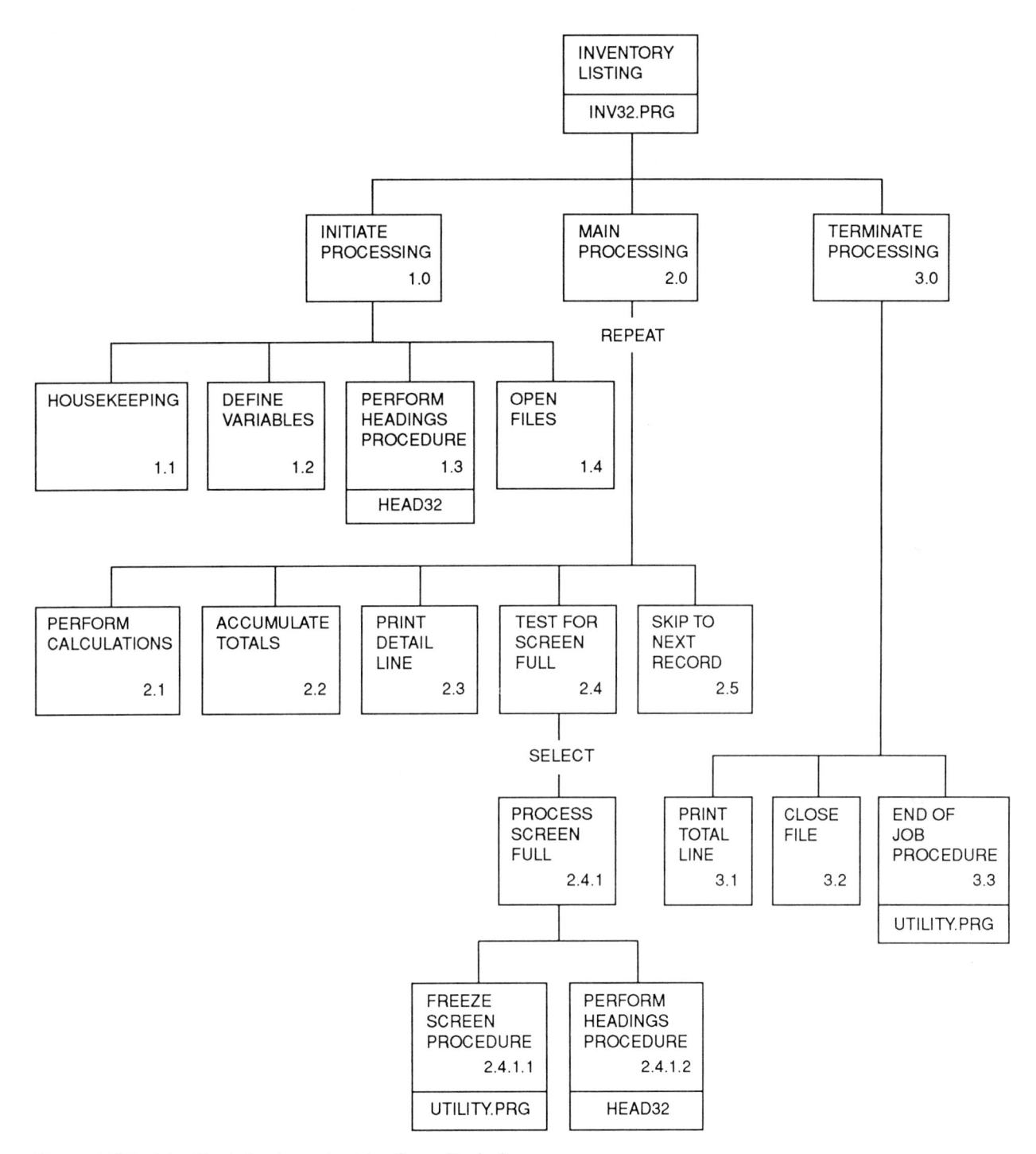

Figure 5.22 Modified structure chart for Case Study 2

Figure 5.23 Modified pseudocode for Case Study 2

```
0.0 INVENTORY LISTING
   1.0 INITIATE PROCESSING
      1.1 HOUSEKEEPING
         CHANGE DEFAULT MODES
            Turn off the dBASE's heading feature
            Turn off the dBASE's user dialogue
            Turn off the dBASE's status bar
         SET PROCEDURE
            Set the procedure to the UTILITY file
      1.2 DEFINE VARIABLES
         DECLARE VARIABLES
            Declare LINECNT as public variable
         DEFINE PROGRAM VARIABLES
            Set Inventory Value = 0
            Set Total Inventory Value = 0
      1.3 PERFORM HEADINGS PROCEDURE
         Perform the headings HEAD32 procedure
      1.4 OPEN FILES
         Open INV database file
   2.0 MAIN PROCESSING
      REPEAT: until end of file
         2.1 PERFORM CALCULATIONS
            Calculate Inventory Value by multiplying
            the quantity and unit cost fields
         2.2 ACCUMULATE TOTALS
            Add inventory value to total inventory value
         2.3 PRINT DETAIL LINE
            PRINT A LINE
               Write Detail Line
            INCREMENT LINE COUNTER
               Add 1 to the Line Counter
         2.4 TEST FOR SCREEN FULL
            SELECT: When screen is full
               2.4.1 PROCESS SCREEN FULL
                  2.4.1.1 FREEZE SCREEN PROCEDURE
                     Perform FREEZE procedure
                  2.4.1.2 PERFORM HEADINGS PROCEDURE
                     Perform the headings HEAD32 procedure
            END SELECT
         2.5 SKIP TO NEXT RECORD
            Skip to the next record of the database
      END REPEAT
   3.0 TERMINATE PROCESSING
      3.1 PRINT TOTAL LINE
         Increment line counter by one
         Print Total line
      3.2 CLOSE FILE
         Close database file
```

Figure 5.23 Continued

```
                    3.3 END OF JOB
                        Perform ENDOFJOB procedure
                PROCEDURE HEAD32
                   PRINT REPORT HEADINGS
                     CLEAR SCREEN
                       Clear the screen
                     PRINT HEADINGS
                       Print Report Main Heading Line 1
                       Print Report Main Heading Line 2
                       Draw a line
                       Print Column Heading Line 1
                       Print Column Heading Line 2
                       Draw a line
                     INITIALIZE LINE COUNTER
                       Set line counter = 8
                   RETURN
```

```
****************************************************************
*                       MINV32                                  *
*               AMERICAN SUPPLY COMPANY                         *
*---------------------------------------------------------------*
* This program produces an Inventory Listing Report for         *
* American Supply Company, containing all the items of          *
* the INV file. The program calculates the inventory            *
* value for each item by multiplying the quantity at hand       *
* by the unit cost. It also calculates the total inventory      *
* value for the whole stock. The heading is also included       *
* in the report.                                                *
*---------------------------------------------------------------*
*             COPYRIGHT (C) . . . SUDESH M. DUGGAL              *
****************************************************************
*
***************************furnish*
* 1.0 INITIATE PROCESSING *
***************************
*
*** 1.1 HOUSEKEEPING ***
   *
   *** CHANGE DEFAULT MODES ***
      *
      SET HEADING OFF
      SET TALK OFF
      SET STATUS OFF
      *
   *** SET PROCEDURES ***
      *
      SET PROCEDURE TO UTILITY
      *
*** 1.2 DEFINE VARIABLES ***
```

Figure 5.24 Modified coding for Case Study 2

```
      *
   *** DECLARE VARIABLES ***
      *
      PUBLIC LINECNT
      *
   *** DEFINE PROGRAM VARIABLES ***
      *
      STORE 0 TO INV_VAL
      STORE 0 TO TOTINV_VAL
      *
*** 1.3 PERFORM HEADINGS PROCEDURE ***
   *
   DO HEAD32
   *
*** 1.4 OPEN FILE ***
   *
   USE INV
   *
***********************
* 2.0 MAIN PROCESSING *
***********************
*
DO WHILE .NOT. EOF ()
   *
   *** 2.1 PERFORM CALCULATIONS ***
      *
      STORE (QUANTITY * UNIT_COST) TO INV_VAL
      *
   *** 2.2 ACCUMULATE TOTALS ***
      *
      TOTINV_VAL = TOTINV_VAL + INV_VAL
      *
   *** 2.3 PRINT DETAIL LINE ***
      *
      *** PRINT A LINE ***
         *
         @ LINECNT,11 SAY ITEM_NUM
         @ LINECNT,19 SAY ITEM_DESC
         @ LINECNT,47 SAY QUANTITY
         @ LINECNT,54 SAY UNIT_COST
         @ LINECNT,60 SAY INV_VAL PICTURE '999,999.99'
         *
      *** INCREMENT LINE COUNTER ***
         *
         LINECNT = LINECNT + 1
         *
   *** 2.4 TEST FOR SCREEN FULL ***
      *
      IF LINECNT = 20
         *
         *** 2.4.1 PROCESS SCREEN FULL ***
            *
            *** 2.4.1.1 FREEZE SCREEN PROCEDURE ***
               *
               DO FREEZE
               *
```

Figure 5.24 Continued

```
                    *** 2.4.1.2 PERFORM HEADINGS PROCEDURE ***
                        *
                        DO HEAD32
                        *
             ENDIF LINECNT = 20
                *
        *** 2.5 SKIP TO NEXT RECORD ***
                *
                SKIP
                *
ENDDO .NOT. EOF ()
*
***************************
* 3.0 TERMINATE PROCESSING *
***************************
*
*** 3.1 PRINT TOTAL LINE ***
        *
        LINECNT = LINECNT + 1
        @ LINECNT,35 SAY 'TOTAL VALUE OF STOCK = '
        @ LINECNT,59 SAY TOTINV_VAL PICTURE '$999,999.99'
        *
*** 3.2 CLOSE FILE ***
        *
        USE
        *
*** 3.3 END OF JOB ***
        *
        DO ENDOFJOB
        *
        *
****************************************************************
*                       PROCEDURE HEAD32                        *
*                     AMERICAN SUPPLY COMPANY                   *
* ------------------------------------------------------------- *
* The function of this procedure is to write headings at the   *
* top of each output screen for the INV32 program. It can be   *
* invoked from anywhere within the program to print the        *
* headings. After printing the headings the control will be    *
* returned to the next command in the program which invoked    *
* this procedure.                                              *
* ------------------------------------------------------------- *
*             COPYRIGHT (C) . . . SUDESH M. DUGGAL             *
****************************************************************
*
PROCEDURE HEAD32
    *
    *** CLEAR SCREEN ***
        *
        CLEAR
        *
    *** PRINT HEADINGS ***
        *
        @  2,29 SAY 'AMERICAN SUPPLY COMPANY'
        @  3,4  SAY DATE ()
        @  3,33 SAY 'INVENTORY REPORT'
```

Figure 5.24 Continued

```
    @  3,70 SAY TIME ()
    @  4,0  TO  4,79
    @  5,6  SAY 'ITEM'
    @  5,42 SAY 'QTY ON'
    @  5,52 SAY 'UNIT'
    @  5,60 SAY 'INVENTORY'
    @  6,5  SAY 'NUMBER'
    @  6,19 SAY 'ITEM DESCRIPTION'
    @  6,43 SAY 'HAND'
    @  6,52 SAY 'PRICE'
    @  6,62 SAY 'VALUE'
    @  7,0  TO  7.79
    *
*** INITIALIZE LINE COUNTER ***
    *
    STORE 8 TO LINECNT
    *
    RETURN
```

Figure 5.24 Continued

5.8 Summary

The ? command, used to print the result of an expression, can make dBASE a simple calculator. This command is also called the CALCULATOR command.

The INT () function is used for converting the numeric values to integer values by truncating the decimal portion.

The memory variables are used to store intermediate results of the calculations in the computer's memory for future use. dBASE IV provides four types of memory variables: character, numeric, date, and logical.

The STORE and ASSIGNMENT commands are used to create memory variables. Memory variables stored in the computer's memory can be displayed by either pressing the F7 Display Memory function key or by typing the DISPLAY MEMORY command.

Memory variables are deleted from the computer's memory as soon as the computer is turned off. These can also be deleted by using the RELEASE command.

Memory variables can be stored in the memory files for future use with the program files. Memory variables so stored can be loaded into the computer's memory by using the RESTORE FROM command.

The COUNT command is used to count the total number of records present or the number of selected records satisfying a particular condition in an active database file.

The SUM command is used to calculate the sum of all or selected numeric fields present in a data record of a database file for all or selected records satisfying a particular condition of a database file.

The AVERAGE command is used to calculate the mean of all or selected numeric fields present in a data record of a database file for all or selected records satisfying a particular condition of a database file.

KEY CONCEPTS

memory variable
private variable
procedure

procedure file
public variable

dBASE COMMANDS AND FUNCTIONS

? command
ASSIGNMENT command
AVERAGE command
COUNT command
DISPLAY MEMORY command
INTEGER function
PROCEDURE command

RELEASE or RELEASE ALL command
RESTORE FROM command
SAVE TO command
SET PROCEDURE TO command
STORE TO command
SUM command

REVIEW QUESTIONS

1. What is the function of the CALCULATOR command?
2. What is the function of the integer function, and how can it be used to round numeric values to two decimal places?
3. What is the purpose of the memory variables, and what types of memory variables are supported by dBASE IV?
4. What are the two commands used in creating memory variables? Give one example of each.
5. Is there any difference between the ASSIGNMENT and STORE commands? If there is, what is it?
6. How can memory variables present in the computer's memory be displayed individually or all together?
7. Explain the difference between a public and private variable.
8. How can the memory variables be saved permanently in a disk file?
9. What is the life span of the memory variables?
10. How can the memory variables be deleted from the computer's memory?
11. How can the memory variables be loaded back to the computer's memory from the disk files? Will this affect the memory variables already in the computer's storage? If so, what can be done to avoid this effect?
12. What is the use of the COUNT command? Explain the function of its different formats.
13. How does the COUNT command differ from the DISPLAY STRUCTURE or GOTO BOTTOM command in providing the count of records in a database file?
14. What is the use of the SUM command? Explain the function of its different formats.
15. What is the use of the AVERAGE command? Explain the function of its different formats.
16. In a multiscreen output, what extra steps are needed as compared to the single-screen output?
17. What is the purpose of the picture function when used with the memory variable?
18. What is meant by a procedure? How many different ways can a procedure be used?
19. What is meant by a procedure file? What extra commands are needed to access the procedure from the program or procedure file?
20. What is the difference between a program and procedure file?
21. How can we tell from the symbol of a structure chart whether it is an internal or external procedure?

HANDS-ON ASSIGNMENT

Programming Assignment 5A

Program Description Write a program ACR32.PRG to produce an accounts receivable report listing for American Supply Company. The report should contain all the records of the database file named ACCREC and calculate the current balance (CURR_BAL) for each record in the ACCREC database file. The current balance can be calculated by subtracting the payment amount (PAY_AMT) from the purchase amount (PUR_AMT) field. Finally, the program should accumulate the current balance to obtain the total current balance (TCURR_BAL) for all receivables due to the company.

Input File(s) The ACCREC database file whose structure is shown in Figure 4.32 is used as an input file.

Output The output of the program should be an accounts receivable report listing, as shown in Figure 5.25. It is a multiscreen report. The headings should be as shown in the accounts receivable report listing, and the detail line should consist of the CUS_NUM, PUR_DATE, PUR_REF, PUR_AMT, PAY_AMT, and CURR_BAL fields only.

Processing Steps Use the following steps to develop the solution of the program:

1. The headings should be printed as shown in the accounts receivable report listing. The date and time should be included in the headings.
2. The column headings should be enclosed between two lines, as shown in Figure 5.25.
3. The current balance (CURR_BAL) for each record in the ACCREC database file should be calculated by subtracting the payment amount (PAY_AMT) from the purchase amount (PUR_AMT) field.
4. The current balance (CURR_BAL) for each record in the ACCREC database file should be accumulated in the TCURR_BAL field.
5. Detail lines should not be printed past row 20.
6. When the screen is full or the final totals have been printed on the final screen, freeze the screen to allow the user to view the output.
7. Print the accumulated current balance, stored in the TCURR_BAL field on the last screen, one row below the last detail line.

Figure 5.25 Accounts receivable report listing: Programming Assignment 5A

```
                    AMERICAN SUPPLY COMPANY
    08/20/89        ACCOUNT RECEIVABLE REPORT              02:29:25
              LISTING OF ALL RECEIVABLE WITH CURRENT BALANCE

    CUSTOMER     PURCHASE    PURCHASE     PURCHASE     PAYMENT     CURRENT
    NUMBER         DATE     REFERENCE      AMOUNT      AMOUNT      BALANCE

    XXXXXXXXXX   99/99/99     9999        9,999.99    99/99/99    9,999.99
    XXXXXXXXXX   99/99/99     9999        9,999.99    99/99/99    9,999.99

                    TOTAL RECEIVABLE FOR THE COMPANY =   $99,999.99

                       *** --- END OF REPORT --- ***




                        PRESS ANY KEY TO CONTINUE . . .
```

8. At the end of the output report, print the message "*** --- END OF REPORT --- ***" to indicate the end of the output report. Then freeze the screen to allow the user to view the output.

9. The whole output should be enclosed in the box, as shown in Figure 5.25.

Programming Assignment 5B

Program Description   Write a program PAY32.PRG to produce a payroll report listing for American Supply Company. The report should contain all the records of the employee database file. It should calculate the gross pay (GROSS_PAY) for each employee in the employee database file by adding the regular pay (REG_PAY) and the overtime pay (OTIME_PAY) fields. Finally, the program should accumulate the gross pay to obtain the total gross pay (TGROSS_PAY) for all company employees.

Input File(s)   The employee database file whose structure is shown in Figure 4.34 is used as an input file.

Output   Program output should be a payroll report listing, as shown in Figure 5.26. It is a multiscreen report. The headings should be as shown in the payroll report listing, and the detail line should consist of the SOC_SC_NUM, EMP_NAME, REG_PAY, OTIME_PAY, and GROSS_PAY.

Processing Steps   Use the following steps to develop the solution of the program:

1. The headings should be printed as shown in the payroll report listing. The date and time should be included in the headings.

2. The column headings should be enclosed between two lines, as shown in Figure 5.26.

3. The gross pay (GROSS_PAY) for each employee in the EMPLOYEE database file should be calculated by adding the regular pay (REG_PAY) and overtime pay (OTIME_PAY) fields.

4. The gross pay (GROSS_PAY) for each employee in the EMPLOYEE database file should be accumulated in the TGROSS_PAY field.

Figure 5.26 Payroll report listing: Programming Assignment 5B

```
                  AMERICAN SUPPLY COMPANY
    08/20/89           PAYROLL REPORT              02:29:25
                     LISTING OF ALL EMPLOYEES

     SOC SEC                          REGULAR   OVERTIME   GROSS
     NUMBER      EMPLOYEE NAME          PAY       PAY       PAY

     XXXXXXXXX   XXXXXXXXXXXXXXXXXXXX  9,999.99  9,999.99  99,999.99
     XXXXXXXXX   XXXXXXXXXXXXXXXXXXXX  9,999.99  9,999.99  99,999.99


                       TOTAL GROSS FOR THE COMPANY = $99,999.99


                  *** --- END OF REPORT --- ***




                     PRESS ANY KEY TO CONTINUE . . .
```

5. Detail lines should not be printed past row 20.
6. When the screen is full or the final totals have been printed on the final screen, freeze the screen to allow the user to view the output.
7. Print the accumulated gross pay, stored in the TGROSS_PAY field on the last screen, one row below the last detail line.
8. At the end of the output report, print the message "*** --- END OF REPORT --- ***" to indicate the end of the output report. Then freeze the screen to allow the user to view the output.
9. The whole output should be enclosed in the box, as shown in Figure 5.26.

Chapter 6

Data Editing and Modifying a Database

LEARNING OBJECTIVES

Upon successfully completing this chapter, you will be able to:

1. Move around in the database files by using
   a. The SKIP command.
   b. The GOTO command.
2. Edit data in the database files by using the EDIT command.
3. Change the structure of the database files by using the MODIFY STRUCTURE command.
4. Analyze, design, and code a program in dBASE programming language in which data in the memory variable file is used in calculations and the result of the calculations is stored in a newly added field of the database file structure using the MODIFY STRUCTURE command.

6.1 Overview

This chapter starts by introducing the SKIP and GOTO commands available in dBASE IV. These are used to move around inside the database file and help locate data there. The LIST or DISPLAY commands used in conjunction with these commands enable us to view the located data for proofreading and provide a means of tracing errors in the database file.

In the second part of the chapter, the EDIT command and its various formats are introduced. These provide a method of editing (correcting the errors) the contents of the database file. The MODIFY STRUCTURE command, which allows us to alter the structure of the database file by adding data fields to, deleting, and modifying the existing data fields in the structure of the database file, is introduced next.

Finally, a simple program, in which the data from the memory variable file are used in calculations and the result of the calculations is stored in a newly created field, is analyzed, designed, coded, tested, and debugged.

6.2 Moving Around in a Database File

In this section, I introduce two dBASE commands that allow you to move around inside the database file. Let us use the database file named FILE2 for this purpose. Open it by typing the following command:

. **USE FILE2**   <Return>

Recall that when a database file is opened, dBASE sets the record pointer to the first physical record of the database file; and the record to which the record pointer is pointing at any particular instance is called the current record. Because the FILE2 database has just been opened, the current record is its first record. To verify this record, display the current record either by pressing the F8 Display function key or by typing the following command:

. **DISPLAY**   <Return>

dBASE will respond by displaying the first record, as shown:

```
Record#  SOC_SC_NUM   CUST_NAME         BALANCE TELEPHONE
      1  605-21-0500  Bernice T. Johnson  75.32 513-234-7560
```

The first command that lets us move around in the database file is the SKIP command.

6.2.1 The SKIP Command

The general format of the SKIP command is

SKIP [<number>]

The optional parameter <number> refers to the number of records the record pointer should move. It can be a positive or a negative number or an expression whose calculated value is a numeric value.

The SKIP command moves the record pointer forward or backward in a database file by a specified number of records from its current location. If no number is specified, it moves the cursor to the next record. Let us now try the simple SKIP command, that is, the SKIP command without the optional <number> parameter. (You have already used this form in section 3.2.6.) The FILE2 database file is already open, and the record pointer is pointing to the first record. If you type the following command:

. **SKIP**   <Return>

dBASE will respond by displaying

Record No.   2

6.2 Moving Around in a Database File

indicating that the record pointer is now pointing to the second record of the FILE2 database file. To verify this result, either press the F8 Display function key or type the following command:

. **DISPLAY**   <Return>

dBASE will respond by displaying the second record, as shown:

```
Record# SOC_SC_NUM   CUST_NAME       BALANCE TELEPHONE
     2  506-97-4200  Jan A. Black     153.75 606-527-4534
```

The SKIP command can also be used to move the record pointer forward by more than one position by specifying the optional <number> parameter along with it. For example, if you type the following command:

. **SKIP 6**   <Return>

the record pointer will move six positions forward from its current position. Because the record pointer in our example was already at the second record, dBASE will respond to this command by displaying:

Record No.   8

indicating that the record pointer is now pointing to the eighth record in the FILE2 database file (in other words, record #8 is now the current record). To display the current record, either press the F8 Display function key or type the following command:

. **DISPLAY**   <Return>

dBASE will respond by displaying the eighth record of the FILE1 database file, as shown:

```
Record# SOC_SC_NUM   CUST_NAME          BALANCE TELEPHONE
     8  562-12-8754  Joseph T. Saxton   1248.60 606-244-1290
```

The SKIP command can also be used to move the record pointer backward by specifying the optional <number> parameter with a negative value. For example, to move the record pointer backward two positions from its current position, you will need the following command:

. **SKIP -2**   <Return>

When this command is executed, dBASE will respond by displaying:

Record No.   6

indicating the the record pointer is now pointing to the sixth record in the FILE2 database file. To display the current record, either press the F8 Display function key or type the following command:

. **DISPLAY**   <Return>

dBASE will respond by displaying the sixth record of the FILE2 database file, as shown:

```
Record# SOC_SC_NUM   CUST_NAME         BALANCE TELEPHONE
     6  452-45-8520  Jill E. Hembree     75.00 513-733-0001
```

As you have seen, the SKIP command alone moves the record pointer forward by one position. In other words, it skips the record pointer to the next record in the database file. But if the database file is indexed (indexes are discussed in Chapter 11), the SKIP command skips the record pointer to the next record defined by the index file.

The second command used to move around in the database file is the GOTO command.

6.2.2 The GOTO Command

The general format of the GOTO command is

```
GOTO/GO [[RECORD]<record number>] [TOP/BOTTOM]
```

where GOTO and GO can be used interchangeably. Their use is optional, the word [RECORD] is also optional, and the <record number> is a number or an expression whose result is a number to which the record pointer should move. This command has two different forms.

The first form of the GOTO command is

```
GOTO/GO [[RECORD]<record number>]
```

The function of this command is to move the record pointer to a specified record number in the active database file. For example, to move the record pointer to the third record of the FILE2 database file, you can use one of the following three commands:

```
. GOTO 3      <Return>
. GO 3        <Return>
. 3           <Return>
```

After executing any of these, dBASE will respond by displaying the dot prompt. Unlike the SKIP command, the GOTO command does not respond by a statement such as record #3. But the record pointer will move to the third record of the FILE2 database file. To verify this result, either press the F8 Display function key or type the following command:

```
. DISPLAY     <Return>
```

dBASE will respond by displaying the third record of the FILE2 database file, as shown:

```
Record# SOC_SC_NUM   CUST_NAME            BALANCE TELEPHONE
     3  120-12-4512  Gregory B. Cardwell    23.50 212-456-8787
```

The second form of the GOTO command is

```
GOTO/GO [TOP/BOTTOM]
```

The function of this command is to move the record pointer to the first or last record in the active database file or to the first and last records determined by the current active index file. (Indexes are covered in Chapter 11.) For example, to move the record pointer to the first record in the FILE2 database file, you can use either of the following commands:

```
. GOTO TOP    <Return>
. GO TOP      <Return>
```

When the dot prompt returns, you can display the current record by either pressing the F8 Display function key or typing the following command:

```
. DISPLAY    <Return>
```

dBASE will respond by displaying the first record of the FILE2 database file, as shown:

```
Record# SOC_SC_NUM   CUST_NAME            BALANCE TELEPHONE
      1 605-21-0500  Bernice T. Johnson     75.32 513-234-7560
```

In addition to the GOTO TOP command, there is an opposite, GOTO BOTTOM, command, the function of which is to move the record pointer to the last record in the database. To move the record pointer to the last record in the FILE2 database file, you can use either of the following commands:

```
. GOTO BOTTOM    <Return>
. GO BOTTOM      <Return>
```

When the dot prompt returns, you can display the current record by either pressing the F8 Display function key or typing the following command:

```
. DISPLAY    <Return>
```

dBASE will respond by displaying the last record of the FILE2 database file, as shown:

```
Record# SOC_SC_NUM   CUST_NAME              BALANCE TELEPHONE
     11 120-21-7895  Jeramiah F. Johnson     276.90 513-733-8871
```

This is the last record in the FILE2 database file. Its record number, 11, indicates that there are 11 records in the FILE2 database file, which tells us that this command can be used to find the number of records present in any database file. You have already learned two other methods for finding the number of records present in a database file: using the DISPLAY STRUCTURE command and using the COUNT command.

6.3 Editing Data in a Database File

The main use of the DISPLAY or LIST commands discussed in Chapter 2 is to proofread the data records of the database files. An appropriate way to do this would be to display the data records on the screen or to print them on the printer and visually check them for the correctness of the data. If errors are found, you can mark them and use the EDIT command to make the corrections. The process of making corrections in the database file is called **editing.**

6.3.1 The EDIT Command

The general format of the EDIT command is

```
EDIT [<record number>]
```

where the optional parameter <record number> is an integer value representing the record number of the database file to be edited. There are two formats of the EDIT command.

The EDIT Format

The simple EDIT command is used to edit the current data record of the active database file. For example, if you type the following sequence of commands:

```
. USE FILE2      <Return>
. EDIT           <Return>
```

dBASE will respond by displaying the edit screen as shown in Figure 6.1.

dBASE is now in the edit mode, and the first data record is displayed on the screen. To start with, the cursor will be in the leftmost position of the first field, that is, the SOC_SC_NUM field. To move around in the data record or to go to the point of error, use the cursor control keys. To make corrections, use the <Del> key, the <Ins> key, or the <Backspace> key. The control keys used with the APPEND command and listed in Table 2.6 can be used with the EDIT command.

Now let's learn how to make a correction. Suppose the customer's name in the first record is entered wrong. It should be Bernice K. Johnson in place of Bernice T. Johnson. To make this correction, first move the cursor to the CUST_NAME field by either pressing the <Return> key or using the <Down Arrow> key. Next use the <Right Arrow> or <Left Arrow> key to position the cursor at the letter "T," as shown in Figure 6.2.

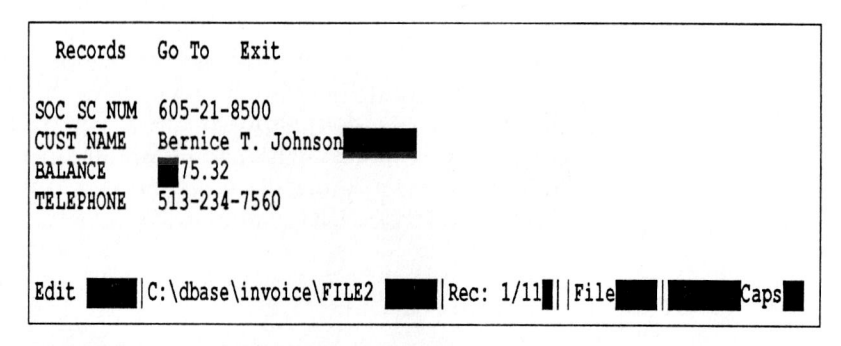

```
Records   Go To   Exit

SOC_SC_NUM  605-21-8500
CUST_NAME   Bernice T. Johnson
BALANCE     75.32
TELEPHONE   513-234-7560


Edit    |C:\dbase\invoice\FILE2   |Rec: 1/11| |File|        |Caps|
```

Figure 6.1 Edit screen for FILE2 database file

6.3 Editing Data in a Database File

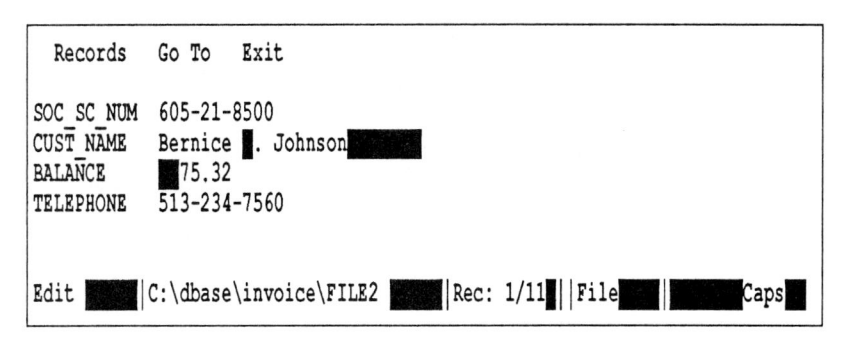

```
┌─────────────────────────────────────────────────────────────┐
│   Records    Go To    Exit                                  │
│                                                             │
│ SOC_SC_NUM   605-21-8500                                    │
│ CUST_NAME    Bernice ▪. Johnson▪▪▪▪                         │
│ BALANCE      ▪75.32                                         │
│ TELEPHONE    513-234-7560                                   │
│                                                             │
│                                                             │
│ Edit ▪▪▪|C:\dbase\invoice\FILE2 ▪▪▪|Rec: 1/11▪||File▪|▪▪Caps▪│
└─────────────────────────────────────────────────────────────┘
```

Figure 6.2 Edit screen 2 for FILE2 database file

Finally, change the "T" to a "K" by pressing the <Shift-K> keys. The edited data record will appear as shown in Figure 6.3.

To save the record and go to the next record after making the corrections, press the <PgDn> key. dBASE will display the next data record in sequence in the database file. The <PgDn> key can be used to save the current data record and go to the next data record in the edit mode. Similarly, the <PgUp> key can be used to save the current data record and go to the previous data record of the database file. The use of the <PgDn> key after the last data record of the database file or the <PgUp> key past the first data record of the database file will terminate the edit process and return the control to the dot prompt.

If you are in the middle of a large database file, you can save the edited data record by terminating the edit process by pressing either the <Ctrl-End> keys or the <Ctrl-W> keys. If after making changes in a particular data record, you realize that you actually do not need these changes, you can exit the edit mode without saving the changes by simply pressing either the <Ctrl-Q> keys or the <Esc> key.

The EDIT <record number> Format

When working with a very large database file and making changes to data records that are far apart, the simple edit format just discussed will not be very useful. In this situation, the second format of the EDIT command becomes very handy.

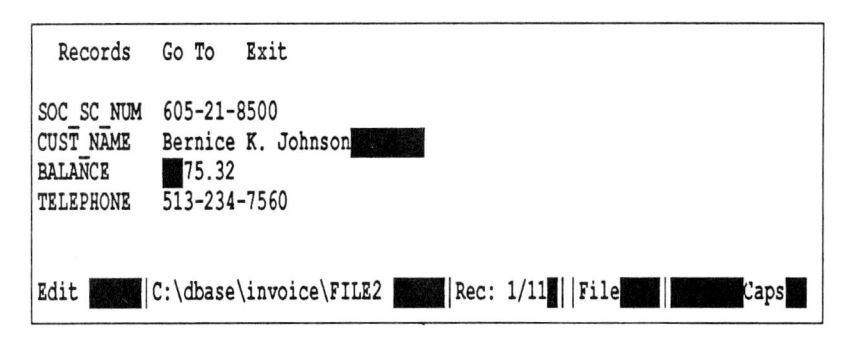

```
┌─────────────────────────────────────────────────────────────┐
│   Records    Go To    Exit                                  │
│                                                             │
│ SOC_SC_NUM   605-21-8500                                    │
│ CUST_NAME    Bernice K. Johnson▪▪▪▪                         │
│ BALANCE      ▪75.32                                         │
│ TELEPHONE    513-234-7560                                   │
│                                                             │
│                                                             │
│ Edit ▪▪▪|C:\dbase\invoice\FILE2 ▪▪▪|Rec: 1/11▪||File▪|▪▪Caps▪│
└─────────────────────────────────────────────────────────────┘
```

Figure 6.3 Edit screen 3 for FILE2 database file

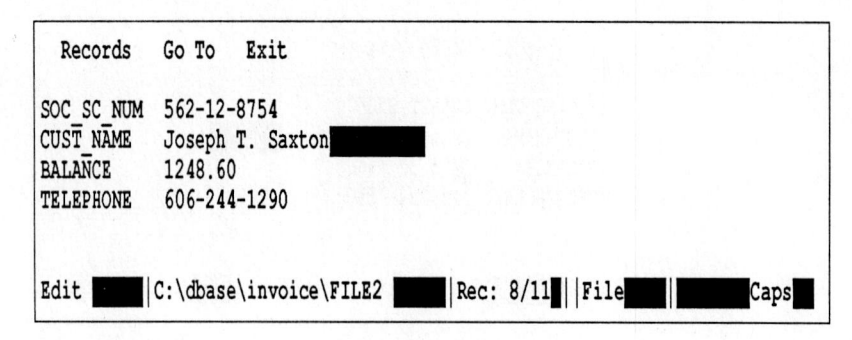

```
 Records   Go To   Exit

SOC_SC_NUM  562-12-8754
CUST_NAME   Joseph T. Saxton
BALANCE     1248.60
TELEPHONE   606-244-1290



Edit    |C:\dbase\invoice\FILE2   |Rec: 8/11| |File|       |Caps
```

Figure 6.4 Edit screen 4 for FILE2 database file

Suppose you want to change a telephone number from 606-244-1290 to 606-234-1290 in the eighth data record of the database file FILE2. You do not have to begin at the first data record and press the <PgDn> key several times to get to the eighth record to make this change. Instead, you can go to that record directly by typing the following command:

```
. USE FILE2      <Return>
. EDIT 8         <Return>
```

dBASE will go into the edit mode and display the eighth data record as shown in Figure 6.4.

First use the <Down Arrow> key to go to the TELEPHONE field, and then use the <Right Arrow> key to move the cursor to the digit to be corrected, that is, the first 4, as shown in Figure 6.5. Now type the new digit 3 in its place. The corrected data record will look as shown in Figure 6.6.

To save the changes and terminate the edit process, press either the <Ctrl-End> keys or <Ctrl-W> keys. Repeat this process to edit any other records in large database files.

To edit the eighth data record in the database file FILE2, we used the following sequence of commands:

```
. USE FILE2      <Return>
. EDIT 8         <Return>
```

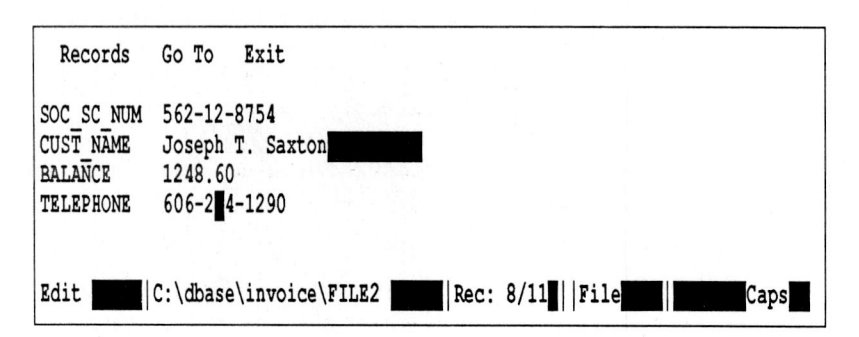

```
 Records   Go To   Exit

SOC_SC_NUM  562-12-8754
CUST_NAME   Joseph T. Saxton
BALANCE     1248.60
TELEPHONE   606-2 4-1290



Edit    |C:\dbase\invoice\FILE2   |Rec: 8/11| |File|       |Caps
```

Figure 6.5 Edit screen 5 for FILE2 database file

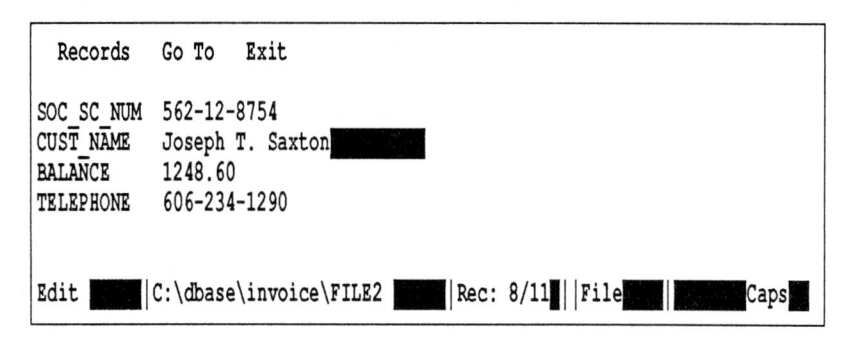

```
   Records   Go To   Exit

SOC_SC_NUM  562-12-8754
CUST_NAME   Joseph T. Saxton
BALANCE     1248.60
TELEPHONE   606-234-1290



Edit     |C:\dbase\invoice\FILE2    |Rec: 8/11||File|        |Caps
```

Figure 6.6 Edit screen 6 for FILE2 database file

We could have achieved the same goal if we had used the following sequence of instructions:

```
. USE FILE2      <Return>
. GOTO 8         <Return>
. EDIT           <Return>
```

6.4 Modifying the Database File Structure

In the previous section, you learned how to edit the data in a database file. In other words, you learned how to change the data within the records of the database file. However, you might need to change the structure of a database file after you have created and populated the database. You might realize that you will need to add some fields, delete some fields, or change the width of an existing field. You can use the dBASE command MODIFY STRUCTURE to make these changes.

6.4.1 The MODIFY STRUCTURE Command

The general format of this command is

```
MODIFY STRUCTURE
```

This command allows you to alter the structure of the existing database file by changing the field name, data type, width, decimal places, and index option on any existing field. You can also add new fields or delete existing fields. The most commonly used control keys used with the CREATE command as listed in Table 2.5 can also be used with this command.

Suppose we want to change the structure of the database file FILE3. The structure and the listing of this database file are given in Figures 6.7 and 6.8.

Two new fields, ORD_DATE and RET_PRICE, are to be added to the existing structure. The ORD_DATE field should be added before the ITEM_NUM field, and the RET_PRICE field should be added at the end of all other fields, that is, after the QUANTITY field in the structure of the FILE3 database file, as shown in Figure 6.7.

To modify the structure of the database file FILE3, type the following commands:

```
. DISPLAY STRUCTURE
Structure for database : C:\DBASE\INVOICE\FILE3.dbf
Number of data records :    12
Date of last update    : 8/11/89
Field  Field name  Type       Width    Dec    Index
    1  ITEM_NUM    Character     4                N
    2  ITEM_DESC   Character    26                N
    3  UNIT_COST   Numeric       6      2         N
    4  QUANTITY    Numeric       3                N
** Total **                     40
```

Figure 6.7 Structure of the database file FILE3

```
. USE FILE3            <Return>
. MODIFY STRUCTURE     <Return>
```

dBASE starts the modification process by creating a backup copy of the database file FILE3 with a .BAK extension. Then dBASE displays the structure of the FILE3.DBF database file for modification, as shown in Figure 6.9.

To add a new ORD_DATE field before the first field, ITEM_NUM, move the cursor to the beginning of the first field. Now create a row for adding the new field by pressing the <Ctrl-N> keys. A blank row will be added to the structure of the database at the position of the first field, and all the existing fields will be pushed down one row, as shown in Figure 6.10.

Now complete the definition of the first field by entering its name, selecting its data type, entering its width, selecting the number of decimal places if needed, and selecting the indexing option. Enter the ORD_DATE for the field name, and select the date data type. dBASE will automatically

```
. USE FILE3
. LIST
Record#  ITEM_NUM  ITEM_DESC                 UNIT_COST  QUANTITY
      1  1136      Bond Paper, Ream              22.99        38
      2  4005      Disks Data Case                5.99        18
      3  1910      Ditto Paper, Ream             19.99        35
      4  4141      Double Sided Disks 10-Pk       8.49        27
      5  2786      Highlighter Pen 10-Box         7.99        86
      6  4012      King Kong Modem 1200         105.99        10
      7  4045      Monochrome Monitor Z-1105     99.99        15
      8  4072      Panasonic Printer KX-P108    269.99         8
      9  3372      Printer Ribbon 10-Box         35.99        19
     10  3375      Typewriter Ribbons 10-Box     23.79        67
     11  1488      Xerographic Paper             19.99        45
     12  4189      Zenith Microcomputer Z-158   829.99         5
```

Figure 6.8 Listing of the database file FILE3

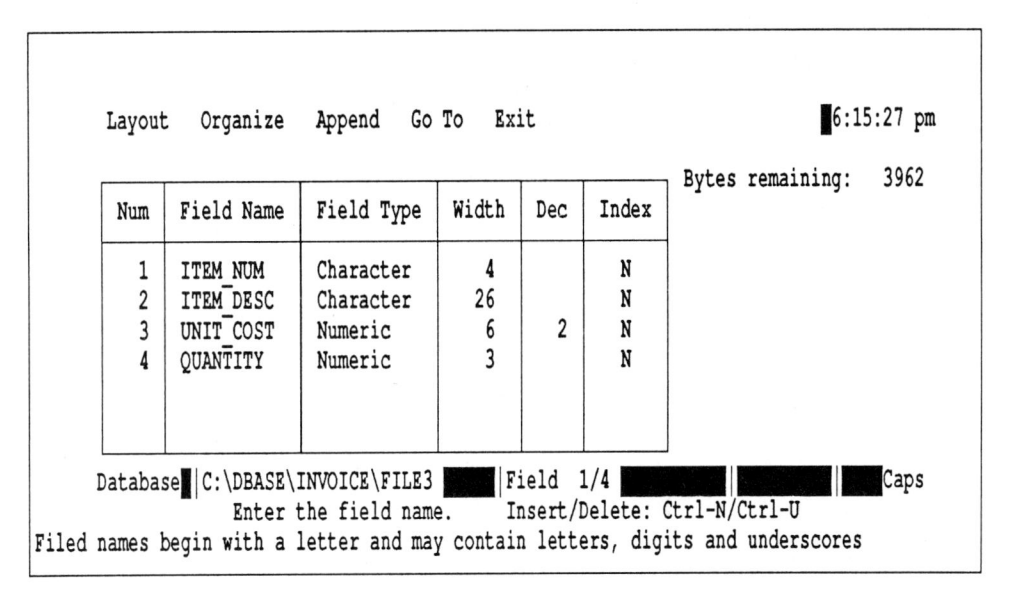

```
Layout   Organize   Append   Go To   Exit            6:15:27 pm

                                              Bytes remaining:   3962
 ┌─────┬────────────┬────────────┬───────┬─────┬───────┐
 │ Num │ Field Name │ Field Type │ Width │ Dec │ Index │
 ├─────┼────────────┼────────────┼───────┼─────┼───────┤
 │  1  │ ITEM_NUM   │ Character  │   4   │     │   N   │
 │  2  │ ITEM_DESC  │ Character  │  26   │     │   N   │
 │  3  │ UNIT_COST  │ Numeric    │   6   │  2  │   N   │
 │  4  │ QUANTITY   │ Numeric    │   3   │     │   N   │
 └─────┴────────────┴────────────┴───────┴─────┴───────┘

Database  C:\DBASE\INVOICE\FILE3    Field 1/4            Caps
          Enter the field name.    Insert/Delete: Ctrl-N/Ctrl-U
Filed names begin with a letter and may contain letters, digits and underscores
```

Figure 6.9 Structure of the database file FILE3

assign a width of eight and skip the next column because the number of decimal places is not required for the date field. Because you do not want to index the database on the ORD_DATE field, make the selection "N" by pressing <Return>. The structure of the database file will look as shown in Figure 6.11.

To add the RET_PRICE field, move the cursor past the last existing field to create an empty row for the sixth field at the end of the structure either by pressing the <PgDn> key once or by using the <Down Arrow> key. The database design screen will look as shown in Figure 6.12.

```
Layout   Organize   Append   Go To   Exit            6:15:27 pm

                                              Bytes remaining:   3962
 ┌─────┬────────────┬────────────┬───────┬─────┬───────┐
 │ Num │ Field Name │ Field Type │ Width │ Dec │ Index │
 ├─────┼────────────┼────────────┼───────┼─────┼───────┤
 │  1  │            │ Character  │       │     │       │
 │  2  │ ITEM_NUM   │ Character  │   4   │     │   N   │
 │  3  │ ITEM_DESC  │ Character  │  26   │     │   N   │
 │  4  │ UNIT_COST  │ Numeric    │   6   │  2  │   N   │
 │  5  │ QUANTITY   │ Numeric    │   3   │     │   N   │
 └─────┴────────────┴────────────┴───────┴─────┴───────┘

Database  C:\DBASE\INVOICE\FILE3    Field 1/5            Caps
          Enter the field name.    Insert/Delete: Ctrl-N/Ctrl-U
Filed names begin with a letter and may contain letters, digits and underscores
```

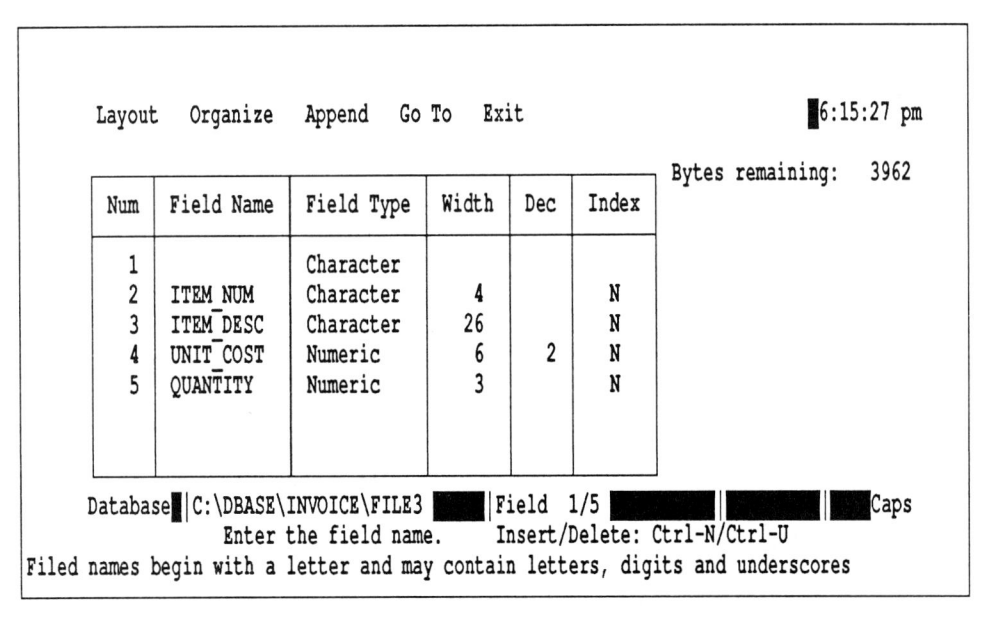

Figure 6.10 Structure of the database file FILE3 with an empty row for adding a new field

```
Layout   Organize   Append   Go To   Exit            ■6:15:27 pm

                                                     Bytes remaining:    3962
 Num | Field Name | Field Type | Width | Dec | Index
  1  | ORD_DATE   | Date       |   8   |     |   N
  2  | ITEM_NUM   | Character  |   4   |     |   N
  3  | ITEM_DESC  | Character  |  26   |     |   N
  4  | UNIT_COST  | Numeric    |   6   |  2  |   N
  5  | QUANTITY   | Numeric    |   3   |     |   N

Database■|C:\DBASE\INVOICE\FILE3   ■|Field  2/5  ■■   ■■   ■■Caps
            Enter the field name.    Insert/Delete: Ctrl-N/Ctrl-U
Filed names begin with a letter and may contain letters, digits and underscores
```

Figure 6.11 Structure of the database file FILE3 with a new field ORD_DATE added to it

Now to complete the definition of this field, enter RET_PRICE for the field name, select numeric for the data type with a width of seven and two decimal places, and select "N" for the Index option. When these selections are entered, the definition of this field is complete; and the database design screen will look as shown in Figure 6.13.

After all the desired changes in the structure of the database file are complete, there are two ways to save the changes.

```
Layout   Organize   Append   Go To   Exit            ■6:15:27 pm

                                                     Bytes remaining:    3962
 Num | Field Name | Field Type | Width | Dec | Index
  1  | ORD_DATE   | Date       |   8   |     |   N
  2  | ITEM_NUM   | Character  |   4   |     |   N
  3  | ITEM_DESC  | Character  |  26   |     |   N
  4  | UNIT_COST  | Numeric    |   6   |  2  |   N
  5  | QUANTITY   | Numeric    |   3   |     |   N
  6  |            | Character  |       |     |

Database■|C:\DBASE\INVOICE\FILE3   ■|Field  6/6  ■■   ■■   ■■Caps
            Enter the field name.    Insert/Delete: Ctrl-N/Ctrl-U
Filed names begin with a letter and may contain letters, digits and underscores
```

Figure 6.12 Structure of the database file FILE3 with an empty row for adding a new field

```
Layout    Organize    Append    Go To    Exit                    6:15:27 pm

                                                    Bytes remaining:   3962

 Num | Field Name | Field Type | Width | Dec | Index
  1  | ORD_DATE   | Date       |   8   |     |   N
  2  | ITEM_NUM   | Character  |   4   |     |   N
  3  | ITEM_DESC  | Character  |  26   |     |   N
  4  | UNIT_COST  | Numeric    |   6   |  2  |   N
  5  | QUANTITY   | Numeric    |   3   |     |   N
  6  | RET_PRICE  | Numeric    |   7   |  2  |   N
  7  |            | Character  |       |     |

Database |C:\DBASE\INVOICE\FILE3    |Field 7/7|                    |Caps
             Enter the field name.     Insert/Delete: Ctrl-N/Ctrl-U
Filed names begin with a letter and may contain letters, digits and underscores
```

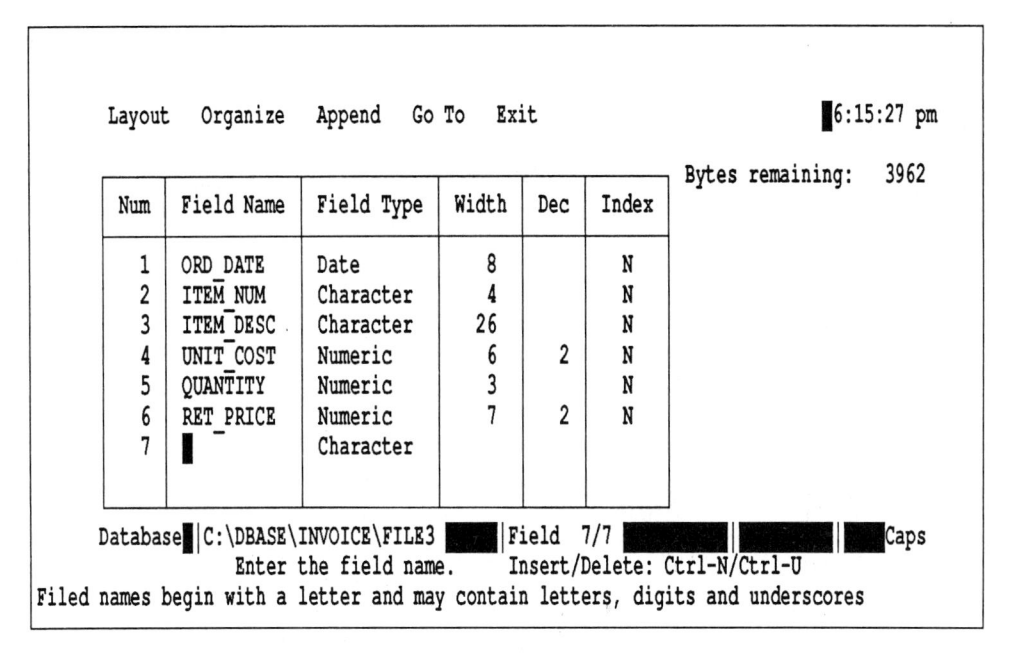

Figure 6.13   Modified structure of the database file FILE3

Saving by the First Method

You can save the modified structure of the database file either by pressing the <Return> key or the <Ctrl-W> keys if the cursor is on an empty row past the last defined field or by pressing the <Ctrl-W> keys if the cursor is on a field in the middle of the structure. For example, in the present case, the cursor is on the empty row past the last defined field of RET_PRICE, as shown in Figure 6.13. You can save the modified structure of the FILE3 database file by pressing either the <Return> key or the <Ctrl-W> keys. But if after making the last change to the structure of the database file, the cursor is positioned on a field in the middle of the structure of the database file, you can save the modified structure of the FILE3 database file by pressing the <Ctrl-W> keys.

To save the changes to the FILE3 database file structure, press either <Return> or <Ctrl-W>. dBASE will respond by displaying a message in the middle of the database design screen, as shown in Figure 6.14.

Notice that the message in the navigation line has also been changed. It reads "Select option and press ENTER, or press first letter of desired option." If you are sure you want to save the changes, select the Yes option using the cursor control keys and press <Return> or simply press the Y key. The modified structure will be saved, and the data records from the FILE3.BAK backup file will be loaded into the modified structure of the FILE3.DBF database file. dBASE will return the control to the dot prompt.

But if you do not want to save the changes, select the No option by using the cursor control keys, and press <Return> or simply the N key. Control will return to the database design screen as shown in Figure 6.13.

Saving by the Second Method

You can also save the modified database file structure by using the menu bar. Press <Alt-E> to highlight the Exit option of the menu bar. The

238 Chapter 6 / Data Editing and Modifying a Database

```
Layout   Organize   Append   Go To   Exit                6:15:27 pm

                                            Bytes remaining:   3962
```

Num	Field Name	Field Type	Width	Dec	Index
1	ORD_DATE	Date			N
2	ITEM_NUM	Character	4		N
3	ITEM_DESC	Character	26		N
4	UNIT_COST	Numeric	6	2	N
5	QUANTITY	Numeric	3		N
6	RET_PRICE	Numeric	7	2	N
7					

> You have made changes to the field structure of this database file. Are you sure you want to save these changes?
>
> [Yes]   [No]

```
Database  C:\DBASE\INVOICE\FILE3      Field 7/7               Caps
       Select option and press ENTER, or press first letter of desired option
       Database records will be APPENDED from backup fields of the same name only!!
```

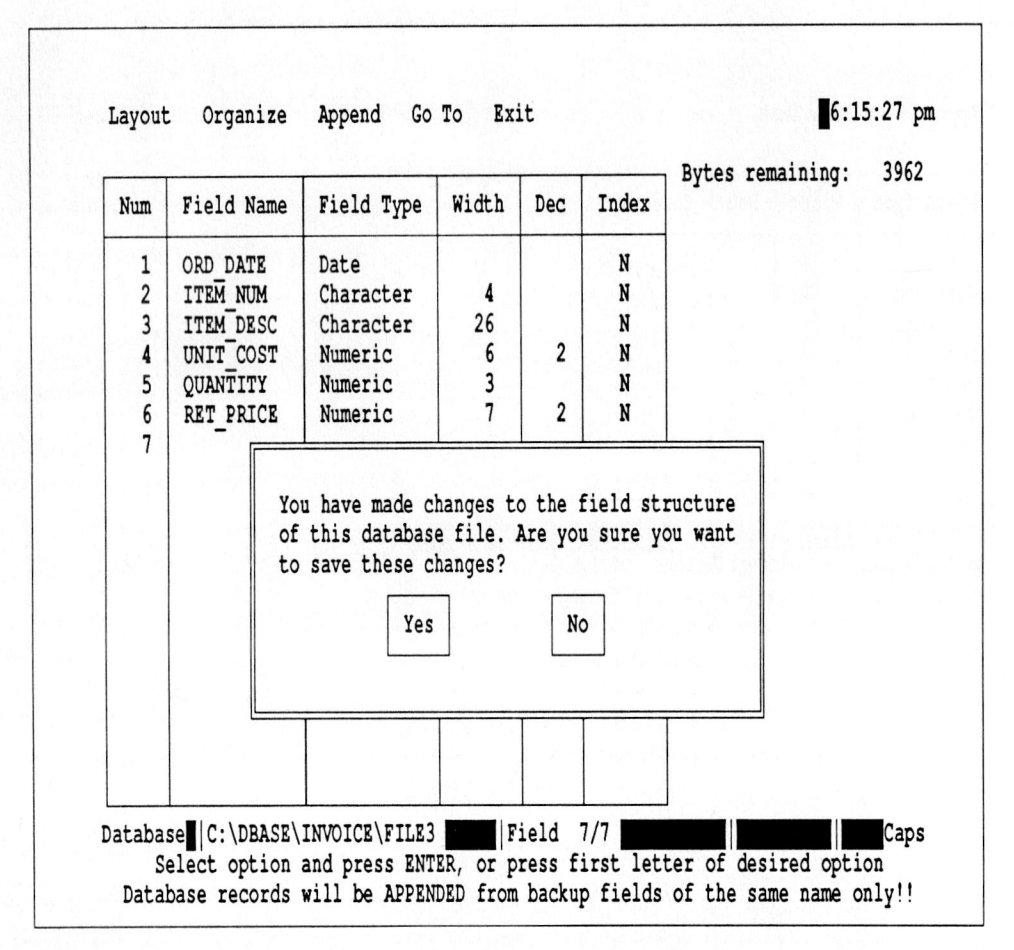

Figure 6.14 Modified structure of the database file FILE3 in the process of being saved

Pull-down Menu for the Exit option will be displayed in a window on the screen, as shown in Figure 6.15.

Use the <Up Arrow> or the <Down Arrow> key to move the cursor up or down the Pull-down Menu choices. Highlight the Save changes and exit option, and then select it by pressing <Return>. The system will display the message in the middle of the screen, as shown in Figure 6.14.

Now you can proceed as explained in "Saving by the First Method" to complete saving the structure of the FILE3 database file.

To examine the structure of the modified FILE3 database file, either press the F5 Display Structure function key or type the following command:

. **DISPLAY STRUCTURE**   <Return>

dBASE will respond by displaying the modified structure, as shown in Figure 6.16.

If at any time while modifying the structure of the database file you decide you do not want to save the changes, you can abandon them and

6.4 Modifying the Database File Structure

```
Layout    Organize    Append    Go To   Exit                    6:15:27 pm
                                                         ining:   3962
  ┌─────┬────────────┬────────────┬─────┬──────────────────────────┐
  │ Num │ Field Name │ Field Type │ Wid │ Save changes and exit    │
  ├─────┼────────────┼────────────┤     │ Abandon changes and exit │
  │  1  │ ITEM_NUM   │ Character  │     └──────────────────────────┘
  │  2  │ ITEM_NUM   │ Character  │  4                N
  │  3  │ ITEM_DESC  │ Character  │ 26                N
  │  4  │ UNIT_COST  │ Numeric    │  6      2         N
  │  5  │ QUANTITY   │ Numeric    │  3                N
  │  6  │ RET_PRICE  │ Numeric    │  7      2         N
  │  7  │            │ Character  │
  └─────┴────────────┴────────────┴─────────────────────────────────┘
Database  C:\DBASE\INVOICE\FILE3        Field 7/7                 Caps
       Select option and press ENTER, or press first letter of desired option
```

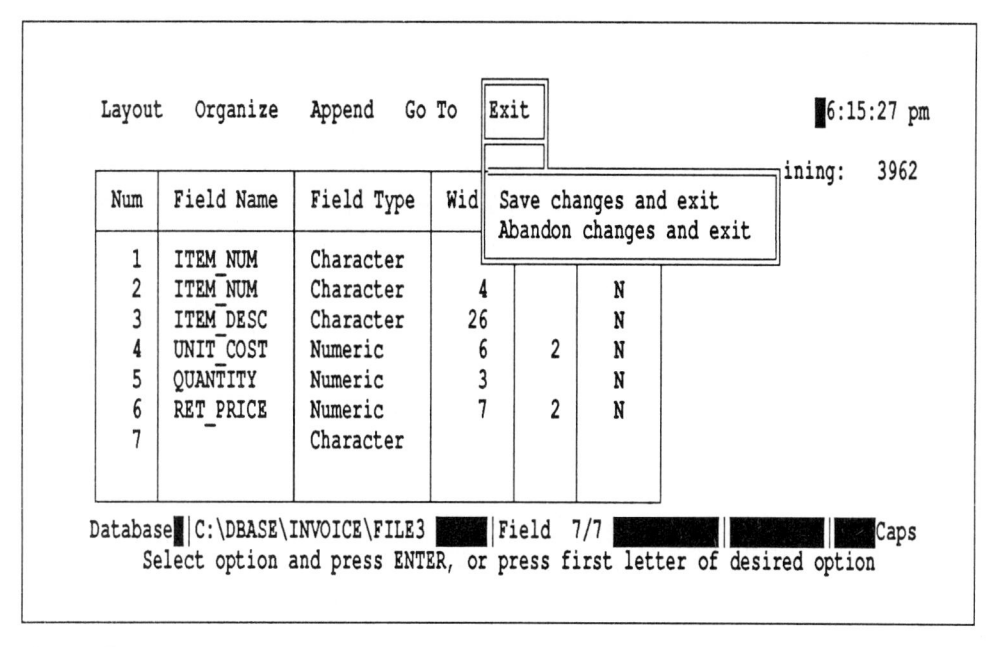

Figure 6.15 Modified structure of the database file FILE3 in the process of being saved using the menu bar

retain the original structure of the database file by simply pressing the <Ctrl-Q> or the <Esc> keys.

dBASE IV has modified the structure of the database file in three steps:

1. Creating a backup copy of the active database file with a .BAK extension
2. Modifying the structure of the database file
3. Restoring the data from the backup file to the modified file

```
. DISPLAY STRUCTURE
Structure for database : C:\DBASE\INVOICE\FILE3.dbf
Number of data records :      12
Date of last update    : 8/11/89
Field  Field name   Type       Width   Dec   Index
    1  ORD_DATE     Date           8           N
    2  ITEM_NUM     Character      4           N
    3  ITEM_DESC    Character     26           N
    4  UNIT_COST    Numeric        6     2     N
    5  QUANTITY     Numeric        3           N
    6  RET_PRICE    Numeric        7     2     N
** Total **                       55
```

Figure 6.16 Modified structure of the database file FILE3

240   Chapter 6 / Data Editing and Modifying a Database

A Word of Caution

In the process of modifying the structure of a database file, if you intend to change both the field name and width, do not do so during a single session because the chances are you will lose some data. To avoid this problem, modify the field name in one session, and immediately save the modified structure. Then start the modify structure process again, change the field width, and save the final modified structure. This procedure will save you hours of labor of entering or recovering the lost data.

Now let us see if the data in the modified FILE3.DBF database file are intact. To do this, either press the F3 List function key or type the following command:

```
. LIST    <Return>
```

dBASE will respond by displaying the listing as shown in Figure 6.17.

The listing of FILE3 as shown in Figure 6.17 consists of six columns (fields), unlike the listing of the same file shown in Figure 6.8. This difference was expected because you modified the structure of the FILE3 database file by adding two fields.

You can use the edit mode and enter the ORD_DATE field data as shown in Figure 6.18 for each record of the database file. I explain how to enter the data for the RET_PRICE field in Case Study 3.

6.5 An Illustrative Example: Case Study 3

Program Description

Write a program to produce a catalog listing for American Supply Company that contains all the records of the INV database file. The program should calculate the retail price for each item of the INV database file in stock and store it in the RET_PRICE data field. The retail price is calculated by multiplying the unit cost of each item (stored in the

```
. LIST
Record#  ORD_DATE  ITEM_NUM  ITEM_DESC                 UNIT_COST  QUANTITY  RET_PRICE
     1    /  /      1136     Bond Paper, Ream              22.99        38
     2    /  /      4005     Disks Data Case                5.99        18
     3    /  /      1910     Ditto Paper, Ream             19.99        35
     4    /  /      4141     Double Sided Disks 10-Pk       8.49        27
     5    /  /      2786     Highlighter Pen 10-Box         7.99        86
     6    /  /      4012     King Kong Modem 1200         105.99        10
     7    /  /      4045     Monochrome Monitor Z-1105     99.99        15
     8    /  /      4072     Panasonic Printer KX-P108    269.99         8
     9    /  /      3372     Printer Ribbon 10-Box         35.99        19
    10    /  /      3375     Typewriter Ribbons 10-Box     23.79        67
    11    /  /      1488     Xerographic Paper             19.99        45
    12    /  /      4189     Zenith Microcomputer  Z-158  829.99         5
```

Figure 6.17   Listing of the modified database file FILE3

```
. LIST
Record#  ORD_DATE  ITEM_NUM  ITEM_DESC                UNIT_COST  QUANTITY  RET_PRICE
     1   01/05/89  1136      Bond Paper, Ream             22.99        38
     2   12/10/88  4005      Disks Data Case               5.99        18
     3   01/05/89  1910      Ditto Paper, Ream            19.99        35
     4   01/05/89  4141      Double Sided Disks 10-Pk      8.49        27
     5   12/10/88  2786      Highlighter Pen 10-Box        7.99        86
     6   01/05/89  4012      King Kong Modem 1200        105.99        10
     7   01/05/89  4045      Monochrome Monitor Z-1105    99.99        15
     8   12/10/88  4072      Panasonic Printer KX-P108   269.99         8
     9   01/05089  3372      Printer Ribbon 10-Box        35.99        19
    10   12/10/88  3375      Typewriter Ribbons 10-Box    23.79        67
    11   12/10/88  1488      Xerographic Paper            19.99        45
    12   12/10/88  4189      Zenith Microcomputer  Z-158 829.99         5
```

Figure 6.18 Listing of the modified database file FILE3 with ORD_DATE data

UNIT_COST field) by its markup factor (1.5 for all items of the database file whose unit cost is less than $100 and 1.4 for items whose unit cost is greater than or equal to $100).

Input File(s)

The INV database file whose structure is shown in Figure 6.19 is used as an input file. The database is populated except for the RET_PRICE field; that is, each field in the database file except the RET_PRICE field contains data.

Output

The output of the program should be a catalog listing, as shown in Figure 6.20. It is a multiscreen report. The headings should be as shown in the catalog listing, and the detail line should consist of the ITEM_NUM, ITEM_DESC, and RET_PRICE fields only.

```
Structure for database : C:\DBASE\INVOICE\INV.DBF
Number of data records :      30
Date of last update    : 12/25/87
Field  Field Name   Type       Width   Dec   Index
    1  ITEM_NUM     Character      4           N
    2  ITEM_DESC    Character     26           N
    3  UNIT_COST    Numeric        6    2      N
    4  QUANTITY     Numeric        3           N
    5  RET_PRICE    Numeric        7    2      N
    6  REOD_POINT   Numeric        3           N
    7  REOD_QTY     Numeric        3           N
    8  DEPT_NUM     Numeric        3           N
** Total **                       56
```

Figure 6.19 Structure of the INV database file

```
              AMERICAN SUPPLY COMPANY
08/27/89           CATALOG LISTING                  14:09:48

        ITEM                                RETAIL
        NUMBER      ITEM DESCRIPTION        PRICE

        1136        Bond Paper, Ream        34.49
        5818        Calendar Refill           .
        5960        Calendar Stands           .
        3802        Correction Fluid 10-Box   .
        3570        Correction Tape 10-Box    .
        4005        Disks Data Case          8.99
        1910        Ditto Paper, Ream       29.99
        2786        Highlighter Pen 10-Box  11.99
        4012        King Kong Modem 1200   148.39
        5130        Letter Opener             .
        1732        Message Pads  10-Pk       .

             *** ---  END OF REPORT  --- ***

              PRESS ANY KEY TO CONTINUE . . .
```

Figure 6.20 Catalog listing: Case Study 3

Processing Steps

The following steps should be used to develop the solution of the program:

1. The headings should be printed as shown in the catalog listing. The date and time should be included in the headings.
2. The column headings should be enclosed between the two lines, as shown in Figure 6.20.
3. The program should calculate the retail price for each record of the INV database file in stock and store it in the RET_PRICE data field.
4. The retail price should be calculated by multiplying the unit cost of each item (stored in the UNIT_COST field) by its markup factor. The markup factor is 1.5 for all items whose unit cost is less than $100 and 1.4 for those whose unit cost is greater than or equal to $100.
5. Detail lines should not be printed past row 20.
6. When the screen is full or the last record of the INV database file has been processed, freeze the screen to allow the user to view the output.
7. At the end of the output report, print the message "*** --- END OF REPORT --- ***" to indicate the end of the report.
8. The whole output should be enclosed in a box, as shown in Figure 6.20.

The five phases of the program development process for Case Study 3 follow.

6.5.1 The Analysis Phase

The analysis phase in the program development process consists of the review and analysis of the program specifications leading to the clear understanding of the output report to be produced, the input database file(s) to be used in the program to produce the required output, and the identification of the processing steps needed to solve the problem.

Analysis of the Output Report

The catalog listing represents the necessary format of the desired output report of Case Study 3, as shown in Figure 6.20. Analysis of the catalog listing reveals that the report is similar to the one produced for Case Study 2. It consists of two heading lines, including the date and time, is single-spaced, and consists of multiple screens. The detail line includes the ITEM_NUM, ITEM_DESC, and RET_PRICE fields, all of which are present in the input database file.

After the analysis of the output report, prepare the screen layout form as shown in Figure 6.21. Because it is similar to the screen layout form of Case Study 1, no further explanation is needed for it.

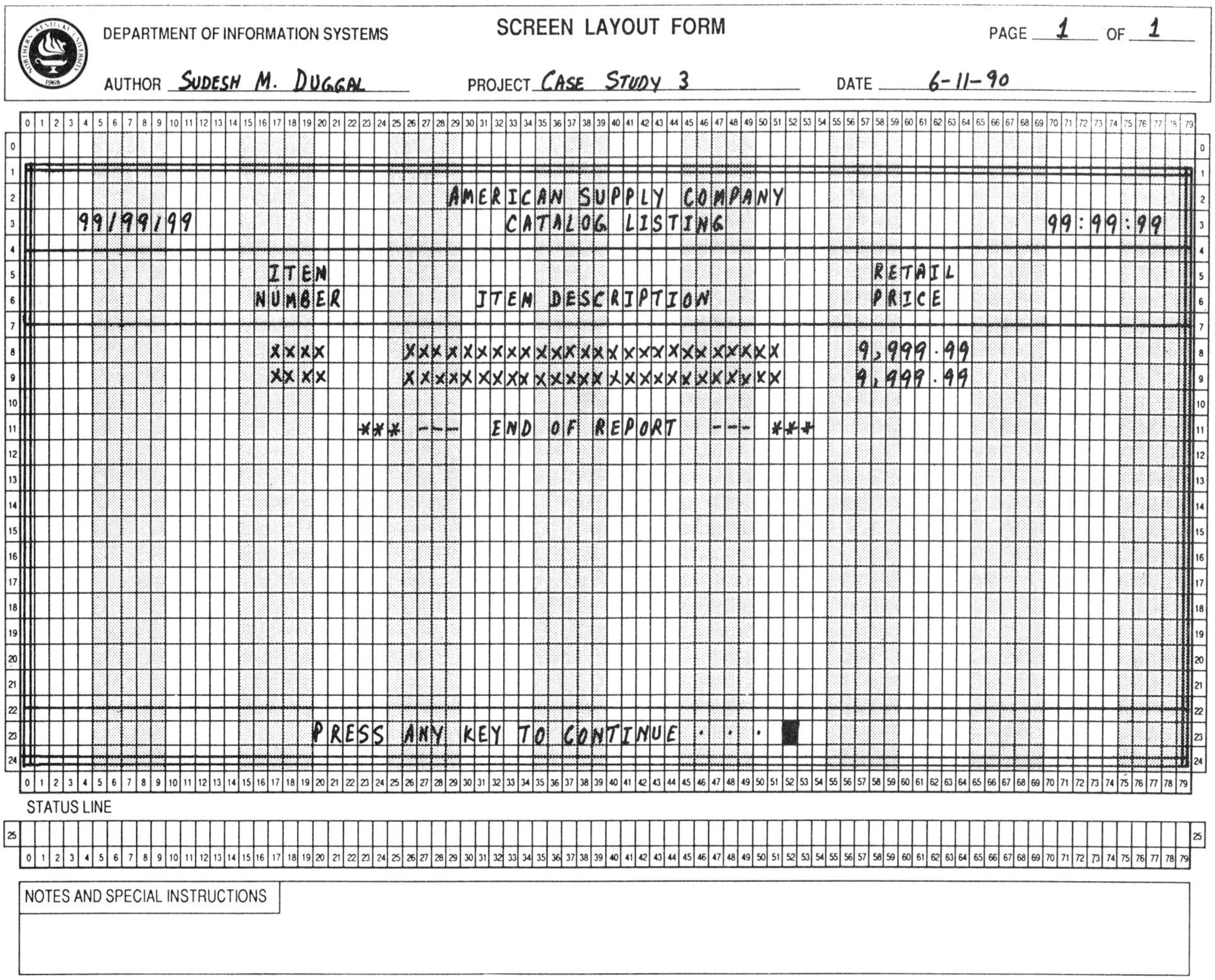

Figure 6.21 Screen layout form for Case Study 3

Analysis of the Input Database File(s)

A review of the structure of the INV database file shown in Figure 6.19 indicates that there are 30 records in the input INV database file, and each consists of 8 fields: ITEM_NUM, ITEM_DESC, UNIT_COST, QUANTITY, RET_PRICE, REOD_POINT, REOD_QTY, and DEPT_NUM. The detail line of the catalog listing consists of only three fields: ITEM_NUM, ITEM_DESC, and RET_PRICE. The data in the RET_PRICE field are not present. They are calculated by multiplying the UNIT_COST and the markup factor, whose value is either 1.5 or 1.4, depending on whether the value of the UNIT_COST is less than, greater than, or equal to $100. The result is stored in the RET_PRICE field.

Analysis of the Processing Steps

The next step in the analysis phase is analyzing the processing steps needed to solve the problem. A review of the program specifications and the output as required (shown in Figure 6.20) reveals that the processing steps needed in this program are similar to those of Case Study 2 except that you do not need to accumulate and print the totals.

The first step needed in the initiate processing part of the program is housekeeping, which includes resetting the default modes and invoking the utility procedure file. The next step is define variables, in which the two markup factors should be defined. The process heading routine should be the next step; finally, the database file INV should be opened. These steps need to be performed once before the main processing part of the program.

In the main processing part of the program, the retail price of each item of the INV database file in stock is calculated and stored in the RET_PRICE field. The retail price is calculated by multiplying the unit cost of each item (stored in the UNIT_COST field) by its markup factor (1.5 or 1.4). After calculating the retail price of each record, print the detail line (Figures 6.22 and 6.23).

After printing the detail line, increase the line counter memory variable LINECNT by one, and check whether the screen is full. If it is, perform the heading routine; otherwise, skip it. Then move the record pointer to the next record. These four steps—calculating the retail price, printing the detail line, testing for screen full, and skipping to the next record—are performed for each record of the INV database file.

The next step in the processing of the program is the terminate process part. The first step is to close the database file. The next step is the end of job, in which the end of report message is printed and the screen is frozen once again to allow the users to view the final screen. Finally, the default modes are reset.

To sum it up, the following processing steps are needed in the solution of Case Study 3:

1. Housekeeping
2. Define variables
3. Process heading routine
4. Open file(s)
5. Perform calculations
6. Print detail line

6.5 An Illustrative Example: Case Study 3

Figure 6.22 Data flow analysis of Case Study 3 (calculation of retail price for items costing less than $100)

```
INV Database File

Record#  ITEM_NUM  ITEM_DESC              UNIT_COST  QUANTITY  ...  DEPT_NUM
   1      1136     Bond Paper, Ream         22.99       38     ...    100
   2      5818     Calendar Refill           4.99       32     ...    500
   3      5960     Calendar Stands           5.69       14     ...    500
   .        .            .                    .          .              .
  10      4012     King Kong Modem 1200    105.99       10     ...    400
   .        .            .                    .          .              .
  29      1488     Xerographic Paper        19.99       45     ...    100
  30      4189     Zenith Microcomputer Z-158  829.99    5     ...    400
```

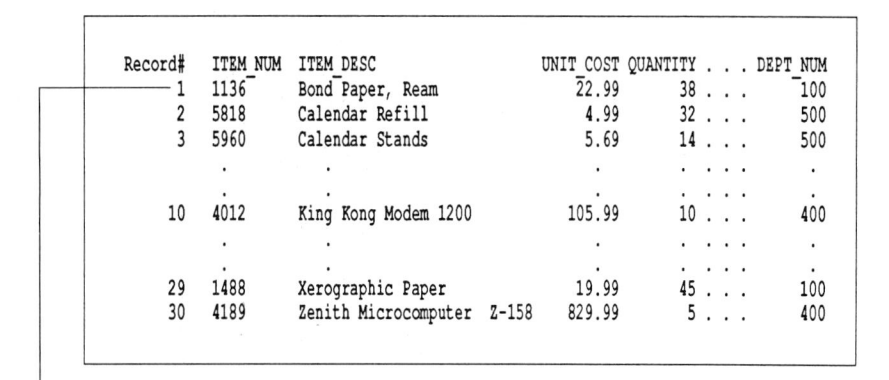

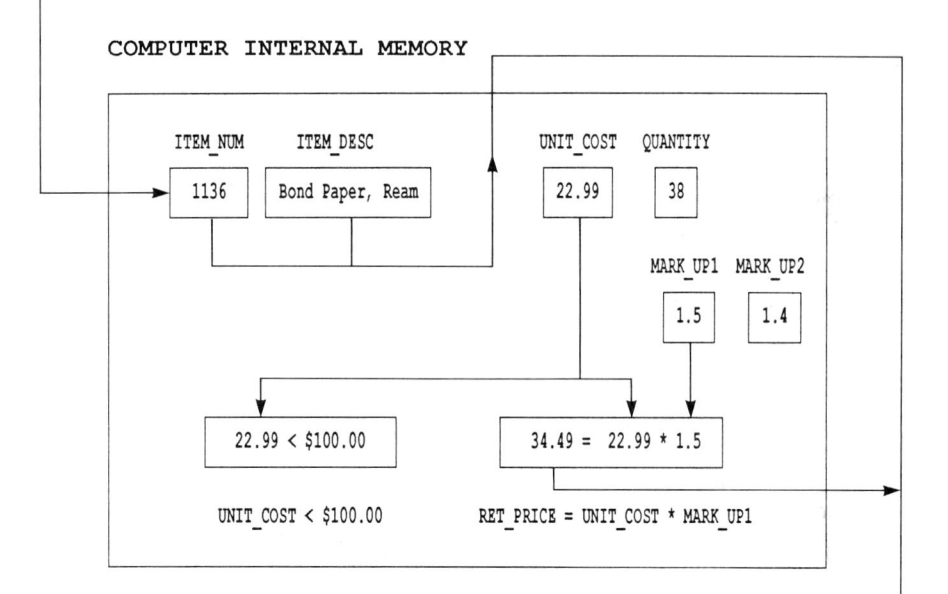

COMPUTER INTERNAL MEMORY

```
ITEM_NUM   ITEM_DESC              UNIT_COST   QUANTITY
 1136      Bond Paper, Ream         22.99        38

                                              MARK_UP1   MARK_UP2
                                                1.5        1.4

   22.99 < $100.00              34.49 = 22.99 * 1.5

   UNIT_COST < $100.00         RET_PRICE = UNIT_COST * MARK_UP1
```

Output

```
                       AMERICAN SUPPLY COMPANY
08/27/89                   CATALOG LISTING                      14:09:48

            ITEM                                   RETAIL
           NUMBER      ITEM DESCRIPTION            PRICE

            1136       Bond Paper, Ream            34.49
```

Figure 6.23 Data flow analysis of Case Study 3 (calculation of retail price for items costing not less than $100)

```
INV Database File

Record#  ITEM_NUM  ITEM_DESC                UNIT_COST  QUANTITY  . . .  DEPT_NUM
   1      1136     Bond Paper, Ream           22.99       38    . . .    100
   2      5818     Calendar Refill             4.99       32    . . .    500
   3      5960     Calendar Stands             5.69       14    . . .    500
                      .                          .          .    . . .     .
                      .                          .          .    . . .     .
  10      4012     King Kong Modem 1200      105.99       10    . . .    400
                      .                          .          .    . . .     .
                      .                          .          .    . . .     .
  29      1488     Xerographic Paper          19.99       45    . . .    100
  30      4189     Zenith Microcomputer Z-158 829.99       5    . . .    400
```

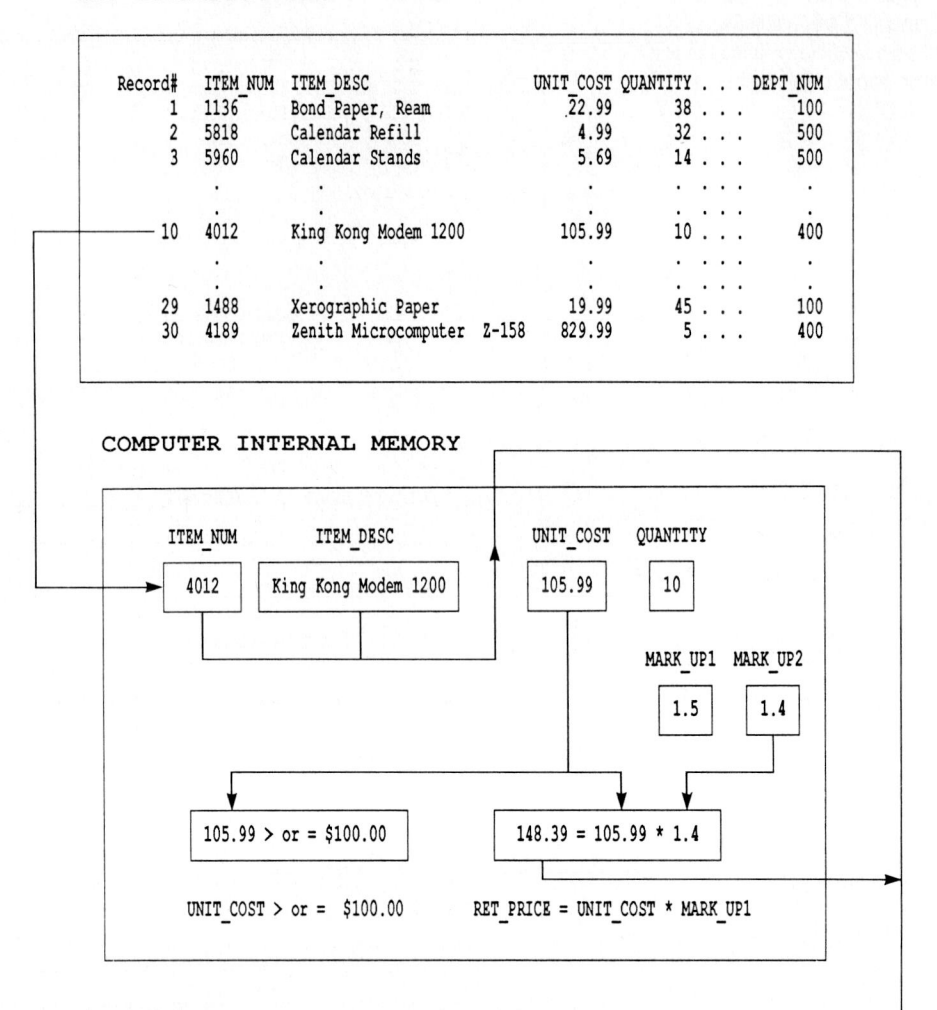

COMPUTER INTERNAL MEMORY

```
ITEM_NUM       ITEM_DESC              UNIT_COST   QUANTITY
  4012      King Kong Modem 1200        105.99       10

                                               MARK_UP1  MARK_UP2
                                                 1.5       1.4

  105.99 > or = $100.00                148.39 = 105.99 * 1.4

  UNIT_COST > or = $100.00             RET_PRICE = UNIT_COST * MARK_UP1
```

Output

```
                        AMERICAN SUPPLY COMPANY
 08/27/89                   CATALOG LISTING                      14:09:48

              ITEM                                    RETAIL
              NUMBER       ITEM DESCRIPTION           PRICE

              1136         Bond Paper, Ream           34.49
              5818         Calendar Refill             7.49
              5960         Calendar Stands             8.54
                .                .                       .
                .                .                       .
              4012         King Kong Modem 1200      148.39
```

7. Test for screen full
8. If screen not full, proceed to step 11
9. Freeze screen
10. Print report headings
11. Skip to next record
12. Close file(s)
13. End of job
    a. Print end of report message
    b. Freeze screen
    c. Reset default modes

6.5.2 The Design Phase

The function of this step is to take the result of the problem analysis (that is, the problem broken down into several smaller, manageable components) and transform it to a structure chart. Using all the tools and techniques discussed in Section 4.4.2 and the 13 processing steps identified in the analysis phase, complete the structure chart for Case Study 3 as shown in Figure 6.24. All the modules in this structure chart are either functionally or highly cohesive. They are also loosely coupled.

The structure chart of Figure 6.24 satisfies the three rules for designing a good structure chart; that is, it consists of highly cohesive, loosely coupled modules with the span of control of any module no more than four. Therefore, it is a well-designed solution of Case Study 3.

6.5.3 The Detailed Design Phase

The function of this step is to take the result of the design phase (the structure chart), identify the actual computer operations required for each program function represented in it, and produce the detailed solution of the problem. Using the translation of the three control structures to pseudocode as given in Figure 4.14, the screen layout form of Figure 6.21, and the method described in section 4.4.3 allows us to translate the structure chart of Figure 6.24 to pseudocode, as given in Figure 6.25.

6.5.4 The Coding Phase

The function of this phase in the program development process is to translate the pseudocode instructions of the solution of the program into programming language instructions. The pseudocode of Figure 6.25 is translated into dBASE commands, and the complete program for Case Study 3 in dBASE language is given in Figure 6.26 (see page 250).

The logic of this program is almost identical to the program of Case Study 2, so it needs no explanation. However, there are two new functions introduced in this program that do need explanation. The first is in the 1.2 Define Variables module:

```
*** 1.2 Define Variables ***
*
MARK_UP1 = 1.5
MARK_UP2 = 1.4
*
```

The markup factors of 1.5 and 1.4 are assigned to the variables MARK_UP1 and MARK_UP2. Of course, we have used constants before in

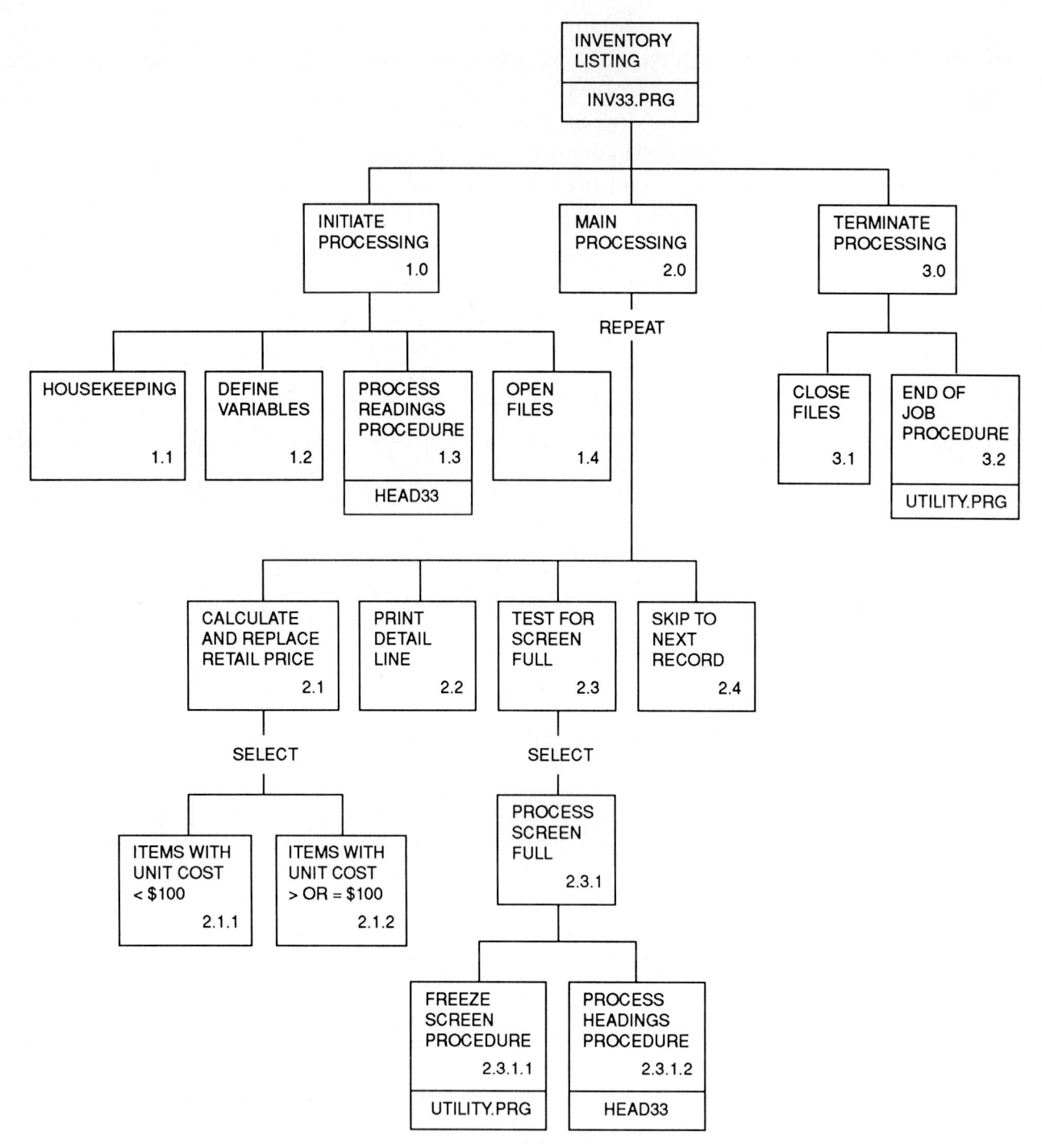

Figure 6.24 Structure chart for Case Study 3

the main processing part of the program, but it is recommended that *you never use constant values* in the main processing part of the program. These values should always be defined as memory variables and assigned the constant value in the initiate processing part of the program under the heading Define Variables, as shown previously. As the values of these constants change, it is easy to locate the variables and make the needed changes.

```
0.0 INVENTORY LISTING
   1.0 INITIATE PROCESSING
      1.1 HOUSEKEEPING
         CHANGE DEFAULT MODES
            Turn off the dBASE's heading feature
            Turn off the dBASE's user dialogue
            Turn off the dBASE's status bar
         SET PROCEDURE
            Set procedure to UTILITY
      1.2 DEFINE VARIABLES
         DECLARE VARIABLES
            Declare LINECNT as public variable
         DEFINE PROGRAM VARIABLES
            Set Mark up1 = 1.5
            Set Mark up2 = 1.4
      1.3 PERFORM HEADING ROUTINE
         Perform headings routine HEAD33
      1.4 OPEN FILES
         Open database file INV
   2.0 MAIN PROCESSING
      REPEAT: until end of file
      2.1 CALCULATE AND REPLACE RETAIL PRICE
         SELECT: Depending on Unit price compared to $100
            2.1.1 ITEMS WITH UNIT COST < $100
               Replace Retail price with the product of
               Unit cost and Mark up1
            2.1.2 ITEMS WITH UNIT COST > OR = $100
               Replace Retail price with the product of
               Unit cost and Mark up2
         END SELECT
      2.2 PRINT DETAIL LINE
         PRINT A LINE
            Write Detail Line
         INCREMENT LINE COUNTER
            Add 1 to the Line Counter
      2.3 TEST FOR SCREEN FULL
         SELECT: When screen is full
            2.3.1 PROCESS SCREEN FULL
               2.3.1.1 PERFORM FREEZE SCREEN PROCEDURE
                  Perform FREEZE procedure
               2.3.1.2 PERFORM HEADING PROCEDURE
                  Perform headings HEAD33 procedure
         END SELECT
      2.4 SKIP TO NEXT RECORD
         Skip to the next record of the database
      END REPEAT
```

Figure 6.25 Pseudocode for Case Study 3

>   3.0 TERMINATE PROCESSING
>   3.1 CLOSE FILE
>   Close database file
>   3.2 END OF JOB
>   Perform ENDOFJOB procedure
>   PROCEDURE HEAD33
>   PRINT REPORT HEADINGS
>   CLEAR SCREEN
>   Clear the screen
>   PRINT HEADINGS
>   Print Report Main Heading Line 1
>   Print Report Main Heading Line 2
>   Draw a line
>   Print Column Heading Line 1
>   Print Column Heading Line 2
>   Draw a line
>   INITIALIZE LINE COUNTER
>   Set line counter = 8
>   RETURN

Figure 6.25 Continued

```
****************************************************************
*                         INV33                                 *
*               AMERICAN SUPPLY COMPANY                         *
*---------------------------------------------------------------*
* This program calculates the retail price for each item        *
* of the Inventory database file called INV3.DBF, and then      *
* stores this value in the database file's field called        *
* RET_PRICE. The retail price is to be obtained by              *
* multiplying the unit cost of each item by its markup          *
* factor. The markup factor of 1.5 is used for all items        *
* of the database file whose unit cost is less than             *
* $100.00, and for items of the database whose unit cost        *
* is equal to or more than $100.00, the markup factor is        *
* 1.4. The listing of the modified database file is also        *
* displayed.                                                    *
*---------------------------------------------------------------*
*           COPYRIGHT (C) . . . SUDESH M. DUGGAL                *
****************************************************************
*
****************************
* 1.0 INITIATE PROCESSING *
****************************
*
*** 1.1 HOUSEKEEPING ***
    *
    *** CHANGE DEFAULT MODES ***
      *
      SET HEADING OFF
```

Figure 6.26 Coding for Case Study 3

```
        SET TALK OFF
        SET STATUS OFF
        *
    *** SET PROCEDURES ***
        *
        SET PROCEDURE TO UTILITY
        *
*** 1.2 DEFINE VARIABLES ***
    *
    *** DECLARE VARIABLES ***
        *
        PUBLIC LINECNT
        *
    *** DEFINE PROGRAM VARIABLES ***
        *
        STORE 0 TO INV_VAL
        STORE 0 TO TOTINV_VAL
        *
*** 1.3 PERFORM HEADINGS PROCEDURE ***
    *
    DO HEAD32
    *
*** 1.4 OPEN FILE ***
    *
    USE INV
    *
***********************
* 2.0 MAIN PROCESSING *
***********************
*
DO WHILE .NOT. EOF ()
    *
    *** 2.1 PERFORM CALCULATIONS ***
        *
        IF UNIT_COST < 100
            *
            *** 2.1.1 ITEMS WITH UNIT COST < $100 ***
            *
            REPLACE RET_PRICE WITH UNIT_COST * MARK_UP1
            *
        ELSE
            *
            *** 2.1.2 ITEMS WITH UNIT_COST > OR = $100 ***
            *
            REPLACE RET_PRICE WITH UNIT_COST * MARK_UP2
            *
        ENDIF UNIT_COST < MARK_RANGE
        *
    *** 2.2 PRINT DETAIL LINE ***
        *
        *** PRINT A LINE ***
            *
            @ LINECNT,17 SAY ITEM_NUM
            @ LINECNT,26 SAY ITEM_DESC
            @ LINECNT,57 SAY RET_PRICE
            *
```

Figure 6.26 Continued

```
            *** INCREMENT LINE COUNTER ***
                *
            LINECNT = LINECNT + 1
                *
        *** 2.3 TEST FOR SCREEN FULL ***
            *
            IF LINECNT = 20
                *
                *** 2.3.1 PROCESS SCREEN FULL ***
                    *
                    *** 2.3.1.1 PROCESS FREEZE SCREEN PROCEDURE ***
                        *
                        DO FREEZE
                        *
                    *** 2.3.1.2 PROCESS HEADINGS PROCEDURE ***
                        *
                        DO HEAD33
                        *
            ENDIF LINECNT = 20
                *
        *** 2.4 SKIP TO NEXT RECORD ***
            *
            SKIP
            *
ENDDO .NOT. EOF ()
*
*****************************
* 3.0 TERMINATE PROCESSING *
*****************************
*
*** 3.1 CLOSE FILES ***
    *
    USE
    *
*** 3.2 END OF JOB ***
    *
    DO ENDOFJOB


***************************************************************
*                    PROCEDURE HEAD33                          *
*                 AMERICAN SUPPLY COMPANY                      *
* ------------------------------------------------------------ *
* The function of this procedure is to write headings at the   *
* top of each output screen for the INV33 program. It can be   *
* invoked from anywhere within the program to print the        *
* headings. After printing the headings the control will be    *
* returned to the next command in the program which invoked    *
* this procedure.                                              *
* ------------------------------------------------------------ *
*           COPYRIGHT (C) . . . SUDESH M. DUGGAL               *
***************************************************************
*
PROCEDURE HEAD33
    *
    *** CLEAR SCREEN ***
        *
```

Figure 6.26 Continued

```
    CLEAR
    *
*** PRINT HEADINGS ***
    *
    @ 2,29 SAY 'AMERICAN SUPPLY COMPANY'
    @ 3,4  SAY DATE ()
    @ 3,33 SAY 'INVENTORY REPORT'
    @ 3,70 SAY TIME ()
    @ 4,0  TO  4,79
    @ 5,17 SAY 'ITEM'
    @ 5,58 SAY 'RETAIL'
    @ 6,16 SAY 'NUMBER'
    @ 6,30 SAY 'ITEM DESCRIPTION'
    @ 6,58 SAY 'PRICE'
    @ 7,0  TO  7,79
    *
*** INITIALIZE LINE COUNTER ***
    *
    STORE 8 TO LINECNT
    *
RETURN
```

Figure 6.26 Continued

We have used the constant before in the main processing part of the program in the IF LINECNT = 20 command, where we compared the constant 20 with the line counter memory variable to test if the screen was full. A better way to test this is to define a memory variable such as PAGE_SIZE = 20 in the 1.2 Define Variables module along with the other variables and replace the IF LINECNT = 20 command with IF LINECNT = PAGE_SIZE. If you want to produce a printed report, you can change the value of the PAGE_SIZE memory variable to 50 or any other value without changing program logic.

One more constant is used in the main processing part of this program in the IF UNIT_COST < 100 command. If the company alters its policy and changes this range from 100 to 150, this modification will require a change in the main processing part of the program, that is, in the program logic. Also, if this constant was being used in more than one place in the program and if a change is needed, the constant has to be changed everywhere it occurs. If we miss a place, the program will produce wrong and unpredictable results. However, we could define this as a memory variable of MARK_RANGE = 100 along with the other variables in the 1.2 Define Variables module and use the memory variable MARK_RANGE in place of 100 in the program. Now whenever a change in this constant value is required, such as to 150, it can be achieved by altering the MARK_RANGE = 100 command to MARK_RANGE = 150. Only one change will be needed, and it will avoid the problem cited previously. Following this recommendation will save much maintenance time and frustration.

So if we make all the recommended alterations, the 1.2 Define Variables module will change as shown:

```
*** 1.2 DEFINE VARIABLES ***
    *
```

```
            MARK_UP1 = 1.5
            MARK_UP2 = 1.4
            PAGE_SIZE = 20
            MARK_RANGE = 100
            *
```

and the corresponding commands will change to IF LINECNT = PAGE_SIZE and IF UNIT_COST < MARK_RANGE.

The next set of commands needing explanation is from the 2.1 Calculate and Replace Retail Price module of the main processing part of the program:

```
     *** 2.1 CALCULATE AND REPLACE RETAIL PRICE ***
       *
     IF UNIT_COST < MARK _RANGE
       *
       *** 2.1.1 ITEMS WITH UNIT COST < $100 ***
         *
         REPLACE RET_PRICE WITH (UNIT_COST * MARK_UP1)
         *
     ELSE
       *
       *** 2.1.2 ITEMS WITH UNIT COST > OR = $100 ***
         *
         REPLACE RET_PRICE WITH (UNIT_COST * MARK_UP2)
         *
     ENDIF UNIT_COST < MARK_RANGE
```

The command IF UNIT_COST < MARK_RANGE performs the selection whether the UNIT_COST is less than, greater than, or equal to MARK_RANGE. If the UNIT_COST is less than MARK_RANGE, then the command

```
REPLACE RET_PRICE WITH (UNIT_COST * MARK_UP1)
```

calculates the retail price using the MARK_UP1 factor and stores this value in the RET_PRICE variable. But if the UNIT_COST is either equal to or greater than MARK_RANGE, then the command

```
REPLACE RET_PRICE WITH (UNIT_COST * MARK_UP2)
```

calculates the retail price using the MARK_UP2 factor and stores this value in the RET_PRICE variable.

We have used a new command in this function, that is, the REPLACE command. I discuss it in detail in Chapter 12, but here is its simple form:

```
REPLACE <field name> WITH <expression>
```

where <field name> is the name of the data field receiving the value of the <expression>. The <expression> may be a constant, a memory variable, a data field, or an expression.

The function of the REPLACE command is to replace the value of the receiving variable with that of a constant, another memory variable, a data field, or the result of an expression. In this case, the value of the RET_PRICE, which is blank, is replaced with the calculated value of the product of the unit cost and the markup factor.

This completes the discussion of the coding of Case Study 3. The next step is to create the program file for this coded program. Use the MODIFY COMMAND command as discussed in section 3.2.1 and create the program file. Call this new file INV33.PRG.

6.5.5 The Testing and Debugging Phase

The last step in program development is the testing and debugging phase, in which the source program is executed and tested for the accuracy of its logic. Execute the program to complete this step, correct the syntactical errors, if any, and execute the program again. Repeat this process until the program is free of syntactical errors. When the output is produced by the program, verify some of the records of the output to ensure its accuracy. If any discrepancies exist, make the needed corrections, and execute the program again. Repeat the execution until the program produces correct and predictable results.

6.6 Modified Version of Case Study 3

You will now modify this program. Instead of defining the MARK_UP1, MARK_UP2, PAGE_SIZE, and MARK_RANGE constants in the program, you can define them as memory variables, save them in the memory file, and then use them in the program.

To do this, first define these variables as memory variables and store them in the disk file called INV33.MEM. The following instructions will perform this function:

```
. MARK_UP1 = 1.5        <Return>
. MARK_UP2 = 1.4        <Return>
. PAGE_SIZE = 20        <Return>
. MARK_RANGE = 100      <Return>
. SAVE TO INV33         <Return>
```

Now clear the computer's memory by using the following command:

```
. RELEASE ALL    <Return>
```

To make sure all memory variables have been erased from the computer's memory, either press the F7 Display Memory function key or simply type the following command:

```
. DISPLAY MEMORY
```

dBASE will respond by displaying the following information:

```
            User Memory Variables

    0 out of 500 memvar defined (and 0 array elements)
```

This response indicates that the memory variables have been deleted from the computer's memory.

To see what information has been saved in the memory variables disk file INV33.MEM, type the following command:

```
. RESTORE FROM INV33     <Return>
```

To display the contents of the computer's memory, either press the F7 Display Memory function key or simply type the following command:

```
. DISPLAY MEMORY     <Return>
```

dBASE will respond as shown:

```
. DISPLAY MEMORY
        User Memory Variables

MARK_UP1    pub N   1.5 (1.50000000000000000)
MARK_UP2    pub N   1.4 (1.40000000000000000)
PAGE_SIZE   pub N    20 (20.00000000000000000)
MARK_RANGE  pub N   100 (100.00000000000000000)

4 out of 500 memvar defined (and 0 array elements)
```

This response indicates that the four memory variables previously mentioned have been stored in the disk file INV33.MEM. You can use these in any program.

To implement these changes, all you need to change is the 1.2 Define Variables module in the coding of your program. This module should look as shown:

```
*** 1.2 DEFINE VARIABLES ***
    *
    RESTORE FROM INV33 ADDITIVE
    *
```

This command will restore the four memory variables previously defined to the computer's memory. Use the ADDITIVE parameter to add the memory variable from the INV33.MEM memory file to the memory variables already present in the computer's memory. If the ADDITIVE parameter is not used, then the memory variables present in the computer's memory will be erased from the computer's memory before loading the memory variables from INV33.MEM memory file. Recall that we have another memory variable, LINECNT, being used in the program, and we do not want to erase it from the computer's memory. Therefore, use of the ADDITIVE command is required in the RESTORE command.

Loading the memory variables from the memory file further helps maintain the program. If a change is needed in the constant values defined as memory variables, you do not have to make any changes in the program itself. You can just change the memory file.

After making the modifications discussed in this section, the program of Case Study 3 will be as shown in Figure 6.27.

```
****************************************************************
*                           INV33                              *
*                   AMERICAN SUPPLY COMPANY                    *
*--------------------------------------------------------------*
* This program calculates the retail price for each item       *
* of the Inventory database file called INV3.DBF, and then     *
* stores this value in the database file's field called        *
* RET_PRICE. The retail price is to be obtained by             *
* multiplying the unit cost of each item by its markup         *
* factor. The markup factor of 1.5 is used for all items       *
* of the database file whose unit cost is less than            *
* $100.00, and for items of the database whose unit cost       *
* is equal to or more than $100.00, the markup factor is       *
* 1.4. The listing of the modified database file is also       *
* displayed.                                                   *
*--------------------------------------------------------------*
*              COPYRIGHT (C) . . . SUDESH M. DUGGAL            *
****************************************************************
*
***************************react***********
* 1.0 INITIATE PROCESSING *
******************************
*
*** 1.1 HOUSEKEEPING ***
   *
   *** CHANGE DEFAULT MODES ***
      *
      SET HEADING OFF
      SET TALK OFF
      SET STATUS OFF
      *
   *** SET PROCEDURES ***
      *
      SET PROCEDURE TO UTILITY
      *
*** 1.2 DEFINE VARIABLES ***
   *
   *** DECLARE VARIABLES ***            *
      *
      PUBLIC LINECNT
      *
   *** DEFINE PROGRAM CONSTANTS ***
      *
      RESTORE FROM INV33 ADDITIVE
      *
*** 1.3 PROCESS HEADINGS PROCEDURE ***
   *
   DO HEAD33
   *
*** 1.4 OPEN FILES ***
   *
   USE INV
   *
```

Figure 6.27 Coding for Case Study 3

```
***********************
* 2.0 MAIN PROCESSING *
***********************
*
DO WHILE .NOT. EOF()
   *
   *** 2.1 CALCULATE AND REPLACE RETAIL PRICE ***
      *
      IF UNIT_COST < 100
         *
         *** 2.1.1 ITEMS WITH UNIT COST < $100 ***
         *
         REPLACE RET_PRICE WITH UNIT_COST * MARK_UP1
         *
      ELSE
         *
         *** 2.1.2 ITEMS WITH UNIT_COST > OR = $100 ***
         *
         REPLACE RET_PRICE WITH UNIT_COST * MARK_UP2
         *
      ENDIF UNIT_COST < MARK_RANGE
      *
   *** 2.2 PRINT DETAIL LINE ***
      *
      *** PRINT A LINE ***
         *
         @ LINECNT,17 SAY ITEM_NUM
         @ LINECNT,26 SAY ITEM_DESC
         @ LINECNT,57 SAY RET_PRICE
         *
      *** INCREMENT LINE COUNTER ***
         *
         LINECNT = LINECNT + 1
         *
   *** 2.3 TEST FOR SCREEN FULL ***
      *
      IF LINECNT = 20
         *
         *** 2.3.1 PROCESS SCREEN FULL ***
            *
            *** 2.3.1.1 PROCESS FREEZE SCREEN PROCEDURE ***
               *
               DO FREEZE
               *
            *** 2.3.1.2 PROCESS HEADINGS PROCEDURE ***
               *
               DO HEAD33
               *
      ENDIF LINECNT = PAGE_SIZE
      *
   *** 2.4 SKIP TO NEXT RECORD ***
      *
      SKIP
      *
ENDDO .NOT. EOF ()
*
```

Figure 6.27 Continued

```
****************************
* 3.0 TERMINATE PROCESSING *
****************************
*
*** 3.1 CLOSE FILES ***
   *
   USE
   *
*** 3.2 END OF JOB ***
   *
   DO ENDOFJOB


*******************************************************************
*                      PROCEDURE HEAD33                            *
*                    AMERICAN SUPPLY COMPANY                       *
* ---------------------------------------------------------------- *
* The function of this procedure is to write headings at the       *
* top of each output screen for the INV33 program. It can be       *
* invoked from anywhere within the program to print the            *
* headings. After printing the headings the control will be        *
* returned to the next command in the program which invoked        *
* this procedure.                                                  *
* ---------------------------------------------------------------- *
*             COPYRIGHT (C) . . . SUDESH M. DUGGAL                 *
*******************************************************************
*
PROCEDURE HEAD33
   *
   *** CLEAR SCREEN ***
      *
      CLEAR
      *
   *** PRINT HEADINGS ***
      *
      @ 2,29 SAY 'AMERICAN SUPPLY COMPANY'
      @ 3,4  SAY DATE ()
      @ 3,33 SAY 'INVENTORY REPORT'
      @ 3,70 SAY TIME ()
      @ 4,0  TO  4,79
      @ 5,17 SAY 'ITEM'
      @ 5,58 SAY 'RETAIL'
      @ 6,16 SAY 'NUMBER'
      @ 6,30 SAY 'ITEM DESCRIPTION'
      @ 6,58 SAY 'PRICE'
      @ 7,0  TO  7,79
      *
   *** INITIALIZE LINE COUNTER ***
      *
      STORE 8 TO LINECNT
      *
   RETURN
```

Figure 6.27 Continued

6.7 Summary

The LIST and DISPLAY commands introduced in Chapter 2 helped display the data record on the screen and/or obtain a printed copy. This output enables you to visually examine the data, which provides a means to locate the errors in the data records of the database file. If errors are found, they are marked and corrected using the EDIT command.

The SKIP and GOTO commands provide the ability to move around inside the database and help locate the data needed for corrections. After the data are located, they are edited or corrected using the EDIT command. The EDIT command also provides a format that takes you directly to the record to be corrected, thus eliminating use of the SKIP and GOTO commands.

The GOTO command also provides two other formats—GOTO TOP and GOTO BOTTOM. The GOTO TOP format is used when all the records present in a database file need to be processed. It moves the record pointer to the first record of the database file. The GOTO BOTTOM format is used to move the record pointer to the last record of the database file. Displaying the last record provides the number of records present in the database file.

The EDIT command provides a method of correcting the data in a database file. The MODIFY STRUCTURE command is used to change the structure of a database file. These changes include adding new data fields to, deleting the existing data fields from, or updating the existing data fields in the structure of the database file.

KEY CONCEPTS

editing

dBASE COMMANDS AND FUNCTIONS

EDIT command
GOTO command
MODIFY STRUCTURE command
SKIP command

REVIEW QUESTIONS

1. List the dBASE commands used to move around inside a database file.
2. List the different formats of the SKIP command.
3. List the different formats of the GOTO command.
4. What dBASE command instructs the record pointer to move to the first record of the database file? When is this command used, and what is its advantage?
5. What dBASE command instructs the record pointer to move to the last record of the database file? When is this command used, and what is its advantage?
6. What dBASE command instructs the record pointer to move to a particular record of the database file?
7. What dBASE command instructs the record pointer to skip a particular number of records from its present position in a database file?
8. List the different formats of the EDIT command.
9. Explain the different situations in which the

various formats of the EDIT command should be used.
10. What is the function of the MODIFY STRUCTURE command?
11. During the process of modifying the structure of a database file, how can a blank row be added between two existing fields for the purpose of adding a new field?
12. List the two methods for saving the modified structure of a database file. Explain each method.
13. List the three steps followed by dBASE in modifying the structure of a database file.
14. Explain any restrictions to be followed while modifying the structure of a database file.
15. What is the reason for not using a constant value in the main processing part of the program?
16. What is the reason for not defining a constant value in the program, as compared to loading one from the memory variables file?
17. How can the memory variables from a memory variables file be added to the computer's memory without deleting the previously set memory variables?

HANDS-ON ASSIGNMENT

Programming Assignment 6A

Program Description Write a program ACR33.PRG to produce an accounts receivable report listing for American Supply Company. The listing should contain all the records of the ACCREC database file. The program should calculate the days lapsed since the last payment date for each record (receivable) in the ACCREC database file and, based on it, indicate the amount due for each receivable in the appropriate column. The number of lapsed days since the last payment date is calculated by subtracting the payment date (PAY_DATE) from the current date (CURR_DATE = 04/15/90) memory variable field.

Input File(s) The ACCREC database file, whose structure is shown in Figure 4.32, is used as an input file.

Output The output of the program should be an aged trial balance report listing, as shown in Figure 6.28. It is a multiscreen report. The headings should be as shown in the aged trial balance report, and the detail line should consist of the CUS_NUM, PUR_DATE, PAY_DATE, and CURR_BAL fields.

Processing Steps Use the following steps in the development of the solution of the program:

1. Print the headings as shown in the aged trial balance report. Include date and time.
2. Enclose column headings between the two lines as shown in Figure 6.28.
3. Calculate the current balance (CURR_BAL) for each record in the ACCREC database file by subtracting the payment amount (PAY_AMT) from the purchase amount (PUR_AMT) field.
4. Calculate the days lapsed since the last payment date for each record (receivable) in the ACCREC database file by subtracting the payment date (PAY_DATE) from the current date (CURR_DATE = 04/15/90) field of each record.
5. Depending on the lapsed days, print the current balance amount in the appropriate column (that is, in AMOUNT 1–30 DAYS OVERDUE, AMOUNT 31–60 DAYS OVERDUE, or AMOUNT 60+ DAYS OVERDUE).
6. Do not print detail lines past row 20.
7. When the screen is full or the final totals have been printed on the last screen, freeze the screen to allow the user to view the output.
8. At the end of the output report, print the message "*** --- END OF REPORT --- ***" to indicate the end of the output report. Then freeze the screen to allow the user to view the output.
9. Enclose the whole output in a box, as shown in Figure 6.28.

Programming Assignment 6B

Program Description Write a program PAY33.PRG to produce a payroll report listing for American Supply Company. The listing should contain all the records of the EMPLOYEE database file. The program should calculate gross pay (GROSS_PAY) for each employee in the EMPLOYEE database file by adding the REG_PAY and the OTIME_PAY fields. Then the total deductions (TOT_DED) should be calculated by

```
                    AMERICAN SUPPLY COMPANY
     08/20/89       ACCOUNT RECEIVABLE REPORT          02:29:25
                    AGED TRAIL BALANCE REPORT

     CUSTOMER    PURCHASE    PAYMENT    AMOUNT 1-30   AMOUNT 31-60   AMOUNT 60 +
      NUMBER       DATE       DATE      DAYS OVERDUE  DAYS OVERDUE   DAYS OVERDUE

     xxxxxxxxxx   99/99/99   99/99/99     9,999.99      9,999.99       9,999.99
     xxxxxxxxxx   99/99/99   99/99/99     9,999.99      9,999.99       9,999.99

                    ***  ---  END OF REPORT  ---  ***




                         PRESS ANY KEY TO CONTINUE . . .
```

Figure 6.28 Accounts receivable report listing: Programming Assignment 6A

adding the FED_TAX, ST_TAX, SC_TAX, and L_TAX fields. Finally, the net pay (NET_PAY) should be calculated by subtracting the total deductions from the gross pay field.

Input File(s) The EMPLOYEE database file, whose structure is shown in Figure 4.34, is used as an input file.

Output Program output should be a payroll report listing. It is a multiscreen report, as shown in Figure 6.29. The headings should be as shown in the payroll report listing. If the employee has worked this pay period, the detail line should consist of the SOC_SC_NUM, EMP_NAME, GROSS_PAY, TOT_DED, and NET_PAY fields. If he or she has not worked this pay period, the detail line should consist of SOC_ SC_NUM, EMP_NAME, and the message "NO PAYCHECK THIS PERIOD."

Processing Steps Use the following steps to develop the solution of the program:

1. Print the headings as shown in the payroll report listing. Include the date and time.
2. Enclose the column headings between the two lines, as shown in Figure 6.29.
3. Calculate the gross pay for each employee in the EMPLOYEE database file by adding the REG_PAY and the OTIME_PAY fields and store it in the NET_PAY memory variable field.
4. Next, calculate the total deductions of each employee by adding the federal tax (FED_TAX), state tax (ST_TAX), city tax (SC_TAX), and local tax (L_TAX) fields and store it in the TOT_DED memory variable field.
5. Finally, calculate the net pay for each employee by subtracting the total deductions from the gross pay and store it in the NET_PAY memory variable field.
6. Do not print detail lines past row 20.
7. When the screen is full or the last record of the EMPLOYEE database file has been processed, freeze the screen to allow the user to view the output.
8. At the end of the output report, print the message "*** --- END OF REPORT --- ***" to indicate the end of the output report. Then freeze the screen to allow the user to view the output.
9. Enclose the whole output in a box, as shown in Figure 6.29.

6.7 Summary

```
┌─────────────────────────────────────────────────────────────┐
│                    AMERICAN SUPPLY COMPANY                  │
│  08/20/89              PAYROLL REPORT              02:29:25 │
│                 LIST OF ALL EMPLOYEES WITH NET PAY          │
├─────────────────────────────────────────────────────────────┤
│    SOC SEC                              GROSS    TOTAL    NET │
│    NUMBER       EMPLOYEE NAME            PAY   DEDUCTIONS  PAY │
│                                                             │
│  xxxxxxxxxx   xxxxxxxxxxxxxxxxxxxxxx   99,999.99  9,999.99  99,999.99 │
│  xxxxxxxxxx   xxxxxxxxxxxxxxxxxxxxxx    NO PAYCHECK THIS PAY PERIOD   │
│                                                             │
│              ***  ---  END OF REPORT  ---  ***             │
│                                                             │
│                                                             │
│                                                             │
│                                                             │
│                                                             │
├─────────────────────────────────────────────────────────────┤
│              PRESS ANY KEY TO CONTINUE . . . ▮              │
└─────────────────────────────────────────────────────────────┘
```

Figure 6.29 Payroll report listing: Programming Assignment 6B

Chapter 7

Sorting and Control Breaks

LEARNING OBJECTIVES

Upon successfully completing this chapter, you will be able to:

1. Sort the database file in ascending or descending order using:
   a. The single field sort.
   b. The multiple field sort.
   c. The conditional sort.

   All these methods use different formats of the SORT command.

2. Create a new database file:
   a. By copying the entire structure as well as the contents of the active database file.
   b. By copying the entire structure and containing only the conditionally selected records of the active database file.
   c. By copying only a portion of the structure and adding to it all the records of the active database file.
   d. By copying only a portion of the structure and containing only the conditionally selected records of the active database file.
   e. By copying only the structure of the active database file but with no data.
   f. By copying only a portion of the structure of the active database but with no data.

   All these methods use the different formats of the COPY command.

3. Identify the key and the control field in a record of the database file.

4. Explain the concept of control break.
5. Analyze, design, and code a control break program and a subroutine program in dBASE programming language.

7.1 Overview

This chapter starts by introducing the SORT command, which is used to arrange the records of the database file in ascending or descending order on a specific data field or fields. This command organizes the data by physically rearranging the records of the database file and creating a new database file. The file can be organized either in full or to contain only selected records. The rules to be used with the SORT command are summarized, and the disadvantages associated with the sorting are discussed.

The most commonly used dBASE command, the COPY command, is introduced next. First, the format of the COPY command used to copy *any* file (such as database, program file, index file, or text file) to another file is discussed. Then the different formats of the COPY command used to copy only the full or partial structure and/or the partial or full contents of the database file to another database file are explained.

In the previous chapters and case studies, we were concerned only with individual records of the database file, not their order or their relationship to the other records in the database file. In this section, I describe one of the most common business applications, in which both the order of records and their relationship to other records in the database file are used.

A control break application requires that the records in the database file be either in ascending or descending order of the control field. The logic of the application program tests the control field of each record in relation to that of the previous record.

In this application, one group of records is processed, and then the next group is processed. This cycle continues until all records in the file have been processed. Each record in the group is identified by the control field, which contains the same value for the control key for all the records in that group. When the end of each group of records is processed, a control break has occurred. The control break triggers the printing of the group subtotal. Obviously, there will be as many subtotals in the report as there are different groups in the whole database file. At the end of the chapter, Case Study 4, which deals with the concept of the control break, is analyzed, designed, coded, tested, and debugged.

7.2 Sorting the Database File

dBASE IV provides two methods for organizing the data of a database file into a specific sequence: sorting and indexing. This chapter deals with the first method, that is, use of a sort operation to arrange the records of a database file in ascending or descending order. The command used for this purpose is explained in section 7.2.1. The second method of arranging the records of a database file, that is, indexing, is covered in Chapter 11.

7.2.1 The SORT Command

The general format of the SORT command is

```
SORT TO <sorted file name> ON <field1>[/A] [/D]
    [,<field2>[/A] [/D] . . .] [<scope>]
    [FOR <condition>] [WHILE <condition>]
```

where <sorted file name> is the name of the database file in which the sorted records will be stored, <field1> is the name of the required primary sort field, and <field2> . . . are the optional secondary fields on which the records are sorted. <Scope> is a dBASE scope option such as Rest or Next, and <condition> is a valid search condition that selects records from the database file to be sorted.

The /A and /D are sorting order options that can be used with each field name to specify the order in which the data should be sorted. If no sorting order option is specified with the field, the default option of ascending order is assumed by dBASE.

The SORT command is used to arrange the records of a database file, either in full or containing only the selected records from the database file, in ascending or descending order, depending on the contents of a specified data field or fields. The data field or fields on which the database file is sorted is called the *sort key*, and the individual fields used in the sort are called *sort field*(*s*).

The SORT command sorts the data by physically rearranging the order of the records of the database file and storing the sorted records in a new database file. The newly created database file is called the target file. The *target database file* should be unopened. The extension .DBF is automatically added by dBASE to the target file name unless you specify your own. You cannot sort a database file to itself or use a logical or memo field as a sort key.

A few of the formats of the SORT commands are discussed next.

Single Field SORT

The format of the SORT command with one sort field is

```
SORT TO <sorted file name> ON <field>[/A] [/D]
```

where <field> is the name of the required sort field, and /A and /D are the sorting order options that can be used with the sort field to indicate the sorting order.

This format of the SORT command is used to arrange the records of the database file in ascending or descending order on a single specified field of the data record. In this case, this single field is called the sort **key field.**

Now use the FILE1 database file created in Chapter 2. Type the following commands to open this file and obtain its listing:

```
. USE FILE1     <Return>
. LIST          <Return>
```

7.2 Sorting the Database File

Figure 7.1 Listing of the database file FILE1

```
. USE FILE1
. LIST
Record#  ITEM_NUM  ITEM_DESC                 UNIT_COST  QUANTITY
     1   1136      Bond Paper, Ream             22.99        38
     2   1910      Ditto Paper, Ream            19.99        35
     3   4012      King Kong Modem 1200        105.99        10
     4   4045      Monochrome Monitor Z-1105    99.99        15
     5   4072      Panasonic Printer KX-P108   269.99         8
     6   3372      Printer Ribbon 10-Box        35.99        19
     7   3375      Typewriter Ribbons 10-Box    23.79        67
     8   1488      Xerographic Paper            19.99        45
     9   4189      Zenith Microcomputer Z-158  829.99         5
```

dBASE will respond by displaying the listing shown in Figure 7.1.

To sort the FILE1 database file in ascending order on the ITEM_NUM field and store the sorted records in the FILE1AS sorted database file, you will need to type the following command:

```
. SORT TO FILE1AS ON ITEM_NUM      <Return>
```

Note that no sorting order option has been used with the sort key, that is, with the ITEM_NUM field. Recall that if no sorting order option is specified with the field, dBASE assumes the default option of ascending order.

When the sorting process is complete, dBASE will respond by displaying the following message:

```
100 % Sorted      9 Records sorted
```

Now check the sorted database file. To obtain the listing of FILE1AS sorted file, you need to type the following commands:

```
. USE FILE1AS     <Return>
. LIST            <Return>
```

dBASE will respond by displaying the listing of the sorted database file as shown in Figure 7.2.

Compare this new listing of Figure 7.2 with the original listing of Figure 7.1. The record numbers assigned to the records in the original database file have been changed by the sorting process in the new database file listing. In other words, the records of the original database file have been physically rearranged.

Let us sort the same database file (FILE1) on the same key (ITEM_NUM) in the descending order sequence and store the sorted records in FILE1DS. To do this, type the following commands:

```
. USE FILE1                         <Return>
. SORT TO FILE1DS ON ITEM_NUM/D     <Return>
```

When the sorting process is complete, dBASE will respond by displaying the following message:

Figure 7.2 Listing of the FILE1AS sorted database file

```
. SORT TO FILE1AS ON ITEM_NUM
100 % Sorted          9 Records sorted

. USE FILE1AS
. LIST
Record#  ITEM_NUM  ITEM_DESC                 UNIT_COST  QUANTITY
      1  1136      Bond Paper, Ream              22.99        38
      2  1488      Xerographic Paper             19.99        45
      3  1910      Ditto Paper, Ream             19.99        35
      4  3372      Printer Ribbon 10-Box         35.99        19
      5  3375      Typewriter Ribbons 10-Box     23.79        67
      6  4012      King Kong Modem 1200         105.99        10
      7  4045      Monochrome Monitor Z-1105     99.99        15
      8  4072      Panasonic Printer KX-P108    269.99         8
      9  4189      Zenith Microcomputer Z-158   829.99         5
```

```
100 % Sorted     9 Records sorted
```

To obtain the listing of the new sorted file, type the following commands:

```
. USE FILE1DS     <Return>
. LIST            <Return>
```

dBASE will respond by displaying the listing of the new sorted file as shown in Figure 7.3.

Compare the listings of the new sorted file (FILE1DS) given in Figure 7.3 with that of the first sorted file (FILE1AS) given in Figure 7.2. The order of the records in the two listings is different. The records in the listing of the FILE1AS sorted file (Figure 7.2) are in the ascending order of the ITEM_NUM field; those in the listing of the FILE1DS sorted file (Figure 7.3) are in the descending order of the ITEM_NUM field.

To obtain the listing of the sorted file in both cases, you had to open the sorted database file before issuing the LIST command. This step is very important; always keep in mind that whenever a database file is sorted, it must be opened first before you perform any function with the sorted file.

Multiple Fields SORT

The format of the SORT command with multiple sort fields is

```
SORT TO <sorted file name> ON <field1>[/A] [/D]
        [,<field2>[/A] [/D] . . .]
```

where <field1> is the name of the required primary sort field, and <field2> . . . are the optional secondary fields on which the records are sorted. /A and /D are the sorting order options that can be used with each sort field to indicate the sorting order.

This format of the SORT command is used to arrange the records of the database file on multiple fields of the data record. When you use

Figure 7.3 Listing of the FILE1DS sorted database file

```
. SORT TO FILE1DS ON ITEM_NUM
100 % Sorted        9 Records sorted

. USE FILE1DS
. LIST
 Record#  ITEM_NUM  ITEM_DESC                   UNIT COST  QUANTITY
       1  4189      Zenith Microcomputer Z-158     829.99         5
       2  4072      Panasonic Printer KX-P108      269.99         8
       3  4045      Monochrome Monitor Z-1105       99.99        15
       4  4012      King Kong Modem 1200           105.99        10
       5  3375      Typewriter Ribbons 10-Box       23.79        67
       6  3372      Printer Ribbon 10-Box           35.99        19
       7  1910      Ditto Paper, Ream               19.99        35
       8  1488      Xerographic Paper               19.99        45
       9  1136      Bond Paper, Ream                22.99        38
```

multiple fields, separate them with a comma. You can include up to ten sort fields in the SORT command. Their order should be that of their importance.

Now use the database file FILE4. Type the following commands to open this file and obtain its listing:

```
. USE FILE4      <Return>
. LIST OFF       <Return>
```

dBASE will respond by displaying the listing as shown in Figure 7.4.

Now sort the FILE4 database file in descending order on the ORD_DATE field and within the ORD_DATE field in ascending order on the ITEM_NUM field. Store the sorted records in the FILE4DAS sorted file. To achieve this, type the following command:

```
. USE FILE4
. LIST OFF
 ORD_DATE  ITEM_NUM  ITEM_DESC                   UNIT_COST  QUANTITY  RET_PRICE
 01/05/89  1136      Bond Paper, Ream               22.99        38       0.00
 12/20/88  4005      Disks Data Case                 5.99        18       0.00
 01/05/89  1910      Ditto Paper, Ream              19.99        35       0.00
 01/05/89  4141      Double Sided Disks 10-Pk        8.49        27       0.00
 12/20/88  2786      Highlighter Pen 10-Box          7.99        86       0.00
 01/05/89  4012      King Kong Modem 1200          105.99        10       0.00
 01/05/89  4045      Monochrome Monitor Z-1105      99.99        15       0.00
 12/20/88  4072      Panasonic Printer KX-P108     269.99         8       0.00
 01/05/89  3372      Printer Ribbon 10-Box          35.99        19       0.00
 12/20/88  3375      Typewriter Ribbons 10-Box      23.79        67       0.00
 12/20/88  1488      Xerographic Paper              19.99        45       0.00
 12/20/88  4189      Zenith Microcomputer Z-158    829.99         5       0.00
```

Figure 7.4 Listing of the FILE4 database file

```
. SORT TO FILE4DAS ON ORD_DATE/D, ITEM_NUM
<Return>
```

When the sorting process is complete, dBASE will respond by displaying the following message:

```
100 % Sorted     12 Records sorted
```

To obtain the listing of the FILE4DAS sorted file, you need to type the following commands:

```
. USE FILE4DAS      <Return>
. LIST OFF          <Return>
```

dBASE will respond by displaying the listing of the sorted file as shown in Figure 7.5. In this listing, all the records appear in descending order on the ORD_DATE field; and within each ORD_DATE field, the records are listed in ascending order on the ITEM_NUM field. For example, all records with ORD_DATE = {01/05/89} are listed first, followed by all records with ORD_DATE = {12/20/88}, which is in descending order of the ORD_DATE field. All records with ORD_DATE = {01/05/89} are further sorted in ascending order on the ITEM_NUM field. The same is true for all the records with ORD_DATE = {12/20/88}.

The ORD_DATE field is called the **primary field**, and the ITEM_NUM field is called the **secondary field.** The records in a database file are first sorted on the primary field in the sort sequence specified with the sort option. Then within the primary field, the records are sorted on the secondary field in the sort sequence specified with the sort option of the secondary field. For example, in the previous case, the records in the FILE4 database file were sorted first on the ORD_DATE field in descending order. Then within the same ORD_DATE field, they were sorted on the ITEM_NUM field in ascending order.

```
. USE FILE4DAS
. LIST OFF
ORD_DATE  ITEM_NUM  ITEM_DESC                  UNIT_COST  QUANTITY  RET_PRICE
01/05/89  1136      Bond Paper, Ream               22.99        38       0.00
01/05/89  1910      Ditto Paper, Ream              19.99        35       0.00
01/05/89  3372      Printer Ribbon 10-Box          35.99        19       0.00
01/05/89  4012      King Kong Modem 1200          105.99        10       0.00
01/05/89  4045      Monochrome Monitor Z-1105      99.99        15       0.00
01/05/89  4141      Double Sided Disks 10-Pk        8.49        27       0.00
12/20/88  1488      Xerographic Paper              19.99        45       0.00
12/20/88  2786      Highlighter Pen 10-Box          7.99        86       0.00
12/20/88  3375      Typewriter Ribbons 10-Box      23.79        67       0.00
12/20/88  4005      Disks Data Case                 5.99        18       0.00
12/20/88  4072      Panasonic Printer KX-P108     269.99         8       0.00
12/20/88  4189      Zenith Microcomputer Z-158    829.99         5       0.00
```

Figure 7.5 Listing of the FILE4DAS sorted database file

7.2 Sorting the Database File

When using multiple sort fields with the SORT command, keep the following rules in mind:

1. The primary field should be mentioned first in the list of sort fields.
2. Each sort field should have its own sort ordering option attached to it. Of course, the /A option can be omitted because it is the default option.
3. In a multiple SORT command, different sort fields can have different sort options. For example, in the previous example, the ORD_DATE field has a /D (descending) sort option, but the ITEM_NUM field has, by default, an /A sort option.

Conditional SORT

The general format of the conditional SORT command is

```
SORT TO <sorted file name> ON <field1>[/A] [/D]
        [,<field2>[/A] [/D] . . .] [FOR <condition>]
```

where <condition> is a valid search condition that selects the records from the database file to be sorted.

The conditional SORT command is used to arrange only the selected records from the database file in ascending or descending order, depending on the contents of a specified data field or fields.

The most useful feature of the SORT command is its ability to create a sorted database of records that satisfies a given condition. For example, if you want to create a sorted database file named FILE1A20 containing all the records of the FILE1 database file in ascending order of the ITEM_NUM field whose UNIT_COST is greater than $20, you will need to type the following commands:

```
. USE FILE1      <Return>
. SORT TO FILE1A20 ON ITEM_NUM FOR UNIT_COST >
20      <Return>
```

When the sorting process is complete, dBASE will respond by displaying the following message:

```
100 % Sorted      7 Records sorted
```

This response indicates that there were only seven records with a UNIT_COST greater than $20 in the FILE1 database file. To obtain the listing of FILE1A20, the new sorted file, you need to type the following commands:

```
. USE FILE1A20    <Return>
. LIST            <Return>
```

dBASE will respond by displaying the listing of the sorted file as shown in Figure 7.6.

Figure 7.6 Listing of the FILE1A20 sorted database file

```
. USE FILE1
. SORT TO FILE1A20 ON ITEM_NUM FOR UNIT_COST > 20
100 % Sorted        7 Records sorted

. USE FILE1A20
. LIST
Record#  ITEM_NUM  ITEM_DESC              UNIT_COST  QUANTITY
     1   1136      Bond Paper, Ream           22.99        38
     2   3372      Printer Ribbon 10-Box      35.99        19
     3   3375      Typewriter Ribbons 10-Box  23.79        67
     4   4012      King Kong Modem 1200      105.99        10
     5   4045      Monochrome Monitor Z-1105  99.99        15
     6   4072      Panasonic Printer KX-P108 269.99         8
     7   4189      Zenith Microcomputer Z-158 829.99         5
```

If you try to sort a database file to an existing database file, dBASE will respond with an error message. For example, you might want to create a database file containing only those records of the FILE1 database file in which QUANTITY is greater than 20 in ascending order of the ITEM_NUM field. But by mistake you name it FILE1A20. (Recall that you have already named a file FILE1A20.) To do this, you will type the following commands:

```
. USE FILE1      <Return>
. SORT TO FILE1A20 ON ITEM_NUM FOR QUANTITY >
20     <Return>
```

dBASE will respond by displaying the error message box as shown in Figure 7.7. When the error message appears, you can make the appropriate selection either to proceed with the sorting process by selecting the Overwrite option or abort the process by selecting the Cancel option. When using the SORT command in the programming mode, avoid displaying such messages by using the SET SAFETY command.

The SET SAFETY Command

The general format of the SET SAFETY command is

```
SET SAFETY [ON/OFF]
```

where ON is the default option.

The function of the SET SAFETY command is to protect against overwriting or destroying a database file. The SET SAFETY is ON by default, and the system will display a warning message, as shown in Figure 7.7, before overwriting or deleting an existing database file.

The SET SAFETY OFF command is used to bypass this safety feature in the programming mode. Once this command is issued, it will remain in effect until you exit dBASE or reset it by using the SET SAFETY ON command.

7.2 Sorting the Database File

```
┌─────────────────────────────────────────────────┐
│  File already exists                            │
│                                                 │
│  SORT TO FILEA20 ON ITEM_NUM FOR QUANTITY > 20  │
│                                                 │
│  Overwrite                          Cancel      │
└─────────────────────────────────────────────────┘

. USE FILE1
. SORT TO FILE1A20 ON ITEM_NUM FOR QUANTITY > 20
Command   c:\dbase\invoice\File1   Rec 1/9   File   Caps
    Type a dBASE command and press the ENTER key (⏎)
```

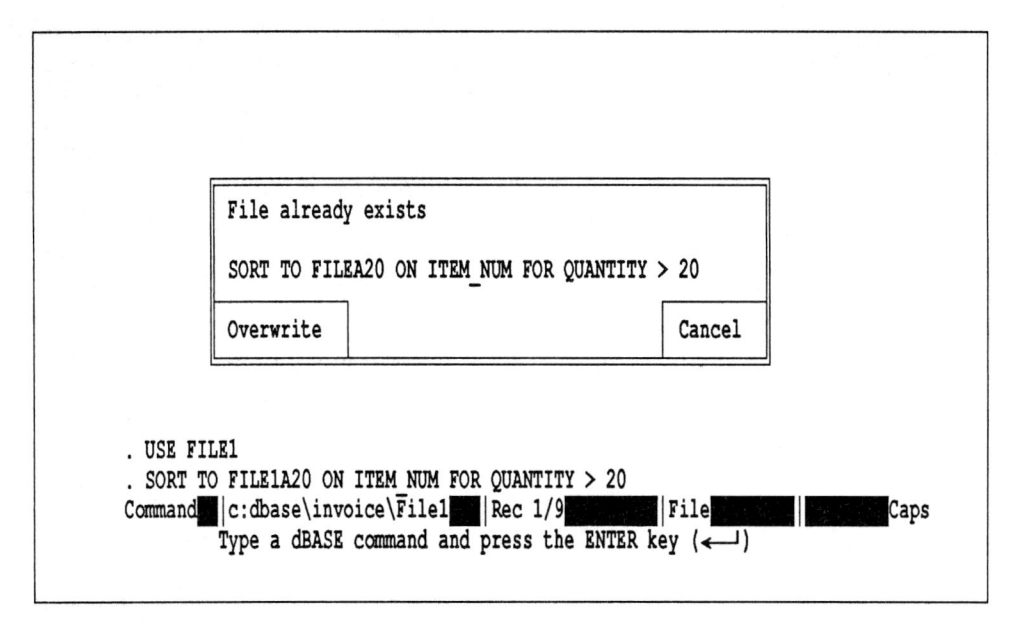

Figure 7.7 Error message box for the SORT command

When using the SORT command, keep the following rules in mind:

1. When all the records of a database file are sorted, dBASE creates a target database file equal to the size of the original database file to store the sorted records.

2. You cannot sort a database file to itself. For example, if you type the following commands:

   ```
   . USE FILE1                           <Return>
   . SORT TO FILE1 ON ITEM_NUM           <Return>
   ```

   dBASE will respond with the error message, as shown in Figure 7.8.

3. The target database file should be an unopened database file. If it is open, the same message as shown in Figure 7.8 will appear.

4. You cannot sort a database file on a logical or memo field. Now use the database file FILE5, whose structure is shown in Figure 7.9.
   Note that the SALE_ITEM field is a logical field, and the COMMENT field is a memo field. Now type the following commands:

   ```
   . USE FILE5                           <Return>
   . SORT TO FILE5A ON SALE_ITEM         <Return>
   ```

Figure 7.8 Error message box

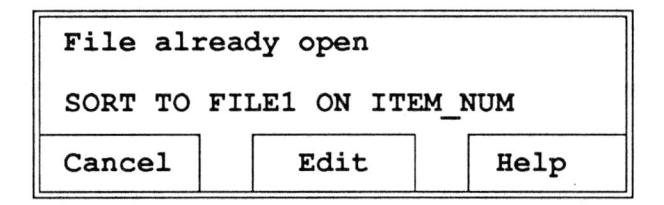

```
┌───────────────────────────────────────┐
│  File already open                    │
│                                       │
│  SORT TO FILE1 ON ITEM_NUM            │
│                                       │
│  Cancel      Edit          Help       │
└───────────────────────────────────────┘
```

Figure 7.9 Structure of the FILE5 database file

```
Structure for database: C:\DBASE\INVOICE\FILE5.DBF
Number of data records:      9
Date of last update   : 12/25/88
Field  Field Name  Type        Width    Dec   Index
    1  ITEM_NUM    Character      4            N
    2  ITEM_DESC   Character     26            N
    3  UNIT_COST   Numeric        6     2      N
    4  QUANTITY    Numeric        3            N
    5  RET_PRICE   Numeric        7     2      N
    6  SALE_ITEM   Logical        1            N
    7  COMMENT     Memo          10            N
** Total **                      58
```

dBASE will respond with the error message shown in Figure 7.10. If you type the following commands:

```
. USE FILE5                          <Return>
. SORT TO FILE5B ON COMMENT          <Return>
```

dBASE will respond with the error message shown in Figure 7.11.

5. After the SORT command, always use the USE <sorted file name> command. Unless you do so, you won't see the effect of the sorting on the data stored in the sorted file.

Sorting can be very useful in certain instances, for example, when you want to permanently change the order of the records in a relatively small database file. But there are a few disadvantages of sorting that you should be aware of:

1. Sorting very large files is time-consuming because the sorted records are physically rearranged into a new database file.
2. Because sorting an entire database file creates another sorted database file of equal size, the disk storage requirements may be a problem for large files.
3. When new records are added to a sorted database file, they are not automatically sorted. The database must be sorted again every time new records are added.

These drawbacks of sorting can be overcome by indexing the database files. Indexing is discussed in Chapter 11.

Figure 7.10 Error message box

```
Operation with Logical field invalid

SORT TO FILE5A ON SALE_ITEM

 Cancel              Edit              Help
```

Figure 7.11 Error message box

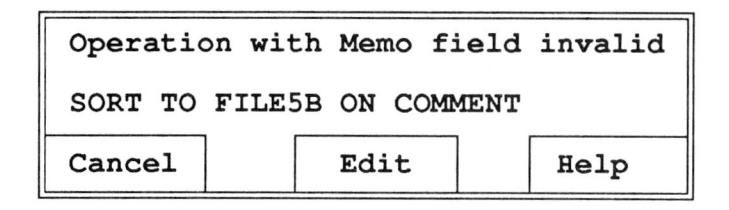

```
┌─────────────────────────────────────────────┐
│  Operation with Memo field invalid          │
│                                             │
│  SORT TO FILE5B ON COMMENT                  │
│  ┌────────┐      ┌────────┐     ┌────────┐  │
│  │ Cancel │      │  Edit  │     │  Help  │  │
│  └────────┘      └────────┘     └────────┘  │
└─────────────────────────────────────────────┘
```

7.3 The COPY Command

There is always a need to create an extra copy of an existing file. It can be kept as a backup, used as a test file in an application, or used to test some features of dBASE IV without changing the original file. Whatever the situation, copying files is a very common function. The dBASE COPY command can be used to do this.

The general format of the COPY command is

```
COPY [FILE <source file name>] [TO <target file
     name>]
     [FIELDS <field list>] [FOR <condition>]
     [WHILE <condition>] [<scope>] [STRUCTURE]
     [TYPE <file type>]
```

where <source file name> is the name of the source file to be copied, <target file name> is the name of the target file to which the source file will be copied, <field list> is a list of the field names, separated by a comma, to be included in the structure of the target database file, <condition> is a valid search condition that selects records from the database file to be copied, <scope> is a dBASE Scope option such as REST or NEXT, and <file type> is the name of a *foreign file*. Foreign files are discussed in Chapter 16.

The [FILE], [TO], [STRUCTURE], and [TYPE] options are alternate versions of the COPY command provided in dBASE. The first three are discussed here and the fourth, [TYPE], in Chapter 16.

In all versions of the COPY command, if a file with the target file name already exists, dBASE will overwrite the existing file provided that SET SAFETY is OFF; or it will display the error message. But if the file with the target file name does not exist, dBASE will create a new file with that name and then perform the copy function.

7.3.1 The COPY FILE TO Command

The first version of the COPY command is COPY FILE TO, and its general format is

```
COPY FILE <source file name> TO <target file
          name>
```

where <source file name> is the name of the source file to be copied, and <target file name> is the name of the target file to which the source file will be copied.

The function of this command is to copy any file (such as a database file, program file, index file, text file, or any other file that is not active) to a new file. This command requires the use of an extension in both the source and the target file names. For example, to create a backup copy of the program file named PROG1.PRG, use the following command:

```
. COPY FILE PROG1.PRG TO PROG1.BAK      <Return>
```

dBASE will respond by displaying the following message:

```
522 bytes copied
```

To verify the effect of the command, type the following command:

```
. DIR PROG1.*     <Return>
```

dBASE will respond by displaying the listing shown in Figure 7.12.

The FOR, WHILE, and FIELDS options are not available for use with this command. This command can also copy an entire database file, but if it contains a memo field, that will have to be copied separately.

7.3.2 The COPY TO Command

The second version of the COPY command is COPY TO, and its general format is

```
COPY [TO <target file name>] [FOR <condition>]
     [FIELDS <field list>] [WHILE <condition>]
```

where <target file name> is the name of the target file to which the source file will be copied, <condition> is a valid search condition that selects records from the database file to be copied, and <field list> is a list of the field names, separated by a comma, to be included in the structure of the target database file.

The function of the COPY TO command is to copy an active database file to a new database file including the structure as well as the data records. There are several different formats of this command available, depending on the parameters used. These are the possible parameters:

```
COPY TO <target file name>
COPY TO <target file name> FOR <condition>
COPY TO <target file name> FIELDS <field list>
COPY TO <target file name> FIELDS <field list>
        FOR <condition>
```

Figure 7.12 Directory listing of PROG1.*

```
. DIR PROG1.*
PROG1.PRG            PROG1.BAK           PROG1.DBO
    1864 bytes in     3 files
3645440 bytes remaining on drive
```

The COPY TO Format

The general form of the COPY TO format is

```
COPY TO <target file name>
```

where <target file name> is the name of the target file to which the source file will be copied.

This simple format of the COPY TO command is used to copy an entire active database file and its structure as well as its data records to a new database file. The main use of this command is to create backup database files.

For example, to create a backup database file named FILE1.BAK of the database file FILE1.DBF, type the following commands:

```
. USE FILE1              <Return>
. COPY TO FILE1.BAK      <Return>
```

dBASE will respond by displaying the following message:

```
9 records copied
```

To verify the results of the last set of instructions, type:

```
. USE FILE1.BAK          <Return>
. DISPLAY STRUCTURE      <Return>
```

dBASE will respond by displaying the structure of the backup database file FILE1.BAK, as shown in Figure 7.13. Compare this listing with that in Figure 2.13, and note that the two database files FILE1.BAK and FILE1.DBF contain exactly the same structure and the same number of records.

If you copy to a file that already exists and SET SAFETY OFF has been issued, the existing file will be overwritten and destroyed without any message to the user. In the default condition (SET SAFETY ON), warning messages are given if an existing file is to be overwritten.

Note: When using the COPY command, SAFETY should be always in the default mode. To be sure, *always* execute the SET SAFETY ON command before using any COPY command.

```
.USE FILE1.BAK
.DISPLAY STRUCTURE
Structure for database : C:\DBASE\INVOICE\FILE1.BAK
Number of data records :      30
Date of last update    :  8/12/89
Field  Field name  Type        Width    Dec    Index
    1  ITEM_NUM    Character       4                N
    2  ITEM_DESC   Character      26                N
    3  UNIT_COST   Numeric         6      2         N
    4  QUANTITY    Numeric         3                N
** TOTAL **                       40
```

Figure 7.13 Structure of the FILE1.BAK file

The COPY TO FOR Format

The general format of the COPY TO FOR command is

```
COPY TO <target file name> FOR <condition>
```

where <target file name> is the name of the target file to which the source file will be copied, and <condition> is a valid search condition that selects records from the database file to be copied.

This format of the COPY TO command is used to create a new database file by copying the full structure and including only the conditionally selected records of the active database file.

Assume that the American Supply Company has a large database file called INV.DBF. For the practical purpose of listing the file in this textbook, the size of this file is kept to 30 records. However, in actuality, it may consist of several thousand records. The listing of this database file is shown in Figure 7.14.

The American Supply Company consists of five departments, each of which is represented by a department number, as indicated in Figure 7.14 by the DEPT_CODE field. The five departments are Department 100, Department 200, Department 300, Department 400, and Department 500. The company needs to subdivide this database file into five smaller database files in such a way that each will contain data pertaining to an individual department.

Name these database files INVD100, INVD200, INVD300, INVD400, and INVD500, respectively. The first three letters (INV) indicate the name of the larger database file (INV.DBF) of which these database files will be a part. "D" is an abbreviation for the word *department*, and the last three digits indicate the department number to which this database file belongs.

To create the database file INVD100.DBF for Department 100, the following commands will be needed:

```
. USE INV                                        <Return>
. COPY TO INVD100 FOR DEPT_CODE = 100            <Return>
```

dBASE will respond by displaying the following message:

```
8 records copied
```

To view the listing of this newly created database file INVD100 for Department 100 of the American Supply Company, type the following commands:

```
. USE INVD100    <Return>
. LIST           <Return>
```

dBASE will respond by displaying the listing shown in Figure 7.15.

In the same way, you can create the database file INVD200 for Department 200 by using the following commands:

```
. USE INV                                        <Return>
. COPY TO INVD200 FOR DEPT_CODE = 200            <Return>
```

7.3 The COPY Command

```
. USE INV
. LIST TO PRINT
Record#  ITEM_NUM  ITEM_DESC                UNIT_COST  QUANTITY  RET_PRICE  REOD_POINT  REOD_QTY  DEPT_CODE
     1    1136     Bond Paper, Ream             22.99        38      34.49          30        30        100
     2    5818     Calendar Refill               4.99        32       7.49          50        50        500
     3    5960     Calendar Stands               5.69        14       8.54          40        40        500
     4    3802     Correction Fluid 10-Box       3.39        65       5.09          50        50        300
     5    3570     Correction Tape 10-Box        4.29        49       6.44          50        50        300
     6    4005     Disks Data Case               5.99        18       8.99          40        40        400
     7    1910     Ditto Paper, Ream            19.99        35      29.99          30        30        100
     8    4141     Double Sided Disks 10-Pk      8.49        27      12.74          40        40        400
     9    2786     Highlighter Pen 10-Box        7.99        86      11.99          50        50        200
    10    4012     King Kong Modem 1200        105.99        10     148.39          10        15        400
    11    5130     Letter Opener                 1.45        49       2.18          50        50        500
    12    1732     Message Pads  10-Pk           2.25        45       3.38          50        50        100
    13    4045     Monochrome Monitor Z-1105    99.99        15     149.99          10        15        400
    14    1975     Notebook Filler               1.79        65       2.69          50        50        100
    15    4072     Panasonic Printer KX-P108   269.99         8     377.99          10        10        400
    16    5890     Paper Puncher                 6.99        22      10.49          40        40        500
    17    2605     Pencil #2 Box                 6.29        54       9.44          50        50        200
    18    2818     Pencil Sharpener              7.99        17      11.99          40        40        200
    19    5000     Plastic Ruler                 0.89        87       1.34          50        50        500
    20    3372     Printer Ribbon 10-Box        35.99        19      53.99          25        25        300
    21    1359     Report Covers 10-Pk           2.79        87       4.19          50        50        100
    22    5225     Rubber Bands 10-Pk            3.45        72       5.18          50        50        500
    23    1536     Ruled Pads 8.5 x 11 10-Pk     4.55        38       6.83          50        50        100
    24    5250     Scissors                      4.99        34       7.49          50        50        500
    25    5370     Staple Remover                1.39        55       2.09          50        50        500
    26    5375     Stapler                       6.29        29       9.44          40        40        500
    27    1060     Steno Notebook 10-Pk          4.55        84       6.83          50        50        100
    28    3375     Typewriter Ribbons 10-Box    23.79        67      35.69          25        25        300
    29    1488     Xerographic Paper            19.99        45      29.99          30        30        100
    30    4189     Zenith Microcomputer  Z-158 829.99         5    1161.99          10        10        400
```

Figure 7.14 Listing of the INV database file

dBASE will respond by displaying the following message:

```
3 records copied
```

To view the listing of this newly created database file INVD200 for Department 200 of the American Supply Company, type the following commands:

```
. USE INVD200    <Return>
. LIST           <Return>
```

dBASE will respond by displaying the listing shown in Figure 7.16.

```
. USE INVD100
. LIST TO PRINT
Record#   ITEM NUM   ITEM DESC              UNIT_COST  QUANTITY  RET_PRICE  REOD_POINT  REOD_QTY  DEPT_CODE
     1      1136     Bond Paper, Ream          22.99       38       34.49        30         30        100
     2      1910     Ditto Paper, Ream         19.99       35       29.99        30         30        100
     3      1732     Message Pads  10-Pk        2.25       45        3.38        50         50        100
     4      1975     Notebook Filler            1.79       65        2.69        50         50        100
     5      1359     Report Covers 10-Pk        2.79       87        4.19        50         50        100
     6      1536     Ruled Pads 8.5 x 11 10-Pk  4.55       38        6.83        50         50        100
     7      1060     Steno Notebook 10-Pk       4.55       84        6.83        50         50        100
     8      1488     Xerographic Paper         19.99       45       29.99        30         30        100
```

Figure 7.15 Listing of the INVD100 database file

The database files INVD300, INVD400, and INVD500 for Departments 300, 400, and 500 can be created using the method just explained. The listings of these database files are given in Figures 7.17, 7.18, and 7.19, respectively.

The two formats of the COPY TO command discussed dealt with copying an entire structure and then adding to it either all the records or only the conditionally selected records of an active database file. The next two formats of the COPY TO command deal with copying only a portion of the structure and then adding to it either all the records or only the conditionally selected records of the active database file.

The COPY TO FIELDS Format

The general format of the COPY TO FIELDS format is

```
COPY [TO <target file name>] [FIELDS <field list>]
```

where <target file name> is the name of the target file to which the source file will be copied, and <field list> is a list of the field names, each separated by a comma, to be included in the structure of the target database file.

This format of the COPY TO command is used to create a new database file by copying only a portion of the structure and then adding to it all the records of an active database file.

```
. USE INVD200
. LIST TO PRINT
Record#   ITEM NUM   ITEM DESC              UNIT_COST  QUANTITY  RET_PRICE  REOD_POINT  REOD_QTY  DEPT_CODE
     1      2786     Highlighter Pen 10-Box     7.99       86       11.99        50         50        200
     2      2605     Pencil #2 Box              6.29       54        9.44        50         50        200
     3      2818     Pencil Sharpener           7.99       17       11.99        40         40        200
```

Figure 7.16 Listing of the INVD200 database file

```
. USE INV
. COPY TO INVD300 FOR DEPT_CODE = 300
    4 records copied
. USE INVD300
. LIST TO PRINT
Record#   ITEM_NUM   ITEM_DESC              UNIT_COST  QUANTITY  RET_PRICE  REOD_POINT  REOD_QTY  DEPT_CODE
     1    3802       Correction Fluid 10-Box     3.39        65       5.09          50        50        300
     2    3570       Correction Tape 10-Box      4.29        49       6.44          50        50        300
     3    3372       Printer Ribbon 10-Box      35.99        19      53.99          25        25        300
     4    3375       Typewriter Ribbons 10-Box  23.79        67      35.69          25        25        300
```

Figure 7.17 Listing of the INVD300 database file

```
. USE INV
. COPY TO INVD400 FOR DEPT_CODE = 400
    6 records copied
. USE INVD400
. LIST TO PRINT
Record#   ITEM_NUM   ITEM_DESC              UNIT_COST  QUANTITY  RET_PRICE  REOD_POINT  REOD_QTY  DEPT_CODE
     1    4005       Disks Data Case             5.99        18       8.99          40        40        400
     2    4141       Double Sided Disks 10-Pk    8.49        27      12.74          40        40        400
     3    4012       King Kong Modem 1200      105.99        10     148.39          10        15        400
     4    4045       Monochrome Monitor Z-1105  99.99        15     149.99          10        15        400
     5    4072       Panasonic Printer KX-P108 269.99         8     377.99          10        10        400
     6    4189       Zenith Microcomputer Z-158 829.99        5    1161.99          10        10        400
```

Figure 7.18 Listing of the INVD400 database file

```
. USE INV
. COPY TO INVD500 FOR DEPT_CODE = 500
    9 records copied
. USE INVD500
. LIST TO PRINT
Record#   ITEM_NUM   ITEM_DESC              UNIT_COST  QUANTITY  RET_PRICE  REOD_POINT  REOD_QTY  DEPT_CODE
     1    5818       Calendar Refill             4.99        32       7.49          50        50        500
     2    5960       Calendar Stands             5.69        14       8.54          40        40        500
     3    5130       Letter Opener               1.45        49       2.18          50        50        500
     4    5890       Paper Puncher               6.99        22      10.49          40        40        500
     5    5000       Plastic Ruler               0.89        87       1.34          50        50        500
     6    5225       Rubber Bands 10-Pk          3.45        72       5.18          50        50        500
     7    5250       Scissors                    4.99        34       7.49          50        50        500
     8    5370       Staple Remover              1.39        55       2.09          50        50        500
     9    5375       Stapler                     6.29        29       9.44          40        40        500
```

Figure 7.19 Listing of the INVD500 database file

Once again consider the INV.DBF database file. The listing of this database file is already shown in Figure 7.14, and its structure is shown in Figure 7.20.

There are 30 records in the INV database file, each consisting of 56 bytes and containing 8 data fields (ITEM_NUM, ITEM_DESC, UNIT_COST, QUANTITY, RET_PRICE, REOD_POINT, REOD_QTY, and DEPT_CODE).

Now suppose you want to create a new database file, such as INV1, containing only a portion of the structure of the INV database file (the ITEM_NUM, ITEM_DESC, UNIT_COST, and QUANTITY fields) but all 30 data records. To do this, type the following commands:

```
. USE INV      <Return>
. COPY TO INV1 FIELDS ITEM_NUM, ITEM_DESC,
       UNIT_COST, QUANTITY    <Return>
```

dBASE will respond by displaying the following message:

```
30 records copied
```

Let us now look at the structure of the newly created database file. Type the following commands:

```
. USE INV1           <Return>
. DISPLAY STRUCTURE  <Return>
```

dBASE will respond by displaying the structure of the INV1 database file as shown in Figure 7.21. There are 30 records in the INV1 database file, each consisting of 40 bytes and containing 4 data fields (ITEM_NUM, ITEM_DESC, UNIT_COST, and QUANTITY). To obtain the listing of this new database file, type:

```
. LIST    <Return>
```

dBASE will respond by displaying the listing of the INV1 database file shown in Figure 7.22 (see page 284).

Figure 7.20 Structure of the INV database file

```
Structure for database: C:\DBASE\INVOICE\INV.DBF
Number of data records:    30
Date of last update   : 12/25/87
Field  Field Name  Type       Width    Dec
    1  ITEM_NUM    Character     4
    2  ITEM_DESC   Character    26
    3  UNIT_COST   Numeric       6       2
    4  QUANTITY    Numeric       3
    5  RET_PRICE   Numeric       7       2
    6  REOD_POINT  Numeric       3
    7  REOD_QTY    Numeric       3
    8  DEPT_CODE   Numeric       3
** Total **                     56
```

Figure 7.21 Structure of the INV1 database file

```
. USE INV1
. DISPLAY STRUCTURE
Structure for database : C:\DBASE\INVOICE\INV1.dbf
Number of data records :      30
Date of last update    : 12/20/87
Field  Field name  Type        Width    Dec
    1  ITEM_NUM    Character       4
    2  ITEM_DESC   Character      26
    3  UNIT_COST   Numeric         6      2
    4  QUANTITY    Numeric         3
** Total **                       40
.
```

The COPY TO FIELDS FOR Format

The general format of the COPY TO FIELDS FOR command is

```
COPY [TO <target file name>] [FIELDS <field list>]
     [FOR <condition>]
```

where <target file name> is the name of the target file to which the source file will be copied, <field list> is a list of the field names, separated by a comma, to be included in the structure of the target database file, and <condition> is a valid search condition that selects records from the database file to be copied.

This format of the COPY TO command is used to create a new database file by copying only a portion of the structure and then adding to it only the conditionally selected records of an active database file.

Now suppose you want to create a new database file, such as INVD500, which is the inventory database file for Department 500, containing only a portion of the structure of the INV database file (the ITEM_NUM, ITEM_DESC, UNIT_COST, and QUANTITY fields) and only those records that belong to Department 500. Recall that the DEPT_CODE for the items belonging to Department 500 is 500. To make these changes, use the following commands:

```
. USE INV       <Return>
. COPY TO INVFD500 FIELDS ITEM_NUM, ITEM_DESC,
        UNIT_COST, QUANTITY FOR DEPT_CODE =
        500     <Return>
```

dBASE will respond by displaying the following message:

```
9 records copied
```

To verify the effect of the last instructions, type the following commands:

```
. USE INVFD500   <Return>
. DISPLAY ALL    <Return>
```

Figure 7.22 Listing of the INV1 database file

```
. LIST
Record#  ITEM_NUM  ITEM_DESC                  UNIT_COST  QUANTITY
      1    1136    Bond Paper, Ream              22.99        38
      2    5818    Calendar Refill                4.99        32
      3    5960    Calendar Stands                5.69        14
      4    3802    Correction Fluid 10-Box        3.39        65
      5    3570    Correction Tape 10-Box         4.29        49
      6    4005    Disks Data Case                5.99        18
      7    1910    Ditto Paper, Ream             19.99        35
      8    4141    Double Sided Disks 10-Pk       8.49        27
      9    2786    Highlighter Pen 10-Box         7.99        86
     10    4012    King Kong Modem 1200         105.99        10
     11    5130    Letter Opener                  1.45        49
     12    1732    Message Pads  10-Pk            2.25        45
     13    4045    Monochrome Monitor Z-1105     99.99        15
     14    1975    Notebook Filler                1.79        65
     15    4072    Panasonic Printer KX-P108    269.99         8
     16    5890    Paper Puncher                  6.99        22
     17    2605    Pencil #2 Box                  6.29        54
     18    2818    Pencil Sharpener               7.99        17
     19    5000    Plastic Ruler                  0.89        87
     20    3372    Printer Ribbon 10-Box         35.99        19
     21    1359    Report Covers 10-Pk            2.79        87
     22    5225    Rubber Bands 10-Pk             3.45        72
     23    1536    Ruled Pads 8.5 x 11 10-Pk      4.55        38
     24    5250    Scissors                       4.99        34
     25    5370    Staple Remover                 1.39        55
     26    5375    Stapler                        6.29        29
     27    1060    Steno Notebook 10-Pk           4.55        84
     28    3375    Typewriter Ribbons 10-Box     23.79        67
     29    1488    Xerographic Paper             19.99        45
     30    4189    Zenith Microcomputer  Z-158  829.99         5
```

dBASE will display the listing of the INVFD500 database file shown in Figure 7.23.

All the formats of the COPY TO command discussed in this section dealt with copying either all or part of the structure and either all or part of the contents of an active database file to a new database file. Now we will proceed with the version of the COPY command that deals with copying either all or part of only the structure of an active database file to a new database file.

7.3.3 The COPY STRUCTURE TO Command

The third version of the COPY command is COPY STRUCTURE TO, and the general format of this command is

```
COPY STRUCTURE TO <target file name>
                 [FIELDS <field list>]
```

where <target file name> is the name of the target file to which the

Figure 7.23 Listing of the INVFD500 database file

```
. USE B:INVFD500
. DISPLAY ALL
Record#   ITEM_NUM   ITEM_DESC           UNIT_COST   QUANTITY
      1       5818   Calendar Refill          4.99         32
      2       5960   Calendar Stands          5.69         14
      3       5130   Letter Opener            1.45         49
      4       5890   Paper Puncher            6.99         22
      5       5000   Plastic Ruler            0.89         87
      6       5225   Rubber Bands 10-Pk       3.45         72
      7       5250   Scissors                 4.99         34
      8       5370   Staple Remover           1.39         55
      9       5375   Stapler                  6.29         29
```

structure of the source file will be copied, and <field list> is a list of the field names, separated by a comma, to be included in the structure of the target database file.

The function of this command is to copy the whole structure or part of an active database file to a new database file. There are two different formats for this command.

The COPY STRUCTURE TO Format

The general format of the COPY STRUCTURE TO command is

```
COPY STRUCTURE TO <target file name>
```

where <target file name> is the name of the target file to which the structure of the source file will be copied.

This format of the COPY STRUCTURE TO command is used to create a new database file by copying only the full structure of the active database file. The resulting database file will be identical to that in use but will contain no data.

Suppose you want to create an empty database file, such as INVX, which is an exact copy of the INV database file; that is, its structure is the same as that of the INV database file. To do this, you will need the following commands:

```
. USE INV                       <Return>
. COPY STRUCTURE TO INVX        <Return>
```

dBASE will respond by displaying the dot prompt.

Now let us display the structure of this newly created database file by typing the following commands:

```
. USE INVX                      <Return>
. DISPLAY STRUCTURE             <Return>
```

dBASE will respond by displaying the structure of the INVX database file, as shown in Figure 7.24. If you compare the structure of the INVX

Figure 7.24 Structure of the INVX database file

```
. USE INVX
. DISPLAY STRUCTURE
Structure for database : C:\DBASE\INVOICE\INVX.dbf
Number of data records :        0
 Date of last update   : 12/25/87
 Field  Field Name  Type        Width    Dec
     1  ITEM_NUM    Character       4
     2  ITEM_DESC   Character      26
     3  UNIT_COST   Numeric         6      2
     4  RET_PRICE   Numeric         7      2
     5  QUANTITY    Numeric         3
     6  REOD_POINT  Numeric         3
     7  REOD_QTY    Numeric         3
     8  DEPT_NUM    Numeric         3
** Total **                        56
```

database file in Figure 7.24 with that of the INV database file given in Figure 7.20, you will notice they are identical. The INV database file contains 30 records, but the INVX database file just created above contains no records.

The COPY STRUCTURE TO FIELDS Format

The general format of the COPY STRUCTURE TO FIELDS command is

```
COPY STRUCTURE TO <target file name>
                 FIELDS <field list>
```

where <target file name> is the name of the target file to which the structure of the source file will be copied, and <field list> is a list of the field names, separated by a comma, to be included in the structure of the target database file.

This format of the COPY STRUCTURE TO command is used to create a new database file by copying only a portion of the structure of the active database file.

Suppose you want to create an empty database file, such as INV1X, containing only part of the structure of the INV database file, that is, the ITEM_NUM, ITEM_DESC, QUANTITY, and UNIT_COST fields. To do this, type the following commands:

```
. USE INV       <Return>
. COPY STRUCTURE TO INV1X FIELDS ITEM_NUM,
             ITEM_DESC, QUANTITY,
             UNIT_COST    <Return>
```

dBASE will respond by displaying the dot prompt.

Now display the structure of this newly created database file by typing the following commands:

```
. USE INV1X              <Return>
. DISPLAY STRUCTURE      <Return>
```

Figure 7.25 Structure of the INV1X database file

```
. USE INV1X
. DISPLAY STRUCTURE
Structure for database : C:\DBASE\INVOICE\INV1X.dbf
Number of data records :        0
 Date of last update   : 12/25/87
 Field  Field Name  Type       Width    Dec
     1  ITEM_NUM    Character      4
     2  ITEM_DESC   Character     26
     3  QUANTITY    Numeric        3
     4  UNIT_COST   Numeric        6      2
** Total **                       40
```

dBASE will respond by displaying the structure of the INV1X database file as shown in Figure 7.25. If you compare the structure of the INV1X database file given in Figure 7.25 with the structure of the INV1 database file given in Figure 7.21, you will notice that by copying the partial structure of the database, you are able to change the order of the fields present in the new database.

7.4 Control Breaks

A couple of new terms must be defined before discussing the control break concept. The first is *key*. In data processing terms, the key is a field in the record that uniquely identifies the record in a file. For example, in the INV database file whose data listing is given in Figure 7.14, the ITEM_NUM field is the key—each record in this database file is uniquely identified by the ITEM_NUM field.

The next term to be defined is the **control field.** The control field is a field in the record of the file that identifies a group of records of the file. Let us sort the INV database file in ascending order on the DEPT_CODE field and store the sorted records in the sorted database file called INVDSORT. To do this, type the following commands:

```
. USE INV                              <Return>
. SORT TO INVDSORT ON DEPT_CODE        <Return>
```

dBASE will respond by displaying the following message:

```
100 % Sorted    30 records sorted
```

You can obtain the listing of this sorted file by typing the following commands:

```
. USE INVDSORT    <Return>
. LIST            <Return>
```

dBASE will respond by displaying the listing of the INVDSORT database file as shown in Figure 7.26. An examination of this listing, particularly the last column (the DEPT_CODE field), reveals that the value of this field is

```
. USE B:INVDSORT
. LIST TO PRINT
```

Record#	ITEM NUM	ITEM DESC	UNIT COST	QUANTITY	RET_PRICE	REOD_POINT	REOD_QTY	DEPT_CODE
1	1136	Bond Paper, Ream	22.99	38	4.19	30	30	100
2	1910	Ditto Paper, Ream	19.99	35	34.49	30	30	100
3	1732	Message Pads 10-Pk	2.25	45	6.83	50	50	100
4	1975	Notebook Filler	1.79	65	2.69	50	50	100
5	1359	Report Covers 10-Pk	2.79	87	3.38	50	50	100
6	1536	Ruled Pads 8.5 x 11 10-Pk	4.55	38	6.83	50	50	100
7	1060	Steno Notebook 10-Pk	4.55	84	29.99	50	50	100
8	1488	Xerographic Paper	19.99	45	29.99	30	30	100
9	2786	Highlighter Pen 10-Box	7.99	86	11.99	50	50	200
10	2605	Pencil #2 Box	6.29	54	9.44	50	50	200
11	2818	Pencil Sharpener	7.99	17	11.99	40	40	200
12	3802	Correction Fluid 10-Box	3.39	65	53.99	50	50	300
13	3570	Correction Tape 10-Box	4.29	49	6.44	50	50	300
14	3372	Printer Ribbon 10-Box	35.99	19	5.09	25	25	300
15	3375	Typewriter Ribbons 10-Box	23.79	67	35.69	25	25	300
16	4005	Disks Data Case	5.99	18	12.74	40	40	400
17	4141	Double Sided Disks 10-Pk	8.49	27	8.99	40	40	400
18	4012	King Kong Modem 1200	105.99	10	149.99	10	15	400
19	4045	Monochrome Monitor Z-1105	99.99	15	148.39	10	15	400
20	4072	Panasonic Printer KX-P108	269.99	8	377.99	10	10	400
21	4189	Zenith Microcomputer Z-158	829.99	5	1161.99	10	10	400
22	5818	Calendar Refill	4.99	32	5.18	50	50	500
23	5960	Calendar Stands	5.69	14	10.49	40	40	500
24	5130	Letter Opener	1.45	49	7.49	50	50	500
25	5890	Paper Puncher	6.99	22	1.34	40	40	500
26	5000	Plastic Ruler	0.89	87	9.44	50	50	500
27	5225	Rubber Bands 10-Pk	3.45	72	2.18	50	50	500
28	5250	Scissors	4.99	34	8.54	50	50	500
29	5370	Staple Remover	1.39	55	7.49	50	50	500
30	5375	Stapler	6.29	29	2.09	40	40	500

Figure 7.26 Listing of the INVDSORT database file

the same for the first eight records. Then the value changes and remains the same for the next three records and so on. In other words, the value of this field identifies a group of records in this database file. This DEPT_CODE field is called the control field for the INVDSORT database file. Records with DEPT_CODE = 100 belong to one group, that is, Department 100. Similarly, the value 200 of the DEPT_CODE control field separates the records belonging to Department 200 and so on. The listing of the INVDSORT database file as shown in Figure 7.26 indicates that there are five different departments in the American Supply Company.

When the records in a database file are arranged like those just described, in ascending or descending order in the control field, then the records belonging to the different values of the control field are grouped together. And when the data records of such a file are processed using an application program, the records belonging to one group are processed before those of any other group, the group subtotals are printed at the end of each group, and then the processing of the next group of records continues until all the records of the database file have been processed.

The method of processing the records of a database file that are in ascending or descending order in a field and the logic of the application program testing the change of the value of this field with respect to the value of this field in the previous record of the database file are termed **control break** application. The example discussed in the next section illustrates this concept.

7.5 An Illustrative Example: Case Study 4

Program Description

Write a program to produce an inventory report listing for American Supply Company. Each listing should contain only the records belonging to a particular department from the database file named INVDSORT, which is obtained by sorting the INV.DBF database file in the ascending order of the DEPT_CODE field. Each listing should also contain the inventory total value for each department, and the final inventory total for the entire stock of the company. The program should calculate the total department inventory and the final total for the entire file by accumulating the inventory value of each item. This inventory value is obtained by multiplying the quantity on hand by the unit cost of each item.

Input File(s)

The INV database file, whose structure is shown in Figure 7.27, is used as an input file. The listing of the data records in the ascending order on the DEPT_CODE field is as shown in Figure 7.26.

Output

Program output should be an inventory report listing. It is a multiscreen report, as shown in Figures 7.28(a)–(f). The headings should be as shown in

Figure 7.27 Structure of the INV database file

```
Structure for database : C:\DBASE\INVOICE\INV.DBF
Number of data records :      30
Date of last update    : 12/25/87
Field  Field Name  Type       Width     Dec    Index
    1  ITEM_NUM    Character    4                 N
    2  ITEM_DESC   Character   26                 N
    3  UNIT_COST   Numeric      6         2       N
    4  QUANTITY    Numeric      3                 N
    5  RET_PRICE   Numeric      7         2       N
    6  REOD_POINT  Numeric      3                 N
    7  REOD_QTY    Numeric      3                 N
    8  DEPT_CODE   Numeric      3                 N
** Total **                    56
```

Figure 7.28 Inventory report listing for Case Study 4

```
                    AMERICAN SUPPLY COMPANY
   08/27/89            INVENTORY REPORT              14:09:48

   ITEM                              QTY ON    UNIT    INVENTORY
   NUMBER    ITEM DESCRIPTION        HAND      PRICE   VALUE

   1359      Report Covers 10-Pk     87        2.79    242.73
     .            .                   .         .        .
     .            .                   .         .        .
   1488      Xerographic Paper       45        19.99   899.55

                          TOTAL FOR DEPT # 100    $3,488.25




          PRESS ANY KEY TO CONTINUE . . . ▮
```
(a)

```
                    AMERICAN SUPPLY COMPANY
   08/27/89            INVENTORY REPORT              14:09:48

   ITEM                              QTY ON    UNIT    INVENTORY
   NUMBER    ITEM DESCRIPTION        HAND      PRICE   VALUE

   2786      Highlighter Pen 10-Box  86        7.99    687.14
     .            .                   .         .        .
     .            .                   .         .        .
   2818      Pencil Sharpner         17        7.99    135.83

                          TOTAL FOR DEPT # 200    $1,162.63




          PRESS ANY KEY TO CONTINUE . . . ▮
```
(b)

the inventory report listing; and the detail line should consist of the ITEM_NUM, ITEM_DESC, QUANTITY, UNIT_COST, and INV_VAL fields. Each department report should end with the department total line, and the next department inventory report should begin on a new screen. The final total should be on a separate screen.

Processing Steps

Use the following steps to develop the solution of the program:

Figure 7.28 Continued

```
                    AMERICAN SUPPLY COMPANY
  08/27/89             INVENTORY REPORT              14:09:48

   ITEM                            QTY ON    UNIT    INVENTORY
  NUMBER     ITEM DESCRIPTION       HAND    PRICE      VALUE

   3372    Printer Ribbon 10-Box     19     35.99     683.81
     .            .                   .       .          .
     .            .                   .       .          .
   3375    Typewriter Ribbons 10-Box 67     23.79    1,593.93

                       TOTAL FOR DEPT # 300        $2,708.30




                 PRESS ANY KEY TO CONTINUE . . . ▮
```
(c)

```
                    AMERICAN SUPPLY COMPANY
  08/27/89             INVENTORY REPORT              14:09:48

   ITEM                            QTY ON    UNIT    INVENTORY
  NUMBER     ITEM DESCRIPTION       HAND    PRICE      VALUE

   4141    Double Sided Disks 10-Pk  27      8.49     229.23
     .            .                   .       .          .
     .            .                   .       .          .
   4189    Zenith Microcomputer Z-158 5    829.99    4,149.95

                       TOTAL FOR DEPT # 400        $9,206.67




                 PRESS ANY KEY TO CONTINUE . . . ▮
```
(d)

1. The headings should be printed as shown in the inventory report listing. The date and time should be included in the headings.
2. The column headings should be enclosed between the two lines as shown in Figure 7.28.
3. The INV database file should be sorted in the ascending order of DEPT_CODE and stored in the INVDSORT database file.
4. The inventory value (INV_VAL) for each record in stock of the INVDSORT database file should be calculated by multiplying the UNIT_COST and the QUANTITY fields.

Figure 7.28 Continued

```
                  AMERICAN SUPPLY COMPANY
   08/27/89        INVENTORY REPORT              14:09:48

   ITEM                                QTY ON   UNIT    INVENTORY
   NUMBER    ITEM DESCRIPTION          HAND     PRICE   VALUE

   5225      Rubber Bands 10-Pk         72      3.45     248.40
     .            .                      .        .         .
     .            .                      .        .         .
     .            .                      .        .         .
   5370      Staple Remover             55      1.39      76.45

                       TOTAL FOR DEPT # 500      $1,218.52



                PRESS ANY KEY TO CONTINUE . . . ▮
```
(e)

```
                  AMERICAN SUPPLY COMPANY
   08/27/89        INVENTORY REPORT              14:09:48

   ITEM                                QTY ON   UNIT    INVENTORY
   NUMBER    ITEM DESCRIPTION          HAND     PRICE   VALUE


          FINAL TOTAL FOR AMERICAN SUPPLY COMPANY    $177,784.37




                *** --- END OF REPORT --- ***


                PRESS ANY KEY TO CONTINUE . . . ▮
```
(f)

5. The inventory value (INV_VAL) for all the records of the INVDSORT database file belonging to a particular department should be accumulated in the DEPINV_TOT memory variable, and the company total should be accumulated in the FININV_TOT memory variable.

6. The inventory value (INV_VAL), department inventory total (DEPINV_TOT), and final inventory total (FININV_TOT) memory variables, and any other constants used in the program, should be loaded from the memory file INVD.MEM.

7. Detail lines should not be printed past row 20.
8. Each department inventory listing should start on a new screen and end with its departmental total line.
9. When the screen is full or the department and/or final totals have been printed, the screen should be frozen to allow the user to view the output.
10. Print the final inventory total on a separate screen.
11. At the end of the output report, print the message "*** --- END OF REPORT ---***" to indicate the end of the report.
12. The whole output should be enclosed in a box, as shown in Figure 7.28.

The five phases of the program development process for Case Study 4 follow.

7.5.1 The Analysis Phase

The analysis phase in the program development process consists of the review and analysis of the program specifications leading to the clear understanding of the output report to be produced, the input database file(s) to be used in the program to produce the required output, and the identification of the processing steps needed in the solution of the problem.

Analysis of the Output Report

The inventory report listing as shown in Figure 7.28 represents the necessary format of the desired output report of Case Study 4. The analysis of the inventory report listing reveals it is similar to the one produced for Case Study 2; that is, it consists of two heading lines, including date and time, it is single-spaced, and the detail line consists of the same five fields. The only difference is that data belonging to different departments is grouped. Each department of the inventory listing starts on a new screen and ends with its departmental total line. The final inventory total is to be printed on a separate screen.

After analyzing the output report, prepare the screen layout form as shown in Figure 7.29. Because it is similar to the screen layout form of Case Study 1, no further explanation is needed for it.

Analysis of the Input Database File(s)

A review of the structure of the INV database file shown in Figure 7.27 indicates that there are 30 records in the input INV database file, each consisting of eight fields: ITEM_NUM, ITEM_DESC, UNIT_COST, QUANTITY, RET_PRICE, REOD_POINT, REOD_QTY, and DEPT_CODE. The detail line of the output report consists of five fields, four of which—ITEM_NUM, ITEM_DESC, QUANTITY, and UNIT_COST—are from the data record of the INVDSORT database file. The fifth field, INV_VAL, is evaluated by multiplying the UNIT_COST and QUANTITY fields. The listing of the INVDSORT database file as shown in Figure 7.26 indicates that the data records are grouped for the same DEPT_CODE value. In other words, the records for the same department appear at one place in the database and are also in ascending order on the DEPT_CODE field.

Analysis of the Processing Steps

The review of the problem specifications and the required output as shown in Figures 7.28(a)–(f) reveals that it is a control break problem. A control break problem is one in which the records are grouped on a particular field, called the control field, and the database file should be arranged in ascending or descending order on that field.

In such a problem, the records belonging to one group are processed, after which the subtotal for that group is printed. The processing then proceeds to the next group of records. This process continues until all the records of the database file have been processed. In our case study problem, the records are grouped in terms of those belonging to different departments. As indicated in the output as shown in Figure 7.28, the records for each department are processed. When the department changes, the subtotal for the department is printed. This process continues until all the records of the database file have been processed. For such a problem, the database file should be sorted in the ascending or descending order of

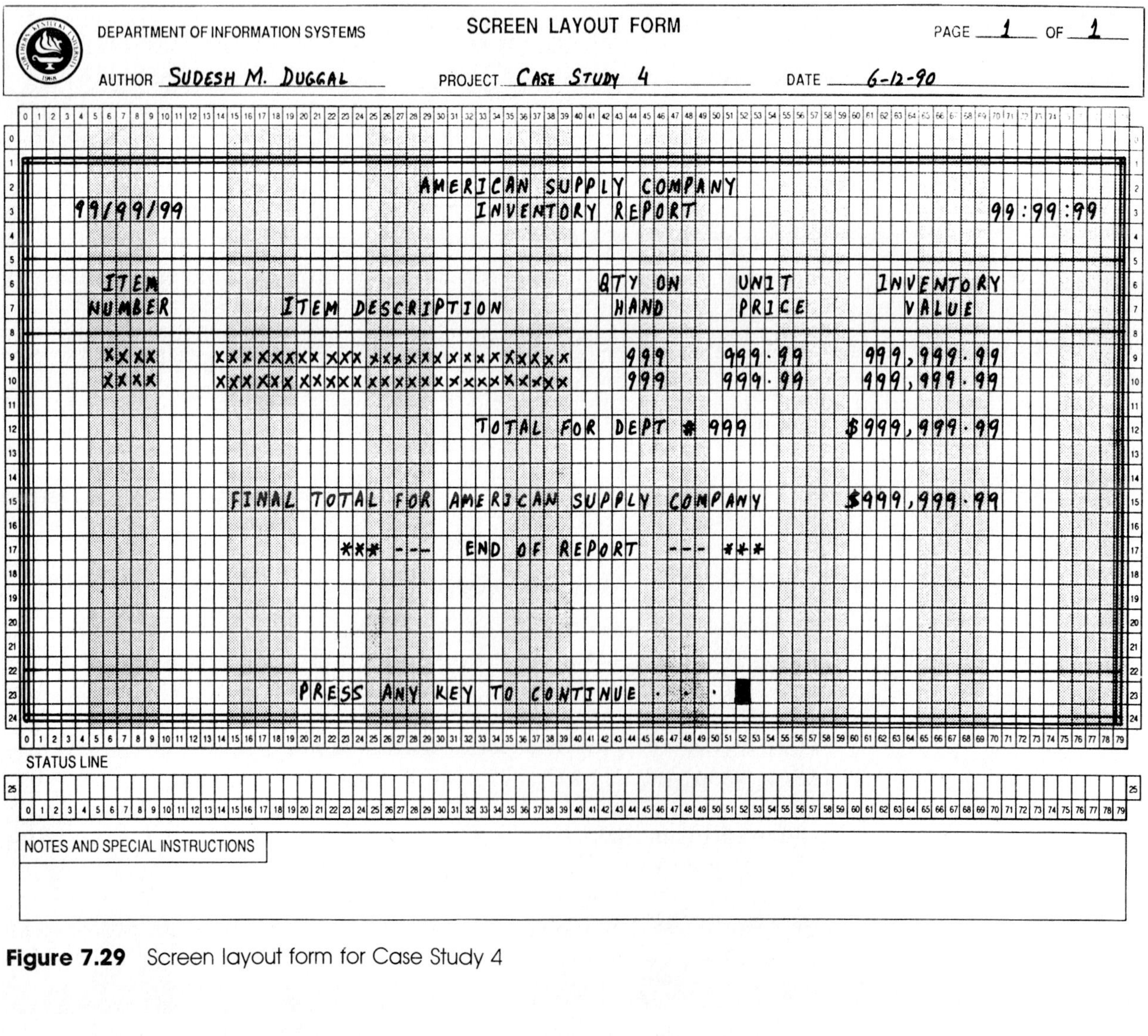

DEPARTMENT OF INFORMATION SYSTEMS — SCREEN LAYOUT FORM — PAGE 1 OF 1

AUTHOR SUDESH M. DUGGAL — PROJECT CASE STUDY 4 — DATE 6-12-90

```
99/99/99                 AMERICAN SUPPLY COMPANY
                            INVENTORY REPORT                        99:99:99

 ITEM                                            QTY ON     UNIT      INVENTORY
NUMBER             ITEM DESCRIPTION               HAND      PRICE       VALUE

 XXXX     XXXXXXXX XXX XXXXXXXXXXXXXXXXXX          999     999.99    999,999.99
 XXXX     XXXXXXXX XXXXXXXXXXXXXXXXXXXXXX          999     999.99    999,999.99

                            TOTAL FOR DEPT # 999                   $999,999.99

          FINAL TOTAL FOR AMERICAN SUPPLY COMPANY                  $999,999.99

                     *** --- END OF REPORT --- ***

                 PRESS ANY KEY TO CONTINUE . . .
```

STATUS LINE

NOTES AND SPECIAL INSTRUCTIONS

Figure 7.29 Screen layout form for Case Study 4

the control field, and fewer additional steps are needed than in the problems discussed in earlier chapters.

Except that this is a control break problem, it is similar to Case Study 2, and the processing steps needed to solve it will be similar to those of Case Study 2. In fact, the first four processing steps of initiate processing, which are housekeeping, define variables, print report headings, and open files, will be the same. Three memory variables will be initialized to zero in the define variables step—the INV_VAL to store the inventory value of each item, the DEPINV_TOT to accumulate the inventory total for the department, and the FININV_TOT to accumulate the final total for the whole file.

Because the subtotal at the end of each group of records belonging to a particular department is to be printed, a method needs to be devised to find out when the department number changes. This can be accomplished by defining a COMP_AREA memory variable in which the value of the DEPT_CODE field, the control field of the file, can be stored and used to test for the change in the department number. In other words, this test for the control break is contained in the main processing step.

For the first time, the value of the DEPT_CODE of the first record, 100, will be stored in the COMP_AREA memory variable. This result is shown in Figure 7.30.

Next, the following processing steps, belonging to main processing, will be performed:

1. The inventory value (INV_VAL) will be calculated by multiplying the UNIT_COST and the QUANTITY fields.
2. INV_VAL will be added to the department inventory total field (DEPINV_TOT).
3. INV_VAL will be added to the final inventory total field (FININV_TOT).
4. The detail line will be printed.
5. The test will be made to see if the screen is full. If it is, the new screen will be made available by clearing the screen and printing the headings; otherwise, the control will go to the next step.
6. The record pointer will skip to the next record.
7. A test will be made to check if the value of the control field has changed by comparing the DEPT_CODE of the next record with the COMP_AREA field, which contains the value of the DEPT_CODE field of the previous record.

Steps 1 through 4 are shown in Figure 7.31 and step 7, in Figure 7.32.

Because there is no change in the two values, you are still processing the records belonging to the same department. The seven steps just given will be repeated for each record of the database file until the values in the two fields, that is, the DEPT_CODE and the COMP_AREA, are not equal, as shown in Figure 7.32 (see page 298). This result indicates that the next record does not belong to the same department as the previous record, thereby signaling the control break.

Because all the records in a single department have been processed, this department subtotal needs to be printed, after which the department inventory total accumulator should be initialized, and the COMP_AREA

INVDSORT Database File

Record#	ITEM_NUM	ITEM_DESC	UNIT_COST	QUANTITY	. . .	DEPT_NUM
1	1136	Bond Paper, Ream	22.99	38	. . .	100
2	1910	Ditto Paper, Ream	19.99	35	. . .	100
3	1732	Message Pads 10-Pk	2.25	45	. . .	100
4	1975	Notebook Filler	1.79	65	. . .	100
5	1359	Report Covers 10-Pk	2.79	87	. . .	100
6	1536	Ruled Pads 8.5 x 11 10-Pk	4.55	38	. . .	100
7	1060	Steno Notebook 10-Pk	4.55	84	. . .	100
8	1488	Xerographic Paper	19.99	45	. . .	100
9	2786	Highlighter Pen 10-Pk	7.99	86	. . .	200
.	.	.	.	.		.
30	5375	Stapler	6.29	29	. . .	500

COMPUTER INTERNAL MEMORY

ITEM_NUM	ITEM_DESC	UNIT_COST	QUANTITY	DEPT_CODE
1136	Bond Paper, Ream	22.99	38	100

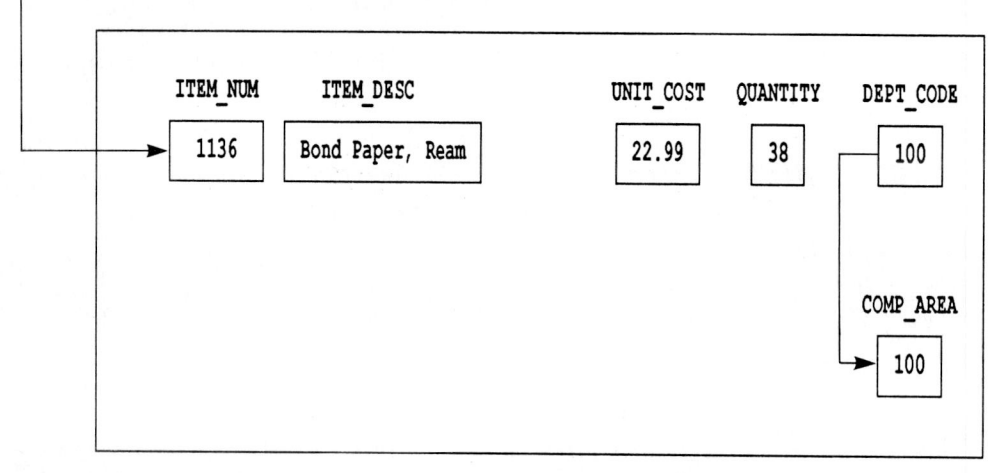

COMP_AREA: 100

Figure 7.30 Storing the DEPT_CODE value to the COMP_AREA memory variable

memory variable should be replaced by the value of the DEPT_CODE of the next record. At this point, the screen should be frozen to allow the user to view the output. Also as requested in the specifications of the case study, the new screen should be prepared for the output of the next department's records. All the steps listed in this paragraph, called the "control break processing" steps, are summarized in Table 7.1 for future reference.

These steps will be repeated until all the department's data are processed. Then the control will proceed to the function to be performed in the terminate processing step. The three steps used in Case Study 2—print the final totals, close file(s), and end of job—will be performed.

COMPUTER INTERNAL MEMORY

ITEM_NUM	ITEM_DESC	UNIT_COST	QUANTITY	DEPT_CODE
1136	Bond Paper, Ream	22.99	38	100

COMP_AREA: 100

① 22.99 × 38 = 873.62
INV_VAL
(= UNIT_COST * QUANTITY)

② 873.62 = 0 + 873.62
DEPINV_TOT
(= DEPINV_TOT + INV_VAL)

③ 873.62 = 0 + 873.62
FININV_TOT
(= FININV_TOT + INV_VAL)

Output

```
                    AMERICAN SUPPLY COMPANY
08/27/89              INVENTORY REPORT              14:09:48

ITEM                            QTY ON    UNIT      INVENTORY
NUMBER    ITEM DESCRIPTION      HAND      PRICE     VALUE

1136      Bond Paper, Ream      38        22.99     873.62
```

④

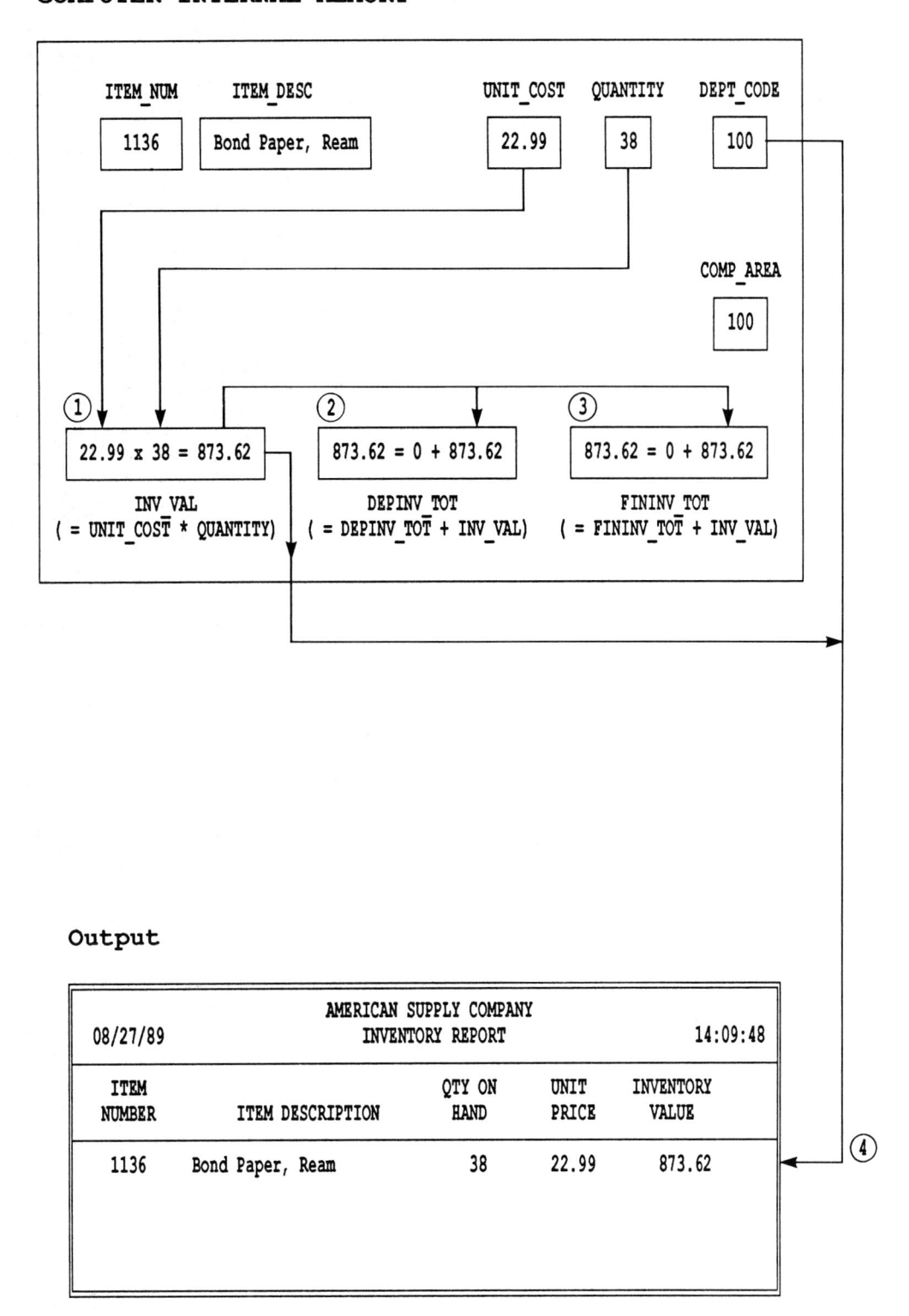

Figure 7.31 Processing of the first record

INVDSORT Database File

Record#	ITEM_NUM	ITEM_DESC	UNIT_COST	QUANTITY	...	DEPT_NUM
1	1136	Bond Paper, Ream	22.99	38	...	100
2	1910	Ditto Paper, Ream	19.99	35	...	100
3	1732	Message Pads 10-Pk	2.25	45	...	100
4	1975	Notebook Filler	1.79	65	...	100
5	1359	Report Covers 10-Pk	2.79	87	...	100
6	1536	Ruled Pads 8.5 x 11 10-Pk	4.55	38	...	100
7	1060	Steno Notebook 10-Pk	4.55	84	...	100
8	1488	Xerographic Paper	19.99	45	...	100
9	2786	Highlighter Pen 10-Pk	7.99	86	...	200
.	.	.	.	.		.
.	.	.	.	.		.
30	5375	Stapler	6.29	29	...	500

COMPUTER INTERNAL MEMORY

ITEM_NUM	ITEM_DESC	UNIT_COST	QUANTITY	DEPT_CODE
2786	Highlighter Pen 10-box	7.99	86	200

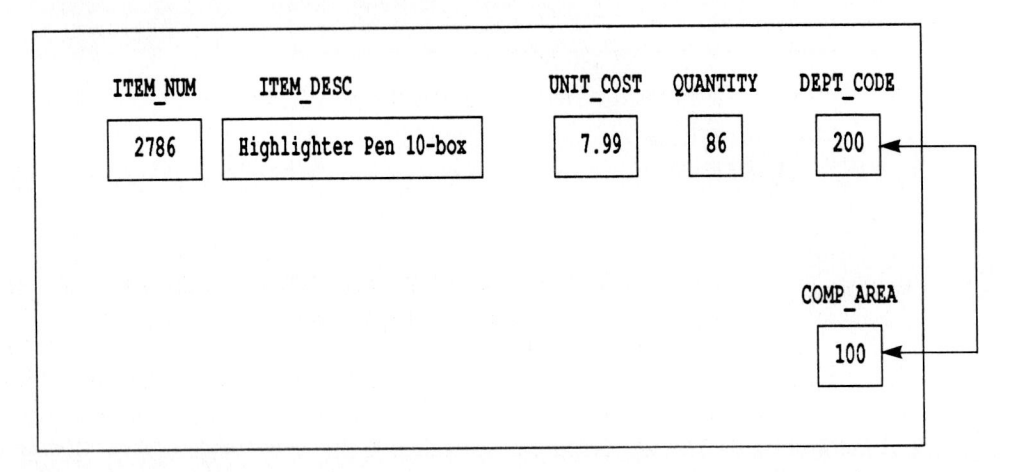

COMP_AREA: 100

Figure 7.32 Testing of the control break

Table 7.1 Control break processing steps

1. Printing the subtotal line
2. Reinitializing the subtotal accumulator
3. Resetting the compare area
4. Freezing the screen
5. Clearing the screen and printing the headings

7.5 An Illustrative Example: Case Study 4

To summarize, the following processing steps will be needed in the solution of Case Study 4.

1. Housekeeping
2. Define variables
3. Print report headings
4. Open file(s)
5. Define control compare areas
6. Perform calculations
7. Accumulate totals
8. Print detail line
9. Test for screen full
10. If screen not full, proceed to step 12
11. Print report headings
12. Skip to next record
13. Test for control break. If control break occurs, perform the following steps:
    a. Print the subtotal line
    b. Reinitialize the subtotal accumulator
    c. Reset the compare area
    d. Freeze the screen
    e. Clear the screen and print the headings
14. Print final total line
15. Close file(s)
16. End of job

The first five steps should be performed only once, at the start of the program. Therefore, they belong to initiate processing. The next eight steps should be performed again and again for each record of the INV database file. Therefore, these steps belong to main processing. The last three steps need to be performed after all the records of the INV database file have been processed. Therefore, they belong to the terminate processing.

7.5.2 The Design Phase

The function of the design phase steps is to take the result of the problem analysis, that is, the problem broken down into several smaller, manageable components, and transform them into a structure chart. Using all the tools and techniques discussed in Section 4.4.2 and the 16 processing steps identified in the analysis phase, complete the structure charts for Case Study 4 and control break procedure CBREAK34, as shown in Figures 7.33 and 7.34.

In these structure charts, all the modules except 1.3 Process Headings Procedure (or 2.4.1.2 Process Headings Procedure, or CB34.5 Process Headings Procedure) and 2.3 Print Detail Line perform one function and, as such, are functionally cohesive. As explained in Chapter 4, these two modules are highly cohesive. Thus, all the modules in these structure

300 Chapter 7 / Sorting and Control Breaks

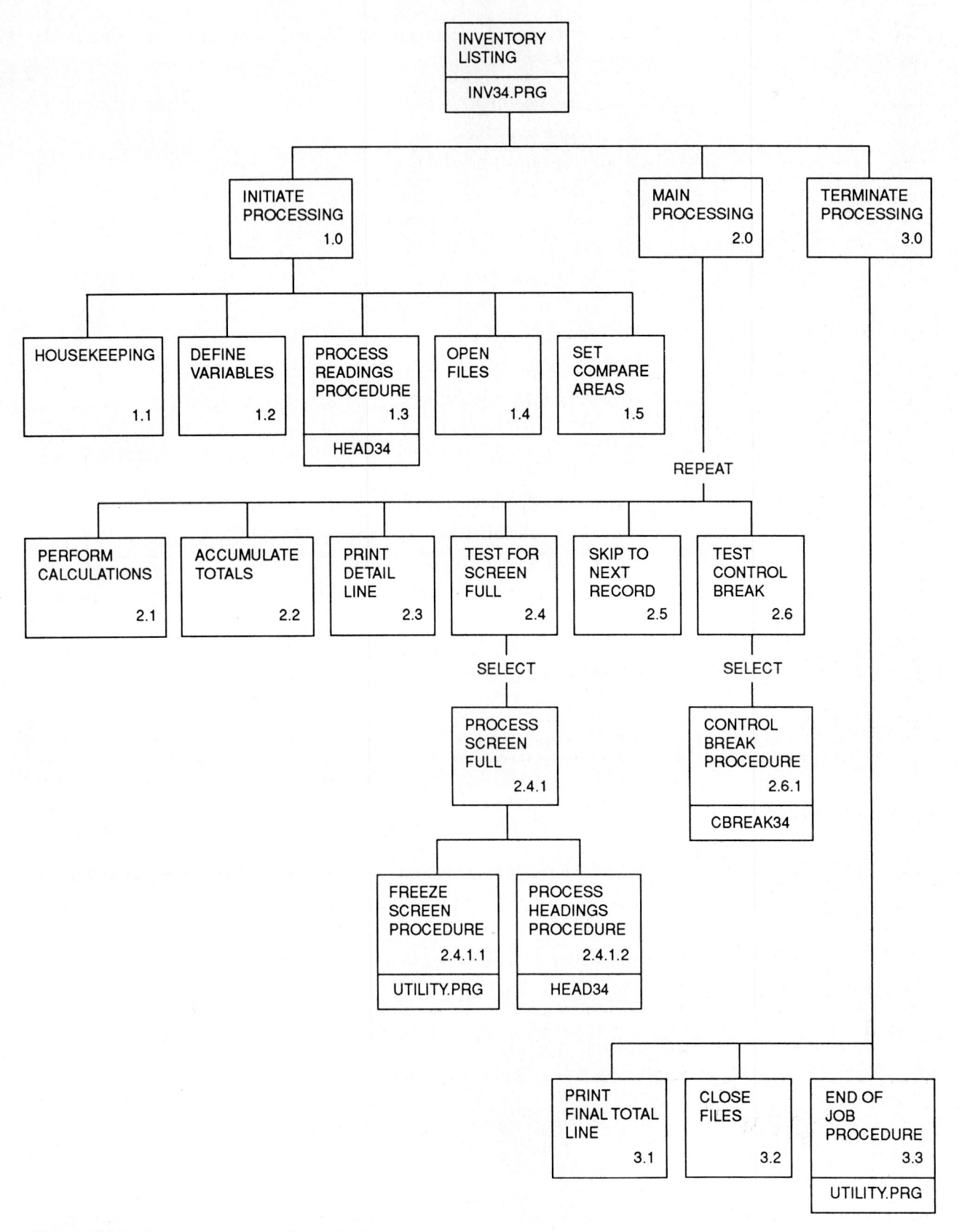

Figure 7.33 Structure chart for Case Study 4

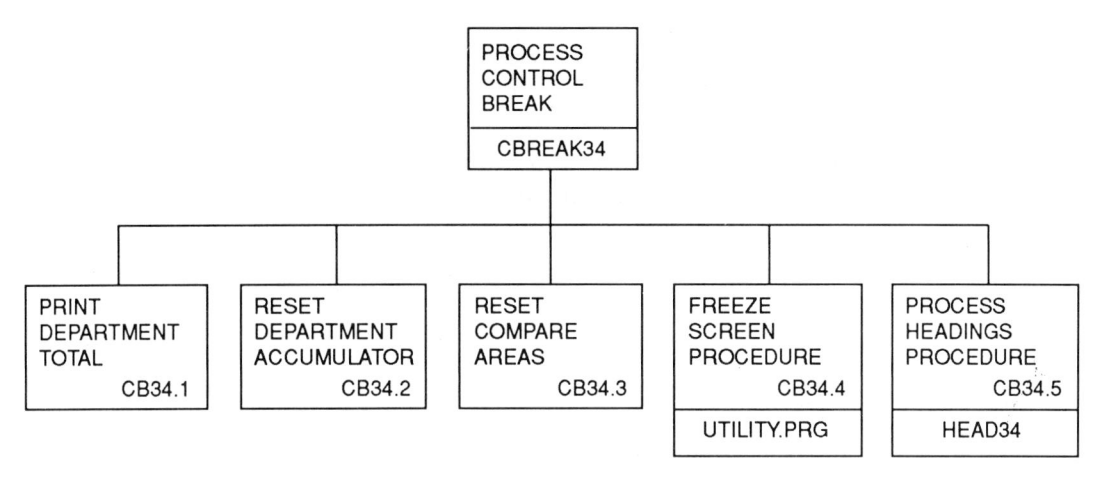

```
                    ┌─────────────┐
                    │  PROCESS    │
                    │  CONTROL    │
                    │  BREAK      │
                    ├─────────────┤
                    │  CBREAK34   │
                    └──────┬──────┘
    ┌──────────┬───────────┼───────────┬──────────┐
┌───┴────┐ ┌───┴────┐ ┌────┴───┐ ┌─────┴────┐ ┌───┴──────┐
│ PRINT  │ │ RESET  │ │ RESET  │ │ FREEZE   │ │ PROCESS  │
│DEPART- │ │DEPART- │ │COMPARE │ │ SCREEN   │ │ HEADINGS │
│MENT    │ │MENT    │ │ AREAS  │ │PROCEDURE │ │PROCEDURE │
│TOTAL   │ │ACCUM.  │ │        │ │          │ │          │
├────────┤ ├────────┤ ├────────┤ ├──────────┤ ├──────────┤
│CB34.1  │ │CB34.2  │ │CB34.3  │ │ CB34.4   │ │ CB34.5   │
└────────┘ └────────┘ └────────┘ └─────┬────┘ └─────┬────┘
                                 ┌─────┴────┐ ┌─────┴────┐
                                 │UTILITY.PRG│ │ HEAD34  │
                                 └──────────┘ └──────────┘
```

Figure 7.34 Structure chart for control break CBREAK34 procedure

charts are either functionally or highly cohesive. The modules are also loosely coupled. The structure charts of Figures 7.33 and 7.34 satisfy the three rules for designing a good structure chart; that is, they consist of highly cohesive, loosely coupled modules none of which has a span of control of more than six. So it is a well-designed solution of Case Study 4.

7.5.3 The Detailed Design Phase

The function of this step is to take the result of the design phase, the structure chart, identify the actual computer operations required for each program function represented in it, and produce the detailed solution of the problem. Using the translation of the three control structures to pseudocode as given in Figure 4.14, the screen layout form of Figure 7.29, and the method described in section 4.4.3 allows us to translate the structure charts of Figures 7.33 and 7.34 to pseudocode, as shown in Figure 7.35 (see page 302).

7.5.4 The Coding Phase

The purpose of this phase in the program development process is to translate the pseudocode instructions of the solution of the program into programming language instructions. The pseudocode of Figure 7.35 is translated into dBASE commands, and the complete program for Case Study 4 in dBASE language is given in Figure 7.36.

7.5.5 The Testing and Debugging Phase

The last step in program development is the testing and debugging phase, in which the source program is executed and tested for the accuracy of its logic. Execute the program to complete this step, correct the syntactical errors, if any, and execute the program again. Repeat this process until the program is free of syntactical errors. When the output is produced by the program, verify some of the records of the output to ensure its accuracy. If any discrepancies exist, make the needed corrections, and execute the program again. Repeat the process of making corrections and executing the program until the program produces correct and predictable results.

```
0.0 INVENTORY LISTING—INV34
   1.0 INITIATE PROCESSING
      1.1 HOUSEKEEPING
         SET DEFAULT MODES
            Turn off the dBASE's heading feature
            Turn off the dBASE's user dialogue
            Turn off the dBASE's status bar
         SET PROCEDURE
            Set procedure to UTILITY procedure
      1.2 DEFINE VARIABLES
         DECLARE VARIABLES
            Declare LINECNT public
         INITIALIZE VARIABLES
            Set Inventory Value = 0
            Set Comp Area = 0
         INITIALIZE ACCUMULATORS
            Set Department Inventory Value = 0
            Set Final Total Inventory Value = 0
      1.3 PROCESS HEADINGS PROCEDURE
         Perform heading HEAD34 procedure
      1.4 OPEN FILES
         Open database file INV
         Sort INV database file to INVDSORT file on DEPT_CODE
         Open INVDSORT file
      1.5 SET COMPARE AREAS
         Set Compare Area = Department Code
   2.0 MAIN PROCESSING
      REPEAT: until end of file
         2.1 PERFORM CALCULATIONS
            Calculate Inventory Value by multiplying
            the quantity and unit cost fields
         2.2 ACCUMULATE TOTALS
            Add Inventory Value to Department Total Inventory Value
            Add Inventory Value to Final Total Inventory Value
         2.3 PRINT DETAIL LINE
            Write Detail Line
         INCREMENT LINE COUNTER
            Add 1 to the Line Counter
         2.4 TEST FOR SCREEN FULL
            SELECT: When screen is full
               2.4.1 PROCESS SCREEN FULL
                  2.4.1.1 FREEZE SCREEN PROCEDURE
                     Perform FREEZE procedure
                  2.4.1.2 PERFORM HEADINGS PROCEDURE
                     Perform heading HEAD34 procedure
         2.5 SKIP TO NEXT RECORD
            Skip to the next record of the database
```

Figure 7.35 Pseudocode for Case Study 4

7.5 An Illustrative Example: Case Study 4

```
        2.6 TEST CONTROL BREAK
              SELECT: When Department Code ≠ Compare Area
                 2.6.1 PROCESS CONTROL BREAK
                        Process control break CBREAK34 procedure
              END SELECT
        END REPEAT
    3.0 TERMINATE PROCESSING
        3.1 PRINT FINAL TOTAL LINE
              Increment LINECNT by one
              Print Final Total Inventory Value
        3.2 CLOSE FILES
              Close database file
        3.3 END OF JOB PROCEDURE
              Perform ENDOFJOB Procedure
PROCEDURE HEAD34
    CLEAR SCREEN
      Clear the screen
    PRINT HEADINGS
      Print Report Main Heading Line 1
      Print Report Main Heading Line 2
      Draw a line
      Print column heading line 1
      Print column heading line 2
      Draw a line
    INITIALIZE LINE COUNTER
      Set line counter = 8
    RETURN
PROCEDURE CBREAK34
    CB34.1 PRINT DEPARTMENT TOTAL
              Print Department Total Inventory Value
    CB34.2 RESET DEPARTMENT ACCUMULATOR
              Rest Department Inventory total = 0
    CB34.3 RESET COMPARE AREAS
              Reset Compare Area = Department Code
    CB34.4 FREEZE SCREEN PROCEDURE
              Perform FREEZE procedure
    CB34.5 PROCESS HEADINGS PROCEDURE
              Perform headings HEAD34 procedure
    RETURN
```

Figure 7.35 Continued

```
**************************************************************
*                         INV34                              *
*               AMERICAN SUPPLY COMPANY                      *
* ---------------------------------------------------------- *
* This program produces an Inventory Listing Report for      *
* American Supply Company, containing all the items of       *
* the INV.DBF file, printing the inventory total value       *
* for each department and also the final inventory total     *
* for the whole stock of the company. The program            *
* calculates the department inventory total by accumulating  *
* the inventory value for each item, which is obtained by    *
* multiplying the quantity at hand by the unit cost. The     *
* heading is also included in the report.                    *
* ---------------------------------------------------------- *
*            COPYRIGHT (C) . . . SUDESH M. DUGGAL            *
**************************************************************
*
***************************
* 1.0 INITIATE PROCESSING *
***************************
*
*** 1.1 HOUSEKEEPING ***
   *
   *** CHANGE DEFAULT MODES ***
      *
      SET HEADING OFF
      SET TALK OFF
      SET STATUS OFF
      *
   *** SET PROCEDURE ***
      *
      SET PROCEDURE TO UTILITY
      *
*** 1.2 DEFINE VARIABLES ***
   *
   *** DECLARE VARIABLES ***
      *
      PUBLIC LINECNT
      *
   *** INITIALIZE VARIABLES ***
      *
      INV_VAL = 0
      COMP_AREA = 0
      *
   *** INITIALIZE ACCUMULATORS ***
      *
      DEPINV_TOT = 0
      FININV_TOT = 0
*** 1.3 PROCESS HEADINGS PROCEDURE ***
   *
   DO HEAD34
   *
*** 1.4 OPEN FILES ***
   *
   USE INV
```

Figure 7.36 Coding for Case Study 4

```
   SORT ON DEPT_CODE TO INVDSORT
   USE INVDSORT
      *
   *** 1.5 SET COMPARE AREAS ***
      *
      STORE DEPT_CODE TO COMP_AREA
      *
***********************
* 2.0 MAIN PROCESSING *
***********************
*
DO WHILE .NOT. EOF()
   *
   *** 2.1 PERFORM CALCULATIONS ***
      *
      INV_VAL = QUANTITY * UNIT_COST
      *
   *** 2.2 ACCUMULATE TOTALS ***
      *
      DEPINV_TOT = DEPINV_TOT + INV_VAL
      FININV_TOT = FININV_TOT + INV_VAL
      *
   *** 2.3 PRINT DETAIL LINE ***
      *
      *** PRINT A LINE ***
         *
         @ LINECNT,6  SAY ITEM_NUM
         @ LINECNT,14 SAY ITEM_DESC
         @ LINECNT,44 SAY QUANTITY
         @ LINECNT,51 SAY UNIT_COST
         @ LINECNT,61 SAY INV_VAL PICTURE '$9,999.99'
         *
      *** INCREMENT LINE COUNTER ***
         *
         LINECNT = LINECNT + 1
         *
   *** 2.4 TEST FOR SCREEN FULL ***
      *
      IF LINECNT = 20
         *
         *** 2.4.1 PROCESS SCREEN FULL ***
            *
            *** 2.4.1.1 FREEZE SCREEN PROCEDURE ***
               *
               DO FREEZE
               *
            *** 2.4.1.2 PROCESS HEADINGS PROCEDURE ***
               *
               DO HEAD34
               *
      ENDIF LINECNT = 20
      *
   *** 2.5 SKIP TO NEXT RECORD ***
      *
      SKIP
      *
```

Figure 7.36 Continued

```
      *** 2.6 TEST CONTROL BREAK ***
         *
         IF .NOT. DEPT_CODE = COMP_AREA
            *
            *** 2.6.1 PROCESS CONTROL BREAK ***
               *
               DO CBREAK34
               *
         ENDIF .NOT. DEPT_CODE = COMP_AREA
         *
ENDDO .NOT. EOF ()
*
****************************
* 3.0 TERMINATE PROCESSING *
****************************
*
*** 3.1 PRINT FINAL TOTAL LINE ***
   *
   LINECNT = LINECNT + 1
   @ LINECNT,10 SAY 'FINAL TOTAL FOR AMERICAN SUPPLY COMPANY'
   @ LINECNT,61 SAY FININV_TOT PICTURE '$99,999.99'
   *
*** 3.2 CLOSE FILES ***
   *
   *** CLOSE DATABASE FILE ***
      *
      USE
      *
   *** DELETE SORTED FILE ***
      *
      ERASE INVDSORT
      *
*** 3.3 END OF JOB PROCEDURE ***
   *
   DO ENDOFJOB
   *
   *
*******************************************************************
*                      PROCEDURE HEAD34                            *
*                   AMERICAN SUPPLY COMPANY                        *
* ---------------------------------------------------------------- *
* The function of this procedure is to write headings at the       *
* top of each output screen for the INV34 program. It can be       *
* invoked from anywhere within the program to print the            *
* headings. After printing the headings the control will be        *
* returned to the next command in the program which invoked        *
* this procedure.                                                  *
* ---------------------------------------------------------------- *
*           COPYRIGHT (C) . . . SUDESH M. DUGGAL                   *
*******************************************************************
*
PROCEDURE HEAD34
   *
   *** CLEAR SCREEN ***
      *
      CLEAR
```

Figure 7.36 Continued

```
      *
   *** PRINT HEADINGS ***
      *
      @ 2,29 SAY 'AMERICAN SUPPLY COMPANY'
      @ 3,4  SAY DATE ()
      @ 3,33 SAY 'INVENTORY REPORT'
      @ 3,70 SAY TIME ()
      @ 4,0  TO  4,79
      @ 5,6  SAY 'ITEM'
      @ 5,42 SAY 'QTY ON'
      @ 5,52 SAY 'UNIT'
      @ 5,60 SAY 'INVENTORY'
      @ 6,5  SAY 'NUMBER'
      @ 6,19 SAY 'ITEM DESCRIPTION'
      @ 6,43 SAY 'HAND'
      @ 6,52 SAY 'PRICE'
      @ 6,62 SAY 'VALUE'
      @ 7,0  TO  7,79
      *
   *** INITIALIZE LINE COUNTER ***
      *
      STORE 8 TO LINECNT
      *
   RETURN
   *
   *
************************************************************
*                  PROCEDURE CBREAK34                       *
*                  AMERICAN SUPPLY COMPANY                  *
* --------------------------------------------------------- *
* The function of this procedure is to perform control break*
* processing. It is invoked by the INV34 program. After     *
* performing the control break processing, the control is   *
* transferred back to the INV34 program.                    *
* --------------------------------------------------------- *
*          COPYRIGHT (C) . . . SUDESH M. DUGGAL             *
************************************************************
*
PROCEDURE CBREAK34
   *
   *** CB34.1 PRINT DEPARTMENT TOTAL ***
      *
      LINECNT = LINECNT + 1
      @ LINECNT,20 SAY 'INVENTORY TOTAL FOR DEPT # '
      @ LINECNT,36 SAY COMP_AREA
      @ LINECNT,61 SAY DEPINV_TOT PICTURE '$99,999.99'
      *
   *** CB34.2 RESET DEPARTMENT ACCUMULATOR ***
      *
      DEPINV_TOT = 0
      *
   *** CB34.3 RESET COMPARE AREAS ***
      *
      STORE DEPT_CODE TO COMP_AREA
      *
   *** CB34.4 FREEZE SCREEN PROCEDURE ***
```

Figure 7.36 Continued

```
    *
    DO FREEZE
    *
*** CB4.5 PROCESS HEADINGS PROCEDURE ***
    *
    DO HEAD4
    *
RETURN
```

Figure 7.36 Continued

7.6 Summary

The SORT command is used to arrange the data by physically rearranging the order of the records of the database file in ascending or descending order in a specific data field or fields and then creating a new database file. When the data are sorted using the multiple fields, the field on which the file will be sorted first is called the primary field; the field on which the records will be sorted within the primary field is called the secondary field. Each sorted field can have its own sorting option attached to it. The ascending option is the default option and, as such, can be omitted.

The most useful feature of the SORT command is its ability to select data records satisfying a given condition and then arrange them in ascending or descending order, depending on a specific field or fields. When using the SORT command, follow these rules:

1. A database file can't be sorted to itself.
2. The sorted database file in which the sorted data records are stored should be an unopened database file.
3. Database files can't be sorted on a logical or memo field.
4. To perform any function on the sorted data records after sorting a database file, you should open the sorted database file.

Although sorting is very useful in certain instances, it has some disadvantages:

1. Sorting a large file is very time-consuming.
2. Because a sorted database file is the same size as the original database file, there can be a storage problem for large files.
3. Every time new records are added to the database file, resorting is required to keep the data in the database file in sequence.

The most commonly used command in any application is the COPY command. It is used to create an extra or a backup copy of any existing file. The COPY FILE TO command is used to copy any file (such as database, program, or index) to a new file. The COPY TO command is used to copy the full or partial contents of an active database file to another database file. Similarly, the COPY STRUCTURE TO command is used to copy only the full or partial structure of an active database file to another database file.

The key is a data field in the record of a database file that uniquely identifies each record of the database file. The control field is a data field in the record of a database file that uniquely identifies a group of records in the database file. When the records of a database file are arranged depending on the control field and are processed in a manner so that those belonging to each control field are processed separately and their total is also obtained, it is termed a control break application.

KEY CONCEPTS

control break
control field
key field

primary field
secondary field

dBASE COMMANDS AND FUNCTIONS

COPY FILE TO command
COPY STRUCTURE TO command
COPY TO command

SET SAFETY command
SORT TO command

REVIEW QUESTIONS

1. What is the function of the SORT command? Name another command used for arranging the data in sequential order.
2. What is the format of the SORT command? What is meant by ascending and descending order?
3. What is the default order in which dBASE IV sorts the data?
4. What is meant by the Sort key? Is it possible to sort a database file on multiple fields? If so, how should the different fields be mentioned in the SORT command?
5. What is meant by the physical order of the records in the database file? Does the physical order remain the same after the database file is sorted?
6. Is it possible to sort a database file to itself?
7. Is it possible to sort the database file on all different types of data fields? If not, name the data types on which the sort is not possible.
8. What is meant by the primary sort field and the secondary sort field? In what order should these fields be present in the SORT command?
9. Is it possible to sort a selected group of records of a database file?
10. What is meant by a target file? Are the records in the target file in the same physical order as in the original database file?
11. What is the function of the SET SAFETY command? What is its default option?
12. What is the size of the sorted file? Should this file be opened before the sort command is issued?
13. After the SORT command, what step is needed to perform any function with the sorted records?
14. List and explain the disadvantages of the SORT command.
15. What are the uses of the COPY command?
16. What format of the COPY command should be used to copy any file to another file?
17. What format of the COPY command should be used to copy the contents as well as the structure of the active database file?
18. What format of the COPY command should be used to copy only the structure of the active database file?
19. What precaution should be used when employing the COPY command?
20. Explain what is meant by the following terms:
    a. Sort key
    b. Control key
    c. Control break

HANDS-ON ASSIGNMENT

Programming Assignment 7A

Program Description Write a program ACR34.PRG to produce an accounts receivable report listing by customer number for American Supply Company. Each listing should contain only the records belonging to a particular customer from the ACCREC database file. Each listing should also contain the total for the purchase amount, amount paid, current balance for each customer, and final total for these fields for all company receivables.

Input File(s) The ACCREC database file, whose structure is shown in Figure 4.32, is used as an input file. The listing of the data records in ascending order on the CUS_NUM field is given in Figure 7.37.

Output Program output should be an accounts receivable report listing by customer number. It is multiscreen output, and its format is shown in Figure 7.38(a) and (b). The headings should be as shown in the accounts receivable report listing; and the detail line should consist of the PUR_DATE, PUR_REF, PUR_AMT, PAY_AMT, and CURR_BAL fields. Each customer report should end with the customer total line, and the next customer accounts receivable report should begin on a new screen. The final total should be on a separate screen.

Figure 7.37 Listing of the ACCREC database file in the ascending order of CUS_NUM

Record #	ACCT_NUM	PUR_DATE	PUR_REF	PUR_AMT	PAY_DATE	PAY_REF	PAY_AMT	CURR_BAL
1	250-21-5560	03/22/90	1057	219.00	03/22/90	0	0.00	219.00
2	250-21-5560	01/08/90	752	133.56	02/02/90	455	39.50	94.06
3	250-21-5560	03/17/90	1006	78.50	03/17/90	0	0.00	78.50
4	250-21-5560	02/12/90	871	345.33	04/05/90	542	125.00	220.33
5	250-21-5560	01/30/90	844	96.00	03/05/90	507	48.00	48.00
6	320-45-1423	01/15/90	795	275.67	03/25/90	906	129.00	146.67
7	320-45-1423	02/26/90	904	504.00	04/12/90	987	250.00	254.00
8	320-45-1423	01/07/90	794	73.50	02/27/90	890	50.00	23.50
9	320-45-1423	03/17/90	1009	84.00	03/17/90	0	0.00	84.00
10	320-45-1423	02/28/90	922	244.50	04/07/90	975	140.00	104.50
11	320-45-1423	01/02/90	739	386.00	02/12/90	866	200.00	186.00
12	401-65-9986	02/02/90	854	395.76	04/05/90	203	57.00	338.76
13	401-65-9986	03/04/90	946	126.00	03/04/90	0	0.00	126.00
14	401-65-9986	03/25/90	1078	145.76	03/25/90	0	0.00	145.76
15	401-65-9986	02/13/90	872	157.25	02/13/90	0	0.00	157.25
16	401-65-9986	01/27/90	835	356.98	02/15/90	1256	150.00	206.98
17	452-45-6767	02/27/90	915	105.00	04/03/90	199	35.00	70.00
18	452-45-6767	03/01/90	935	505.00	03/01/90	0	0.00	505.00
19	452-45-6767	03/12/90	984	167.45	03/12/90	0	0.00	167.45
20	452-45-6767	01/16/90	799	50.00	02/17/90	135	25.00	25.00
21	452-45-6767	02/05/90	859	292.00	04/06/90	205	146.00	146.00
22	605-21-2345	03/04/90	948	297.50	03/04/90	1002	125.00	172.50
23	605-21-2345	02/25/90	898	129.97	04/08/90	1108	65.00	64.97
24	605-21-2345	03/15/90	997	215.89	03/15/90	1059	100.00	115.89
25	605-21-2345	02/10/90	862	137.85	04/08/90	1109	75.00	62.85
26	605-21-2345	01/12/90	790	405.00	04/02/90	1088	135.00	270.00
27	605-21-2345	01/27/90	836	167.50	01/27/90	0	0.00	167.50
28	605-21-2345	03/12/90	983	354.67	03/12/90	1043	140.00	214.67

7.6 Summary

```
                    AMERICAN SUPPLY COMPANY
   08/20/89         ACCOUNT RECEIVABLE REPORT              02:29:25
              LISTING OF ALL RECEIVABLE WITH CURRENT BALANCE

      PURCHASE     PURCHASE      PURCHASE      PAYMENT      CURRENT
        DATE       REFERENCE      AMOUNT       AMOUNT       BALANCE

       99/99/99      9999        9,999.99     9,999.99     9,999.99
       99/99/99      9999        9,999.99     9,999.99     9,999.99

   TOTALS FOR     XXXXXXXXXX    $9,999.99    $9,999.99    $9,999.99




                  PRESS ANY KEY TO CONTINUE . . . ▮
```
(a)

```
                    AMERICAN SUPPLY COMPANY
   08/20/89         ACCOUNT RECEIVABLE REPORT              02:29:25
              LISTING OF ALL RECEIVABLE WITH CURRENT BALANCE

      PURCHASE     PURCHASE      PURCHASE      PAYMENT      CURRENT
        DATE       REFERENCE      AMOUNT       AMOUNT       BALANCE


          FINAL TOTALS           $9,999.99    $9,999.99    $9,999.99

                  ***  ---  END OF REPORT  ---  ***




                  PRESS ANY KEY TO CONTINUE . . . ▮
```
(b)

Figure 7.38 Accounts receivable report listing: Programming Assignment 7A

Processing Steps Use the following steps to develop the solution of the program:

1. The headings should be printed as shown in the accounts receivable report. The date and time should be included in the headings.
2. The column headings should be enclosed between the two lines as shown in Figure 7.38.
3. The ACCREC database file should be sorted in the ascending order of CUST_NUM and stored in the ARECSORT database file.
4. The program should calculate the current balance for each customer in the ACCREC database file by subtracting the payment amount (PAY_AMT) from the purchase amount (PUR_AMT) and store it in the CURR_BAL memory variable field.
5. The purchase amount (PUR_AMT), payment amount (PAY_AMT), and current balance (CURR_BAL) fields for all the records of the ARECSORT database file belonging to a particular customer should be accumulated in the DPUR_AMT, DPAY_AMT, and DCURR_BAL memory variables. The company total should be accumulated in the FPUR_AMT, FPAY_AMT, and FCURR_BAL memory variables.
6. The PUR_AMT, PAY_AMT, CURR_BAL, DPUR_AMT, DPAY_AMT, DCURR_BAL, FPUR_AMT, FPAY_AMT, and FCURR_BAL memory variables, and any other constants used in the program, should be loaded from the memory file ACR34.MEM.
7. Detail lines should not be printed past row 20.
8. Each customer account receivable listing should start on a new screen and end with its customer total line.
9. When the screen is full or the customer and/or final totals have been printed, the screen should be frozen to allow the user to view the output.
10. Print the final accounts receivable totals on a separate screen.
11. At the end of the output report, print the message "*** --- END OF REPORT --- ***" to indicate the end of the output report. Then freeze the screen to allow the user to view the output.
12. The whole output should be enclosed in a box, as shown in Figure 7.38.

Programming Assignment 7B

Program Description Write a program PAY34.PRG to produce a payroll report listing by department for American Supply Company. Each listing should contain only the records belonging to a particular department from the EMPLOYEE database file, the total for the gross pay, total deductions, and net pay for each department, and the final total for these fields for all company employees.

Input File(s) The EMPLOYEE database file, whose structure is shown in Figure 4.34, is used as an input file. The listing of the data records in ascending order on the DEPT_CODE field is given in Figure 7.39.

Output Program output should be a payroll report listing by department. The format of this multiscreen report is shown in Figure 7.40(a) and (b) (see page 316). The headings should be as shown in the payroll report listing; and the detail line should consist of the SOC_SEC_NUM, EMP_NAME, GROSS_PAY, TOT_DED, and NET_PAY fields. Each department report should end with the department total line, and the next department payroll report should begin on a new screen. The final total should be on a separate screen.

Processing Steps Use the following steps to develop the solution of the program:

1. The headings should be printed as shown in the inventory report listing. The date and time should be included in the headings.
2. The column headings should be enclosed between the two lines, as shown in Figure 7.40.
3. The EMPLOYEE database file should be sorted in the ascending order of DEPT_CODE and stored in the EMPDSORT database file.
4. The program should calculate the net pay for each employee in the EMPDSORT database file by subtracting the total deductions (TOT_DED) from the gross pay (GROSS_PAY). The gross-pay is obtained by adding REG_PAY and OTIME _PAY fields, and the total deductions by adding the federal tax (FED_TAX), state tax (ST_TAX), city tax (SC_TAX), and local tax (L_TAX) fields.
5. The gross pay (GROSS_PAY), total deductions (TOT_DED), and net pay (NET_PAY) fields for all the records of the EMPDSORT database file belonging to a particular department should be accumulated in the DGROSS_PAY, DTOT_DED, and DNET_PAY memory variables. The com-

pany total should be accumulated in the FGROSS_PAY, FTOT_DED, and FNET_PAY memory variables.

6. The GROSS_PAY, TOT_DED, DGROSS_PAY, DTOT_DED, DNET_PAY, FGROSS_PAY, FTOT_DED, and FNET_PAY memory variables, and any other constants used in the program, should be loaded from the memory file PAY34.MEM.

7. Detail lines should not be printed past row 20.

8. Each department payroll listing should start on a new screen and end with its departmental total line.

9. When the screen is full or the department and/or final totals have been printed, the screen should be frozen to allow the user to view the output.

10. Print the final payroll totals on a separate screen.

11. At the end of the output report, print the message "*** --- END OF REPORT --- ***" to indicate the end of the output report. Then freeze the screen to allow the user to view the output.

12. The whole output should be enclosed in a box, as shown in Figure 7.40.

```
Record #  SOC_SC_NUM    EMP_NAME              DEPT_CODE  PAY_CODE  M_STATUS  N_DEP  REG_PAY  OVT_PAY
      1   215-67-9802   John W. Mussick           101       70         1       0    329.64     0.00
      2   063-77-5151   Suzy P. Chapstick         101       90         1       0    685.60    90.02
      3   082-69-7021   Harvey S. Wallbanger      101       69         2       3    540.00     0.00
      4   102-50-6099   Scott N. Sichak           101       49         2       5    573.50     0.00
      5   111-21-7942   Carol J. Ungrahe          101       57         2       2    660.00   160.94
      6   123-56-9042   Debbie E. Stamper         101       43         1       0    600.00     0.00
      7   021-67-9201   Bill K. Whitkar           101       17         1       0    420.00     0.00
      8   273-46-9884   Paul L. McCartney         102       41         1       0    476.37    53.35
      9   288-74-7667   John A. Dilenger          102       29         2      15      0.00     0.00
     10   345-67-8912   Sherrill P. Milnes        102       52         4       4    627.90     0.00
     11   364-89-1212   Bernardo A Garcia         102       17         2       1    420.00    78.80
     12   372-64-8984   Christine D. Lippman      102       69         2       2    405.00     0.00
     13   415-00-6501   Roger B. Abernathy        102       57         3      13      0.00     0.00
     14   452-67-9235   Plins C. Designori        102       49         1       0    507.50     0.00
     15   491-64-8338   Malcome E. Smyth          103       43         1       0    600.00     0.00
     16   505-62-9001   David H. Vanderpool       103       90         1       0    685.60    64.30
     17   506-92-3447   Lisa W. Smerhuriski       103       70         2       3    393.60    14.76
     18   572-67-3924   Vicki M. Lawerence        103       29         5       4      0.00     0.00
     19   689-11-0020   Benson I. Dubois          103       17         1       0    420.00     0.00
     20   645-89-1357   Tommy T. Tutone           103       41         2       3    483.48     0.00
     21   675-93-2739   Jessica N. Lange          103       52         2       4    644.00    72.48
     22   777-01-1919   Tonya T. Peace            104       69         3      12      0.00     0.00
     23   783-92-1065   Julie A. Andrew           104       43         2       3    600.00     0.00
     24   800-47-9911   Peter J. Benatar          104       49         2       5    620.00   139.56
     25   867-00-5309   Alexander R. Haig         104       90         1       0    565.62     0.00
     26   891-01-3079   Donna S. Saylor           104       57         1       0    660.00     0.00
     27   916-14-8736   George W. London          104       41         1       0    568.80    21.34
     28   942-78-8210   Sara L. Berhart           104       70         2       4    354.24     0.00
     29   987-65-4321   Linda G. Holbrook         104       52         2       3    644.00    84.56
     30   601-62-1115   Herb F. Tarleck           105       24         2       2    500.00     0.00
```

Figure 7.39 Listing of the EMPLOYEE database file in the ascending order of DEPT_CODE

FED_TAX	ST_TAX	SC_TAX	L_TAX	YTD_GPAY	YTD_FTAX	YTD_STAX	YTD_CTAX	YTD_LTAX
55.49	1.44	21.59	6.59	2307.48	388.43	10.08	151.13	46.13
177.47	8.89	50.80	15.51	5429.34	1242.29	62.23	355.60	108.57
72.76	4.30	35.37	10.80	3780.00	509.32	30.10	247.59	75.60
73.56	4.97	37.56	11.47	4014.50	514.92	34.79	262.92	80.29
148.70	10.02	53.77	16.42	5746.58	1040.90	70.14	376.39	114.94
120.60	4.50	39.30	12.00	4200.00	844.20	31.50	275.10	84.00
75.17	2.80	27.51	8.40	2940.00	526.19	19.60	192.57	58.80
100.65	4.09	34.70	10.59	3708.04	704.55	28.63	242.90	74.13
0.00	0.00	0.00	0.00	0.00	446.46	0.00	0.00	0.00
88.56	5.20	41.13	12.56	4395.30	619.92	36.40	287.91	87.92
70.65	3.48	32.67	9.98	3491.60	494.55	24.36	228.69	69.86
52.25	2.58	26.53	8.10	2835.00	365.75	18.06	185.71	56.70
0.00	0.00	0.00	0.00	0.00	701.26	0.00	0.00	0.00
94.87	3.65	33.24	10.15	3552.50	664.09	25.55	232.68	71.05
120.60	4.50	39.30	12.00	4200.00	844.20	31.50	275.10	84.00
168.47	8.25	49.12	15.00	5249.30	1179.29	57.75	343.84	105.00
21.15	2.63	26.75	8.17	2858.52	148.05	18.41	187.25	57.19
0.00	0.00	0.00	0.00	0.00	425.25	0.00	0.00	0.00
75.17	2.80	27.51	8.40	2940.00	526.19	19.60	192.57	58.80
63.15	3.17	31.67	9.67	3384.36	442.05	22.19	221.69	67.69
110.70	7.41	46.93	14.33	5015.36	774.90	51.87	328.51	100.31
0.00	0.00	0.00	0.00	0.00	320.32	0.00	0.00	0.00
85.18	4.50	39.30	12.00	4200.00	596.26	31.50	275.10	84.00
117.37	8.49	49.75	15.19	5316.92	821.59	59.43	348.25	106.33
110.29	4.81	37.05	11.31	3959.34	772.03	33.67	259.35	79.16
138.60	6.00	43.23	13.20	4620.00	970.20	42.00	302.61	92.40
117.64	5.30	38.65	11.80	4130.98	823.48	37.10	270.55	82.60
37.25	1.81	23.20	7.08	2479.68	260.75	12.67	162.40	49.56
117.32	7.71	47.72	14.57	5099.92	821.24	53.97	334.04	101.99
68.40	3.50	32.75	10.00	3500.00	478.80	24.50	229.25	70.00

Figure 7.39 Continued

```
╔══════════════════════════════════════════════════════════════════╗
║              AMERICAN SUPPLY COMPANY                             ║
║  08/27/89        PAYROLL REPORT                       14:09:48   ║
║              LISTINGS BY DEPARTMENTS                             ║
╠══════════════════════════════════════════════════════════════════╣
║   SOC SEC                              GROSS     TOTAL      NET  ║
║   NUMBER     EMPLOYEE NAME              PAY   DEDUCTIONS    PAY  ║
╟──────────────────────────────────────────────────────────────────╢
║  XXXXXXXXX   XXXXXXXXXXXXXXXXXXXXXX   99,999.99  9,999.99  99,999.99 ║
║  XXXXXXXXX   XXXXXXXXXXXXXXXXXXXXXX   99,999.99  9,999.99  99,999.99 ║
║                                                                  ║
║              TOTAL FOR DEPT # 101    $99,999.99 $9,999.99 $99,999.99 ║
║                                                                  ║
╠══════════════════════════════════════════════════════════════════╣
║              PRESS ANY KEY TO CONTINUE . . . ▮                   ║
╚══════════════════════════════════════════════════════════════════╝
```

(a)

```
╔══════════════════════════════════════════════════════════════════╗
║              AMERICAN SUPPLY COMPANY                             ║
║  08/27/89        PAYROLL REPORT                       14:09:48   ║
║              LISTINGS BY DEPARTMENTS                             ║
╠══════════════════════════════════════════════════════════════════╣
║   SOC SEC                              GROSS     TOTAL      NET  ║
║   NUMBER     EMPLOYEE NAME              PAY   DEDUCTIONS    PAY  ║
╟──────────────────────────────────────────────────────────────────╢
║                                                                  ║
║              FINAL TOTALS         $999,999.99 $999,999.99 $999,999.99 ║
║                                                                  ║
║              ***  ---  END OF REPORT  ---  ***                   ║
║                                                                  ║
╠══════════════════════════════════════════════════════════════════╣
║              PRESS ANY KEY TO CONTINUE . . . ▮                   ║
╚══════════════════════════════════════════════════════════════════╝
```

(b)

Figure 7.40 Payroll report listing: Programming Assignment 7B

Chapter 8

Case Structure and Menu Driven Program

LEARNING OBJECTIVES

Upon successfully completing this chapter, you will be able to:

1. Use the IF-ENDIF command, which is the partial version of the IF-ELSE-ENDIF command.
2. Use the full version of the IF-ELSE-ENDIF command.
3. Use the nested IF-ELSE-ENDIF command.
4. Explain the concept of a case control structure.
5. Use the DO CASE-ENDCASE command.
6. Analyze, design, and code any menu program that will display a menu with different processing options, accept a valid value for the selection from the user, and execute the associated processing function.

8.1 Overview

The partial format IF-ENDIF of the IF-ELSE-ENDIF command was introduced in Chapter 3. This format is used with the selection control structure with only one option available, which can be selected or not, depending on the selection criteria. The full version of the IF-ELSE-ENDIF command was used in Chapter 6. This version is used with the selection control structure with two options available, depending on the selection criteria.

This chapter introduces the concept of the nested IF-ELSE-ENDIF command. The nesting of this command is required when it is necessary to test a condition only after testing a previous condition regardless of the result of the first testing. The nested IF-ELSE-ENDIF command is also used with the selection control structure in which more than two possible options are available and only one is to be selected, depending on the selection criteria.

This type of situation arises in the menu program in which several processing options are made available to the user, and the user selects one. Depending on the selection, the function associated with the selected option is processed. When the number of possible options becomes large, the level of nesting, which is directly proportional to the number of options available, increases, making the coding more complex.

The dBASE command DO CASE-ENDCASE is used with the case control structure, which is an extension of the selection control structure. When there are more than three options available in the selection control structure, it is termed a case control structure. The chapter ends with the complete solution of a menu program using the program development process.

8.2 The IF-ELSE-ENDIF Command Revisited

You were introduced to the decision-making command IF-ELSE-ENDIF in section 3.2.8. This command provides a means for selecting one out of two given choices. The general format of this command is

```
IF <condition>
   <commands set I>
[ELSE
   <commands set II>]
ENDIF
```

where <condition> is a dBASE logical expression, <commands set I> and <commands set II> are a set of any number of dBASE IV commands, ELSE is an optional part of the command, and ENDIF is the required command to end the IF command structure.

If the <condition> is true, <commands set I> is executed; if the <condition> is false, <commands set II> is executed. This process selects one of the two sets of commands, depending on whether the <condition> is true or not. This possibility is further discussed in section 8.2.2.

There are two other possible situations. The first is when there are no commands in the <commands set II>; that is, there are no commands between the ELSE and ENDIF parts of the IF-ELSE-ENDIF command. In this situation, the ELSE part can be omitted, and the command reduces to:

```
IF <condition>
   <commands set I>
ENDIF
```

In this situation, the <commands set I> is executed when the <condition> is true, and no action is taken if the <condition> is false. This is referred to as the IF-ENDIF format. In this case, the optional ELSE component is not present in the command.

The second situation is when there are no commands in the <commands set I>; that is, there are no commands between the IF and

ELSE parts of the IF-ELSE-ENDIF command. In this situation, the IF-ELSE-ENDIF command will reduce to:

```
IF <condition>
ELSE
   <commands set II>
ENDIF
```

In this case, the <commands set II> will be executed when the <condition> is false, and no action is taken if it is true. But this format can be reduced to the IF-ENDIF format by negating the <condition>. For example, if a late fee is charged for payment received after the due date, this can be represented as shown:

```
IF DATE_PAID <= DUE_DATE
ELSE
    CALCULATE LATE_CHARGE
ENDIF
```

This format means that if the payment is received on or before the due date, no action is needed. But if the payment is not received on or before the due date, then the late charge is calculated. This situation can also be represented in another form:

```
IF .NOT. (DATE_PAID <= DUE_DATE)
    CALCULATE LATE_CHARGE
ENDIF
```

Both forms will produce identical results. But the one in which there are no commands between the IF and ELSE parts of the command, that is, in which no action is taken when the <condition> is true, is not recommended. You can negate the <condition> and use the IF-ENDIF format as demonstrated in the previous example.

When there are no commands in either the <commands set I> or the <commands set II>, the situation can be represented by the IF-ENDIF command.

8.2.1 The IF-ENDIF Command

The general format of the IF-ENDIF command is

```
IF <condition>
    <commands set>
ENDIF
```

where <condition> is a dBASE logical expression, <commands set> is a set of any number of dBASE IV commands, and ENDIF is the required command to end the IF command structure.

If the <condition> is true, then the <commands set> is executed; if the <condition> is false, no action is taken. Therefore, no commands are executed. In other words, you are given only one choice, which you can accept or reject. This situation is also represented by the selection control structure given in Figure 8.1. There is only one module under SELECT of this selection control structure. In this situation, module 2.1.1 Process Step A is either selected or not, depending on the selection criteria. When the IF-ENDIF command is applied to this type of selection control structure, the following coding is produced:

```
IF <condition>
    Process Step A
ENDIF
```

We have already used this form of the selection control structure in Case Study 1 (Chapter 4). The selection control structure for it, which is part of Figure 4.12, is given in Figure 8.2. In this example, if the <condition> UNIT_COST > 10 for the record in question is true, then module 2.1.1 Print Detail Line will be selected, thus printing the record and incrementing the line count. But if the <condition> is not true, the record will not be printed; and the line count will not be increased. In other words, the function of the selection control structure of Figure 8.2 is to select and print only those records of the database file for which the value of the UNIT_COST field is greater than $10.

The pseudocode for the structure chart of Figure 8.2 is given in Figure 8.3.

The coding using the IF-ENDIF command and the internal documentation are shown in Figure 8.4.

The format IF-ENDIF of the IF-ELSE-ENDIF command is used with the selection control structure with only one option available, which can be selected or rejected, depending on the selection criteria.

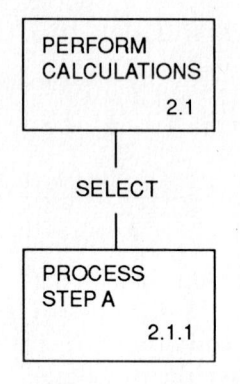

Figure 8.1 Selection control structure with only one choice

8.2.2 The IF-ELSE-ENDIF Command

The general format of the full version of the IF-ELSE-ENDIF command is shown in section 8.2. The full version of the IF-ELSE-ENDIF command is used to select one of the two given options. This selection method is also represented by the selection control structure given in Figure 8.5.

There are two modules under SELECT of this selection control structure. In this situation, either module 2.1.1 Process Step A or module 2.1.2 Process Step B is selected, depending on the selection criteria. When the IF-ELSE-ENDIF command is applied to this type of selection control structure, the following coding is produced:

```
IF <condition>
    Process Step A
ELSE
    Process Step B
ENDIF
```

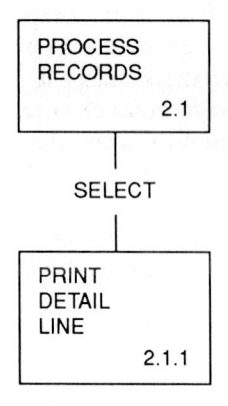

Figure 8.2 Selection control structure part of Case Study 1

```
2.1 PROCESS RECORDS
    SELECT: Records with unit price more than $10.00
        2.1.1 PRINT DETAIL LINE
            PRINT A LINE
                Write Detail LIne
            INCREMENT LINE COUNTER
                Add 1 to the Line Counter
    END SELECT
```

Figure 8.3 Pseudocode for structure chart of Figure 8.2

Figure 8.4 Coding for structure chart of Figure 8.2

```
*** 2.1 PROCESS RECORDS ***
   *
   IF UNIT_COST > 10
      *
      *** 2.1.1 PRINT DETAIL LINE ***
         *
         *** PRINT A LINE ***
            *
            @ LINECNT,14 SAY ITEM_NUM
            @ LINECNT,23 SAY ITEM_DESC
            @ LINECNT,54 SAY QUANTITY
            @ LINECNT,63 SAY UNIT_COST
            *
         *** INCREMENT LINE COUNT ***
            *
            LINECNT = LINECNT + 1
            *
   ENDIF   UNIT_COST > 10
```

We have already used this form of the selection control structure in Case Study 3 (Chapter 6). The selection control structure for it, which is part of Figure 6.24, is given in Figure 8.6.

In the previous example, if the <condition> UNIT_COST < 100 for the record in question is true, then module 2.1.1 Items with Unit Cost < $100 is executed. This module calculates and replaces the retail price of the items representing the record in question. The retail price is determined by multiplying the UNIT_COST field by the markup factor MARK_UP1. But if the <condition> is false, then module 2.1.2 Items with Unit Cost > OR = $100 is executed. This command also calculates and replaces the retail price of the item representing the record in question. The retail price in this case is evaluated by multiplying the UNIT_COST field by the markup factor MARK_UP2.

In other words, the format of the selection control structure of Figure 8.6 is used to select one module out of the two given. It then calculates and

Figure 8.5 Selection control structure with two choices

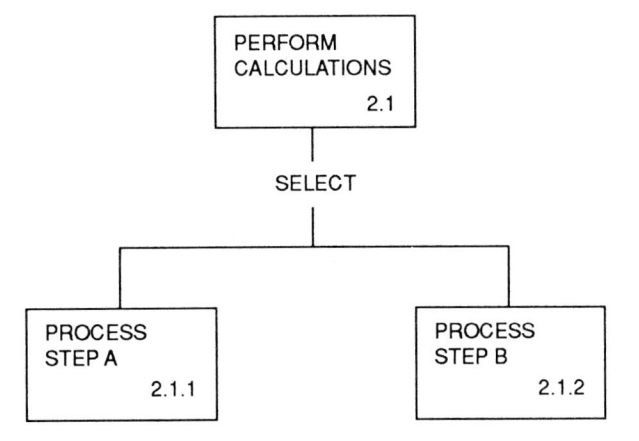

Figure 8.6 Selection control structure part of Case Study 3

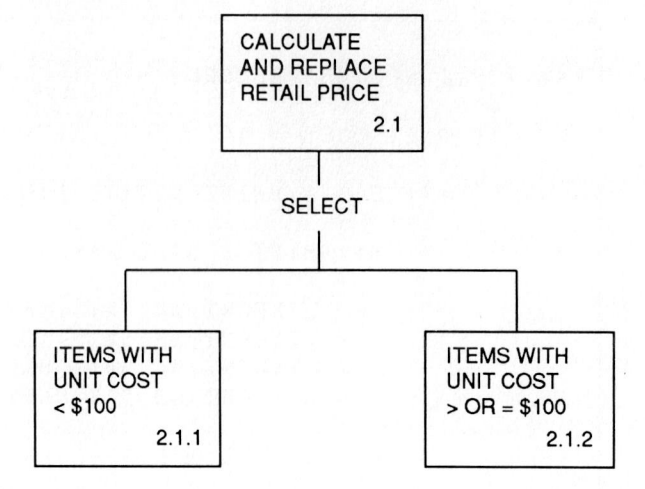

```
          ┌─────────────┐
          │  CALCULATE  │
          │ AND REPLACE │
          │ RETAIL PRICE│
          │         2.1 │
          └──────┬──────┘
                 │
               SELECT
          ┌──────┴──────┐
  ┌───────┴────┐   ┌────┴───────┐
  │ ITEMS WITH │   │ ITEMS WITH │
  │ UNIT COST  │   │ UNIT COST  │
  │  < $100    │   │ > OR = $100│
  │      2.1.1 │   │      2.1.2 │
  └────────────┘   └────────────┘
```

replaces the retail price of the item, depending on the criteria of the <condition>, that is, whether the unit cost of the item is less than $100 or not.

The pseudocode for the structure chart of Figure 8.6 is given in Figure 8.7.

The coding using the IF-ENDIF command and the internal documentation are shown in Figure 8.8.

The two formats of the IF-ELSE-ENDIF command discussed in sections 8.2.1 and 8.2.2 deal with the selection of one option out of those available in the selection control structure. The IF-ENDIF format was used in a situation where the selection control structure had only one possible option available, and it could either select or reject this option, depending on the selection criteria. The full version of the IF-ELSE-ENDIF format was used in a situation where the selection control structure had two possible options available, and it could select either one of these, depending on the selection criteria. But what if you have a situation in which you have more than two possible options available in the selection control structure, and you want to select only one, depending on the selection criteria? To handle this situation, you'll need the nested form of the IF-ELSE-ENDIF command.

Figure 8.7 Pseudocode for structure chart of Figure 8.6

2.1 CALCULATE AND REPLACE RETAIL PRICE
    SELECT: Items with Unit price compared with $100.00
        2.1.1 ITEMS WITH UNIT COST < $100
            Replace Retail price with the product of
            Unit cost and Mark up1
        2.1.2 ITEMS WITH UNIT COST > OR = $100
            Replace Retail price with the product of
            Unit cost and Mark up2
    END SELECT

```
*** 2.1 CALCULATE AND REPLACE RETAIL PRICE ***
   *
   IF UNIT_COST < 100
      *
      *** 2.1.1 ITEMS WITH UNIT COST < $100 ***
         *
         REPLACE RET_PRICE WITH UNIT_COST * MARK_UP1
         *
   ELSE
      *
      *** 2.1.2 ITEMS WITH UNIT COST > OR = $100 ***
         *
         REPLACE RET_PRICE WITH UNIT_COST * MARK_UP2
         *
   ENDIF UNIT_COST < 100
   *
```

Figure 8.8 Coding for structure chart of Figure 8.6

8.2.3 The Nested IF-ELSE-ENDIF Command

The general format of the nested IF-ELSE-ENDIF command is

```
IF <condition 1>
   IF <condition 2>
      Process Step 1
   ELSE
      Process Step 2
   ENDIF
ELSE
   IF <condition 3>
      Process Step 3
   ELSE
      Process Step 4
   ENDIF
ENDIF
```

<Condition 1>, <condition 2>, and <condition 3> are logical dBASE expressions. Process Step 1, Process Step 2, Process Step 3, and Process Step 4 are a set of any number of dBASE IV commands. ELSE is an optional part of the command, and ENDIF is the required command to end the IF command structure.

In business applications, it is common to have a situation in which the first command between the IF and ELSE or ELSE and ENDIF parts of the IF-ELSE-ENDIF command is another IF-ELSE-ENDIF command. This situation arises when it is necessary to test a condition only after testing a previous condition regardless of the result of the first testing (either true or false). To code such a situation, the IF-ELSE-ENDIF command is nested or included between the IF and ELSE or ELSE and ENDIF parts of the outer IF-ELSE-ENDIF command. The structure chart representing the nested IF-ELSE-ENDIF command is shown in Figure 8.9.

Figure 8.9 Structure chart representing nested IF-ELSE-ENDIF structure

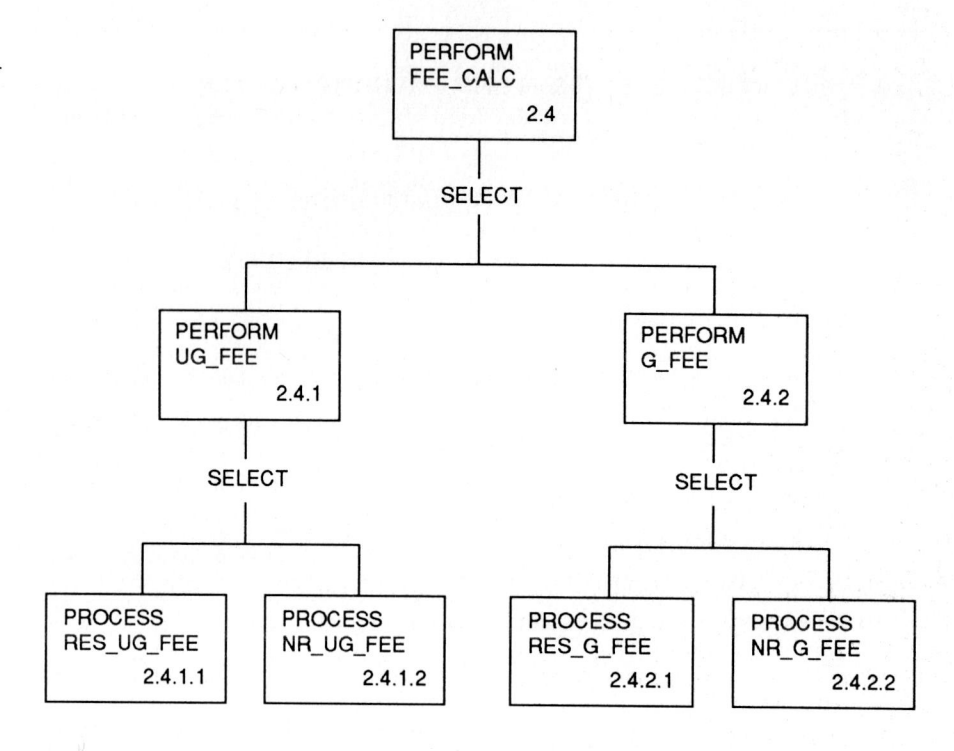

```
                    PERFORM
                    FEE_CALC
                         2.4
                         |
                      SELECT
              _____|_____
             |                       |
         PERFORM                 PERFORM
         UG_FEE                  G_FEE
            2.4.1                  2.4.2
             |                      |
          SELECT                 SELECT
         ____|____              ____|____
        |         |            |         |
     PROCESS   PROCESS      PROCESS   PROCESS
     RES_UG_   NR_UG_       RES_G_    NR_G_
     FEE       FEE          FEE       FEE
     2.4.1.1   2.4.1.2      2.4.2.1   2.4.2.2
```

The pseudocode for the structure chart of Figure 8.9 is given in Figure 8.10.

This example illustrates the steps needed to calculate a student's fee depending on his or her status (graduate or undergraduate) and place of residence. The first test is made when module 2.4 Perform FEE_CALC is executed to calculate the student's fee. This test determines whether the student is an undergraduate or a graduate student.

The second test is made to determine the student's residency status. If the student is an undergraduate, module 2.4.1 Perform UG_FEE is executed. If the student is a resident, then module 2.4.1.1 Process RES_UG_FEE is executed to calculate the resident undergraduate fee. But if the student is a nonresident, then module 2.4.1.2 Process NR_UG_FEE is executed to calculate the nonresident undergraduate fee. If this is a graduate student, module 2.4.2 Perform G_FEE is executed. Further, if the student is a resident, then module 2.4.2.1 Process RES_G_FEE is executed to calculate the resident graduate fee. But if the student is a nonresident, then module 2.4.2.2 Process NR_G_FEE is executed to calculate the nonresident graduate fee.

The coding using the IF-ELSE-ENDIF command and the internal documentation are shown in Figure 8.11.

These examples deal with the first level of nesting; that is, the IF-ELSE-ENDIF command is nested in another IF-ELSE-ENDIF command. But this process of nesting can continue for more than one level, giving rise to second, third, and higher levels of nesting.

As mentioned earlier, the nested IF-ELSE-ENDIF command is also used with the selection control structure in which more than two possible options are available and one option is to be selected, depending on the selection criteria. For example, consider the selection control structure

Figure 8.10 Pseudocode for structure chart of Figure 8.9

```
2.4 PERFORM FEE_CALC
    SELECT: Depending on student's undergraduate or graduate status
        2.4.1 PERFORM UG_FEE
            SELECT: Depending on student's residency status
                2.4.1.1 PROCESS RES_UG_FEE
                    Calculate the resident undergraduate fee
                2.4.1.2 PROCESS NR_UG_FEE
                    Calculate the nonresident undergraduate fee
            ENDSELECT
        2.4.2 PERFORM G_FEE
            SELECT: Depending on student's residency status
                2.4.2.1 PROCESS RES_G_FEE
                    Calculate the resident graduate fee
                2.4.2.2 PROCESS NR_G_FEE
                    Calculate the nonresident graduate fee
            ENDSELECT
    END SELECT
```

shown in Figure 8.12, with four modules out of which one is to be executed, depending on the user's selection. The function performed by module 2.5 Process Selection is typical of a **menu program.** In a menu program, several different processing options are made available to the user. Depending on which the user selects, the program performs the particular processing associated with the selection.

The processing of a menu program consists of the following tasks:

1. A menu with several choices in it is presented to the user.
2. The user selects one of the available choices.
3. The process reflecting the user's choice is performed.

Processing a choice usually involves executing another program, which either performs certain processing functions or presents another menu.

The selection control structure presented in Figure 8.12 is part of a menu program that presents four different options, accepts valid input from the user, and then depending on the user's selection, performs the associated processing function. The four possible functions are modules 2.5.1 Process Selection 1, 2.5.2 Process Selection 2, 2.5.3 Process Selection 3, and 2.5.4 Process Selection 4.

In this example, processing a selection involves executing programs INV31 (Case Study 1), INV32 (Case Study 2), INV33 (Case Study 3), and INV34 (Case Study 4), which have already been developed in previous chapters.

The pseudocode for the structure chart of Figure 8.12 is given in Figure 8.13.

Figure 8.11 Coding for structure chart of Figure 8.9

```
*** 2.4 PERFORM FEE_CALC ***
   *
   IF STUD_STAT = 'UG'
      *
      *** 2.4.1 PERFORM UG_FEE ***
         *
         IF STUD_RES = 'R'
            *
            *** 2.4.1.1 PROCESS RES_UG_FEE ***
            *
            PROCESS RES_UG_FEE ROUTINE
            *
         ELSE
            *
            *** 2.4.1.2 PROCESS NR_UG_FEE ***
            *
            PROCESS NR_UG_FEE ROUTINE
            *
         ENDIF
         *
   ELSE
      *
      *** 2.4.2 PERFORM G_FEE ***
         *
         IF STUD_RES = 'R'
            *
            *** 2.4.2.1 PROCESS RES_G_FEE ***
            *
            *PROCESS RES_G_FEE ROUTINE
            *
         ELSE
            *
            *** 2.4.2.2 PROCESS NR_G_FEE ***
            *
            PROCESS NR_G_FEE ROUTINE
            *
         ENDIF
         *
   ENDIF
```

The coding using the nested IF-ELSE-ENDIF command and the internal documentation are shown in Figure 8.14.

When module 2.5 Process Selection is executed, it tests for the value of the variable CHOICE. If its value is equal to one, the instructions contained between the IF and ELSE commands will be executed. In other words, the module 2.5.1 Process Selection 1 is processed and executes the program INV31. But if the value of the variable CHOICE is not equal to one, then the instructions contained between the ELSE and ENDIF commands will be performed. The first command in this is another IF-ELSE-ENDIF command, which is nested between the outer IF-ELSE-ENDIF commands. It tests for the value of the variable CHOICE. If its value is equal to two, then module 2.5.2 Process Selection 2 is processed

Figure 8.12 Selection control structure with four choices

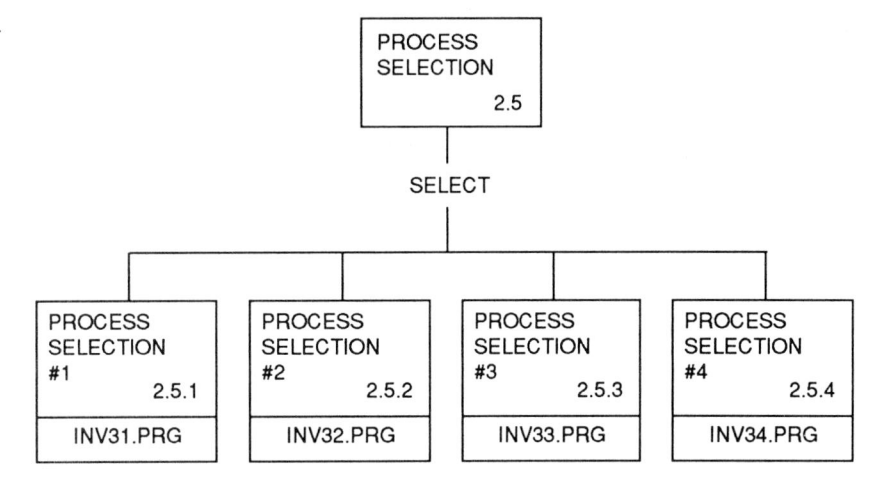

```
                    PROCESS
                   SELECTION
                         2.5
                          |
                       SELECT
    ┌─────────────┬──────┴──────┬─────────────┐
 PROCESS       PROCESS       PROCESS       PROCESS
 SELECTION     SELECTION     SELECTION     SELECTION
    #1            #2            #3            #4
       2.5.1         2.5.2         2.5.3         2.5.4
 INV31.PRG     INV32.PRG     INV33.PRG     INV34.PRG
```

and executes the program INV32. But if the value of the variable CHOICE is not equal to two, then the ELSE part of the nested IF-ELSE-ENDIF command will be executed. This part tests for the value of the variable CHOICE to see if it is equal to three. This process continues until all possible values of the variable CHOICE have been tested.

In this example, there are only four possible values of the variable CHOICE; thus, it has three levels of nesting of the IF-ELSE-ENDIF command. But if there are more possible values, the level of nesting will increase, thus increasing the complexity and readability of the coding.

8.2.4 The Case Control Structure

Chapter 4 stated that only three control structures (sequence, repeat, and selection) are needed for the solution of any programming problem. But the previously discussed example indicates that when there are several possible options available in a selection control structure, its coding becomes complex and difficult and complicated to read and understand.

In such cases, a fourth control structure, which is an extension of the selection control structure, should be used. Called **case control structure,** this is actually a selection control structure with more than three possible options. In dBASE programming, a command is available for this structure: the DO CASE-ENDCASE command.

Figure 8.13 Pseudocode for structure chart of Figure 8.12

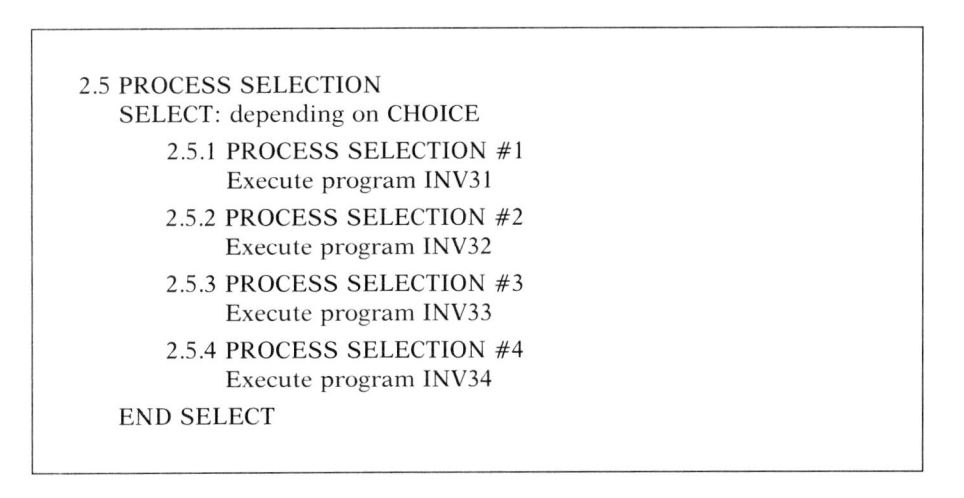

```
2.5 PROCESS SELECTION
    SELECT: depending on CHOICE
        2.5.1 PROCESS SELECTION #1
            Execute program INV31
        2.5.2 PROCESS SELECTION #2
            Execute program INV32
        2.5.3 PROCESS SELECTION #3
            Execute program INV33
        2.5.4 PROCESS SELECTION #4
            Execute program INV34
    END SELECT
```

Figure 8.14 Coding for selection control structure of Figure 8.12 using nested IF-ELSE-ENDIF commands

```
*** 2.5 PROCESS SELECTION ***
*
IF CHOICE = 1
   *
   *** 2.5.1 PROCESS SELECTION #1 ***
      *
      DO INV31
      *
ELSE
   *
   IF CHOICE = 2
      *
      *** 2.5.2 PROCESS SELECTION #2 ***
         *
         DO INV32
         *
      ELSE
         *
         IF CHOICE = 3
            *
            *** 2.5.3 PROCESS SELECTION #3 ***
               *
               DO INV33
               *
            ELSE
               *
               IF CHOICE = 4
                  *
                  *** 2.5.4 PROCESS SELECTION #4 ***
                     *
                     DO INV34
                     *
                  ENDIF CHOICE = 4
                  *
            ENDIF CHOICE = 3
            *
      ENDIF CHOICE = 2
   *
ENDIF CHOICE = 1
```

The DO CASE-ENDCASE Command

The general format of the DO CASE-ENDCASE command is

```
DO CASE
   CASE <condition 1>
        <commands set 1>
   [CASE <condition 2>
        <commands set 2>
      .
      .
      .]
```

```
        [OTHERWISE
                <commands set>]
        ENDCASE
```

where <condition 1>, <condition 2>, . . . and <condition N> are dBASE logical expressions. <Commands set 1>, <commands set 2>, . . . and <commands set> are a set of any number of dBASE IV commands. The DO CASE and ENDCASE commands must always be used in pairs. The DO CASE command marks the beginning and the ENDCASE command marks the end of a case control structure. There can be any number of CASE commands between these. The OTHERWISE command is optional.

The DO CASE-ENDCASE command is normally used with the case control structure. Each of the CASE commands between the DO CASE and ENDCASE commands is evaluated until one is determined to be true. Then dBASE executes all the commands between this CASE command and the next CASE command; that is, the command set associated with the CASE command evaluated to be true is executed. The command sets used in the DO CASE-ENDCASE command are usually other dBASE programs. After execution of the command set associated with the CASE command, which was evaluated to be true, dBASE skips all remaining CASE commands up to ENDCASE and transfers control of the program to the first command after the ENDCASE command. This means that the CASE commands in the DO CASE-ENDCASE command are mutually exclusive.

If none of the CASE commands is true, then the command listed between the optional OTHERWISE command and the ENDCASE command is executed. If the optional OTHERWISE command is not present, then control is transferred to the first command after the ENDCASE command.

The coding for the selection control structure of Figure 8.12, translated from the pseudocode of Figure 8.13, using the DO CASE-ENDCASE command, is given in Figure 8.15. Compare the coding of Figures 8.14 and 8.15. The coding of Figure 8.15 is much simpler and easier to read and understand than that of Figure 8.14.

8.3 An Illustrative Example: Case Study 5

Program Description

Write a report generating submenu program for the American Supply Company. It should display the report generating menu consisting of different options available and instructions for the users as shown in Figure 8.16. It should accept valid input from the user and then, depending on the user's selection, execute the processing function associated with the selection.

Processing Steps

Use the following processing steps to develop the solution of the program:

1. The menu screen, consisting of five options and instructions for the user as shown in Figure 8.16, should be displayed.

Figure 8.15 Coding for case control structure of Figure 8.12 using the DO CASE-ENDCASE command

```
*** 2.5 PROCESS SELECTION ***
*
DO CASE
   *
   *** 2.5.1 PROCESS SELECTION #1 ***
      *
      CASE CHOICE = 1
      DO INV31
      *
   *** 2.5.2 PROCESS SELECTION #2 ***
      *
      CASE CHOICE = 2
      DO INV32
      *
   *** 2.5.3 PROCESS SELECTION #3 ***
      *
      CASE CHOICE = 3
      DO INV33
      *
   *** 2.5.4 PROCESS SELECTION #4 ***
      *
      CASE CHOICE = 4
      DO INV34
      *
ENDCASE
```

2. The screen should be frozen (paused) until the user selects one of the valid options.
3. After the user's selection, the processing function associated with the selection should be executed as follows:
    a. For the first selection, Case Study 1, the program INV31 (List items over $10.00) should be executed.
    b. For the second selection, Case Study 2, the program INV32 (List whole file with totals) should be executed.
    c. For the third selection, Case Study 3, the program INV33 (List whole file with retail price) should be executed.
    d. For the fourth selection, Case Study 4, the program INV34 (List whole file with control breaks) should be executed.
    e. For the the fifth selection, the program should exit back to the dBASE prompt.
4. Make the modifications needed in programs INV31.PRG, INV32.PRG, INV33.PRG, and INV34.PRG so they can be invoked and executed under the control of this (INV3.PRG) program.

The five phases of the program development process for Case Study 5 follow.

Figure 8.16 Menu screen for Case Study 5

```
                    AMERICAN SUPPLY COMPANY
    09/15/89       INVOICE GENERATING SYSTEM              11:23:57
                     REPORT GENERATING MENU



                  1. List items over $10.00
                  2. List whole file with totals
                  3. List whole file with retail price

                  4. List whole file with control breaks

                  5. Exit to dBASE




            ENTER YOUR SELECTION, PLEASE (1-5) ==>:5
```

8.3.1 The Analysis Phase

In this first step in the program development process, review and analysis of the program specifications lead to the identification of the processing steps needed to solve the problem. As with every problem, the usual housekeeping step will be needed. We will also need to define the control field required to control the loop in which the menu screen will be displayed repeatedly. The function of this control will be to exit from the loop when the user instructs it to do so. These are the only two steps needed in the initiate processing function of the solution of the problem.

The processing steps needed in the main processing function should include displaying the menu screen, accepting the user's selection, and processing the selection. These three steps should be repeated until the user wishes to terminate the program. At that point, the control should move to the terminate processing function.

In the terminate processing function, the default modes should be reset, and program control should exit to the dBASE prompt.

To sum up, you'll need the following processing steps for the solution of Case Study 5:

1. Housekeeping
2. Define control variables
3. Display menu screen
4. Accept user's selection
5. Process one of these selections:
   a. Process selection 1
   b. Process selection 2
   c. Process selection 3

d. Process selection 4
e. Process selection 5
6. Reset default modes

The first two steps should be performed only once, at the start of the program. Therefore, they belong to initiate processing. The next three steps should be performed again and again until the user indicates his or her wish by selecting choice 5 to exit to dBASE prompt. Therefore, these steps belong to main processing. The last step needs to be performed only once before terminating the execution of the program. Therefore, it belongs to terminate processing.

8.3.2 The Design Phase

The function of this step is to take the result of the problem analysis, that is, the processing steps identified in the analysis phase, and transform them into a structure chart. The shell structure chart given in Figure 8.17 is the starting point for almost any menu program.

Major Processing Steps of a Menu Program

As with the batch programs, the solution of any menu problem is also divided into three major processing steps:

1. Initiate processing
2. Main processing
3. Terminate processing

Initiate Processing The activities included in this part of the solution of the problem are the ones that occur only once, at the beginning of program processing, and are not needed anywhere else in the program. These activities include:

1. Housekeeping (changing default modes and setting procedures)
2. Define variables (declaring variables, defining program constants, defining control variables, and loading memory variables)
3. Displaying of introduction screen (needed only with the main menu)

These activities can occur in any sequence in the solution of the problem in the initiate processing function.

Main Processing Main processing consists of activities that occur repeatedly, usually once for each selection until no more selections need to be processed. The activities include:

1. Display menu screen
2. Accept user selection
3. Process selection

Figure 8.17 Shell structure chart for menu program

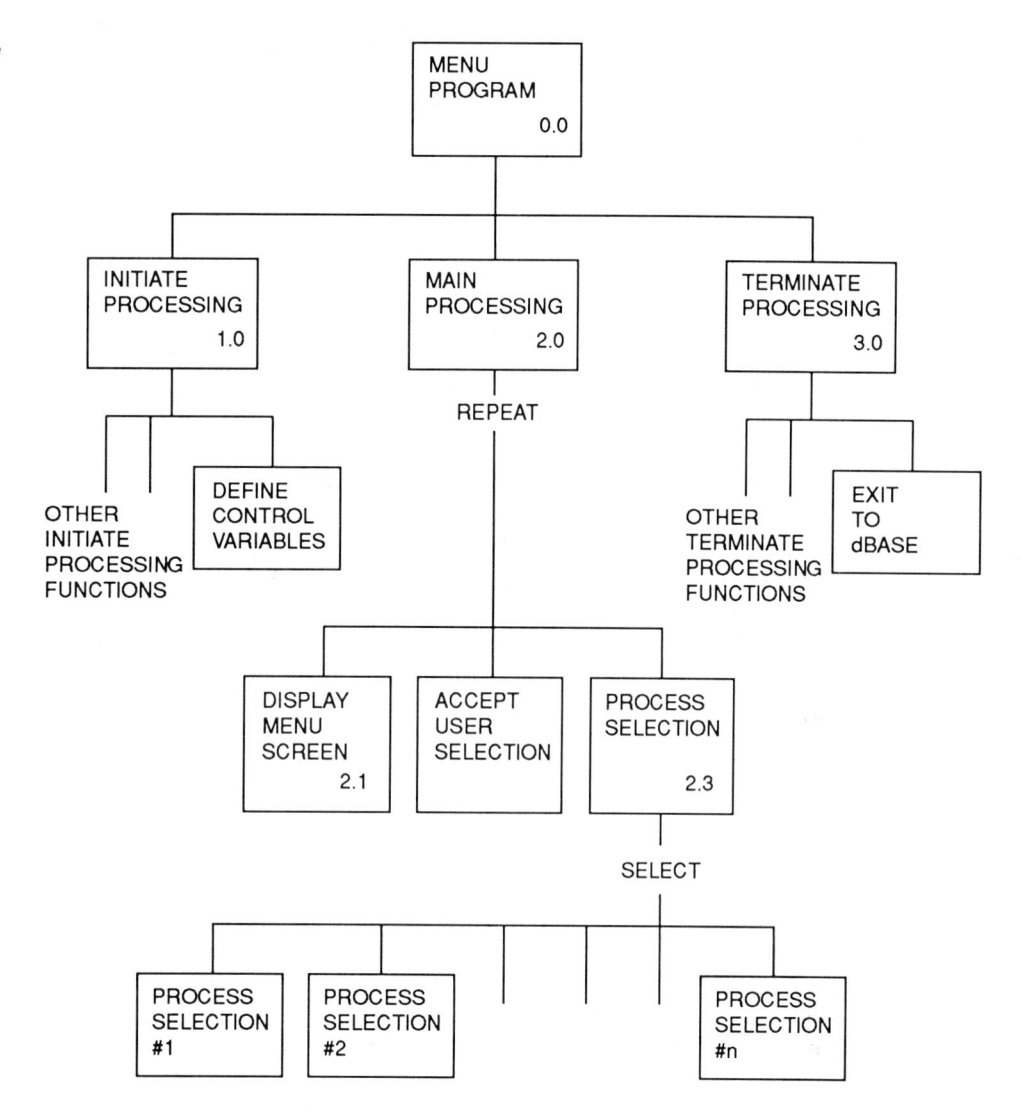

All these activities are needed in the solution of any menu problem and should be present in the same sequence as just listed.

Terminate Processing   The activities included in this part of the solution of the problem are the ones that occur only once, at the end of program processing, and are not needed anywhere else in the program. These activities include:

1. Exit to DOS or exit to dBASE or return to calling program or return to main menu
2. Reset default modes or reset procedures

These activities should occur in the same sequence as just listed.

In the solution of any problem, all the activities from each of the processing categories listed may not be needed. But if they are, they should be in the sequence listed.

Table 8.1 Processing steps needed in a menu program

Initiate Processing	1. Housekeeping: including changing default modes and setting procedures
	2. Define variables: including declaring variables, defining program constants, defining control variables, and loading memory variables
	3. Display introductory screen; needed only with the main menu
Main Processing	1. Display menu screen
	2. Accept user selection
	3. Process selection
Terminate Processing	1. Exit to DOS or exit to dBASE or return to calling program or return to main menu
	2. Reset default modes or reset procedures

The processing steps needed in the solution of a menu program are shown in Table 8.1 for future reference.

Using the shell structure chart of Figure 8.17 and the tools and techniques discussed in section 4.4.2, transform the six steps identified in the analysis phase into a structure chart for Case Study 5 as shown in Figure 8.18. All the modules in this structure chart are either functionally or highly cohesive. They are also loosely coupled. Thus, the structure chart of Figure 8.18 satisfies the three rules for designing a good structure chart: highly cohesive, loosely coupled modules with the span of control of any module no more than five. So it is a well-designed solution to Case Study 5.

8.3.3 The Detailed Design Phase

The function of this step is to take the result of the design phase, that is, the structure chart, and identify the actual computer operations required for each program function represented in it, producing the detailed solution of the problem. Using the translation of the three control structures to pseudocode as given in Figure 4.14, the screen format of Figure 8.16, and the method described in section 4.4.3 produces Figure 8.19, the structure chart of Figure 8.18 as translated to pseudocode.

In this pseudocode, there is a new step. In module 1.2 Define Control Variables, a switch named REPEAT3 is set to a value of T. It is used with the DO WHILE command in the main processing to repeatedly display the menu, accept the user's choice, and execute the associated processing function. These three steps are repeated again and again until the user wants to exit to the dBASE prompt. In that case, the user selects the fifth choice, and sets the REPEAT3 switch to the F value. This value causes the program control to exit from the DO WHILE-ENDDO loop and then execute the terminate processing.

8.3.4 The Coding Phase

The purpose of this phase in the program development process is to translate the pseudocode instructions of the solution of the program into programming language instructions. The pseudocode of Figure 8.19 is

8.3 An Illustrative Example: Case Study 5

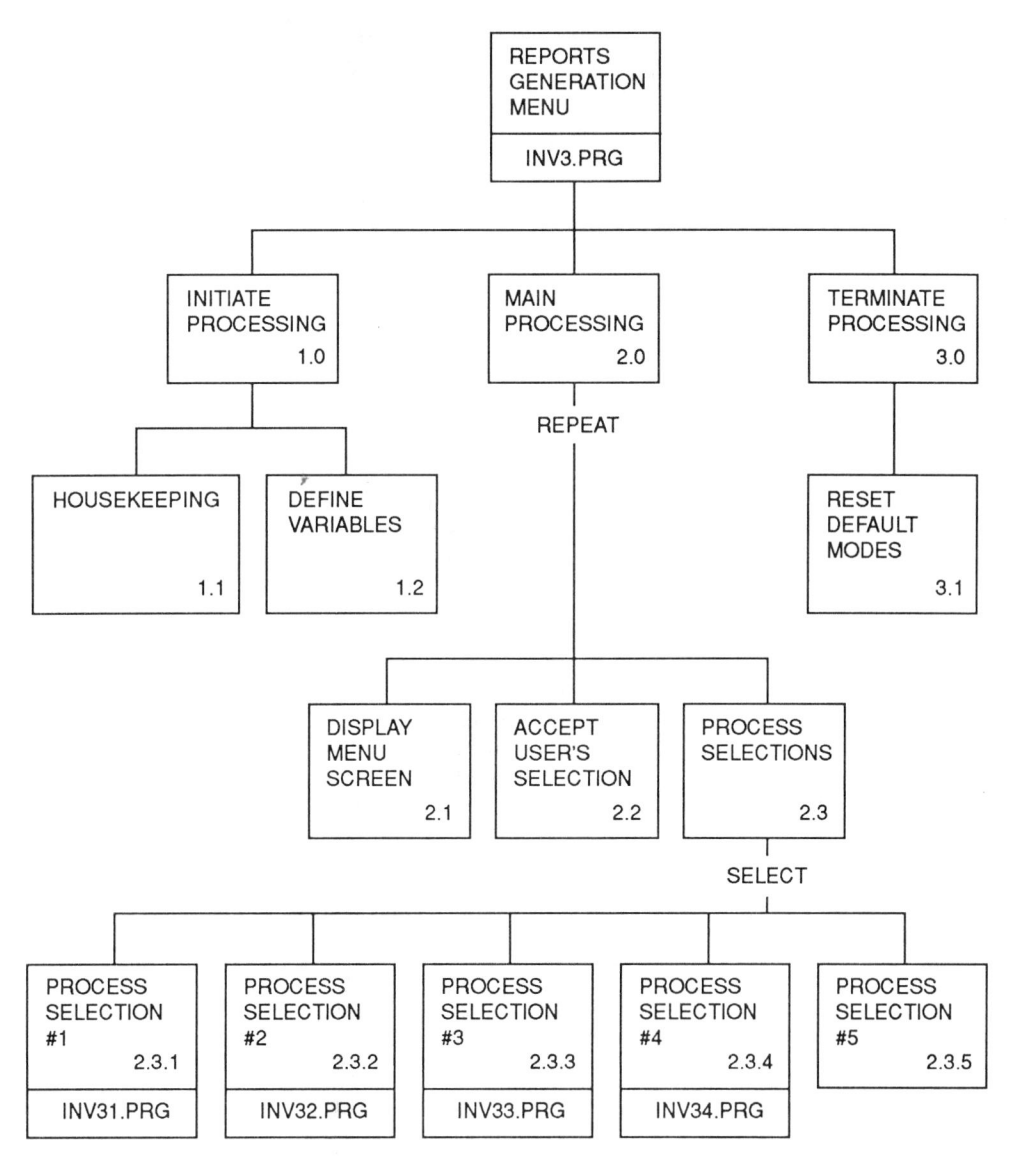

Figure 8.18 Structure chart for Case Study 5

translated into dBASE commands, and the complete program for Case Study 5 in dBASE language is given in Figure 8.20.

In this coding, there are two new concepts. One is the use of the logical variable named REPEAT3 in module 1.2 Define Control Variables. Assigned a value of T, this variable is used with the DO WHILE-ENDDO command in the main processing to repeatedly display the menu, accept the user's choice, and execute the associated processing function. These steps are repeated until the user wants to exit to the dBASE prompt, when the user selects the fifth choice, setting the REPEAT3 memory variable to F value in module 2.3.5 Process Selection 5. This setting causes the program control to exit from the DO WHILE-ENDDO loop.

The second new item used in this coding is the RANGE 1, 5 with the GET command to accept the value of the selection memory variable from

```
0.0 REPORT GENERATING MENU: INV3
    1.0 INITIATE PROCESSING
        1.1 HOUSEKEEPING
            CHANGE DEFAULT MODES
                Turn off the dBASE's heading feature
                Turn off the dBASE's user dialogue
                Turn off the dBASE's status bar
        1.2 DEFINE VARIABLES
            DEFINE CONTROL VARIABLES
                Set REPEAT3 Switch = T
    2.0 MAIN PROCESSING
        REPEAT: While the REPEAT3 switch = T
            2.1 DISPLAY MENU SCREEN
                CLEAR SCREEN
                    Clear the screen
                DISPLAY REPORT GENERATING MENU
                    Display heading #1
                    Display heading #2
                    Display heading #3
                    Display Option #1 List items over $10.00
                    Display Option #2 List whole file with Totals
                    Display Option #3 List whole file with Retail price
                    Display Option #4 List whole file with Control Breaks
                    Display Option #5 Exit to dBASE
                    Draw box and Display Instructions
            2.2 ACCEPT USER SELECTION
                Accept selection in the range of 1-5
            2.3 PROCESS SELECTION
                SELECT: Depending on SELECTION
                    2.3.1 PROCESS SELECTION #1
                        Execute program INV31
                    2.3.2 PROCESS SELECTION #2
                        Execute program INV32
                    2.3.3 PROCESS SELECTION #3
                        Execute program INV33
                    2.3.4 PROCESS SELECTION #4
                        Execute program INV34
                    2.3.5 PROCESS SELECTION #5
                        Set REPEAT3 Switch = F
                END SELECT
        END REPEAT
    3.0 TERMINATE PROCESSING
        3.1 RESET DEFAULT MODES
            Turn on the dBASE's heading feature
            Turn on the dBASE's user dialogue
            Turn on the dBASE's status bar
```

Figure 8.19 Pseudocode for Case Study 5

```
****************************************************************
*                        INV3.PRG                               *
*                 AMERICAN SUPPLY COMPANY                       *
*                 INVOICE GENERATING SYSTEM                     *
*                  REPORTS GENERATING MENU                      *
*---------------------------------------------------------------*
* This is the Report Generating Menu subprogram. It is          *
* invoked by the Main Menu program INV.PRG of the Invoice       *
* Generating System for American Supply Company. The            *
* function of this program is to display the Reports            *
* Generating Menu, accept the user's choice, and then           *
* execute the program corresponding to the user's choice.       *
*                                                                *
* Menu Choices are:                                             *
*                                                                *
* 1. INV31.PRG - List items over $10.00                         *
* 2. INV32.PRG - List whole file with Totals                    *
* 3. INV33.PRG - List whole file with Retail Price              *
* 4. INV34.PRG - List whole file with Control Breaks            *
* 5.           - Exit to dBASE                                  *
*---------------------------------------------------------------*
*             COPYRIGHT (C) . . . SUDESH M. DUGGAL              *
****************************************************************
*
***************************
* 1.0 INITIATE PROCESSING *
***************************
*
*** 1.1 HOUSEKEEPING ***
    *
    *** CHANGE DEFAULT MODES ***
        *
        SET HEADING OFF
        SET TALK OFF
        SET STATUS OFF
        *
*** 1.2 DEFINE VARIABLES ***
    *
    *** DEFINE CONTROL VARIABLES ***
        *
        STORE [T] TO REPEAT3
        *
***********************
* 2.0 MAIN PROCESSING *
***********************
*
DO WHILE REPEAT3 = [T]
    *
    *** 2.1 DISPLAY MENU SCREEN ***
        *
        *** CLEAR SCREEN ***
            *
            CLEAR
```

Figure 8.20 Coding for Case Study 5

```
            *
            *** DISPLAY REPORT GENERATING MENU3 ***
            *
            @  2,29 SAY 'AMERICAN SUPPLY COMPANY'
            @  3,4  SAY DATE ()
            @  3,30 SAY 'REPORT GENERATING MENU'
            @  3,70 SAY TIME ()
            @  4,34 SAY 'MENU3'
            @  5,0  TO   5,79
            @ 10,24 SAY '1. List items over $10.00'
            @ 11,24 SAY '2. List whole file with Totals'
            @ 12,24 SAY '3. List whole file with Retail price'
            @ 14,24 SAY '4. Listing with Control Breaks'
            @ 16,24 SAY '5. Exit to dBASE'
            @ 22,0  TO  22,79
            @  1,0  TO  24,79 DOUBLE
            *
       *** 2.2 ACCEPT USER SELECTION ***
            *
            @ 23,24 SAY 'ENTER YOUR SELECTION, PLEASE (1-5) ==>:'
            STORE 5 TO SELECTION3
            @ 23,59 GET SELECTION3 PICTURE '9' RANGE 1,5
            READ
            *
       *** 2.3 PROCESS SELECTION ***
            *
            DO CASE
                *
                *** 2.3.1 PROCESS SELECTION #1 ***
                *
                CASE SELECTION3 = 1
                DO INV31
                *
                *** 2.3.2 PROCESS SELECTION #2 ***
                *
                CASE SELECTION3 = 2
                DO INV32
                *
                *** 2.3.3 PROCESS SELECTION #3 ***
                *
                CASE SELECTION3 = 3
                DO INV33
                *
                *** 2.3.4 PROCESS SELECTION #4 ***
                *
                CASE SELECTION3 = 4
                DO INV34
                *
                *** 2.3.5 PROCESS SELECTION #5
                *
                CASE SELECTION3 = 5
```

Figure 8.20 Continued

```
                    STORE [F] TO REPEAT3
                         *
            ENDCASE
                 *
ENDDO REPEAT3 = [T]
*
***************************
* 3.0 TERMINATE PROCESSING *
***************************
*
*** 3.1 RESET DEFAULT MODES ***
        *
    SET TALK ON
    SET HEADING ON
    SET STATUS ON
```

Figure 8.20 Continued

the user. Because there are only five options available in the menu, this parameter with the GET command allows the user to enter only the numbers from one through five inclusively.

The rest of the commands have already been discussed and need no further explanation.

8.3.5 The Testing and Debugging Phase

Next you need to make the required changes in the INV31.PRG, INV32.PRG, INV33.PRG, and INV34.PRG programs so they can be invoked by the INV3.PRG program. To do this, you need to delete the setting and resetting of default mode commands and add the RETURN command to all these programs. Make the required changes and test the INV3.PRG program by executing it and selecting each of its options, which in turn should invoke the INV31.PRG, INV32.PRG, INV33.PRG, and INV34.PRG programs.

8.4 Summary

The partial format IF-ENDIF of the IF-ELSE-ENDIF command is used with the selection control structure with only one option available, which can be selected or not, depending on the selection criteria. The full version of the IF-ELSE-ENDIF command is used with the selection control structure with two options available. Which is selected depends on the selection criteria.

The IF-ELSE-ENDIF command is nested when it is necessary to test a condition only after testing a previous condition regardless of the result of the first testing. The nested IF-ELSE-ENDIF command is also used with the selection control structure in which more than two possible options are available and only one is to be selected, depending on the selection criteria.

The selection control structure in which there are more than three options available is termed case control structure. This is commonly used in the menu programs, and the dBASE command DO CASE-ENDCASE is used with it.

The processing steps for a menu program in the initiate processing function are

1. Housekeeping
2. Define control variables
3. Display introduction screen

The processing steps for a menu program in the main processing function are

1. Display menu screen
2. Accept user selection
3. Process selection

The processing steps for a menu program in the terminate processing function are

1. Exit to DOS, exit to dBASE, return to calling program, or return to main menu
2. Reset default modes

KEY CONCEPTS

case control structure   menu program

dBASE COMMANDS AND FUNCTIONS

DO CASE-ENDCASE command   IF-ENDIF command
IF-ELSE-ENDIF command

REVIEW QUESTIONS

1. When is the partial format IF-ENDIF of the IF-ELSE-ENDIF command used?
2. When is the full version of the IF-ELSE-ENDIF command used?
3. List two different uses of the nested IF-ELSE-ENDIF command.
4. When should the DO CASE-ENDCASE command be preferred over the nested IF-ELSE-ENDIF command?
5. Explain what is meant by the term *level of nesting*.
6. Explain what is meant by a menu program.

7. What are the processing tasks performed by a menu program?
8. What is meant by case control structure?
9. What is meant by the statement that the CASE commands in the DO CASE-ENDCASE command are mutually exclusive?
10. What action is taken if none of the CASE command is true?
11. List all the possible steps needed in the initiate processing step of a menu program.
12. List all the possible steps needed in the main processing step of a menu program.
13. List all the possible steps needed in the terminate processing step of a menu program.
14. What is the function of the range parameter in the GET command?

HANDS-ON ASSIGNMENT

Programming Assignment 8A

Program Description Write a report generating menu program ACR3.PRG for the American Supply Company. It should display the report generating menu as shown in Figure 8.21, accept the valid user's choice, and then execute the corresponding program.

Processing Steps Use the following steps to develop the solution of the program:

1. The menu screen consisting of five options and instructions for the user, as shown in Figure 8.21, should be displayed.
2. The screen should be frozen (paused) until the user selects one of the valid options.
3. After the user makes a selection, the processing function associated with the selection should be executed as follows:
   a. For the first selection, the program ACR31.PRG (List receivables with payment in April 1990) should be executed.
   b. For the second selection, the program ACR32.PRG (List receivables with current balance) should be executed.

Figure 8.21 Menu screen for ACR3.PRG program

```
                    AMERICAN SUPPLY COMPANY
 09/15/89           ACCOUNT RECEIVABLE REPORT            11:23:54
                    REPORT GENERATING MENU


              1. List receivables with payment in April 1990
              2. List receivables with current balance
              3. List aged trial balance report

              4. List whole file with control breaks

              5. Exit to dBASE




                ENTER YOUR SELECTION, PLEASE (1-5) ==>:5
```

c. For the third selection, the program ACR33.PRG (List aged trial balance report) should be executed.
d. For the fourth selection, the program ACR34.PRG (List whole file with control breaks) should be executed.
e. For the fifth selection, the program should exit to the dBASE prompt.

4. Make any modifications needed in the programs ACR31.PRG, ACR32.PRG, ACR33.PRG, and ACR34.PRG so that these can be invoked and executed under the control of the ACR3.PRG program.

Programming Assignment 8B

Program Description Write a report generating menu program PAY3.PRG for the American Supply Company. It should display the report generating menu as shown in Figure 8.22, accept the valid user's choice, and then execute the corresponding program.

Processing Steps Use the following steps in the development of the solution of the program:

1. The menu screen consisting of five options and instructions for the user, as shown in Figure 8.22, should be displayed.
2. The screen should be frozen (paused) until the user selects one of the valid options.
3. After the user makes a selection, the processing function associated with the selection should be executed as follows:

a. For the first selection, the program PAY31.PRG (List all employees with overtime pay) should be executed.
b. For the second selection, the program PAY32.PRG (List all employees with gross pay with totals) should be executed.
c. For the third selection, the program PAY33.PRG (List all employees with net pay with totals) should be executed.
d. For the fourth selection, the program PAY34.PRG (List whole file with control breaks) should be executed.
e. For the fifth selection, the program should exit to the dBASE prompt.

4. Make any modifications needed in the programs PAY31.PRG, PAY32.PRG, PAY33.PRG, and PAY34.PRG so that these can be invoked and executed under the control of the PAY3.PRG program.

Figure 8.22 Menu screen for PAY3.PRG program

```
┌─────────────────────────────────────────────────────────────────┐
│                       AMERICAN SUPPLY COMPANY                   │
│    09/15/89              PAYROLL SYSTEM              11:23:57   │
│                       REPORT GENERATING MENU                    │
├─────────────────────────────────────────────────────────────────┤
│                                                                 │
│                                                                 │
│           1. List all employees with overtime pay               │
│           2. List all employees with gross pay with totals      │
│           3. List all employees with net pay with totals        │
│                                                                 │
│           4. List whole file with control breaks                │
│                                                                 │
│           5. Exit to dBASE                                      │
│                                                                 │
│                                                                 │
├─────────────────────────────────────────────────────────────────┤
│              ENTER YOUR SELECTION, PLEASE (1-5) ==>:5           │
└─────────────────────────────────────────────────────────────────┘
```

PART 3

SYSTEM DEVELOPMENT USING dBASE IV PROGRAMMING

Chapter 9 starts by defining the system and then explains the difference between physical and business application systems. Next, the structured system approach to system development, which consists of the structured system analysis phase, the structured system design phase, and the structured system implementation phase, is described. The structured system implementation phase is applied to fully develop a business application system, called the invoice generating system. The concept of stub programming is introduced and applied in the development of this system. The main menu program and the other menu programs needed in this system are also developed. The invoice generating system is developed in Chapters 4–13.

The maintenance programs for the inventory database file INV.DBF are developed in Chapters 10–12, and the maintenance programs for the customer database file CUSTOMER.DBF, left as assignments, are present as stub programs in the invoice generating system, which is otherwise fully developed. The report generating programs have already been developed in Chapters 4–7, and the invoice generating program is developed in Chapter 13.

The dBASE commands used to delete, add, and update the data records of the database files are presented in Chapters 10–12. Indexing, an alternative to the SORT command to organize the data of the database file into a specific sequence, is introduced in Chapter 11. The use of index tags and of the production multiple index file in dBASE IV, in place of index files as used in dBASE III PLUS, is explained next. The use of the SET ORDER and the SET INDEX commands to activate the index tags and the nonproduction multiple index files and the method of creating the multiple field indexes are also explained. Finally, the FIND and SEEK commands, used for searching the indexed database files, and the LOCATE and CONTINUE commands, used in pairs for searching the nonindexed or indexed files, are introduced.

The BROWSE command, along with the detailed discussion of all the optional clauses available with it using the illustrative examples, is presented in Chapter 12. Different methods of case-by-case conditional editing, the editing of only those records of the database file that satisfy the specified criteria, the EDIT FOR format of the EDIT command, the LOCATE and the EDIT commands, and the LOCATE and EDIT WHILE commands are also discussed. Different methods of global editing, in which several data records in a file can be edited at one time rather than editing on a case-by-case basis, are also introduced.

The concept of accessing data from multiple database files at the same time using the SELECT command is introduced in Chapter 13. The SELECT command allows you to open up to ten work areas at a time and to select an already open work area. The use of prefixes and aliases is introduced to permit the access of data from the different database files open in different work areas. Finally, the concept of defining the relationships among the database files sharing a field is introduced. This allows you to obtain related data from different database files.

Chapter 9

System Development

LEARNING OBJECTIVES

Upon successfully completing this chapter, you will be able to:

1. Explain the terms *system*, *subsystem*, and *suprasystem*.
2. Explain the difference between physical and business application systems.
3. Describe the structured approach to system development.
4. Design the system structure chart for a business application system.
5. Describe the function of the structured system implementation phase of the structured approach to system development.
6. Analyze, design, and code a main menu program for a business application system that will display a menu with different processing options, accept a valid value for the selection from the user, and process the associated processing function.
7. Understand the concept of stub programming.
8. Develop a stub program.

9.1 Overview

This chapter begins by defining the terms *system*, *subsystem*, and *suprasystem*. The difference between physical and business application systems is explained. The structured approach to system development is described and illustrated by designing a business application system, called invoice generating system. The structured system implementation phase is applied to fully develop the invoice generating system. The concept of stub programming is introduced and applied in the development of the invoice generating system.

The main menu program and the other menu programs needed in the invoice generating system are developed in this chapter. The maintenance programs for the inventory database file INV.DBF are developed in Chapters 10–12. Because the maintenance programs for the customer database file CUSTOMER.DBF are similar to those for the inventory database file INV.DBF, they are left as assignments and are present as stub programs in the invoice generating system, which is otherwise fully developed in this book. The report generating programs have already been developed in Chapters 4–7. The invoice generating program is developed in Chapter 13.

9.2 What Is a System?

A **system** is a collection of components integrated to achieve a common goal. For example, a car is a collection of components integrated to provide transportation. Thus, the car itself is a system, and it is made up of several components (a mechanical component, an electrical component, and so on). Each has its own interacting elements that function together to contribute toward meeting the overall objectives. According to the definition of system stated above, each car component is also a system; and is called a **subsystem** of the car system. Thus, a car system consists of several subsystems (the mechanical subsystem, the electrical subsystem, and so on).

But the car is only one device that provides transportation. Others are bicycles, buses, trains, and airplanes. All of these together form a transportation system, called a **suprasystem** of the car system. Thus, each system may be part of the suprasystem and may consist of several subsystems. The difference between a system, a suprasystem, and a subsystem is a matter of perspective.

A system may be a **physical system,** as in the previous examples, or it may be a typical business application system. A **business application system** is a collection of computer programs working together to solve a particular business problem, such as the inventory control system, the payroll system, the accounts payable system, or the accounts receivable system. All of these are part of the suprasystem called the accounting system, and each one may consist of several subsystems.

To develop a system, you follow a set of orderly steps in a process termed the structured approach to system development, which is the topic of the next section. I confine the discussion to business application systems.

9.3 The Structured Approach to System Development

The **structured approach to system development** for a typical business application system consists of a set of orderly phases and includes the following steps:

1. Structured system analysis phase
2. Structured system design phase
3. Structured system implementation phase

In the **structured system analysis phase,** the problem necessitating system development is identified. The current system is analyzed to find out how it works. The objectives for the new system are defined. The solution to the stated problem and ways of meeting the objectives are proposed. Finally, the requirements for the new system to be used in the structured system design approach are specified.

In the **structured system design phase,** the system is subdivided into subsystems, subsubsystems, and so on until the system has been subdivided into simple subsystems that can be developed independently by different people.

The structure design tools and techniques (such as a structure chart, cohesion, coupling, and span of control as used in developing programs in previous chapters) are applied in the subdivision of the systems. These tools and techniques have already been described in Chapter 4. Each subsystem is analyzed and designed as explained in earlier chapters, and when all the subsystems have been developed, the whole system is implemented.

In the **structured system implementation phase,** the individual subsystems are designed, coded, and tested. However, detailed discussion of this topic is beyond the scope of this book.

To illustrate the concept of the structured approach to system development, I introduce a business application system called the invoice generating system in the next section and fully develop it in the rest of this book.

9.4 The Invoice Generating System

Design for the American Supply Company an invoice generating system the main function of which is to accept orders from customers and prepare invoices for the orders. The system should be able to produce various inventory reports and handle the maintenance of the database files used in the system.

Two database files will be used in this system. The first is the inventory database file INV.DBF, containing all the items in the American Supply Company stock. The structure of the INV.DBF database file is shown in Figure 9.1. The second file is the customer database file CUSTOMER.DBF, containing the information about all company customers. The structure of the CUSTOMER.DBF database file is shown in Figure 9.2

The invoice generating system should consist of the following four subsystems:

Figure 9.1 Structure of the INV.DBF database file

```
Structure for database : C:\DBASE\INVOICE\INV.DBF
Number of data records :      30
Date of last update    : 12/20/87
Field  Field Name  Type       Width    Dec   Index
    1  ITEM_NUM    Character    4              N
    2  ITEM_DESC   Character   26              N
    3  UNIT_COST   Numeric      6       2      N
    4  QUANTITY    Numeric      3              N
    5  RET_PRICE   Numeric      7       2      N
    6  REOD_POINT  Numeric      3              N
    7  REOD_QTY    Numeric      3              N
    8  DEPT_CODE   Numeric      3              N
** Total **                    56
```

1. Inventory file maintenance subsystem
2. Customer file maintenance subsystem
3. Report generating subsystem
4. Invoice generating subsystem

Each of these performs several functions, which are explained in the following sections.

Inventory File Maintenance Subsystem

The function of the inventory file maintenance subsystem is to maintain the inventory database file INV.DBF, which consists of the following three functions:

1. To delete an existing record from the INV.DBF database file
2. To add a new record to the INV.DBF database file
3. To update an existing record of the INV.DBF database file

Customer File Maintenance Subsystem

The function of the customer file maintenance subsystem is to maintain the customer database file CUSTOMER.DBF, which consists of the following three functions:

Figure 9.2 Structure of the CUSTOMER.DBF database file

```
.USE CUSTOMER
.DISPLAY STRUCTURE
Structure for database : C:\DBASE\INVOICE\CUSTOMER.DBF
Number of data records :      11
Date of last update    : 01/12/88
Field  Field name  Type       Width   Dec
    1  SOC_SC_NUM  Character   11
    2  CUST_NAME   Character   25
    3  BALANCE     Numeric      7      2
    4  TELEPHONE   Character   12
** TOTAL **                    56
```

1. To delete an existing record from the CUSTOMER.DBF database file
2. To add a new record to the CUSTOMER.DBF database file
3. To update an existing record of the CUSTOMER.DBF database file

Report Generating Subsystem

The function of the report generating subsystem is to produce various inventory reports. The following four reports should be produced by this subsystem:

1. An inventory report listing for American Supply Company consisting of only those records of the INV.DBF database file whose UNIT_COST field value is greater than $10
2. An inventory report listing for American Supply Company that contains all the records of the INV.DBF database file (The program should calculate the inventory value for each item of the INV.DBF database file in stock. The listing should also contain the total inventory value of all the items contained in the database file.)
3. A catalog listing for American Supply Company containing all the records of the INV.DBF database file (The program should calculate the retail price for each item in the stock of the INV.DBF database file and store it in the RET_PRICE data field.)
4. The inventory report listings for American Supply Company containing the records belonging to a particular department from the sorted inventory database file INVDSORT.DBF, the department's total inventory value, and the total inventory value for the entire stock of the company

Invoice Generating Subsystem

This subsystem is the heart of the system. The invoice generating system uses both database files (INV.DBF and CUSTOMER.DBF). It accepts orders from the customer, verifies the information by checking the inventory for the item in stock, and then produces the invoices. The items ordered reduce the numbers in the inventory database file INV.DBF. The invoice is printed and sent to the shipping department for the shipment of the items.

System Structure Chart

The structure chart for the invoice generating system, having the specifications previously described, is shown in Figure 9.3. This chart consists of 15 programs:

1. The main menu program (INV.PRG) for the invoice generating system. The function of this program is to initiate processing of the system by displaying the Main Menu. It accepts the user's choice and then executes the program chosen.
2. An inventory file maintenance submenu program (INV1.PRG). This program is invoked by the main menu program INV.PRG of

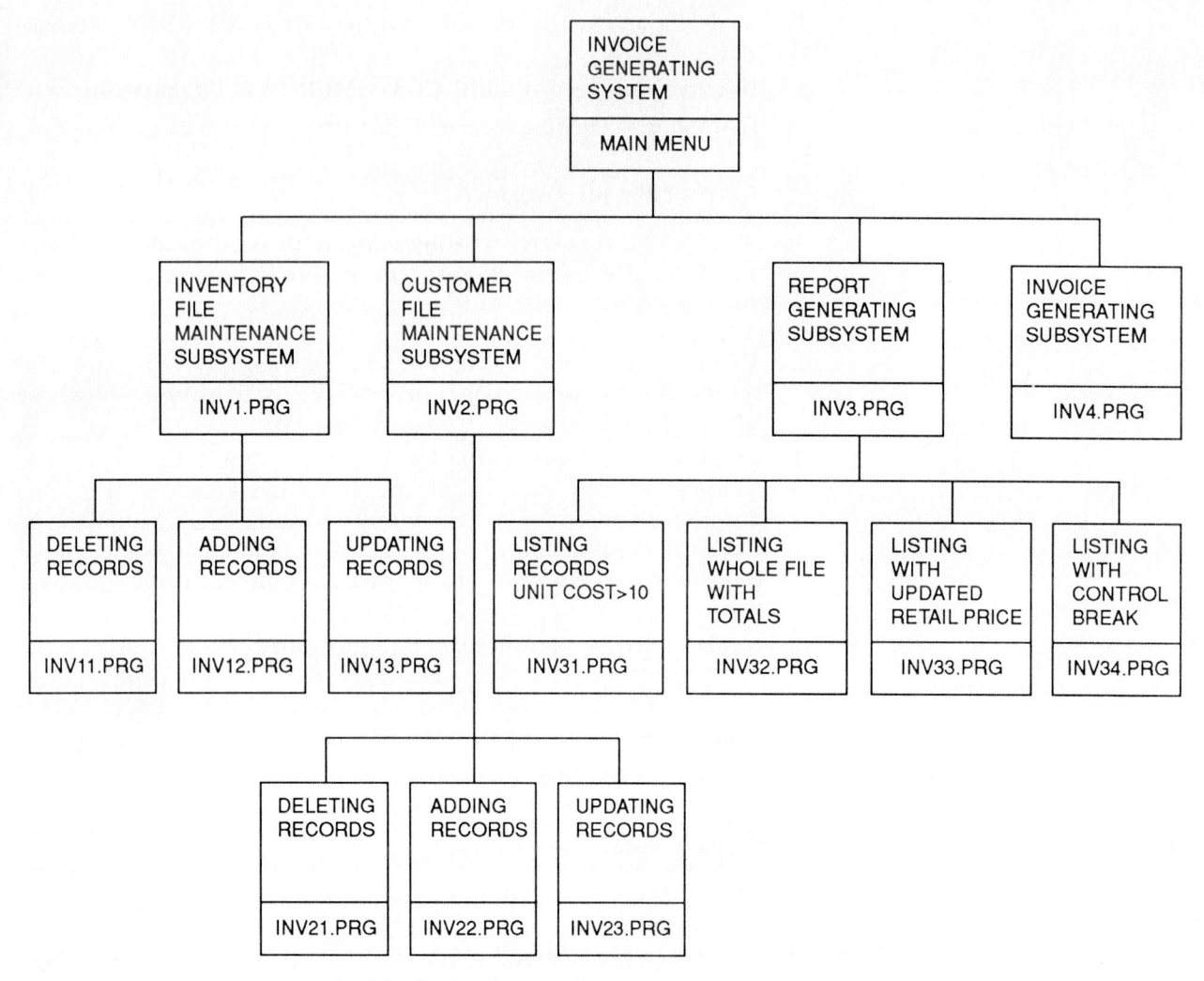

Figure 9.3 System structure chart for the Invoice generating system

the invoice generating system. The function of this program is to display the Inventory File Maintenance Menu, accept the user's choice, and then execute the corresponding program.

3. An inventory file maintenance program (INV11.PRG). This program is invoked by the inventory file maintenance submenu program INV1.PRG of the invoice generating system. The function of this program is to delete the records of discontinued items from the INV.DBF database file.

4. An inventory file maintenance program (INV12.PRG). This program is invoked by the inventory file maintenance submenu program INV1.PRG of the invoice generating system. The function of this program is to add new records to the INV.DBF database file.

5. An inventory file maintenance program (INV13.PRG). This program is invoked by the inventory file maintenance submenu program INV1.PRG of the invoice generating system. The function of this program is to update the existing records of the INV.DBF database file.

9.4 The Invoice Generating System

6. A customer file maintenance submenu program (INV2.PRG). This program is invoked by the main menu program INV.PRG of the invoice generating system. The function of this program is to display the Customer File Maintenance Menu, accept the user's choice, and then execute the corresponding program.

7. A customer file maintenance program (INV21.PRG). This program is invoked by the customer file maintenance submenu program INV2.PRG of the invoice generating system. The function of this program is to delete the records of discontinued items from the CUSTOMER.DBF database file.

8. A customer file maintenance program (INV22.PRG). This program is invoked by the customer file maintenance submenu program INV2.PRG of the invoice generating system. The function of this program is to add new records to the CUSTOMER.DBF database file.

9. A customer file maintenance program (INV23.PRG). This program is invoked by the customer file maintenance submenu program INV2.PRG of the invoice generating system. The function of this program is to update the existing records of the CUSTOMER.DBF database file.

10. A report generating submenu program (INV3.PRG). This program is invoked by the main menu program INV.PRG of the invoice generating system. The function of this program is to display the Report Generating Menu, accept the user's choice, and then execute the corresponding program.

11. A report generating program (INV31.PRG). This program is invoked by the report generating submenu program INV3.PRG of the invoice generating system. The function of this program is to produce an inventory report listing for American Supply Company consisting of only those records of the INV.DBF database file whose UNIT_COST field value is greater than $10.

12. A report generating program (INV32.PRG). This program is invoked by the report generating submenu program INV3.PRG of the invoice generating system. The function of this program is to produce an inventory report listing for American Supply Company that contains all the records of the INV.DBF database file. The program should calculate the inventory value for each item of the INV.DBF database file in stock. The listing should also contain the total inventory value of all the items contained in the database file.

13. A report generating program (INV33.PRG). This program is invoked by the report generating submenu program INV3.PRG of the invoice generating system. The function of this program is to produce a catalog listing for American Supply Company containing all the records of the INV.DBF database file. The program should calculate the retail price for each item in the stock of the INV.DBF database file and store it in the RET_PRICE data field.

14. A report generating program (INV34.PRG). This program is invoked by the report generating submenu program INV3.PRG of the invoice generating system. The function of this program is to produce inventory report listings. Each listing should contain

only the records belonging to a particular department from the sorted inventory database file INVDSORT.DBF. Each listing should also contain each department's total inventory value and the total inventory value for the entire stock of the company.

15. An invoice generating subsystem program (INV4.PRG). This program is invoked by the main menu program INV.PRG of the invoice generating system. The function of this program is to accept orders from customers, verify the information by checking the inventory for the item in stock, and then produce the invoices. The items ordered reduce the number in the inventory database file. The invoice is printed and sent to the shipping department for the shipment of the items.

The functions of the structured system implementation phase are to design, code, and test the individual programs of the business application system, which is the objective of this book. So let's proceed with the development of the programs of the invoice generating system following the top-down approach, in which we go from top to bottom and from left to right. Thus, the first program we will be developing is the main menu program INV.PRG, which is given as Case Study 6.

9.5 An Illustrative Example: Case Study 6

Program Description

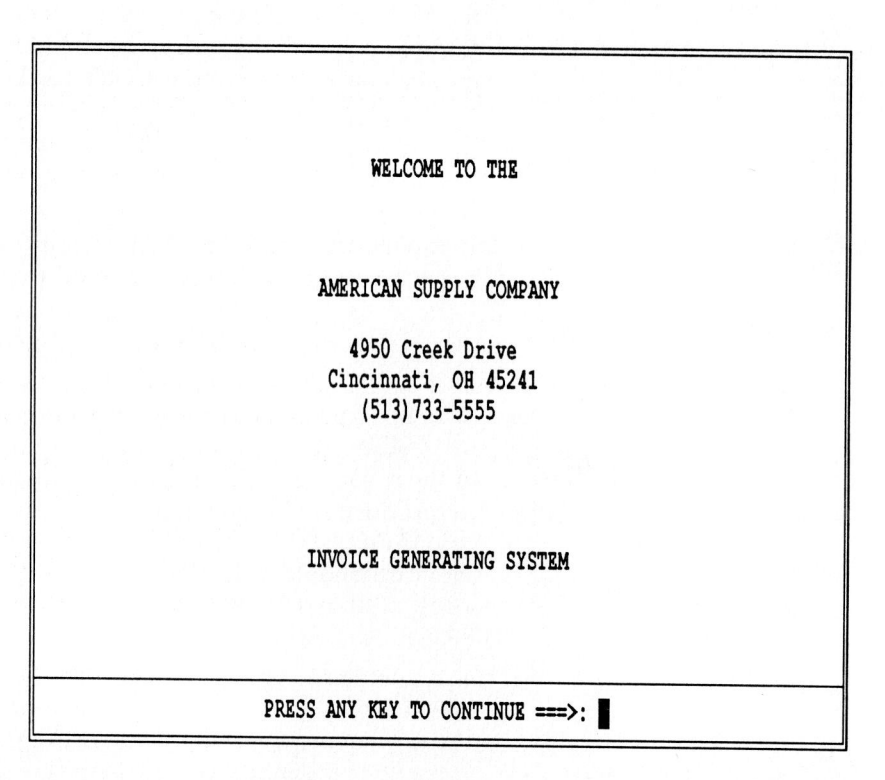

Write a main menu program for the invoice generating system for the American Supply Company. It should display the introductory welcome screen, including the name of the system, as shown in Figure 9.4.

Figure 9.4 Introductory welcome screen for the invoice generating system

```
┌─────────────────────────────────────────────┐
│                                             │
│                                             │
│              WELCOME TO THE                 │
│                                             │
│                                             │
│           AMERICAN SUPPLY COMPANY           │
│                                             │
│              4950 Creek Drive               │
│            Cincinnati, OH 45241             │
│               (513) 733-5555                │
│                                             │
│                                             │
│                                             │
│           INVOICE GENERATING SYSTEM         │
│                                             │
│                                             │
│                                             │
├─────────────────────────────────────────────┤
│         PRESS ANY KEY TO CONTINUE ===>:  █  │
└─────────────────────────────────────────────┘
```

Figure 9.5 Main Menu for the invoice generating system

```
                    AMERICAN SUPPLY COMPANY
  09/15/89         INVOICE GENERATING SYSTEM              11:23:57
                          MAIN MENU



                    1. Maintain Inventory File
                    2. Maintain Customer File

                    3. Generate Reports
                    4. Produce Invoices

                    5. Exit to DOS
                    6. Exit to dBASE




            ENTER YOUR SELECTION, PLEASE (1-6)  =>:6
```

After the introductory screen is displayed, the program should display the Main Menu for the system, as shown in Figure 9.5, accept the valid user's choice, and then, depending on the user's selection, execute the corresponding subsystem program.

Processing Steps

Use the following steps to develop the solution of the program:

1. The main menu screen, consisting of six options and instructions for the user, as shown in Figure 9.5, should be displayed.
2. The screen should be frozen (paused) until the user selects one of the valid options.
3. After the user makes a selection, the processing function corresponding to the selection made should be executed as follows:
   a. For the first selection, the subsystem program INV1.PRG (maintain inventory file) should be executed.
   b. For the second selection, the subsystem program INV2.PRG (maintain customer file) should be executed.
   c. For the third selection, the subsystem program INV3.PRG (generate reports) should be executed.
   d. For the fourth selection, the subsystem program INV4.PRG (produce invoices) should be executed.
   e. For the fifth selection, the program should exit to the DOS prompt.
   f. For the sixth selection, the program should exit to the dBASE prompt.
4. Because the subsystem programs INV1.PRG, INV2.PRG,

INV3.PRG, and INV4.PRG have not yet been developed, you can create the **stub programs** for these subsystem programs. The stub program is a dummy program that should contain four main functions: (1) clear the screen, (2) display the message that the stub program has been processed, (3) freeze the screen and wait for a response to continue processing, and (4) return to the calling program. When executed, each stub program should simply display the message that the subsystem program has been processed, as shown in Figure 9.6.

The five phases of the program development process for Case Study 6 follow.

9.5.1 The Analysis Phase

In the analysis phase, the first step in the program development process, review and analysis of the program specifications lead to the identification of the processing steps needed to solve the problem. As with every problem, the usual housekeeping step will be needed. We will also need to define two control variables. One is needed for control of the loop, in which the main menu screen will be displayed repeatedly. The function of this control variable will be to exit from the loop when instructed to do so by the user. The second control variable will be used to decide whether the program should exit to DOS or to the dBASE prompt. The introductory screen should be displayed next. These steps are the only three needed in the initiate processing function.

The processing steps needed in the main processing function should include displaying the main menu screen, accepting the user's selection, and processing the selection. These three steps should be repeated until

Figure 9.6 Stub program for INV1.PRG program

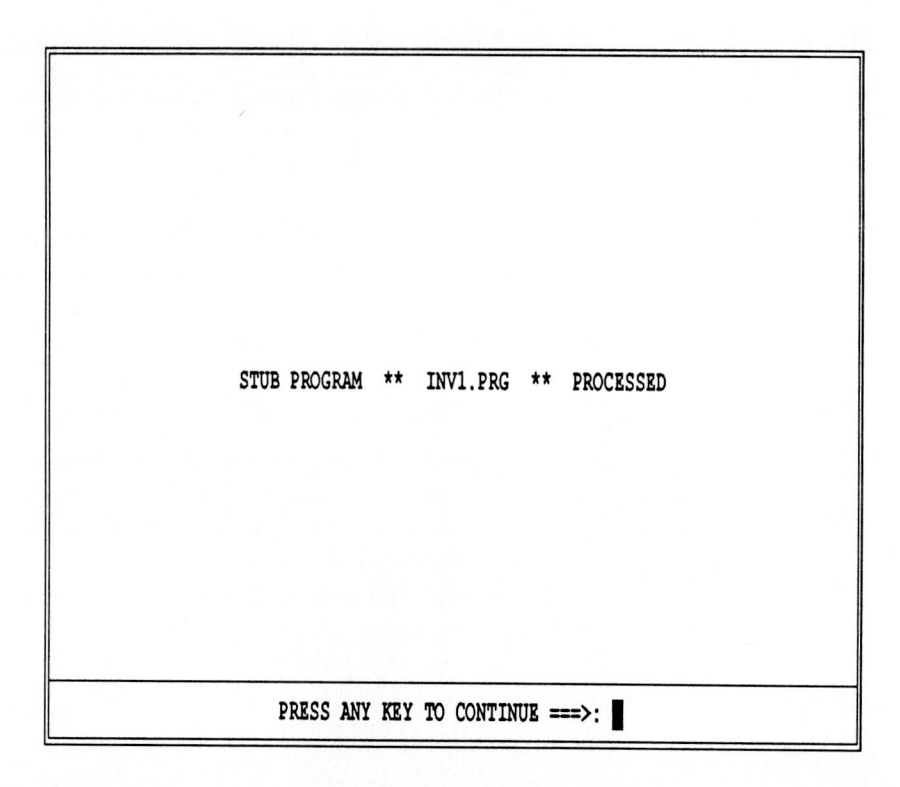

```
                STUB PROGRAM  **  INV1.PRG  **  PROCESSED




              PRESS ANY KEY TO CONTINUE ===>: ▮
```

9.5 An Illustrative Example: Case Study 6

the user wishes to terminate the program, at which point program control should move to the terminate processing function.

In the terminate processing function, depending on the user's choice, the program should exit to either DOS or the dBASE prompt.

To summarize, you'll need the following processing steps to solve Case Study 6:

1. Housekeeping
2. Define control variables
3. Display introductory screen
4. Display main menu screen
5. Accept user's selection
6. One of the following process selections:
   a. Process selection 1
   b. Process selection 2
   c. Process selection 3
   d. Process selection 4
   e. Process selection 5
   f. Process selection 6
7. Depending on the user's selection, either
   a. Exit to DOS
   b. Exit to dBASE

Perform the first three steps only once, at the start of the program. Therefore, these steps belong to initiate processing. The next three steps should be performed again and again until the user indicates his or her wish by selecting either choice 5 or choice 6. Therefore, these steps belong to main processing. The last step needs to be performed only once before terminating the execution of the program. Therefore, this step belongs to the terminate processing.

9.5.2 The Design Phase

The function of this step is to take the result of the problem analysis, that is, the processing steps identified in the analysis phase, and transform them into a structure chart. Using the shell structure chart of Figure 8.17 and the tools and techniques discussed in section 4.4.2, transform the seven steps identified in the analysis phase into a structure chart for Case Study 6 as shown in Figure 9.7.

All the modules in this structure chart are either functionally or highly cohesive. They are also loosely coupled. Thus, the structure chart of Figure 9.7 satisfies the three rules for designing a good structure chart; that is, it consists of highly cohesive, loosely coupled modules with the span of control of any one not more than six. Therefore, this chart is a well-designed solution to Case Study 6.

9.5.3 The Detailed Design Phase

The function of this step is to take the result of the design phase (the structure chart) and identify the actual computer operations required for each program function represented in it, thereby producing the detailed solution of the problem. Using the translation of the three control structures to pseudocode as given in Figure 4.14, the Main Menu format as

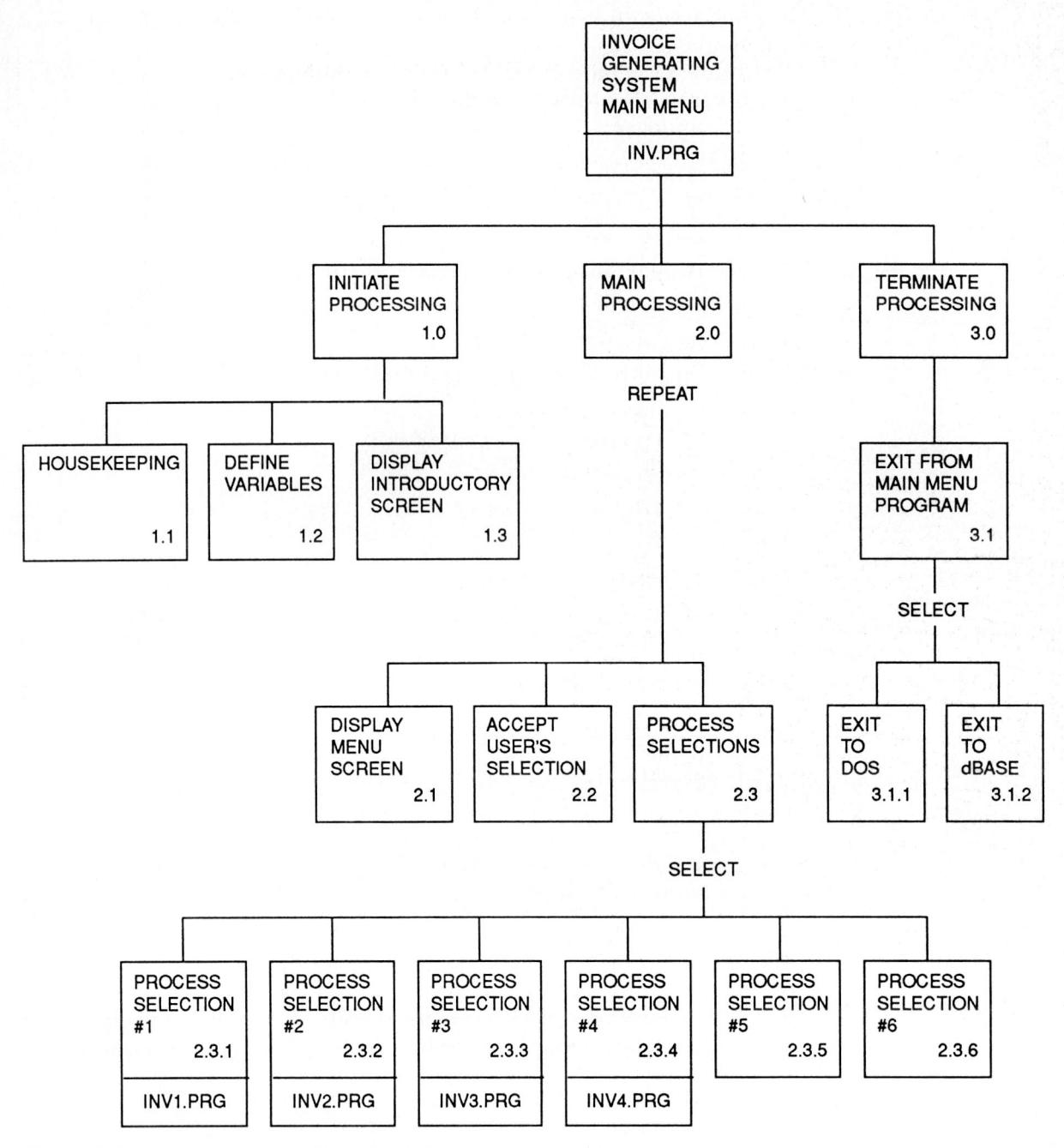

Figure 9.7 Structure chart for Case Study 6

shown in Figure 9.5, and the method described in section 4.4.3, we arrive at the structure chart of Figure 9.7 as translated to pseudocode and given in Figure 9.8.

In this pseudocode, two control variables, REPEAT and EXITDOS, have been defined in the 1.2 Define Control Variables module. The values of "T" and "F" are assigned to the REPEAT and EXITDOS variables, respectively. The first control variable REPEAT is used with the DO WHILE-ENDDO command in the main processing step to repeatedly

Figure 9.8 Pseudocode for Case Study 6

```
0.0 INVOICE GENERATING SYSTEM—MAIN MENU
   1.0 INITIATE PROCESSING
      1.1 HOUSEKEEPING
         CHANGE DEFAULT MODES
            Turn off the dBASE's heading feature
            Turn off the dBASE's user dialogue
            Turn off the dBASE's status bar
         SET PROCEDURES
            Set procedure to UTILITY
      1.2 DEFINE VARIABLES
         DEFINE CONTROL VARIABLES
            Set REPEAT Switch = T
            Set EXITDOS Switch = F
      1.3 DISPLAY INTRODUCTORY SCREEN
         CLEAR SCREEN
            Clear the screen
         DISPLAY INTRODUCTORY SCREEN
            Display Welcome line
            Display Company's name
            Display Company's address
            Display Company's city, state, zip
            Display Company's telephone number
            Display the system name
         FREEZE SCREEN
            Perform FREEZE procedure
   2.0 MAIN PROCESSING
      REPEAT: While the REPEAT switch = T
         2.1 DISPLAY MAIN MENU SCREEN
            CLEAR SCREEN
               Clear the screen
            DISPLAY MAIN MENU
               Display Option #1 Maintain Inventory File
               Display Option #2 Maintain Customer File
               Display Option #3 Generate Reports
               Display Option #4 Produce Invoices
               Display Option #5 Exit to DOS
               Display Option #6 Exit to dBASE
               Draw box and Display Instructions
         2.2 ACCEPT USER'S SELECTION
            Accept SELECTION in the range of 1-6
         2.3 PROCESS SELECTIONS
            SELECT: Depending on SELECTION
               2.3.1 PROCESS SELECTION #1
                  Execute program INV1
               2.3.2 PROCESS SELECTION #2
                  Execute program INV2
               2.3.3 PROCESS SELECTION #3
                  Execute program INV3
               2.3.4 PROCESS SELECTION #4
                  Execute program INV4
```

Figure 9.8 Continued

```
                    2.3.5 PROCESS SELECTION #5
                          Set REPEAT Switch = F
                          Set EXITDOS Switch = T
                    2.3.6 PROCESS SELECTION #6
                          Set REPEAT Switch = F
              END SELECT
         END REPEAT
         3.0 TERMINATE PROCESSING
              3.1 EXIT FROM MAIN MENU PROGRAM
                  SELECT: On EXITDOS switch value
                       3.1.1 EXIT TO DOS
                             Exit to DOS
                       3.1.2 EXIT TO dBASE
                             Turn on the dBASE's heading feature
                             Turn on the dBASE's user dialogue
                             Turn on the dBASE's status bar
                             Reset procedure back to normal
              END SELECT
```

display the Main Menu, to accept the user's choice, and then to execute the associated processing function.

The process of displaying the Main Menu, accepting the user's choice, and executing the associated processing function is repeated again and again until the user wants to exit from the invoice generating system main menu program. In that case, the user selects either the fifth or the sixth choice from the Main Menu. Then the REPEAT switch is set to "F" value, which causes the program control to exit from the DO WHILE-ENDDO loop and proceed to the terminate processing step.

The second control variable, EXITDOS, is used to decide whether the program should exit to DOS or to dBASE. If the user selects the fifth choice in the main processing step, the EXITDOS control variable is set to a "T" value. A test is made in the terminate processing step to determine the value of the EXITDOS control variable. If it is "T," the program will exit to DOS, and the system prompt C:\> will be displayed. But if the value of the EXITDOS control variable is "F," the program will exit to dBASE, the default modes will be reset, and the dBASE dot prompt will be displayed.

9.5.4 The Coding Phase

The purpose of this phase in the program development process is to translate the pseudocode instructions of the solution of the program into programming language instructions. The pseudocode of Figure 9.8 is translated into dBASE commands, and the complete program for Case Study 6 in dBASE language is given in Figure 9.9.

9.5.5 The Testing and Debugging Phase

The next (and last) step in program development is to test the program. Because this program invokes four subprograms, we need to have those programs developed. The question is, "Should we wait until we develop these programs, namely, INV1.PRG, INV2.PRG, INV3.PRG, and

```
****************************************************************
*                          INV.PRG                              *
*                   AMERICAN SUPPLY COMPANY                     *
*                   INVOICE GENERATING SYSTEM                   *
*                      MAIN MENU PROGRAM                        *
* ------------------------------------------------------------- *
* This is a Main Menu program for the Invoice Generating        *
* System for American Supply Company. The function of this      *
* program is to initiate processing by displaying the Main      *
* Menu, accepting the user's choice, and then executing the     *
* program corresponding to the user's choice.                   *
*                                                                *
* Main Menu Choices are:                                        *
*                                                                *
*    1. INV1.PRG - Inventory File Maintenance Subsystem         *
*    2. INV2.PRG - Customer File Maintenance Subsystem          *
*    3. INV3.PRG - Reports Generating Subsystem                 *
*    4. INV4.PRG - Invoices Generating Subsystem                *
*    5.         - Exit to DOS                                   *
*    6.         - Exit to dBASE                                 *
* ------------------------------------------------------------- *
*            COPYRIGHT (C) . . . SUDESH M. DUGGAL               *
****************************************************************
*
****************************床***********
* 1.0 INITIATE PROCESSING *
*****************************************
*
*** 1.1 HOUSEKEEPING ***
    *
    *** CHANGE DEFAULT MODES ***
        *
        SET HEADING OFF
        SET TALK OFF
        SET STATUS OFF
        *
    *** SET PROCEDURES ***
        *
        SET PROCEDURE TO UTILITY
        *
*** 1.2 DEFINE VARIABLES ***
    *
    *** DEFINE CONTROL VARIABLES ***
        *
        STORE [T] TO REPEAT
        STORE [F] TO EXITDOS
        *
*** 1.3 DISPLAY INTRODUCTORY SCREEN ***
    *
    *** CLEAR SCREEN ***
        *
        CLEAR
        *
    *** DISPLAY INTRODUCTORY SCREEN ***
        *
```

Figure 9.9 Coding for Case Study 6

```
            @  5,25 SAY '     WELCOME TO THE'
            @  9,25 SAY ' AMERICAN SUPPLY COMPANY'
            @ 11,25 SAY '    4950 Creek Drive'
            @ 12,25 SAY '   Cincinnati, OH 45241'
            @ 13,25 SAY '     (513)733-5555'
            @ 18,25 SAY 'INVOICE GENERATING SYSTEM'
            *
*** 1.4 FREEZE SCREEN **
    *
    DO FREEZE
    *
***********************
* 2.0 MAIN PROCESSING *
***********************
*
DO WHILE REPEAT = [T]
    *
    *** 2.1 DISPLAY MAIN MENU SCREEN ***
        *
        *** CLEAR SCREEN ***
            *
            CLEAR
            *
        *** DISPLAY MAIN MENU ***
            *
            @  2,29 SAY 'AMERICAN SUPPLY COMPANY'
            @  3,4  SAY DATE ()
            @  3,28 SAY 'INVOICE GENERATING SYSTEM'
            @  3,70 SAY TIME ()
            @  4,36 SAY 'MAIN MENU'
            @  5,0  TO   5,79
            @ 10,25 SAY ' 1. Maintain Inventory File'
            @ 11,25 SAY ' 2. Maintain Customers File'
            @ 13,25 SAY ' 3. Generate Reports'
            @ 14,25 SAY ' 4. Produce Invoices'
            @ 16,25 SAY ' 5. Exit to DOS'
            @ 17,25 SAY ' 6. Exit to dBASE'
            @ 22,0  TO  22,79
            @  1,0  TO  24,79 DOUBLE
            *
    *** 2.2 ACCEPT USER'S SELECTION ***
        *
        @ 23,24 SAY ' ENTER YOUR SELECTION, PLEASE (1-6) =>:'
        STORE 6 TO SELECTION
        @ 23,65 GET SELECTION PICTURE '9' RANGE 1,6
        READ
        *
    *** 2.3 PROCESS SELECTIONS ***
        *
        DO CASE
            *
            *** 2.3.1 PROCESS SELECTION #1 ***
                *
                CASE SELECTION = 1
                DO INV1
                *
```

Figure 9.9 Continued

```
                *** 2.3.2 PROCESS SELECTION #2 ***
                    *
                    CASE SELECTION = 2
                    DO INV2
                    *
                *** 2.3.3 PROCESS SELECTION #3 ***
                    *
                    CASE SELECTION = 3
                    DO INV3
                    *
                *** 2.3.4 PROCESS SELECTION #4 ***
                    *
                    CASE SELECTION = 4
                    DO INV4
                    *
                *** 2.3.5 PROCESS SELECTION #5 ***
                    *
                    CASE SELECTION = 5
                    STORE [F] TO REPEAT
                    STORE [T] TO EXITDOS
                    *
                *** 2.3.6 PROCESS SELECTION #6 ***
                    *
                    CASE SELECTION = 6
                    STORE [F] TO REPEAT
                    *
            ENDCASE
            *
ENDDO REPEAT = [T]
*
****************************
* 3.0 TERMINATE PROCESSING *
****************************
*
*** 3.1 EXIT FROM MAIN MENU PROGRAM ***
    *
    IF EXITDOS = [T]
        *
        *** 3.1.1 EXIT TO DOS ***
            *
            QUIT
            *
    ELSE
        *
        *** 3.1.2 EXIT TO dBASE ***
            *
            SET TALK ON
            SET HEADING ON
            SET STATUS ON
            SET PROCEDURE TO
            *
    ENDIF EXITDOS = [T]
```

Figure 9.9 Continued

INV4.PRG, to test INV.PRG main menu program?" We do not have to wait for the development of these programs. Instead, we can use stub programs in their place.

Such programs can be coded in less than five minutes. Therefore, we do not have to await the development of the invoked programs to test the main menu program. The stub program for INV1.PRG is given in Figure 9.10. The stub programs for INV2.PRG, INV3.PRG, and INV4.PRG can be written similarly.

When the main menu program INV.PRG is executed, it will display the introductory screen as given in Figure 9.4. Then the Main Menu as shown in Figure 9.5 will be displayed. If choice 1 is selected, the stub program INV1.PRG will be invoked and executed. It will display the result as shown in Figure 9.6. Pressing any key on the keyboard will return the control to the main menu program INV.PRG, and the Main Menu of Figure 9.5 will be displayed again.

In the same way, when choices 2, 3, and 4 are selected, their corresponding stub programs will be executed; and screens similar to Figure 9.6 will be displayed, indicating that the program has been invoked and processed. But when choice 5 is selected, the control will be transferred to DOS prompt; and if choice 6 is selected, the control will be transferred to the dBASE prompt.

Figure 9.10 Stub program for INV1.PRG

```
*****************************************************************
*                         INV1.PRG                               *
*----------------------------------------------------------------*
*                                                                *
*                 This is a STUB program.                        *
*                                                                *
*----------------------------------------------------------------*
*          COPYRIGHT (C)  . . .   SUDESH M. DUGGAL               *
*****************************************************************
*
*** CLEAR SCREEN ***
    *
    CLEAR
    *
*** DISPLAY MESSAGE ***
    *
    @  1,2  TO 24,79 DOUBLE
    @ 14,20 SAY ' STUB PROGRAM  **  INV1.PRG  **  EXECUTED'
    *
*** FREEZE SCREEN ***
    *
    STORE ' ' TO RESPONSE
    @ 23,20 SAY 'PRESS ANY KEY TO CONTINUE ===>:' GET RESPONSE
    READ
    *
*** RETURN TO CALLING PROGRAM ***
    *
    RETURN
```

9.6 Development of Other Programs of the System

Let us now develop the rest of the programs of the invoice generating system. Subsystem programs INV1.PRG, INV2.PRG, and INV3.PRG also are menu programs. They can be developed following the instructions in this chapter. In fact, the menu program INV3.PRG has already been developed as Case Study 5 in Chapter 8. It can be modified so that it can work as a subsystem for the main menu program INV.PRG. All these programs are given on the following pages of this chapter along with their menu screens, structure charts, pseudocodes, and codings.

The maintenance programs INV11.PRG, INV12.PRG, and INV13.PRG for the inventory database file INV.DBF will be developed in Chapters 10–12. The maintenance programs INV21.PRG, INV22.PRG, and INV23.PRG for the customer database file CUSTOMER.DBF are left as assignments.

The report generating subsystem programs INV31.PRG, INV32.PRG, INV33.PRG, and INV34.PRG have already been developed in Chapters 4–7. Modify these programs so that they can work as subprograms for the subsystem program INV3.PRG. The invoice generating subsystem program INV4.PRG will be developed in Chapter 13.

9.6.1 Subprogram INV1.PRG

Program Description

Write an inventory file maintenance submenu program. It should be invoked by main menu program INV.PRG of the invoice generating system for the American Supply Company. The program should display the Inventory File Maintenance Menu as shown in Figure 9.11, accept the user's valid choice, and then execute the corresponding program.

Figure 9.11 Menu screen for INV1.PRG program

```
                    AMERICAN SUPPLY COMPANY
     09/15/89       INVOICE GENERATING SYSTEM          11:23:57
                   INVENTORY FILE MAINTENANCE MENU




                        1. Delete A Record
                        2. Add a record
                        3. Update a Record

                        4. Exit to dBASE
                        5. Return to Main Menu




               ENTER YOUR SELECTION, PLEASE (1-5) ==>:5
```

Chapter 9 / System Development

Processing Steps

The following steps should be used to develop the solution of the program:

1. The menu screen consisting of five options and instructions for the user, as shown in Figure 9.11, should be displayed.
2. The screen should be frozen (paused) until the user selects one of the valid options.
3. After the user makes a selection, the processing function associated with the selection should be executed as follows:
   a. For the first selection, the maintenance program INV11.PRG (delete a record) should be executed.

Figure 9.12 Structure chart for INV1.PRG program

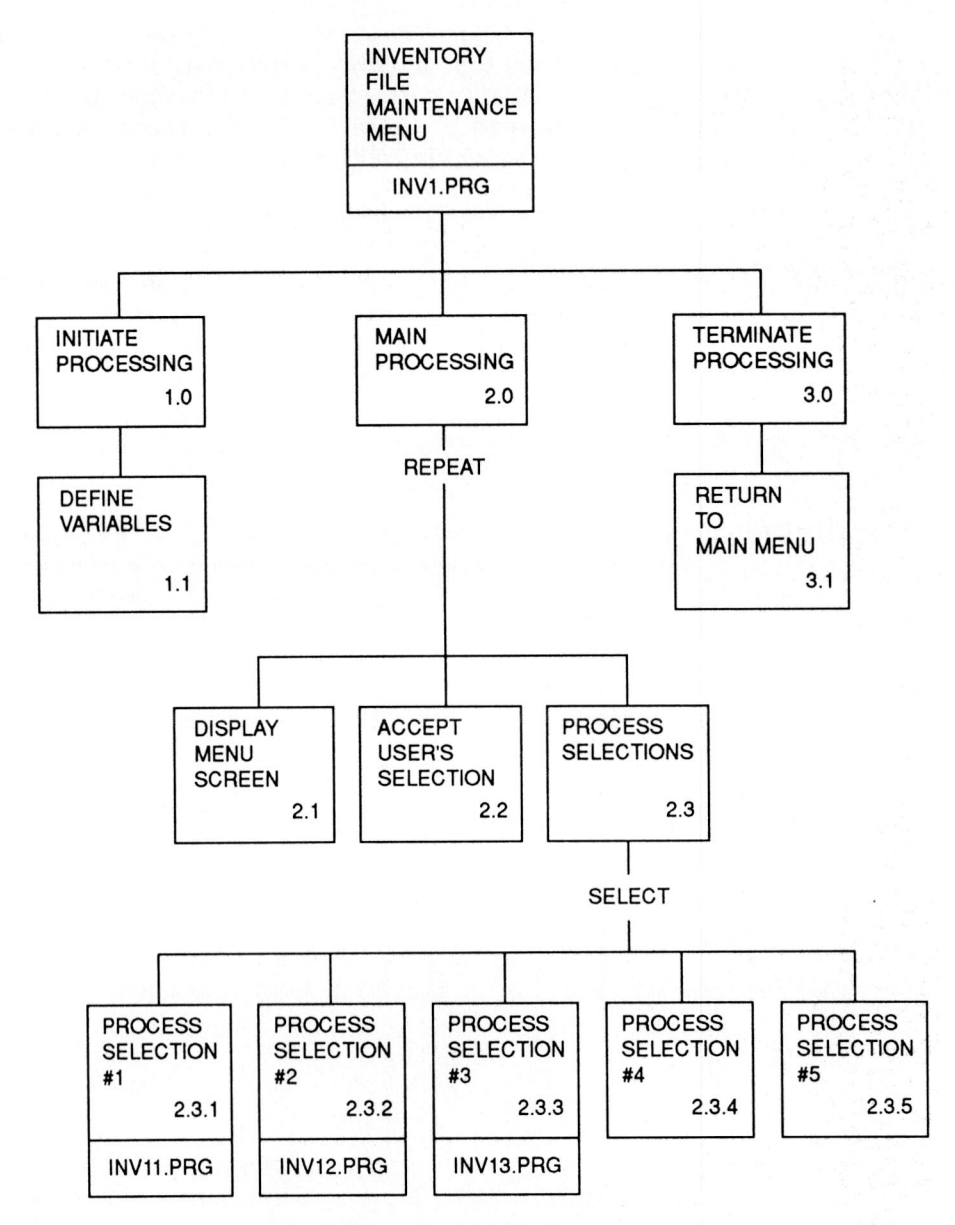

9.6 Development of Other Programs of the System

b. For the second selection, the maintenance program INV12.PRG (add a record) should be executed.
c. For the third selection, the maintenance program INV13.PRG (update a record) should be executed.
d. For the fourth selection, the program should exit to the dBASE prompt.
e. For the fifth selection, the program should return to the Main Menu.

The solution of this subprogram is similar to that of the main menu program of Case Study 6, except for three differences:

1. There is no need to set or reset the default modes because these are set at the start of the main menu program that invokes this submenu program and are reset at the end of the main menu program.
2. No introduction screen need be displayed in the submenu program.
3. There is no direct exit to DOS from the submenu program, but program control is returned to the main menu program.

Following the steps of the analysis and design phase of the program development process as used in Case Study 6, develop the structure chart, pseudocode, and coding of the program INV1.PRG. These solutions are given in Figure 9.12, 9.13, and 9.14, respectively. A complete dBASE program for the menu program INV1.PRG is given in Figure 9.14.

9.6.2 Subprogram INV2.PRG

Program Description

Write a customer file maintenance submenu program. It should be invoked by the main menu program INV.PRG of the invoice generating system for the American Supply Company. The program should display the Customer File Maintenance Menu as shown in Figure 9.15 (see page 369), accept the user's valid choice, and then execute the corresponding program.

Processing Steps

The following steps should be used to develop the solution of the program:

1. The menu screen consisting of five options and instructions for the user as shown in Figure 9.15 should be displayed.
2. The screen should be frozen (paused) until the user selects one of the valid options.
3. After the user makes a selection, the processing function associated with the selection should be executed as follows:
   a. For the first selection, the maintenance program INV21.PRG (delete a record) should be executed.
   b. For the second selection, the maintenance program INV22.PRG (add a record) should be executed.

Figure 9.13 Pseudocode for menu program INV1.PRG

```
0.0 INVENTORY FILE MAINTENANCE—SUBMENU
  1.0 INITIATE PROCESSING
    1.1 DEFINE VARIABLES
      DEFINE CONTROL VARIABLES
        Set REPEAT1 Switch = T
  2.0 MAIN PROCESSING
    REPEAT: While the REPEAT1 switch = T
      2.1 DISPLAY MENU SCREEN
        CLEAR SCREEN
          Clear the screen
        DISPLAY MENU
          Display Option #1 Add a Record
          Display Option #2 Delete a Record
          Display Option #3 Update a Record
          Display Option #4 Exit to dBASE
          Display Option #5 Return to Main Menu
          Draw a box and Display Instructions
      2.2 ACCEPT USER'S SELECTION
        Accept SELECTION1 in the range of 1-5
      2.3 PROCESS SELECTIONS
        SELECT: Depending on SELECTION1
          2.3.1 PROCESS SELECTION #1
            Execute program INV11
          2.3.2 PROCESS SELECTION #2
            Execute program INV12
          2.3.3 PROCESS SELECTION #3
            Execute program INV13
          2.3.4 PROCESS SELECTION #4
            Set REPEAT Switch = F
            Set REPEAT1 Switch = F
          2.3.5 PROCESS SELECTION #5
            Set REPEAT1 Switch = F
        END SELECT
    END REPEAT
  3.0 TERMINATE PROCESSING
    3.1 RETURN TO MAIN MENU
      Return to calling program
```

    c. For the third selection, the maintenance program INV23.PRG (update a record) should be executed.

    d. For the fourth selection, the program should exit to the dBASE prompt.

    e. For the fifth selection, the program should return to the Main Menu.

The solution of this submenu program is similar to that of submenu program INV1.PRG. Following the steps of the solution of the submenu

```
****************************************************************
*                   AMERICAN SUPPLY COMPANY                     *
*                   INVOICE GENERATING SYSTEM                   *
*                   CUSTOMER FILE MAINTENANCE MENU              *
*                          INV2.PRG                             *
* ------------------------------------------------------------- *
* This is a Customer File Maintenance Menu subprogram. It       *
* is invoked by the Main Menu program INV.PRG of the            *
* Invoice Generating System for American Supply Company.        *
* The function of this program is to display the Customer       *
* File Maintenance Menu, accept the user's choice, and then     *
* execute the program corresponding to the user's choice.       *
*                                                               *
* Menu Choices are:                                             *
*                                                               *
*       1. INV21.PRG - Delete a Record                          *
*       2. INV22.PRG - Add a Record                             *
*       3. INV23.PRG - Update a Record                          *
*       4.          - Exit to dBASE                             *
*       5.          - Return to Main Menu                       *
* ------------------------------------------------------------- *
*            COPYRIGHT (C) . . . SUDESH M. DUGGAL               *
****************************************************************
*
***************************
* 1.0 INITIATE PROCESSING *
***************************
*
*** 1.1 DEFINE VARIABLES ***
    *
    *** DEFINE CONTROL VARIABLES ***
        *
        STORE [T] TO REPEAT2
        *
***********************
* 2.0 MAIN PROCESSING *
***********************
*
DO WHILE REPEAT2 = [T]
    *
    *** 2.1 DISPLAY MENU SCREEN ***
        *
        *** CLEAR SCREEN ***
            *
            CLEAR
            *
        *** DISPLAY MENU ***
            *
            @  2,29 SAY 'AMERICAN SUPPLY COMPANY'
            @  3,4  SAY DATE ()
            @  3,28 SAY 'INVOICE GENERATING SYSTEM'
            @  3,70 SAY TIME ()
            @  4,25 SAY 'CUSTOMER FILE MAINTENANCE MENU'
            @  5,0  TO  5,79
            @  9,25 SAY ' 1. Delete a Record'
```

Figure 9.14 Coding for menu program INV1.PRG

```
                @ 10,25 SAY ' 2. Add a Record'
                @ 11,25 SAY ' 3. Update a Record'
                @ 13,25 SAY ' 4. Exit to dBASE'
                @ 14,25 SAY ' 5. Return to Main Menu'
                @ 22,0  TO  22,79
                @ 1,0   TO  24,79 DOUBLE
                *
        *** 2.2 ACCEPT USER'S SELECTION ***
            *
            @ 23,24 SAY 'ENTER YOUR SELECTION, PLEASE (1-5) =>:'
            STORE 5 TO SELECTION1
            @ 23,65 GET SELECTION1 PICTURE '9' RANGE 1,5
            READ
            *
        *** 2.3 PROCESS SELECTIONS ***
            *
            DO CASE
                *
                *** 2.3.1 PROCESS SELECTION #1 ***
                    *
                    CASE SELECTION1 = 1
                    DO INV11
                    *
                *** 2.3.2 PROCESS SELECTION #2 ***
                    *
                    CASE SELECTION1 = 2
                    DO INV12
                    *
                *** 2.3.3 PROCESS SELECTION #3 ***
                    *
                    CASE SELECTION1 = 3
                    DO INV13
                    *
                *** 2.3.4 PROCESS SELECTION #4 ***
                    *
                    CASE SELECTION1 = 4
                    STORE [F] TO REPEAT
                    STORE [F] TO REPEAT1
                    *
                *** 2.3.5 PROCESS SELECTION #5 ***
                    *
                    CASE SELECTION1 = 5
                    STORE [F] TO REPEAT1
                    *
            ENDCASE
            *
ENDDO REPEAT1 = [T]
*
***************************
* 3.0 TERMINATE PROCESSING *
***************************
*
*** 3.1 RETURN TO MAIN MENU ***
    *
    RETURN
```

Figure 9.14 Continued

Figure 9.15 Menu screen for INV2.PRG program

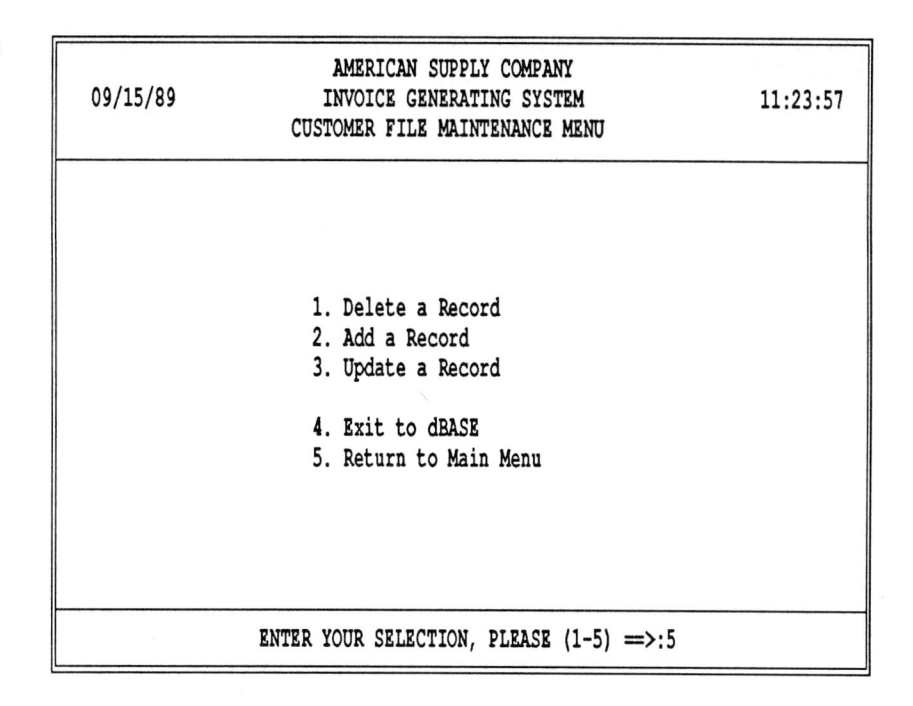

```
                      AMERICAN SUPPLY COMPANY
    09/15/89          INVOICE GENERATING SYSTEM              11:23:57
                    CUSTOMER FILE MAINTENANCE MENU




                       1. Delete a Record
                       2. Add a Record
                       3. Update a Record

                       4. Exit to dBASE
                       5. Return to Main Menu




              ENTER YOUR SELECTION, PLEASE (1-5) =>:5
```

program INV1.PRG, develop the structure chart, pseudocode, and coding of the subprogram INV2.PRG. These solutions are given in Figures 9.16, 9.17, and 9.18, respectively. A complete dBASE program for the menu program INV2.PRG is given in Figure 9.18 (see page 372).

9.6.3 Subprogram INV3.PRG

Program Description

Write a report generating submenu program. It should be invoked by the main menu program INV.PRG of the invoice generating system for the American Supply Company. The program should display the Report Generating Menu as shown in Figure 9.19, accept the user's valid choice, and then execute the corresponding program.

Processing Steps

The following steps should be used to develop the solution of the program:

1. The menu screen consisting of six options and instructions for the user as shown in Figure 9.19 should be displayed.
2. The screen should be frozen (paused) until the user selects one of the valid options.
3. After the user makes a selection, the processing function associated with the selection should be executed as follows:
   a. For the first selection, the program INV31.PRG (list items over $10) should be executed.
   b. For the second selection, the program INV32.PRG (list whole file with totals) should be executed.
   c. For the third selection, the program INV33.PRG (list whole file with retail price) should be executed.

Figure 9.16 Structure chart for INV2.PRG program

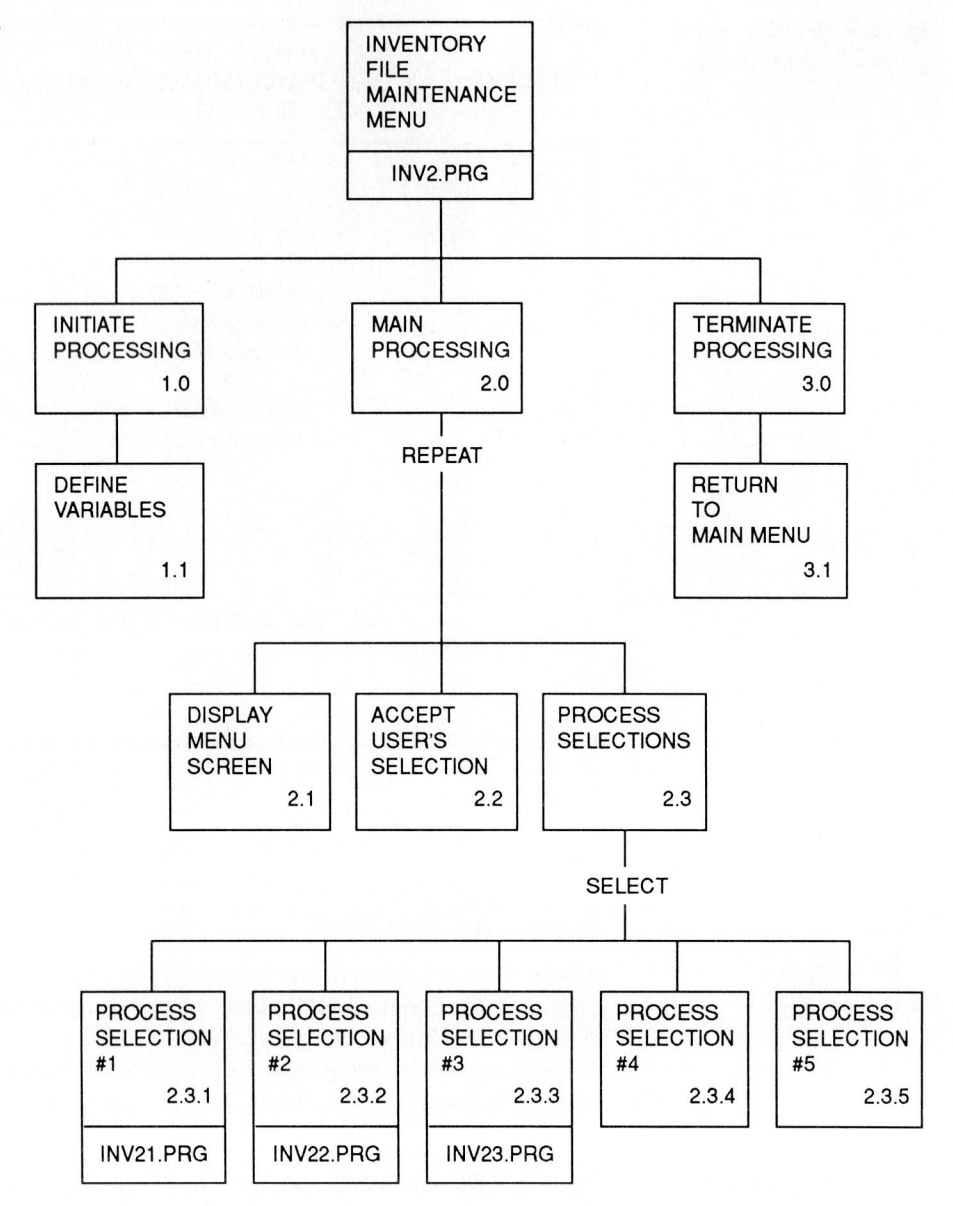

```
                    INVENTORY
                    FILE
                    MAINTENANCE
                    MENU
                    ────────────
                    INV2.PRG
       ┌───────────────┼───────────────┐
   INITIATE         MAIN            TERMINATE
   PROCESSING       PROCESSING      PROCESSING
        1.0             2.0             3.0
       │             REPEAT              │
   DEFINE              │               RETURN
   VARIABLES           │               TO
                       │               MAIN MENU
         1.1           │                   3.1
         ┌─────────────┼─────────────┐
      DISPLAY       ACCEPT        PROCESS
      MENU          USER'S        SELECTIONS
      SCREEN        SELECTION
           2.1          2.2            2.3
                                     SELECT
         ┌──────┬──────┼──────┬──────┐
      PROCESS PROCESS PROCESS PROCESS PROCESS
      SELECTION SELECTION SELECTION SELECTION SELECTION
      #1      #2      #3      #4      #5
        2.3.1   2.3.2   2.3.3   2.3.4   2.3.5
      ────── ────── ──────
      INV21.PRG INV22.PRG INV23.PRG
```

d. For the fourth selection, the program INV34.PRG (list whole file with control breaks) should be executed.

e. For the fifth selection, the program should exit to the dBASE prompt.

f. For the sixth selection, the program should return to the Main Menu.

The solution of this submenu program is similar to that of submenu program INV1.PRG. Following the steps of the solution of the submenu program INV1.PRG, develop the structure chart, pseudocode, and coding of the subprogram INV3.PRG. These solutions are given in Figures 9.20, 9.21, and 9.22, respectively.

Figure 9.17 Pseudocode for menu program INV2.PRG

```
0.0 CUSTOMER FILE MAINTENANCE—SUBMENU
    1.0 INITIATE PROCESSING
        1.1 DEFINE VARIABLES
            DEFINE CONTROL VARIABLES
                Set REPEAT2 switch = T
    2.0 MAIN PROCESSING
        REPEAT: While the REPEAT2 switch = T
            2.1 DISPLAY MENU SCREEN
                CLEAR SCREEN
                    Clear the screen
                DISPLAY MENU
                    Display Option #1 Add a Record
                    Display Option #2 Delete a Record
                    Display Option #3 Update a Record
                    Display Option #4 Exit to dBASE
                    Display Option #5 Return to Main Menu
                    Draw a box and Display the Instructions
            2.2 ACCEPT USER'S SELECTION
                Accept SELECTION2 in the range of 1-5
            2.3 PROCESS SELECTIONS
                SELECT: Depending on SELECTION2
                    2.3.1 PROCESS SELECTION #1
                        Execute program INV21
                    2.3.2 PROCESS SELECTION #2
                        Execute program INV22
                    2.3.3 PROCESS SELECTION #3
                        Execute program INV23
                    2.3.4 PROCESS SELECTION #4
                        Set REPEAT switch = F
                        Set REPEAT2 switch = F
                    2.3.5 PROCESS SELECTION #5
                        Set REPEAT2 switch = F
                END SELECT
        END REPEAT
    3.0 TERMINATE PROCESSING
        3.1 RETURN TO MAIN MENU
            Return to calling program
```

You have already developed the submenu program INV3.PRG in Chapter 8. Compare the structure charts of Figure 8.18 and 9.20. You will notice three changes. First, in Figure 9.20, you do not need housekeeping because the submenu program INV3.PRG is invoked by the main menu program INV.PRG. And because the default modes have already been set in the main menu program, you do not need to set them again in the submenu program.

```
****************************************************************
*                  AMERICAN SUPPLY COMPANY                      *
*                  INVOICE GENERATING SYSTEM                    *
*                CUSTOMER FILE MAINTENANCE MENU                 *
*                         INV2.PRG                              *
*---------------------------------------------------------------*
* This is a Customer File Maintenance Menu subprogram. It       *
* is invoked by the Main Menu program INV.PRG of the            *
* Invoice Generating System for American Supply Company.        *
* The function of this program is to display the Customer       *
* File Maintenance Menu, accept the user's choice, and then     *
* execute the program corresponding to the user's choice.       *
*                                                               *
* Menu Choices are:                                             *
*                                                               *
*      1. INV21.PRG - Delete a Record                           *
*      2. INV22.PRG - Add a Record                              *
*      3. INV23.PRG - Update a Record                           *
*      4.          - Exit to dBASE                              *
*      5.          - Return to Main Menu                        *
*---------------------------------------------------------------*
*           COPYRIGHT (C) . . . SUDESH M. DUGGAL                *
****************************************************************
*
**************************originaria
* 1.0 INITIATE PROCESSING *
***************************
*
*** 1.1 DEFINE VARIABLES ***
    *
    *** DEFINE CONTROL VARIABLES ***
        *
        STORE [T] TO REPEAT2
        *
***********************
* 2.0 MAIN PROCESSING *
***********************
*
DO WHILE REPEAT2 = [T]
    *
    *** 2.1 DISPLAY MENU SCREEN ***
        *
        *** CLEAR SCREEN ***
            *
            CLEAR
            *
        *** DISPLAY MENU ***
            *
            @  2,29 SAY 'AMERICAN SUPPLY COMPANY'
            @  3,4  SAY DATE ()
            @  3,28 SAY 'INVOICE GENERATING SYSTEM'
            @  3,70 SAY TIME ()
            @  4,25 SAY 'CUSTOMER FILE MAINTENANCE MENU'
            @  5,0  TO  5,79
            @  9,25 SAY ' 1. Delete a Record'
```

Figure 9.18 Coding for menu program INV2.PRG

```
            @ 10,25 SAY ' 2. Add a record'
            @ 11,25 SAY ' 3. Update a Record'
            @ 13,25 SAY ' 4. Exit to dBASE'
            @ 14,25 SAY ' 5. Return to Main Menu'
            @ 22,0  TO  22,79
            @  1,0  TO  24,79 DOUBLE
            *
    *** 2.2 ACCEPT USER'S SELECTION ***
        *
        @ 23,24 SAY ' ENTER YOUR SELECTION, PLEASE (1-5) =>:'
        STORE 5 TO SELECTION2
        @ 23,65 GET SELECTION2 PICTURE '9' RANGE 1,5
        READ
        *
    *** 2.3 PROCESS SELECTIONS ***
        *
        DO CASE
            *
            *** 2.3.1 PROCESS SELECTION #1 ***
                *
                CASE SELECTION2 = 1
                DO INV21
                *
            *** 2.3.2 PROCESS SELECTION #2 ***
                *
                CASE SELECTION2 = 2
                DO INV22
                *
            *** 2.3.3 PROCESS SELECTION #3 ***
                *
                CASE SELECTION2 = 3
                DO INV23
                *
            *** 2.3.4 PROCESS SELECTION #4 ***
                *
                CASE SELECTION2 = 4
                STORE [F] TO REPEAT
                STORE [F] TO REPEAT2
                *
            *** 2.3.5 PROCESS SELECTION #5 ***
                *
                CASE SELECTION2 = 5
                STORE [F] TO REPEAT2
                *
        ENDCASE
        *
ENDDO REPEAT2 = [T]
*
***************************
* 3.0 TERMINATE PROCESSING *
***************************
*
*** 3.1 RETURN TO MAIN MENU ***
    *
    RETURN
```

Figure 9.18 Continued

Figure 9.19 Menu screen for INV3.PRG program

```
┌─────────────────────────────────────────────────────────────┐
│                    AMERICAN SUPPLY COMPANY                  │
│   09/15/89         INVOICE GENERATING SYSTEM      11:23:57  │
│                     REPORT GENERATING MENU                  │
├─────────────────────────────────────────────────────────────┤
│                                                             │
│                                                             │
│                                                             │
│              1. List items over $10.00                      │
│              2. List whole file with totals                 │
│              3. List whole file with retail price           │
│                                                             │
│              4. List whole file with control breaks         │
│                                                             │
│              5. Exit to dBASE                               │
│              6. Return to Main Menu                         │
│                                                             │
│                                                             │
│                                                             │
├─────────────────────────────────────────────────────────────┤
│         ENTER YOUR SELECTION, PLEASE (1-6)  =>:6            │
└─────────────────────────────────────────────────────────────┘
```

Second, there is an extra option available in Figure 9.20: return to Main Menu. Because the submenu program INV3.PRG is invoked by the main menu program INV.PRG, its control should be returned to the main menu program after the execution of the INV3.PRG submenu program. Thus, this step is needed here, whereas it was not needed in Chapter 8, where the submenu program INV3.PRG was executed independently.

Third, the step reset default modes is replaced by the Return to Main Menu module. As already mentioned, the submenu program INV3.PRG is invoked by the main menu program INV.PRG, so the default modes have not been set. Therefore, there is no need for resetting them, and we do not need the Reset Default Mode module. But because the submenu program INV3.PRG is invoked by the main menu program, its control should be returned to the calling program after the execution of this submenu program. Thus, the Return to Calling Program module has been added to terminate processing of the submenu program INV3.PRG.

Make the required changes in the pseudocode and coding of Figures 8.19 and 8.20, respectively, to obtain the modified pseudocode and coding for the INV3.PRG submenu program as shown in Figures 9.21 and 9.22, respectively. A complete dBASE program for the menu program INV3.PRG is given in Figure 9.22.

Having developed the main menu program INV.PRG and submenu programs INV1.PRG, INV2.PRG, and INV3.PRG, we now test run the system. To do this, if you type the command

    . DO INV   <Return>

the system will respond by displaying the introductory screen as shown in Figure 9.4.

Press any key to continue with the execution of the system processing. The Main Menu of the invoice generating system as shown in Figure 9.5 will be displayed.

9.6 Development of Other Programs of the System

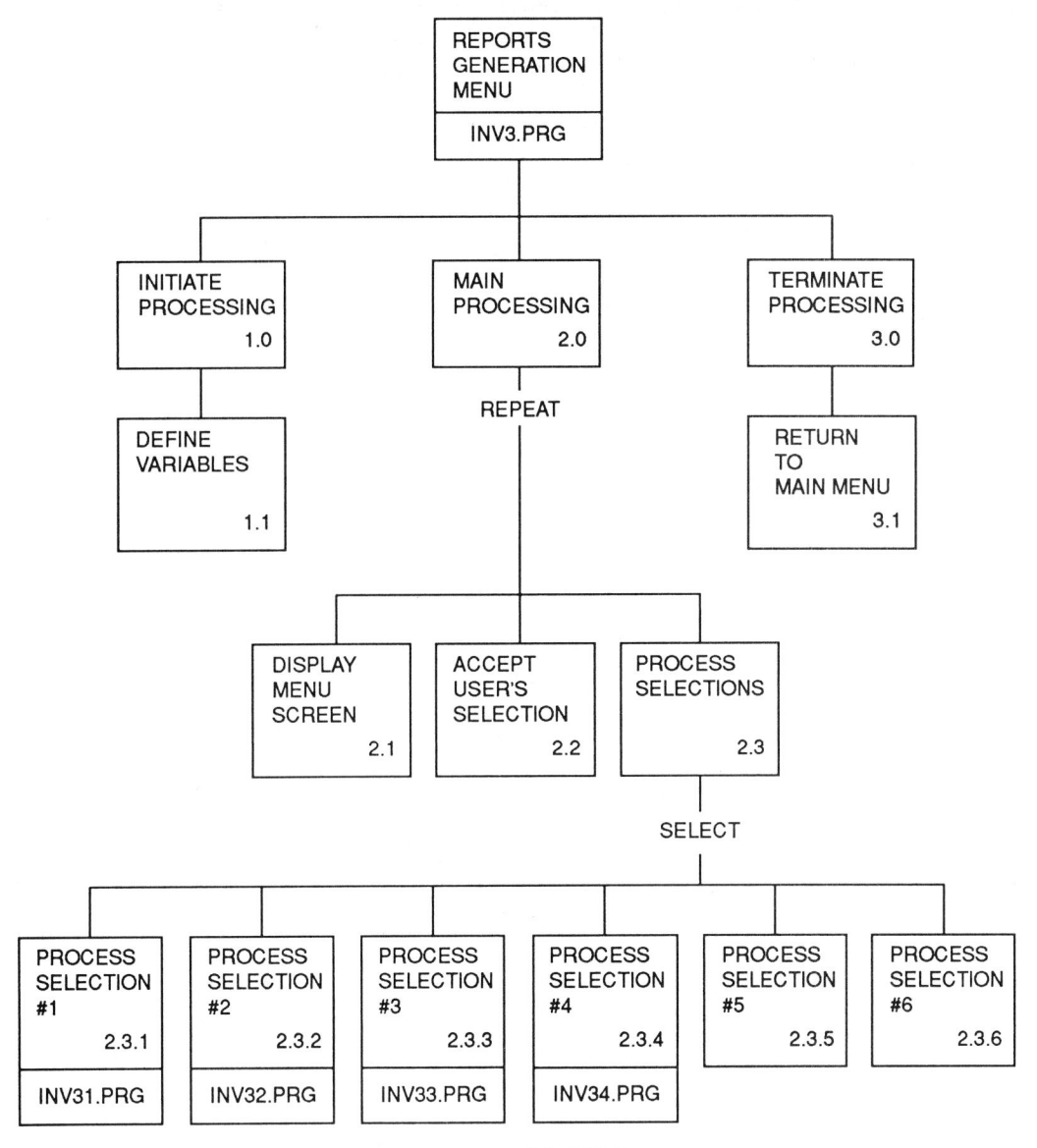

Figure 9.20 Structure chart for menu program INV3.PRG

Test each of the options of this menu. If you select the first, the system will respond by displaying the submenu for maintaining the inventory file as shown in Figure 9.11. Test each option of this submenu program; stub programs should be supplied for the first three. The programs corresponding to these options will be developed in Chapters 10–12.

Next, select the second option from the Main Menu; the system will respond by displaying the submenu for maintaining the customer file as shown in Figure 9.15. Test each of the options of this submenu program. Stub programs should be supplied for the first three. The programs corresponding to these options will not be developed and are left as assignments to be completed by you.

Now select the third option from the Main Menu; the system will respond by displaying the Report Generating Submenu as shown in Figure 9.19. Further test each of the options of this subsystem program. Programs

Figure 9.21 Pseudocode for menu program INV3.PRG

```
0.0 REPORTS GENERATING—SUBMENU
    1.0 INITIATE PROCESSING
        1.1 DEFINE VARIABLES
            DEFINE CONTROL VARIABLES
                Set REPEAT3 switch = T
    2.0 MAIN PROCESSING
        REPEAT: While the REPEAT3 switch = T
            2.1 DISPLAY MENU SCREEN
                CLEAR SCREEN
                    Clear the screen
                DISPLAY MENU
                    Display Option #1 List items over $10.00
                    Display Option #2 List whole file with Totals
                    Display Option #3 List whole file with Retail price
                    Display Option #4 List whole file with Control Breaks
                    Display Option #5 Exit to dBASE
                    Display Option #6 Return to Main Menu
                    Draw a box and Display the Instructions
            2.2 ACCEPT USER'S SELECTION
                Accept SELECTION3 in the range of 1-6
            2.3 PROCESS SELECTIONS
                SELECT: Depending on SELECTION3
                    2.3.1 PROCESS SELECTION #1
                        Execute program INV31
                    2.3.2 PROCESS SELECTION #2
                        Execute program INV32
                    2.3.3 PROCESS SELECTION #3
                        Execute program INV33
                    2.3.4 PROCESS SELECTION #4
                        Execute program INV34
                    2.3.5 PROCESS SELECTION #5
                        Set REPEAT switch = F
                        Set REPEAT3 switch = F
                    2.3.6 PROCESS SELECTION #6
                        Set REPEAT3 switch = F
                END SELECT
        END REPEAT
    3.0 TERMINATE PROCESSING
        3.1 RETURN TO MAIN MENU
            Return to calling program
```

INV31.PRG, INV32.PRG, INV33.PRG, and INV34.PRG corresponding to the first four options have already been developed in Case Studies 1, 2, 3, and 4 in Chapters 4, 5, 6, and 7, respectively.

The fourth option should be selected next. A stub program should be provided to respond to this selection. The program corresponding to this option will be developed in Chapter 13. Finally, test the last two options.

```
*****************************************************************
*                   AMERICAN SUPPLY COMPANY                      *
*                   INVOICE GENERATING SYSTEM                    *
*                   REPORTS GENERATING MENU                      *
*                          INV3.PRG                              *
* -------------------------------------------------------------- *
* This is the Reports Generating Menu subprogram. It is          *
* invoked by the Main Menu program INV.PRG of the Invoice        *
* Generating System for American Supply Company. The             *
* function of this program is to display the Reports             *
* Generating Menu, accept the user's choice, and then            *
* execute the program corresponding to the user's choice.        *
*                                                                *
* Menu Choices are:                                              *
*                                                                *
*       1. INV31.PRG - List items over $10.00                    *
*       2. INV32.PRG - List whole file with Totals               *
*       3. INV33.PRG - List whole file with Retail Price         *
*       4. INV34.PRG - List whole file with Control Breaks       *
*       5.          - Exit to dBASE                              *
*       6.          - Return to Main Menu                        *
* -------------------------------------------------------------- *
*             COPYRIGHT (C) . . . SUDESH M. DUGGAL               *
*****************************************************************
*
**************************
* 1.0 INITIATE PROCESSING *
**************************
*
*** 1.1 DEFINE VARIABLES ***
    *
    *** DEFINE CONTROL VARIABLES ***
        *
        STORE [T] TO REPEAT3
        *
***********************
* 2.0 MAIN PROCESSING *
***********************
*
DO WHILE REPEAT3 = [T]
    *
    *** 2.1 DISPLAY MENU SCREEN ***
        *
        *** CLEAR SCREEN ***
            *
            CLEAR
            *
        *** DISPLAY MENU ***
            *
            @ 2,29 SAY 'AMERICAN SUPPLY COMPANY'
            @ 3,4  SAY DATE ()
            @ 3,28 SAY 'INVOICE GENERATING SYSTEM'
            @ 4,29 SAY 'REPORT GENERATING MENU'
            @ 5,0  TO  5,79
```

Figure 9.22 Coding for menu program INV3.PRG

```
            @  9,25 SAY ' 1. List items over $10.00'
            @ 10,25 SAY ' 2. List whole file with Totals'
            @ 11,25 SAY ' 3. List whole file with Retail price'
            @ 12,25 SAY ' 4. List whole file with Control Breaks'
            @ 14,25 SAY ' 5. Exit to dBASE'
            @ 15,25 SAY ' 6. Return to Main Menu'
            @ 22,0  TO  22,79
            @  1,0  TO  24,79 DOUBLE
            *
    *** 2.2 ACCEPT USER'S SELECTION ***
            *
        @ 23,25 SAY 'ENTER YOUR SELECTION, PLEASE (1-6) =>:'
        STORE 6 TO SELECTION3
        @ 23,65 GET SELECTION3 PICTURE '9' RANGE 1,6
        READ
        *
    *** 2.3 PROCESS SELECTIONS ***
            *
        DO CASE
            *
            *** 2.3.1 PROCESS SELECTION #1 ***
                *
                CASE SELECTION3 = 1
                DO INV31
                *
            *** 2.3.2 PROCESS SELECTION #2 ***
                *
                CASE SELECTION3 = 2
                DO INV32
                *
            *** 2.3.3 PROCESS SELECTION #3 ***
                *
                CASE SELECTION3 = 3
                DO INV33
                *
            *** 2.3.4 PROCESS SELECTION #4 ***
                *
                CASE SELECTION3 = 4
                DO INV34
                *
            *** 2.3.5 PROCESS SELECTION #5 ***
                *
                CASE SELECTION3 = 5
                STORE [F] TO REPEAT
                STORE [F] TO REPEAT3
                *
            *** 2.3.6 PROCESS SELECTION #6 ***
                *
                CASE SELECTION3 = 6
                STORE [F] TO REPEAT3
                *
        ENDCASE
        *
ENDDO REPEAT3 = [T]
*
```

Figure 9.22 Continued

```
****************************
* 3.0 TERMINATE PROCESSING *
****************************
*
*** 3.1 RETURN TO MAIN MENU ***
    *
    RETURN
```

Figure 9.22 Continued

When selected, these will provide exit to DOS and exit to dBASE, respectively.

9.7 Summary

A system is a collection of components integrated for the purpose of achieving a common goal. Each system is part of a suprasystem, and each system consists of several subsystems. A business application system is a collection of computer programs working together to solve a particular business problem.

The structured approach to system development consists of the following three steps:

1. Structured system analysis phase
2. Structured system design phase
3. Structured system implementation phase

In the structured system analysis phase, the need for the system development is identified, the current system is analyzed, the objectives for the new system are defined, the solution to the needs and ways of meeting the objectives are proposed, and the requirements for the new system to be used in the structured system design approach are specified.

In the structured system design phase, the system is subdivided into subsystems using the structure chart design tools. These tools are the structure chart, cohesion, coupling, and span of control. Each subsystem is developed using the program development process as explained in Chapter 4.

In the structured system implementation phase, the individual programs of the system are designed, coded, and tested.

A stub program is a dummy program used in place of any subsystem to test the main system program. Use the stub program instead of waiting for the individual subsystem to be developed to test the main system program.

KEY CONCEPTS

business application system
physical system
structured approach to system development
structured system analysis phase
structured system design phase

structured system implementation phase
stub programs
subsystem
suprasystem
system

REVIEW QUESTIONS

1. Define the following terms:
   a. System
   b. Subsystem
   c. Suprasystem
   d. Physical system
   e. Business application system
2. What is the difference between a physical system and a business application system?
3. List three different steps for the structured approach to system development.
4. What is the function of the structured system analysis phase?
5. What is the function of the structured system design phase?
6. What is the function of the structured system implementation phase?
7. What is a stub program? What is its use?
8. List the four functions performed by a stub program.

HANDS-ON ASSIGNMENT

Programming Assignment 9A

Program Description Write a main menu program ACR.PRG for the accounts receivable system for the American Supply Company. It should display the introductory welcome screen, including the name of the system, as shown in Figure 9.23.

After the introductory screen is displayed, the program should display the Main Menu for the accounts receivable system as shown in Figure 9.24, accept the user's valid choice, and then, depending on the user's selection, execute the corresponding subsystem program.

Figure 9.23 Introductory welcome screen for the accounts receivable system

```
               WELCOME TO THE


           AMERICAN SUPPLY COMPANY

              4950 Creek Drive
            Cincinnati, OH 45241
                (513) 733-5555




           ACCOUNTS RECEIVABLE SYSTEM




        PRESS ANY KEY TO CONTINUE ===>:
```

Figure 9.24 Main Menu for the accounts receivable system

```
                      AMERICAN SUPPLY COMPANY
      09/15/89       ACCOUNTS RECEIVABLE SYSTEM              11:23:57
                             MAIN  MENU


                     1. Maintain Customer File
                     2. Maintain Receivable File

                     3. Generate Receivable Reports
                     4. Process Receivable Bills

                     5. Exit to DOS
                     6. Exit to dBASE




                ENTER YOUR SELECTION, PLEASE (1-6) ==>:6
```

Processing Steps The following steps should be used to develop the solution of the program:

1. The main menu screen consisting of six options and instructions for the user, as shown in Figure 9.24, should be displayed.
2. The screen should be frozen (paused) until the user selects one of the valid options.
3. After the user makes a selection, the processing function corresponding to the selection made should be executed as follows:
    a. For the first selection, the subsystem program ACR1.PRG (maintain customer file) should be executed.
    b. For the second selection, the subsystem program ACR2.PRG (maintain receivable file) should be executed.
    c. For the third selection, the subsystem program ACR3.PRG (generate receivable reports) should be executed.
    d. For the fourth selection, the subsystem program ACR4.PRG (process receivable bills) should be executed.
    e. For the fifth selection, the program should exit to the DOS prompt.
    f. For the sixth selection, the program should exit to the dBASE prompt.
4. Because subsystem programs ACR1.PRG, ACR2.PRG, ACR3.PRG, and ACR4.PRG have not yet been developed, you can create the stub programs for these subsystem programs. When executed, each stub program should simply display the message that the subsystem program has been processed, as shown in Figure 9.25.

Now develop the rest of the menu subsystem programs ACR1.PRG, ACR2.PRG, and ACR3.PRG, which are described in the following sections.

Submenu Program ACR1.PRG

Program Description Write a customer file maintenance submenu program ACR1.PRG. It should be invoked by the main menu program ACR.PRG of the accounts receivable system for the American Supply Company. The program should display the Customer File Maintenance Menu as shown in Figure 9.26, accept the user's valid choice, and then execute the corresponding program.

Processing Steps The following steps should be used to develop the solution of the program:

1. The menu screen consisting of five options and instructions for the user as shown in Figure 9.26 should be displayed.
2. The screen should be frozen (paused) until the user selects one of the valid options.

Figure 9.25 Stub program for the ACR1.PRG program

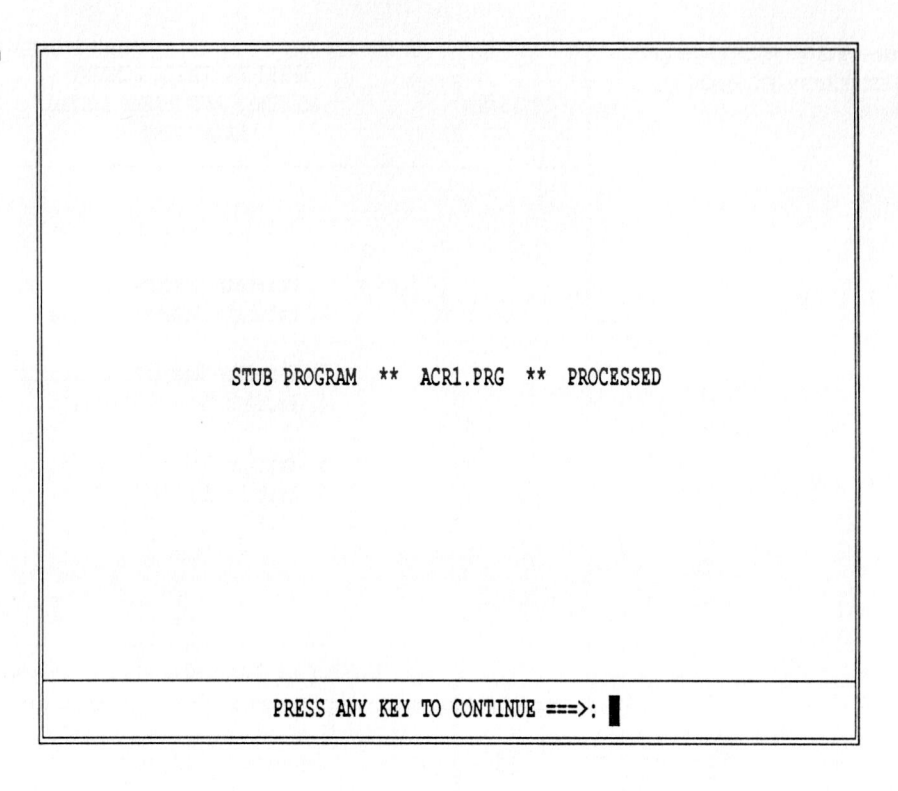

```
          STUB PROGRAM  **  ACR1.PRG  **  PROCESSED




          PRESS ANY KEY TO CONTINUE ===>: ▋
```

3. After the user makes a selection, the processing function associated with the selection should be executed as follows:
   a. For the first selection, the maintenance program ACR11.PRG (delete a record) should be executed.
   b. For the second selection, the maintenance program ACR12.PRG (add a record) should be executed.
   c. For the third selection, the maintenance program ACR13.PRG (update a record) should be executed.
   d. For the fourth selection, the program should exit to the dBASE prompt.

Figure 9.26 Menu screen for the ACR1.PRG program

```
                    AMERICAN SUPPLY COMPANY
   09/15/89         ACCOUNTS RECEIVABLE SYSTEM          11:23:57
                   CUSTOMER FILE MAINTENANCE MENU



                      1. Delete a Record
                      2. Add a Record
                      3. Update a Record

                      4. Exit to dBASE
                      5. Return to Main Menu




            ENTER YOUR SELECTION, PLEASE (1-5) ==>:5
```

Figure 9.27 Stub program for the ACR11.PRG program

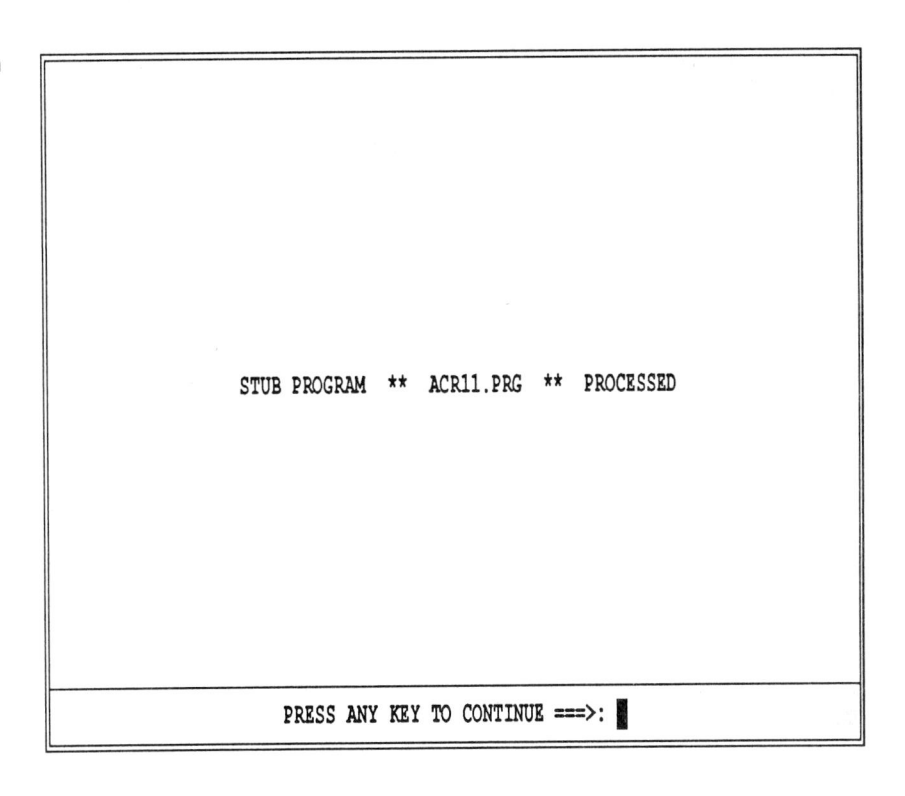

```
┌──────────────────────────────────────────────────┐
│                                                  │
│                                                  │
│                                                  │
│                                                  │
│         STUB PROGRAM  **  ACR11.PRG  **  PROCESSED │
│                                                  │
│                                                  │
│                                                  │
│                                                  │
│                                                  │
│                                                  │
│              PRESS ANY KEY TO CONTINUE ===>: ▌   │
└──────────────────────────────────────────────────┘
```

    e. For the fifth selection, the program should return to the Main Menu.

4. Because the subsystem programs ACR11.PRG, ACR12.PRG, and ACR13.PRG have not yet been developed, you can create the stub programs for these. When executed, each stub program should simply display the message that the subsystem program has been processed, as shown in Figure 9.27.

Submenu Program ACR2.PRG

Program Description Write an accounts receivable file maintenance submenu program ACR2.PRG. It should be invoked by the main menu program ACR.PRG of the accounts receivable system for the American Supply Company. The program should display the Accounts Receivable File Maintenance Menu as shown in Figure 9.28, accept the valid user's choice, and then execute the corresponding program.

Processing Steps The following steps should be used to develop the solution of the program:

1. The menu screen consisting of five options and instructions for the user as shown in Figure 9.28 should be displayed.
2. The screen should be frozen (paused) until the user selects one of the valid options.
3. After the user makes a selection, the processing function associated with the selection should be executed as follows:

    a. For the first selection, the maintenance program ACR21.PRG (delete a record) should be executed.
    b. For the second selection, the maintenance program ACR22.PRG (add a record) should be executed.
    c. For the third selection, the maintenance program ACR23.PRG (update a record) should be executed.
    d. For the fourth selection, the program should exit to the dBASE prompt.
    e. For the fifth selection, the program should return to the Main Menu.

4. Because the subsystem programs ACR21.PRG, ACR22.PRG, and ACR23.PRG have not yet been developed, you can create the stub programs for these. When executed, each stub program should simply display the message that the subsystem program has been processed, as shown in Figure 9.29.

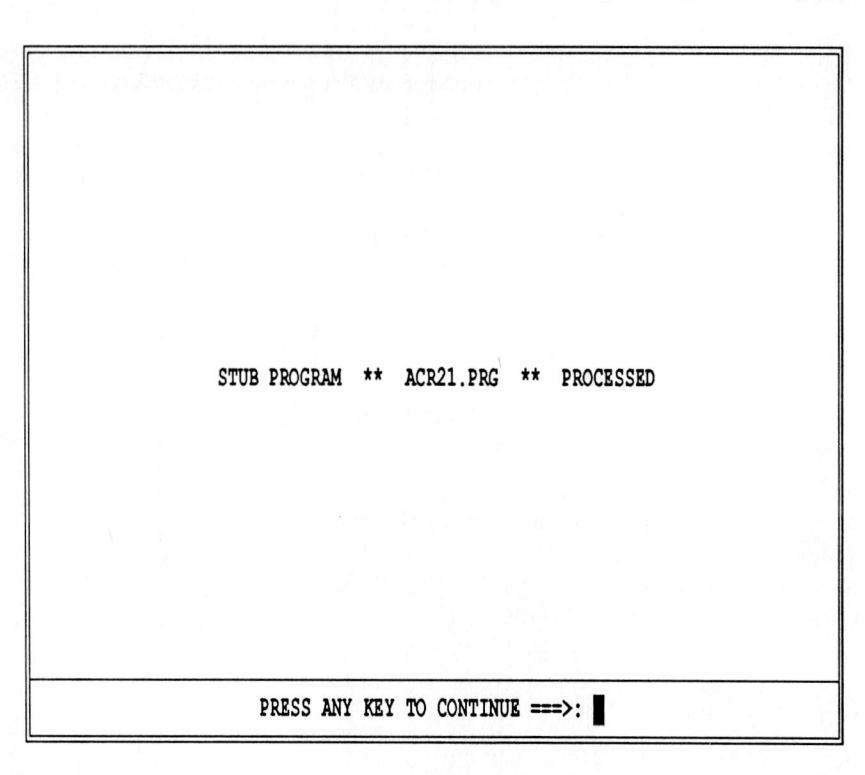

Figure 9.28 Menu screen for the ACR2.PRG program

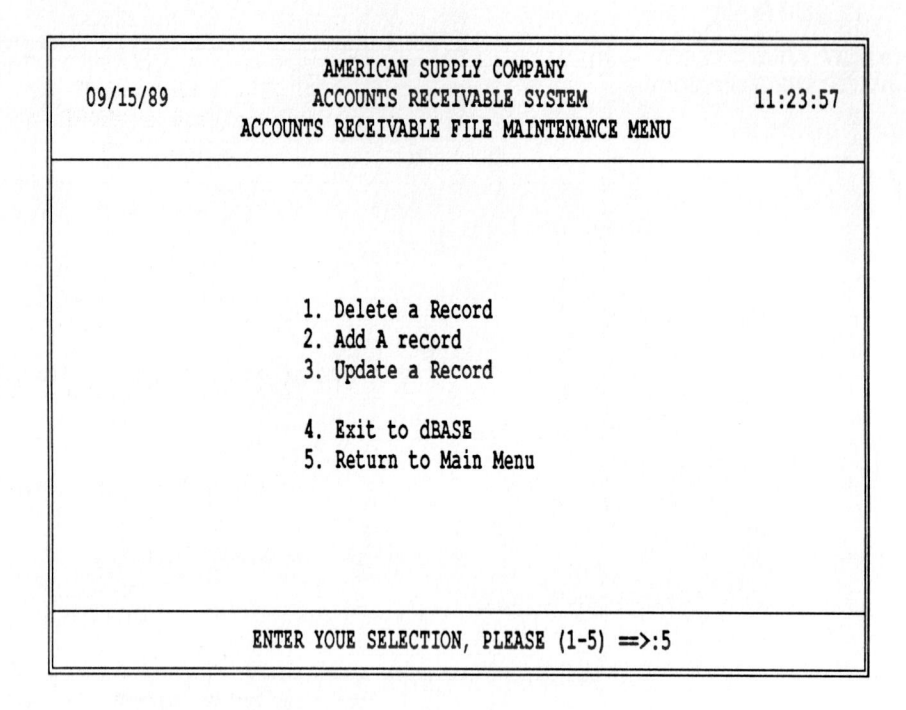

```
                    AMERICAN SUPPLY COMPANY
  09/15/89          ACCOUNTS RECEIVABLE SYSTEM              11:23:57
              ACCOUNTS RECEIVABLE FILE MAINTENANCE MENU




                     1. Delete a Record
                     2. Add A record
                     3. Update a Record

                     4. Exit to dBASE
                     5. Return to Main Menu




              ENTER YOUE SELECTION, PLEASE (1-5) ==>:5
```

Submenu Program ACR3.PRG

Program Description Write a report generating submenu program ACR3.PRG. It should be invoked by the main menu program ACR.PRG of the accounts receivable system for the American Supply Company. The program should display the Report Generating Menu as shown in Figure 9.30, accept the valid user's choice, and then execute the corresponding program.

Processing Steps The following steps should be used to develop the solution of the program:

1. The menu screen consisting of six options and

Figure 9.29 Stub program for the ACR21.PRG program

```





              STUB PROGRAM  **  ACR21.PRG  **  PROCESSED






              PRESS ANY KEY TO CONTINUE ===>:
```

Figure 9.30 Menu screen for the ACR3.PRG program

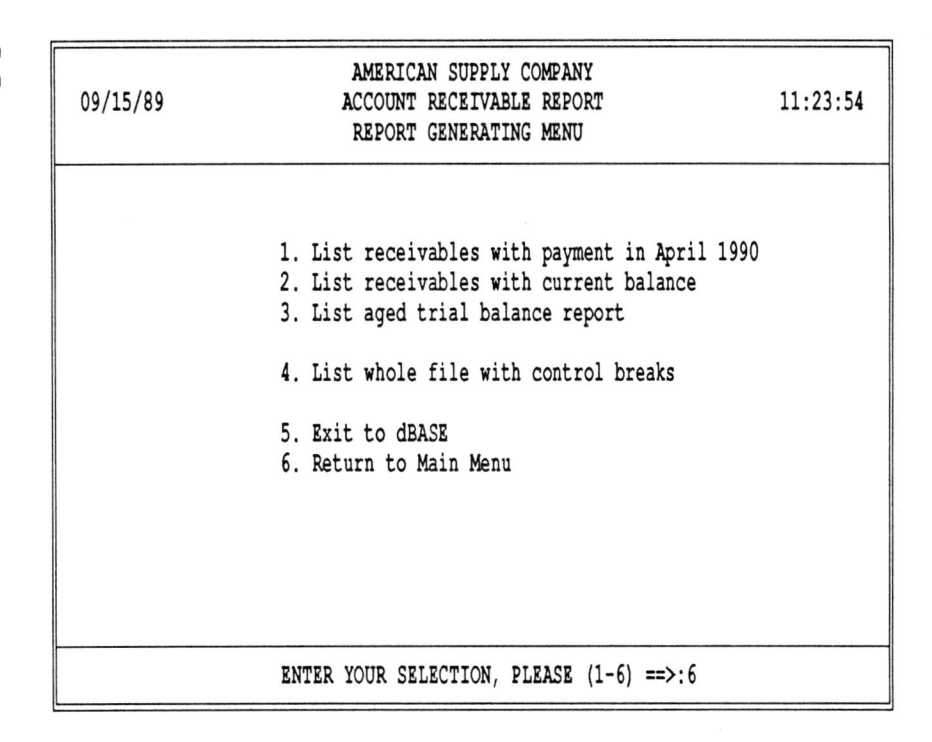

```
┌─────────────────────────────────────────────────────────────────┐
│                       AMERICAN SUPPLY COMPANY                   │
│  09/15/89            ACCOUNT RECEIVABLE REPORT         11:23:54 │
│                       REPORT GENERATING MENU                    │
├─────────────────────────────────────────────────────────────────┤
│                                                                 │
│         1. List receivables with payment in April 1990          │
│         2. List receivables with current balance                │
│         3. List aged trial balance report                       │
│                                                                 │
│         4. List whole file with control breaks                  │
│                                                                 │
│         5. Exit to dBASE                                        │
│         6. Return to Main Menu                                  │
│                                                                 │
│                                                                 │
├─────────────────────────────────────────────────────────────────┤
│              ENTER YOUR SELECTION, PLEASE (1-6) ==>:6           │
└─────────────────────────────────────────────────────────────────┘
```

instructions for the user as shown in Figure 9.30 should be displayed.

2. The screen should be frozen (paused) until the user selects one of the valid options.
3. After the user makes a selection, the processing function associated with the selection should be executed as follows:
   a. For the first selection, the program ACR31.PRG (List receivables with payment in April 1990) should be executed.
   b. For the second selection, the program ACR32.PRG (List receivables with current balance) should be executed.
   c. For the third selection, the program ACR33.PRG (List aged trial balance report) should be executed.
   d. For the fourth selection, the program ACR34.PRG (List whole file with control breaks) should be executed.
   e. For the fifth selection, the program should exit to the dBASE prompt.
   f. For the sixth selection, the program should return to the Main Menu.

Note: The subsystem program ACR3.PRG has already been developed in Chapter 8 (Programming Assignment 8A). You need to modify it so that it can be invoked by the main menu program ACR.PRG of the accounts receivable system for the American Supply Company.

Programming Assignment 9B

Program Description Write a main menu program PAY.PRG for the payroll system for the American Supply Company. It should display the introductory welcome screen, including the name of the system, as shown in Figure 9.31.

After the introductory screen is displayed, the program should display the Main Menu for the payroll system as shown in Figure 9.32, accept the user's valid choice, and then, depending on the user's selection, execute the corresponding subsystem program.

Processing Steps The following steps should be used to develop the solution of the program:

1. The main menu screen consisting of six options and instructions for the user as shown in Figure 9.32 should be displayed.
2. The screen should be frozen (paused) until the user selects one of the valid options.
3. After the user makes a selection, the processing

Figure 9.31 Introductory welcome screen for the payroll system

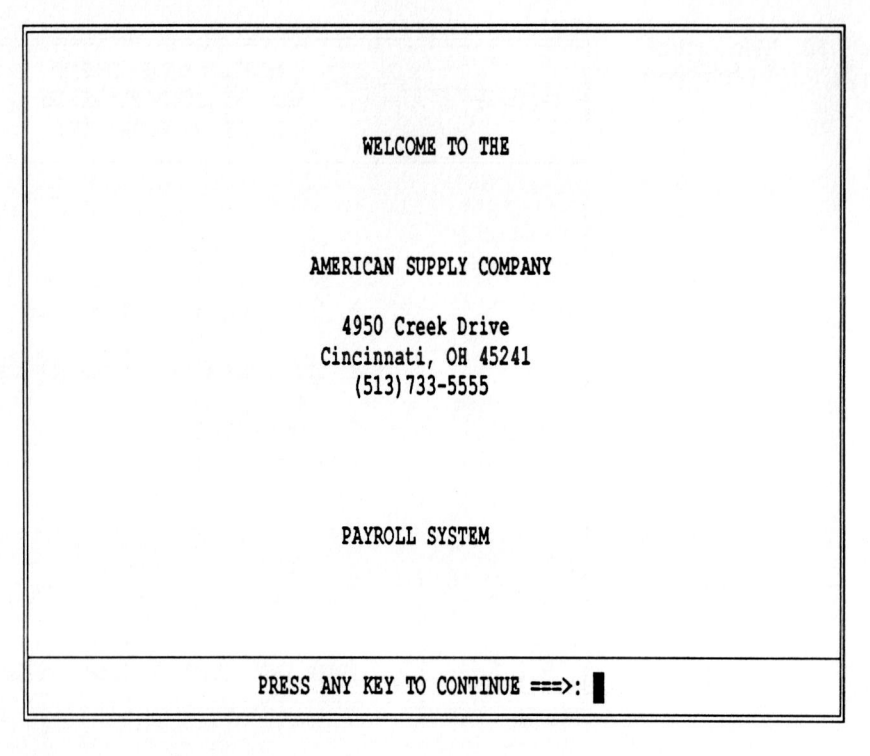

```
                    WELCOME TO THE


               AMERICAN SUPPLY COMPANY

                   4950 Creek Drive
                  Cincinnati, OH 45241
                    (513) 733-5555




                    PAYROLL SYSTEM




          PRESS ANY KEY TO CONTINUE ===>: ▌
```

function corresponding to the selection made should be executed as follows:

a. For the first selection, the subsystem program PAY1.PRG (maintain employee file) should be executed.
b. For the second selection, the subsystem program PAY2.PRG (maintain hours file) should be executed.
c. For the third selection, the subsystem program PAY3.PRG (generate payroll reports) should be executed.
d. For the fourth selection, the subsystem program PAY4.PRG (process payroll) should be executed.
e. For the fifth selection, the program should exit to the DOS prompt.

Figure 9.32 Main Menu for the payroll system

```
                    AMERICAN SUPPLY COMPANY
  09/15/89              PAYROLL SYSTEM              11:23:57
                          MAIN  MENU
_____

               1. Maintain Employee File
               2. Maintain Hours File

               3. Generate Payroll Reports
               4. Process Payroll

               5. Exit to DOS
               6. Exit to dBASE



_____
          ENTER YOUR SELECTION, PLEASE (1-6) ==>:6
```

Figure 9.33 Stub program for the PAY1.PRG program

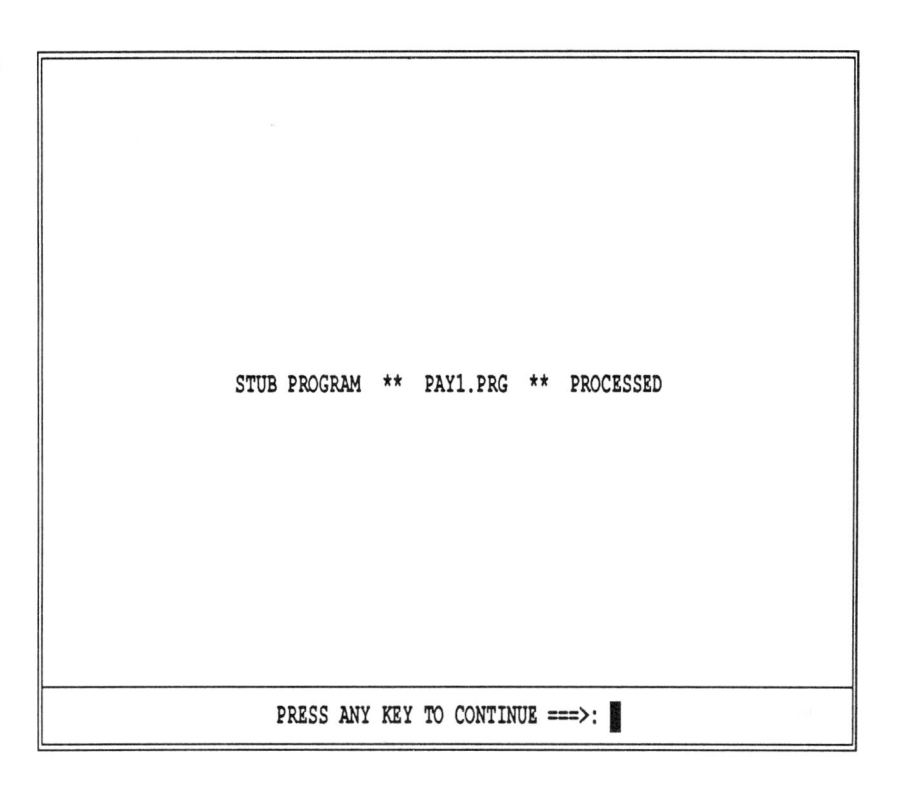

```
STUB PROGRAM ** PAY1.PRG ** PROCESSED




                    PRESS ANY KEY TO CONTINUE ===>: █
```

f. For the sixth selection, the program should exit to the dBASE prompt.

4. Because the subsystem programs PAY1.PRG, PAY2.PRG, PAY3.PRG, and PAY4.PRG have not yet been developed, you can create the stub programs for these. When executed, each stub program should simply display the message that the subsystem program has been processed, as shown in Figure 9.33.

Now develop the rest of the menu subsystem programs PAY1.PRG, PAY2.PRG, and PAY3.PRG, which are described in the following sections.

Submenu Program PAY1.PRG

Program Description Write an employee file maintenance submenu program PAY1.PRG. It should be invoked by the main menu program PAY.PRG of the payroll system for the American Supply Company. The program should display the Employee File Maintenance Menu as shown in Figure 9.34, accept the user's valid choice, and then execute the corresponding program.

Processing Steps The following steps should be used to develop the solution of the program:

1. The menu screen consisting of five options and instructions for the user as shown in Figure 9.34 should be displayed.
2. The screen should be frozen (paused) until the user selects one of the valid options.
3. After the user makes a selection, the processing function associated with the selection should be executed as follows:

   a. For the first selection, the maintenance program PAY11.PRG (delete a record) should be executed.
   b. For the second selection, the maintenance program PAY12.PRG (add a record) should be executed.
   c. For the third selection, the maintenance program PAY13.PRG (update a record) should be executed.
   d. For the fourth selection, the program should exit to the dBASE prompt.
   e. For the fifth selection, the program should return to the Main Menu.

4. Because the subsystem programs PAY11.PRG, PAY12.PRG, and PAY13.PRG have not yet been developed, you can create the stub programs for these. When executed, each stub program should simply display the message that the subsystem program has been processed, as shown in Figure 9.35.

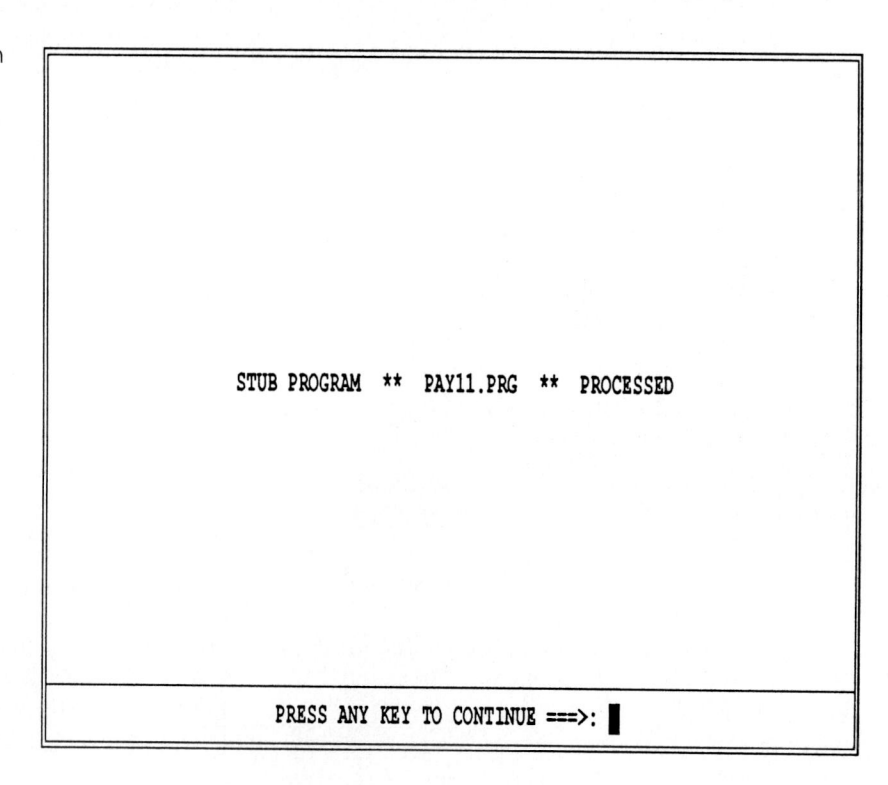

Figure 9.34 Menu screen for the PAY1.PRG program

```
┌─────────────────────────────────────────────────────────────┐
│                    AMERICAN SUPPLY COMPANY                  │
│   09/15/89            PAYROLL SYSTEM              11:23:57  │
│                EMPLOYEE FILE MAINTENANCE MENU               │
├─────────────────────────────────────────────────────────────┤
│                                                             │
│                                                             │
│                                                             │
│                    1. Delete a Record                       │
│                    2. Add a Record                          │
│                    3. Update a Record                       │
│                                                             │
│                    4. Exit to dBASE                         │
│                    5. Return to Main Menu                   │
│                                                             │
│                                                             │
│                                                             │
├─────────────────────────────────────────────────────────────┤
│             ENTER YOUR SELECTION, PLEASE (1-5) ==>:5        │
└─────────────────────────────────────────────────────────────┘
```

Submenu Program PAY2.PRG

Program Description   Write an hours file maintenance submenu program PAY2.PRG. It should be invoked by the main menu program PAY.PRG of the payroll system for the American Supply Company. The program should display the Hours File Maintenance Menu as shown in Figure 9.36, accept the user's valid choice, and then execute the corresponding program.

Processing Steps   The following steps should be used to develop the solution of the program:

Figure 9.35 Stub program for the PAY11.PRG program

```
┌─────────────────────────────────────────────────────────────┐
│                                                             │
│                                                             │
│                                                             │
│                                                             │
│                                                             │
│                                                             │
│            STUB PROGRAM  **  PAY11.PRG  **  PROCESSED       │
│                                                             │
│                                                             │
│                                                             │
│                                                             │
│                                                             │
│                                                             │
├─────────────────────────────────────────────────────────────┤
│              PRESS ANY KEY TO CONTINUE ===>:                │
└─────────────────────────────────────────────────────────────┘
```

Figure 9.36 Menu screen for the PAY2.PRG program

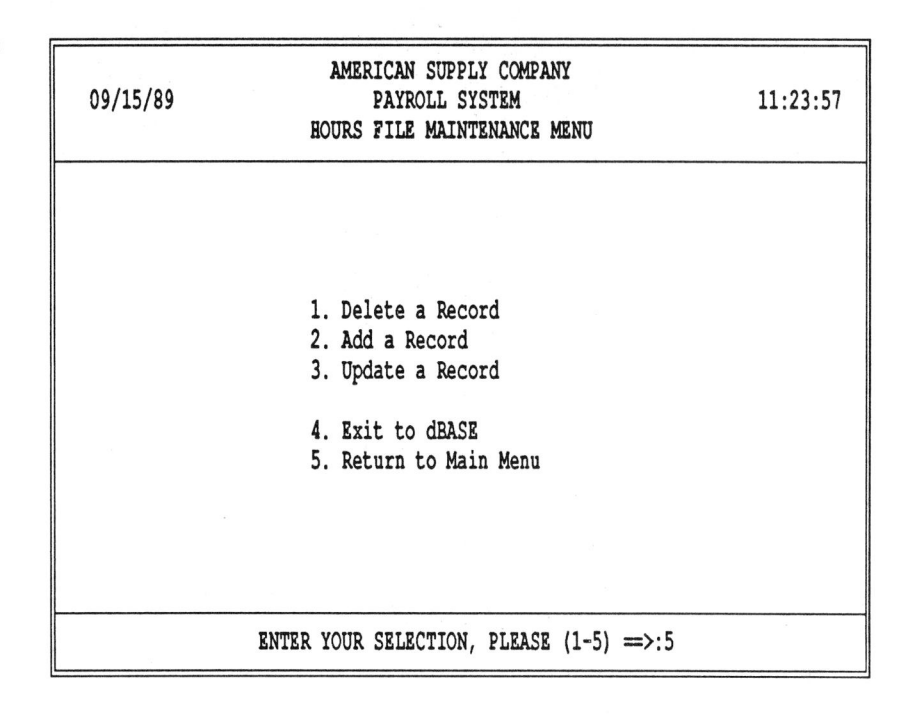

```
┌─────────────────────────────────────────────────────────────┐
│                    AMERICAN SUPPLY COMPANY                  │
│    09/15/89            PAYROLL SYSTEM           11:23:57    │
│                 HOURS FILE MAINTENANCE MENU                 │
├─────────────────────────────────────────────────────────────┤
│                                                             │
│                                                             │
│                                                             │
│                    1. Delete a Record                       │
│                    2. Add a Record                          │
│                    3. Update a Record                       │
│                                                             │
│                    4. Exit to dBASE                         │
│                    5. Return to Main Menu                   │
│                                                             │
│                                                             │
│                                                             │
├─────────────────────────────────────────────────────────────┤
│            ENTER YOUR SELECTION, PLEASE (1-5)  =>:5         │
└─────────────────────────────────────────────────────────────┘
```

1. The menu screen consisting of five options and instructions for the user as shown in Figure 9.36 should be displayed.
2. The screen should be frozen (paused) until the user selects one of the valid options.
3. After the user makes a selection, the processing function associated with the selection should be executed as follows:
   a. For the first selection, the maintenance program PAY21.PRG (delete a record) should be executed.
   b. For the second selection, the maintenance program PAY22.PRG (add a record) should be executed.
   c. For the third selection, the maintenance program PAY23.PRG (update a record) should be executed.
   d. For the fourth selection, the program should exit to the dBASE prompt.
   e. For the fifth selection, the program should return to the Main Menu.
4. Because the subsystem programs PAY21.PRG, PAY22.PRG, and PAY23.PRG have not yet been developed, you can create the stub programs for these. When executed, each stub program should simply display the message that the subsystem program has been processed, as shown in Figure 9.37 (see page 390).

Submenu Program PAY3.PRG

Program Description Write a report generating submenu program PAY3.PRG. It should be invoked by the main menu program PAY.PRG of the payroll system for the American Supply Company. The program should display the Report Generating Menu as shown in Figure 9.38, accept the valid user's choice, and then execute the corresponding program.

Processing Steps The following steps should be used to develop the solution of the program:

1. The menu screen consisting of six options and instructions for the user as shown in Figure 9.38 should be displayed.
2. The screen should be frozen (paused) until the user selects one of the valid options.
3. After the user makes a selection, the processing function associated with the selection should be executed as follows:
   a. For the first selection, the program PAY31.PRG (list all employees with overtime pay) should be executed.
   b. For the second selection, the program PAY32.PRG (list all employees with gross pay & its totals) should be executed.
   c. For the third selection, the program PAY33.PRG (list all employees with net pay & its totals) should be executed.

Figure 9.37 Stub program for the PAY21.PRG program

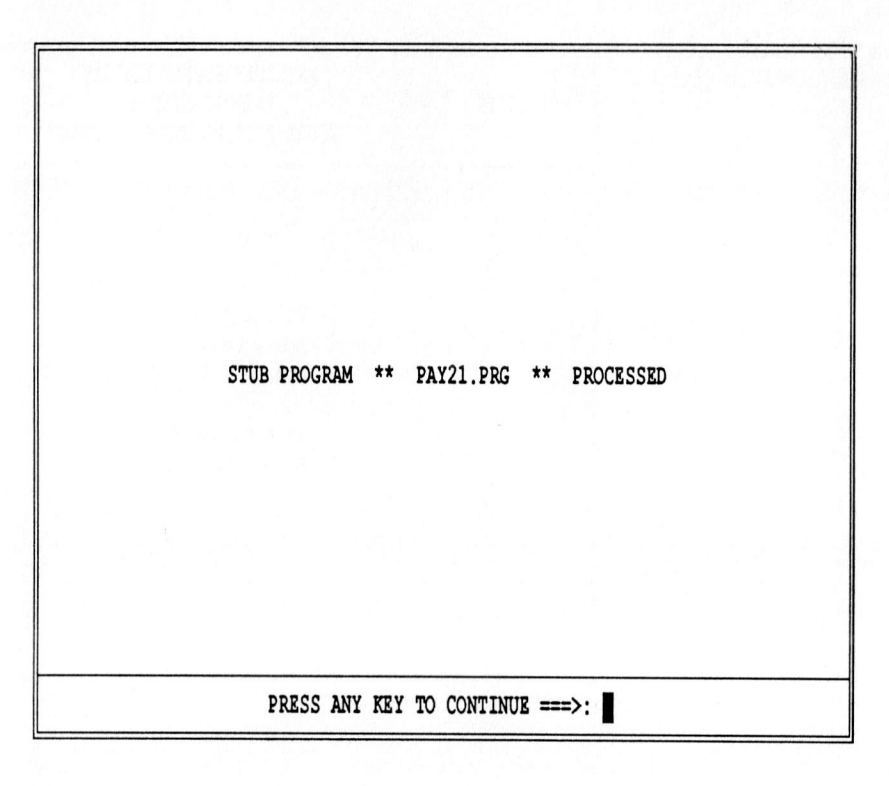

```
                STUB PROGRAM  **  PAY21.PRG  **  PROCESSED




                        PRESS ANY KEY TO CONTINUE ===>:  ▮
```

d. For the fourth selection, the program PAY34.PRG (list whole file with control breaks) should be executed.
e. For the fifth selection, the program should exit to the dBASE prompt.
f. For the sixth selection, the program should return to the Main Menu.

Note: The subsystem program PAY3.PRG has already been developed in Chapter 8 (Programming Assignment 8B). You need to modify it so that it can be invoked by the main menu program PAY.PRG of the payroll system for the American Supply Company.

Figure 9.38 Menu screen for the PAY3.PRG program

```
                    AMERICAN SUPPLY COMPANY
  09/15/89              PAYROLL SYSTEM              11:23:57
                     REPORT GENERATING MENU


            1. List all employees with overtime pay
            2. List all employees with gross pay & its totals
            3. List all employees with net pay & its totals

            4. List whole file with control breaks

            5. Exit to dBASE
            6. Return to Main Menu




                ENTER YOUR SELECTION, PLEASE (1-6) ==>:6
```

Chapter 10

File Maintenance: Deleting a Record

LEARNING OBJECTIVES

Upon successfully completing this chapter, you will be able to:

1. Mark records for deletion using the EDIT command.
2. Mark records for deletion using the DELETE command.
3. List all the records of the database file, including flagged records (that is, records marked for deletion).
4. List only those records of the database file that have been flagged (use the DELETE () function).
5. List only those records of the database file that have not been flagged (use the SET DELETED ON command).
6. Recall all the flagged records (that is, remove the deletion marker from the records marked for deletion (use the RECALL or RECALL ALL commands).
7. Recall a set of flagged records satisfying a condition (use the RECALL ALL FOR command).
8. Physically remove the flagged records from the database file (use the PACK command or the SET DELETED ON and the COPY commands).
9. Analyze, design, and code a file maintenance program that can delete records from the database file.

10.1 Overview

In Chapter 6, you were introduced to data editing—a method of correcting the errors in the contents of the database file. In that chapter, you also learned how to alter the structure of the database file by adding data fields, deleting data fields, and modifying the existing data fields in the structure of the database file. But maintenance of the database files, a method of adding new records to, deleting old records from, and updating the existing records of the database files, has not been discussed so far.

The method of deleting data records from the database files will be discussed in this chapter. The methods of adding data records to and updating the existing records of the database files will be presented in Chapter 11 and Chapter 12, respectively.

Deleting unwanted records from the database file consists of two steps. In the first, the records are marked for deletion. This process helps hide the records without physically removing them from the database file. In the second step, the records are physically removed from the database file.

When the records are marked for deletion, they remain in the database file, but they are flagged. Marking the records for deletion serves two purposes. First, they are temporarily "invisible" to the database inquiries without being permanently eliminated from the database file. Second, this is a preliminary step to physically removing the records. The main advantage of deleting the records in two steps is that the flagged records (those marked for deletion) can be recalled. In other words, you can remove the deleting marker from the flagged records *before* performing the second step.

In the discussion of the rest of this chapter, the phrase "deleting records from the database files" means that the records will be marked for deletion. They will be flagged, but they will not be physically removed from the database file. The terms "records marked for deletion," "flagged records," and "deleted records" are identical in this sense and are used interchangeably in this chapter.

10.2 Deleting Records from the Database Files

dBASE IV provides two methods of deleting records from the database files. These are described in the following sections.

10.2.1 Deleting Records Within the Edit Mode

The first method of deleting records from the database file is by using the EDIT command, which was introduced in section 6.3. When you are in the edit mode, you can delete the record currently being examined simply by pressing the <Ctrl-U> keys. Suppose, for example, you want to delete the fourth record from the database file FILE2. To display the fourth record in the edit mode, you will need the following commands:

```
. USE FILE2      <Return>
. EDIT 4         <Return>
```

If you type these commands, dBASE will respond by displaying the edit screen as shown in Figure 10.1. dBASE is in the edit mode, and the record being displayed on the screen is the fourth record of the database file

Figure 10.1 Edit screen for database file FILE2 displaying the fourth record

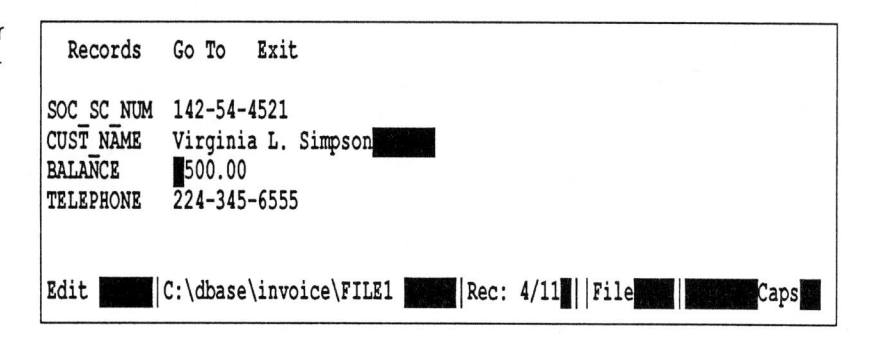

```
 Records   Go To   Exit

SOC_SC_NUM  142-54-4521
CUST_NAME   Virginia L. Simpson
BALANCE     500.00
TELEPHONE   224-345-6555



Edit      |C:\dbase\invoice\FILE1    |Rec: 4/11||File|     |Caps
```

FILE2. To delete this record, you will need to press the <Ctrl-U> keys. If you do so, you will notice that the word "Del" appears on the lower right corner of the status line, as shown in Figure 10.2, indicating that this record has been marked for deletion. In other words, the fourth record of the database file FILE2 has been flagged.

To save this change and exit from the edit mode, press the <Ctrl-W> keys. dBASE will respond by displaying the dot prompt. To see the effect of the previous change, you will need to obtain the listing of the database file FILE2. To do this, either press the F3 List function key or type the following command:

. LIST   <Return>

dBASE will respond by displaying the listing as shown in Figure 10.3. The presence of "*" (asterisk) in Figure 10.3 between the record number and the social security number of the fourth record indicates that this record has been flagged (or marked for deletion).

Now suppose that after some time you change your mind and want to remove the mark from this **flagged record.** This change can be achieved by following the same steps as used for flagging the record. To actually do this, first you will need to type the following commands:

. USE FILE2   <Return>
. EDIT 4   <Return>

If you do so, dBASE will respond by displaying the edit screen as shown in Figure 10.2. The fourth record of the database file FILE2 is displayed on the screen. Observe that the word "Del" appears on the right corner of the status line, which indicates that this record has been flagged. If you press the <Ctrl-U> keys, the "Del" marker will be removed from the

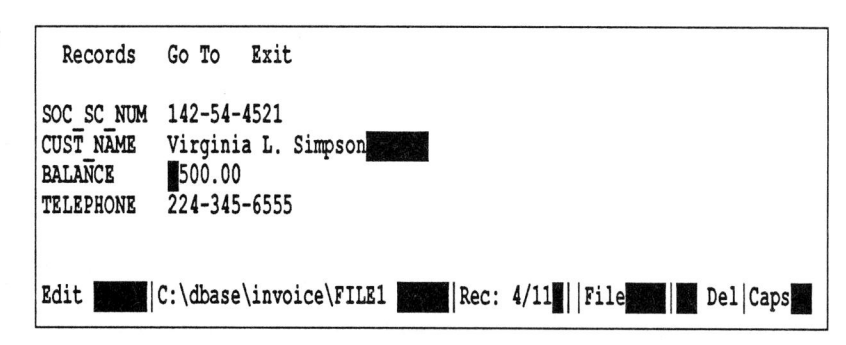

Figure 10.2 Edit screen for database file FILE2 with fourth record as deleted record

```
 Records   Go To   Exit

SOC_SC_NUM  142-54-4521
CUST_NAME   Virginia L. Simpson
BALANCE     500.00
TELEPHONE   224-345-6555



Edit      |C:\dbase\invoice\FILE1    |Rec: 4/11||File|  | Del|Caps
```

Figure 10.3 Listing of database file FILE2 with fourth record as deleted record

```
. LIST
Record#  SOC_SC_NUM   CUST_NAME              BALANCE  TELEPHONE
      1  605-21-0500  Bernice T. Johnson       75.32  513-234-7560
      2  506-97-4200  Jan A. Black            153.75  606-527-4534
      3  120-12-4512  Gregory B. Cardwell      23.50  212-456-8787
      4 *142-54-4521  Virginia L. Simpson     500.00  224-345-6555
      5  350-20-5454  Timothy G. Carlson      107.98  934-766-3344
      6  452-45-8520  Jill E. Hembree          75.00  513-733-0001
      7  124-45-1254  Cindy E. Northland      205.56  212-750-1982
      8  562-12-8754  Joseph T. Saxton       1248.60  606-244-1290
      9  320-45-5241  Marguerite A. Samuelson 354.70  513-355-6420
     10  452-12-9852  Jim A. Jackson           78.45  606-277-5546
     11  120-21-7895  Jeramiah F. Johnson     276.90  513-733-8871
```

status line; and the screen will look as shown in Figure 10.1. The absence of "Del" from the status line indicates that the current record (that is, the fourth record of the database file FILE2) is no longer flagged.

To save the change and exit from the edit mode, press the <Ctrl-W> keys. dBASE will respond by displaying the dot prompt. To see the effect of this change, you will need to obtain the listing of the database file FILE2 once again. To do this, either press the F3 List function key or type the following command:

. **LIST**   <Return>

dBASE will respond by displaying the listing as shown in Figure 10.4. The absence of the "*" (asterisk) in Figure 10.4 between the record number and the social security number of the fourth record indicates that this record is no longer flagged (or marked for deletion).

10.2.2 Deleting Records with the DELETE Command

The second method of deleting records from the database file is by using the DELETE command.

The DELETE Command

The general format of the DELETE command is

Figure 10.4 Listing of database file FILE2 with no deleted record

```
. LIST
Record#  SOC_SC_NUM   CUST_NAME              BALANCE  TELEPHONE
      1  605-21-0500  Bernice T. Johnson       75.32  513-234-7560
      2  506-97-4200  Jan A. Black            153.75  606-527-4534
      3  120-12-4512  Gregory B. Cardwell      23.50  212-456-8787
      4  142-54-4521  Virginia L. Simpson     500.00  224-345-6555
      5  350-20-5454  Timothy G. Carlson      107.98  934-766-3344
      6  452-45-8520  Jill E. Hembree          75.00  513-733-0001
      7  124-45-1254  Cindy E. Northland      205.56  212-750-1982
      8  562-12-8754  Joseph T. Saxton       1248.60  606-244-1290
      9  320-45-5241  Marguerite A. Samuelson 354.70  513-355-6420
     10  452-12-9852  Jim A. Jackson           78.45  606-277-5546
     11  120-21-7895  Jeramiah F. Johnson     276.90  513-733-8871
```

10.2 Deleting Records from the Database Files

```
DELETE [<scope>] [FOR <condition>] [WHILE <condition>]
```

where <scope> specifies the part of the database file being affected by the DELETE command, and the <condition> is a valid search condition that selects the records from the database file to be deleted.

The DELETE command has several different options available, depending on the parameters used. Two formats of the DELETE commands are discussed in the following sections.

The DELETE Format

The first format of the DELETE command is

```
DELETE [<scope>]
```

where the <scope> parameter is optional.
Two forms of this command exist. The first is

```
DELETE
```

The simple DELETE command without any parameters will delete the current record from the active database file.
The second form of the DELETE command is

```
DELETE <scope>
```

This form of the DELETE command is used to delete the records from the active database file as specified in the <scope> parameter. The most commonly used value of the <scope> parameter with the DELETE command is RECORD <number>.

The DELETE RECORD <number> Format

The DELETE RECORD <number> format of the DELETE command is used to delete a single record from the database file. For example, to delete the fourth record from the database file FILE2, you will need to type the following commands:

```
. USE FILE2            <Return>
. DELETE RECORD 4      <Return>
```

If you type these commands, dBASE will respond by displaying:

```
1 record deleted
```

Now, if you obtain the listing of the database file FILE2 by using the LIST command, the listing will be as shown in Figure 10.3.
The presence of "*" (asterisk) in this listing between the record number and the social security number of the fourth record indicates that this record has been flagged (or marked for deletion).

The DELETE FOR Format

The format of the DELETE FOR command is

```
DELETE [<scope>] [FOR <condition>]
```

This format of the DELETE command can be used to mark for deletion a group of records that meet a particular condition. For example, to mark for deletion all the records of the database file FILE2 for which the value of the balance field is less than $100, you will need the following commands:

```
. USE FILE2                           <Return>
. DELETE ALL FOR BALANCE < 100        <Return>
```

If you type these two commands, dBASE will respond by displaying:

```
4 records deleted
```

Once again, you can obtain the listing of all the records of the database file FILE2 either by pressing the F3 List function key or by typing the following command:

```
. LIST      <Return>
```

dBASE will respond by displaying the listing shown in Figure 10.5.

An examination of the listing in Figure 10.5 reveals that there are five flagged records. Of these, four have a balance of less than $100. These records were deleted in the previous step. The fifth record was previously deleted using the DELETE RECORD 4 format of the DELETE command. All the flagged records have a "*" mark between the record number and the social security number data fields.

The "*" mark will appear only in the displayed or listed reports and not in the formatted reports, such as those produced by the REPORT command, which is discussed in Chapter 15.

10.3 Listing Including or Excluding the Deleted Records

The DELETED ( ) function and the SET DELETED ON/OFF command provide two methods of including or excluding the **deleted** (flagged) **records** from the listing of the database file.

Figure 10.5 Listing of database file FILE2 with several deleted records

```
. LIST
Record#  SOC_SC_NUM   CUST_NAME               BALANCE  TELEPHONE
      1 *605-21-0500  Bernice T. Johnson        75.32  513-234-7560
      2  506-97-4200  Jan A. Black             153.75  606-527-4534
      3 *120-12-4512  Gregory B. Cardwell       23.50  212-456-8787
      4 *142-54-4521  Virginia L. Simpson      500.00  224-345-6555
      5  350-20-5454  Timothy G. Carlson       107.98  934-766-3344
      6 *452-45-8520  Jill E. Hembree           75.00  513-733-0001
      7  124-45-1254  Cindy E. Northland       205.56  212-750-1982
      8  562-12-8754  Joseph T. Saxton        1248.60  606-244-1290
      9  320-45-5241  Marguerite A. Samuelson  354.70  513-355-6420
     10 *452-12-9852  Jim A. Jackson            78.45  606-277-5546
     11  120-21-7895  Jeramiah F. Johnson      276.90  513-733-8871
```

10.3.1 The DELETED ( ) Function

The format of the DELETED ( ) function is

```
DELETED ([<alias of the database file>])
```

where the parameter [<alias of the database file>] is optional.

The simple form of the DELETED () function is used to test if the current record of the active database file has been deleted or not. If it has, dBASE will return a logical true (.T.) value; otherwise, it will return a logical false (.F.) value.

The DELETED () function can also be used as a condition for including or excluding those deleted records from the listing of the database file. This function can be chosen by including the DELETED () function or .NOT. DELETED () function, respectively, as a condition in the DISPLAY or LIST commands.

For example, if you want to display only those records of the database file FILE2 that have been deleted, you will need the following commands:

```
. USE FILE2                          <Return>
. DISPLAY ALL FOR DELETED ()         <Return>
```

If you type these, dBASE will respond by displaying the five records of the database file FILE2 that have been deleted, as shown in Figure 10.6.

If you want to list only those records of the database file FILE2 that have not been deleted, you can use the .NOT. operator with the DELETED () function. You will need to type the following commands:

```
. USE FILE2                          <Return>
. LIST FOR .NOT. DELETED ()          <Return>
```

dBASE will respond by displaying the listing of only those records of the database file FILE2 that have not been deleted, as shown in Figure 10.7.

At times, it may be advantageous to make certain records temporarily "invisible" to database inquiries without eliminating them permanently from the database file. This effect can be achieved by the SET DELETED ON/OFF command.

10.3.2 The SET DELETED ON/OFF Command

The SET DELETED command is OFF by default in dBASE IV. In the OFF mode, all deleted records of the database file will be visible to all dBASE commands and queries. But the SET DELETED ON command makes all the deleted records of the database file invisible to all dBASE commands and queries (except, of course, to the INDEX command, which is discussed in Chapter 11). For example, the following sequence of instructions

Figure 10.6 Listing of database file FILE2 displaying only the deleted records

```
. USE FILE1
. DISPLAY ALL FOR DELETED ()
Record#  SOC_SC_NUM    CUST_NAME              BALANCE  TELEPHONE
      1  *605-21-0500  Bernice T. Johnson       75.32  513-234-7560
      3  *120-12-4512  Gregory B. Cardwell      23.50  212-456-8787
      4  *142-54-4521  Virginia L. Simpson     500.00  224-345-6555
      6  *452-45-8520  Jill E. Hembree          75.00  513-733-0001
     10  *452-12-9852  Jim A. Jackson           78.45  606-277-5546
```

Figure 10.7 Listing of database file FILE2 displaying only the nondeleted records

```
. USE FILE1
. LIST FOR .NOT. DELETED ()
Record#  SOC_SC_NUM   CUST_NAME              BALANCE TELEPHONE
      2  506-97-4200  Jan A. Black            153.75 606-527-4534
      5  350-20-5454  Timothy G. Carlson      107.98 934-766-3344
      7  124-45-1254  Cindy E. Northland      205.56 212-750-1982
      8  562-12-8754  Joseph T. Saxton       1248.60 606-244-1290
      9  320-45-5241  Marguerite A. Samuelson 354.70 513-355-6420
     11  120-21-7895  Jeramiah F. Johnson     276.90 513-733-8871
```

```
. USE FILE2        <Return>
. SET DELETED ON   <Return>
. LIST             <Return>
```

will produce the listing similar to the one shown in Figure 10.7.

Because the SET DELETED command is ON, the LIST command will list only those records of the database file FILE2 that have not been marked for deletion. Now, let us see the effect of the SET DELETED ON command on the COUNT command. Type the following commands:

```
. SET DELETED ON   <Return>
. COUNT            <Return>
```

dBASE will respond by displaying the following message:

```
      6 records
.
```

This result indicates that the COUNT command has counted only those records of the database file FILE2 that are not marked for deletion because the SET DELETED ON command makes the deleted records temporarily invisible to all dBASE commands. To count the total number of records present in the database file FILE2, whether they are marked for deletion or not, type the following commands:

```
. SET DELETED OFF  <Return>
. COUNT            <Return>
```

dBASE will respond by displaying the following message:

```
     11 records
.
```

This result indicates that the COUNT command has counted all the records present in database file FILE2, regardless of whether they are marked for deletion.

10.4 Recalling Deleted Records

It has been discussed earlier (section 10.2.1) that in the edit mode, the deletion marker from a particular record of the database file can be removed by pressing the <Ctrl-U> keys. But to remove the deletion marker from all the records of the database file satisfying a given condition, dBASE provides a command that works exactly opposite to that of the DELETE command. The process of removing the mark from the deleted record is called **recalling deleted records,** and it uses the RECALL command.

10.4.1 The RECALL Command

The general format of the RECALL command is

```
RECALL [<scope>] [FOR <condition>] [WHILE <condition>]
```

where <scope> specifies the parts of the database file being affected by the RECALL command, and <condition> is a valid search condition that selects the records to be recalled from the database file.

Because the SET DELETED ON command makes all the deleted records of the database file invisible to all dBASE commands and queries, the RECALL command will not have any effect unless the SET DELETED command is OFF. Therefore, it is recommended that the SET DELETED OFF command always be used *before* using the RECALL command.

The RECALL command has several different options available, depending on the parameters used. Two formats of the RECALL command are discussed.

The RECALL Format

The first format of the RECALL command is

```
RECALL [<scope>]
```

where the <scope> parameter is optional.

Two forms of the RECALL command exist. The first is

```
RECALL
```

The simple RECALL command without any parameters will unmark the current record if it is marked for deletion in the active database file. If the current record is not marked for deletion, this command will have no effect on it.

The second form of the RECALL command is

```
RECALL <scope>
```

This form of the RECALL command is used to unmark the **records marked for deletion** in the active database file as specified in the <scope> parameter. The RECALL command will not have any effect on those records not marked for deletion. Two values of the <scope> parameter are commonly used with the RECALL command.

The RECALL RECORD <number> Format The RECALL RECORD <number> format of the RECALL command is used to unmark a single deleted record. For example, to unmark the fourth record of the database file FILE2, you will need to type the following commands:

```
. USE FILE2            <Return>
. RECALL RECORD 4      <Return>
```

If you type these, dBASE will respond by displaying:

```
1 record recalled
```

Now if you obtain the listing of the database file FILE2 by using the LIST command, the listing will be as shown in Figure 10.8. The absence of the "*" in front of the fourth record indicates that this record is no longer marked for deletion. In other words, the fourth record has been recalled.

Before you proceed, you should understand the difference between the RECALL RECORD <number> command and the use of the <Ctrl-U> keys in the edit mode to unmark the deleted record. As you have seen, the RECALL RECORD <number> command can be used to unmark a deleted record, but it has no effect on the record if it is not already marked for deletion. Use of the <Ctrl-U> keys in the edit mode will also unmark the marked record. However, if the record is not already marked for deletion, it will now be so.

Similarly, the DELETE RECORD <number> command can be used to delete a record, but it will not have any effect on the record if it is already deleted. Use of the <Ctrl-U> keys in the edit mode will also delete the record if it is not already deleted. However, if the record is already marked for deletion, it will unmark it.

These two cases indicate that use of the edit mode to mark the records for deletion or to unmark the deleted records is not safe. Therefore, it is recommended that use of the <Ctrl-U> keys in the edit mode, either to mark the record for deletion or to unmark the deleted record, be reserved for the interactive mode. This method should not be used in the programming mode, where the DELETE RECORD or the RECALL RECORD command should be used to mark the record for deletion or to unmark the deleted record, respectively.

The second commonly used value of the <scope> parameter with the RECALL command is ALL.

The RECALL ALL Format This format of the RECALL command can be used to unmark all the deleted records in a database file. For example, to unmark all the deleted records from database file FILE2, you will need to type the following commands:

```
. USE FILE2      <Return>
. RECALL ALL     <Return>
```

Figure 10.8 Listing of database file FILE2 with four records marked for deletion

```
. LIST
Record#  SOC_SC_NUM    CUST_NAME               BALANCE  TELEPHONE
     1  *605-21-0500  Bernice T. Johnson         75.32  513-234-7560
     2   506-97-4200  Jan A. Black              153.75  606-527-4534
     3  *120-12-4512  Gregory B. Cardwell        23.50  212-456-8787
     4   142-54-4521  Virginia L. Simpson       500.00  224-345-6555
     5   350-20-5454  Timothy G. Carlson        107.98  934-766-3344
     6  *452-45-8520  Jill E. Hembree            75.00  513-733-0001
     7   124-45-1254  Cindy E. Northland        205.56  212-750-1982
     8   562-12-8754  Joseph T. Saxton         1248.60  606-244-1290
     9   320-45-5241  Marguerite A. Samuelson   354.70  513-355-6420
    10  *452-12-9852  Jim A. Jackson             78.45  606-277-5546
    11   120-21-7895  Jeramiah F. Johnson       276.90  513-733-8871
```

10.4 Recalling Deleted Records

If you type these, dBASE will respond by displaying:

```
4 records recalled
```

To verify the effect of these commands, you can obtain the listing of database file FILE2 either by pressing the F3 List function key or simply by typing:

```
. LIST     <Return>
```

dBASE will respond by displaying the listing as shown in Figure 10.4. Notice that all the "*" marks have disappeared, indicating that all the records marked for deletion have been unmarked, or recalled, as it is referred to in dBASE language.

10.4.2 The RECALL FOR Command

The format of the RECALL FOR command is

```
RECALL [<scope>] [FOR <condition>]
```

This format of the RECALL command can be used to unmark all the records marked for deletion that meet a particular condition.

For this purpose, first mark for deletion all the records from file FILE2 that have a balance of less than $500. To achieve this result, you will need to type the following commands:

```
. USE FILE2                              <Return>
. DELETE ALL FOR BALANCE < 500           <Return>
```

dBASE will respond by displaying:

```
9 records deleted
```

Now we can obtain the listing of database file FILE2 by either pressing the F3 List function key or by typing the following command:

```
. LIST     <Return>
```

dBASE will respond by displaying the listing as shown in Figure 10.9. The listing consists of 11 records, 9 of which are marked for deletion.

Now if we want to unmark from database file FILE2 all those records that have a balance greater than $100, the following command will do the job:

```
. RECALL ALL FOR BALANCE > 100     <Return>
```

If this command is typed, dBASE will respond by displaying:

```
5 records recalled
```

Once again, you can obtain the listing of database file FILE2 by either pressing the F3 List function key or typing the LIST command. dBASE will display the listing as shown in Figure 10.10. The listing consists of 11

Figure 10.9 Listing of database file FILE2 with records marked for deletion with BALANCE < $500

```
. LIST
Record#  SOC_SC_NUM    CUST_NAME              BALANCE  TELEPHONE
     1  *605-21-0500  Bernice T. Johnson        75.32  513-234-7560
     2  *506-97-4200  Jan A. Black             153.75  606-527-4534
     3  *120-12-4512  Gregory B. Cardwell       23.50  212-456-8787
     4   142-54-4521  Virginia L. Simpson      500.00  224-345-6555
     5  *350-20-5454  Timothy G. Carlson       107.98  934-766-3344
     6  *452-45-8520  Jill E. Hembree           75.00  513-733-0001
     7  *124-45-1254  Cindy E. Northland       205.56  212-750-1982
     8   562-12-8754  Joseph T. Saxton        1248.60  606-244-1290
     9  *320-45-5241  Marguerite A. Samuelson  354.70  513-355-6420
    10  *452-12-9852  Jim A. Jackson            78.45  606-277-5546
    11  *120-21-7895  Jeramiah F. Johnson      276.90  513-733-8871
```

records, 4 of which are marked for deletion. A comparison of the listings of Figure 10.9 and Figure 10.10 indicates that records with a balance of greater than $100 have been recalled.

10.5 Purging Deleted Records

Purging deleted records means permanently removing from the database file all the records that have been marked for deletion. These records will not be available after they are purged, so this step should be performed only after making sure they will not be needed in the future. If there is any doubt about this, store them in a backup file before purging them from the database file.

The process of purging can be accomplished in two different ways. The first is by using the PACK command; the second is by using the SET DELETED ON command followed by the COPY command.

10.5.1 The PACK Command

The PACK command is used for permanently physically removing the records marked for deletion from the database file and then renumbering all remaining records.

Let us create another database file, called FILE2A, to be used in the

Figure 10.10 Listing of database file FILE2 with records marked for deletion for BALANCE < or = $100

```
. LIST
Record#  SOC_SC_NUM    CUST_NAME              BALANCE  TELEPHONE
     1  *605-21-0500  Bernice T. Johnson        75.32  513-234-7560
     2   506-97-4200  Jan A. Black             153.75  606-527-4534
     3  *120-12-4512  Gregory B. Cardwell       23.50  212-456-8787
     4   142-54-4521  Virginia L. Simpson      500.00  224-345-6555
     5   350-20-5454  Timothy G. Carlson       107.98  934-766-3344
     6  *452-45-8520  Jill E. Hembree           75.00  513-733-0001
     7   124-45-1254  Cindy E. Northland       205.56  212-750-1982
     8   562-12-8754  Joseph T. Saxton        1248.60  606-244-1290
     9   320-45-5241  Marguerite A. Samuelson  354.70  513-355-6420
    10  *452-12-9852  Jim A. Jackson            78.45  606-277-5546
    11   120-21-7895  Jeramiah F. Johnson      276.90  513-733-8871
```

following example by copying database FILE2. This result can be achieved by using the following command:

```
COPY FILE <source file name> TO <target file name>
```

This command has already been discussed in section 7.3.1. Recall that it can be used only if the database file is closed. The database file FILE2 is already open, so it should be closed by typing the following command:

```
. USE      <Return>
```

If you type this command, the database file FILE2 will be closed.

Now copy the database file FILE2 to the new database file FILE2A. The following command will be needed for this purpose:

```
. COPY FILE FILE2.DBF TO FILE2A.DBF    <Return>
```

If you type this command, dBASE will respond by displaying:

```
1024 bytes copied
```

A new database file FILE2A has been created. Now open this file, and obtain its listing by using the following commands:

```
. USE FILE2A    <Return>
. LIST          <Return>
```

The listing will be exactly the same as shown in Figure 10.10.

Note that there are 11 records present in the listing of database file FILE2A, 4 of which have been marked for deletion. You can purge these deleted records by using the PACK command. To do this, type the following command:

```
. PACK    <Return>
```

dBASE will respond by displaying:

```
7 records copied
```

The PACK command has physically removed the four records marked for deletion from database file FILE2A and copied the rest of the records onto itself.

To see the effect of the PACK command, obtain the listing of database file FILE2A either by pressing the F3 List function key or by typing LIST. dBASE will respond by displaying the listing as shown in Figure 10.11. The listing consists of seven records. Comparison of the listings of Figure 10.10 and Figure 10.11 indicates that four deleted records have been purged.

The process of purging the deleted records using the PACK command physically removes the deleted records from the database file and copies the nondeleted records onto itself. A sudden loss of power while the file is only partially through packing can cause the data to be lost. Therefore, it is recommended that you should make a backup copy of your file *before* using the PACK command.

Figure 10.11 Listing of database file FILE2A after purging the deleted records

```
. SET DELETED ON
. PACK
      7 records copied
. LIST
Record#  SOC_SC_NUM   CUST_NAME                BALANCE  TELEPHONE
      1  506-97-4200  Jan A. Black              153.75  606-527-4534
      2  142-54-4521  Virginia L. Simpson       500.00  224-345-6555
      3  350-20-5454  Timothy G. Carlson        107.98  934-766-3344
      4  124-45-1254  Cindy E. Northland        205.56  212-750-1982
      5  562-12-8754  Joseph T. Saxton         1248.60  606-244-1290
      6  320-45-5241  Marguerite A. Samuelson   354.70  513-355-6420
      7  120-21-7895  Jeramiah F. Johnson       276.90  513-733-8871
```

The main advantage of the PACK command is that it automatically rebuilds all the index tags (discussed in Section 11.2.1). The other advantage of the PACK command is that it frees the disk space occupied by the records marked for deletion.

10.5.2 The SET DELETED ON and COPY Commands

The alternative method of permanently physically removing the records marked for deletion from the database file is by using the SET DELETED ON command followed by the COPY command. As you have seen in section 10.3.2, the SET DELETED ON command makes the records marked for deletion temporarily invisible to all dBASE commands and queries. After the SET DELETED command has been set to ON, the COPY command will copy only those records of the database file that have not been marked for deletion. This process will create a copy of the database file containing only those records of the original database file that have not been marked for deletion.

Let us go back to our original database file, FILE2. To open and obtain the listing of this database file, you will need the following commands:

```
. USE FILE2      <Return>
. LIST           <Return>
```

If you type these commands, dBASE will display the listing as shown in Figure 10.10. The listing consists of 11 records, 4 of which have been marked for deletion.

To create a new database file called FILE2B consisting of only nondeleted records of database file FILE2, you need the following commands:

```
. SET DELETED ON     <Return>
. COPY TO FILE2B     <Return>
```

If you type these commands, dBASE will respond by displaying:

```
7 records copied
```

A new database file FILE2B has been created. Now open it, and obtain its listing by using the following commands:

```
. USE FILE2B      <Return>
. LIST            <Return>
```

The listing identical to the one shown in Figure 10.11 will be displayed. It consists of seven records. Comparison of the listings of Figure 10.10 and Figure 10.11 indicates that four deleted records have been recalled.

10.6 An Illustrative Example: Case Study 7

Program Description

Write an inventory file maintenance program. It should be invoked by the inventory file maintenance submenu program INV1.PRG of the invoice generating system. The function of the program is to delete the records of the discontinued items belonging to the inventory database file INV.DBF.

Processing Steps

Use the following steps in developing the solution of the program:

1. Display the inventory file maintenance screen as shown in Figure 10.12 with the message "ENTER THE ITEM NUMBER, PLEASE ===> :" requesting the user to enter the item number of the record to be deleted.
2. Freeze or pause the screen to allow the user to respond to the request.
3. After accepting the entry from the user, test the value of the item

Figure 10.12 Inventory database file maintenance screen

```
┌─────────────────────────────────────────────────────────────────┐
│               AMERICAN SUPPLY COMPANY                           │
│  01/12/90     INVOICE GENERATING SYSTEM            14:25:40     │
│            INVENTORY DATABASE FILE MAINTENANCE                  │
│                   DELETING A RECORD                             │
├─────────────────────────────────────────────────────────────────┤
│                                                                 │
│        ENTER THE ITEM NUMBER, PLEASE ===>:  ▮                   │
│                                                                 │
│                                                                 │
│                                                                 │
│                                                                 │
│                                                                 │
│                                                                 │
│                                                                 │
│                                                                 │
│                                                                 │
├─────────────────────────────────────────────────────────────────┤
│                                                                 │
└─────────────────────────────────────────────────────────────────┘
```

number supplied by the user to see if it is a blank value or a nonblank value.

4. If the value of the item number supplied by the user is blank, the user wants to terminate the process of deleting records from the database file. Therefore, proceed to step 12.
5. For the nonblank value of the item number, search the inventory database file to find the matching record.
6. If the match is not found, display the message indicating that the match was not found, and proceed to step 11.
7. If the match is found, display the matching record on the screen.
8. Request confirmation to delete the record.
9. Check for the validity of the confirmation. If the confirmation is valid, delete the record from the database file.
10. If the confirmation is invalid, indicate this result by displaying the message.
11. Repeat steps 1–10 to delete the next discontinued record.
12. After all the desired records have been deleted, pack the database file, and return to the calling program INV1.PRG.

The five phases of the program development process for Case Study 7 follow.

10.6.1 The Analysis Phase

In this first step in the program development process, the review and analysis of program specifications lead to the identification of the processing steps needed to solve the problem. Because a set of instructions will be needed to delete a record from the database file, these steps should be repeated for each record to be deleted. Therefore, a control switch needs to be defined to control this loop and a memory variable defined to store the value of the item number value for the record to be deleted. Of course, the database file in which the records to be deleted belong should be opened. These are the only three steps needed in the initiate processing function of the solution of the problem.

The processing steps needed in the main processing function should include:

1. Accept the item number to be deleted.
2. Test for a blank item number.
3. Process the blank item number, that is, change the loop control switch to indicate termination of the loop, and proceed to step 7.
4. Process the nonblank item number, that is, search for the matching record in the inventory database file.
5. Process match found:
   a. Display the matching record.
   b. Accept confirmation for deleting the record.
   c. If confirmation is valid, delete the record, and proceed to step 7.
   d. If confirmation is invalid, proceed to step 7.

6. Process no match found.
7. Freeze the screen and blank item number.

Repeat these seven steps until you wish to terminate the program by supplying a blank value to the item number in step 1. At that point, the control should move to the terminate processing function.

In the terminate processing function, the database file should be packed, and program control should exit to the calling program.

To sum up, the following processing steps will be needed for the solution of Case Study 7:

1. Define the variables.
2. Open the database file.
3. Accept the item number to be deleted.
4. Test for a blank item number.
5. Process the blank item number, that is, change the loop control switch to indicate termination of the loop, and proceed to step 9.
6. Process the nonblank item number, that is, search for the matching record in the inventory database file.
7. Process match found:
   a. Display the matching record.
   b. Accept confirmation for deleting the record.
   c. If confirmation is valid, delete the record, and proceed to step 9.
   d. If confirmation is invalid, proceed to step 9.
8. Process no match found.
9. Freeze the screen and blank item number.
10. Close and pack the database file.
11. Return to calling program.

The first two steps should be performed only once, at the start of the program. Therefore, they belong to initiate processing. The next seven steps should be performed again and again until the user supplies a blank value for the item number. Therefore, these belong to main processing. The last two steps need to be performed only once before terminating the execution of the program. Therefore, these belong to terminate processing.

10.6.2 The Design Phase

The function of this step is to take the result of the problem analysis, that is, the processing steps identified in the analysis phase, and transform it into a structure chart. The design of the structure chart of an interactive program is similar to that of a batch program except few steps requesting user input are added. But the interactive maintenance needs some explanation. Note that maintenance can also be done in a batch mode. The shell structure chart given in Figure 10.13 is the starting point for almost any maintenance program.

Figure 10.13 Shell structure chart for the maintenance program

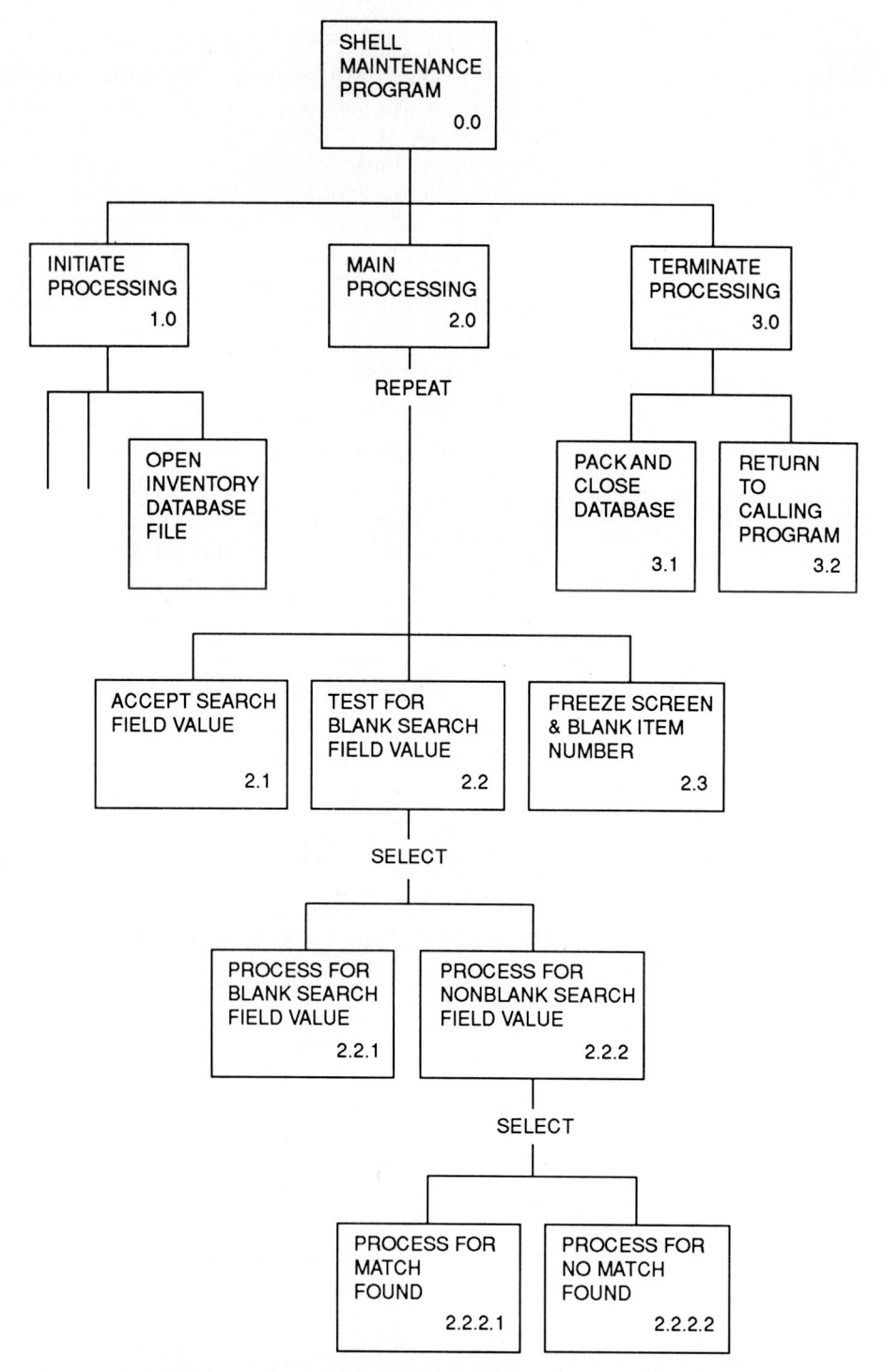

```
                    SHELL
                    MAINTENANCE
                    PROGRAM
                                0.0

        ┌───────────────┼───────────────┐
   INITIATE          MAIN           TERMINATE
   PROCESSING        PROCESSING     PROCESSING
              1.0              2.0             3.0
        │              REPEAT              │
        │                                  │
      OPEN                           ┌─────┴─────┐
      INVENTORY                   PACK AND    RETURN
      DATABASE                    CLOSE       TO
      FILE                        DATABASE    CALLING
                                              PROGRAM
                                        3.1         3.2

        ┌──────────────┼──────────────┐
   ACCEPT SEARCH   TEST FOR        FREEZE SCREEN
   FIELD VALUE     BLANK SEARCH    & BLANK ITEM
                   FIELD VALUE     NUMBER
              2.1            2.2              2.3
                        SELECT
                  ┌───────┴───────┐
             PROCESS FOR     PROCESS FOR
             BLANK SEARCH    NONBLANK SEARCH
             FIELD VALUE     FIELD VALUE
                    2.2.1              2.2.2
                               SELECT
                         ┌───────┴───────┐
                    PROCESS FOR    PROCESS FOR
                    MATCH          NO MATCH
                    FOUND          FOUND
                         2.2.2.1         2.2.2.2
```

Major Processing Steps of a Maintenance Program

As with batch and menu programs, the solution of any maintenance program is also divided into three major processing steps:

1. Initiate processing
2. Main processing
3. Terminate processing

10.6 An Illustrative Example: Case Study 7

Initiate Processing The activities included in this part of the solution of the problem are the ones that occur only once, at the beginning of program processing, and are not needed anywhere else. These include the following:

1. Housekeeping, including changing default modes and setting procedures
2. Define variables, including declaring variables, defining program constants, defining control variables, and loading memory variables
3. Open database file(s) and set active index tags

These activities can occur in any sequence in the solution of the problem in the initiate processing function.

Main Processing Main processing consists of activities that occur repeatedly, usually once for each update (add, delete, or change) of the record of the database file. The activities include:

1. Accept the search field value.
2. Test for a blank search field.
3. Process the blank search field, that is, change the loop control switch to indicate termination of the loop, and proceed to step 7.
4. Process the nonblank search field, that is, search for a matching record in the inventory database file.
5. Process match found.
6. Process no match found.
7. Freeze the screen and blank item number.

The function performed by steps 5 and 6 depends on the type of maintenance function being performed by the program. If it is to delete records from the database file, then steps 5 and 6 perform the following steps:

5. Process match found:
   a. Display the matching record.
   b. Accept confirmation for deleting the record.
   c. If confirmation is valid, delete the record, and proceed to step 7.
   d. If confirmation is invalid, display the message indicating so, and proceed to step 7.
6. Process no match found: Display the message indicating that the record does not exist and so can't delete.

If the function of the maintenance program is to add records to the database file, then steps 5 and 6 perform the following steps:

5. Process match found: Display the message indicating that the record already exists and so can't add duplicate record.

6. Process no match found:
   a. Accept the new record.
   b. Append the blank record.
   c. Replace the blank record with a new record.
   d. Reinitialize the variables.

If the function of the maintenance program is to change the records of the database file, then steps 5 and 6 perform the following steps:

5. Process match found:
   a. Display the matching record, and accept the changes to be made.
   b. Accept confirmation for updating the record.
   c. If confirmation is valid, update the record, and proceed to step 7.
   d. If confirmation is invalid, display the message indicating so, and proceed to step 7.
6. Process no match found: Display the message indicating that the record does not exist and so changes can't be made.

All these activities are needed in the solution of any maintenance program and should be present in the sequence listed.

Terminate Processing The activities included in this part of the solution of the problem are the ones that occur only once, at the end of program processing, and are not needed anywhere else. These are

1. Close the database file, including creating a backup file and packing the database files.
2. Return control to the calling program.

They should occur in the sequence listed.

In the solution of any problem, all the activities from each of the processing categories listed may not be needed. But if they are, they should be performed in the sequence given. The processing steps needed in the solution of a maintenance program are listed in Table 10.1 for future reference.

Using the shell structure chart of Figure 10.13 and the tools and techniques discussed in Section 4.4.2, transform the 11 steps identified in the analysis phase into a structure chart for Case Study 7 as shown in Figure 10.14. All the modules in this structure chart are either functionally or highly cohesive. They are also loosely coupled. Thus, the structure chart of Figure 10.14 satisfies the three rules for designing a good structure chart; that is, it consists of highly cohesive, loosely coupled modules none of which has a span of control of more than three. Therefore, it is a well-designed solution to Case Study 7.

10.6.3 The Detailed Design Phase

The function of this step is to take the result of the design phase—the structure chart—and identify the actual computer operations required for each program function represented in it, thereby producing the detailed solution of the problem. Using the translation of the three control

Table 10.1 Processing steps needed in a maintenance program

Initiate Processing	1. Housekeeping, including changing default modes and setting procedures
	2. Define variables, including declaring variables, defining program constants, defining control variables, and loading memory variables
	3. Open file(s) and set active index tags
Main Processing	1. Accept search field
	2. Test for blank search field
	3. Process blank search field, that is, change loop control switch to indicate the termination of the loop, and proceed to step 7
	4. Process nonblank search field, that is, search for matching record in the inventory database file
	*5. Process match found:
	*6. Process no match found:
	7. Freeze screen and blank item number
Terminate Processing	1. Close database file, including creating backup file and packing database files
	2. Return control to calling program

For Delete Function	5. Process match found:
	  a. Display matching record
	  b. Accept confirmation for deleting record
	  c. If confirmation is valid, delete the record and proceed to step 7
	  d. If confirmation is invalid, display the message indicating so, and proceed to step 7

	6. Process no match found: Display message indicating that record does not exist and so can't delete
For Add Function	5. Process match found: Display message indicating that the record already exists and so can't add duplicate record

	6. Process no match found:
	  a. Accept new record
	  b. Append blank record
	  c. Replace blank record with new record
	  d. Reinitialize variables

For Update Function	5. Process match found:
	  a. Display matching record and accept changes to be made
	  b. Accept confirmation for updating record
	  c. If confirmation is valid, update record, and proceed to step 7
	  d. If confirmation is invalid, display message indicating so, and proceed to step 7

	6. Process no match found: Display message indicating that record does not exist and so can't make any changes

*Steps 5 and 6 vary, depending on the function performed by the maintenance program, and are listed separately along with the function being performed.

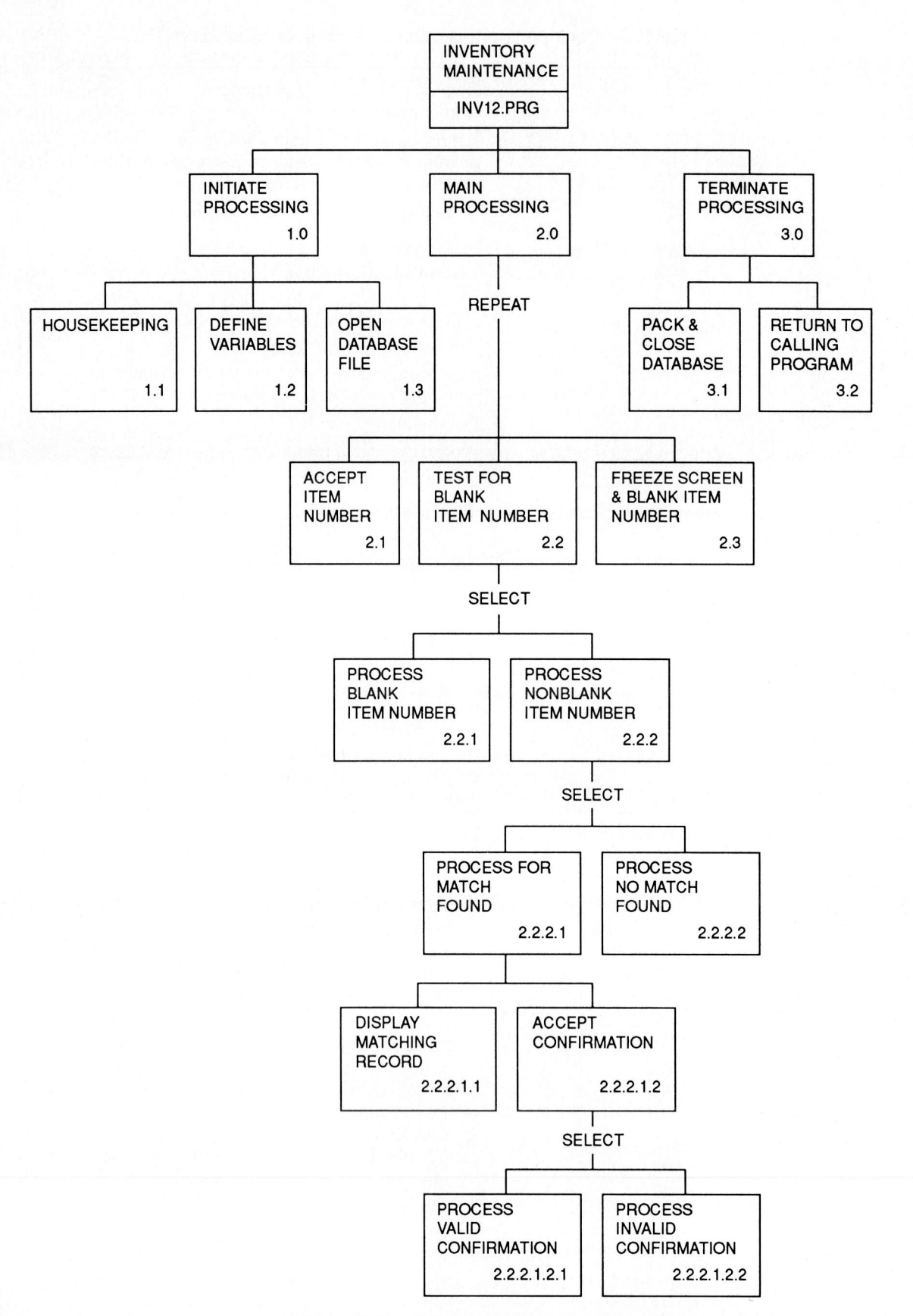

Figure 10.14 Structure chart for Case Study 7

structures to pseudocode as given in Figure 4.14 and the method described in section 4.4.3, we translate the structure chart of Figure 10.14 to pseudocode, as shown in Figure 10.15.

10.6.4 The Coding Phase

The purpose of this phase is to translate the pseudocode instructions of the solution of the program into programming language instructions. The

```
0.0 INVENTORY MAINTENANCE—DELETION
    1.0 INITIATE PROCESSING
        1.1 HOUSEKEEPING
            Turn on the DELETED function
        1.2 DEFINE VARIABLE
            DEFINE CONTROL VARIABLE
              Set REPEAT11 switch = T
            INITIALIZE VARIABLES
              Set ITEMNUM = blank
        1.3 OPEN DATABASE FILE
            Open the database file INV.DBF
    2.0 MAIN PROCESSING
        REPEAT: While the REPEAT11 switch = T
        2.1 ACCEPT ITEM NUMBER
            CLEAR SCREEN
            Clear the screen
            REQUEST AND ACCEPT ITEM NUMBER
            Display Heading #1
            Display Heading #2
            Display Heading #3
            Display Heading #4
            Display Prompt
            Request and accept item number
        2.2 TEST FOR BLANK ITEM NUMBER
            SELECT: If ITEMNUM is blank
            2.2.1  PROCESS BLANK ITEM NUMBER
                   Reset switch REPEAT11 = F
            2.2.2  PROCESS NONBLANK ITEM NUMBER
                   Find matching record in the database file
                   SELECT: If match found
                   2.2.2.1 PROCESS FOR MATCH FOUND
                       2.2.2.1.1 DISPLAY MATCHING RECORD
                                 Display the matching record
                       2.2.2.1.2 ACCEPT CONFIRMATION
                                 SELECT: If valid confirmation
                                 2.2.2.1.2.1 PROCESS VALID CONFIRMATION
                                             Mark record for deletion
                                             Display message
                                 2.2.2.1.2.2 PROCESS INVALID CONFIRMATION
                                             Display message
                                 END SELECT
```

Figure 10.15 Pseudocode for Case Study 7

```
            2.2.2.2 PROCESS FOR NO MATCH FOUND
                   Display message
            END SELECT
         END SELECT
      2.3 FREEZE SCREEN AND BLANK ITEM NUMBER
          Process FREEZE procedure
          Reset ITEMNUM to BLANK
   END REPEAT
 3.0 TERMINATE PROCESSING
    3.1 PACK AND CLOSE DATABASE
        Create backup file
        Pack the database file
        Delete backup file
        Close the database file
        Turn off the DELETED function
    3.2 RETURN TO CALLING PROGRAM
        Return to calling program
```

Figure 10.15 Continued

pseudocode of Figure 10.15 is translated into dBASE commands, and the complete program for Case Study 7 in dBASE language is given in Figure 10.16.

10.6.5 The Testing and Debugging Phase

The last step in program development is the testing and debugging phase, in which the source program is executed and tested for the accuracy of its logic. Execute the program to complete this step, correct the syntactical errors, if any, and execute the program again. Repeat this process until the program is free of syntactical errors. When the output is produced by the program, verify some of the records of the output to ensure its accuracy. If any discrepancies exist, make the needed corrections, and execute the program again. Repeat the process of making corrections and executing the program until the program produces correct and predictable results.

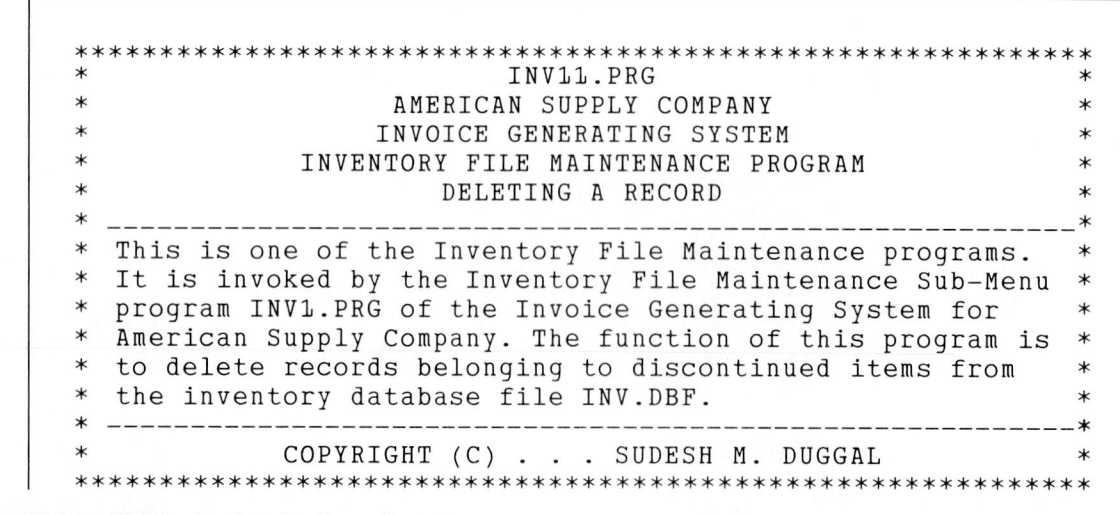

```
***************************************************************
*                        INV11.PRG                             *
*                  AMERICAN SUPPLY COMPANY                     *
*                 INVOICE GENERATING SYSTEM                    *
*             INVENTORY FILE MAINTENANCE PROGRAM               *
*                     DELETING A RECORD                        *
*--------------------------------------------------------------*
* This is one of the Inventory File Maintenance programs.      *
* It is invoked by the Inventory File Maintenance Sub-Menu     *
* program INV1.PRG of the Invoice Generating System for        *
* American Supply Company. The function of this program is     *
* to delete records belonging to discontinued items from       *
* the inventory database file INV.DBF.                         *
*--------------------------------------------------------------*
*           COPYRIGHT (C) . . . SUDESH M. DUGGAL               *
***************************************************************
```

Figure 10.16 Coding for Case Study 7

```
*
****************************
*  1.0 INITIATE PROCESSING  *
****************************
*
*** 1.1 HOUSEKEEPING ***
   *
   SET DELETED ON
   *
*** 1.2 DEFINE VARIABLES ***
   *
   *** DEFINE CONTROL VARIABLES ***
      *
      STORE [T] TO REPEAT11
      *
   *** INITIALIZE VARIABLES ***
      *
      STORE '    ' TO ITEMNUM
      *
*** 1.3 OPEN DATABASE FILE ***
   *
   USE INV
   *
***********************
*  2.0 MAIN PROCESSING  *
***********************
*
DO WHILE REPEAT11 = [T]
   *
   *** 2.1 ACCEPT ITEM NUMBER ***
      *
      *** CLEAR SCREEN ***
         *
         CLEAR
         *
      *** REQUEST AND ACCEPT ITEM NUMBER ***
         *
         @  2,20 SAY '           AMERICAN SUPPLY COMPANY'
         @  3,4  SAY DATE ()
         @  3,20 SAY '          INVOICE GENERATING SYSTEM'
         @  3,70 SAY TIME ()
         @  4,20 SAY '      INVENTORY FILE MAINTENANCE PROGRAM'
         @  5,20 SAY '              DELETING A RECORD'
         @  6,0  TO  6,79
         @ 22,0  TO 22,79
         @  1,2  TO 24,79 DOUBLE
         @  8,20 SAY 'ENTER THE ITEM NUMBER, PLEASE ===>:'
         @  8,56 GET ITEMNUM PICTURE 'XXXX'
         READ
         *
   *** 2.2 TEST FOR BLANK ITEM NUMBER ***
      *
      IF ITEMNUM = '    '
         *
         *** 2.2.1 PROCESS BLANK ITEM NUMBER ***
            *
```

Figure 10.16 Continued

```
                    STORE [F] TO REPEAT11
                    *
            ELSE
                *
                *** 2.2.2 PROCESS NONBLANK ITEM NUMBER ***
                *
                LOCATE FOR ITEM_NUM = ITEMNUM
                *
                IF .NOT. (EOF () .OR. BOF())
                    *
                    *** 2.2.2.1 PROCESS FOR MATCH FOUND ***
                        *
                        *** 2.2.2.1.1 DISPLAY MATCHING RECORD ***
                            *
                            @ 10,15 SAY [ITEM DESCRIPTION:]
                            @ 10,45 SAY ITEM_DESC
                            @ 12,15 SAY [QUANTITY         :]
                            @ 12,45 SAY QUANTITY
                            @ 14,15 SAY [UNIT COST        :]
                            @ 14,45 SAY UNIT_COST
                            @ 16,15 SAY [DEPT CODE        :]
                            @ 16,35 SAY DEPT_CODE
                            @ 18,15 SAY [REORDER POINT    :]
                            @ 18,35 SAY REOD_POINT
                            @ 20,15 SAY [REORDER QUANTITY:]
                            @ 20,35 SAY REOD_QTY
                            *
                        *** 2.2.2.1.2 ACCEPT CONFIRMATION ***
                            *
                            STORE ' ' TO CONFIRM
                            @ 23,22 SAY 'ENTER ''D'' TO CONFIRM DELETE:' GET
                            CONFIRM
                            READ
                            *
                            IF UPPER(CONFIRM) = 'D'
                                *
                                *** 2.2.2.1.2.1 PROCESS VALID CONFIRMATION ***
                                    *
                                    DELETE
                                    @ 23,22 SAY '        *****     RECORD
                                    *****     '
                                    DELETED
                                    *
                            ELSE
                                *
                                *** 2.2.2.1.2.2 PROCESS INVALID
                                    CONFIRMATION ***
                                    *
                                    @ 23,22 SAY '** RECORD NOT DELETED -- WRONG
                                    DELETE CODE **'
                                    *
                            ENDIF UPPER (CONFIRM) = 'D'
                                *
                ELSE
                    *
                    *** 2.2.2.2 PROCESS FOR NO MATCH FOUND ***
                        *
```

Figure 10.16 Continued

```
                              @ 23,22 SAY '        *****    RECORD NOT
                                      FOUND    *****'
                              *
                      ENDIF .NOT. (EOF () .OR. BOF ())
                      *
              ENDIF ITEMNUM ='    '
              *
      *** 2.3 FREEZE SCREEN AND BLANK ITEM NUMBER ***
              *
              DO FREEZE
              *
              STORE '    ' TO ITEMNUM
              *
ENDDO REPEAT11 = [T]
*
****************************
* 3.0 TERMINATE PROCESSING *
****************************
*
*** 3.1 PACK AND CLOSE DATABASE ***
      *
      *** CREATE BACKUP FILE ***
              *
              COPY TO INV.BAK
              *
      *** PACK DATABASE FILE ***
              *
              PACK
              *
      *** DELETE BACKUP FILE ***
              *
              DELETE FILE INV.BAK
           **
      *** CLOSE DATABASE FILE ***
              *
              USE
              *
      *** RESET DELETED FUNCTION ***
              *
              SET DELETED OFF
              *
*** 3.2 RETURN TO CALLING PROGRAM ***
      *
      RETURN
```

Figure 10.16 Continued

10.7 Summary

The deletion of the records of the database file consists of two steps. First, the records are marked for deletion. The marked records are temporarily "invisible" to the dBASE commands and queries, although they have not been removed from the database file. In the second step, the records are physically and permanently removed from the database file.

The records of the database file can be marked for deletion by two different methods. They can be deleted within the edit mode by pressing the <Ctrl-U> keys. The deleted records can be recalled or unmarked by pressing the <Ctrl-U> keys once again. Multiple records satisfying a particular condition are deleted by using the DELETE command. This option is not available with the edit mode, in which only single records can be deleted.

The deleted records are marked by placing a "*" mark in front of them. Recall that the structure of the database file FILE1 was created in Section 2.2.1, and its structure was displayed as shown in Figure 2.13. It was pointed out there that the total number of bytes in the record length is one more than the length of the record. The extra byte is used by dBASE to mark the deleted records by placing a "*" mark before them. The "*" mark appears in the listing of the database file.

dBASE provides two methods of hiding the deleted records from dBASE commands or queries. The SET DELETED command can be used to hide the deleted records temporarily. The SET DELETED command is OFF by default. As such, both deleted and nondeleted records are visible to all dBASE commands and queries. When you change the default mode of the SET DELETED command to ON, the records marked for deletion become temporarily "invisible" to all dBASE commands and queries (except, of course, to the INDEX and the REINDEX commands). Another way to hide the deleted records is by using the DELETED () function as a condition with the dBASE command and queries.

The deleted records can be recalled either in the edit mode as mentioned earlier or by using the RECALL command. In the edit mode, only one record at a time can be recalled; the RECALL command can recall one, all, or a group of records satisfying a particular condition.

dBASE also provides two methods of purging the deleted records: the PACK command and the SET DELETED ON and COPY commands. The latter method creates a new file consisting of only the nondeleted records while leaving the original file intact. The former method deletes the marked records from the file and compresses the nondeleted records onto the original file. The former method has the advantage of saving the space occupied by the deleted records and making it available for other uses. But it has the disadvantage that a break of the electric power to the system during the packing can cause data to be lost.

KEY CONCEPTS

deleted records
flagged record
purging deleted records

recalling deleted records
records marked for deletion

dBASE COMMANDS AND FUNCTIONS

DELETE command
DELETED () function
PACK command

RECALL command
SET DELETED ON/OFF command

REVIEW QUESTIONS

1. What is the advantage of the two-step deletion method used by dBASE to remove records from the database file?
2. Name two different methods of marking records for deletion.
3. Explain how records can be marked for deletion by using the edit mode.
4. What are the two advantages of deleting records by using the edit mode?
5. How can you tell whether a record has been marked for deletion?
6. What are the advantages of using the DELETE command rather than the edit mode method to delete records?
7. How can you hide the deleted records from the dBASE commands?
8. Explain how you can obtain the listing of only the deleted records of the database file.
9. Explain how you can obtain the listing of only the nondeleted records of the database file.
10. What is the default mode of the SET DELETED command? How can it be changed?
11. Name two different methods of recalling the deleted records from the database file.
12. What is the drawback in using the edit mode to recall deleted records?
13. What are the advantages of the RECALL command over the edit mode method of recalling deleted records?
14. Name two different methods of physically removing records from the database file.
15. What is the advantage of the PACK command over the SET DELETED and COPY command method for purging deleted records?
16. What is the disadvantage of using the PACK command for purging deleted records?

HANDS-ON ASSIGNMENT

Programming Assignment 10A

Program Description   Write a customer file maintenance program ACR11.PRG. It should be invoked by the customer file maintenance submenu program ACR1.PRG of the accounts receivable system. The function of the program is to delete the records of the discontinued customers from the CUSTACR.DBF database file, whose structure is given in Figure 10.17 (see page 420).

Processing Steps   Use the following steps to develop the solution of the program:

1. The customer file maintenance screen as shown in Figure 10.18 with the message "ENTER THE CUSTOMER NUMBER, PLEASE ===> :" requesting the user to enter the customer number of the record to be deleted should be displayed.
2. The screen should be frozen or paused to allow the user to respond to the request.
3. After accepting the entry from the user, the value of the customer number supplied by the user should be tested to see if it is a blank or a nonblank value.
4. If it is blank, the user wants to terminate the process of deleting records from the database file. Therefore, proceed to step 12.
5. For a nonblank value of the customer number, search the CUSTACR.DBF database file to find the matching record.
6. If the match is not found, display the message indicating that it was not found, and proceed to step 11.
7. If the match is found, the matching record should be displayed on the screen.
8. Confirmation to delete the record should be requested from the user.
9. Check for the validity of the confirmation. If the confirmation is valid, delete the record from the database file.
10. If the confirmation is invalid, indicate this result by displaying the message.
11. Repeat steps 1–10 to delete the next discontinued record.
12. After all the desired records have been deleted, pack the database file, and return to the calling program ACR1.PRG.

The list of the records to be deleted from the CUSTACR.DBF database file is given in Figure 10.19 (see page 421).

Figure 10.17 Structure of the CUSTACR.DBF database file

```
Structure for database: C:\CUSTACR.DBF
Number of data records:      26
Date of last update   : 06/13/88
Field  Field Name  Type       Width    Dec
    1  CUST_NUM    Character    11
    2  CUST_NAME                25
    3  CUST_ADDR                20
    4  CUST_CITY                20
    5  CUST_STATE                2
    6  CUST_ZIP                  5
    7  CUST_PHONE               12
** Total **                    96
```

Requirements Submit the following items as part of the assignment:

1. Structure chart
2. Listing of program
3. Listing of the CUSTACR.DBF database file before and after deletes (use compressed print)
4. The following three screens printed using <Shift PrtSc> keys:
   a. Screen showing Jan A. Black being deleted with valid confirmation
   b. Screen showing attempt to delete Marguerite M. Jones with invalid confirmation
   c. Screen showing attempt to delete (your name) with record not found error message

Programming Assignment 10B

Program Description Write an employee file maintenance program PAY11.PRG. It should be invoked by the employee file maintenance submenu program PAY1.PRG of the payroll system. The function of the program is to delete the records of employees who are not working with the American Supply Company

Figure 10.18 Customer database file maintenance screen

```
                AMERICAN SUPPLY COMPANY
 01/12/90      ACCOUNTS RECEIVABLE SYSTEM              14:25:40
             CUSTOMER DATABASE FILE MAINTENANCE
                    DELETING A RECORD


       ENTER THE CUSTOMER NUMBER, PLEASE ===>: ▮










              Press ⏎ key to Terminate Processing
```

CUST_NUM	CUST_NAME	CUST_ADDR	CUST_CITY	CUST_STATE	CUST_ZIP	CUST_PHONE
506-97-3421	Jan A. Black	8900 Terwilligers Dr	Burlington	KY	41005	606-431-4534
124-45-7972	Cindy E. Northland	5555 Lovers Lane	Loveland	OH	45140	513-683-1982
401-94-1242	Mary J. Nordman	1200 Immaculate Lane	Sharonville	OH	45241	513-733-7869
404-92-5278	Cindy A. Pollard	10020 Gold Circle Rd	Taylor Mill	KY	41015	606-356-9876
302-54-7281	Ann M. Moss	8000 Reservoir St	Delhi	OH	45012	513-563-6469
632-02-4144	Marguerite M. Jones	1073 Go Go Drive	Newport	KY	41010	606-245-4322

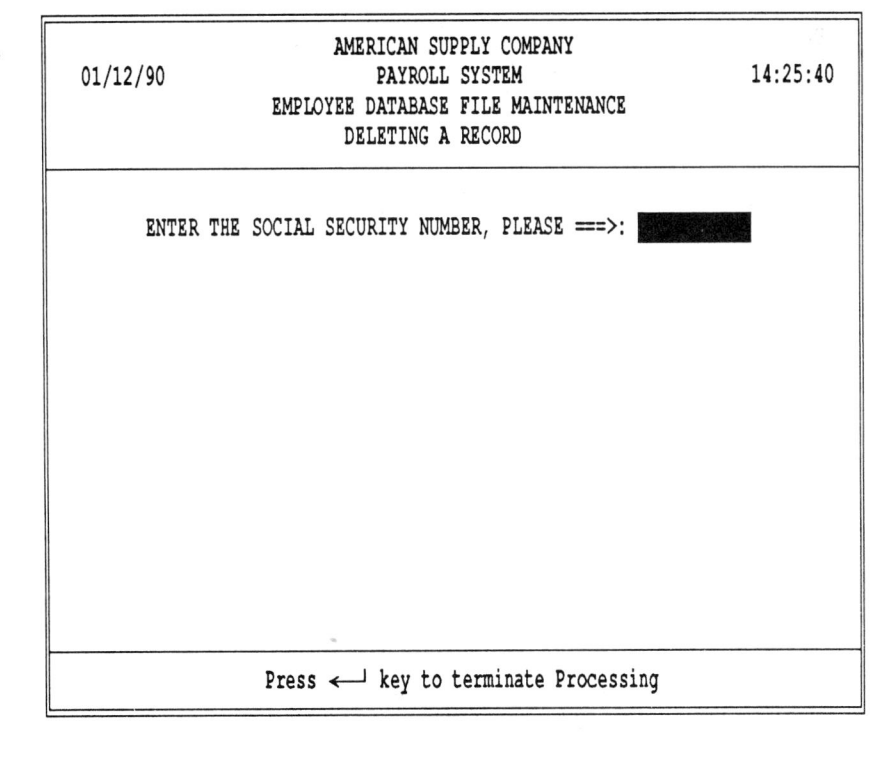

Figure 10.19 Records to be deleted from the CUSTACR.DBF database file

from the employee database file EMPLOYEE.DBF, whose structure is given in Figure 4.33.

Processing Steps Use the following steps to develop the solution of the program:

1. The employee file maintenance screen as shown in Figure 10.20 with the message "ENTER THE SOCIAL SECURITY NUMBER, PLEASE ===> :" requesting the user to enter the social security number of the record to be deleted should be displayed.

2. The screen should be frozen or paused to allow the user to respond to the request.

3. After accepting the entry from the user, the value of the social security number supplied by the user should be tested to see if it is a blank or a nonblank value.

4. If the value of the social security number sup-

Figure 10.20 Employee database file maintenance screen

```
                    AMERICAN SUPPLY COMPANY
01/12/90              PAYROLL SYSTEM                14:25:40
                EMPLOYEE DATABASE FILE MAINTENANCE
                       DELETING A RECORD

     ENTER THE SOCIAL SECURITY NUMBER, PLEASE ===>: ▮▮▮▮▮▮▮▮




                  Press ⏎ key to terminate Processing
```

Figure 10.21 Records to be deleted from the EMPLOYEE.DBF database file

SOC_SC_NUM	EMP_NAME	DEPT_CODE	PAY_CODE	M_STATUS	N_DEP
288-74-7667	John A. Dilenger	102	29	2	15
345-67-8912	Sherril P. Milnes	102	52	4	4
415-00-6501	Roger B. Abernathy	102	57	3	13
572-67-3924	Vicki M. Lawerence	103	29	5	4
601-62-1115	Herb F. Tarleck	105	24	2	2
777-01-1919	Tonya T. Peace	104	69	3	12

plied by the user is blank, the user wants to terminate the process of deleting records from the database file. Therefore, proceed to step 12.

5. For the nonblank value of the social security number, search the EMPLOYEE.DBF database file to find the matching record.

6. If the match is not found, display the message indicating that it was not found, and proceed to step 11.

7. If the match is found, the matching record should be displayed on the screen.

8. Confirmation to delete the record should be requested from the user.

9. Check for the validity of the confirmation. If the confirmation is valid, delete the record from the database file.

10. If the confirmation is invalid, indicate this result by displaying the message.

11. Repeat steps 1–10 to delete the next discontinued record.

12. After all the desired records have been deleted, pack the database file, and return to the calling program PAY1.PRG.

The list of the records to be deleted from the EMPLOYEE.DBF database file is given in Figure 10.21.

Requirements Submit the following items as part of the assignment:

1. Structure chart
2. Listing of program
3. Listing of the EMPLOYEE.DBF database file before and after deletes (containing first six fields only)
4. The following three screens printed using <Shift PrtSc> keys:
   a. Screen showing John Dilenger being deleted with valid confirmation
   b. Screen showing attempt to delete Tonya Peace with invalid confirmation
   c. Screen showing attempt to delete (your name) with record not found error message

Chapter 11

File Maintenance: Adding a Record

LEARNING OBJECTIVES

Upon successfully completing this chapter, you will be able to:

1. Explain the concept of indexing a database file.
2. Explain the conditions under which indexing would be preferred over sorting.
3. Create single field index tags for the database file by using the CREATE STRUCTURE command.
4. Create single field index tags for the database file by using the MODIFY STRUCTURE command.
5. Create single field index tags for the database file by using the INDEX command.
6. Modify the order of the index tags created by using the MODIFY STRUCTURE command or the INDEX command.
7. Explain the concept of the production multiple index file as used in dBASE IV.
8. Describe the advantages of the index tags used in dBASE IV over the individual index file used in dBASE III PLUS.
9. Explain the need of extra multiple index files and describe how to create them.
10. Describe how the index tags can be activated.
11. Describe how the multiple index files can be activated.
12. Define the term *controlling index tag*.
13. Create the multiple field index tags for the database file by using the INDEX command.

14. Copy the individual index files created in dBASE III PLUS to index tags used in dBASE IV.
15. Delete the index tags, individual index files, and multiple index files.
16. Use the DTOS ( ) function to convert the date data type field to the character data type field.
17. Describe the method of searching the indexed database files using the FIND or SEEK command.
18. Describe the method of searching the nonindexed database files using the LOCATE command.
19. Explain the advantage of the LOCATE and CONTINUE commands used as a pair over the FIND and SEEK commands.
20. Analyze, design, and code a file maintenance program that can add records to the database file.

11.1 Overview

This chapter starts by introducing the INDEX command as an alternate to the SORT command to organize the data of the database file into a specific sequence. The concept of indexing, that is, how indexes are used to organize the data, is explained by the use of two examples.

The use of index tags and the production multiple index file in dBASE IV, in place of index files as used in dBASE III PLUS, is justified. Three different methods of creating the single field index tags (the use of the CREATE STRUCTURE command, the use of the MODIFY STRUCTURE command, and the use of the INDEX command) are introduced next. The method of creating the nonproduction multiple index files is also discussed.

The use of the SET ORDER and SET INDEX commands to activate the index tags and the nonproduction multiple index files is described. Creating multiple field indexes is also explained. The introduction of the new DTOS () function to take care of the drawbacks of the old DTOC () function is explained. The drawbacks of the new DTOS () function, when used in creating the multiple field indexes and used in the search of the indexed file, are pointed out. The method of converting the index files created in dBASE III PLUS to the index tags used in dBASE IV is presented along with the commands used to delete the index tags and multiple index files.

The FIND and SEEK commands are introduced next. These are used for searching the indexed database files. Their limitation necessitates introducing the LOCATE and CONTINUE commands, which are used in pairs for searching the nonindexed or indexed files. The use of indexed files is not required with these commands.

11.2 Indexing the Database File

dBASE IV provides two methods for organizing the data of a database file into a specific sequence. The first method, *sorting*, was discussed in section 7.2. The second method, **indexing,** an alternative to sorting, is the topic of this section.

11.2 Indexing the Database File

In section 7.2.1, it was pointed out that sorting is useful only in two cases: when there is a need for permanently changing the order of the records of the database file and when the database file consists of a relatively small number of records. But in other cases, sorting has some problems:

1. Sorting large files takes a long time.
2. Sorting creates a sorted database file equal in size to the original database file.
3. New records added to the database file are not automatically sorted.

Indexing, an alternative method of organizing the data of a database file, solves these problems. First, indexing of large files is much faster than sorting. Second, indexing does not create a new database file to store the sorted data records. Instead, it creates an index tag. The **index tag** is a file containing only the data field to be indexed, which is called the **index key**, and the corresponding record number of the original database file. The index tag file is much smaller than the original database file. Third, when the new records are added to the database file, the indexes are automatically updated.

To sum up, indexing, which saves space and is faster than sorting, is a more efficient method of organizing the database file. Therefore, indexing is always preferable to sorting for organizing the database file, except when the files are small or there is a need to save the sorted records.

Here are two examples to clarify the concept of indexing and how the indexing operation works to organize the data of the database file. First, consider the database file FILE1, which was created in section 2.2.1. The listing and the structure of this database file are given in Figures 11.1 and 11.2, respectively.

The listing of the FILE1 database file, as shown in Figure 11.1, indicates that there are nine records present, not arranged in any particular order. The structure of this database file, as shown in Figure 11.2, indicates that none of the four data fields present in the data records is indexed. Recall that an "N" in the index column indicates that the data field is not indexed.

Now suppose you want to use the method of indexing to arrange the records of this database file in ascending order on the ITEM_NUM field. An index tag named ITEM_NUM.NDX, consisting of the ITEM_NUM field and the corresponding data record number of the original FILE1 database

Figure 11.1 Listing of the FILE1 database file

Record#	ITEM_NUM	ITEM_DESC	UNIT_COST	QUANTITY
1	1136	Bond Paper, Ream	22.99	38
2	1910	Ditto Paper, Ream	19.99	35
3	4012	King Kong Modem 1200	105.99	10
4	4045	Monochrome Monitor Z-1105	99.99	15
5	4072	Panasonic Printer KX-P108	269.99	8
6	3372	Printer Ribbon 10-Box	35.99	19
7	3375	Typewriter Ribbons 10-Box	23.79	67
8	1488	Xerographic Paper	19.99	45
9	4189	Zenith Microcomputer Z-158	829.99	5

```
.DISPLAY STRUCTURE
Structure for database : C:\DBASE\INVOICE\FILE1.DBF
Number of data records :      9
Date of last update    : 1/12/89
Field  Field name   Type          Width    Dec     Index
    1  ITEM_NUM     Character        4                N
    2  ITEM_DESC    Character       26                N
    3  UNIT_COST    Numeric          6      2         N
    4  QUANTITY     Numeric          3                N
** TOTAL **                         40
```

Figure 11.2 Structure of the FILE1 database file

file, will be created. The ITEM_NUM.NDX index tag will look as shown in Figure 11.3.

Observe that the data records in the ITEM_NUM.NDX index tag are in ascending order of the index key, that is, the ITEM_NUM data field. But the sequence of the data records in the original FILE1 database file remains unchanged. When a listing of the FILE1 database file is produced using the ITEM_NUM.NDX index tag, the index key from the index tag dictates the sequence; and the corresponding record number provides the link with the data records of the original database file FILE1. The listing of the database file FILE1 using the ITEM_NUM.NDX index tag will be as shown in Figure 11.4.

As a second example, suppose you also want to arrange the records of the database file FILE1 in descending order on the UNIT_COST data field. Another index tag named UNIT_COST.NDX, consisting of the UNIT_COST field and the corresponding data record number of the original FILE1 database file, will also be created. It will look as shown in Figure 11.5.

Observe that the data records in the UNIT_COST.NDX index tag are in descending order of the index key, that is, the UNIT_COST data field. But the sequence of the data records in the original FILE1 database file still remains unchanged. When a listing of the FILE1 database file is produced using the UNIT_COST.NDX index tag, the index key from the index tag dictates the sequence; and the corresponding record number

Figure 11.3
ITEM_NUM.NDX index tag

FIELD NUMBER	INDEX KEY	RECORD NUMBER
1	1136	1
2	1488	8
3	1910	2
4	3372	6
5	3375	7
6	4012	3
7	4045	4
8	4072	5
9	4189	9

Figure 11.4 Listing of database file FILE1 using the ITEM_NUM.NDX index tag

Record#	ITEM NUM	ITEM DESC	UNIT COST	QUANTITY
1	1136	Bond Paper, Ream	22.99	38
8	1488	Xerographic Paper	19.99	45
2	1910	Ditto Paper, Ream	19.99	35
6	3372	Printer Ribbon 10-Box	35.99	19
7	3375	Typewriter Ribbons 10-Box	23.79	67
3	4012	King Kong Modem 1200	105.99	10
4	4045	Monochrome Monitor Z-1105	99.99	15
5	4072	Panasonic Printer KX-P108	269.99	8
9	4189	Zenith Microcomputer Z-158	829.99	5

provides the link with the data records of the original FILE1 database file. The listing of the FILE1 database file using the UNIT_COST.NDX index tag will be as shown in Figure 11.6.

11.2.1 Creating the Single Field Index Tags

There are three methods of creating single field index tags. The first is by using the CREATE STRUCTURE command, the second is by using the MODIFY STRUCTURE command, and the third is by using the INDEX command.

First Method: Using the CREATE STRUCTURE Command

The first method of creating single field index tags is by using the CREATE STRUCTURE command. This method is used to create the index tags while creating the structure of the database file. The CREATE STRUCTURE command is employed to create the structure of the database file, which is defined by completing the database design form. The completed structure of database file FILE1 as discussed in section 2.2.1 is shown in Figure 11.7.

Each row of the database design form defines a data field of the data record of the database file and consists of six columns labeled num, field name, field type, width, dec, and index. Each data field is defined by supplying the information for each column as described in section 2.2.1.

Figure 11.5 UNIT_COST.NDX index tag

FIELD NUMBER	INDEX KEY	RECORD NUMBER
1	829.99	9
2	269.99	5
3	105.99	3
4	99.99	4
5	35.99	6
6	23.79	7
7	22.99	1
8	19.99	2
9	19.99	8

Figure 11.6 Listing of database file FILE1 using the UNIT_COST.NDX index tag

```
Record#  ITEM NUM  ITEM DESC                    UNIT_COST  QUANTITY
     9   4189      Zenith Microcomputer Z-158      829.99         5
     5   4072      Panasonic Printer KX-P108       269.99         8
     3   4012      King Kong Modem 1200            105.99        10
     4   4045      Monochrome Monitor Z-1105        99.99        15
     6   3372      Printer Ribbon 10-Box            35.99        19
     7   3375      Typewriter Ribbons 10-Box        23.79        67
     1   1136      Bond Paper, Ream                 22.99        38
     2   1488      Xerographic Paper                19.99        45
     8   1910      Ditto Paper, Ream                19.99        35
```

The last column, labeled index, is used to inform dBASE whether the field being defined is to be used as an indexed field or not. There are only two options for indexing a field: Y or N. The default option of N is always displayed in that column. It can be changed to Y by simply pressing the space bar. After the appropriate option (N for not indexing the field and Y for indexing the field) is displayed in that column, press the <Return> key to make the selection. *None* of the four data fields defined in the structure of the FILE1 database file as shown in Figure 11.7 is indexed.

A value of Y in the index column creates an index tag for each field defined in the structure of the database. The name of the field is assigned to the index tag with an extension of .NDX. When a database file is indexed for the first time, a multiple index file is automatically created by default for the database file. Each indexed database file has by default a multiple index file called a **production multiple index file** in which all the index tags created for a database file are stored. The name of the database file is assigned to this multiple index file with an extension of .MDX.

The concept of the index tags and the multiple index (.MDX) file is new

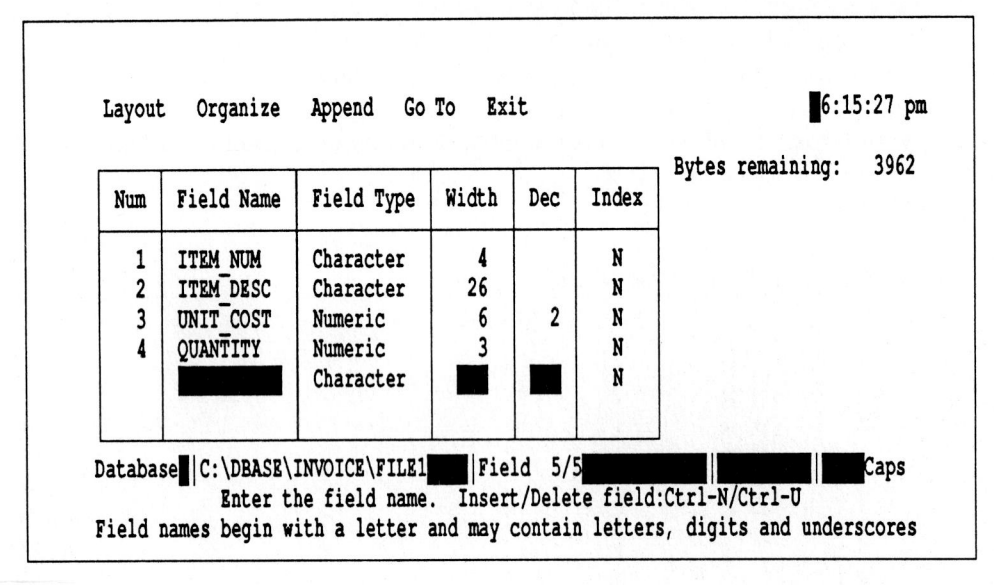

```
Layout    Organize    Append    Go To    Exit              6:15:27 pm

                                              Bytes remaining:   3962
┌─────┬────────────┬────────────┬───────┬─────┬───────┐
│ Num │ Field Name │ Field Type │ Width │ Dec │ Index │
├─────┼────────────┼────────────┼───────┼─────┼───────┤
│  1  │ ITEM NUM   │ Character  │   4   │     │   N   │
│  2  │ ITEM_DESC  │ Character  │  26   │     │   N   │
│  3  │ UNIT_COST  │ Numeric    │   6   │  2  │   N   │
│  4  │ QUANTITY   │ Numeric    │   3   │     │   N   │
│     │            │ Character  │       │     │   N   │
└─────┴────────────┴────────────┴───────┴─────┴───────┘

Database  C:\DBASE\INVOICE\FILE1    Field 5/5              Caps
          Enter the field name.  Insert/Delete field:Ctrl-N/Ctrl-U
Field names begin with a letter and may contain letters, digits and underscores
```

Figure 11.7 Database design screen with completed database design form for the structure of the database file FILE1

in dBASE IV. In the earlier versions of dBASE, individual **index** (.NDX) **files** were used for indexing the database files. The individual index (.NDX) files created with the earlier versions of dBASE can still be used in dBASE IV. But using index tags is more efficient than using the index files, for two reasons. First, because all the index tags are contained in one file, it is easier to maintain them. But this is not true with the index files because each index file is stored as a separate file.

Second, as soon as you open the database file, the corresponding multiple index (.MDX) file is automatically opened, and all the indexes are automatically adjusted to the changes made in the database file. This result is also not true with the index files; that is, the index files are not automatically opened and not automatically adjusted when the changes are made to the database files.

Two methods can be used to update the indexes when the changes are made in the database file using the index files. In the first method, before making the changes to the database file, you can open the database file with the index files needed at the same time. This step requires some extra commands. In the second method, after the changes have been made to the database file, you can reindex all the index files. This procedure also will require a few extra commands. Both methods require some additional work and, as such, indicate that use of the index files is not as efficient as use of the tag files. Therefore, try to avoid using the index files. If you have some index files from the earlier versions of dBASE, you can convert them to the index tags as explained later in section 11.2.5.

Now let us return to the two examples discussed in section 11.2. Two index tags were created for the FILE1 database file—the ITEM_NUM.NDX index tag, which indexed the file in ascending order on the ITEM_NUM field, and the UNIT_COST.NDX index tag, which indexed the file in descending order on the UNIT_COST field.

We can create both of these by applying the first method: using the MODIFY STRUCTURE command while creating the structure of the database file. That is, selecting the option Y for both the ITEM_NUM and the UNIT_COST fields will create the ITEM_NUM.NDX and the UNIT_COST.NDX index tags.

Because the default of dBASE IV for indexing is in ascending order, both of these index tags will be in ascending order on the index key. But we need the UNIT_COST.NDX index tag in descending order, as used in the second example. We can modify this to change its order from ascending to descending by using the MODIFY STRUCTURE command.

Second Method: Using the MODIFY STRUCTURE Command

The second method of creating the single field index tag, by using the MODIFY STRUCTURE command, is used for the database file whose structure has already been created.

The two examples discussed previously employed the database file FILE1, whose structure was created in section 2.2.1. As observed earlier and also shown in Figure 11.7, none of the four data fields used in that database file has been indexed. We can apply the second method of using the MODIFY STRUCTURE command to create the index tags ITEM_NUM and UNIT_COST needed in these two examples.

The following commands will be needed to start the process of indexing the database file FILE1:

```
. USE FILE1              <Return>
. MODIFY STRUCTURE       <Return>
```

dBASE will respond by displaying the structure of the database file FILE1 as shown in Figure 11.7. Move the cursor to the index column of the ITEM_NUM field. The option N will be displayed there. Press the space bar as indicated in the message line, and the option will change to Y. Now press the <Return> key to select this option. Repeat this process for the UNIT_COST field. The screen will look as shown in Figure 11.8.

Both the ITEM_NUM and UNIT_COST fields have been indexed. If these changes are saved, dBASE IV will first create the FILE1.MDX multiple index file. Then the ITEM_NUM.NDX and UNIT_COST.NDX index tags will be created and saved in the FILE1.MDX multiple index file.

But as indicated earlier, both index tags will be in ascending order. Therefore, before we save these changes to the structure of the FILE1 database file, we should modify the UNIT_COST index tag to descending order, as needed in the second example.

Modifying the Order of the Index Tag After creating the single field index tags, you can modify their order by following these steps:

1. Highlight the Organize option of the menu bar by pressing the <Alt-O> keys (or by pressing the F10 key and then using the <Right Arrow> or <Left Arrow> keys as needed to highlight the Organize option).
2. Press the <Return> key to select this option. The Pull-down Menu for the Organize option will be displayed as shown in Figure 11.9.

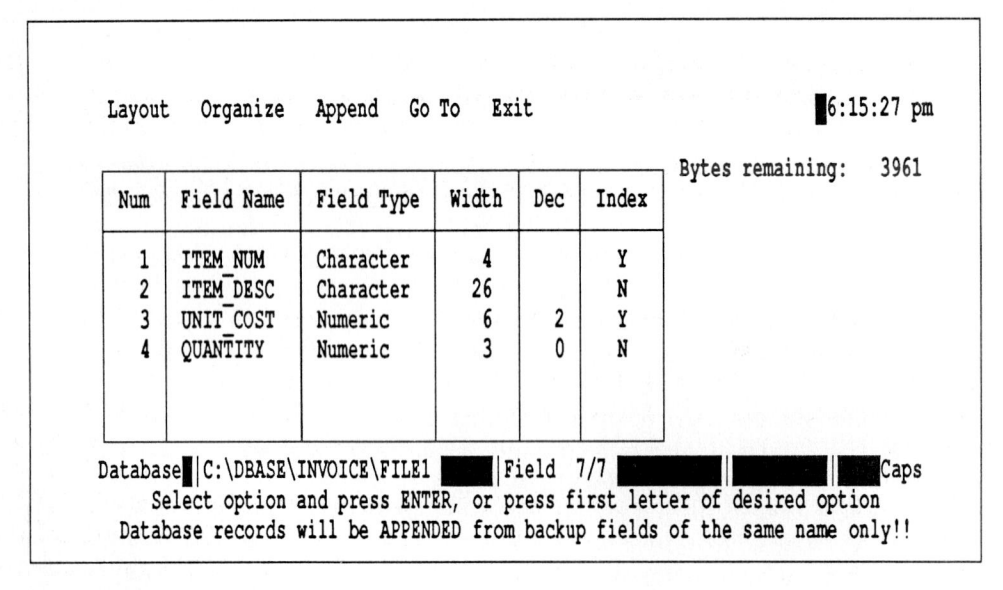

```
 Layout   Organize   Append   Go To   Exit              6:15:27 pm

                                              Bytes remaining:   3961
 ┌─────┬────────────┬────────────┬───────┬─────┬───────┐
 │ Num │ Field Name │ Field Type │ Width │ Dec │ Index │
 ├─────┼────────────┼────────────┼───────┼─────┼───────┤
 │  1  │ ITEM_NUM   │ Character  │   4   │     │   Y   │
 │  2  │ ITEM_DESC  │ Character  │  26   │     │   N   │
 │  3  │ UNIT_COST  │ Numeric    │   6   │  2  │   Y   │
 │  4  │ QUANTITY   │ Numeric    │   3   │  0  │   N   │
 └─────┴────────────┴────────────┴───────┴─────┴───────┘

 Database  C:\DBASE\INVOICE\FILE1    Field 7/7              Caps
     Select option and press ENTER, or press first letter of desired option
     Database records will be APPENDED from backup fields of the same name only!!
```

Figure 11.8 Structure of the database file FILE1 with the ITEM_NUM and the UNIT_COST fields indexed

11.2 Indexing the Database File **431**

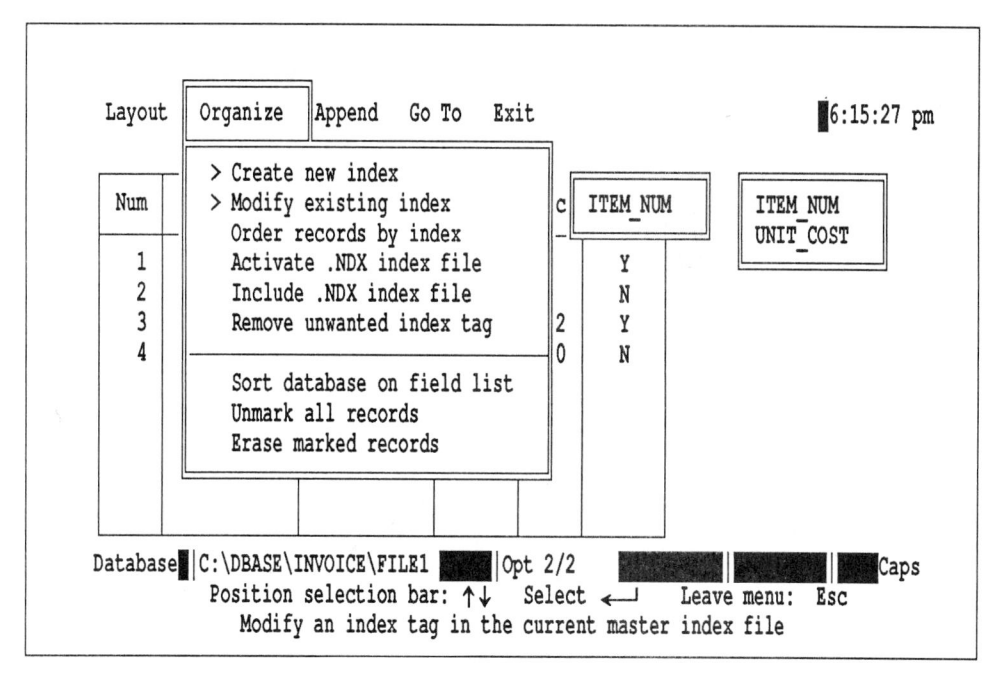

```
  Layout  Organize  Append  Go To  Exit            6:15:27 pm
          > Create new index
   Num    > Modify existing index        C  ITEM_NUM      ITEM_NUM
            Order records by index                        UNIT_COST
    1       Activate .NDX index file        Y
    2       Include .NDX index file         N
    3       Remove unwanted index tag    2  Y
    4                                    0  N
            Sort database on field list
            Unmark all records
            Erase marked records


  Database  C:\DBASE\INVOICE\FILE1    Opt 2/2                   Caps
            Position selection bar: ↑↓  Select ↵  Leave menu: Esc
            Modify an index tag in the current master index file
```

Figure 11.9 Structure of database file FILE1 during the modification of the UNIT_COST.NDX index tag

3. Highlight the Modify existing index option by using the <Down Arrow> key, and select this option by pressing the <Return> key. All the fields on which the database file FILE1 is indexed will be displayed in a window, as shown in Figure 11.9.

4. Highlight and select the UNIT_COST field from this list. The submenu of the Modify existing index option will be displayed as shown in Figure 11.10.

5. Highlight and select the order of index option from this submenu. Observe that the default option of the order of indexing, that is, ASCENDING, is present there.

6. To change the order of indexing to descending, press the space bar. The ASCENDING option will be changed to the DESCENDING option.

7. When the DESCENDING option is displayed, press the <Ctrl-W> or <Ctrl-End> keys to save the changes.

dBASE will respond by displaying the modified structure of the database file FILE1 as given in Figure 11.8. Now to save these changes in the structure of the database file FILE1, press the <Ctrl-W> keys. dBASE will respond by displaying the message as shown in Figure 11.11. This message will be skipped if the indexes are not modified.

Select the Yes option, and press the <Return> key. The following two messages will flash on the screen:

```
INDEX ON ITEM_NUM TAG ITEM_NUM
100% indexed            9 records indexed
```

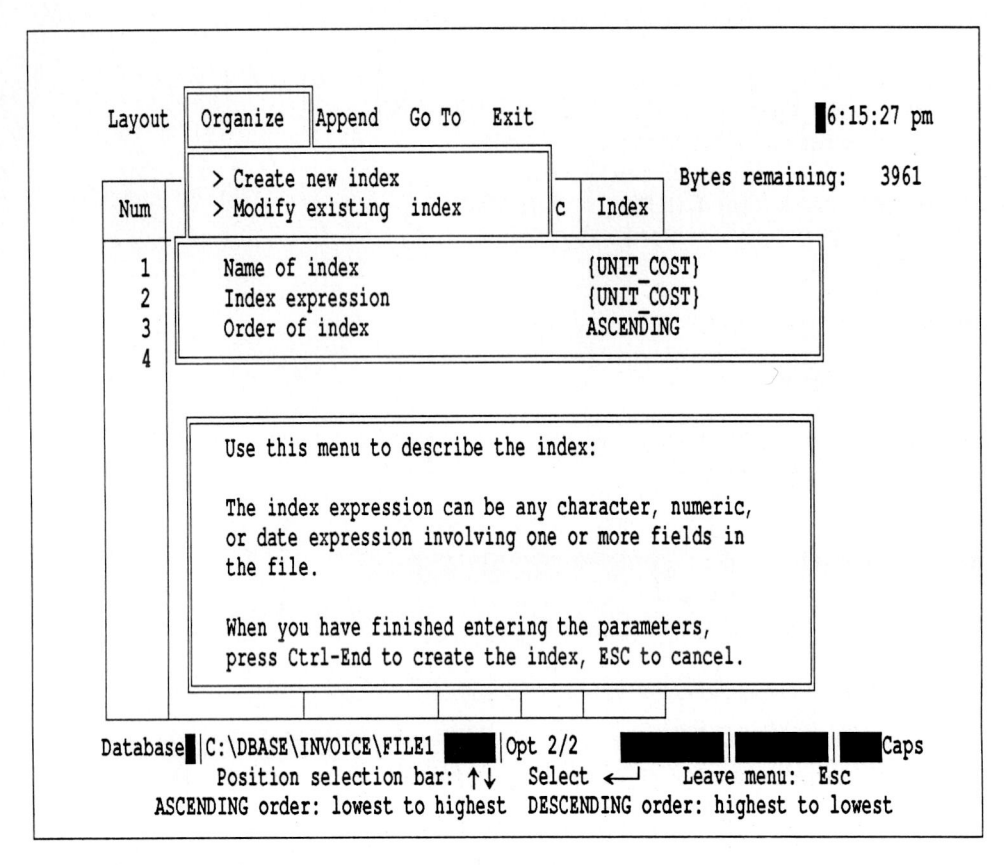

```
            Layout  Organize   Append   Go To   Exit                    ▍6:15:27 pm
                    ┌──────────────────────────┐
                    │ > Create new index       │         Bytes remaining:    3961
              ┌─────┤ > Modify existing index  ├─┬─────────┐
              │ Num │                          │c│ Index   │
              ├─────┤┌─────────────────────────┴─┴─────┐   │
              │  1  ││ Name of index        {UNIT_COST}│   │
              │  2  ││ Index expression     {UNIT_COST}│   │
              │  3  ││ Order of index       ASCENDING  │   │
              │  4  │└─────────────────────────────────┘   │
              │     │                                   ?  │
                    ┌─────────────────────────────────────────┐
                    │ Use this menu to describe the index:    │
                    │                                         │
                    │ The index expression can be any character, numeric,
                    │ or date expression involving one or more fields in
                    │ the file.                               │
                    │                                         │
                    │ When you have finished entering the parameters,
                    │ press Ctrl-End to create the index, ESC to cancel.
                    └─────────────────────────────────────────┘

       Database▊C:\DBASE\INVOICE\FILE1    │Opt 2/2                       │Caps
              Position selection bar: ↑↓    Select ←┘    Leave menu:  Esc
         ASCENDING order: lowest to highest  DESCENDING order: highest to lowest
```

Figure 11.10 Structure of database file FILE1 during the modification of the UNIT_COST.NDX index tag

```
INDEX ON UNIT_COST TAG UNIT_COST DESCENDING
100% indexed            9 records indexed
```

These indicate that the index tags ITEM_NUM.NDX and UNIT_COST.NDX have been created and stored in the FILE1.MDX multiple index file.

Third Method: Using the INDEX Command

The third method of creating single field index tags is by using the INDEX command at the dot prompt.

The INDEX Command   The general format of the INDEX command is

```
INDEX ON <index key/expression> TO <.NDX file name>
       /TAG <index tag name> [OF <.MDX file name>]
       [DESCENDING]
```

where <index key/expression> is the name of the index key or the index expression that is a combination of the index fields, <.NDX file name> is the name of the index file, <index tag name> is the name of the index tag, and <.MDX file name> is the name of the multiple index file.

The INDEX command can be used to create either the index file with

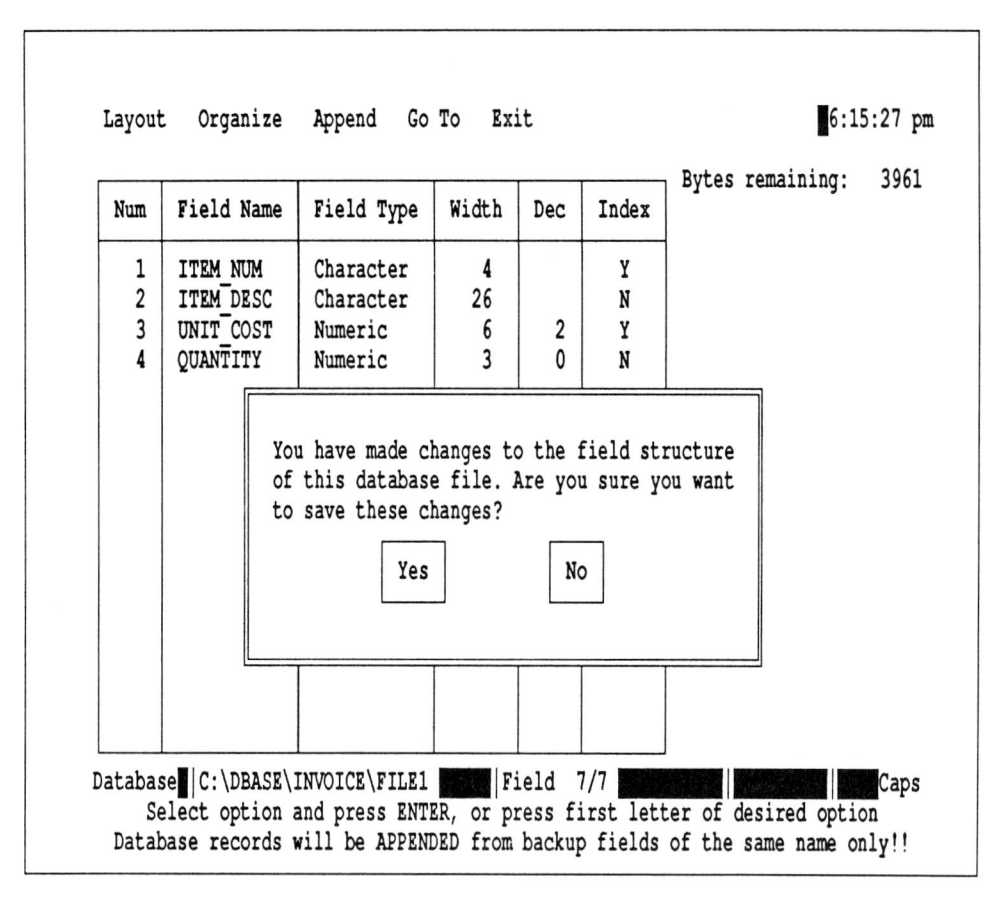

```
       Layout   Organize   Append   Go To   Exit                    6:15:27 pm

                                                        Bytes remaining:   3961
      ┌─────┬────────────┬────────────┬───────┬─────┬───────┐
      │ Num │ Field Name │ Field Type │ Width │ Dec │ Index │
      ├─────┼────────────┼────────────┼───────┼─────┼───────┤
      │  1  │ ITEM_NUM   │ Character  │   4   │     │   Y   │
      │  2  │ ITEM_DESC  │ Character  │  26   │     │   N   │
      │  3  │ UNIT_COST  │ Numeric    │   6   │  2  │   Y   │
      │  4  │ QUANTITY   │ Numeric    │   3   │  0  │   N   │

           ┌──────────────────────────────────────────────┐
           │ You have made changes to the field structure │
           │ of this database file. Are you sure you want │
           │ to save these changes?                       │
           │                                              │
           │          ┌─────┐          ┌─────┐            │
           │          │ Yes │          │ No  │            │
           │          └─────┘          └─────┘            │
           └──────────────────────────────────────────────┘


   Database  C:\DBASE\INVOICE\FILE1      Field 7/7                     Caps
       Select option and press ENTER, or press first letter of desired option
       Database records will be APPENDED from backup fields of the same name only!!
```

Figure 11.11 Structure of database file FILE1 with the ITEM_NUM and the UNIT_COST fields indexed in the process of being saved

the .NDX extension if the TO option is specified or the index tag if the TAG option is specified. This discussion is restricted to index tags.

The default option of the indexing order is ascending. The optional descending clause can be added at the end of the INDEX command to change the default order of indexing.

The format of the INDEX command used for creating the single field index tag is

```
INDEX ON <index key> TAG <index tag name>
        [OF <.MDX file name>] [DESCENDING]
```

where <index key> is the name of the index field, which can be any field of the database file except the memo or logical fields; <index tag name> is the name of the index tag, which can be up to ten characters long and consist of letters, digits, and the underscore (_). When the index tags are created using a single field as the index key, it is recommended that the tag file name be the same as that of the index field. <.MDX file name> is the name of the multiple index file.

If no multiple index (.MDX) file is specified in the INDEX command, then the index tags created are stored in the production multiple index file (.MDX) whose name is the same as that of the database file. If the production multiple index file does not exist, it is created; and the index tags are saved in it. But if it is specified in the INDEX command, then the index tags are stored in the specified multiple index file. If the specified multiple index (.MDX) file does not exist, it is first created, and then the index tags are created and stored in it. The discussions in this and the next section are restricted to the multiple index files.

Now let us create the tag files for the two examples discussed in section 11.2. We are assuming that these tag files have not been created using either the CREATE STRUCTURE command method or the MODIFY STRUCTURE command method discussed previously.

To index database file FILE1 on the ITEM_NUM field in ascending order, the following commands will be needed:

```
. USE FILE1                           <Return>
. INDEX ON ITEM_NUM TAG ITEM_NUM      <Return>
```

If you type these commands, dBASE will respond by displaying the following message:

```
100% indexed     9 records indexed
```

dBASE will create the FILE1.MDX multiple index file if it does not already exist. Then dBASE will create the ITEM_NUM.NDX index tag and save it in the FILE1.MDX multiple index file.

To index the database file FILE1 on the UNIT_COST field in descending order, you'll need the following command. We don't need the USE FILE1 command because the file is already open.

```
. INDEX ON UNIT_COST TAG UNIT_COST
  DESCENDING    <Return>
```

If you type this command, dBASE will respond by displaying the following message:

```
100% indexed     9 records indexed
```

dBASE will create the UNIT_COST.NDX index tag and save it in the FILE1.MDX multiple index file.

11.2.2 Creating Multiple Index Files

The index tags created by all three methods of creating the single field index tags discussed in the previous section were stored in the production multiple index file. The production multiple index file for a database file is automatically created when the first index tag is created for the database file and assumes the name of the database file. An extension of .MDX is supplied by dBASE. A maximum of 47 index tags can be stored in a multiple index file, which is enough for most applications. However, if you need more than 47 index tags, if you need to group index tags for a database file in more than one category, or if you need to create two index tags for the same field in different orders, you can create an additional multiple index file.

You can create a multiple index file, other than the production multiple index file, by using the OF option in the INDEX command to

11.2 Indexing the Database File

specify the name of the multiple index file. The format of the INDEX command for this purpose is

```
INDEX ON <index key/expression> TAG <index tag
    name>
    [OF <.MDX file name>]    [DESCENDING]
```

where <index key/expression> is the name of the index key or the index expression that is the combination of the index fields. <Index tag name> is the name of the index tag. The OF option allows you to save the index tags in the specified multiple index file, and <.MDX file name> is the name of the designated multiple index file.

To index the FILE1 database file in ascending order on the quantity field and store the index tag in the **nonproduction multiple index file** named FILE1QTY, use the following commands:

```
. USE FILE1    <Return>
. INDEX ON QUANTITY TAG QUANTITY OF FILE1QTY
    <Return>
```

dBASE will respond by displaying the following message:

```
100% indexed    9 records indexed
```

When these commands are executed, dBASE will create the QUANTITY.NDX index tag and store it in the FILE1QTY.MDX multiple index file if the FILE1QTY.MDX multiple index file already exists. But if it does not, dBASE will first create it, then create the QUANTITY.NDX index tag, and save it in the newly created multiple index file.

Now let us index the FILE1 database file in ascending order on the UNIT_COST field and store the index tag in the nonproduction multiple index file named FILE1QTY. Recall that we have already indexed the FILE1 database file in descending order on the UNIT_COST field and stored the index tag in the production multiple index file. To complete this step, type the following command:

```
. INDEX ON UNIT_COST TAG UNIT_COST OF
    FILE1QTY    <Return>
```

dBASE will respond by displaying the following message:

```
100% indexed    9 records indexed
```

When this command is executed, dBASE will create the UNIT_COST.NDX index tag and store it in the FILE1QTY.MDX multiple index file.

11.2.3 Using Index Tags

When a database file is opened, all the index tags saved in the production multiple index file are also opened. If the records in the database file are updated, dBASE will automatically update all the index tags. Except for the purpose of updating the index tags automatically when the contents of the database files are updated, the index tags remain inactive until they are activated.

In section 11.2.1, the database file FILE1 was indexed on two fields—ITEM_NUM and UNIT_COST. Two index tags, ITEM_NUM.NDX and UNIT_COST.NDX, were created and stored in the production multiple index file. You can open this database file and obtain its listing by typing the following commands:

```
. USE FILE1     <Return>
. LIST          <Return>
```

dBASE will respond by displaying the listing as shown in Figure 11.1. An examination of the listing indicates that the records in the listing are not in any particular order. In other words, they are in natural order, that in which they are physically present in the database file. You have indexed the file on two different fields. You also know that when the file is opened, the index tags are also opened. However, it is still not producing the listing in the order of the indexed fields because the index tags are not active. To activate the index tags, use the SET ORDER TO command.

The SET ORDER TO Command

The general format of the SET ORDER TO command is

```
SET ORDER TO <index tag name> [OF <.MDX file name>]
```

where <index tag name> is the name of the index tag that designates the controlling index, OF is an optional clause that indicates the multiple index file in which the index tag resides, and <.MDX file name> is the name of the multiple index file.

The SET ORDER TO command is used to designate or activate the index tag of the specified multiple index file. The designated index tag, which controls the sort order of the records of the database file, is called the **controlling index tag.** This index tag is used to obtain the listing of the database file arranged in a particular order. It also determines the field that will be used to search, employing the FIND or SEEK command.

The SET ORDER TO command is used only after opening the database file. If the optional clause OF is not specified with it, the default production multiple index file is assumed. If no index tag file name is specified with the SET ORDER TO command, the natural sort order will be set; that is, no index tag will be in control. In other words, the records of the database file will be available in the natural order, that is, the physical order in which they are stored in the database file. The controlling index can be changed by issuing another SET ORDER TO command.

To obtain the listing of the FILE1 database file in ascending order on the ITEM_NUM field, you will need to activate the ITEM_NUM.NDX index tag. To do this, use the following commands:

```
. USE FILE1                  <Return>
. SET ORDER TO ITEM_NUM      <Return>
```

dBASE will respond by displaying the following message:

```
Master Index: ITEM_NUM
```

11.2 Indexing the Database File

This message indicates that the index tag ITEM_NUM.NDX is active. The records of the FILE1 database file are available in ascending order on the ITEM_NUM field, which is the sort order specified by the ITEM_NUM.NDX index tag for listing or search purposes.

If you obtain the listing of the FILE1 database file by typing the LIST command, the listing will appear as shown in Figure 11.4. The listing is in ascending order on the ITEM_NUM field.

If you wish to change the sort order of the database file FILE1 to descending order on the UNIT_COST field, you can do so by changing the controlling index tag. To do this, you need the following command. Recall that the database file FILE1 is already open, so you do not need the USE FILE1 command.

```
. SET ORDER TO UNIT_COST    <Return>
```

dBASE will respond by displaying the following message:

```
Master Index: UNIT_COST
```

This message indicates that the index tag UNIT_COST.NDX is active. The records of the FILE1 database file are available in descending order on the UNIT_COST field, which is the sort order specified by the UNIT_COST.NDX index tag for listing or search purposes.

If you obtain the listing of the FILE1 database file by typing the LIST command, the listing will appear as shown in Figure 11.6. This listing is in descending order on the UNIT_COST field.

Once again, if you wish to change the sort order of the FILE1 database file to ascending order on the QUANTITY field, you can do so by changing the controlling index tag. To activate the QUANTITY.NDX index tag, which is stored in the FILE1QTY.NDX multiple index file, you need first to open the QUANTITY.NDX index tag. The index tags stored in nonproduction multiple files can be opened by using the SET INDEX TO command.

The SET INDEX TO Command

The general format of the SET INDEX TO command is

```
SET INDEX TO <.MDX file names>
```

where <.MDX file names> is the names of the nonproduction multiple index files of a database file.

Recall that when a database file is opened, all the index tags of the productive multiple index file are also automatically opened, but those of the nonproduction multiple index file are not. The SET INDEX TO command is used to open these latter index tags and are added to the list of already open index tags of the productive multiple index file. The SET INDEX TO command also deactivates the currently active index tag and sets the database file in the natural order.

If a database file has more than one multiple index file, the nonproduction multiple index file should be opened using the SET INDEX TO command before any updating is done to the records of the database file. Otherwise, the index tags present in the nonproduction multiple index file will not be automatically adjusted.

To activate the index tags of the nonproduction multiple index file FILE1QTY.MDX of the FILE1 database file, type the following command:

```
. SET INDEX TO FILE1QTY      <Return>
```

dBASE will respond by displaying the message:

```
Database is in natural order.
```

This message indicates that the index tags UNIT_COST and QUANTITY of the nonproduction multiple index file FILE1QTY.MDX are now open and have been added to the list of already open index tags, ITEM_NUM and UNIT_COST, of the production multiple index file FILE1.MDX. Also, the records of the FILE1 database file are now in the natural order.

Because the FILE1QTY.MDX multiple index file has been opened, you can now activate the QUANTITY.NDX index tag. To do this, you will need the following command:

```
. SET ORDER TO QUANTITY       <Return>
```

If you type this command, dBASE will respond by displaying the following message:

```
Master Index: QUANTITY
```

This message indicates that the index tag QUANTITY.NDX is active, and the records of the FILE1 database file are available in ascending order on the quantity field, which is the sort order specified by the QUANTITY.NDX index tag for listing or search purposes.

If you obtain the listing of the FILE1 database file by typing the LIST command, the listing will appear as shown in Figure 11.12. The listing is in ascending order on the quantity field.

If you wish to change the sort order of the database file FILE1 to ascending order on the UNIT_COST field, you can do so by changing the controlling index tag by using the following command:

```
. SET ORDER TO UNIT_COST OF FILE1QTY     <Return>
```

You now have two index tags named UNIT_COST. The first sets the sort order of the records of the database file in descending order of the

Figure 11.12 Listing of database file FILE1 using the QUANTITY index tag

Record#	ITEM NUM	ITEM DESC	UNIT COST	QUANTITY
9	4189	Zenith Microcomputer Z-158	829.99	5
5	4072	Panasonic Printer KX-P108	269.99	8
3	4012	King Kong Modem 1200	105.99	10
4	4045	Monochrome Monitor Z-1105	99.99	15
6	3372	Printer Ribbon 10-Box	35.99	19
2	1910	Ditto Paper, Ream	19.99	35
1	1136	Bond Paper, Ream	22.99	38
8	1488	Xerographic Paper	19.99	45
7	3375	Typewriter Ribbons 10-Box	23.79	67

11.2 Indexing the Database File

UNIT_COST field and resides in the production multiple index file FILE1.MDX. The second sets the sort order of the records of the database file in ascending order on the UNIT_COST field and resides in the nonproduction multiple index file FILE1QTY.MDX. Because both files are open, both UNIT_COST index tags are also open. To activate the UNIT_COST index tag of the nonproduction multiple index file FILE1QTY.MDX, you must include the option OF FILE1QTY in the SET ORDER TO command as shown previously. If you don't, the UNIT_COST index tag of the default production multiple index file FILE1.MDX will be activated.

Now if you type this command, dBASE will respond by displaying the following message:

```
Master Index: UNIT_COST
```

This message indicates that the index tag UNIT_COST.NDX of the FILE1QTY.MDX is active. The records of the FILE1 database file are available in ascending order on the UNIT_COST field, which is the sort order specified by the UNIT_COST.NDX index tag, for listing or search purposes.

If you obtain the listing of the FILE1 database file by typing the LIST command, the listing will appear as shown in Figure 11.13. The listing is in ascending order on the UNIT_COST field.

Finally, to change the sort order of the database file FILE1 back to the natural order, that is, the order in which the records of the database file are physically arranged, type the following command:

```
. SET ORDER TO      <Return>
```

You can achieve the same result by simply opening the database file again by typing the following command:

```
. USE FILE1     <Return>
```

Or you can reissue the SET INDEX TO command:

```
. SET INDEX TO FILE1QTY      <Return>
```

You can obtain the listing of all the .MDX files and the index tags in each for an active database file by using the DISPLAY STATUS command.

Figure 11.13 Listing of database file FILE1 using the UNIT_COST index tag of the FILE1QTY.MDX multiple index file

```
Record#  ITEM_NUM  ITEM_DESC                  UNIT_COST  QUANTITY
      8  1488      Xerographic Paper              19.99        45
      2  1910      Ditto Paper, Ream              19.99        35
      1  1136      Bond Paper, Ream               22.99        38
      7  3375      Typewriter Ribbons 10-Box      23.79        67
      6  3372      Printer Ribbon 10-Box          35.99        19
      4  4045      Monochrome Monitor Z-1105      99.99        15
      3  4012      King Kong Modem 1200          105.99        10
      5  4072      Panasonic Printer KX-P108     269.99         8
      9  4189      Zenith Microcomputer Z-158    829.99         5
```

Because the FILE1 database file is active, either press the F6 Display Status function key or type the DISPLAY STATUS command at the dot prompt to obtain the listing of all the .MDX files and the index tags contained in each. If you do so, dBASE will respond by displaying the information shown in Figure 11.14.

The second line of the listing indicates the database in use, that is, FILE1.DBF. The third line indicates the name of the production .MDX file, that is, FILE1.MDX. The fourth and the fifth lines list the index tag files belonging to the production .MDX file. These index tags are ITEM_NUM and UNIT_COST (descending), respectively. The word *descending* after the name of the UNIT_COST index tag indicates that it is in descending order on this field. The sixth line indicates the name of the nonproduction MDX file, that is, FILE1QTY.MDX. The seventh and the eighth lines list the index tag files belonging to the nonproduction FILE1QTY.MDX file (QUANTITY and UNIT_COST, respectively).

11.2.4 Creating the Multiple Field Index Tags

Section 11.2.1 discussed three methods of creating single field index tags. These can also be used to create multiple field index tags, but only the third method, using the INDEX command from the dot prompt, is discussed in this section.

The format of the INDEX command used for creating the multiple field index tag is:

```
INDEX ON <index expression> TAG <index tag name>
        [OF <.MDX file name>] [DESCENDING]
```

where <index expression> is the combination of the index fields obtained by joining the index fields with the "+" symbol so that the expression should evaluate to a single data type. Logical and memo field are not allowed in the index expression.

When a database file is indexed on an index expression, the first field in the index expression is considered the *primary index key*, and the second, the *secondary index key*. The listing obtained by using the multiple field index tag will be organized in ascending (or alphabetic) order on the primary index key. Within the primary index key, the records will be arranged in ascending (or alphabetic) order on the secondary index key.

Let us consider the FILE4 database file whose structure and listing are given in Figures 11.15 and 11.16, respectively.

To index this database file using the ORD_DATE field as the primary

```
Currently Selected Database:
Select area:  1, Datbase in Use: C:\DBASE\INVOICE\FILE 1.DBF    Alias: FILE1
Production   MDX file: C:\DBASE\INVOICE\FILE1.MDX
         Index TAG:    ITEM_NUM  Key: ITEM_NUM
         Index TAG:    UNIT_COST Key: UNIT_COST  (Descending)
           MDX file: C:\DBASE\INVOICE\FILE1QTY.MDX
         Index TAG:4   QUANTITY  Key: QUANTITY
         Index TAG:3   UNIT_COST Key:  UNIT_COST
```

Figure 11.14 Listing of the DISPLAY STATUS command for the active database file FILE1

Figure 11.15 Structure of the FILE4 database file

```
. DISPLAY STRUCTURE
Structure for database : C:\DBASE\INVOICE\FILE4.DBF
Number of data records :    12
Date of last update     : 01/20/88
Field  Field name  Type        Width    Dec  Index
    1  ORD_DATE    Date            8              N
    2  ITEM_NUM    Character       4              N
    3  ITEM_DESC   Character      26              N
    4  UNIT_COST   Numeric         6      2       N
    5  QUANTITY    Numeric         3      0       N
    6  RET_PRICE   Numeric         7      2       N
** Total **                       55              N
.                                                 N
```

index key and the ITEM_NUM field as the secondary index key, you'll need the following commands:

```
. USE FILE4        <Return>
. INDEX ON DTOS(ORD_DATE) + ITEM_NUM
  TAG DATE_NUM    <Return>
```

Because the two fields, ORD_DATE and ITEM_NUM, to be used in the creation of the multiple field index tag are of different data types, they cannot be used as such. Therefore, the data type of one has to be changed to that of the other. The DTOS () function used in the INDEX command performs this function.

The DTOS () Function

The general format of the DTOS () function is

```
DTOS (<date expression>)
```

where <date expression> is the date in the MM/DD/YY form.

```
. USE FILE4
. LIST
Record#  ORD_DATE  ITEM_NUM  ITEM_DESC                UNIT_COST  QUANTITY  RET_PRICE
     1   01/05/89  1136      Bond Paper, Ream             22.99        38       0.00
     2   12/20/88  4005      Disks Data Case               5.99        18       0.00
     3   01/05/89  1910      Ditto Paper, Ream            19.99        35       0.00
     4   01/05/89  4141      Double Sided Disks 10-Pk      8.49        27       0.00
     5   12/20/88  2786      Highlighter Pen 10-Box        7.99        86       0.00
     6   01/05/89  4012      King Kong Modem 1200        105.99        10       0.00
     7   01/05/89  4045      Monochrome Monitor Z-1105    99.99        15       0.00
     8   12/20/88  4072      Panasonic Printer KX-P108   269.99         8       0.00
     9   01/05/89  3372      Printer Ribbon 10-Box        35.99        19       0.00
    10   12/20/88  3375      Typewriter Ribbons 10-Box    23.79        67       0.00
    11   12/20/88  1488      Xerographic Paper            19.99        45       0.00
    12   12/20/88  4189      Zenith Microcomputer  Z-158 829.99         5       0.00
```

Figure 11.16 Listing of the FILE4 database file

442   Chapter 11 / File Maintenance: Adding a Record

The DTOS () function, called "date to string," converts the date field in MM/DD/YY form to the character string in YYYYMMDD form. To ensure the proper sort order for the date field, it should always be converted to a character string by using the DTOS () function before using as an index key.

Now if you type the two commands given previously, dBASE will respond by displaying the following message:

```
100% indexed    12 records indexed
```

dBASE will first create the FILE4.MDX production multiple index file, then create the DATE_NUM index tag, and finally save the index tag in the multiple index file.

To obtain the listing of the FILE4 database file using the DATE_NUM index tag, type the following commands:

```
. USE FILE4                      <Return>
. SET ORDER TO DATE_NUM          <Return>
. LIST                           <Return>
```

dBASE will respond by displaying the listing shown in Figure 11.17.

The database file is ordered by the primary key index ORD_DATE. Within this field, it is ordered by the secondary key index ITEM_NUM.

When an index consists of multiple fields, specify the most important field first, then the next most important one, down to the least important field. When using the date field in the INDEX command, you must use the DTOS () function to convert the date field to a character string to ensure proper sort order.

11.2.5 Converting Index Files to Index Tags

Suppose you have a dBASE III PLUS file called FILE4.DBF with three individual index files named ITEM_NUM.NDX, UNIT_COST.NDX, and DATE_NUM.NDX. To convert these to the index tags used in dBASE IV, the following steps will be needed:

```
. USE FILE4
. LIST
Record#  ORD_DATE  ITEM_NUM  ITEM_DESC                  UNIT_COST  QUANTITY  RET_PRICE
    11   12/20/88  1488      Xerographic Paper              19.99       45       0.00
     5   12/20/88  2786      Highlighter Pen 10-Box          7.99       86       0.00
    10   12/20/88  3375      Typewriter Ribbons 10-Box      23.79       67       0.00
     2   12/20/88  4005      Disks Data Case                 5.99       18       0.00
     8   12/20/88  4072      Panasonic Printer KX-P108     269.99        8       0.00
    12   12/20/88  4189      Zenith Microcomputer Z-158    829.99        5       0.00
     1   01/05/89  1136      Bond Paper, Ream               22.99       38       0.00
     3   01/05/89  1910      Ditto Paper, Ream              19.99       35       0.00
     9   01/05/89  3372      Printer Ribbon 10-Box          35.99       19       0.00
     6   01/05/89  4012      King Kong Modem 1200          105.99       10       0.00
     7   01/05/89  4045      Monochrome Monitor Z-1105      99.99       15       0.00
     4   01/05/89  4141      Double Sided Disks 10-Pk        8.49       27       0.00
```

Figure 11.17   Listing of the FILE4 database file using the DATE_NUM index tag

11.2 Indexing the Database File

1. Load dBASE IV into the computer's memory using the steps of either Table 2.1 or Table 2.2.
2. Open the FILE4 database file, and activate all three index files by typing the following commands:

   ```
   . USE FILE4      <Return>
   . SET ORDER TO ITEM_NUM, UNIT_COST,
   DATE_NUM    <Return>
   ```

3. Copy the individual index files to the index tags. The following command will perform this function:

   ```
   . COPY INDEXES ITEM_NUM, UNIT_COST,
   DATE_NUM    <Return>
   ```

   The COPY INDEXES command is discussed later in this section. When it is executed, dBASE IV will first create the FILE4.MDX production multiple index file, then create the three index tags, and finally store them in the multiple index file.

4. Delete the individual index files. To do this, first close all the index files. Recall that no open files can be deleted. Then delete the individual index files by using the ERASE command. To complete this step, type the following four commands:

   ```
   . CLOSE ALL              <Return>
   . ERASE ITEM_NUM.NDX     <Return>
   . ERASE UNIT_COST.NDX    <Return>
   . ERASE DATE_NUM.NDX     <Return>
   ```

These steps complete the process of converting the individual index files to the index tags for the FILE4 database file. Repeat this process to convert individual index files to index tags for the other database files.

A few other commands are used with the INDEX command. These are discussed in the following sections.

The COPY INDEXES Command

The general format of the COPY INDEXES command is

```
COPY INDEXES <.NDX file names> [TO <.MDX file name>]
```

where <.NDX file names> are the names of the individual index files created with dBASE III PLUS to be copied to index tags used in dBASE IV. The list of individual index file names should be separated by commas. <.MDX file name> is the name of the multiple index file in which the index tags will be saved. The TO clause is optional. If it is not specified with the COPY INDEXES command, the index tags will be saved in the default production multiple index file.

The COPY INDEXES command is used to convert individual index files created with dBASE III PLUS to index tags used in dBASE IV and to save the index tags in the multiple index file.

The CLOSE Command

The general format of the CLOSE command is

```
CLOSE [ALL] [DATABASES] [FORMAT] [INDEX] [PROCEDURE]
```

Table 11.1 Formats of the CLOSE command

Format	Function
CLOSE ALL	Closes all the open files
CLOSE DATABASES	Closes all the open databases and their associated index (.NDX, .MDX) and format (.FMT) files
CLOSE INDEX	Closes all the open index (.NDX, .MDX) files
CLOSE FORMAT	Closes all the open format (.FMT) files
CLOSE PROCEDURE	Closes all the open procedure files

The CLOSE command is used to close the files that are not needed for processing in the immediate future. The CLOSE command has no effect on memory variables.

A few formats of the CLOSE command along with their functions are listed in Table 11.1.

The DELETE TAG Command

The general format of the DELETE TAG command is

```
DELETE TAG <index tag name> [OF <.MDX file name>]
```

where <index tag name> is the name of the index tag to be deleted, and <.MDX file name> is the name of the multiple index file in which the index tag to be deleted belongs.

The DELETE TAG command is used to delete an existing index tag. If the optional clause OF is not specified with the command, the index tag to be deleted belongs to the default production multiple index file. But if the index tag belongs to a nonproduction multiple index file, the OF clause must be specified. When the optional clause OF is used with the DELETE TAG command, the multiple index file which contains the index tag to be deleted should be opened by the SET INDEX command *before* the DELETE TAG command is issued.

The ERASE Command

The general format of the ERASE command is

```
ERASE <file name>
```

where <file name> is the name of the file to be deleted.

The ERASE command can be used to delete any type of file supported by dBASE IV. Recall that an open file can't be deleted. Therefore, *before* issuing the ERASE command, close the file to be deleted by using the appropriate CLOSE command. Don't forget to add the extension with the file name to be deleted. The dBASE ERASE command does not support wild card characters.

The ERASE command can be used to delete a multiple index file. *But you should never delete the production multiple index file.* If you do, you will no longer be able to open the database file.

The DELETE FILE Command

The general format of the DELETE FILE command is

```
DELETE FILE <file name>
```

where <file name> is the name of the file to be deleted.

The DELETE FILE command works identically to the ERASE command.

11.3 Searching the Indexed Database Files

There are two commonly used commands for searching for data in an indexed database file.

11.3.1 The FIND Command

The general format of the FIND command is

```
FIND <character string>
```

where <character string> is a string of characters that are part of the index key of the database file. The character string doesn't need to be enclosed in quotes except when it contains leading blank spaces. If the character string used in the search is a memory variable, the macro symbol "&" should precede it.

The FIND command will search for the first record in the indexed database file in use whose index key matches the character string *exactly*. This command will work only if the database file has been indexed and the index tag has been activated by use of the SET ORDER command.

If the FIND command is not successful, that is, if no match is found, then the FOUND () function is set to .F., the EOF () function is set to .T., and a "Not successful" message is displayed.

Let us once again consider the database file FILE1. Its listing is given in Figure 11.1. Now open this file with the index set to the ITEM_NUM field. To do this, type the following commands:

```
. USE FILE1                    <Return>
. SET ORDER TO ITEM_NUM        <Return>
```

dBASE will respond by displaying the following message:

```
Master index:    ITEM_NUM
```

The database file FILE1 is open, and the active index tag is ITEM_NUM.NDX. To search for a record in the database file with the value of the ITEM_NUM field equal to 4072, type the following command:

```
. FIND 4072      <Return>
```

dBASE will respond by displaying the dot prompt, indicating that the match has been found and that the record pointer is now pointing to the matching record. To display this record, either press the F8 Display function key or type the following command:

. **DISPLAY**   <Return>

dBASE will respond by displaying the matching record as shown:

```
Record# ITEM_NUM ITEM_DESC                UNIT_COST QUANTITY
      5 4072     Panasonic Ribbon 10-Box     269.99        8
```

Note that if the FIND command is unsuccessful in locating a match in the indexed field of the database file, dBASE will indicate this by displaying the proper message. For example, if you type the following command:

. **FIND 4000**   <Return>

dBASE will respond by displaying this message:

```
Find not successful
```

Use of Partial Index Key with FIND Command

You do not have to supply more characters in the character string of the FIND command than are necessary to reach the required record. For example, to find the record whose ITEM_NUM is equal to 4189, if you know that there is no other record in the database with ITEM_NUM in the range of 4100 to 4199, the following command will be enough:

. **FIND 41**   <Return>

The database file is already open with the order set to the index tag ITEM_NUM.NDX. After the execution of this command when the dot prompt appears, either press the F8 Display function key or type the following command:

. **DISPLAY**   <Return>

dBASE will respond by displaying the matching record as shown:

```
Record# ITEM_NUM ITEM_DESC                   UNIT_COST QUANTITY
      9 4189     Zenith Microcomputer Z-158     829.99        5
```

Use of the partial index key with the FIND command will be successful in the search only if the SET EXACT option of dBASE is set to OFF. This is so by default; but *before* you use the partial index key with the FIND command, include the SET EXACT OFF command before the FIND command.

11.3.2 The SEEK Command

The general format of the SEEK command is

SEEK <expression>

11.3 Searching the Indexed Database Files

where <expression> is the literal data to be searched. The expression can be the name of the memory variable or a string of characters that are part of the index key of the database file. The character string should be enclosed in quotation marks and the date data value, in curly brackets. But the numeric field should appear without any quotation marks or brackets.

The SEEK command will search for the first record in the indexed database file in use whose index key matches the character string exactly. This command will work only if the database file has been indexed and the index tag has been activated by use of the SET ORDER command.

If the SEEK command is not successful, that is, if no match is found, then the FOUND () function is set to .F., the EOF() function is set to .T., and a "Not successful" message is displayed.

Let us once again consider the database file FILE1. Remember that it is already open with the index set to the ITEM_NUM field. (If it is not, you can open it and set the index to ITEM_NUM by typing the USE FILE1 and SET ORDER TO ITEM_NUM commands.) To search for a record in the database file with a value of the ITEM_NUM field equal to 3372, type the following command:

. **SEEK "3372"**   <Return>

dBASE will respond by displaying the dot prompt, indicating that the match has been found and that the record pointer is now pointing to the matching record. To display this record, either press the F8 Display function key or type the following command:

. **DISPLAY**   <Return>

dBASE will respond by displaying the matching record as shown:

```
Record#  ITEM_NUM  ITEM_DESC              UNIT_COST  QUANTITY
      6  3372      Printer Ribbons 10-Box     35.99        19
```

The value of the ITEM_NUM field, that is, 3372, is enclosed in the quotation marks. If you had not enclosed it in quotation marks, dBASE would respond by displaying a window with a "Data type mismatch" message. The window will offer three options: Cancel, Edit, and Help. Select the Edit option, correct the command by enclosing the value 3372 in quotes, and continue by pressing the <Return> key.

Note that if the SEEK command is unsuccessful in locating a match in the indexed field of the database file, dBASE will indicate this result by displaying the proper message. For example, if you type the following command:

. **SEEK "4141"**   <Return>

dBASE will respond by displaying this message:

    Find not successful

The SEEK and FIND commands work exactly the same way except that the latter can be used only with the character field. The SEEK command can be used with the character, numeric, and date fields.

11.4 Searching the Nonindexed Database Files

Both the FIND and SEEK commands, used for searching the indexed database files, have a disadvantage. They can be used only to find the *first* occurrence of the matching record; there is no option available to continue the search. However, the LOCATE and CONTINUE commands when used in pairs provide this option.

11.4.1 The LOCATE and CONTINUE Commands

The general format of the LOCATE and CONTINUE commands is

```
LOCATE [FOR <condition>] [<scope>] [WHILE
<condition>]
<dBASE commands>
CONTINUE
```

where <condition> is a valid search condition that chooses the records to be selected, <scope> specifies the part of the database file used for the search by the LOCATE command, and <dBASE commands> are any dBASE commands executed before the CONTINUE command resumes the search started by the LOCATE command to find the next matching record.

The LOCATE command works similar to the FIND and SEEK commands except that it does not require an indexed database. The LOCATE command is also not as fast as the FIND and SEEK commands.

The LOCATE command starts at the first record (or the first indexed record) of the database file and searches through the database file until it finds a record for which the specified condition in the FOR or WHILE part of the command is true. When the match is found, dBASE responds by displaying the record number of the matched record.

When the dBASE commands mentioned after the LOCATE command have been processed, the CONTINUE command resumes the search started by the LOCATE command to find the next matching record. If another match is found, dBASE will respond by displaying the new record number. The dBASE commands specified after the LOCATE command are once again processed, and the CONTINUE command resumes the search. This process is repeated until there are no more records that satisfy the specified condition. When the LOCATE command fails to find a matching record, the FOUND () function is set to .F., the EOF () function is set to .T., and a "End of LOCATE scope" message is displayed.

The CONTINUE command works only with the LOCATE command; it is not available with the FIND or SEEK commands. Thus, the CONTINUE command cannot be used with the FIND or SEEK commands to resume the search started by these commands to find the next matching record.

Once again consider the database file FILE4, whose structure and listing are given in Figures 11.15 and 11.16, respectively. To search this database file for the record whose ITEM_DESC is equal to "Disks Data Case," type the following commands:

```
. USE FILE4     <Return>
. LOCATE FOR ITEM_DESC = 'Disks Data Case'
<Return>
```

dBASE will respond by displaying the message:

```
Record =      2
```

Figure 11.18 Use of LOCATE command with the database file FILE4

```
. USE FILE4
. LOCATE FOR ITEM_DESC = 'Disks Data Case'
Record =       2
. DISPLAY
Record#  ITEM_NUM  ITEM_DESC              UNIT_COST  QUANTITY
      2    4005    Disks Data Case             5.99        18
. CONTINUE
End of LOCATE scope
.
```

This message indicates that the matching record is the second record in the database file. To display it, either press the F8 Display function key or type the following command:

. **DISPLAY** <Return>

dBASE will respond by displaying the second record, as shown in Figure 11.18.

Now if you type the CONTINUE command, dBASE will respond by displaying the "End of LOCATE scope" message, as shown in Figure 11.18. This message indicates that there are no more records satisfying the specified condition.

When you are specifying the descriptive information in the search condition, supply the value of the field to be searched *exactly* as it appears in the database file. The uppercase and lowercase letters should match perfectly, there should be no extra spaces between the words, and the items must be spelled exactly the same way. However, supplying extra blank spaces at the end of the information or omitting the extra blank space from the end of the information causes no problem.

Recall that the LOCATE command does not require an indexed database file. This fact can be verified from Figure 11.18. The command USE FILE4 is employed to open the database file, but there is no SET ORDER command used to activate the index tag(s).

The LOCATE command requires quotation marks around the character data and curly brackets around the date data type used in the search condition. The partial key can also be utilized as long as it is enclosed in either quotation marks or brackets, depending on the data type.

The main difference between the LOCATE and FIND (or SEEK) commands, other than that the LOCATE command is used with nonindexed files, is that the search condition does not require an exact match. That is, operators other than the "=" symbol, such as "<" or ">," can also be used in the search condition. This is illustrated in Figure 11.19.

The LOCATE and CONTINUE commands are used in two particular instances:

1. when you need to find more than the first occurrence of the criteria
2. when you need to find a record that meets a particular criterion, but that criterion is not suitable as an index key.

For example, you might want to search for something that may be contained anywhere in the search field. To find all the records in the

Figure 11.19 Use of the LOCATE command using the ">" operator in the search condition

```
. USE FILE4
. LOCATE FOR UNIT_COST > 100
Record =        6
. DISPLAY
Record#  ITEM_NUM  ITEM_DESC                 UNIT_COST  QUANTITY
      6  4012      King Kong Modem 1200         105.99        10
. CONTINUE
Record =        8
. DISPLAY
Record#  ITEM_NUM  ITEM_DESC                 UNIT_COST  QUANTITY
      8  4072      Panasonic Printer KX-P108    269.99         8
. CONTINUE
Record =       12
. DISPLAY
Record#  ITEM_NUM  ITEM_DESC                 UNIT_COST  QUANTITY
     12  4189      Zenith Microcomputer Z-158   829.99         5
. CONTINUE
End of LOCATE scope
.
```

database file FILE4 that contain the word *paper* in the ITEM_DESC field, you'll need the following sequence of commands:

```
. USE FILE4                              <Return>
. LOCATE FOR "Paper" $ITEM_DESC          <Return>
. DISPLAY                                <Return>
. CONTINUE                               <Return>
```

If you type the first two commands and repeat the last two until the end of the file is reached, dBASE will display the results shown in Figure 11.20. The substring operator ($) is used in the LOCATE command, and no other operator is needed between the literal "paper" and the substring $ITEM_DESC.

Figure 11.20 Use of the LOCATE command using the substring operator "$" in the search condition

```
. USE FILE4
. LOCATE FOR "Paper" $ITEM_DESC
Record =        1
. DISPLAY
Record#  ITEM_NUM  ITEM_DESC              UNIT_COST  QUANTITY
      1  1136      Bond Paper, Ream           22.99        38
. CONTINUE
Record =        3
. DISPLAY
Record#  ITEM_NUM  ITEM_DESC              UNIT_COST  QUANTITY
      3  1910      Ditto Paper, Ream          19.99        35
. CONTINUE
Record =       11
. DISPLAY
Record#  ITEM_NUM  ITEM_DESC              UNIT_COST  QUANTITY
     11  1488      Xerographic Paper          19.99        45
. CONTINUE
End of LOCATE scope
.
```

11.5 An Illustrative Example: Case Study 8

Program Description

Write an inventory file maintenance program. It should be invoked by the inventory file maintenance submenu program INV1.PRG of the invoice generating system. The function of the program is to add the records of the new items to the inventory database file INV.DBF.

Processing Steps

The following steps should be used to develop the solution of the program:

1. The inventory file maintenance screen as shown in Figure 11.21 with the message "ENTER THE ITEM NUMBER, PLEASE ===> :" requesting the user to enter the item number of the record to be added should be displayed.
2. The screen should be frozen or paused to allow the user to respond to the request.
3. After accepting the entry from the user, the value of the item number supplied by the user should be tested to see if it is a blank value or a nonblank value.
4. If the value of the item number is blank, it indicates that the user wants to terminate the process of adding records to the database file. Therefore, proceed to step 11.
5. For the nonblank value of the item number, search the inventory database file to find out if the record already exists there.

Figure 11.21 Inventory database file maintenance screen

```
                    AMERICAN SUPPLY COMPANY
  01/12/90         INVOICE GENERATING SYSTEM              14:25:40
                 INVENTORY DATABASE FILE MAINTENANCE
                          ADDING A RECORD


         ENTER THE ITEM NUMBER, PLEASE ===>: ▓
```

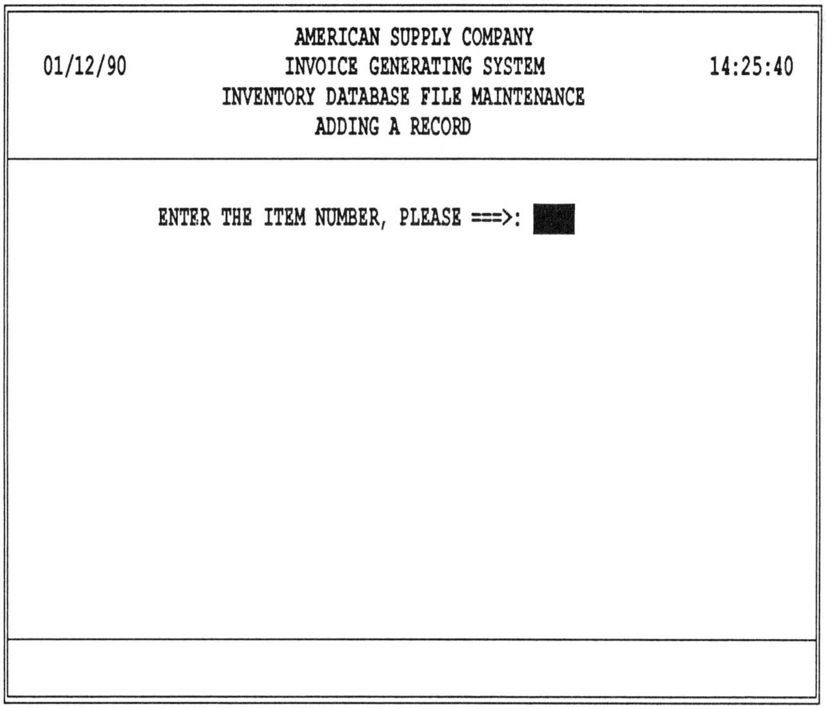

6. If the match is found, display the message indicating that the record already exists in the file. Therefore, the record can't be added. Now proceed to step 10.
7. If the match is not found, accept the data for the record to be added.
8. Append a blank record at the end of the database file.
9. Replace the blank record with the data obtained for the record to be added in step 7.
10. Repeat steps 1–9 to add the next record.
11. After all the records have been added, close the database file, and return the control to the calling program INV1.PRG.

The five phases of the program development process for Case Study 8 are discussed in the following sections.

11.5.1 The Analysis Phase

In the analysis phase, the first step in the program development process, review and analysis of program specifications identify the processing steps needed to solve the problem. A set of instructions will be needed to add a record to the database file, and these steps should be repeated for each record to be added. Therefore, a control switch needs to be defined to control this loop. Also, we will need to define the memory variables for each field in the record to store their values before adding them to the database file. Of course, the database file to which the records are to be added should be opened. These three steps are the only ones needed in the initiate processing function of the problem solution.

The processing steps needed in the main processing function include:

1. Accept the item number to be added.
2. Test for a blank item number.
3. Process the blank item number, that is, change the loop control switch to indicate termination of the loop, and proceed to step 7.
4. Process the nonblank item number, that is, search the inventory database file to check if the record already exists there.
5. Process no match found:
   a. Accept new record data.
   b. Append the blank record.
   c. Replace the blank record with new record data.
   d. Initialize the memory variables, and proceed to step 7.
6. Process match found.
7. Freeze the screen and blank item number.

These seven steps should be repeated until the user wishes to terminate the program, which is accomplished by supplying a blank value to the item number in step 1. At that point, the control should move to the terminate processing function.

In the terminate processing function, the database file should be closed, and program control should exit to the calling program.

To sum up, you'll need the following processing steps for the solution of Case Study 8:

1. Define the variables.
2. Open the indexed database file.
3. Accept the item number to be added.
4. Test for a blank item number.
5. Process the blank item number, that is, change the loop control switch to indicate termination of the loop, and proceed to step 9.
6. Process the nonblank item number, that is, search the inventory database file to check if the record already exists there.
7. Process no match found:
   a. Accept the new record data.
   b. Append the blank record.
   c. Replace the blank record with the new record data.
   d. Initialize the memory variables, and proceed to step 9.
8. Process match found.
9. Freeze the screen and blank item number.
10. Close the database file.
11. Return to calling program.

The first two steps should be performed only once, at the start of the program. Therefore, these belong to initiate processing. The next seven steps should be performed again and again until the user supplies a blank value for the item number. Therefore, these steps belong to main processing. The last two steps need to be performed only once, before terminating the execution of the program. Therefore, these belong to terminate processing.

11.5.2 The Design Phase

The function of this step is to take the result of the problem analysis, that is, the processing steps identified in the analysis phase, and transform them into a structure chart. Using the shell structure chart of Figure 10.12 and the tools and techniques discussed in section 4.4.2, transform the 11 steps identified in the analysis phase into a structure chart for Case Study 8, as shown in Figure 11.22.

All the modules in this structure chart are either functionally or highly cohesive. They are also loosely coupled. Thus, the structure chart of Figure 11.22 satisfies the three rules for designing a good structure chart; that is, it consists of highly cohesive, loosely coupled modules with a span of control of not more than four. Therefore, this chart is a well-designed solution to Case Study 8.

11.5.3 The Detailed Design Phase

The function of this step is to take the result of the design phase, that is, the structure chart, and identify the actual computer operations required for each program function represented in it. This will produce the detailed solution of the problem. Using the translation of the three control structures to pseudocode as given in Figure 4.14 and the method described in section 4.4.3, we translate the structure chart of Figure 11.22 to pseudocode, as shown in Figure 11.23.

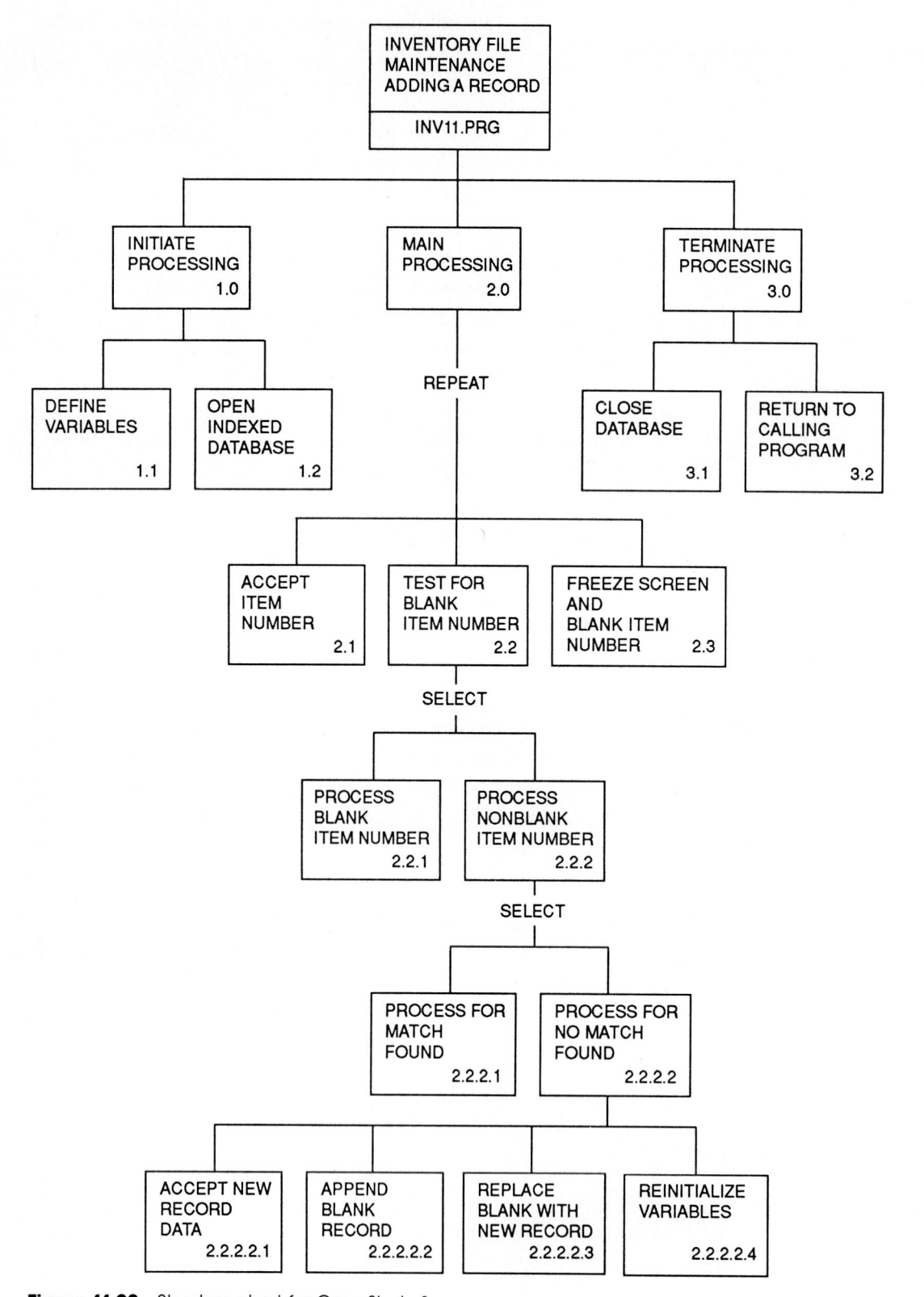

Figure 11.22 Structure chart for Case Study 8

```
0.0 INVENTORY MAINTENANCE—ADDITION
    1.0 INITIATE PROCESSING
        1.1 DEFINE VARIABLE
            DEFINE CONTROL VARIABLE
                Set REPEAT12 switch = T
            INITIALIZE VARIABLES
                Load memory variables from INV12.MEM file
        1.2 OPEN INDEXED DATABASE
            Open INV.DBF database file with index set to ITEM_NUM
    2.0 MAIN PROCESSING
        REPEAT: While the REPEAT12 switch = T
            2.1 ACCEPT ITEM NUMBER
                CLEAR SCREEN
                Clear the screen
                REQUEST AND ACCEPT ITEM NUMBER
                Display Heading # 1
                Display Heading # 2
                Display Heading # 3
                Display Heading # 4
                Display Prompt
                Request and accept item number
            2.2 TEST FOR BLANK ITEM NUMBER
                SELECT: If ITEMNUM is BLANK
                    2.2.1 PROCESS BLANK ITEM NUMBER
                        Reset switch REPEAT12 = F
                    2.2.2 PROCESS NONBLANK ITEM NUMBER
                        Search the database file for a match
                        SELECT: If match found
                            2.2.2.1 PROCESS FOR MATCH FOUND
                                Display message record already on file
                            2.2.2.2 PROCESS FOR NO MATCH FOUND
                                2.2.2.2.1 ACCEPT NEW RECORD DATA
                                    Accept new record data
                                2.2.2.2.2 APPEND BLANK RECORD
                                    Append blank record at the end
                                    of the database file
                                2.2.2.2.3 REPLACE BLANK RECORD WITH NEW RECORD
                                    Replace the fields of the blank record
                                    with the fields of the new record
                                2.2.2.2.4 REINITIALIZE VARIABLES
                                    Reload the memory variables from the
                                    INV12.MEM file
                        END SELECT
                END SELECT
            2.3 FREEZE SCREEN AND BLANK ITEM NUMBER
                Process FREEZE procedure
                Reset ITEMNUM to BLANK
        END REPEAT
```

Figure 11.23 Pseudocode for Case Study 8

3.0 TERMINATE PROCESSING
   3.1 CLOSE DATABASE
      Close the database file
   3.2 RETURN TO CALLING PROGRAM
      Return to calling program

Figure 11.23 Continued

Now define the variables needed in this program as memory variables, and store them in disk file INV12.MEM. To achieve this, type the following commands:

```
. STORE '    ' TO ITEMNUM
. STORE SPACE(25) TO ITEMDESC
. STORE 0 TO QTY
. STORE 0 TO UNITCOST
. STORE 0 TO DEPTCODE
. STORE 0 TO REODPOINT
. STORE 0 TO REODQTY
. STORE 0 TO RETPRICE
. STORE 1.5 TO MARK_UP1
. STORE 1.4 TO MARK_UP2
. SAVE TO INV12
```

These variables can be loaded into computer memory by using the RESTORE FROM . . . ADDITIVE command in any program.

11.5.4 The Coding Phase

The purpose of this phase in program development is to translate the pseudocode instructions of the program solution into programming language instructions. The pseudocode of Figure 11.23 is translated into dBASE commands, and the complete program for Case Study 8 in dBASE language is given in Figure 11.24.

```
**************************************************************
*                         INV12.PRG                           *
*                    AMERICAN SUPPLY COMPANY                  *
*                   INVOICE GENERATING SYSTEM                 *
*              INVENTORY FILE MAINTENANCE PROGRAM             *
*                        ADDING A RECORD                      *
*-------------------------------------------------------------*
* This is one of the Inventory File Maintenance programs.     *
* It is invoked by the Inventory File Maintenance Sub-Menu    *
* program INV1.PRG of the Invoice Generating System for       *
* American Supply Company. The function of this program       *
* is to add new records to the inventory database file INV.DBF.*
*-------------------------------------------------------------*
*            COPYRIGHT (C) . . . SUDESH M. DUGGAL             *
**************************************************************
*
```

Figure 11.24 Coding for Case Study 8

```
*************************
* 1.0 INITIATE PROCESSING *
*************************
*
*** 1.1 DEFINE VARIABLES ***
   *
   *** DEFINE CONTROL VARIABLES ***
      *
      STORE [T] TO REPEAT12
      *
   *** INITIALIZE VARIABLES ***
      *
      RESTORE FROM INV12 ADDITIVE
      *
*** 1.2 OPEN INDEXED DATABASE ***
   *
   USE INV
   SET ORDER TO ITEM_NUM
   *
*************************
* 2.0 MAIN PROCESSING *
*************************
*
DO WHILE REPEAT12 = 'T'
   *
*** 2.1 ACCEPT ITEM NUMBER ***
      *
      *** CLEAR SCREEN ***
         *
         CLEAR
         *
      *** REQUEST AND ACCEPT ITEM NUMBER ***
         *
         @ 2,20 SAY '          AMERICAN SUPPLY COMPANY'
         @ 3,4  SAY DATE ()
         @ 3,20 SAY '          INVOICE GENERATING SYSTEM'
         @ 3,70 SAY TIME ()
         @ 4,20 SAY '      INVENTORY FILE MAINTENANCE PROGRAM'
         @ 5,20 SAY '              ADDING A RECORD'
         @ 6,0  TO  6,79
         @ 22,0 TO 22,79
         @ 1,2  TO 24,79 DOUBLE
         @ 8,20 SAY 'ENTER THE ITEM NUMBER, PLEASE ===>:'
         @ 8,56 GET ITEMNUM PICTURE 'XXXX'
         READ
         *
*** 2.2 TEST FOR BLANK ITEM NUMBER ***
   *
   IF ITEMNUM =' '
   *
   *** 2.2.1 PROCESS BLANK ITEM NUMBER ***
      *
      STORE [F] TO REPEAT12
      *
   ELSE
   *
```

Figure 11.24 Continued

```
*** 2.2.2 PROCESS NONBLANK ITEM NUMBER ***
*
FIND &ITEMNUM
*
IF .NOT. (EOF () .OR. BOF ())
    *
    *** 2.2.2.1 PROCESS FOR MATCH FOUND ***
    *
        @ 22,20 SAY '*** RECORD ALREADY ON FILE ***'
    *
ELSE
    *
    *** 2.2.2.2 PROCESS FOR NO MATCH FOUND ***
    *
        *** 2.2.2.2.1 ACCEPT NEW RECORD DATA ***
        *
            @ 10,15 SAY [ITEM DESCRIPTION:]
            @ 10,35 GET ITEMDESC
            @ 12,15 SAY [QUANTITY        :]
            @ 12,35 GET QTY PICTURE '999'
            @ 14,15 SAY [UNIT COST       :]
            @ 14,35 GET UNITCOST PICTURE '999.99'
            @ 16,15 SAY [DEPT CODE       :]
            @ 16,35 GET DEPTCODE PICTURE '999'
            @ 18,15 SAY [REORDER POINT   :]
            @ 18,35 GET REODPOINT PICTURE '999'
            @ 20,15 SAY [REORDER QUANTITY:]
            @ 20,35 GET REODQTY PICTURE '999'
            READ
        *
        *** 2.2.2.2.2 APPEND BLANK RECORD ***
        *
            APPEND BLANK
        *
        *** 2.2.2.2.3 REPLACE BLANK RECORD WITH NEW RECORD ***
        *
            REPLACE ITEM_NUM WITH ITEMNUM
            REPLACE ITEM_DESC WITH ITEMDESC
            REPLACE QUANTITY WITH QTY
            REPLACE UNIT_COST WITH UNITCOST
            REPLACE DEPT_CODE WITH DEPTCODE
            REPLACE REOD_POINT WITH REODPOINT
            REPLACE REOD_QTY WITH REODQTY
            *
            IF UNITCOST < MARK_RANGE
            *
                RETPRICE = UNITCOST *MARK_UP1
            *
        ELSE
            *
                RETPRICE = UNITCOST *MARK_UP2
            *
        ENDIF UNIT_COST < MARK_RANGE
        *
        REPLACE RET_PRICE WITH RETPRICE
        *
        @ 22,17 SAY ' *** RECORD ADDED TO THE DATABASE ***'
```

Figure 11.24 Continued

```
                         *
                  *** 2.2.2.2.4 REINITIATE VARIABLES ***
                         *
                         RESTORE FROM INV12 ADDITIVE
                         *
                  ENDIF .NOT. (EOF () .OR. BOF ())
                  *
         ENDIF ITEMNUM = '    '
         *
     *** 2.3 FREEZE SCREEN AND BLANK ITEM NUMBER ***
         *
         DO FREEZE
         *
         STORE '    ' TO ITEMNUM
         *
ENDDO REPEAT12 = [T]
*
***************************
* 3.0 TERMINATE PROCESSING *
***************************
*
*** 3.1 CLOSE DATABASE ***
    *
    USE
    *
*** 3.2 RETURN TO CALLING PROGRAM ***
    *
    RETURN
```

Figure 11.24 Continued

Note: The customer file maintenance program INV21.PRG for adding a record to the CUSTOMER.DBF database file can be developed similarly to Case Study 8.

11.5.5 The Testing and Debugging Phase

The last step in program development is the testing and debugging phase, in which the source program is executed and tested for the accuracy of its logic. Execute the program to complete this step, correct the syntactical errors, if any, and execute the program again. Repeat this process until the program is free of syntactical errors. When the output is produced by the program, verify some of the records of the output to ensure its accuracy. If any discrepancies exist, make the needed corrections, and execute the program again. Repeat the process of making corrections and executing the program until the program produces correct and predictable results.

11.6 Summary

Indexing the database files, which is an alternative method to sorting for organizing the records of a database file into a specific sequence, has the following advantages:

1. Indexing works faster with larger files.
2. Indexing saves storage space by not creating separate sorted files. Instead, it creates index tags, which occupy much less space than the whole sorted file.

3. Records newly added to the database files are automatically updated in the indexed files.

In dBASE IV, when a database file is indexed, index tags are created and later used to organize the records of the database file. These can be created in several different ways. Three methods of creating single field index tags are presented in this chapter: by using the CREATE STRUCTURE command, by using the MODIFY STRUCTURE command, and by using the INDEX command. A method of creating multiple field index tags using the INDEX command is also described.

The first method of creating the single field index tags using the CREATE STRUCTURE command is employed during the creation of the structure of the database file. The second method using the MODIFY STRUCTURE command and the third method using the INDEX command are utilized when the database files have already been created.

When a database file is indexed, index tags are created and are stored in the production multiple index file, which is automatically created when the database file is indexed for the first time. The production multiple index file assumes the name of the database file with an extension of .MDX. The index tags assume the name of the fields being indexed with an extension of .NDX unless a different name is specified with the INDEX command.

A maximum of 47 index tags can be stored in a multiple index file. If more than 47 are needed for a database file, if the index tags of a database file need to be grouped in more than one category, or if two index tags on the same data field in a different order of sequencing are needed, additional multiple index files can be created with the INDEX command.

When an indexed database file is opened, all the index tags saved in the production multiple index file are also opened. These are updated automatically when the records of the database file are updated. But the index tags saved in the nonproduction multiple index file should be opened with the SET INDEX TO command *before* updating the records of the database file. Otherwise, the index tags stored in the nonproduction multiple index file will not be updated.

Opening the indexed database file or using the SET INDEX TO command simply opens the index tags but does not activate them. The index tags can be activated by using the SET ORDER TO command. Only one index tag is the controlling index at a particular time. The controlling index tag can be changed by issuing another SET ORDER TO command. When an index tag present in a nonproduction file is to be activated, the name of the multiple index file should be specified in the SET ORDER TO command.

The list of all the index tags and the multiple index files of an active database file can be obtained with the DISPLAY STATUS command. When indexing a database file on multiple fields, the fields used in the index expression should be of the same data type. If they are not, they should be made so by using the appropriate functions. This change can be accomplished either before using the fields in the expression or by having the function used to change the data type present in the expression itself. The DTOS () function is used to convert the date data type field to the character data type field.

The individual index files created by dBASE III PLUS can be converted to index tags used in dBASE IV by using the COPY INDEXES command. After converting the individual index files to index tags, delete the individual index files using the ERASE command. Because open files cannot be deleted, use the CLOSE ALL command to close the individual index files before attempting to delete them. The DELETE TAG command is used to delete the index tags. The ERASE command can be used to delete any type of file except the index tag file. When using the ERASE command to delete files other than database files, specify the extension of the file to be deleted along with the file name. Never delete the production multiple index file because you will then not be able to open the database file.

The FIND and SEEK commands are used to search the indexed database files. These two commands work in exactly the same way except the FIND command is used only with the character data type fields. The SEEK command can also be used with the character, numeric, and date data type fields. The main disadvantage of the FIND and SEEK commands is that they can be used only to search for the first occurrence of the matching record. If there is more than one record in the database file satisfying the search criteria, these commands have no option available to further search the records in the file. The LOCATE and CONTINUE commands used in pairs solve this problem. The LOCATE command also does not require that the database file be indexed, but it can be used with the indexed database files. However, the FIND and SEEK commands cannot be used with nonindexed files.

KEY CONCEPTS

controlling index tag
index files
index key
index tag

indexing
nonproduction multiple index file
production multiple index file

dBASE COMMANDS AND FUNCTIONS

CLOSE ALL command
COPY INDEXES command
DELETE TAGS command
DTOS ( ) function
ERASE command
FIND command

INDEX command
LOCATE and CONTINUE commands
SEEK command
SET INDEX TO command
SET ORDER TO command

REVIEW QUESTIONS

1. List the advantages of indexing over sorting.
2. List the conditions under which sorting would be preferred to indexing.
3. List the conditions under which indexing would be preferred to sorting.
4. What are the contents of an index tag file?
5. What will be the effect of indexing a database file on the order of its records?
6. Explain the concept of indexing by using an example.

7. List three different methods of creating single field index tags.
8. Describe the method of creating single field index tags using the CREATE STRUCTURE command. When should this method be used?
9. Describe the method of creating single field index tags using the MODIFY STRUCTURE command. When should this method be used?
10. Describe the method of modifying the order of the index tags created by the MODIFY STRUCTURE command method or by the CREATE STRUCTURE command method.
11. Describe the method of creating single field index tags using the INDEX command. When should this method be used?
12. Describe the concept of production multiple index files as used in dBASE IV. What are its advantages over the individual index files used in the earlier versions of dBASE?
13. What are the advantages of index tags used in dBASE IV over the individual index files used in dBASE III PLUS?
14. What is the maximum number of index tags that can be saved in a multiple index file?
15. Explain the circumstances under which additional multiple index files should be created.
16. Describe the method of creating nonproduction multiple index files.
17. What is the use of the SET ORDER TO command? When should it be employed?
18. What is the use of the SET INDEX TO command? When should it be employed?
19. How many index tags can be active at a time? What is meant by the term *controlling index*?
20. Describe the method of creating multiple field index tags using the INDEX command. What are the restrictions on the index expression used in the INDEX command for creating the multiple field index tags?
21. Describe the method of converting index files created with dBASE III PLUS to index tags used in dBASE IV.
22. Explain the steps needed to delete the index tags.
23. Explain the steps needed to delete the individual index files.
24. Explain the steps needed to delete the multiple index files.
25. Explain why the production multiple index file should not be deleted.
26. Explain the use of the DTOS () function.
27. What are the restrictions on the use of the FIND command for searching the indexed database file?
28. What are the restrictions on the use of the SEEK command for searching the indexed database file?
29. Explain the advantage of the LOCATE and CONTINUE commands used as a pair over the FIND and SEEK commands.
30. Compare the FIND, SEEK, and LOCATE commands, indicating the different features of each.

HANDS-ON ASSIGNMENT

Programming Assignment 11A

Program Description Write a customer file maintenance program ACR12.PRG. It should be invoked by the customer file maintenance submenu program ACR1.PRG of the accounts receivable system. The function of the program is to add new customers' records to the CUSTACR.DBF database file, whose structure is given in Figure 10.17.

Processing Steps The following steps should be used to develop the solution of the program:

1. The customer file maintenance screen as shown in Figure 11.25, with the message "ENTER THE CUSTOMER NUMBER, PLEASE ===> :," requesting the user to enter the customer number of the record to be added, should be displayed.
2. The screen should be frozen or paused to allow the user to respond to the request.
3. After accepting the entry from the user, the value of the customer number supplied by the user should be tested to see if it is a blank or a nonblank value.
4. If the value is blank, the user wants to terminate the process of adding records to the database file. Therefore, proceed to step 11.

Figure 11.25 Customer database file maintenance screen

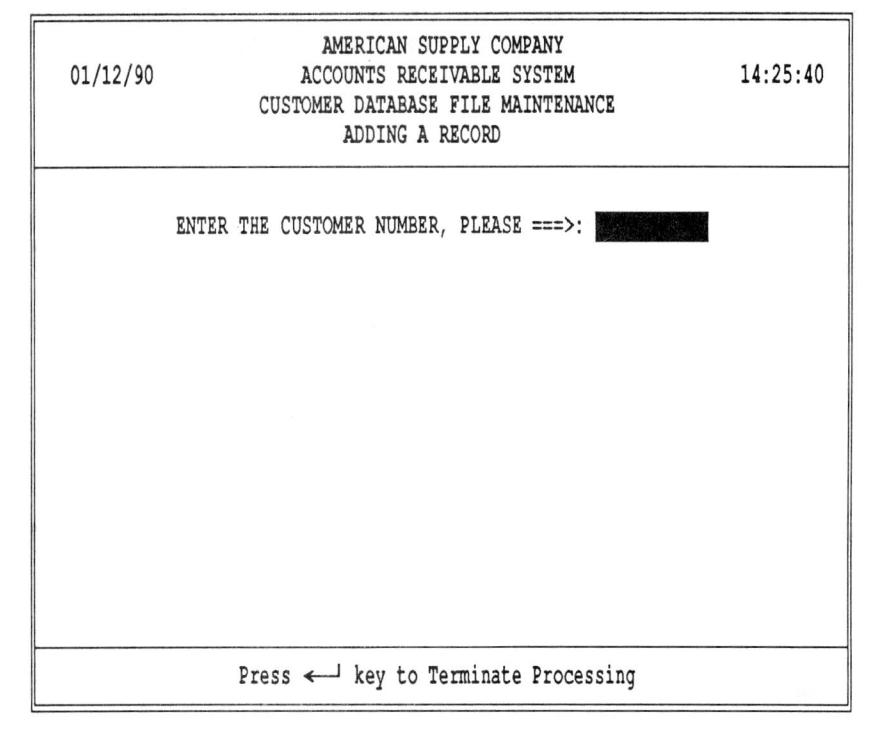

```
┌─────────────────────────────────────────────────────────────────┐
│                     AMERICAN SUPPLY COMPANY                     │
│   01/12/90         ACCOUNTS RECEIVABLE SYSTEM          14:25:40 │
│                  CUSTOMER DATABASE FILE MAINTENANCE             │
│                         ADDING A RECORD                         │
├─────────────────────────────────────────────────────────────────┤
│                                                                 │
│          ENTER THE CUSTOMER NUMBER, PLEASE ===>:  ███████       │
│                                                                 │
│                                                                 │
│                                                                 │
│                                                                 │
│                                                                 │
│                                                                 │
│                                                                 │
│                                                                 │
│                                                                 │
├─────────────────────────────────────────────────────────────────┤
│              Press ←┘ key to Terminate Processing               │
└─────────────────────────────────────────────────────────────────┘
```

5. For the nonblank value of the customer number, search the CUSTACR.DBF database file to find out if the record already exists there.

6. If the match is found, display the message indicating that the record already exists in the file. Therefore, the record can't be added. Now proceed to step 10.

7. If the match is not found, accept the data for the record to be added.

8. Append a blank record at the end of the database file.

9. Replace the blank record with the data obtained for the record to be added in step 7.

10. Repeat steps 1–9 to add the next record.

11. After all the records have been added, close the database file, and return the control to the calling program ACR1.PRG.

The list of the records to be added to the CUSTACR.DBF database file is given in Figure 11.26.

Requirements Submit the following items as part of the assignment:

1. Structure chart
2. Listing of the program
3. Listing of the CUSTACR.DBF database file before and after the additions of the records (use compressed print)

CUST_NUM	CUST_NAME	CUST_ADDR	CUST_CITY	CUST_STATE	CUST_ZIP	CUST_PHONE
289-47-4561	Herb F. Dilenger	1200 Immaculate Lane	Sharonville	OH	45241	513-733-7869
315-66-3744	Vicki E. Tarleck	8900 Terwilligers Dr	Burlington	KY	41005	606-431-4534
455-11-2991	Tonya M. Milnes	10020 Gold Circle Rd	Taylor Mill	KY	41015	606-356-9876
404-92-5277	Roger P. Abernathy	5555 Lovers Lane	Loveland	OH	45140	513-683-1982

Figure 11.26 Records to be added to the CUSTACR.DBF database file

4. The following two screens printed using <Shift PrtSc> keys:
   a. Showing Vicki E. Tarleck being added to the file
   b. Showing an attempt to add a record already in the file to generate the "Record Already Present Can't Add" error message

Programming Assignment 11B

Program Description   Write an employee file maintenance program PAY12.PRG. It should be invoked by the employee file maintenance submenu program PAY1.PRG of the payroll system. The function of the program is to add the records of a new employee to the EMPLOYEE.DBF database file, whose structure is given in Figure 4.33.

Processing Steps   The following steps should be used to develop the solution of the program:

1. The employee file maintenance screen as shown in Figure 11.27, with the message "ENTER THE SOCIAL SECURITY NUMBER, PLEASE ===> :," requesting the user to enter the social security number of the customer to be added, should be displayed.
2. The screen should be frozen or paused to allow the user to respond to the request.
3. After accepting the entry from the user, the value of the social security number supplied by the user should be tested to see if it is a blank or a nonblank value.
4. If the value is blank, the user wants to terminate the process of adding records to the database file. Therefore, proceed to step 11.
5. For the nonblank value, search the EMPLOYEE.DBF database file to find out if the record already exists there.
6. If the match is found, display the message indicating that the record already exists in the file. Therefore, the record can't be added. Now proceed to step 10.
7. If the match is not found, accept the data for the record to be added.
8. Append a blank record at the end of the database file.
9. Replace the blank record with the data obtained for the record to be added in step 7.
10. Repeat steps 1–9 to add the next record.
11. After all the records have been added, close the database file, and return the control to the calling program PAY1.PRG.

Figure 11.27   Employee database file maintenance screen

```
                    AMERICAN SUPPLY COMPANY
  01/12/90              PAYROLL SYSTEM                    14:25:40
                 EMPLOYEE DATABASE FILE MAINTENANCE
                          ADDING A RECORD

         ENTER THE SOCIAL SECURITY NUMBER, PLEASE ==>: ▓▓▓▓▓▓▓▓




                  Press ←┘ key to terminate Processing
```

Figure 11.28 Records to be added to the EMPLOYEE.DBF database file

```
SOC_SC_NUM    EMP_NAME           DEPT_CODE  PAY_CODE  M_STATUS  N_DEP

298-47-6667   Vicki K. Dilenger    102        29         2        15

315-66-8212   Roger P. Milnes      102        52         4         4

455-11-0501   Herb F. Abernathy    102        57         3        13

631-22-1515   Tonya M. Tarleck     105        24         2         2
```

The list of the records to be added to the EMPLOYEE.DBF database file is given in Figure 11.28.

Requirements Submit the following items as part of the assignment:

1. Structure chart
2. Listing of the program
3. Listing of the EMPLOYEE.DBF database file before and after the additions of the records (containing the first six fields only)
4. The following two screens printed using <Shift PrtSc> keys:
   a. Showing Vicki Dilenger being added to the file
   b. Showing an attempt to add a record already in the file to generate the "Record Already Present Can't Add" error message

Chapter 12

File Maintenance: Updating a Record

LEARNING OBJECTIVES

Upon successfully completing this chapter, you will be able to:

1. Edit data in the database file on a case-by-case basis using the EDIT command.
2. Edit data in the database file on a case-by-case basis using the BROWSE command.
3. Utilize the LOCK, FREEZE, and FIELDS options with the BROWSE command for efficient editing.
4. Use the WIDTH option of the BROWSE command to view more fields on the screen at a time.
5. Edit the conditionally selected records in a database file on a case-by-case basis using the EDIT FOR format of the EDIT command.
6. Edit the conditionally selected records in a database file on a case-by-case basis using the LOCATE and EDIT commands.
7. Edit the conditionally selected records in a database file on a case-by-case basis using the LOCATE and EDIT WHILE formats of the EDIT command.
8. Replace the content of a field by an expression in either all records or only the conditionally selected records of the database file using the REPLACE command.
9. Edit the conditionally selected records in a database file on a global basis using the LOCATE and other dBASE commands.
10. Analyze, design, and code a file maintenance program that can update records of the database file.

12.1 Overview

The concept of data editing as introduced in Chapter 6 is presented again in this chapter. The three most commonly used dBASE commands for data editing are the EDIT, BROWSE, and REPLACE commands, which are discussed in this chapter.

The chapter starts by introducing the general format of the EDIT command and reviewing the two formats of it already discussed in Chapter 6. This section is followed by the introduction of the BROWSE command and the optional clauses available with it. The usage and advantages of these optional clauses of the BROWSE command are illustrated by examples.

The concept of conditional editing—the editing of only those records of the database file that satisfy the specified criteria—is introduced next. Three different methods of case-by-case conditional editing using the EDIT FOR format of the EDIT command, the LOCATE and EDIT commands, and the LOCATE and EDIT WHILE commands are also discussed. The editing of either all the records or only the conditionally selected records of the database file on the global basis, which is the method where several records can be edited at one time, as compared to the case-by-case basis, is also introduced. In addition, two different methods of global editing are discussed.

Finally, a file maintenance program that can update the existing records of the inventory database file INV.DBF is analyzed, designed, and coded.

12.2 Data Editing Revisited

The process of correcting errors in the contents of the database file is called **editing.** dBASE provides three commands for editing: the EDIT, BROWSE, and REPLACE commands. The first two are discussed in this section. The REPLACE command is discussed in section 12.4.1.

12.2.1 The EDIT Command

The general format of the EDIT command is

```
EDIT [<scope>] [FIELDS <field names>]
    [FOR <condition>] [WHILE <condition>]
```

where <scope> is an optional qualifier specifying the range of the records in the database file (for example, ALL, NEXT, RECORD, and REST), <field names> specifies the names of the fields to be displayed on the edit screen, and <condition> is any valid condition used with the optional FOR or WHILE clause to limit the records of the database file to be edited.

The EDIT command is a full-screen command that allows data to be edited in the current record of the active database file. It displays the default edit screen containing the current record along with all its fields if these fields can fit on one screen. Otherwise, multiple screens will be used.

The optional FIELDS clause allows the user to choose the fields to be included in the edit screen.

The default edit screen can be replaced by the customized form, in which case it should be opened using the SET FORMAT command *before* issuing the EDIT command. In that situation, the EDIT command will invoke the customized form instead of the default edit screen. However, the design and use of the customized screen is beyond the scope of this book.

Editing was discussed in Chapter 6, where two formats of the EDIT command were discussed in section 6.3.1: the simple EDIT format, which is used to edit the current record of the active database file, and the EDIT <record number> format, which allows you to edit any record in the database file by simply specifying its record number. The latter format is useful in large database files. Further discussion of the EDIT command is postponed until section 12.3.

12.2.2 The BROWSE Command

The general format of the BROWSE command is

```
BROWSE [FIELDS <field names>] [FREEZE <field name>]
       [LOCK <numeric expression>]
       [WIDTH <field width>]
```

where <field names> specifies the names of the fields to be displayed on the edit screen, <field name> is the name of the single field on which the editing of the data is allowed, <numeric expression> specifies the number of fields on the left-hand side of the screen that are to be locked, and <field width> is the maximum width allowed for all the fields.

BROWSE is a full-screen command that allows editing or appending of records in a currently active database file. It displays 17 records at a time with as many fields as will fit across the screen.

The optional FIELDS clause allows you to choose the fields to be included in the edit screen.

The FREEZE clause allows you to specify the name of a single field on which data editing is allowed.

The LOCK clause allows you to specify the number of fields on the left of the screen to be locked. These fields remain locked when you move the cursor to the right of the screen to view the other fields.

The WIDTH clause allows you to specify the maximum width for all the fields or those specified in the BROWSE command.

A few examples of the BROWSE command with different optional clauses follow to help you understand the use and importance of the optional clauses available with the BROWSE command. The ADDRESS .DBF database file, the structure of which is given in Figure 12.1, is used in all the examples.

Example 1: Browse Mode with No Options

To display the browse edit screen without using any optional clauses, you will need the following command:

```
. BROWSE     <Return>
```

Figure 12.1 Structure of the ADDRESS.DBF database file

```
Structure for database : C:\DBASE\INVOICE\ADDRESS.DBF
Number of data records :      26
Date of last update    : 12/24/89
Field  Field Name   Type        Width    Dec    Index
    1  CUST_NUM     Character      6              Y
    2  CUST_NAME    Character     25              N
    3  CUST_ADDR    Character     20              N
    4  CUST_CITY    Character     20              N
    5  CUST_STATE   Character      2              N
    6  CUST_ZIP     Character      5              N
    7  CUST_BAL     Numeric        7      2       N
    8  CUST_PHONE   Character     12              N
** Total **                       98
```

If you type this command, dBASE will respond by displaying the browse edit screen, as shown in Figure 12.2. This screen consists of 17 records of the database file, each one showing the first four fields and the first letter of the fifth field.

To start with, the cursor will be in the first field. Move it to the fifth field, which is partially visible, by pressing the <Tab> key as many times

```
    Records    Fields    Go To    Exit                   6:15:27 pm

   CUST_NUM CUST_NAME             CUST_ADDR           CUST_CITY          C

   605-21   Bernice T. Johnson    1205 Whispering Way Cincinnati         O
   506-97   Jan A. Black          8900 Terwilligers Dr Burlington        K
   120-12   Gregory B. Cardwell   6250 Benninghofen Av Milford           O
   142-54   Virginia L. Simpson   3478 Assisiknoll Ct Lawrenceburg       I
   350-20   Timothy G. Carlson    9942 Flamigo Drive  Highland Heights   K
   452-45   Jill E. Hembree       12 Devil Backnone Rd Cincinnati        O
   124-45   Cindy E. Northland    5555 Lovers Lane    Loveland           O
   562-12   Joseph T. Saxton      6700 Happy Doll Rd  Covington          K
   320-45   Marguerite A. Samuelson 4550 My Farm Land Cincinnati         O
   452-12   Jim A. Jackson        2432 Crazy Bum Drive Florence          K
   120-21   Jeramiah F. Johnson   9876 Oilve Branch Rd Blue Ash          O
   401-94   Mary J. Nordman       1200 Immaculate Lane Sharonville       O
   250-21   Jessica A. Timbers    3450 Koll Breeze Rd Burlington         K
   201-21   Barry L. Tucker       7865 Japonica Drive Cincinnati         O
   404-92   Cindy A. Pollard      10020 Gold Circle Rd Taylor Mill       K
   406-03   Marge C. Marian       4280 Heavenly Lane  Finney Town        O
   305-25   Marty P. Jones        12455 Gatehouse Dr  Villa Hill         K

   Browse  C:\...INVOICE\ADDRESS    Rec 1/26       File              Ins
                          View and Edit fields
```

Figure 12.2 Browse screen for the ADDRESS.DBF database file without any optional clause

as is needed to reach that field. You will notice that all the fields will move one field toward the left. The CUST_NUM field will disappear from the screen, and the CUST_STATE field will appear on the right end of the screen, as shown in Figure 12.3.

When the BROWSE command is used without locking any fields, as in the present example, and you move the cursor to the next field to the right, the field on the left side of the screen will disappear. The field or fields (depending on the size of the fields on the right side of the screen, which are not visible) on the right side of the screen will now appear on the screen.

In this form of the browse mode, you can move freely to any field of any record and make the necessary changes. However, much time will be wasted in moving from one field to another. Also, to make changes in a field not originally in view, you must move to that field, causing the fields on the left side of the screen to disappear. You will not be able to tell by looking at only part of the screen whether the corrections being made are in the correct record or not. To make sure, you will have to move to the left side to verify by the customer name field or the customer number field that you are in the correct record. Then you must move back to the field to be

```
 Records      Fields      Go To      Exit                        6:15:27 pm

┌─────────────────────┬─────────────────────┬─────────────────┬────────────┐
│ CUST_NAME           │ CUST_ADDR           │ CUST_CITY       │ CUST_STATE │
├─────────────────────┼─────────────────────┼─────────────────┼────────────┤
│ Bernice T. Johnson  │ 1205 Whispering Way │ Cincinnati      │ OH         │
│ Jan A. Black        │ 8900 Terwilligers Dr│ Burlington      │ KY         │
│ Gregory B. Cardwell │ 6250 Benninghofen Av│ Milford         │ OH         │
│ Virginia L. Simpson │ 3478 Assisiknoll Ct │ Lawrenceburg    │ IN         │
│ Timothy G. Carlson  │ 9942 Flamigo Drive  │ Highland Heights│ KY         │
│ Jill E. Hembree     │ 12 Devil Backnone Rd│ Cincinnati      │ OH         │
│ Cindy E. Northland  │ 5555 Lovers Lane    │ Loveland        │ OH         │
│ Joseph T. Saxton    │ 6700 Happy Doll Rd  │ Covington       │ KY         │
│ Marguerite A. Samuelson │ 4550 My Farm Land │ Cincinnati    │ OH         │
│ Jim A. Jackson      │ 2432 Crazy Bum Drive│ Florence        │ KY         │
│ Jeramiah F. Johnson │ 9876 Oilve Branch Rd│ Blue Ash        │ OH         │
│ Mary J. Nordman     │ 1200 Immaculate Lane│ Sharonville     │ OH         │
│ Jessica A. Timbers  │ 3450 Koll Breeze Rd │ Burlington      │ KY         │
│ Barry L. Tucker     │ 7865 Japonica Drive │ Cincinnati      │ OH         │
│ Cindy A. Pollard    │ 10020 Gold Circle Rd│ Taylor Mill     │ KY         │
│ Marge C. Marian     │ 4280 Heavenly Lane  │ Finney Town     │ OH         │
│ Marty P. Jones      │ 12455 Gatehouse Dr  │ Villa Hill      │ KY         │
└─────────────────────┴─────────────────────┴─────────────────┴────────────┘
 Browse  C:\...INVOICE\ADDRESS   Rec 1/26           File              Ins
                          View and Edit fields
```

Figure 12.3 Browse screen for the ADDRESS.DBF database file after moving the cursor to the fifth field without locking any field

altered and make the required changes. Thus, the simple browse mode is not very efficient.

Recall that you have already worked with the browse mode before, in section 2.2.2. After creating the structure of the database file FILE1 and adding the first record to it in the append mode, you switched to the browse mode by pressing the F2 Browse function key. The rest of the records of the database file were added using the browse mode. This indicates that, in addition to editing, the browse mode can be used for adding records to a database file.

When you are using the edit mode for editing, you can switch from it to the browse mode by pressing the F2 Browse function key, as already discussed. (Note that the append mode is an edit mode; refer to Figure 2.15.)

To terminate the process of the browse mode, first select the Exit option of the menu bar by pressing the <Alt-E> keys. Then select the Exit option from the Pull-down Menu. Finally, press the <Return> key. dBASE will return to the dot prompt mode.

Example 2: Browse Mode with LOCK Option

One of the problems encountered in example 1 was that when editing a field on the right side of the screen, some of the identifying fields present on the left side were not visible. This problem can be solved in several different ways. The first is by locking the identifying field(s).

Suppose we want to lock two fields on the left side of the screen, that is, the CUST_NUM and the CUST_NAME fields. To do this, type the following command:

```
. BROWSE LOCK 2     <Return>
```

dBASE will respond by displaying the browse mode screen (Figure 12.2). At this point, the cursor will be in the first field. Move it to the fifth field, which is partially visible, as discussed in example 1. You will notice that the third field of CUST_ADDR will disappear from the screen, and the two fields of CUST_STATE and CUST_ZIP will appear on the right end of the screen, as shown in Figure 12.4. The first two fields, CUST_NUM and CUST_NAME, will remain locked in their positions. This results from adding the optional LOCK 2 clause to the BROWSE command.

Now you can make the required changes in any field after moving the cursor to it. Still, much time will be wasted in moving from one field to another. The only advantage of locking the identifying field is that when you are making changes in a field, the identifying fields are still in view. Simply moving your eyes across the row will let you know whether you are changing the right record. This method will save the time of moving back and forth to make sure you are in the right record before making the changes.

To save the time wasted in moving from one field to another, make changes to one field during one session of the browse mode. In other words, if the corrections are needed in more than one field, use more browse sessions.

```
Records     Fields      Go To     Exit                      ▌6:15:27 pm

┌────────┬─────────────────────┬──────────────────┬────────────┬──────────┬────┐
│CUST_NUM│CUST_NAME            │CUST_CITY         │CUST_STATE  │CUST_ZIP  │CU  │
├────────┼─────────────────────┼──────────────────┼────────────┼──────────┼────┤
│605-21  │Bernice T. Johnson   │Cincinnati        │OH          │45245     │    │
│506-97  │Jan A. Black         │Burlington        │KY          │41005     │1   │
│120-12  │Gregory B. Cardwell  │Milford           │OH          │45150     │    │
│142-54  │Virginia L. Simpson  │Lawrenceburg      │IN          │47025     │5   │
│350-20  │Timothy G. Carlson   │Highland Heights  │KY          │41076     │1   │
│452-45  │Jill E. Hembree      │Cincinnati        │OH          │45239     │    │
│124-45  │Cindy E. Northland   │Loveland          │OH          │45140     │2   │
│562-12  │Joseph T. Saxton     │Covington         │KY          │41015     │12  │
│320-45  │Marguerite A. Samuelson│Cincinnati      │OH          │45236     │3   │
│452-12  │Jim A. Jackson       │Florence          │KY          │41042     │    │
│120-21  │Jeramiah F. Johnson  │Blue Ash          │OH          │45241     │2   │
│401-94  │Mary J. Nordman      │Sharonville       │OH          │45241     │32  │
│250-21  │Jessica A. Timbers   │Burlington        │KY          │41005     │    │
│201-21  │Barry L. Tucker      │Cincinnati        │OH          │45230     │4   │
│404-92  │Cindy A. Pollard     │Taylor Mill       │KY          │41015     │    │
│406-03  │Marge C. Marian      │Finney Town       │OH          │45238     │1   │
│305-25  │Marty P. Jones       │Villa Hill        │KY          │41018     │2   │
└────────┴─────────────────────┴──────────────────┴────────────┴──────────┴────┘
Browse ▌C:\...INVOICE\ADDRESS▌Rec 1/26       ▌File▌              ▌      Ins
                          View and Edit fields
```

Figure 12.4 Browse screen for the ADDRESS.DBF database file after moving the cursor to the fifth field with locking the first two fields

Example 3: Browse Mode with LOCK and FREEZE Options

Use the FREEZE clause in the browse mode to restrict the editing to the one field specified in it. To lock the first two fields and allow editing only in the CUST_PHONE field, type the following command:

. BROWSE LOCK 2 FREEZE CUST_PHONE   <Return>

dBASE will respond by displaying the edit screen shown in Figure 12.5. The screen consists of two locked fields on the left and four other fields. The cursor is located in the CUST_PHONE field, which is specified with the FREEZE clause in the BROWSE command. You cannot move the cursor to any other field.

The LOCK and FREEZE combination in the BROWSE command allows you to verify visually the exactness of the record in which the corrections should be made. It also saves time by not moving from one field to another.

```
Records     Fields     Go To     Exit                    6:15:27 pm
```

CUST_NUM	CUST_NAME	CUST_STATE	CUST_ZIP	CUST_BAL	CUST_PHONE
605-21	Bernice T. Johnson	OH	45245	75.32	513-752-7560
506-97	Jan A. Black	KY	41005	153.75	606-431-4534
120-12	Gregory B. Cardwell	OH	45150	23.50	513-831-8787
142-54	Virginia L. Simpson	IN	47025	500.00	812-637-6555
350-20	Timothy G. Carlson	KY	41076	107.98	606-635-3344
452-45	Jill E. Hembree	OH	45239	75.00	513-741-0001
124-45	Cindy E. Northland	OH	45140	205.56	513-683-1982
562-12	Joseph T. Saxton	KY	41015	1248.60	606-291-1290
320-45	Marguerite A. Samuelson	OH	45236	354.70	513-793-6420
452-12	Jim A. Jackson	KY	41042	78.45	606-586-5546
120-21	Jeramiah F. Johnson	OH	45241	276.90	513-733-8871
401-94	Mary J. Nordman	OH	45241	3278.65	513-733-7869
250-21	Jessica A. Timbers	KY	41005	45.23	606-586-6542
201-21	Barry L. Tucker	OH	45230	450.00	513-231-8900
404-92	Cindy A. Pollard	KY	41015	78.55	606-356-9876
406-03	Marge C. Marian	OH	45238	107.40	513-234-6654
305-25	Marty P. Jones	KY	41018	284.67	606-342-7677

```
Browse   C:\...INVOICE\ADDRESS   Rec 1/26          File                  Ins
                              View and Edit fields
```

Figure 12.5 Browse screen for the ADDRESS.DBF database file with first two fields locked and the CUST_PHONE field frozen

Example 4: Browse Mode with FIELDS and FREEZE Options

There is a better way to use the method discussed in example 3, where the CUST_NAME field was used for identification purposes, and the changes were allowed only in the CUST_PHONE field. This change can also be accomplished by including only the CUST_NAME and the CUST_PHONE fields in the edit screen by using the FIELDS clause in the BROWSE command. Add the FREEZE clause with the CUST_PHONE field to restrict the editing to this field. To do this, type the following command:

```
. BROWSE FIELDS CUST_NAME, CUST_PHONE
  FREEZE CUST_PHONE
```

dBASE will respond by displaying the edit screen shown in Figure 12.6. The screen consists of only two fields: CUST_NAME and CUST_PHONE. The cursor will be positioned in the CUST_PHONE field, the only one in which editing will be allowed.

Including fewer fields in the edit screen, as in Figure 12.6, makes the screen less cluttered and easier to work with. Having the verifying field

```
┌─────────────────────────────────────────────────────────────────────┐
│  Records     Fields    Go To    Exit                    ▌6:15:27 pm │
│ ┌─────────────────────────────┬───────────────────────────────────┐ │
│ │ CUST_NAME                   │ CUST_PHONE                        │ │
│ ├─────────────────────────────┼───────────────────────────────────┤ │
│ │ Bernice T. Johnson          │ 513-752-7560                      │ │
│ │ Jan A. Black                │ 606-431-4534                      │ │
│ │ Gregory B. Cardwell         │ 513-831-8787                      │ │
│ │ Virginia L. Simpson         │ 812-637-6555                      │ │
│ │ Timothy G. Carlson          │ 606-635-3344                      │ │
│ │ Jill E. Hembree             │ 513-741-0001                      │ │
│ │ Cindy E. Northland          │ 513-683-1982                      │ │
│ │ Joseph T. Saxton            │ 606-291-1290                      │ │
│ │ Marguerite A. Samuelson     │ 513-793-6420                      │ │
│ │ Jim A. Jackson              │ 606-586-5546                      │ │
│ │ Jeramiah F. Johnson         │ 513-733-8871                      │ │
│ │ Mary J. Nordman             │ 513-733-7869                      │ │
│ │ Jessica A. Timbers          │ 606-586-6542                      │ │
│ │ Barry L. Tucker             │ 513-231-8900                      │ │
│ │ Cindy A. Pollard            │ 606-356-9876                      │ │
│ │ Marge C. Marian             │ 513-234-6654                      │ │
│ │ Marty P. Jones              │ 606-342-7677                      │ │
│ └─────────────────────────────┴───────────────────────────────────┘ │
│  Browse ▌C:\...INVOICE\ADDRESS ▌Rec 1/26 ▌        ▌File▌      ▌ Ins│
│                          View and Edit fields                       │
└─────────────────────────────────────────────────────────────────────┘
```

Figure 12.6 Browse screen for the ADDRESS.DBF database file with CUST_NAME and CUST_PHONE fields and the CUST_PHONE field frozen

and the field to be edited next to each other also saves the time needed to move your eyes across the screen for verification. These two features definitely make this method more efficient than that of example 3.

Example 5: Browse Mode with FIELDS and WIDTH Options

The WIDTH clause allows you to specify the maximum width for all the fields or the fields specified in the BROWSE command using the FIELDS clause. By restricting field widths, you can include more fields in the edit screen. An example of the use of the WIDTH clause in the BROWSE command follows:

```
. BROWSE FIELDS CUST_NAME, CUST_PHONE, CUST_ADDR,
  CUST_CITY, CUST_STATE, CUST_ZIP WIDTH 15
```

If you type this command, dBASE will respond by displaying the edit screen shown in Figure 12.7.

The screen consists of six fields. This screen contains the complete address information, including the telephone number, for each customer in one screen row. The restrictions put on field width help the user view all

```
           Records     Fields     Go To     Exit                    6:15:27 pm

        ┌─────────────┬─────────────┬─────────────┬─────────────┬───────────┬────────┐
        │ CUST_NAME   │ CUST_PHONE  │ CUST_ADDR   │ CUST_CITY   │CUST_STATE │CUST_Z  │
        ├─────────────┼─────────────┼─────────────┼─────────────┼───────────┼────────┤
        │ Bernice T. John │513-752-7560│1205 Whispering│Cincinnati    │OH │45245│
        │ Jan A. Black    │606-431-4534│8900 Terwillige│Burlington    │KY │41005│
        │ Gregory B. Card │513-831-8787│6250 Benninghof│Milford       │OH │45150│
        │ Virginia L. Sim │812-637-6555│3478 Assisiknol│Lawrenceburg  │IN │47025│
        │ Timothy G. Carl │606-635-3344│9942 Flamigo Dr│Highland Heights│KY│41076│
        │ Jill E. Hembree │513-741-0001│12 Devil Backno│Cincinnati    │OH │45239│
        │ Cindy E. Northl │513-683-1982│5555 Lovers Lan│Loveland      │OH │45140│
        │ Joseph T. Saxto │606-291-1290│6700 Happy Doll│Covington     │KY │41015│
        │ Marguerite A. S │513-793-6420│4550 My Farm La│Cincinnati    │OH │45236│
        │ Jim A. Jackson  │606-586-5546│2432 Crazy Bum │Florence      │KY │41042│
        │ Jeramiah F. Joh │513-733-8871│9876 Oilve Bran│Blue Ash      │OH │45241│
        │ Mary J. Nordman │513-733-7869│1200 Immaculate│Sharonville   │OH │45214│
        │ Jessica A. Timb │606-586-6542│3450 Koll Breez│Burlington    │KY │41005│
        │ Barry L. Tucker │513-231-8900│7865 Japonica D│Cincinnati    │OH │45230│
        │ Cindy A. Pollar │606-356-9876│10020 Gold Circ│Taylor Mill   │KY │41015│
        │ Marge C. Marian │513-234-6654│4280 Heavenly L│Finney Town   │OH │45238│
        │ Marty P. Jones  │606-342-7677│12455 Gatehouse│Villa Hill    │KY │41018│
        └─────────────────┴────────────┴───────────────┴──────────────┴───┴─────┘
        Browse  C:\...INVOICE\ADDRESS   Rec 1/26            File              Ins

                              View and Edit fields
```

Figure 12.7 Browse screen for the ADDRESS.DBF database with first record

the information on one screen rather than moving around the screen to find the needed information.

The part of the information not visible in the displayed fields on the screen is not lost. It is still there, and you can view it without disturbing the whole screen. For example, to find the last name of the customer of the first record, move the cursor to the CUST_NAME field, and position it at the letter "n," the last letter in "John." Now press the <Right Arrow> key once. The letter "s" will appear at the cursor position, and the rest of the information in that field will move one position to the left. Every time you press the <Right Arrow> key, an additional letter will appear at the cursor position and will move the rest of the information one position to the left. You can repeat this process until you reach the end of the field. If you try this, you will have changed the information in this field to "nice T. Johnson."

12.3 Conditional Editing

Conditional editing is editing only those records of the database file that satisfy a particular condition. Three methods of conditional editing are presented in this section.

12.3.1 The EDIT FOR Format

The use of the FOR clause and the optional qualifier ALL with the EDIT command allows you to edit the conditionally selected records. (The general format of the EDIT command is given in section 12.2.1.) This command gives you the option of changing the values of all the fields or only those specified with the FIELDS clause on a case-by-case basis. When the EDIT command is executed, only the specified fields will be displayed and can be edited. Make the required changes, if any, in those fields, and press <PgDn> to proceed to the next record satisfying the search criteria. If no changes are needed, simply press <PgDn> to proceed to the next record. When dBASE finds no more records satisfying the search criteria, the dot prompt is displayed.

As an example, consider the database file FILE4, whose listing is given in Figure 11.16.

When the company received its new shipment, it was found that the unit cost of some items had changed. So the appropriate changes should be made to update the database file FILE4 for which the ORD_DATE is equal to "01/05/89." The following commands will be needed to perform this function:

```
. USE FILE4      <Return>
. EDIT ALL FIELDS UNIT_COST FOR
ORD_DATE = {01/05/89}    <Return>
```

If you type these, dBASE will respond by displaying the value of the UNIT_COST field for the first record satisfying the search condition, as shown in Figure 12.8.

Make the required change in the value of the UNIT_COST field, if any, and press the <PgDn> key. dBASE will display the next record satisfying the search condition. Continue making the changes until all the records satisfying the search condition have been taken care of. When there are no more records satisfying the search condition, dBASE will return to the dot prompt.

You can cancel the changes made in the record being edited by pressing the <Ctrl-Q> keys and the effect of the EDIT function by pressing the <Esc> key.

The listing of the database file FILE4 after the changes have been made is shown in Figure 12.9. Compare the listings of Figures 11.16 and 12.9. You will notice that the value of the UNIT_COST field in five records has been changed.

12.3.2 The LOCATE and EDIT Commands

As discussed in section 11.4.1, the LOCATE command can be used to search the records that meet the specified condition. After these records have been located by the LOCATE command, the EDIT command can be used to edit them. Thus, the combination of these commands can be used for editing the conditionally selected records in dBASE IV.

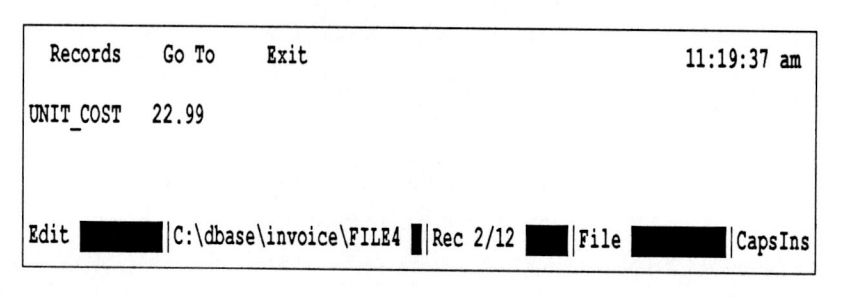

Figure 12.8 Edit screen for database file FILE4

```
Records    Go To    Exit                              11:19:37 am

UNIT_COST   22.99




Edit       |C:\dbase\invoice\FILE4 |Rec 2/12   |File        |CapsIns
```

12.3 Conditional Editing

```
. LIST
Record#  ORD DATE  ITEM NUM  ITEM DESC                UNIT_COST  QUANTITY  RET_PRICE
     1   01/05/89  1136      Bond Paper, Ream             22.99        38       0.00
     2   12/10/88  4005      Disks Data Case               5.99        18       0.00
     3   01/05/89  1910      Ditto Paper, Ream            18.99        35       0.00
     4   01/05/89  4141      Double Sided Disks 10-Pk      6.99        27       0.00
     5   12/10/88  2786      Highlighter Pen 10-Box        7.99        86       0.00
     6   01/05/89  4012      King Kong Modem 1200         99.99        10       0.00
     7   01/05/89  4045      Monochrome Monitor Z-1105    89.99        15       0.00
     8   12/10/88  4072      Panasonic Printer KX-P108   269.99         8       0.00
     9   01/05/89  3372      Printer Ribbon 10-Box        32.99        19       0.00
    10   12/10/88  3375      Typewriter Ribbons 10-Box    23.79        67       0.00
    11   12/10/88  1488      Xerographic Paper            19.99        45       0.00
    12   12/10/88  4189      Zenith Microcomputer Z-158  829.99         5       0.00
```

Figure 12.9 Listing of database file FILE4 after the editing process is complete

Suppose you have a database file in which several records have been marked for deletion. If you want to remove all the deletion markers, use the RECALL command. But suppose you want to remove the deletion marker from only some records, and you must view each record marked for deletion to determine which ones. The combination of the LOCATE and EDIT commands can be used to perform this function.

Consider the database file INV5.DBF, whose listing is given in Figure 12.10. Note that there are five records marked for deletion: the first, third, fifth, tenth, and eleventh. You want to view each of these and remove the deletion marker from those whose ITEM_DESC field contains the word *paper*. To do this, follow these steps:

1. Open the database file, and search for the first record marked for deletion by typing the following commands:

   ```
   . USE INV5                      <Return>
   . LOCATE FOR DELETED ()         <Return>
   ```

Figure 12.10 Listing of database file INV5.DBF

```
. USE INV5
. DISPLAY ALL
Record#  ITEM NUM  ITEM DESC                 UNIT_COST  QUANTITY
     1   *1136     Bond Paper, Ream              22.99        38
     2    4005     Disks Data Case                5.99        18
     3   *1910     Ditto Paper, Ream             19.99        35
     4    4141     Double Sided Disks 10-Pk       8.49        27
     5   *2786     Highlighter Pen 10-Box         7.99        86
     6    4012     King Kong Modem 1200         105.99        10
     7    4045     Monochrome Monitor Z-1105     99.99        15
     8    4072     Panasonic Printer KX-P108    269.99         8
     9    3372     Printer Ribbon 10-Box         35.99        19
    10   *3375     Typewriter Ribbons 10-Box     23.79        67
    11   *1488     Xerographic Paper             19.99        45
    12    4189     Zenith Microcomputer Z-158   829.99         5
```

Figure 12.11 Edit screen for database file INV5.DBF displaying the first located record

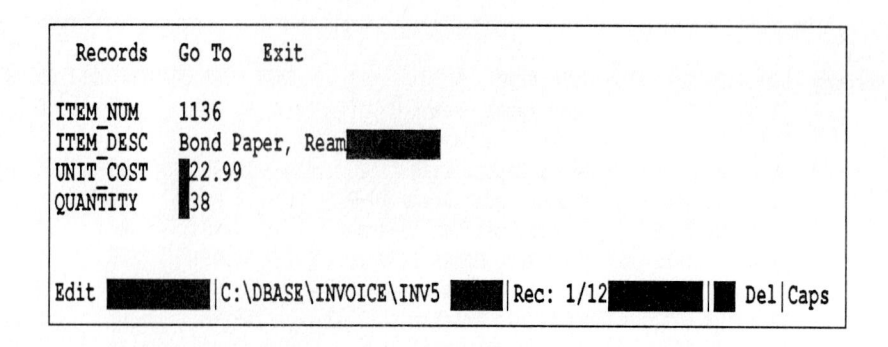

```
 Records   Go To   Exit

 ITEM_NUM    1136
 ITEM_DESC   Bond Paper, Ream
 UNIT_COST   22.99
 QUANTITY    38



 Edit            |C:\DBASE\INVOICE\INV5    |Rec: 1/12       | Del|Caps
```

dBASE will respond by displaying the following message:

`Record = 1`

This message indicates that the first record marked for deletion is record 1.

2. To see if this record is to be recalled or not, you should view it by typing the EDIT command. dBASE will then go into the edit mode and respond by displaying the first record, as shown in Figure 12.11. Note that the delete marker "DEL" appears in the lower right corner of the status bar.

3. An examination of the ITEM_DESC field indicates that the word *paper* is present in this field. Therefore, the delete marker should be removed from this record. To do this, press the <Ctrl-U> keys, and the delete marker "DEL" will disappear from the status bar, as shown in Figure 12.12.

4. To save this edited record, press the <Ctrl-W> keys. dBASE will respond by displaying the dot prompt.

5. Now search for the next record marked for deletion by typing the CONTINUE command. dBASE will respond by displaying the message:

`Record = 3`

This message indicates that the next record marked for deletion in the database file is the third one.

The process of viewing the searched record, editing it if needed, saving it, and searching for the next record marked for deletion, as given in steps 2–5, should be repeated until the "End of locate scope" message is displayed by dBASE as a response to the CONTINUE command.

Figure 12.12 Edit screen for database file INV5.DBF displaying the first located record after removing the mark for deletion

```
 Records   Go To   Exit

 ITEM_NUM    1136
 ITEM_DESC   Bond Paper, Ream
 UNIT_COST   22.99
 QUANTITY    38



 Edit            |C:\DBASE\INVOICE\INV5    |Rec: 1/12       |    |Caps
```

Figure 12.13 Listing of database file INV5.DBF after editing the conditionally selected records

```
. USE INV5
. DISPLAY ALL
Record#  ITEM_NUM  ITEM_DESC                 UNIT_COST  QUANTITY
      1  1136      Bond Paper, Ream              22.99        38
      2  4005      Disks Data Case                5.99        18
      3  1910      Ditto Paper, Ream             19.99        35
      4  4141      Double Sided Disks 10-Pk       8.49        27
      5 *2786      Highlighter Pen 10-Box         7.99        86
      6  4012      King Kong Modem 1200         105.99        10
      7  4045      Monochrome Monitor Z-1105     99.99        15
      8  4072      Panasonic Printer KX-P108    269.99         8
      9  3372      Printer Ribbon 10-Box         35.99        19
     10 *3375      Typewriter Ribbons 10-Box     23.79        67
     11  1488      Xerographic Paper             19.99        45
     12  4189      Zenith Microcomputer Z-158   829.99         5
```

These steps complete the process of editing the conditionally selected records. If you get the listing of database file INV5.DBF, it will be as shown in Figure 12.13. A comparison of the listings of database file INV5.DBF of Figures 12.10 and 12.13 indicates that the records marked for deletion and containing the word *paper* in the ITEM_DESC field have been recalled.

12.3.3 The LOCATE and EDIT WHILE Commands

The LOCATE and EDIT commands used in section 12.3.2 helped you edit conditionally selected records. The LOCATE command searched the records satisfying the specified condition; the EDIT command allowed you to edit the searched record. This method can be used with a database file in which records satisfying the condition are scattered.

But if the records satisfying the condition are grouped in the database file, which is possible only when the records of the database file are sorted or indexed on the field used in the search condition, then you can use the LOCATE and EDIT WHILE commands in place of the LOCATE and EDIT commands. This method is more efficient, but you can apply the LOCATE and EDIT WHILE commands *only* if the database file is sorted or indexed on the search field and the index tag of that field is activated.

For example, consider the example discussed in section 12.3.1, where the value of the UNIT_COST field was changed for all the records of the database file in which ORD_DATE is equal to "01/05/89." Suppose that the database file is indexed on the ORD_DATE field, and the database file is open with the ORD_DATE index as an active index tag. This step can be achieved by typing the following commands:

```
. USE FILE6                <Return>
. SET ORDER TO ORD_DATE    <Return>
```

dBASE will respond by displaying this message:

```
Master index: ORD_DATE
```

indicating that the ORD_DATE index tag is active. To search for the first occurrence of the record for which ORD_DATE is equal to "01/05/89," type the following command:

```
. LOCATE FOR ORD_DATE = {01/05/89}    <Return>
```

dBASE will respond by displaying the message:

```
Record no. 2
```

indicating that the first record satisfying the condition (in the indexed sequence) is the second one of the database file. To edit all the records of the database file with ORD_DATE equal to "01/05/89," you'll need the following command:

```
. EDIT WHILE ORD_DATE = {01/05/89}    <Return>
```

If you type this, dBASE will respond by displaying the edit screen shown in Figure 12.14. After editing this record, press the <PgDn> key; the next record with the ORD_DATE equal to "01/05/89" will be displayed. You can continue this process of editing until all the records of the database satisfying the condition have been edited and dBASE responds by displaying the dot prompt.

Using this method, you do not have to save each edited record by pressing the <Ctrl-W> keys, typing the CONTINUE command to search the next record, and then typing the EDIT command to display the edit screen, as in the method using the LOCATE and EDIT commands in section 12.3.2. Not having to type the CONTINUE and EDIT commands for each record satisfying the condition saves time and makes this method faster and more efficient.

12.4 Global Editing

The editing methods discussed in the three previous sections dealt with editing the records of the database file on a case-by-case basis. This required each record of the database file to be edited individually. Such methods work fine with the database files that have a small number of records, but they are not efficient for larger files.

Global editing is the answer to this problem. This is the process by which all or all the conditionally selected records of the database file are edited by the use of a dBASE command rather than being edited manually. Two such methods are discussed in this section.

Figure 12.14 Edit screen for database file FILE6 with selected record in which ORD_DATE = {01/05/89}

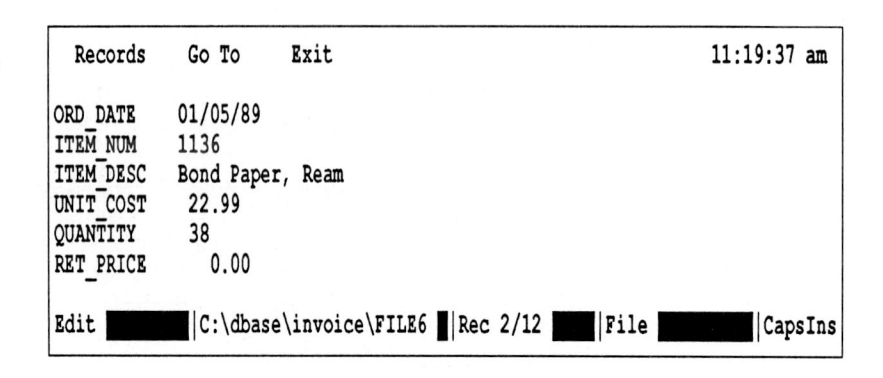

```
Records    Go To    Exit                              11:19:37 am

ORD_DATE    01/05/89
ITEM_NUM    1136
ITEM_DESC   Bond Paper, Ream
UNIT_COST   22.99
QUANTITY    38
RET_PRICE    0.00

Edit         |C:\dbase\invoice\FILE6 |Rec 2/12   |File      |CapsIns
```

12.4.1 The REPLACE Command

The general format of the REPLACE command is

```
REPLACE [<scope>] <field name> WITH <expression>
        [FOR <condition>] [WHILE <condition>]
```

where <scope> specifies which part of the database file is affected by the command, <field name> is the name of the field receiving the new data, <expression> is the new data being placed into the receiving field, and <condition> is a valid query condition.

The REPLACE command is used to replace the contents of a database field with a new value, which can be a literal data item, data stored in a memory variable, or the result of an expression. The receiving field and the replacing data must be of the same type. That is, you cannot replace a numeric data field with a character data field.

The REPLACE command is very fast and powerful. It is used to replace the contents of a database field with the value of an expression in all the records of the database file or those satisfying a specific condition. Its most efficient use is when global replacement is needed, that is, to replace the value of a field by an expression in all the records of the database file.

Consider the database file INV6.DBF, whose listing is given in Figure 12.15. The RET_PRICE field contains no data. Suppose the value of this field can be obtained by multiplying the value of UNIT_COST by the markup factor of 1.5. Then the data in the RET_PRICE field of the whole database file can be entered by using the following command:

```
. REPLACE ALL RET_PRICE WITH UNIT_COST * 1.5
<Return>
```

dBASE will respond by displaying the message:

```
12 records replaced
```

Figure 12.15 Listing of database file INV6.DBF

```
. USE INV6
. DISPLAY ALL
Record#  ITEM_NUM  ITEM_DESC                  UNIT_COST  RET_PRICE
     1   1136      Bond Paper, Ream               22.99
     2   4005      Disks Data Case                 5.99
     3   1910      Ditto Paper, Ream              19.99
     4   4141      Double Sided Disks 10-Pk        8.49
     5   2786      Highlighter Pen 10-Box          7.99
     6   4012      King Kong Modem 1200          105.99
     7   4045      Monochrome Monitor Z-1105      99.99
     8   4072      Panasonic Printer KX-P108     269.99
     9   3372      Printer Ribbon 10-Box          35.99
    10   3375      Typewriter Ribbons 10-Box      23.79
    11   1488      Xerographic Paper              19.99
    12   4189      Zenith Microcomputer Z-158    829.99
```

Figure 12.16 Listing of database file INV6.DBF including the RET_PRICE field data

```
. USE INV6
. DISPLAY ALL
Record#  ITEM NUM  ITEM DESC                    UNIT COST  RET PRICE
      1  1136      Bond Paper, Ream                 22.99      34.48
      2  4005      Disks Data Case                   5.99       8.98
      3  1910      Ditto Paper, Ream                19.99      29.98
      4  4141      Double Sided Disks 10-Pk          8.49      12.73
      5  2786      Highlighter Pen 10-Box            7.99      11.98
      6  4012      King Kong Modem 1200            105.99     158.98
      7  4045      Monochrome Monitor Z-1105        99.99     149.98
      8  4072      Panasonic Printer KX-P108       269.99     404.98
      9  3372      Printer Ribbon 10-Box            35.99      53.98
     10  3375      Typewriter Ribbons 10-Box        23.79      35.68
     11  1488      Xerographic Paper                19.99      29.98
     12  4189      Zenith Microcomputer Z-158      829.99    1244.98
```

If you obtain the listing of the database file INV6.DBF either by pressing the F3 List function key or by typing the following command:

. **LIST**   <Return>

dBASE will respond by displaying the listing shown in Figure 12.16.

Conditional REPLACE

Suppose the company changes its policy for the calculation of the RET_PRICE field value. The markup factor of 1.5 is still used to calculate the value of the RET_PRICE field for items whose UNIT_COST is less than or equal to $100. But the markup factor of 1.4 is used to calculate the value of the RET_PRICE field for items whose UNIT_COST is greater than $100. To make this change, type the following REPLACE command:

. **REPLACE ALL RET_PRICE WITH UNIT_COST * 1.4 FOR UNIT_COST > or = 100**   <Return>

Figure 12.17 Listing of database file INV6.DBF including the modified value of the RET_PRICE field data

```
. USE INV6
. LIST
Record#  ITEM NUM  ITEM DESC                    UNIT COST  RET PRICE
      1  1136      Bond Paper, Ream                 22.99      34.48
      2  4005      Disks Data Case                   5.99       8.98
      3  1910      Ditto Paper, Ream                19.99      29.98
      4  4141      Double Sided Disks 10-Pk          8.49      12.73
      5  2786      Highlighter Pen 10-Box            7.99      11.98
      6  4012      King Kong Modem 1200            105.99     148.38
      7  4045      Monochrome Monitor Z-1105        99.99     149.98
      8  4072      Panasonic Printer KX-P108       269.99     377.98
      9  3372      Printer Ribbon 10-Box            35.99      53.98
     10  3375      Typewriter Ribbons 10-Box        23.79      35.68
     11  1488      Xerographic Paper                19.99      29.98
     12  4189      Zenith Microcomputer Z-158      829.99    1161.98
```

dBASE will respond by displaying the following message:

```
3 records replaced
```

Now again obtain the listing of the database file INV6.DBF either by pressing the F3 List function key or by typing the following command:

```
. LIST    <Return>
```

dBASE will respond by displaying the listing shown in Figure 12.17. Notice the change in the value of the RET_PRICE field in Figure 12.17 for records 6, 8, and 12.

12.4.2 The LOCATE and CONTINUE Commands

The example discussed in section 12.3.2 dealt with recalling the deleted records whose item description contained the word *paper*. This result was achieved in three steps. First, the deleted record was searched by the use of the LOCATE command. Then the EDIT command was used to recall the record. The searched record was examined to see if its item description contained the word *paper*. If it did, the record was recalled; otherwise, it was not recalled. Then the search for the next deleted record was resumed by the use of the CONTINUE command. This process went on until the LOCATE command could not find any more records satisfying the specified condition. These steps were completed by the LOCATE command displaying the "End of locate scope" message.

But this processing was done on a case-by-case basis. Each searched record was visually examined and recalled if its item description contained the word *paper*. This method is not applicable for large database files. What would you do if you had to perform this problem on a global basis, that is, recall all the deleted records from the large database file whose item description contains the word *paper*? The method explained in section 12.3.2 cannot accomplish this because the EDIT command used therein is not programmable. But you can achieve global editing by using the dBASE commands shown in Figure 12.18. If you create a program with these commands and execute it, you will obtain the same result as in section 12.3.2, but on a global rather than a case-by-case basis.

The first command in Figure 12.18 will open the database file INV5.DBF. The next one will search the record whose item description field contains the word *paper*. The next one will test whether the record is deleted. If it is, it will be recalled. If it is not a deleted record, the control will transfer to the command after the ENDIF command; that is, the CONTINUE command will be executed next. This command tells the

Figure 12.18 A program to recall all the deleted records from the database file whose item description contains the word *paper*

```
USE INV5
LOCATE FOR "Paper" $ITEM_DESC
    DO WHILE FOUND ()
        IF DELETED ()
            RECALL
        ENDIF
        CONTINUE
    ENDDO
```

LOCATE command to search the next record satisfying the condition specified in the LOCATE command. This process will continue until the LOCATE command finds a record satisfying the specified condition. When no more records satisfying the condition specified in the LOCATE command are available, dBASE will respond by displaying the "End of locate scope" message.

You cannot use the EDIT command in a program; it is not a programmable command. You can use the REPLACE command or combinations of other dBASE commands as done previously to perform the global editing.

12.5 An Illustrative Example: Case Study 9

Program Description

Write an inventory file maintenance program. It should be invoked by the inventory file maintenance submenu program INV1.PRG of the invoice generating system. The function of the program is to update the records of the inventory database file INV.DBF.

Processing Steps

Use the following steps to develop the solution of the program:

1. The inventory file maintenance screen as shown in Figure 12.19 with the message "ENTER THE ITEM NUMBER, PLEASE ===> :," requesting the user to enter the item number of the record to be updated, should be displayed.

Figure 12.19 Inventory database file maintenance screen

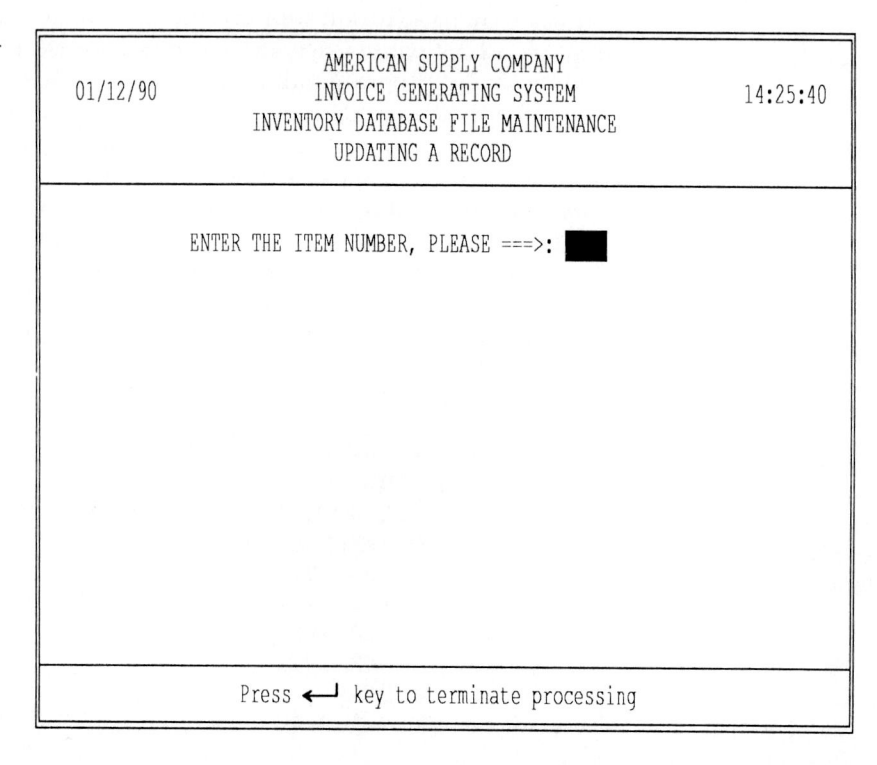

```
                    AMERICAN SUPPLY COMPANY
  01/12/90          INVOICE GENERATING SYSTEM              14:25:40
                 INVENTORY DATABASE FILE MAINTENANCE
                         UPDATING A RECORD

         ENTER THE ITEM NUMBER, PLEASE ===>: ■




                   Press ⏎ key to terminate processing
```

2. The screen should be frozen or paused to allow the user to respond to the request.
3. After user entry is accepted, the value of the item number supplied by the user should be tested to see if it is a blank or a nonblank value.
4. A blank value indicates that the user wants to terminate the process of updating database file records. Therefore, proceed to step 13.
5. For the nonblank value of the item number, search the inventory database file to find the matching record.
6. If the match is not found, display the message indicating that, and proceed to step 12.
7. If the match is found, the matching record should be displayed on the screen.
8. Accept the changes to be made.
9. Confirmation to update the record should be requested from the user.
10. Check for the validity of the confirmation. If the confirmation is valid, update the record.
11. If the confirmation is invalid, indicate this by displaying the proper message.
12. Repeat steps 1–11 to update the next record.
13. After all the desired records have been updated, close the database file, and return the control to the calling program INV1.PRG.

The five phases of the program development process for Case Study 9 follow.

12.5.1 The Analysis Phase

In the analysis phase, the first step in the program development process, review and analysis of the program specifications lead to the identification of the processing steps needed to solve the problem. First, the housekeeping step will be needed to declare public variables. Because a set of instructions will be needed to update a record from the database file, these steps should be repeated for each record to be updated. Thus, a control switch needs to be defined to control this loop. Also, we will need to define the memory variables for each field in the record to store their updated value before updating the record. Of course, the database file to which the records to be deleted belong should be opened. These three steps are the only ones needed in the initiate processing function of the solution of the problem.

The processing steps needed in the main processing function should include:

1. Accept the item number to be updated.
2. Test for a blank item number.
3. Process the blank item number, that is, change the loop control switch to indicate termination of the loop, and proceed to step 7.

4. Process the nonblank item number, that is, search for a matching record in the inventory database file.
5. Process match found:
    a. Display the matching record.
    b. Accept the changes.
    c. Accept confirmation for updating the record.
    d. If confirmation is valid, perform the record update routine, and proceed to step 7.
    e. If confirmation is invalid, proceed to step 7.
6. Process no match found.
7. Freeze the screen and blank item number.

Repeat these seven steps until the user wishes to terminate the program, which is done by supplying a blank value to the item number in step 1. At that point, the control should move to the terminate processing function.

In the terminate processing function, the database file should be closed, and program control should be transferred to the calling program.

Summing up, the following processing steps will be needed for the solution of Case Study 9:

1. Define the variables.
2. Open the database file.
3. Accept the item number to be updated.
4. Test for a blank item number.
5. Process the blank item number, that is, change the loop control switch to indicate the termination of the loop, and proceed to step 9.
6. Process the nonblank item number, that is, search for a matching record in the inventory database file.
7. Process match found:
    a. Display the matching record.
    b. Accept the changes.
    c. Accept confirmation for updating the record.
    d. If confirmation is valid, perform the record update routine, and proceed to step 9.
    e. If confirmation is invalid, proceed to step 9.
8. Process no match found.
9. Freeze the screen and blank item number.
10. Close the database file.
11. Return to the calling program.

The first two steps should be performed only once, at the start of the program. Therefore, these belong to initiate processing. The next seven steps should be performed again and again until the user indicates his or her wish by supplying a blank value for the item number. Therefore, these steps belong to main processing. The last two steps need to be performed only once before terminating the execution of the program. Therefore, these belong to terminate processing.

12.5 An Illustrative Example: Case Study 9

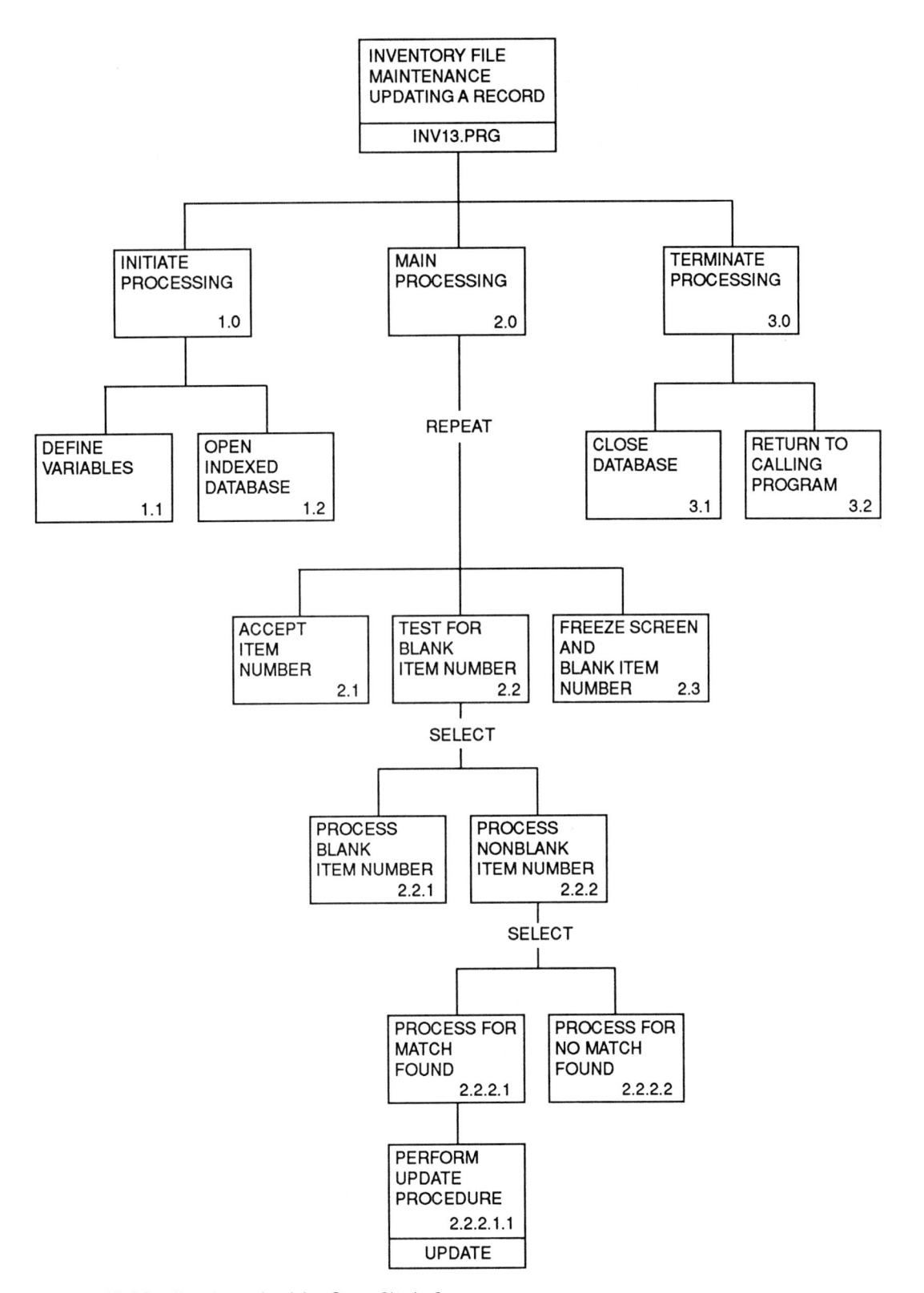

Figure 12.20 Structure chart for Case Study 9

12.5.2 The Design Phase

The function of this step is to take the result of the problem analysis, that is, the processing steps identified in the analysis phase, and transform them into a structure chart. Using the shell structure chart of Figure 10.12 and the tools and techniques discussed in section 4.4.2, transform the 11 steps identified in the analysis phase into a structure chart for Case Study 9, as shown in Figure 12.20.

All the modules in this structure chart are either functionally or highly cohesive. They are also loosely coupled. Thus, the structure chart of Figure 12.20 satisfies the three rules for designing a good structure chart; that is, it consists of highly cohesive, loosely coupled modules with the span of control of any module no more than three. Therefore, it is a well-designed solution to Case Study 9.

12.5.3 The Detailed Design Phase

The function of this step is to take the result of the design phase, the structure chart, and identify the actual computer operations required for each program function represented in the structure chart, thereby producing the detailed solution of the problem. Using the translation of the three control structures to pseudocode as given in Figure 4.14 and the method described in section 4.4.3, we can translate the structure chart of Figure 12.20 to pseudocode, as shown in Figure 12.21.

Figure 12.21 Pseudocode for Case Study 9

```
0.0 INVENTORY FILE MAINTENANCE—UPDATING
   1.0 INITIATE PROCESSING
      1.1 DEFINE VARIABLES
         DEFINE CONTROL VARIABLES
            Set REPEAT13 switch = T
         INITIALIZE VARIABLES
            Load memory variables from INV12.MEM file
      1.2 OPEN INDEXED DATABASE
         Open INV.DBF database file with index set to ITEM_NUM
   2.0 MAIN PROCESSING
      REPEAT: While REPEAT13 switch = T
         2.1 ACCEPT ITEM NUMBER
            CLEAR SCREEN
            Clear the screen
            REQUEST AND ACCEPT ITEM NUMBER
            Display Heading #1
            Display Heading #2
            Display Heading #3
            Display Heading #4
            Display Prompt
            Request and accept item number
         2.2 TEST FOR BLANK ITEM NUMBER
            SELECT: if ITEMNUM is BLANK
               2.2.1 PROCESS BLANK ITEM NUMBER
                  Reset switch REPEAT13 = F
               2.2.2 PROCESS NONBLANK ITEM NUMBER
                  Find matching record in database file
```

Figure 12.21 Continued

```
                        SELECT: if match found
                        2.2.2.1 PROCESS FOR MATCH FOUND
                                2.2.2.1.1 PERFORM UPDATE PROCEDURE
                                          Perform the UPDATE procedure
                        2.2.2.2 PROCESS FOR NO MATCH FOUND
                                Display message record already on file
                     END SELECT
                 END SELECT
             2.3 FREEZE SCREEN AND BLANK ITEM NUMBER
                 Process FREEZE procedure
                 Reset ITEMNUM to BLANK
         END REPEAT
    3.0 TERMINATE PROCESSING
        3.1 CLOSE DATABASE FILE
            Close the database file
        3.2 RETURN TO CALLING PROGRAM
            Return to calling program
```

12.5.4 The Coding Phase

The purpose of this phase in the program development process is to translate the pseudocode instructions of the solution of the program into programming language instructions. The pseudocode of Figure 12.21 is translated into dBASE commands, and the complete program for Case Study 9 in dBASE language is given in Figure 12.22.

```
************************************************************
*                       INV13.PRG                          *
*                  AMERICAN SUPPLY COMPANY                 *
*                 INVOICE GENERATING SYSTEM                *
*             INVENTORY FILE MAINTENANCE PROGRAM           *
*                     UPDATING A RECORD                    *
*----------------------------------------------------------*
* This is one of the Inventory File Maintenance programs.  *
* It is invoked by the Inventory File Maintenance Sub-Menu *
**program INV1.PRG of the Invoice Generating System for    *
* American Supply Company. The function of this program is *
* to update the records of the inventory database file INV.DBF. *
*----------------------------------------------------------*
*           COPYRIGHT (C) . . . SUDESH M. DUGGAL           *
************************************************************
*
*****************************
* 1.0 INITIATE PROCESSING *
*****************************
*
*** 1.1 DEFINE VARIABLES ***
    *
    *** DEFINE CONTROL VARIABLES ***
        *
```

Figure 12.22 Coding for Case Study 9

```
            STORE [T] TO REPEAT13
            *
         *** INITIALIZE VARIABLES ***
            *
            RESTORE FROM INV12 ADDITIVE
            *
*** 1.2 OPEN INDEXED DATABASE ***
     *
     USE INV
     SET ORDER TO ITEM_NUM
     *
**********************
* 2.0 MAIN PROCESSING *
**********************
*
DO WHILE REPEAT13 = 'T'
   *
   *** 2.1 ACCEPT ITEM NUMBER ***
       *
       *** CLEAR SCREEN ***
          *
          CLEAR
          *
       *** REQUEST AND ACCEPT ITEM NUMBER ***
          *
          @ 2,20 SAY '          AMERICAN SUPPLY COMPANY'
          @ 3,4  SAY DATE ()
          @ 3,20 SAY '          INVOICE GENERATING SYSTEM'
          @ 3,70 SAY TIME ()
          @ 4,20 SAY '       INVENTORY FILE MAINTENANCE PROGRAM'
          @ 5,20 SAY '             UPDATING A RECORD'
          @ 6,0  TO  6,79
          @ 22,0 TO 22,79
          @ 1,2  TO 24,79 DOUBLE
          @ 8,20 SAY 'ENTER THE ITEM NUMBER, PLEASE ===>:'
          @ 8,56 GET ITEMNUM PICTURE 'XXXX'
          READ
          *
   *** 2.2 TEST FOR BLANK ITEM NUMBER ***
       *
       IF ITEMNUM = '    '
          *
          *** 2.2.1 PROCESS BLANK ITEM NUMBER ***
             *
             STORE  [F] TO REPEAT13
             *
       ELSE
          *
          *** 2.2.2 PROCESS NONBLANK ITEM NUMBER ***
             *
             FIND &ITEMNUM
             *
             IF .NOT. (EOF () .OR. BOF())
                *
                *** 2.2.2.1 PROCESS FOR MATCH FOUND ***
                   *
```

Figure 12.22 Continued

```
                        *** 2.2.2.1.1 PERFORM UPDATE PROCEDURE ***
                            *
                            DO UPDATE
                            *
                ELSE
                    *
                    *** 2.2.2.2 PROCESS FOR NO MATCH ***
                        *
                        @ 21,20 SAY '****        RECORD NOT FOUND        *****'
                        *
                ENDIF .NOT. (EOF () .OR. BOF ())
                *
        ENDIF ITEMNUM = '    '
        *
        *** 2.3 FREEZE SCREEN AND BLANK ITEM NUMBER ***
            *
            DO FREEZE
            *
            STORE '    ' TO ITEMNUM
            *
ENDDO REPEAT13 = [T]
*
***************************
* 3.0 TERMINATE PROCESSING *
***************************
*
*** 3.1 CLOSE DATABASE ***
    *
    USE
    *
*** 3.2 RETURN TO CALLING PROGRAM ***
    *
    RETURN
```

Figure 12.22 Continued

12.5.5 The Testing and Debugging Phase

The last step in program development is the testing and debugging phase, in which the source program is executed and tested for the accuracy of its logic. Execute the program to complete this step, correct the syntactical errors, if any, and execute the program again. Repeat this process until the program is free of syntactical errors. When the output is produced by the program, verify some of the records of the output to ensure its accuracy. If any discrepancies exist, make the needed corrections and execute the program again. Repeat the process of making corrections and executing the program until the program produces correct and predictable results.

12.6 Update Procedure for Case Study 9

The function of the update procedure is to display the old record, accept the changes, accept the confirmation for updating the record, and then check for the validity of the confirmation. If the confirmation is valid, the changes will be made as requested; but if the confirmation is not valid, no changes will be made.

Figure 12.23 Structure chart for UPDATE procedure

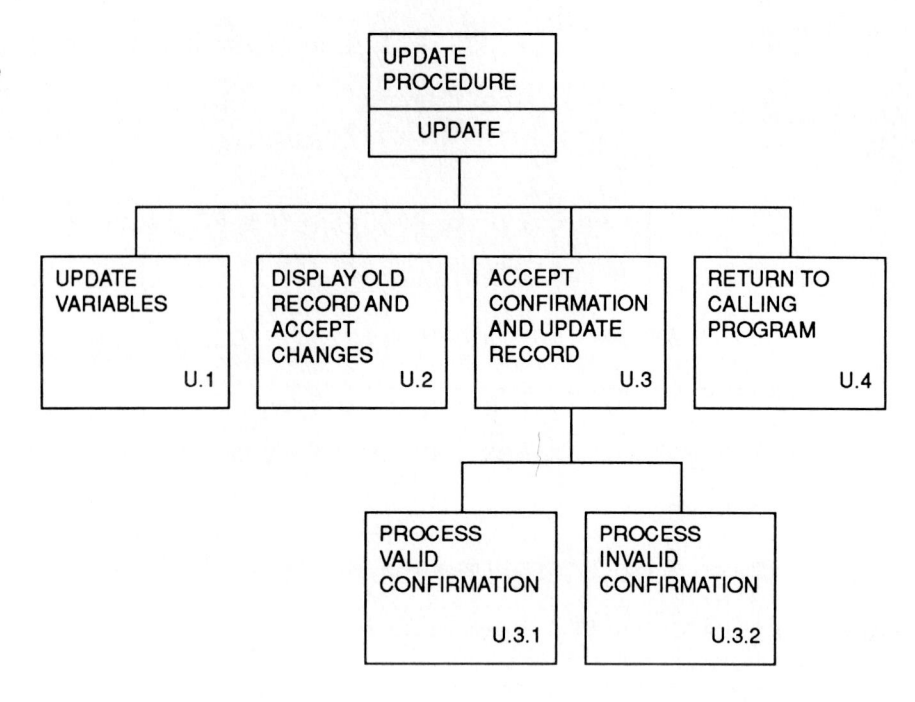

```
                        ┌──────────────┐
                        │   UPDATE     │
                        │  PROCEDURE   │
                        ├──────────────┤
                        │   UPDATE     │
                        └──────┬───────┘
         ┌─────────────┬───────┴────────┬─────────────┐
  ┌──────┴──────┐ ┌────┴──────┐  ┌──────┴──────┐ ┌────┴──────┐
  │   UPDATE    │ │DISPLAY OLD│  │   ACCEPT    │ │ RETURN TO │
  │  VARIABLES  │ │RECORD AND │  │CONFIRMATION │ │  CALLING  │
  │             │ │  ACCEPT   │  │ AND UPDATE  │ │  PROGRAM  │
  │             │ │  CHANGES  │  │   RECORD    │ │           │
  │         U.1 │ │       U.2 │  │         U.3 │ │       U.4 │
  └─────────────┘ └───────────┘  └──────┬──────┘ └───────────┘
                                  ┌─────┴──────┐
                           ┌──────┴─────┐ ┌────┴──────┐
                           │  PROCESS   │ │  PROCESS  │
                           │   VALID    │ │  INVALID  │
                           │CONFIRMATION│ │CONFIRMATION│
                           │      U.3.1 │ │     U.3.2 │
                           └────────────┘ └───────────┘
```

When this process is complete, program control will be transferred to the calling program. The structure chart of the update procedure is given in Figure 12.23. The pseudocode for the update procedure is given in Figure 12.24. The coding for the update procedure is given in Figure 12.25.

Figure 12.24 Pseudocode for UPDATE procedure

```
0.0 INVENTORY FILE MAINTENANCE—UPDATE PROCEDURE
    U.1 UPDATE VARIABLES
            Set ITEM_DESC  = ITEMDESC
            Set QUANTITY   = QTY
            Set UNIT_COST  = UNITCOST
            Set DEPT_CODE  = DEPTCODE
            Set REOD_POINT = REODPOINT
            Set REOD_QTY   = REODQTY
    U.2 DISPLAY OLD RECORD AND ACCEPT CHANGES
            Display the old record
            Accept the changes
    U.3 ACCEPT CONFIRMATION AND UPDATE RECORD
            Accept confirmation for changes
            SELECT: On confirmation
                U.3.1 PROCESS VALID CONFIRMATION
                        Update changes
                        Display message indicating record changed
                        Reinitialize variables
                U.3.2 PROCESS INVALID CONFIRMATION
                        Display message indicating record not changed
    U.4 RETURN TO CALLING PROGRAM
            Return to calling program
```

```
***************************************************************
*                       UPDATE                                 *
*                AMERICAN SUPPLY COMPANY                       *
*--------------------------------------------------------------*
* This is a subroutine program invoked by the program          *
* INV13.PRG of Case Study 9 to update the requested            *
* fields of the inventory database file INV.DBF.               *
*--------------------------------------------------------------*
*           COPYRIGHT (C) . . . SUDESH M. DUGGAL               *
***************************************************************
*
PROCEDURE UPDATE
*
*** U.1 UPDATE VARIABLES ***
    *
    STORE ITEM_DESC    TO ITEMDESC
    STORE QUANTITY     TO QTY
    STORE UNIT_COST    TO UNITCOST
    STORE DEPT_CODE    TO DEPTCODE
    STORE REOD_POINT   TO REODPOINT
    STORE REOD_QTY     TO REODQTY
    *
*** U.2 DISPLAY OLD RECORD AND ACCEPT CHANGES ***
    *
    @ 10,15 SAY [ITEM DESCRIPTION:]
    @ 10,45 GET ITEMDESC
    @ 12,15 SAY [QUANTITY         :]
    @ 12,45 GET QTY
    @ 14,15 SAY [UNIT COST        :]
    @ 14,45 GET UNITCOST
    @ 16,15 SAY [DEPT CODE        :]
    @ 16,45 GET DEPTCODE
    @ 18,15 SAY [REORDER POINT    :]
    @ 18,45 GET REODPOINT
    @ 20,15 SAY [REORDER QUANTITY:]
    @ 20,45 GET REODQTY
    *
    @ 21,15 SAY 'ENTER ONLY THE FIELDS TO BE CHANGED'
    READ
    *
*** U.3 ACCEPT CONFIRMATION AND UPDATE RECORD ***
    *
    STORE ' ' TO CONFIRM
    @ 21,15 SAY 'ENTER "C" TO CONFIRM THE CHANGE ===>:'
    @ 21,55 GET CONFIRM
    READ
    *
    IF UPPER (CONFIRM) = 'C'
        *
        *** U.3.1 PROCESS VALID CONFIRMATION ***
            *
            *** UPDATE CHANGES ***
                *
                REPLACE ITEM_DESC   WITH ITEMDESC
                REPLACE QUANTITY    WITH QTY
```

Figure 12.25 Coding for UPDATE procedure

```
            REPLACE UNIT_COST   WITH UNITCOST
            REPLACE DEPT_CODE   WITH DEPTCODE
            REPLACE REOD_POINT  WITH REODPOINT
            REPLACE REOD_QTY    WITH REODQTY
            *
            IF UNIT_COST < MARK_RANGE
                *
                RETPRICE = UNITCOST * MARK_UP1
                *
            ELSE
                *
                RETPRICE = UNITCOST * MARK_UP2
                *
            ENDIF UNITCOST < MARK_RANGE
            *
            REPLACE RET_PRICE WITH RETPRICE
            *
         *** RECORD CHANGED MESSAGE ***
            *
            @ 21,15 SAY '****   RECORD CHANGED   *****'
            *
         *** REINITIALIZE VARIABLES ***
            *
            RESTORE FROM INV12 ADDITIVE
            *
      ELSE
         *
      *** U.3.2 PROCESS INVALID CONFIRMATION ***
         *
         @ 21,15 SAY '** WRONG CONFIRM CODE - RECORD NOT DELETED **'
         *
   ENDIF UPPER (CONFIRM) = 'C'
   *
*** U.4 RETURN TO CALLING PROGRAM ***
   *
   RETURN
```

Figure 12.25 Continued

Note: The customer file maintenance program INV23.PRG for updating the records of the CUSTOMER.DBF database file can be developed similarly to Case Study 9.

12.7 Summary

Three commands are commonly used for data editing: EDIT, BROWSE, and REPLACE.

The EDIT command is a full-screen command that allows data to be edited in the current record of the active database file. The default edit screen is invoked by the EDIT command, which displays all the fields present in the record of the database file unless the FIELDS option is used to restrict them. The customized form can be invoked in place of the default edit screen if this form is created and opened *before* the use of the EDIT command with the SET FORMAT command.

The BROWSE command is also a full-screen command. It displays 17 records at a time with as many fields as will fit on the screen. Fields not on the screen can be brought into view by moving the cursor to the right beyond the right side of the screen. The LOCK option allows you to lock a certain number of fields on the left-hand side of the screen. The FREEZE option allows you to restrict the editing of only one field specified with the FREEZE option. The FIELDS option allows you to restrict the fields to be present in the edit screen. The WIDTH option allows you to specify the maximum width for each field to be displayed in the edit screen. This option helps display more fields, thus providing more information on the screen for each record.

Conditionally selected records can be edited in several ways. The EDIT FOR format of the EDIT command can be used, and the LOCATE and EDIT commands can be combined to conditionally select the records and then edit them. The LOCATE command and EDIT WHILE format of the EDIT command can also be combined for conditional editing. But the database should be either sorted or indexed and the index tag activated on the field used in the search condition.

The main shortcomings of the EDIT and BROWSE commands are that they are not programmable. In other words, they are useful only on a case-by-case basis. But the REPLACE command can be used for global editing, that is, to replace field content by an expression in either all records or in the conditionally selected records of the database file. Global editing can also be performed by the combination of the LOCATE and CONTINUE commands with other dBASE commands, except the EDIT and BROWSE commands.

KEY CONCEPTS

conditional editing
editing

global editing

dBASE COMMANDS AND FUNCTIONS

BROWSE command
CONTINUE command
EDIT command

LOCATE command
REPLACE command

REVIEW QUESTIONS

1. Name the three most commonly used commands in data editing.
2. How can the default edit screen invoked by the EDIT command be replaced by the customized form?
3. What is the advantage of the BROWSE command over the EDIT command?
4. What is the disadvantage of the BROWSE command over the EDIT command?

5. What is the function of the FIELDS option in the BROWSE command? Explain this function by giving an example.

6. What is the function of the WIDTH option in the BROWSE command? Explain this function by giving an example.

7. What is the function of the LOCK option in the BROWSE command? Explain this function by giving an example.

8. What is the function of the FREEZE option in the BROWSE command? Explain this function by giving an example.

9. What combination of the optional clauses of the BROWSE command makes it most efficient for data editing?

10. Name the different methods available for conditional editing.

11. How can the EDIT FOR format of the EDIT command be used for conditional editing? What are the advantages and disadvantages of including only the field to be edited in the edit screen used with the EDIT FOR command?

12. Explain how the combination of the LOCATE and EDIT commands can be used for conditional editing.

13. Explain how the combination of the LOCATE command and the EDIT WHILE format of the EDIT command can be used for conditional editing. What are the special requirements for using these two commands together?

14. What are the shortcomings of the EDIT and BROWSE commands?

15. What is meant by global editing? Explain the term by an example. List a set of commands that can perform global editing.

16. Explain the use of the REPLACE command. Give an example where this command is most useful.

17. What is the advantage of the REPLACE command over the EDIT and BROWSE commands?

HANDS-ON ASSIGNMENT

Programming Assignment 12A

Program Description Write a customer file maintenance program ACR13.PRG. It should be invoked by the customer file maintenance submenu program ACR1.PRG of the accounts receivable system. The function of the program is to update the records of the CUSTACR.DBF database file, whose structure is given in Figure 10.17.

Processing Steps The following steps should be used to develop the solution of the program:

1. The customer file maintenance screen as shown in Figure 12.26 with the message "ENTER THE CUSTOMER NUMBER, PLEASE ===> :," requesting the user to enter the customer number of the record to be updated, should be displayed.

2. The screen should be frozen or paused to allow the user to respond to the request.

3. After the user entry has been accepted, the value of the customer number should be tested to see if it is a blank or a nonblank value.

4. If the value is blank, it indicates that the user wants to terminate the process of updating records of the database file. Therefore, proceed to step 13.

5. For the nonblank value of the customer number, search the CUSTACR.DBF database file to find the matching record.

6. If the match is not found, display the message indicating this, and proceed to step 12.

7. If the match is found, the matching record should be displayed on the screen.

8. The program should accept the changes to be made.

9. Confirmation to update the record should be requested from the user.

10. Check for the validity of the confirmation. If the confirmation is valid, update the record.

11. If the confirmation is invalid, indicate this by displaying the proper message.

12. Repeat steps 1–11 to update the next record.

13. After all the desired records have been updated, close the database file, and return the control to the calling program ACR1.PRG.

The list of the records to be updated in the CUSTACR.DBF database file is given in Figure 12.27.

Figure 12.26 Customer database file maintenance screen

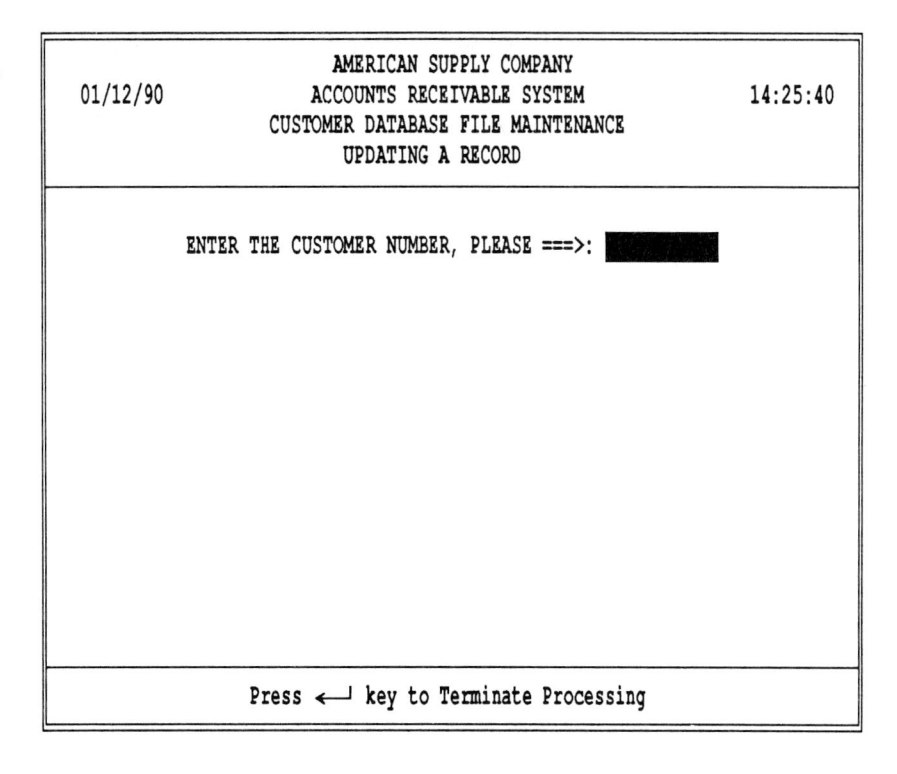

```
                    AMERICAN SUPPLY COMPANY
   01/12/90         ACCOUNTS RECEIVABLE SYSTEM              14:25:40
                  CUSTOMER DATABASE FILE MAINTENANCE
                         UPDATING A RECORD


            ENTER THE CUSTOMER NUMBER, PLEASE ===>:  ▇▇▇▇▇▇▇▇








                    Press ←┘ key to Terminate Processing
```

Requirements Submit the following items as part of the assignment:

1. Structure chart
2. Listing of the program
3. Listing of the CUSTACR.DBF database file before and after updating the records (use compressed print) with the changed fields circled and the customer numbers underlined
4. Use <Shift PrtSc> keys to print the five screens showing the changes outlined previously.

CUST_NUM	CUST_NAME	CUST_ADDR	CUST_CITY	CUST_STATE	CUST_ZIP	CUST_PHONE
120-12-5612						513-523-0044
562-12-1256		1073 Go Go Drive	Newport	KY	41010	606-431-4455
406-03-4063	Marge C. Nordman					
302-24-2433					45020	
9999-999-99			Blue Ash			

Figure 12.27 Records to be updated in the CUSTACR.DBF database file

Programming Assignment 12B

Program Description   Write an employee file maintenance program PAY13.PRG. It should be invoked by the employee file maintenance submenu program PAY1.PRG of the payroll system. The function of the program is to update the records of the EMPLOYEE.DBF database file, whose structure is given in Figure 4.33.

Processing Steps   The following steps should be used to develop the solution of the program:

1. The employee file maintenance screen as shown in Figure 12.28 with the message "ENTER THE SOCIAL SECURITY NUMBER, PLEASE ===> :," requesting the user to enter the social security number of the record to be updated, should be displayed.
2. The screen should be frozen or paused to allow the user to respond to the request.
3. After the user entry has been accepted, the value of the social security number supplied should be tested to see if it is a blank or a nonblank value.
4. If the value of the social security number is blank, it indicates that the user wants to terminate the process of updating records of the database file. Therefore, proceed to step 13.
5. For the nonblank value, search the EMPLOYEE.DBF database file to find the matching record.
6. If the match is not found, display the message indicating that, and proceed to step 12.
7. If the match is found, the matching record should be displayed on the screen.
8. Accept the changes to be made.
9. Confirmation to update the record should be requested from the user.
10. Check for the validity of the confirmation. If the confirmation is valid, update the record.
11. If the confirmation is invalid, indicate this by displaying the proper message, and proceed without updating the record.
12. Repeat steps 1–11 to update the next record.
13. After all the desired records have been updated, close the database file, and return the control to the calling program PAY1.PRG.

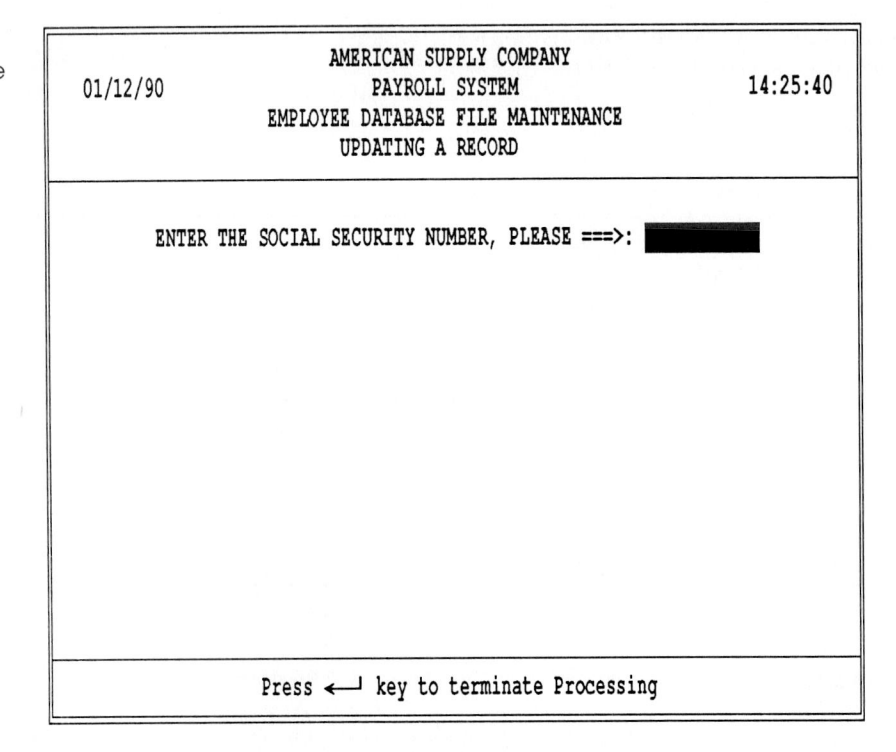

The list of the records to be updated in the EMPLOYEE.DBF database file is given in Figure 12.29.

Figure 12.28   Employee database file maintenance screen

```
+------------------------------------------------------------------+
|                     AMERICAN SUPPLY COMPANY                      |
| 01/12/90                 PAYROLL SYSTEM                 14:25:40 |
|               EMPLOYEE DATABASE FILE MAINTENANCE                 |
|                       UPDATING A RECORD                          |
|------------------------------------------------------------------|
|                                                                  |
|       ENTER THE SOCIAL SECURITY NUMBER, PLEASE ===>: ■■■■■■■     |
|                                                                  |
|                                                                  |
|                                                                  |
|                                                                  |
|                                                                  |
|                                                                  |
|                                                                  |
|                                                                  |
|------------------------------------------------------------------|
|               Press ←┘ key to terminate Processing               |
+------------------------------------------------------------------+
```

12.7 Summary

Figure 12.29 Records to be updated in the EMPLOYEE.DBF database file

SOC_NUM	EMP_NAME	DEPT_CODE	PAY_CODE	M_STATUS	N_DEP
298-47-6667					5
315-66-8212				2	
455-11-0501					3
631-22-1515		104			
(YOUR SS N)					

Requirements Submit the following items as part of the assignment:

1. Structure chart
2. Listing of the program
3. Listing of the EMPLOYEE.DBF database file before and after updating the records (containing the first six fields only) with the changed fields circled and the social security numbers underlined
4. Use <Shift PrtSc> keys to print the five screens showing the changes outlined previously.

Chapter 13

Multiple Files

LEARNING OBJECTIVES

Upon successfully completing this chapter, you will be able to:

1. Open and use multiple database files simultaneously.
2. Use prefixes and aliases to access the data from the multiple database files.
3. Distinguish between the open and active database files.
4. Define the relationship among multiple database files having a common field.
5. Access the related data from the multiple files.
6. Analyze, design, and code a program using multiple files.

13.1 Overview

The chapter starts with accessing data from multiple database files at the same time. The SELECT command, which allows you to open up to ten work areas at a time and select an already open work area, is introduced. One database file can be opened in each open work area. The use of prefixes and aliases, which permits the access of data from various open database files in different work areas, is described.

Defining the relationship among the database files having a field in common is introduced next. This allows you to obtain related data from different database files. Finally, an invoice generating program using multiple database files is analyzed, designed, and coded. The function of the program is to accept an on-line order from the customer, update the inventory database file, and print the invoice for the order.

13.2 Accessing Multiple Database Files

All the programs developed so far used only one database file. But most business applications are not that simple and require more than one database file. In fact, the program to be developed as the case study in this chapter requires the use of three database files, which necessitates *accessing multiple database files*.

So far you have opened a database file, performed the necessary processing functions using the dBASE commands, and then opened another database file by issuing the USE command. Issuing the USE command to open a new database file closes the previously open database file; therefore, after opening a new database file, you have only the data of the currently open file available. If you want the data of the first database file available with that of the currently open file, it would not be possible because that file is already closed. This limitation raises the question of how we can have multiple files open at the same time.

13.2.1 Opening Multiple Database Files

dBASE IV allows you to have up to ten database files open at one time by assigning a database file to a separate **work area** using the SELECT command.

The SELECT Command

The general format of the SELECT command is

```
SELECT <work area/alias>
```

where <work area/alias> can be a number from 1 through 10 inclusively or a letter A through J inclusively. It can also be the name of a database file or an alias defined in the USE command.

The SELECT command allows you to open up to ten work areas, select a work area and open a database file in it, or specify a work area in which

Figure 13.1 Structure of the FILE1.DBF database file

```
.DISPLAY STRUCTURE
Structure for database : C:\DBASE\INVOICE\FILE1.DBF
Number of data records :      9
Date of last update    : 1/12/89
Field  Field name  Type        Width  Dec  Index
    1  ITEM_NUM    Character       4        N
    2  ITEM_DESC   Character      26        N
    3  UNIT_COST   Numeric         6    2   N
    4  QUANTITY    Numeric         3        N
** TOTAL **                       40
```

a database file is already open. After you've selected a work area, all the dBASE commands issued will pertain to it. This procedure can be altered by using the prefixes or the aliases, discussed later in this section.

Suppose you want to work with two database files, FILE1.DBF and ORDERS.DBF, simultaneously. Their structures are given in Figures 13.1 and 13.2, respectively.

First, close all the open database files, and release all the memory variables from the computer's memory. To do this, type the following command.

```
. CLEAR ALL     <Return>
```

dBASE will be reset; that is, all the open database files will be closed, and all the memory variables will be deleted from the computer's memory. In dBASE terms, all the memory variables will be released from the computer's memory, and dBASE will respond by displaying the dot prompt.

Now open work area A, and then open the FILE1.DBF database file in this work area. These steps can be performed by typing the following commands:

```
. SELECT A      <Return>
. USE FILE1     <Return>
```

dBASE will respond by displaying the dot prompt. The first command, SELECT A, will open work area A. All the dBASE commands (except the SELECT command) issued after this command will be directed to this work area. But using another SELECT command can change this situation. The second command, USE FILE1, will open the FILE1.DBF database file in work area A already opened by the SELECT command.

Figure 13.2 Structure of the ORDERS.DBF database file

```
.DISPLAY STRUCTURE
Structure for database : C:\DBASE\INVOICE\ORDERS.DBF
Number of data records :      4
Date of last update    : 1/12/89
Field  Field name  Type        Width  Dec  Index
    1  ITEM_NUM    Character       4        Y
    2  ITEM_QTY    Numeric         3        N
** TOTAL **                        8
```

13.2 Accessing Multiple Database Files

Now you can obtain the listing of the FILE1.DBF database file either by pressing the F3 List function key or typing the following command:

```
. LIST        <Return>
. GOTO TOP    <Return>
```

If you type this command, dBASE will respond by displaying the listing shown in Figure 13.3.

Now open work area B, and then open the ORDERS.DBF database file in this work area. This step can be done by typing the following commands:

```
. SELECT B    <Return>
. USE ORDERS  <Return>
```

dBASE will respond by displaying the dot prompt. The first command, SELECT B, will open work area B. All the dBASE commands (except the SELECT command) issued after this command will be directed to this work area, that is, work area B. But using another SELECT command can change this situation. The second command, USE ORDERS, will open the ORDERS.DBF database file in work area B already opened by the SELECT command.

Recall that earlier whenever a new database file was opened by issuing a USE command, it closed the previously open database file. But that was the case when you were working in only one work area. In the previous example, FILE1.DBF was opened in work area A, and the ORDERS.DBF database file was opened in work area B. Issuing the USE command in work area B will not have any effect on the database file in work area A; that is, the previously opened FILE1.DBF database file in work area A will not be closed by the USE ORDERS command issued in work area B to open the ORDERS.DBF database file.

At present, you have two open database files, FILE1.DBF and ORDERS.DBF, in their respective work areas A and B. Although you can have ten different database files open simultaneously in ten different work areas, only one database file can be active at a time. The **active database file** will be the one that belongs to the currently selected work area. Other files will still be open in the background, but they will not be active.

In the previous example, the last SELECT command chose work area B as the active work area; therefore, the ORDERS.DBF database file open

Figure 13.3 Listing of the FILE1.DBF database file

```
. LIST
Record#  ITEM_NUM  ITEM_DESC                 UNIT_COST  QUANTITY
      1  1136      Bond Paper, Ream              22.99        38
      2  1910      Ditto Paper, Ream             19.99        35
      3  4012      King Kong Modem 1200         105.99        10
      4  4045      Monochrome Monitor Z-1105     99.99        15
      5  4072      Panasonic Printer KX-P108    269.99         8
      6  3372      Printer Ribbon 10-Box         35.99        19
      7  3375      Typewriter Ribbons 10-Box     23.79        67
      8  1488      Xerographic Paper             19.99        45
      9  4189      Zenith Microcomputer Z-158   829.99         5
```

Figure 13.4 Listing of the ORDERS.DBF database file

```
. LIST
Record#  ITEM_NUM    ITEM_QTY
      1  1910               4
      2  4072               1
      3  1488               5
      4  3375               2
```

in that area is the only active file at the present time. *All the commands after the SELECT B command will be directed to the database file opened in work area B* unless prefixes or aliases are used. Prefixes and aliases are discussed later in this section.

Now obtain the listing of the ORDERS.DBF database file. Because work area B has been selected and the ORDERS.DBF database file is open in it, you can obtain its listing either by pressing the F3 List function key or by typing the following command:

```
. LIST       <Return>
. GOTO TOP   <Return>
```

If you type this command, dBASE will respond by displaying the listing shown in Figure 13.4.

You can open multiple database files simultaneously, but only one is active at a given time. The active file belongs to the currently selected work area, and all the dBASE commands issued are directed to it. You can eliminate this limitation by using prefixes or aliases.

Use of Prefixes In order to refer to fields of a database file in a work area different from that currently selected, you can add prefixes before the names of the fields. For example, you have the FILE1.DBF database file open in work area A and the ORDERS.DBF database file open in work area B. Because work area B is currently selected, you will need the prefix before the names of the fields of the FILE1.DBF database file open in the unselected work area to display the fields from both database files. The **prefix** can be either the number or the name of the unselected work area or the name or the alias (discussed later in this section) of the database file in the unselected work area. To display the ITEM_NUM field of the ORDERS.DBF database file, the ITEM_DESC and UNIT_COST fields of the FILE1.DBF database file, and the ITEM_QTY field of the ORDERS.DBF database file in one line, type the following command:

```
. DISPLAY ITEM_NUM, A->ITEM_DESC,
  A->UNIT_COST, ITEM_QTY    <Return>
```

dBASE will respond by displaying the information shown in Figure 13.5. The prefix A before the field names ITEM_DESC and UNIT_COST

Figure 13.5 Listing of fields from two database files

```
. DISPLAY ITEM_NUM, A->ITEM_DESC, A->UNIT_COST, ITEM_QTY
Record# ITEM_NUM  A->ITEM_DESC           A->UNIT_COST ITEM_QTY
      1 1910      Bond Paper, Ream              22.99        4
```

indicates that these fields belong to the database file from the unselected work area A. The prefix –> is formed by the combination of the hyphen (–) and the greater than (>) signs.

When you have finished using the database files, close all the open files in all the work areas by typing the following command:

```
. CLOSE DATABASES      <Return>
```

Use of Aliases   The same result as achieved by the use of prefixes can also be achieved by using **aliases.** An alias is an abbreviated name assigned by using the ALIAS option with the USE command when opening the database files.

Once again open these two database files, FILE1 and ORDERS, in work areas A and B, respectively. However, this time use aliases. To do this, type the following commands:

```
. SELECT A                <Return>
. USE FILE1 ALIAS F1      <Return>
. SELECT B                <Return>
. USE ORDERS ALIAS O2     <Return>
```

dBASE will respond by displaying the dot prompt. To obtain the result shown in Figure 13.5 using aliases, you need the DISPLAY command:

```
. DISPLAY ITEM_NUM, F1->ITEM_DESC,
  F1->UNIT_COST, ITEM_QTY    <Return>
```

If you type this command, dBASE will respond by displaying the information as already shown in Figure 13.5.

These two examples of the DISPLAY command demonstrate that you can use either the work area name or the alias as a prefix when working with several database files in different work areas. But if no alias is defined for a file, dBASE automatically assigns the database file name as an alias. Thus, the database file name can also be used as the alias. For example, the following DISPLAY command will have the same effect as that of the previous DISPLAY command:

```
. DISPLAY ITEM_NUM, FILE1->ITEM_DESC,
  FILE1->UNIT_COST, ITEM_QTY    <Return>
```

In other words, the prefix can be the work area name, the name of the database file, or the alias of the database file as defined by the USE command. Thus, these three DISPLAY commands produced the result shown in Figure 13.5:

```
. DISPLAY ITEM_NUM, A->ITEM_DESC, A->UNIT_COST,
  ITEM_QTY    <Return>
. DISPLAY ITEM_NUM, F1->ITEM_DESC, F1->UNIT_COST,
  ITEM_QTY    <Return>
. DISPLAY ITEM_NUM, FILE1->ITEM_DESC,
  FILE1->UNIT_COST, ITEM_QTY    <Return>
```

When the alias is used in the DISPLAY command, it should be defined in the USE command when opening the database file. Use of the prefix or alias to access data from different database files opened in different work areas is allowed only with the DISPLAY command. The use of prefixes or aliases with the dBASE commands used to change the data of the database file, such as the APPEND, EDIT, and BROWSE commands, is not allowed. That is, you cannot change the contents of a database file in an unselected work area by a command issued from the currently selected work area.

To review briefly, the SELECT command, which allows us to open up to ten work areas, helps open multiple database files by assigning each to a separate work area. Use of the prefix or alias helps access data from multiple database files. They can combine data from different database files by use of the DISPLAY command. The result of the DISPLAY command is given in Figure 13.5.

A comparison of Figures 13.5 and 13.3 reveals that the listing of the data in Figure 13.5 is not correct. It shows item number 1910 as "Bond Paper, Ream." The listing of the FILE1 database file indicates that item number 1910 is "Ditto Paper, Ream," which is the description for the record with item number 1136, the first record in the FILE1 database file. The same problem exists with the unit price value in the result of the DISPLAY command as shown in Figure 13.5. Why are these two values inconsistent?

To answer this question, trace the commands used to achieve the result shown in Figure 13.5. The sequence of the commands used to access the data from the two database files, FILE1.DBF and ORDERS.DBF, is as follows:

```
. SELECT A        <Return>
. USE FILE1       <Return>
. SELECT B        <Return>
. USE ORDERS      <Return>
. DISPLAY ITEM_NUM, A->ITEM_DESC,
A->UNIT_COST, ITEM_QTY    <Return>
```

The first command opened work area A. The second opened the FILE1.DBF database file in work area A. When a database file is opened, the record pointer points to the first record in it. This is called the **active data record** of the FILE1.DBF database file. The third command opened work area B. The fourth command opened the ORDERS.DBF database file in work area B. The first record is the active data record of the ORDERS.DBF database file. The DISPLAY command displayed the ITEM_NUM field of the active data record of the ORDERS.DBF database file, which is 1910. The second field in the DISPLAY command is the ITEM_DESC field of the active data record of the FILE1.DBF database file, which is "Bond Paper, Ream"; and this is the description for item number 1136, which is the first record of the FILE1 database file. The same problem exists for the UNIT_COST field.

To get the right description and correct the unit cost value, we need the description and the UNIT_COST field values for the record whose item number is 1910, which is the active data record of the ORDERS.DBF database file. We need first to find the matching record in the FILE1.DBF database file and then to pick up the values of the ITEM_DESC and UNIT_COST fields of the matching record. The solution to this problem is discussed in the next section.

13.2.2 Defining the Relationship Among Database Files

When two or more database files contain a common field, you can use the SET RELATION TO command to define the relationship between them. After defining the relationship, you can obtain the data from the different files belonging to the common field by using the DISPLAY command. For example, the two database files of FILE1.DBF and ORDERS.DBF used in the previous section contained the common field ITEM_NUM. If we had defined the relationship between these two files using the ITEM_NUM field and had used the DISPLAY command as in the previous section, we would not have had the inconsistent data shown in Figure 13.5.

The SET RELATION TO Command

The general format of the SET RELATION TO command is

```
SET RELATION TO <key field name>
            INTO <file name/alias>
```

where <key field name> is the name of the key field common to both files, and <file name/alias> is the name, or the alias name, of the database file being linked.

The SET RELATION TO command is used to define the relationship between two database files using the common field. Both database files should be open to define the relationship. The link should be defined from the active database file to the database file in the unselected work area. The database file in the unselected work area should be indexed on the common field, and the index must be active.

To explain the concept of a relationship between the two database files, let us once again consider the FILE1.DBF and the ORDERS.DBF database files used in the previous section.

As before, open work area A, and then open the FILE1.DBF database file in it. Also activate the index tag of the ITEM_NUM field. These steps can be accomplished by typing the following commands:

```
. SELECT A                    <Return>
. USE FILE1                   <Return>
. SET ORDER TO ITEM_NUM       <Return>
```

dBASE will respond by displaying the dot prompt. The first command, SELECT A, will open work area A. The second command, USE FILE1, will open the FILE1.DBF database file in work area A already opened by the SELECT command. The third command will activate the ITEM_NUM index tag.

Now open work area B, and then open the ORDERS.DBF database file in it and set relation to database file FILE1.DBF using the ITEM_NUM field. This step can be done by typing the following commands:

```
. SELECT B                                      <Return>
. USE ORDERS                                    <Return>
. SET RELATION TO ITEM_NUM INTO FILE1           <Return>
```

dBASE will respond by displaying the dot prompt. The first command, SELECT B, will open work area B. The second command, USE ORDERS,

Figure 13.6 Listing of fields from two database files with the relation set between them

```
. DISPLAY ITEM_NUM, A->ITEM_DESC, A->UNIT_COST, ITEM_QTY
Record# ITEM_NUM  A->ITEM_DESC           A->UNIT_COST ITEM_QTY
      1 1910      Ditto Paper, Ream            19.99        4
```

will open the ORDERS.DBF database file in work area B already opened by the SELECT command.

You now have two open database files: the FILE1.DBF database file with the index set to the ITEM_NUM field and the ORDERS.DBF database file in work area A and B, respectively. The ORDERS.DBF database file is the active file. Now to display the ITEM_NUM field of the ORDERS.DBF database file, the ITEM_DESC and UNIT_COST fields of the *corresponding* record of the FILE1.DBF database file, and the ITEM_QTY field of the ORDERS.DBF database file in one line, type the following command:

```
. DISPLAY ITEM_NUM, A->ITEM_DESC,
  A->UNIT_COST, ITEM_QTY    <Return>
```

dBASE will respond by displaying the information as shown in Figure 13.6.

Comparing Figures 13.5 and 13.6 indicates that the results are different. Comparing Figures 13.6 and 13.3 reveals that the listings in the figures represent the correct item description and the unit cost for item number 1910. In others words, the SET RELATION TO command helped find the corresponding record in the FILE1 database file whose ITEM_NUM field matched the ITEM_NUM field of the active data record of the ORDERS.DBF database file. This command supplied the ITEM_DESC field and the UNIT_COST field of the corresponding record from the FILE1.DBF database file to the DISPLAY command. Thus, it provided the correct information for the order for item number 1910.

13.3 An Illustrative Example: Case Study 10

Program Description

Write an invoice generating subsystem program. It should be invoked by the main menu program INV.PRG of the invoice generating system for the American Supply Company. The program should be able to accept customer orders by telephone or in person and verify the information by checking the inventory database file INV.DBF for the items in stock. The items ordered should be reduced from the inventory database file. When the order is complete, program control should be transferred to the INV41.PRG file to print the invoices. After printing the invoice, return the control to this program.

Processing Steps

The following steps should be used to develop the solution of the program:

1. The program should start by displaying the customer information screen of the order receiving system as shown in Figure 13.7. The screen should consist of the company's name, address, the next order number, and the order date.

Figure 13.7 Customer information screen for the order receiving system program

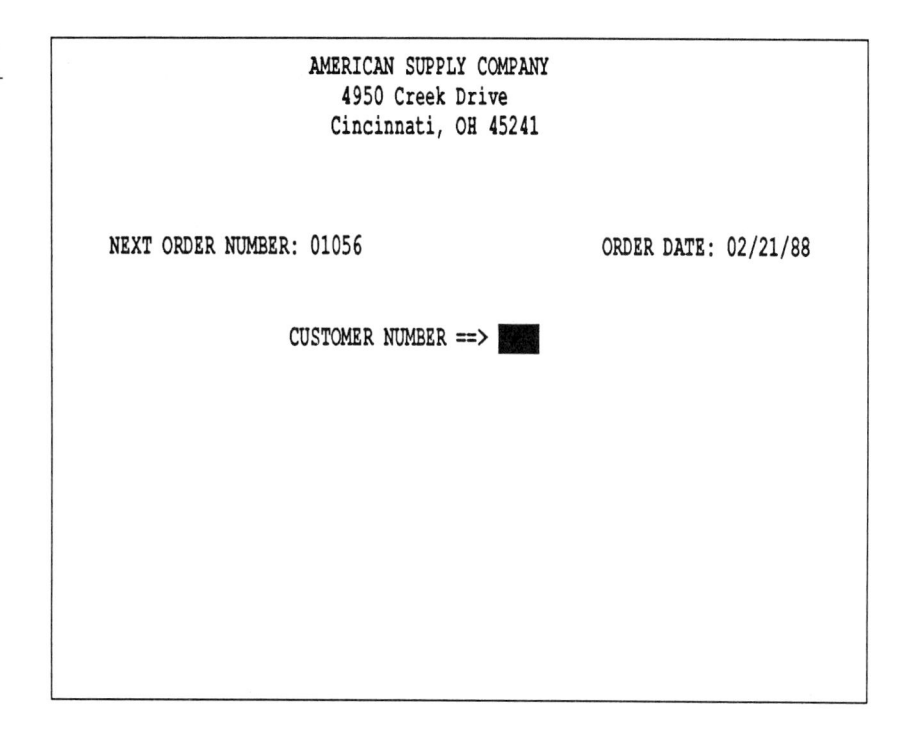

```
                    AMERICAN SUPPLY COMPANY
                         4950 Creek Drive
                       Cincinnati, OH 45241



    NEXT ORDER NUMBER: 01056                    ORDER DATE: 02/21/88


                    CUSTOMER NUMBER ==>  ▆
```

2. The next order number should be loaded from the memory variable NEXT_ORDN saved in the INV4.MEM file. Whenever this program is executed, the value of the next order number should be loaded into it. Its value should be increased by one for every order processed, and the updated value should be used for the next order.
3. At the termination of the program, the value of the NEXT_ORDN field should be saved in the INV4.MEM file.
4. The order date should be obtained from the computer clock.
5. The customer information screen should display the message for requesting the customer number. When the customer number is supplied, the program will search the CUSTOMER.DBF database file to find the match. The program assumes that the match will exist.
6. After the match is obtained, the rest of the customer information from the CUSTOMER.DBF database file should be displayed on the screen, as shown in Figure 13.8.
7. After the customer information is verified with the customer, the program should display the order receiving screen, as shown in Figure 13.9.
8. The order for each item ordered will be shown on the screen. The item number should be requested and entered. After the item number is received, the quantity ordered for the item number should be requested and entered.
9. When these values have been entered, the program should search the INV.DBF database file for the matching item number. Again, we assume the match will be found.

Figure 13.8 Customer information screen displaying the complete information for a customer

```
                    AMERICAN SUPPLY COMPANY
                        4950 Creek Drive
                      Cincinnati, OH 45241



      NEXT ORDER NUMBER: 01056              ORDER DATE: 02/21/88


                   CUSTOMER NUMBER ==>  ▓▓▓


                   Marguerite A. Samuelson
                   4550 My Farm Land
                   Cincinnati, OH 45236
                   513-793-6420




                   PRESS ANY KEY TO CONTINUE ===>:▓
```

10. When the match is found, the corresponding item description, its list price, and the net price (obtained by multiplying the quantity ordered by the list price) should be displayed on the screen, as shown in Figure 13.10.

11. If the quantity of an item ordered by the customer is not available, the program should indicate this by displaying the "ONLY n ITEMS AVAILABLE" message in the description field of the order receiving screen, as shown in Figure 13.10.

Figure 13.9 Order receiving screen

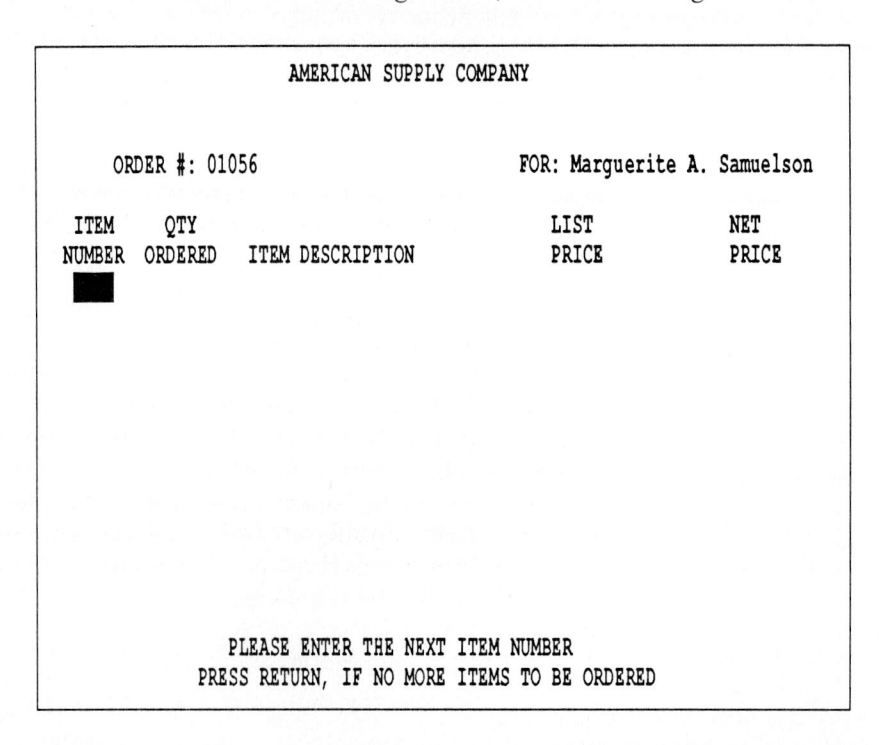

```
                      AMERICAN SUPPLY COMPANY


       ORDER #: 01056                  FOR: Marguerite A. Samuelson

       ITEM    QTY                             LIST         NET
       NUMBER  ORDERED   ITEM DESCRIPTION      PRICE        PRICE
       ▓▓






                   PLEASE ENTER THE NEXT ITEM NUMBER
                PRESS RETURN, IF NO MORE ITEMS TO BE ORDERED
```

Figure 13.10 Order receiving screen with the message that the number of items ordered is not in stock

```
              AMERICAN SUPPLY COMPANY

   ORDER #: 01056                    FOR: Marguerite A. Samuelson

   ITEM    QTY                              LIST         NET
   NUMBER  ORDERED  ITEM DESCRIPTION        PRICE        PRICE
   5130    1        Letter Opener           2.17         2.17
   4012    1        King Kong Modem 1200    148.39       148.39
   4189    10       ONLY n ITEMS AVAILABLE




              ORDER AS MANY AVAILABLE OR CANCEL THIS ITEM'S ORDER
              PRESS ANY KEY, OR PRESS "C" TO CANCEL THIS ITEM ===>
```

12. A message permitting the choice to either cancel the order for the item in question or to process the order for as many items as are available in stock should be displayed at the bottom of the screen. This message is also shown in Figure 13.10.

13. The process of requesting the item number and the quantity needed should continue until the end of the order, which should be indicated by a blank item number.

14. At this point, control of the program should be transferred to the program INV41.PRG, where the invoices will be printed.

The five phases of the program development process for Case Study 10 follow.

13.3.1 The Analysis Phase

In the analysis phase, the first step in the program development process, review and analysis of program specifications lead to the identification of the processing steps needed to solve the problem. First, a step is needed to declare public variables. A set of instructions will be needed to accept orders from customers, and these steps should be repeated for each order received. As such, a control switch needs to be defined to control this loop. We will also need to define the memory variables for the item number field and the quantity ordered by the customer. Of course, the customer database file, the inventory database file, and the order database file should be opened. These two steps are the only ones needed in the initiate processing function of the solution of the problem.

The processing steps needed in the main processing function should include:

1. Accept the customer number.
2. Test for a blank customer number.

3. Process the blank customer number, that is, change the loop control switch to indicate termination of the loop, and proceed to step 7.
4. Process the nonblank customer number, that is, search for a matching record in the CUSTOMER.DBF database file.
5. Process match found:
   a. Display the matching record; that is, display the customer name, address, etc., and confirm their validity with the customer.
   b. Display the order receiving screen.
   c. Process the order subroutine, and proceed to step 7.
6. Process no match found.
7. Freeze the screen and blank customer number.

These seven steps should be repeated for each customer order. The program should be terminated at the end of the day by the user supplying a blank value to the customer number in step 1. At that point, the control should move to the terminate processing function.

In the terminate processing function, all the database files should be closed, and program control should be transferred to the calling program.

To sum up, the following processing steps will be needed for the solution of Case Study 10:

1. Define the variables.
2. Open the database files.
3. Accept the customer number.
4. Test for a blank customer number.
5. Process the blank customer number; that is, change the loop control switch to indicate termination of the loop, and proceed to step 9.
6. Process the nonblank customer number; that is, search for a matching record in the CUSTOMER.DBF database file.
7. Process match found:
   a. Display the matching record; that is, display the customer name, address, etc., and confirm their validity with the customer.
   b. Display the order receiving screen.
   c. Process the order subroutine, and proceed to step 9.
8. Process no match found.
9. Freeze the screen and blank customer number.
10. Close the database files.
11. Return to the calling program.

The first two steps should be performed only once, at the start of the program. Therefore, these belong to initiate processing. The next seven steps should be performed for each customer order until the end of the day, when you want to terminate the processing of the program. Do so by supplying a blank value for the customer number. Therefore, these steps

13.3 An Illustrative Example: Case Study 10   **513**

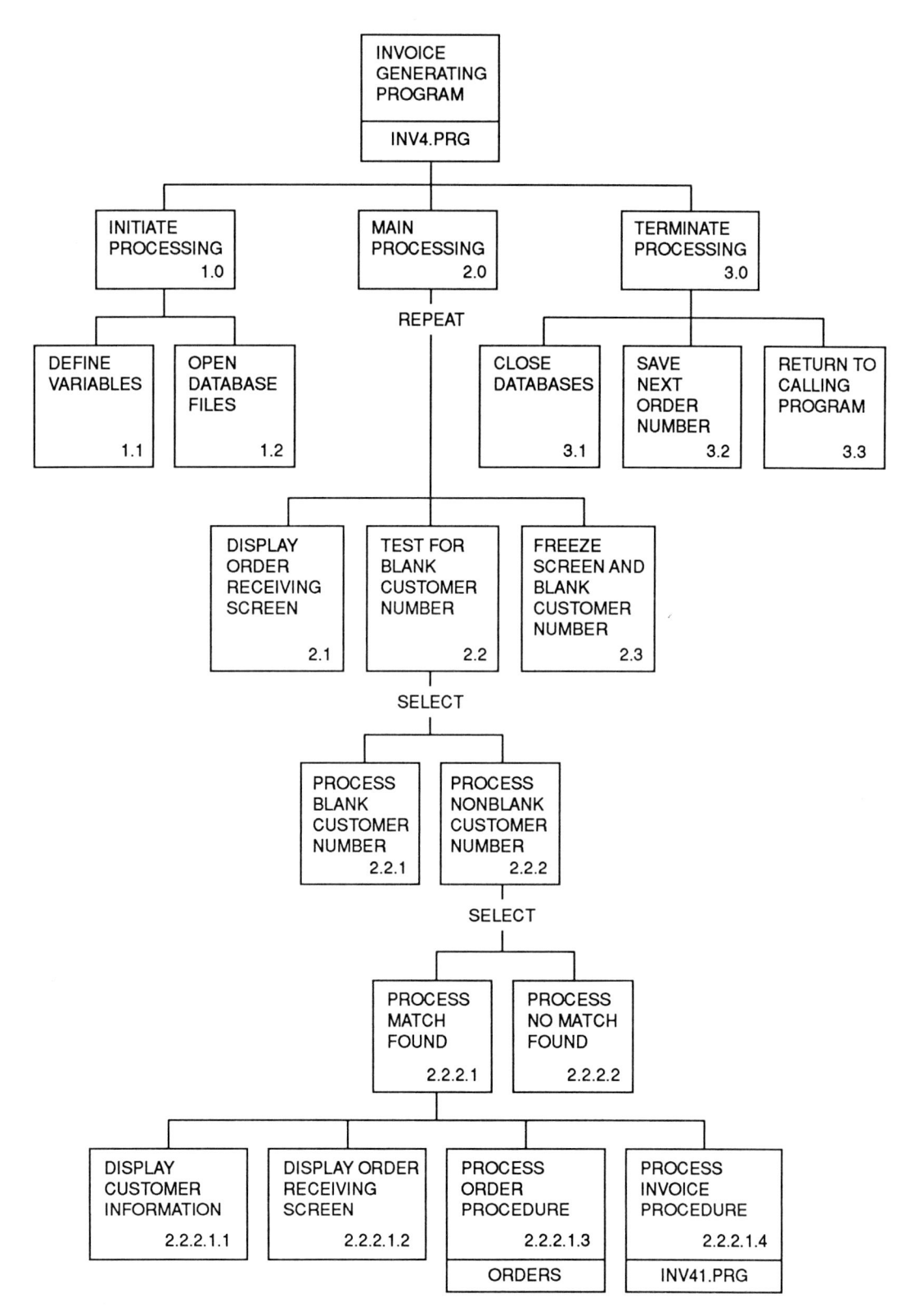

Figure 13.11 Structure chart for Case Study 10

belong to main processing. The last two steps need to be performed only once, before terminating the execution of the program. Therefore, these belong to terminate processing.

13.3.2 The Design Phase

The function of this step is to take the result of the problem analysis, that is, the processing steps identified in the analysis phase, and transform them into a structure chart. Using the shell structure chart of Figure 10.12 and the tools and techniques discussed in section 4.4.2, transform the 11 steps identified in the analysis phase into a structure chart for Case Study 10, as shown in Figure 13.11 (see page 513).

All the modules in this structure chart are either functionally or highly cohesive. They are also loosely coupled. Thus, the structure chart of Figure 13.11 satisfies the three rules for designing a good structure chart; that is, it consists of highly cohesive, loosely coupled modules none of which has a span of control of more than four. Therefore, this chart is a well-designed solution to Case Study 10.

13.3.3 The Detailed Design Phase

The function of this step is to take the result of the design phase, that is, the structure chart, and identify the actual computer operations required for each program function represented in it, thereby producing the detailed solution of the problem. Using the translation of the three control structures to pseudocode as given in Figure 4.14 and the method described in section 4.4.3, we arrive at the structure chart of Figure 13.11 as translated to pseudocode shown in Figure 13.12.

```
0.0 INVOICE GENERATING SYSTEM
   1.0 HOUSEKEEPING
      1.1 DEFINE VARIABLES
         DECLARE PUBLIC VARIABLES
            Declare NEXT_ORDN, BLANKLINE Public Variable
         DEFINE CONTROL VARIABLES
            Set REPEAT4 switch = T
         INITIALIZE VARIABLES
            Set CUSTNUM to BLANK
            Set ITEMNUM to BLANK
            Set QTY = 0
            Set BLANKLINE to BLANK
         LOAD NEXT ORDER NUMBER
            Load next order number from the INV4.MEM file
      1.2 OPEN DATABASE FILES
         Open CUSTOMER file in work area A
         Set Index to CUST_NUM
         Open INV file in work area B
         Set Index to ITEM_NUM
         Open ORDERS file in work area C
   2.0 MAIN PROCESSING
      REPEAT: While the REPEAT4 switch = T
      2.1 DISPLAY ORDER RECEIVING SCREEN
         CLEAR SCREEN
            Clear the screen
```

Figure 13.12 Pseudocode for Case Study 10

```
        REQUEST AND ACCEPT CUSTOMER NUMBER
            Display Heading #1
            Display Heading #2
            Display Heading #3
            Display Order number and Order date
            Display Prompt
            Request and accept customer number
    2.2 TEST FOR BLANK CUSTOMER NUMBER
        SELECT: if customer number is blank
            2.2.1 PROCESS BLANK CUSTOMER NUMBER
                Reset switch REPEAT4 = F
            2.2.2 PROCESS NONBLANK CUSTOMER NUMBER
                Find matching record in CUSTOMER.DBF database file
                SELECT: if match found
                    2.2.2.1 PROCESS MATCH FOUND
                        2.2.2.1.1 DISPLAY CUSTOMER INFORMATION
                            Display customer name
                            Display customer address
                            Display customer city, state, and zip
                            Display customer telephone
                            FREEZE SCREEN
                                Freeze screen
                        2.2.2.1.2 DISPLAY ORDER RECEIVING SCREEN
                            CLEAR SCREEN
                                Clear Screen
                            DISPLAY ORDER SCREEN
                                Display Heading
                                Display order number and Customer name
                                Display column heading 1
                                Display column heading 2
                                Set LINECNT = 10
                        2.2.2.1.3 PROCESS ORDERS PROCEDURE
                            Process ORDERS procedure
                        2.2.2.1.4 PROCESS INVOICE PROCEDURE
                            Process Invoice procedure INV41.PRG
                    2.2.2.2 PROCESS NO MATCH FOUND
                        Display message 'CUSTOMER NOT FOUND'
            END SELECT
    2.3 FREEZE SCREEN & BLANK CUSTOMER NUMBER
        FREEZE SCREEN
            Freeze screen
        INITIALIZE CUSTOMER NUMBER
            Set CUSTNUM to BLANK
    END REPEAT
3.0 TERMINATE PROCESSING
    3.1 CLOSE DATABASE FILE
        Close the database files
    3.2 SAVE NEXT ORDER NUMBER
        Save next order number to INV4.MEM file
    3.3 RETURN TO CALLING PROGRAM
        Return to calling program
```

Figure 13.12 Continued

13.3.4 The Coding Phase

The purpose of this phase in the program development process is to translate the pseudocode instructions for the solution of the program into programming language instructions. The pseudocode of Figure 13.12 is translated into dBASE commands, and the complete program for Case Study 10 in dBASE language is given in Figure 13.13.

```
****************************************************************
*                         INV4.PRG                              *
*                  AMERICAN SUPPLY COMPANY                      *
*                  INVOICE GENERATING SYSTEM                    *
*                  INVOICE GENERATING PROGRAM                   *
* ------------------------------------------------------------- *
* This is an Invoice Generating Subsystem program which is      *
* invoked by the Main Menu program INV.PRG of the Invoice       *
* Generating System for American Supply Company. The            *
* function of this program is to accept orders from the         *
* customer, verify the information by checking the              *
* inventory database file INV.DBF for the items in stock.       *
* The items ordered should be reduced from the inventory        *
* database file. When the order is complete, program            *
* control should be transferred to the INV41.PRG program        *
* to print the invoice. After printing the invoice the          *
* control should be returned to this program.                   *
* ------------------------------------------------------------- *
*             COPYRIGHT (C) . . . SUDESH M. DUGGAL              *
****************************************************************
*
***************************
* 1.0 INITIATE PROCESSING *
***************************
*
*** 1.1 DEFINE VARIABLES ***
   *
   *** DECLARE PUBLIC VARIABLES ***
      *
      PUBLIC NEXT_ORDN, BLANKLINE
      *
   *** DEFINE CONTROL VARIABLES ***
      *
      STORE [T] TO REPEAT4
      *
   *** INITIALIZE VARIABLES ***
      *
      STORE SPACE(6) TO CUSTNUM
      STORE SPACE(4) TO ITEMNUM
      STORE 0 TO QTY
      STORE SPACE(60) TO BLANKLINE
      *
   *** LOAD NEXT ORDER NUMBER ***
      *
      RESTORE FROM INV4 ADDITIVE
      *
```

Figure 13.13 Coding for Case Study 10

13.3 An Illustrative Example: Case Study 10

```
*** 1.2 OPEN DATABASE FILES ***
    *
    SELECT A
    USE CUSTOMER
    SET ORDER TO CUST_NUM
    SELECT B
    USE INV
    SET ORDER TO ITEM_NUM
    SELECT C
    USE ORDERS
*
***********************
* 2.0 MAIN PROCESSING *
***********************
*
DO WHILE REPEAT4 = 'T'
    *
    *** 2.1 DISPLAY ORDER RECEIVING SCREEN ***
        *
        *** CLEAR SCREEN ***
            *
            CLEAR
            *
        *** REQUEST AND ACCEPT CUSTOMER NUMBER ***
            *
            @  1,2  TO  24,79 DOUBLE
            @  2,25 SAY ' AMERICAN SUPPLY COMPANY'
            @  3,25 SAY '     4950 Creek Drive'
            @  4,25 SAY '  Cincinnati, OH 45241'
            @  7,5  SAY 'NEXT ORDER NUMBER:'
            @  7,24 SAY ORDNUM
            @  7,57 SAY 'ORDER DATE:'
            @  7,69 SAY DATE ()
            @ 10,25 SAY 'CUSTOMER NUMBER ==>'
            @ 10,45 GET CUSTNUM
            READ
            *
    *** 2.2 TEST FOR BLANK CUSTOMER NUMBER ***
        *
        IF CUSTNUM = '    '
            *
            *** 2.2.1 PROCESS BLANK CUSTOMER NUMBER ***
                *
                STORE [F] TO REPEAT4
                *
        ELSE
            *
            *** 2.2.2 PROCESS NONBLANK CUSTOMER NUMBER ***
                *
                SELECT A
                FIND &CUSTNUM
                *
                IF .NOT. (EOF () .OR. BOF())
                    *
                    *** 2.2.2.1 PROCESS MATCH FOUND ***
                        *
```

Figure 13.13 Continued

```
              *** 2.2.2.1.1 DISPLAY CUSTOMER INFORMATION ***
                 *
                 @ 12,25 SAY CUST_NAME
                 @ 13,25 SAY CUST_ADDR
                 @ 14,25 SAY TRIM(CUST_CITY)+',
                 '+CUST_STATE+' '+CUST_ZIP
                 @ 15,25 SAY CUST_PHONE
                 *
                 *** FREEZE SCREEN ***
                    *
                    DO FREEZE
                    *
              *** 2.2.2.1.2 DISPLAY ORDER RECEIVING SCREEN ***
                 *
                 *** CLEAR SCREEN ***
                    *
                    CLEAR
                    *
                 *** DISPLAY ORDER SCREEN ***
                    *
                    @ 1,2  TO  24,79 DOUBLE
                    @ 3,12 SAY '             AMERICAN SUPPLY COMPANY'
                    @ 5,12 SAY 'ORDER #:'
                    @ 5,21 SAY ORDNUM
                    @ 5,45 SAY 'FOR :'
                    @ 5,50 SAY CUST_NAME
                    @ 7,6  SAY 'ITEM'
                    @ 7,15 SAY 'QTY'
                    @ 7,54 SAY 'LIST'
                    @ 7,66 SAY 'NET'
                    @ 8,5  SAY 'NUMBER'
                    @ 8,13 SAY 'ORDERED'
                    @ 8,27 SAY 'ITEM DESCRIPTION'
                    @ 8,54 SAY 'PRICE'
                    @ 8,65 SAY 'PRICE'
                    *
                 *** INITIALIZE LINE COUNTER ***
                    *
                    STORE 10 TO LINECNT
                    *
              *** 2.2.2.1.3 PROCESS ORDER PROCEDURE ***
                 *
                 DO ORDERS
                 *
              *** 2.2.2.1.4 PROCESS INVOICE PROCEDURE ***
                 *
                 DO INV41
                 *
        ELSE
           *
           *
           *** 2.2.2.2 PROCESS NO MATCH FOUND ***
              *
              @ 12,25 SAY '**** CUSTOMER NOT FOUND ****'
              *
```

Figure 13.13 Continued

```
                    ENDIF .NOT. (EOF () .OR. BOF ())
                 *
            ENDIF CUSTNUM = '      '
         *
    *** 2.3 FREEZE SCREEN & BLANK CUSTOMER NUMBER ***
         *
         *** FREEZE SCREEN ***
             *
             DO FREEZE
             *
         *** INITIALIZE CUSTOMER NUMBER ***
             *
             STORE SPACE(6) TO CUSTNUM
             *
ENDDO  REPEAT4 = 'T'
*
***************************
* 3.0 TERMINATE PROCESSING *
***************************
*
*** 3.1 CLOSE DATABASES ***
    *
    CLOSE DATABASES
    *
*** 3.2 SAVE NEXT ORDER NUMBER ***
    *
    SAVE ALL LIKE NEXT_ORDN TO INV4
    *
*** 3.3 RETURN TO CALLING PROGRAM ***
    *
    RETURN
```

Figure 13.13 Continued

13.3.5 The Testing and Debugging Phase

The last step in program development is the testing and debugging phase, in which the source program is executed and tested for the accuracy of its logic. Execute the program to complete this step, correct the syntactical errors, if any, and execute the program again. Repeat this process until the program is free of syntactical errors. When the output is produced by the program, verify some of the records of the output to ensure its accuracy. If any discrepancies exist, make the needed corrections, and execute the program again. Repeat the process of making corrections and executing the program until the program produces correct and predictable results.

13.4 Orders Procedure for Case Study 10

The ORDERS procedure is a part of Case Study 10. It is an internal procedure, and its function is to accept orders from the customer for each item ordered and verify from the inventory database file whether the quantity ordered is available or not. If it is, the order will be processed; otherwise, the customer will be given the choice to order as many items as are available in stock or cancel the order for that item. The process of accepting the order for each item will continue until no more items are to be ordered. This decision is indicated by returning a blank value for the item number.

Because this procedure is by itself a program, the five phases of the program development process will be applied for its development.

13.4.1 The Analysis Phase

In the analysis phase, the first step in the program development process, review and analysis of program specifications lead to the identification of the processing steps needed to solve the problem. Because each order will consist of several items, a set of steps will be needed to accept an order for each item. In addition, these steps should be repeated for each item of the order; therefore, a control switch needs to be defined to control this loop. This step is the only one needed in the initiate processing function of the solution of the orders procedure.

The processing steps needed in the main processing function should include:

1. Accept the item number.
2. Test for a blank item number.
3. Process the blank item number; that is, change the loop control switch to indicate termination of the loop, and proceed to step 9.
4. Process the nonblank item number.
5. Accept the quantity ordered.
6. Test for quantity available; that is, select the inventory database file, and search for a matching record.
7. Process the quantity available:
   a. Print a line for item ordered.
   b. Select the ORDER.DBF database file.
   c. Add a record to the ORDER.DBF database file.
8. Process the quantity not available:
   a. Print a message indicating how many items are in stock.
   b. Accept the customer choice either to cancel this item from the order or to order as many items as are available, depending on the response process in steps 8c and 8d.
   c. Process the cancel for this item.
   d. Process the order for as many items as are available.
9. Freeze the screen and blank item number.

These nine steps should be repeated for each item ordered. The procedure should be terminated by supplying a blank value to the item number in step 1. At that point, the control should move to the terminate processing function.

In the terminate processing function, the program control should be transferred to the calling program.

To sum up, the following processing steps will be needed for the solution of Case Study 10:

1. Define the variables.
2. Accept the item number.

13.4 Orders Procedure for Case Study 10

3. Test for a blank item number.
4. Process the blank item number; that is, change the loop control switch to indicate termination of the loop, and proceed to step 10.
5. Process the nonblank item number.
6. Accept the quantity ordered.
7. Test for the quantity available; that is, select the inventory database file, and search for a matching record.
8. Process the quantity available:
   a. Print a line for the item ordered.
   b. Select the ORDER.DBF database file.
   c. Add a record to the ORDER.DBF database file.
9. Process the quantity not available:
   a. Print a message indicating how many items are in stock.
   b. Accept the customer choice either to cancel this item from the order or to order as many items as are available, depending on the response process in steps 9c and 9d.
   c. Process the cancel for this item.
   d. Process the order for as many items as are available.
10. Freeze the screen and blank item number.
11. Return to the calling program.

The first step should be performed only once, at the start of the program. Therefore, it belongs to initiate processing. The next nine steps should be performed for each item ordered until a blank value for the item number is supplied. At that point, control of the subroutine should be transferred to terminate processing. Therefore, these steps belong to main processing. The last step needs to be performed only once, before terminating the execution of the subroutine. Therefore, this step belongs to the terminate processing.

13.4.2 The Design Phase

The function of this step is to take the result of the problem analysis, that is, the processing steps identified in the analysis phase, and transform them into a structure chart. Using the shell structure chart of Figure 10.12 and the tools and techniques discussed in section 4.4.2, transform the 11 steps identified in the analysis phase into a structure chart for the order subroutine as shown in Figure 13.14.

All the modules in this structure chart are either functionally or highly cohesive. They are also loosely coupled. Thus, the structure chart of Figure 13.14 satisfies the three rules for designing a good structure chart; that is, it consists of highly cohesive, loosely coupled modules with the span of control of any module no more than three. Therefore, it is a well-designed solution for the orders procedure.

13.4.3 The Detailed Design Phase

The function of this step is to take the result of the design phase, that is, the structure chart, and identify the actual computer operations required for each program function represented in it, thereby producing the detailed solution of the problem. If we use the translation of the three control structures to pseudocode as given in Figure 4.14 and the method described

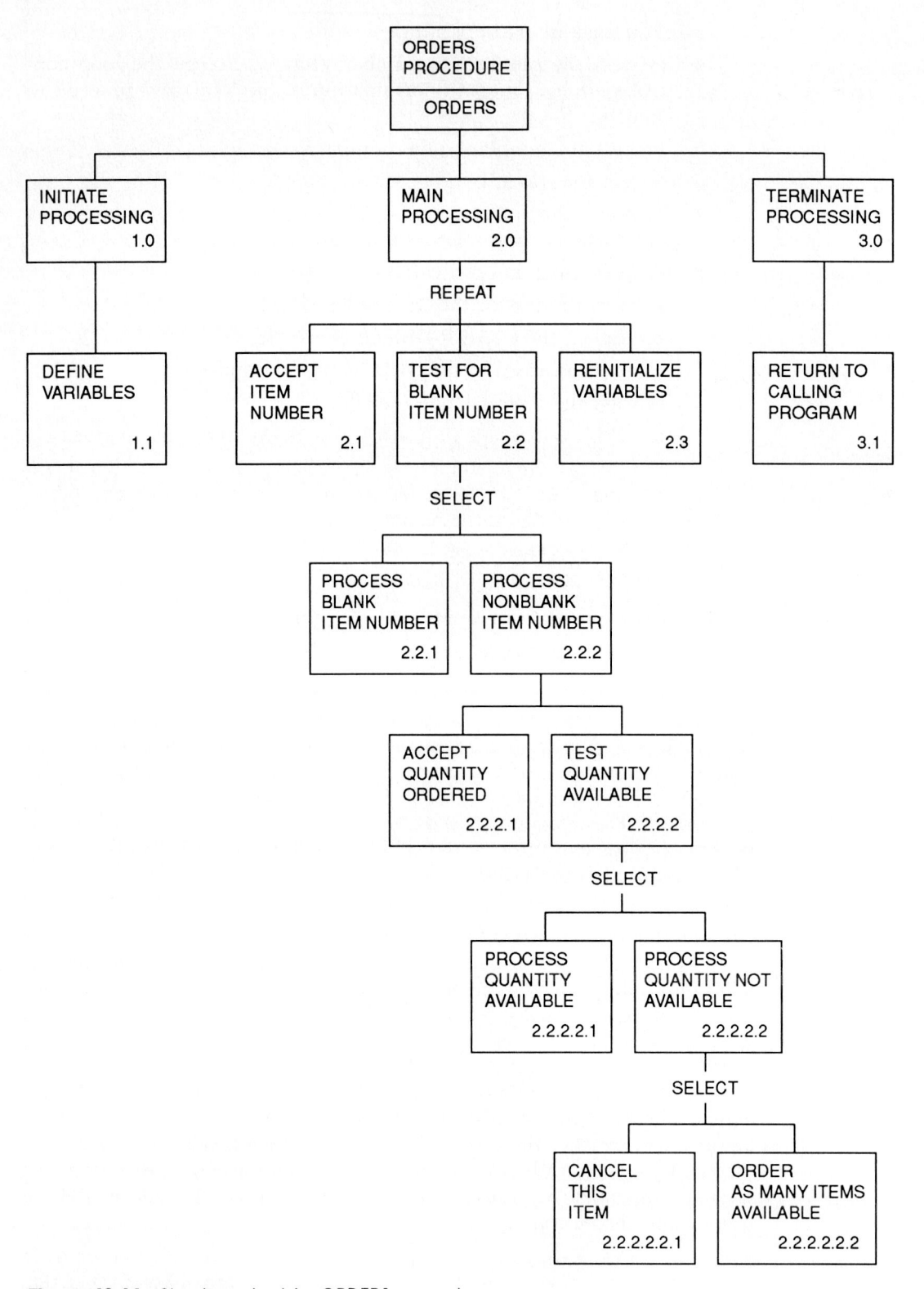

Figure 13.14 Structure chart for ORDERS procedure

in section 4.4.3, the structure chart of Figure 13.14 is translated to pseudocode as given in Figure 13.15.

13.4.4 The Coding Phase

The purpose of this phase in the program development process is to translate the pseudocode instructions of the solution of the subroutine into programming language instructions. The pseudocode of Figure 13.15 is

```
0.0 ORDERS PROCEDURE
    1.0 INITIATE PROCESSING
        1.1 DEFINE VARIABLES
            DEFINE CONTROL VARIABLES
                Set GOBACK = T
    2.0 MAIN PROCESSING
        REPEAT: While the GOBACK switch = T
            2.1 ACCEPT ITEM NUMBER
                Request and accept item number
            2.2 TEST FOR BLANK ITEM NUMBER
                SELECT: On item number
                    2.2.1 PROCESS BLANK ITEM NUMBER
                        Set GOBACK = F
                    2.2.2 PROCESS NONBLANK ITEM NUMBER
                        2.2.2.1 ACCEPT QUANTITY ORDERED
                            Accept quantity ordered
                        2.2.2.2 TEST QUANTITY AVAILABLE
                            Select INV database file
                            Find matching record
                            SELECT: On quantity available
                                2.2.2.2.1 PROCESS QUANTITY AVAILABLE
                                    Print a line for item
                                    Subtract quantity ordered
                                            from quantity in stock
                                    Select ORDERS database file
                                    Add a record to ORDERS file
                                2.2.2.2.2 PROCESS QUANTITY NOT AVAILABLE
                                    Print message "ONLY n ITEMS AVAILABLE"
                                    Accept "cancel" or "order as many available"
                                    SELECT: On response
                                        2.2.2.2.2.1 CANCEL THIS ITEM
                                            Subtract 1 from LINECNT
                                        2.2.2.2.2.2 ORDER AS MANY AVAILABLE
                                            Print a line for item
                                            Subtract quantity ordered
                                                    from quantity in stock
                                            Select ORDERS database file
                                            Add a record to ORDERS file
                                    END SELECT
                END SELECT
                Increment LINECNT by 1
```

Figure 13.15 Pseudocode for the ORDERS procedure

```
        END SELECT
    2.3 REINITIALIZE ITEM NUMBER
        Reinitialize item number and QTY
        Increment NEXT_ORDN by 1
    END REPEAT
3.0 TERMINATE PROCESSING
    3.1 RETURN TO CALLING PROGRAM
        Return to calling program
```

Figure 13.15 Continued

translated into dBASE commands, and the complete program for the orders procedure in dBASE language is given in Figure 13.16.

13.4.5 The Testing and Debugging Phase

The last step in program development is the testing and debugging phase, in which the source program is executed and tested for the accuracy of its logic. Execute the program to complete this step, correct the syntactical errors, if any, and execute the program again. Repeat this process until the program is free of syntactical errors. When the output is produced by the program, verify some of the records of the output to ensure its accuracy. If any discrepancies exist, make the needed corrections, and execute the program again. Repeat the process of making corrections and executing the program until the program produces correct and predictable results.

```
****************************************************************
*                      ORDERS PROCEDURE                         *
*                   AMERICAN SUPPLY COMPANY                     *
*                  INVOICE GENERATING PROGRAM                   *
*---------------------------------------------------------------*
* This is an internal procedure which is invoked by the         *
* Invoice Generating Subsystem program INV4.PRG of the          *
* Invoice Generating System for American Supply Company.        *
* The function of this program is to accept orders from         *
* the customer, verify the information from the INV.DBF         *
* database file for each item ordered. After the                *
* verification, item description, its list price, and the       *
* net price (obtained by multiplying the quantity ordered       *
* by the list price) is displayed on the screen. At the         *
* end of the order the control is returned to the INV4.PRG      *
* program.                                                      *
*---------------------------------------------------------------*
*           COPYRIGHT (C) . . . SUDESH M. DUGGAL                *
****************************************************************
*
PROCEDURE ORDERS
*
***************************████
* 1.0 INITIATE PROCESSING *
***************************████
*
```

Figure 13.16 Coding for the ORDERS procedure

```
   *** 1.1 DEFINE VARIABLES ***
      *
      *** DEFINE CONTROL VARIABLES ***
         *
         STORE [T] TO GOBACK
         *
***********************
* 2.0 MAIN PROCESSING *
***********************
*
DO WHILE GOBACK = 'T'
   *
   *** 2.1 ACCEPT ITEM NUMBER ***
      *
      @ LINECNT,6 GET ITEMNUM
      @ 22,15 SAY '   PLEASE ENTER THE NEXT ITEM NUMBER'
      @ 23,15 SAY 'PRESS RETURN, IF NO MORE ITEMS TO BE ORDERED'
      READ
      *
   *** 2.2 TEST FOR BLANK ITEM NUMBER ***
      *
      IF ITEMNUM = '    '
         *
         *** 2.2.1 PROCESS BLANK ITEM NUMBER ***
            *
            STORE [F] TO GOBACK
            *
      ELSE
         *
         *** 2.2.2 PROCESS NONBLANK ITEM NUMBER ***
            *
            *** 2.2.2.1 ACCEPT QUANTITY ORDERED ***
               *
               @ LINECNT,15 GET QTY PICTURE '999'
               @ 22,15 SAY '       PLEASE ENTER THE QUANTITY TO BE
               ORDERED'
               @ 23,15 SAY BLANKLINE
               READ
               *
            *** 2.2.2.2 TEST QUANTITY AVAILABLE ***
               *
               SELECT B
               FIND &ITEMNUM
               *
               IF QTY < QUANTITY
                  *
                  *** 2.2.2.2.1 PROCESS QUANTITY AVAILABLE ***
                     *
                     @ LINECNT,23 SAY ITEM_DESC
                     @ LINECNT,52 SAY RET_PRICE
                     @ LINECNT,61 SAY (QTY*RET_PRICE)
                     REPLACE QUANTITY WITH QUANTITY-QTY
                     *
                     SELECT C
                     APPEND BLANK
                     REPLACE ITEM_NUM WITH ITEMNUM, ITEM_QTY WITH QTY
                     *
```

Figure 13.16 Continued

```
                    ELSE
                        *
                    *** 2.2.2.2.2 PROCESS QUANTITY NOT AVAILABLE ***
                        *
                        @ LINECNT,25 SAY 'ONLY'
                        @ LINECNT,29 SAY QUANTITY
                        @ LINECNT,33 SAY 'ITEMS AVAILABLE'
                        @ 22,15 SAY BLANKLINE
                        @ 22,15 SAY [ORDER AS MANY AVAILABLE OR CANCEL
                             THIS]
                        @ 22,52 SAY [ITEM'S ORDER]
                        STORE ' ' TO RESPONSE
                        @ 23,15 SAY 'PRESS ANY KEY, OR PRESS "C" TO
                             CANCEL'
                        @ 23,50 SAY 'THIS ITEM ==>' GET RESPONSE
                        READ
                        *
                        IF UPPER(RESPONSE) = 'C'
                            *
                        *** 2.2.2.2.2.1 CANCEL THIS ITEM ***
                            *
                            LINECNT = LINECNT - 1
                            *
                        ELSE
                            *
                        *** 2.2.2.2.2.2 ORDER AS MANY AVAILABLE ***
                            *
                            @ LINECNT,15 SAY QUANTITY
                            @ LINECNT,23 SAY ITEM_DESC
                            @ LINECNT,52 SAY RET_PRICE
                            @ LINECNT,61 SAY (QUANTITY*RET_PRICE)
                              PICTURE '99,999.99'
                            REPLACE QUANTITY WITH 0
                            *
                            SELECT C
                            APPEND BLANK
                            REPLACE ITEM_NUM WITH ITEMNUM, ITEM_QTY
                            WITH B ->QUANTITY
                            *
                        ENDIF UPPER (RESPONSE) = 'C'
                        *
                        @ 22,15 SAY BLANKLINE
                        @ 23,15 SAY BLANKLINE
                        *
                    ENDIF QTY < QUANTITY
                    *
                    LINECNT = LINECNT + 1
                    *
        ENDIF ITEMNUM = '    '
            *
    *** 2.3 REINITIALIZE ITEM NUMBER ***
        *
        STORE SPACE(4) TO ITEMNUM
        STORE 0 TO QTY
        NEXT_ORDN = NEXT_ORDN + 1
        *
```

Figure 13.16 Continued

```
ENDDO GOBACK = 'T'
*
*****************************
* 3.0 TERMINATE PROCESSING *
*****************************
*
*** 3.1 RETURN TO CALLING PROGRAM ***
    *
    RETURN
```

Figure 13.16 Continued

13.5 Invoice Procedure for Case Study 10

The INVOICE procedure is a part of Case Study 10. It is an external procedure, and its function is to print the invoice after a customer order is complete. The company name, address, etc., and the order date should be printed at the top of the invoice, followed by the customer and shipping information. The headings should be printed next, followed by a line for each item ordered, including item number, item description, list price, and net price. After all the items ordered have been listed, the total sale amount should be printed, followed by the sales tax. Finally, the total amount due from the customer should be printed. The printed invoice should look like that in Figure 13.17. The invoice should be printed and sent to the shipping department for the shipment of the items.

Because this procedure is by itself a program, the five phases of the program development process will be applied for its development.

Figure 13.17 Sample printed invoice

```
                    AMERICAN SUPPLY COMPANY
                        4950 Creek Drive           ORDER DATE: 02/21/88
                       Cincinnati, OH 45241
    CUSTOMER  NUMBER:   320-45                     ORDER NUMBER:  01056
    SOLD TO:  Marguerite A. Samuels       SHIP TO: Marguerite A. Samuels
              4550 My Farm Land                    4550 My Farm Land
              Cincinnati, OH 45230                 Cincinnati, OH 45230
              513-793-6420                         513-793-6420

    ITEM     QTY                             LIST           NET
    NUMBER   ORDERED  ITEM DESCRIPTION       PRICE          PRICE

    5130     1        Letter Opener            2.17           2.17
    4012     1        King Kong Modem 1200   148.39         148.39
    2786     5        Highlighter Pen 10-Box  11.99          59.95
                                   TOTAL SALE ==>:         210.51
                                          TAX ==>:          11.58
                                    TOTAL DUE ==>:         222.09


                    PRESS ANY KEY TO CONTINUE ==>:
```

13.5.1 The Analysis Phase

In the analysis phase, the first step in the program development process, review and analysis of program specifications lead to the identification of the processing steps needed to solve the problem.

Because each order will consist of several items, a set of steps will be needed to accept the order for each. These steps should also be repeated for each item in the order, so a control switch needs to be defined to control this loop. The memory variable for net price and sales tax, the accumulators for the total sales amount, and the total amount due need to be initialized. Defining the control variables and initializing the memory variables and the accumulator memory variables can be accomplished in one step, which is called define variables. The invoice containing the company information and the order date is displayed in the next step. Customer information, shipping information, and headings lines can be printed in the third step. These three steps are the only ones needed in the initiate processing function of the solution of the invoice procedure.

The processing steps needed in the main processing function should include:

1. Process the order file. If no more records are in the file, proceed to the next step; otherwise, proceed to step 3.
2. Process no more records. Change the loop control switch to indicate termination of the loop, and skip step 3.
3. Process the next item:
   a. Print the item number and quantity.
   b. Find a match in the inventory database file.
   c. Print the item description and the retail price.
   d. Calculate and print the net price.
   e. Calculate the total sale amount.
   f. Increment the line counter.
   g. Skip to the next record.

These three steps should be repeated for each item ordered. The subroutine should be terminated when the end of the file is reached. At that point, the control should move to the terminate processing function.

In the terminate processing function, the total lines should be processed, the order file should be cleared and packed, and the control of the procedure should be transferred to the calling program.

To sum up, the following processing steps will be needed for the solution of Case Study 10:

1. Define the variables.
2. Display the invoice screen.
3. Print the customer information.
4. Process the order file. If no more records are in the file, proceed to the next step; otherwise, proceed to step 6.
5. Process no more records. Change the loop control switch to indicate termination of the loop, and skip step 6.

13.5 Invoice Procedure for Case Study 10

6. Process the next item:
   a. Print the item number and quantity.
   b. Find a match in the inventory database file.
   c. Print the item description and the retail price.
   d. Calculate and print the net price.
   e. Calculate the total sale amount.
   f. Increment the line counter.
   g. Skip to the next record.
7. Process the total lines.
8. Clear the ORDERS.DBF database file and pack it.
9. Return to the calling program.

The first three steps should be performed only once, at the start of the program. Therefore, these belong to initiate processing. The next three steps should be performed for each item ordered until the end of the file is reached. At that point, control of the procedure should be transferred to terminate processing. Therefore, these steps belong to main processing. The last three steps need to be performed only once, before terminating the execution of the procedure. Therefore, these belong to terminate processing.

13.5.2 The Design Phase

The function of this step is to take the results of the problem analysis, that is, the processing steps identified in the analysis phase, and transform them into a structure chart. Using the shell structure chart of Figure 10.12 and the tools and techniques discussed in section 4.4.2, transform the 9 steps identified in the analysis phase into a structure chart for the invoice procedure, as shown in Figure 13.18.

All the modules in this structure chart are either functionally or highly cohesive. They are also loosely coupled. Thus, the structure chart of Figure 13.18 satisfies the three rules for designing a good structure chart. It consists of highly cohesive, loosely coupled modules with the span of control of any module no more than three. Therefore, this chart is a well-designed solution for the invoice procedure.

13.5.3 The Detailed Design Phase

The function of this step is to take the result of the design phase, that is, the structure chart, and identify the actual computer operations required for each program function represented in it, thereby producing the detailed solution of the problem. Using the translation of the three control structures to pseudocode as given in Figure 4.14 and the method described in section 4.4.3, we arrive at the structure chart of Figure 13.18 translated to pseudocode as given in Figure 13.19.

13.5.4 The Coding Phase

The purpose of this phase in the program development process is to translate the pseudocode instructions of the solution of the subroutine into programming language instructions. The pseudocode of Figure 13.19 is translated into dBASE commands, and the complete program for the invoice procedure in dBASE language is given in Figure 13.20 (see page 533).

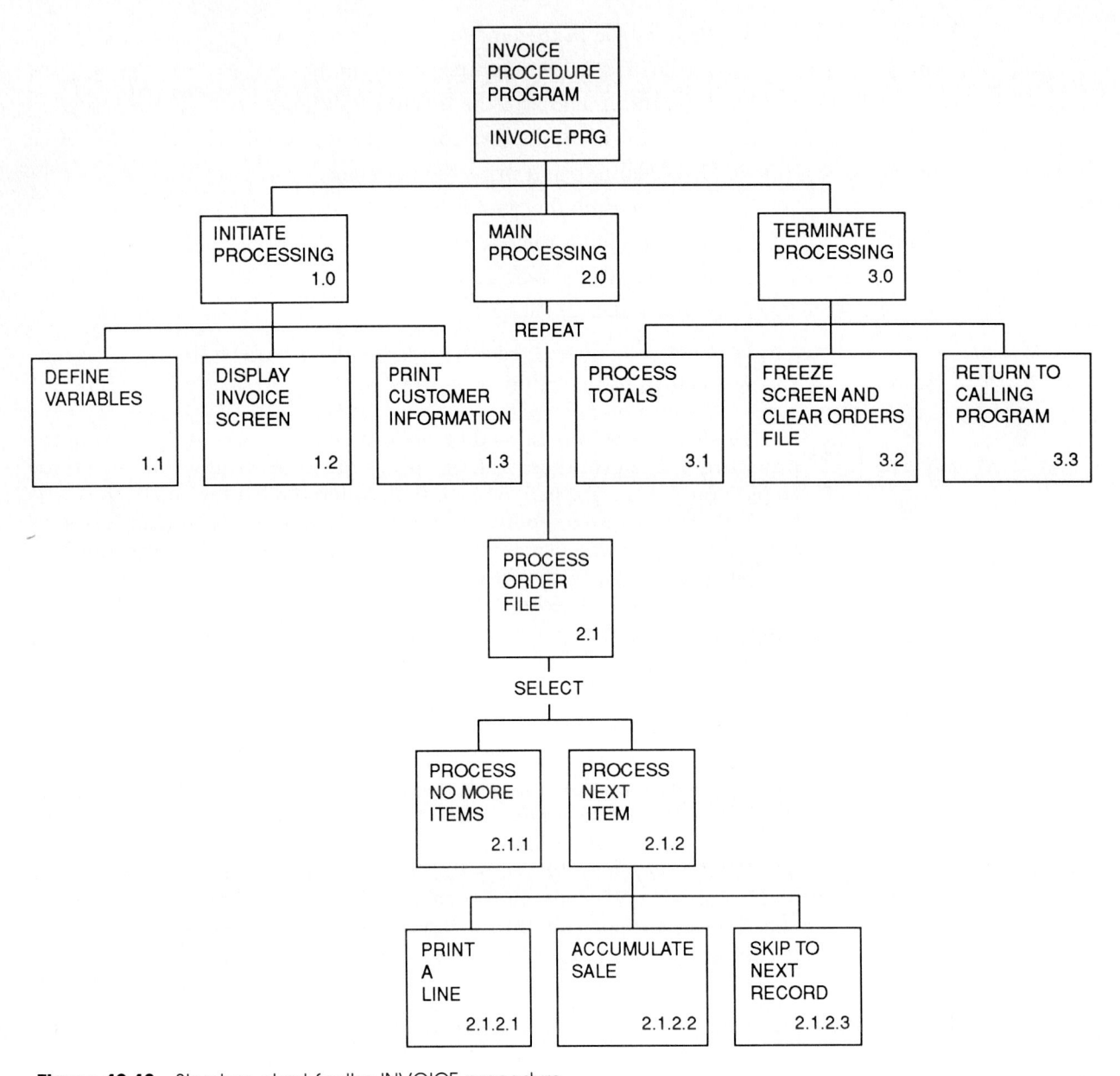

Figure 13.18 Structure chart for the INVOICE procedure

13.5.5 The Testing and Debugging Phase

The last step in program development is the testing and debugging phase, in which the source program is executed and tested for the accuracy of its logic. Execute the program to complete this step, correct the syntactical errors, if any, and execute the program again. Repeat this process until the program is free of syntactical errors. When the output is produced by the program, verify some of the records of the output to ensure its accuracy. If any discrepancies exist, make the needed corrections, and execute the program again. Repeat the process of making corrections and executing the program until the program produces correct and predictable results.

```
0.0 INVOICE GENERATING PROGRAM—INVOICE PROCEDURE
    1.0 INITIATE PROCESSING
        1.1 DEFINE VARIABLES
            DEFINE CONTROL VARIABLES
                Set REPEAT41 switch = T
            INITIALIZE VARIABLES
                Set COST = 0
                Set TAX = 0
            INITIALIZE ACCUMULATORS
                Set TOTSAL = 0
                Set TOTDUE = 0
        1.2 DISPLAY INVOICE SCREEN
            CLEAR SCREEN
                Clear screen
            DISPLAY COMPANY INFORMATION
                Display Company name
                Display Company address
                Display Company city, state and zip code
                Display Company telephone
                Display Customer number and Order number
        1.3 PRINT CUSTOMER INFORMATION
            FIND MATCHING CUSTOMER
                Select work area A
                Find matching record in the customer file
            PRINT CUSTOMER ADDRESS
                Display Customer name, address etc.
                Display Shipping address etc.
            PRINT COLUMN HEADINGS
                Display column headings for the item detail line
            INITIALIZE LINE COUNTER
                Set LINECNT = 14
                Select work area C
                Go to first record
    2.0 MAIN PROCESSING
        REPEAT: While the REPEAT41 switch = T
            2.1 PROCESS ORDER FILE
                OPEN ORDER FILE
                    Open ORDERS file
                    SELECT: On end of file
                        2.1.1 PROCESS NO MORE ITEMS
                            Set REPEAT41 switch = F
                        2.1.2 PROCESS NEXT ITEM
                            2.1.2.1 PRINT A LINE
                                PRINT ITEM NUMBER & QUANTITY
                                    Print item number and item quantity
                                FIND MATCH IN INV FILE
                                    Select work area B
                                    Find match for item ordered in INV file
```

Figure 13.19 Pseudocode for the INVOICE procedure

     PRINT ITEM DESCRIPTION & RETAIL PRICE
      Print item description, list price
     CALCULATE & PRINT NET PRICE
      Calculate Net price
      Print Net price
     INCREMENT LINE COUNTER
      Increment LINECNT by one
    2.1.2.2 ACCUMULATE SALE
     ACCUMULATE TOTAL SALE
      Accumulate Net price
    2.1.2.3 SKIP TO NEXT RECORD
     SKIP TO NEXT RECORD
      Select work area C
      Skip to next record
   END SELECT
  END REPEAT
3.0 TERMINATE PROCESSING
  3.1 PROCESS TOTALS
    PRINT TOTAL SALE
     Print Total sale amount
     Increment LINECNT by one
    CALCULATE & PRINT TAX
     Calculate Tax amount
     Print Tax amount
     Increment LINECNT by one
    CALCULATE & PRINT TOTAL DUE
     Calculate Total due
     Print Total due
  3.2 FREEZE SCREEN AND CLEAR ORDER FILE
    FREEZE SCREEN
     Wait for response to continue processing
    CLEAR ORDERS FILE
     Select work area C
     Delete all records from the ORDERS file
     Pack the ORDERS file
  3.3 RETURN TO CALLING PROGRAM
    Return to calling program

Figure 13.19 Continued

```
****************************************************************
*                        INV41.PRG                              *
*                   INVOICE PROCEDURE                           *
*                INVOICE GENERATING PROGRAM                     *
*---------------------------------------------------------------*
* This is an external procedure invoked by the program          *
* INV4.PRG of the Invoice Generating System for American        *
* Supply Company. The function of this program is to            *
* print the invoices for the orders received in the             *
* Invoice Generating Program INV4.PRG.                          *
*---------------------------------------------------------------*
*            COPYRIGHT (C) . . . SUDESH M. DUGGAL               *
****************************************************************
*
***************************
* 1.0 INITIATE PROCESSING *
***************************
*
*** 1.1 DEFINE VARIABLES ***
   *
   *** DEFINE CONTROL VARIABLES ***
      *
      STORE [T] TO REPEAT41
      *
   *** INITIALIZE VARIABLES ***
      *
      COST = 0
      TAX = 0
      *
   *** INITIALIZE ACCUMULATORS ***
      *
      TOTSAL = 0
      TOTDUE = 0
      *
*** 1.2 DISPLAY INVOICE SCREEN ***
   *
   *** CLEAR SCREEN ***
      *
      CLEAR
      *
   *** DISPLAY COMPANY INFORMATION ***
      *
      @ 2,25 SAY '  AMERICAN SUPPLY COMPANY'
      @ 3,57 SAY 'ORDER DATE:'
      @ 3,25 SAY '     4950 Creek Drive'
      @ 3,69 SAY DATE ()
      @ 4,25 SAY '    Cincinnati, OH 45241'
      @ 5,5  SAY 'CUSTOMER NUMBER:'
      @ 5,24 SAY CUSTNUM
      @ 5,55 SAY 'ORDER NUMBER:'
      @ 5,70 SAY NEXT_ORDN PICTURE '9999'
      *
*** 1.3 PRINT CUSTOMER INFORMATION ***
   *
   *** FIND MATCHING CUSTOMER ***
```

Figure 13.20 Coding for the INVOICE procedure

```
        *
        SELECT A
        FIND &CUSTNUM
        *
   *** PRINT CUSTOMER ADDRESS ***
        *
        @  6,5   SAY 'SOLD TO:'
        @  6,15  SAY CUST_NAME
        @  7,15  SAY CUST_ADDR
        @  8,15  SAY TRIM(CUST_CITY)+' '+CUST_STATE+' '+CUST_ZIP
        @  9,15  SAY CUST_PHONE
        *
        @  6,40  SAY 'SHIP TO:'
        @  6,50  SAY CUST_NAME
        @  7,50  SAY CUST_ADDR
        @  8,50  SAY TRIM(CUST_CITY)+' '+CUST_STATE+' '+CUST_ZIP
        @  9,50  SAY CUST_PHONE
        *
   *** PRINT COLUMN HEADINGS ***
        *
        @ 10,0   TO   10,79
        @ 11,6   SAY 'ITEM'
        @ 11,15  SAY 'QTY'
        @ 11,56  SAY 'LIST'
        @ 11,68  SAY 'NET'
        @ 12,5   SAY 'NUMBER'
        @ 12,13  SAY 'ORDERED'
        @ 12,23  SAY 'ITEM DESCRIPTION'
        @ 12,56  SAY 'PRICE'
        @ 12,69  SAY 'PRICE'
        @ 13,0   TO   13,79
        @  1,0   TO   24,79 DOUBLE
        *
   *** INITIALIZE LINE COUNTER ***
        *
        STORE 14 TO LINENUM
        *
        SELECT C
        GOTO TOP
        *
***********************
* 2.0 MAIN PROCESSING *
***********************
*
DO WHILE REPEAT41 = 'T'
   *
   *** 2.1 PROCESS ORDER FILE ***
      *
      IF EOF () .OR. BOF ()
         *
         *** 2.1.1 PROCESS NO MORE ITEMS ***
             STORE 'F' TO REPEAT41
             *
      ELSE
         *
         *** 2.1.2 PROCESS NEXT ITEM ***
```

Figure 13.20 Continued

13.5 Invoice Procedure for Case Study 10

```
              *
              *** PRINT ITEM NUMBER & QUANTITY ***
                  *
                  @ LINENUM,5  ITEM_NUM
                  @ LINENUM,15 SAY ITEM_QTY
                  *
              *** SET RELATION TO INV.DBF FILE ***
                  *
                  SET RELATION TO ITEM_NUM INTO INV
                  *
              *** PRINT ITEM DESCRIPTION & RETAIL PRICE ***
                  *
                  @ LINENUM,25 SAY B->ITEM_DESC
                  @ LINENUM,54 SAY B->RET_PRICE
                  *
              *** CALCULATE & PRINT NET COST ***
                  *
                  COST = ITEM_QTY * B->RET_PRICE
                  @ LINENUM,65 SAY COST PICTURE '99,999.99'
                  *
              *** INCREMENT LINE COUNTER ***
                  *
                  LINENUM = LINENUM + 1
                  *
              *** ACCUMULATE SALE ***
                  *
                  TOTSAL = TOTSAL + COST
                  *
              *** SKIP TO NEXT LINE ***
                  *
                  SKIP
                  *
         ENDIF EOF ()
         *
ENDDO REPEAT41 = 'T'
*
***************************
* 3.0 TERMINATE PROCESSING *
***************************
*
*** 3.1 PROCESS TOTALS ***
    *
    *** PRINT TOTAL SALE ***
        *
        @ LINENUM,40 SAY 'TOTAL SALE ==>:'
        @ LINENUM,65 SAY TOTSAL PICTURE '99,999.99'
        LINENUM = LINENUM + 1
    *** CALCULATE & PRINT TAX ***
        *
        TAX = TOTSAL * 0.055
        @ LINENUM,47 SAY 'TAX ==>:'
        @ LINENUM,65 SAY TAX PICTURE '99,999.99'
        LINENUM = LINENUM + 1
        *
    *** CALCULATE & PRINT TOTAL DUE ***
        *
```

Figure 13.20 Continued

```
            @ LINENUM,40 SAY 'TOTAL DUE ==>:'
            TOTDUE = TOTSAL + TAX
            @ LINENUM,65 SAY TOTDUE PICTURE '99,999.99'
            *
*** 3.2 FREEZE SCREEN & CLEAR ORDER FILE ***
      **
      *** FREEZE SCREEN ***
            *
            DO FREEZE
            *
      *** CLEAR ORDER FILE ***
            *
            DELETE ALL
            PACK
            *
*** 3.3 RETURN TO CALLING PROGRAM ***
      *
            RETURN
```

Figure 13.20 Continued

13.6 Summary

The SELECT command allows you to open up to ten different work areas named A through J or numbered 1 through 10. It also allows you to select a work area and open a database file. You can have up to ten different database files open at one time in ten different work areas, but only one can be active at a time. The active database file belongs to the currently selected work area.

After a work area has been selected, all dBASE commands issued after this command except the SELECT command pertain to this work area. The use of prefixes and aliases can alter the effect of some of the commands and can be used to access the data from the database files open in different work areas.

Use of the prefixes and aliases is restricted to the DISPLAY and LIST commands. Any dBASE command used to change the contents of the database file affects only the database file open in the current work area, that is, the active database file.

The SET RELATION TO command is issued to define the relationship among the database files having a field in common. This command allows you to obtain the related data from different files open in different work areas.

KEY CONCEPTS

active database file
active data record
aliases

prefix
work area

dBASE COMMANDS AND FUNCTIONS

SELECT command

SET RELATION TO command

REVIEW QUESTIONS

1. Explain the concept of the work area. What is its advantage?
2. How many different work areas can be open at one time?
3. What is meant by the term *active database file*? How many files can be active at one time?
4. What is the function of the SELECT command?
5. What is the function of the prefix and/or alias? What values can be used as a prefix? What values can be used as an alias?
6. What is the function of the SET RELATION TO command? What are the requirements for its use?
7. What is the advantage of defining the relationship between the database files? What is/are the condition(s) for defining the relationship?
8. What types of dBASE commands can affect only the currently selected work area?
9. Explain the difference between open and active database files.
10. Explain what is meant by the term *active data record*.

HANDS-ON ASSIGNMENT

Programming Assignment 13A

Program Description Design and write an accounts receivable subsystem program ACR4.PRG. It should be invoked by the main menu program ACR.PRG of the accounts receivable system for the American Supply Company. The program should be able to produce the monthly statements for all customers in the CUSTACR.DBF database file who owe any amount to the company. The monthly statement should consist of the previous balance, the interest due on it, and current transactions. The previous balance should be obtained by adding the current balance from all unpaid invoices stored in the ACCREC.DBF database file. The interest due on the previous balance should be calculated by using the rate of 8 percent for a balance less than $1000 and 6 percent for one greater than or equal to $1000. The current transactions are stored in the INVOICES.DBF database file. The last line in the monthly statements should be the total amount due from the customer, which is the sum of the previous balance, interest on the previous balance, and the total of the invoice amount from all new transactions.

Input File(s) The CUSTACR.DBF, ACCREC.DBF, and INVOICES.DBF database files, whose structures are given in Figures 13.21, 13.22, and 13.23, respectively, are the three input files to be used in the program.

Output The output from this program should be the monthly statements, shown in Figure 13.24, which may consist of a variable number of screens.

Processing Steps The following steps should be used to develop the solution of the program:

1. The company's information containing the telephone number and the date of billing should be included in the statements, as shown in Figure 13.24.
2. The customer's information and customer number should be included in the statement.
3. The column headings should be enclosed in two lines.

Figure 13.21 Structure of the CUSTACR.DBF database file

```
Structure for database: C:\DBASE\ACCREC\CUSTACR.DBF
Number of data records:      26
Date of last update   : 06/13/88
Field  Field Name   Type       Width    Dec
    1  CUST_NUM     Character     11
    2  CUST_NAME    Character     25
    3  CUST_ADDR    Character     20
    4  CUST_CITY    Character     20
    5  CUST_STATE   Character      2
    6  CUST_ZIP     Character      5
    7  CUST_PHONE   Character     12
** Total **                       96
```

Figure 13.22 Structure of the ACCREC.DBF database file

```
Structure for database : C:\DBASE\ACCREC\ACCREC.DBF
Number of data records :     30
Date of last update    : 05/18/90
Field  Field Name   Type       Width    Dec   Index
    1  CUS_NUM      Character     11                N
    2  PUR_DATE     Date           8                N
    3  PUR_REF      Numeric        4      0         N
    4  PUR_AMT      Numeric        8      2         N
    5  PAY_DATE     Date           8                N
    6  PAY_REF      Numeric        4      0         N
    7  PAY_AMT      Numeric        8      2         N
** Total **                       52
```

Figure 13.23 Structure of the INVOICES.DBF database file

```
Structure for database : C:\DBASE\ACCREC\INVOICES.DBF
Number of data records :     30
Date of last update    : 05/18/90
Field  Field Name   Type       Width    Dec   Index
    1  C_NUM        Character     11                N
    2  INV_NUM      Character      8                N
    3  INV_DATE     Date           8                N
    4  INV_AMT      Numeric        8      2         N
** Total **                       36
```

Figure 13.24 Monthly statement

```
┌─────────────────────────────────────────────────────────────────┐
│      Telephone        AMERICAN SUPPLY COMPANY     Billing Date  │
│    (513) 733-5555        4950 Creek Drive          06/21/90     │
│                        Cincinnati, OH 45241                     │
│                                                                 │
│   SOLD TO:  Marguerite A. Samuelson                             │
│             4550 My Farm Land                                   │
│             Cincinnati, OH 45230      Customer Number: 320-45-1423 │
│             513-793-6420                                        │
│  ┌──────────────────────────────────────────────────────────┐   │
│  │ INVOICE     INVOICE      INVOICE                         │   │
│  │ NUMBER      DATE         AMOUNT                          │   │
│  ├──────────────────────────────────────────────────────────┤   │
│  │                                  Previous Balance  99,999.99 │
│  │                                  Interest on Balance   99.99 │
│  │  xxxxxx    xx/xx/xx    99,999.99                         │   │
│  │  xxxxxx    xx/xx/xx    99,999.99                         │   │
│  │                                                   99,999.99 │
│  │         Current Total  99,999.99                         │   │
│  │                                  Total Due       99,999.99 │
│  │                                                          │   │
│  │            PRESS ANY KEY TO CONTINUE ===>: ▌             │   │
│  └──────────────────────────────────────────────────────────┘   │
└─────────────────────────────────────────────────────────────────┘
```

4. The previous balance for each customer should be obtained by adding the current balance due of all the unpaid invoices due from the customer. The unpaid invoices are stored in the ACCREC database file. The previous balance thus obtained should be printed as the first line of the monthly statement.

5. The interest should be calculated on the previous balance by using the interest rate of 8 percent for a balance less than $1000 and 6 percent for one greater than or equal to $1000.

6. Next, all the current transactions stored in the INVOICES.DBF database file belonging to the customer in question should be printed on the monthly statement. If all the transactions cannot be accommodated on one screen, use a second screen and as many more as are needed to complete the statement.

7. After all the transactions have been printed, the total amount due from the customer should be calculated by adding the previous balance due, interest on it, and the total amount of all the new transactions. This total should be printed as the last line of the statement.

8. The whole output should be enclosed in a box, as shown in Figure 13.24.

Programming Assignment 13B

Program Description Design and write a payroll subsystem program PAY4.PRG. It should be invoked by the main menu program PAY.PRG of the payroll system for the American Supply Company. The program should be able to process the payroll for all the employees in the EMPLOYEE.DBF database file using the hours worked for this biweekly pay period stored in the HOURS.DBF database file. The processing should consist of calculating the regular and overtime hours worked, regular and overtime pay, gross pay, federal tax, state tax, social security tax, and local tax for this biweekly pay period for all company employees. Next, the net pay should be calculated by subtracting the total deductions (the sum of federal tax, state tax, social security tax, and local tax) from the gross pay. The gross pay, federal tax, state tax, social security tax, and local tax should also be accumulated in the year to date (YTD) fields of the EMPLOYEE.DBF database file. Finally, the payroll report and the listing of the updated EMPLOYEE.DBF database file should be obtained.

Input File(s) The database files EMPLOYEE.DBF and HOURS.DBF, whose structures are given in Figures 13.25 and 13.26, respectively, are the two input files to be used in the program.

Figure 13.25 Structure of the EMPLOYEE.DBF database file

```
Structure for database: B:EMPLOYEE.dbf
Number of data records:       30
Date of last update   : 06/13/88
Field  Field Name  Type       Width    Dec    Index
    1  SOC_SC_NUM  Character    11             Y
    2  EMP_NAME    Character    25             N
    3  DEPT_CODE   Numeric       3             N
    4  PAY_CODE    Numeric       2             N
    5  M_STATUS    Numeric       1             N
    6  N_DEP       Numeric       2             N
    7  REG_PAY     Numeric       8      2      N
    8  OTIME_PAY   Numeric       8      2      N
    9  FED_TAX     Numeric       6      2      N
   10  ST_TAX      Numeric       6      2      N
   11  SC_TAX      Numeric       6      2      N
   12  L_TAX       Numeric       6      2      N
   13  YTD_GPAY    Numeric       9      2      N
   14  YTD_FTAX    Numeric       8      2      N
   15  YTD_STAX    Numeric       8      2      N
   16  YTD_CTAX    Numeric       8      2      N
   17  YTD_LTAX    Numeric       8      2      N
** Total **                    126
```

Output There should be two output reports from this program:

1. The payroll report, consisting of only those employees in the EMPLOYEE.DBF database file who have worked during this pay period, that is, all employees in the EMPLOYEE.DBF database file for whom the gross pay for this pay period is nonzero. The report should also contain the main heading, column headings, and SOC_SC_NUM, EMP_NAME, total hours worked, PAY_RATE, gross pay, FED_TAX, ST_TAX, L_TAX, SC_TAX, total deductions, and NET_PAY fields. These should take 130 columns using the compressed print.

2. A listing of the updated EMPLOYEE.DBF database file containing the SOC_SC_NUM, EMP_NAME, YTD_GPAY, YTD_FTAX, YTD_STAX, YTD_CTAX, and YTD_LTAX fields. The headings and the column headings should also be added.

Processing Steps The following steps should be used to develop the solution of the program:

1. Calculate the regular and overtime hours worked for each week, and then add them to obtain the regular and overtime hours worked by each employee.

2. Use the pay code of the employee record being processed to obtain the corresponding pay rate from the PAYRATE.DBF database file, whose structure is shown in Figure 13.27.

3. Calculate the regular pay by multiplying the total regular hours worked by the pay rate and overtime pay by multiplying the total overtime hours worked by (1.5*pay rate). Finally, add the regular and overtime pay to get the weekly gross pay.

4. Now calculate the taxes as follows:
   a. Social security tax (SC_TAX) and local tax (L_TAX) are to be calculated at 6.55 percent

Figure 13.26 Structure of the HOURS.DBF database file

```
Structure for database: B:HOURS.dbf
Number of data records:      28
Date of last update   : 06/13/88
Field  Field Name  Type       Width    Dec    Index
    1  SS_NUM      Character    11             N
    2  HOURS_W1    Numeric       2             N
    3  HOURS_W2    Numeric       2             N
** Total **                     16
```

Figure 13.27 Structure of the PAYRATE.DBF database file

```
Structure for database: B:PAYRATE.DBF
Number of data records:      12
Date of last update    : 06/13/88
   Field   Field Name    Type       Width    Dec   Index
     1     P_CODE        Numeric      3              Y
     2     P_RATE        Numeric      4       2      N
** Total **                           8
```

Figure 13.28 State tax table

	Gross Pay Range	Amount of Tax
1	$0 to $150	$0.0
2	$150 to $300	1% of excess over $150
3	$300 to $450	$1.00 plus 1-1/2% of excess over $300
4	$450 to $600	$2.50 plus 2% of excess over $450
5	$600 to above	$4.50 plus 2-1/2% of excess over $600

and 2.00 percent of the weekly gross pay, respectively.

b. State tax (ST_TAX) is to be calculated using the table of Figure 13.28 and using nested IF commands. Do not use these constant values in your program. Store them in the memory variables, and save them in the STATE.MEM database file. Load this file in your program.

After finding the weekly gross pay, find the income range for the employee from the table. Then subtract the low limit from the gross pay to find excess earnings. Multiply the excess earnings by the percentage associated with the entry, giving the proportional tax. Add the base tax and the proportional tax, giving the total state tax due.

c. Finally, calculate the federal tax (FED_TAX) as follows:

i. After the biweekly gross pay is obtained, compute the taxable income, which is obtained by subtracting $14.40 times the number of dependents from the gross pay.

ii. Using this taxable income, find the corresponding base tax, percentage tax, and bracket base in the tax table (single or married person table, as shown in Figures 13.29 and 13.30, respectively). If the M_STATUS code is 1, use the single tax table; for any other value (2, 3, or 4), use the married tax table.

iii. Using these numbers, compute the amount of federal tax.

5. Now store the REG_PAY, OTIME_PAY, FED_TAX, ST_TAX, SC_TAX, and L_TAX in the EMPLOYEE.DBF database file, and update the corre-

Figure 13.29 Single person, including head of household

	Wages less allowances:	Income tax to be withheld:	
1	Not over $50	0	
	Over -- but not over --		of excess over
2	$ 50 -- $135	16%	$ 50
3	$135 -- $231	$ 13.60 plus 20%	$135
4	$231 -- $365	$ 32.80 plus 23%	$231
5	$365 -- $481	$ 63.62 plus 21%	$365
6	$481 -- $558	$ 87.98 plus 26%	$481
7	$558 -- $692	$108.00 plus 30%	$558
8	$692 -- above	$148.20 plus 35%	$692

Figure 13.30 Married person, including head of household

	Wages less allowances:	Income tax to be withheld:	
1	Not over $96	0	
	Over -- but not over --		of excess over
2	$ 96 -- $192	17%	$ 96
3	$ 192 -- $346	$ 16.32 plus 20%	$ 192
4	$ 346 -- $529	$ 47.12 plus 17%	$ 346
5	$ 529 -- $692	$ 78.23 plus 25%	$ 529
6	$ 692 -- $865	$118.98 plus 28%	$ 692
7	$ 865 -- $1,000	$167.42 plus 32%	$ 865
8	$1,000 -- above	$210.62 plus 36%	$1,000

sponding YTD fields by adding the current pay period data.

6. After all the records of the EMPLOYEE.DBF database file have been processed, produce the payroll report and the listing of the updated EMPLOYEE.DBF database file.

The single person table of Figure 13.29 redefined for dBASE use as a SINGLE.DBF database file is shown in Figure 13.31. The married person table of Figure 13.30 can also be redefined for dBASE use as a MARRIED.DBF database file.

Figure 13.31 Single person table defined as SINGLE.DBF database file

Record	B_BASE	B_LIMIT	PER_TAX	BASE_TAX
1	0	50	0	0
2	50	135	16	0
3	135	231	20	13.60
4	231	365	23	32.80
5	365	481	21	63.62
6	481	558	26	87.98
7	558	692	30	108.00
8	692	9,999	35	148.20

PART 4

dBASE IV UTILITIES

A few of the most commonly used dBASE IV utilities are presented in Part 4. It consists of three chapters.

The dBASE IV label utility is introduced in Chapter 14. Two commands used to create and produce customized mailing labels, the CREATE LABEL and the LABEL FORM, are introduced in this chapter. The first is used to design the label format and the second, to produce the labels. Use of the LABEL FORM command, either to print the labels or to create the label text files, is also presented.

The dBASE IV report generator utility is introduced in Chapter 15. Two commands used for the creation and production of reports, the CREATE REPORT and the REPORT FORM, are introduced in this chapter. The first is used to design the report format, and the latter is used to produce the reports using the report format designed by the first command. Use of the REPORT FORM command, either to print the reports or to create the report text files, is also presented.

Chapter 16 covers exporting dBASE file data to foreign files (those not in dBASE format) and importing data from foreign files into dBASE files. The data from the foreign files can be directly used by other software packages such as word processors, spreadsheets, or even programming languages like BASIC and COBOL.

Chapter 14

Creating Labels

LEARNING OBJECTIVES

Upon successfully completing this chapter, you will be able to:

1. Use the built-in dBASE IV label generator utility.
2. Design the label format using the CREATE LABEL command.
3. Modify the already existing label format using the MODIFY LABEL command.
4. Produce labels using the LABEL FORM command.
5. Produce labels from the conditionally selected records of a database file using the LABEL FORM command.
6. Produce printed labels using the LABEL FORM command.
7. Produce labels text file using the LABEL FORM command.

14.1 Overview

This chapter deals with the creation and production of customized mailing labels using the dBASE IV label utility. It starts by introducing the CREATE LABEL command, which is used to design the label format. The label format design process consists of selecting the label dimensions from the predefined sizes supplied by dBASE IV, placing the data fields to be printed in the labels on the label form, and defining the display attributes for the fields. The use of the trim function, to trim off the leading and the trailing blank spaces from the data fields, is illustrated.

The LABEL FORM command, used to produce the labels with the help of the label format designed with the CREATE LABEL command, is introduced next. How this command can be used to produce the labels, for either all records or only selected records of a database file, is illustrated with examples. Use of this command to print the labels and create the label text files is also presented.

14.2 Label Generation

The label utility provided by dBASE IV allows you to design the label format, which you can use to print the contents of a database file in a mailing label form. The label utility not only allows you to design and print any type of mailing labels, but you can design and print envelopes, Rolodex cards, identification tags, and price tags. Sample labels are shown in Figure 14.1.

Label generation is a two-step process. In the first step, the label format is designed; in the second step, this format is used to print the contents of the database file in the form of customized mailing labels.

Figure 14.1 Sample labels

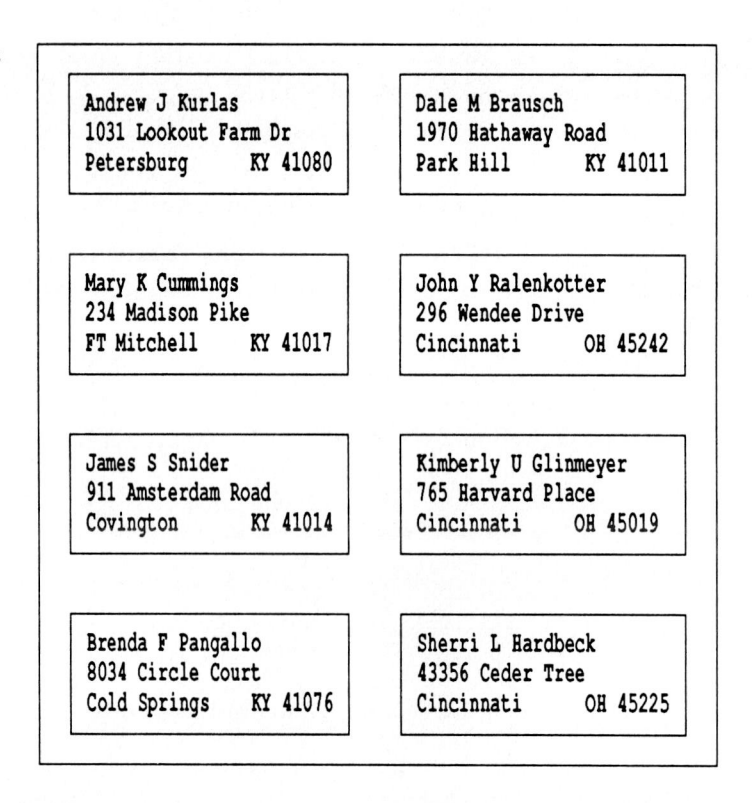

```
┌─────────────────────────┐  ┌─────────────────────────┐
│ Andrew J Kurlas         │  │ Dale M Brausch          │
│ 1031 Lookout Farm Dr    │  │ 1970 Hathaway Road      │
│ Petersburg     KY 41080 │  │ Park Hill      KY 41011 │
└─────────────────────────┘  └─────────────────────────┘

┌─────────────────────────┐  ┌─────────────────────────┐
│ Mary K Cummings         │  │ John Y Ralenkotter      │
│ 234 Madison Pike        │  │ 296 Wendee Drive        │
│ FT Mitchell    KY 41017 │  │ Cincinnati     OH 45242 │
└─────────────────────────┘  └─────────────────────────┘

┌─────────────────────────┐  ┌─────────────────────────┐
│ James S Snider          │  │ Kimberly U Glinmeyer    │
│ 911 Amsterdam Road      │  │ 765 Harvard Place       │
│ Covington      KY 41014 │  │ Cincinnati     OH 45019 │
└─────────────────────────┘  └─────────────────────────┘

┌─────────────────────────┐  ┌─────────────────────────┐
│ Brenda F Pangallo       │  │ Sherri L Hardbeck       │
│ 8034 Circle Court       │  │ 43356 Ceder Tree        │
│ Cold Springs   KY 41076 │  │ Cincinnati     OH 45225 │
└─────────────────────────┘  └─────────────────────────┘
```

14.2.1 Designing a Label Format

The first step of label generation is designing the label format. The dBASE command used for this purpose is the CREATE LABEL command.

The CREATE LABEL Command

The general format of the CREATE LABEL command is

```
CREATE LABEL <label format file name>
```

where <label format file name> is the name of the file in which the label format is stored on the computer disk for future use.

The CREATE LABEL command provides interactive techniques for designing the label format. It displays a label design screen consisting of a label design form and seven Pull-down menu options. The Pull-down Menus are used to design the label format using the label design form for the currently active database file. The label format is stored in a disk file with a default extension of .LBL.

If the specified label format file already exists on the disk when the CREATE LABEL command is issued, dBASE will ask if you want to modify it. In fact, the MODIFY LABEL command, which works like the CREATE LABEL command, should be used to modify the already existing label format.

Consider the CUSTOMER.DBF database file whose structure is shown in Figure 14.2. To design a label format named CUSTOMER.LBL for the CUSTOMER.DBF database file, you will need the following commands:

```
. USE CUSTOMER              <Return>
. CREATE LABEL CUSTOMER     <Return>
```

The first command will open the CUSTOMER.DBF database file, and the second will start the process for designing the CUSTOMER.LBL label format. If you type these commands, dBASE IV will respond by displaying the label design screen shown in Figure 14.3.

The label design screen consists of a menu bar at the top of the screen with seven Pull-down menu options used to design the label format. In the

Figure 14.2 Structure of the CUSTOMER.DBF database file

```
. USE CUSTOMER
. DISPLAY STRUCTURE
Structure for database : C:\DBASE\INVOICE\CUSTOMER.DBF
Number of data records :      26
Date of last update    : 01/12/88
Field  Field name  Type       Width  Dec  Index
    1  CUST_NUM    Character      6         N
    2  CUST_NAME   Character     25         N
    3  CUST_ADDR   Character     20         N
    4  CUST_CITY   Character     20         N
    5  CUST_STATE  Character      2         N
    6  CUST_ZIP    Character      5         N
    7  CUST_BAL    Numeric        7    2    N
    8  CUST_PHONE  Character     12         N
** TOTAL **                     98
```

Figure 14.3 Label design screen

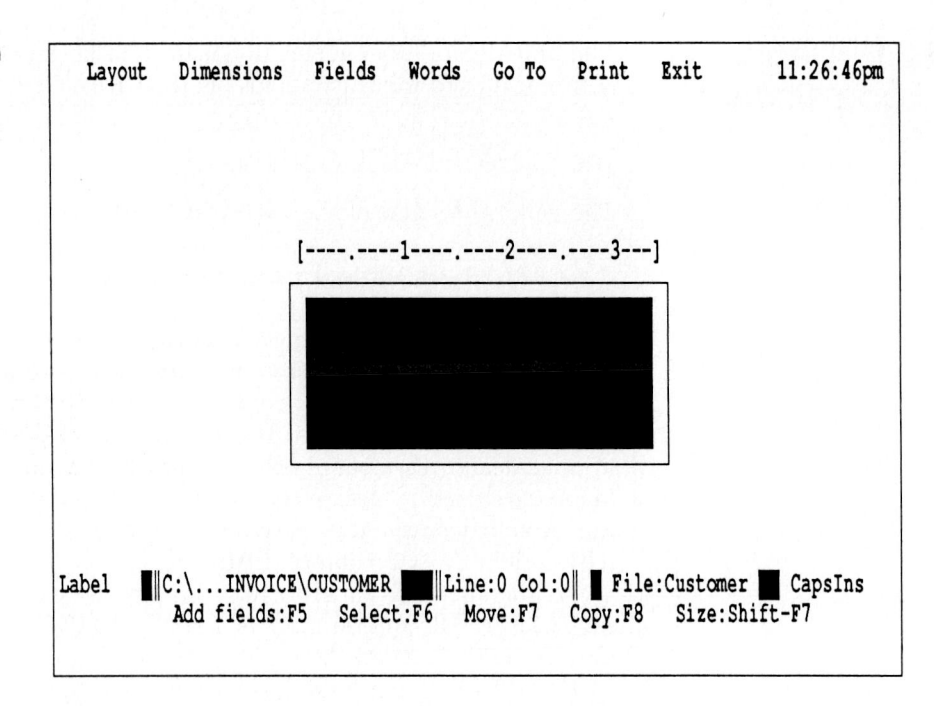

```
Layout   Dimensions   Fields   Words   Go To   Print   Exit        11:26:46pm



                      [----.----1----.----2----.----3---]




















Label    ‖C:\...INVOICE\CUSTOMER ‖‖Line:0 Col:0‖ File:Customer  CapsIns
              Add fields:F5   Select:F6   Move:F7   Copy:F8   Size:Shift-F7
```

center of the screen is a label design form where the label format can be designed. The status bar displaying the current operation, drive name, file currently in use, and other information and the navigation line that helps you design the label form are displayed at the bottom of the screen.

Selecting Label Dimensions Labels are usually created on a special computer form consisting of self-adhesive labels on a perforated backing with one to four labels across the horizontal row. A typical label size is $3\frac{7}{16}$ inches wide by $\frac{15}{16}$ inch high. With a print pitch of 10 characters and six

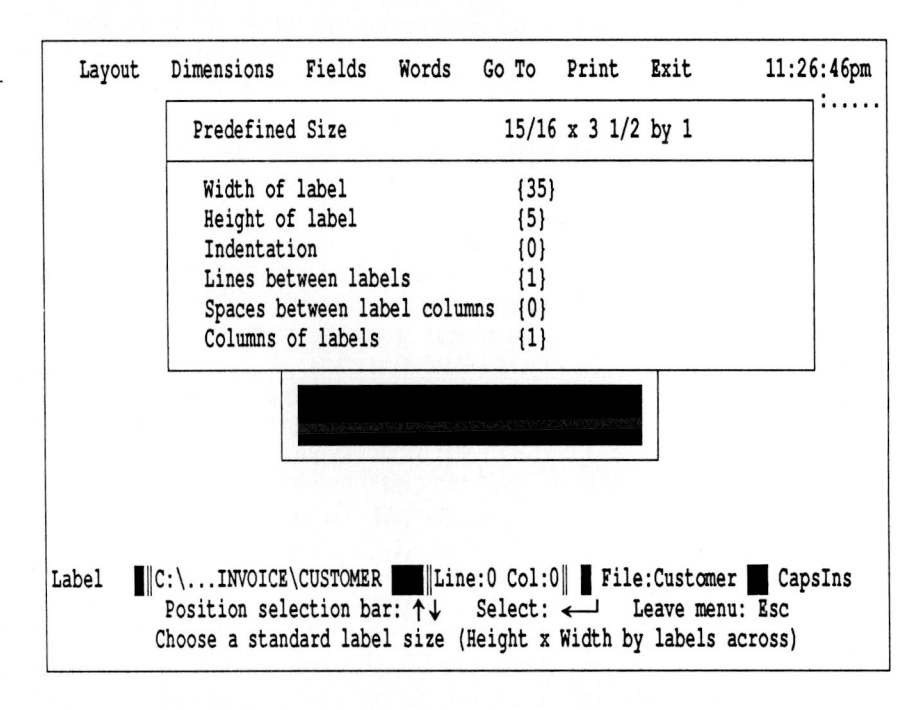

Figure 14.4 Label design screen with Dimensions Pull-down Menu

```
Layout   Dimensions   Fields   Words   Go To   Print   Exit       11:26:46pm
         ┌─────────────────────────────────────────────┐
         │ Predefined Size            15/16 x 3 1/2 by 1│
         ├─────────────────────────────────────────────┤
         │   Width of label                      {35}  │
         │   Height of label                     {5}   │
         │   Indentation                         {0}   │
         │   Lines between labels                {1}   │
         │   Spaces between label columns        {0}   │
         │   Columns of labels                   {1}   │
         └─────────────────────────────────────────────┘




Label    ‖C:\...INVOICE\CUSTOMER ‖‖Line:0 Col:0‖ File:Customer  CapsIns
              Position selection bar: ↑↓   Select: ←   Leave menu: Esc
           Choose a standard label size (Height x Width by labels across)
```

Figure 14.5 Label design screen with a listing of predefined label sizes

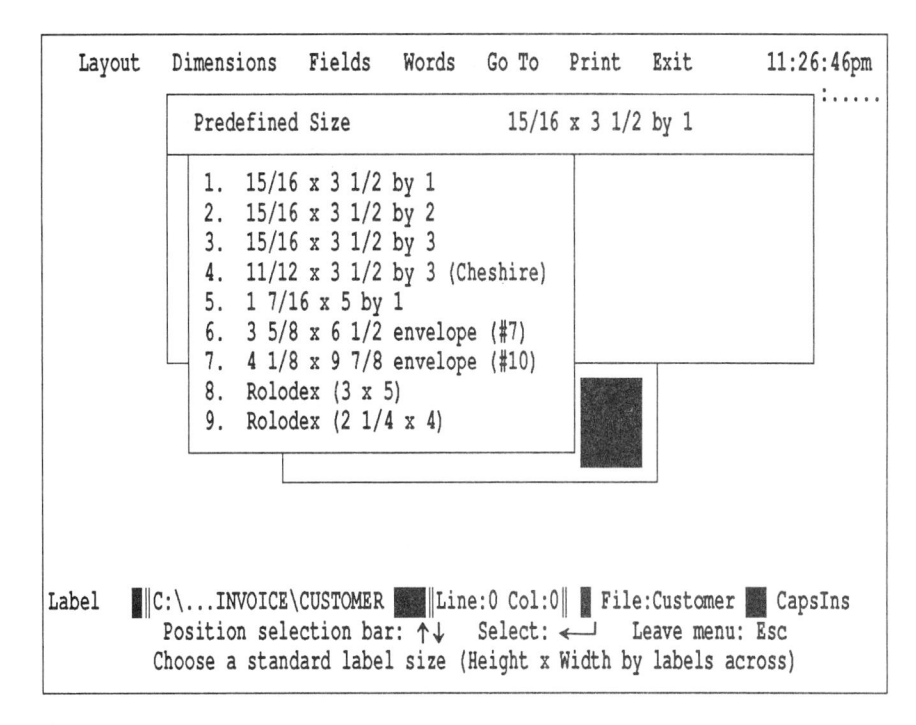

```
 Layout   Dimensions   Fields   Words   Go To   Print   Exit        11:26:46pm
 ┌──────────────────────────────────────────────┐
 │ Predefined Size              15/16 x 3 1/2 by 1
 │  ┌────────────────────────────────────┐
 │  │ 1. 15/16 x 3 1/2 by 1              │
 │  │ 2. 15/16 x 3 1/2 by 2              │
 │  │ 3. 15/16 x 3 1/2 by 3              │
 │  │ 4. 11/12 x 3 1/2 by 3 (Cheshire)   │
 │  │ 5. 1 7/16 x 5 by 1                 │
 │  │ 6. 3 5/8 x 6 1/2 envelope (#7)     │
 │  │ 7. 4 1/8 x 9 7/8 envelope (#10)    │
 │  │ 8. Rolodex (3 x 5)                 │
 │  │ 9. Rolodex (2 1/4 x 4)             │
 │  └────────────────────────────────────┘


 Label   ‖C:\...INVOICE\CUSTOMER ‖Line:0 Col:0‖ File:Customer   CapsIns
         Position selection bar: ↑↓   Select: ←┘   Leave menu: Esc
         Choose a standard label size (Height x Width by labels across)
```

lines per inch, this label size can accommodate five lines of print of up to 35 characters each.

You must define the label dimensions before designing the format. You can do this by invoking the Dimensions pull-down option of the menu bar. To do this, press the <Alt-D> keys. The Dimensions Pull-down Menu will be displayed, as shown in Figure 14.4. The Dimensions Pull-down Menu helps you select one of the nine predefined label sizes provided by dBASE IV or define your own label size. The default predefined size of $\frac{15}{16}$ x $3\frac{1}{2}$ by 1 inch is displayed in Figure 14.4. To select other predefined sizes, highlight the Predefined size option and select by pressing the <Return> key. A submenu of the predefined label sizes will be displayed, as shown in Figure 14.5.

To select any one of the predefined label sizes, highlight your choice and select it by pressing the <Return> key. For example, if you highlight the second option ($\frac{15}{16}$ x $3\frac{1}{2}$ by 2 inches, which is two labels across) and press the <Return> key, dBASE will respond by displaying the label design screen of Figure 14.3.

To define any label size other than the predefined ones, you can use the bottom half of the Dimensions Pull-down Menu shown in Figure 14.4. First highlight the option to be defined, and then select it by pressing the <Return> key. A window displaying the default value will be displayed with the navigation line indicating how to change the default value and the message line displaying the instructions and the acceptable range values. An example of changing the Lines between the labels option is shown in Figure 14.6.

The default value of 1 is displayed in the window. The navigation line indicates that this value can be increased or decreased by using the <Up Arrow> or the <Down Arrow> keys, and when the desired value is displayed, it can be accepted by pressing the <Return> key. The message line indicates that the acceptable range for the number of lines that can be left blank between the labels is 0–16.

Figure 14.6 Label design screen while defining the Lines between the labels option

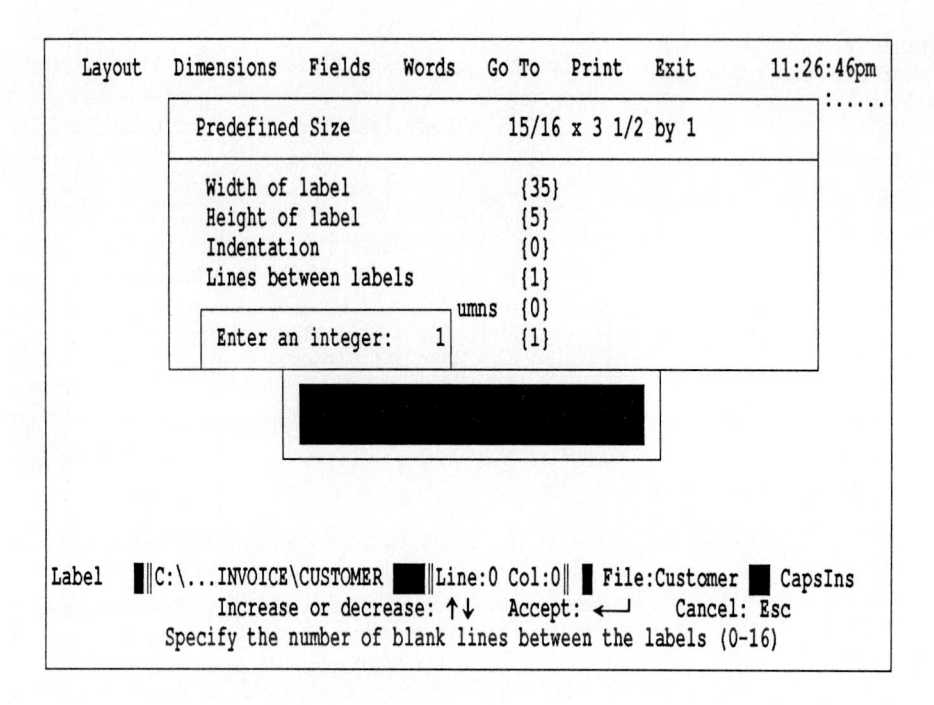

```
Layout    Dimensions    Fields    Words    Go To    Print    Exit        11:26:46pm

         ┌─────────────────────────────────────────────────────────┐
         │  Predefined Size              15/16 x 3 1/2 by 1        │
         │                                                         │
         │     Width of label                {35}                  │
         │     Height of label               {5}                   │
         │     Indentation                   {0}                   │
         │     Lines between labels          {1}                   │
         │                          ┌──umns  {0}                   │
         │    Enter an integer:   1 │        {1}                   │
         │                          └──                            │
         │                                                         │
         │              ████████████████████████████               │
         │                                                         │
         └─────────────────────────────────────────────────────────┘

 Label    ║C:\...INVOICE\CUSTOMER║ ║Line:0 Col:0║ File:Customer  CapsIns
              Increase or decrease: ↑↓     Accept: ←┘     Cancel: Esc
              Specify the number of blank lines between the labels (0-16)
```

The other options can be defined similarly. After they have all been defined, press the <Ctrl-End> keys to continue. dBASE will respond by displaying the label design screen of Figure 14.3.

Placing Fields on the Label Form After you have defined the label dimensions, place the fields from the active database file on the label form. Before you proceed with this step, it is recommended that you prepare a rough draft of the label to be printed. Suppose you want to create a label format as shown in Figure 14.7, which consists of three lines: customer name on the first line, customer address on the second, and city, state, and zip code on the third line. Because the label form consists of five rows and the actual label consists of only three, you should print the label on the second, third, and fourth rows, leaving the first and the fifth rows blank, to center the label on the label form.

To proceed with the design of the label format, move the cursor to the first position of the second row of the label form (Line: 1 Col: 0, as shown on the status bar), and press the F5 Add Fields function key as indicated in the navigation line. The system will display the Fields Submenu, as shown in Figure 14.8.

The Fields Submenu consists of three columns. The first, headed "CUSTOMER," contains the fields of the CUSTOMER.DBF database file. The third column, named "PREDEFINED," contains the predefined fields supplied by dBASE IV. The fields of the CUSTOMER.DBF database file or the predefined fields from the first and the third columns of the Fields Submenu can be used as they are individually in the design of the label form. These can be combined to create an expression in the second column of the Fields Submenu.

Figure 14.7 Rough draft of the label

```
┌─────────────────────────────┐
│  Andrew J Kurlas            │
│  1031 Lookout Farm Dr       │
│  Petersburg, KY 41080       │
└─────────────────────────────┘
```

Figure 14.8 Label design screen with the Fields Submenu

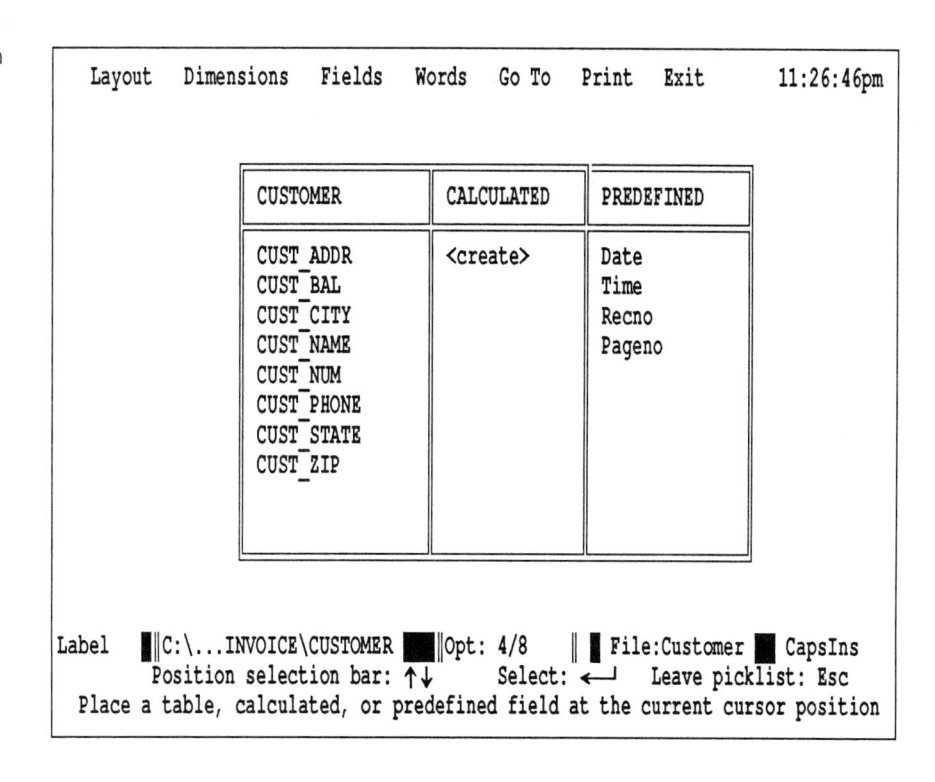

```
 Layout   Dimensions   Fields   Words   Go To   Print   Exit        11:26:46pm


        ┌─────────────────┬────────────┬─────────────┐
        │ CUSTOMER        │ CALCULATED │ PREDEFINED  │
        ├─────────────────┼────────────┼─────────────┤
        │ CUST_ADDR       │ <create>   │ Date        │
        │ CUST_BAL        │            │ Time        │
        │ CUST_CITY       │            │ Recno       │
        │ CUST_NAME       │            │ Pageno      │
        │ CUST_NUM        │            │             │
        │ CUST_PHONE      │            │             │
        │ CUST_STATE      │            │             │
        │ CUST_ZIP        │            │             │
        └─────────────────┴────────────┴─────────────┘


 Label    ║C:\...INVOICE\CUSTOMER  ║Opt: 4/8 ║ File:Customer   CapsIns
              Position selection bar: ↑↓    Select: ↵    Leave picklist: Esc
        Place a table, calculated, or predefined field at the current cursor position
```

Because we need to place the CUST_NAME field in the first line of the label, select it from the first column of the Fields Submenu by highlighting and then pressing the <Return> key. dBASE will respond by displaying the menu for specifying the display attributes for this field, as shown in Figure 14.9.

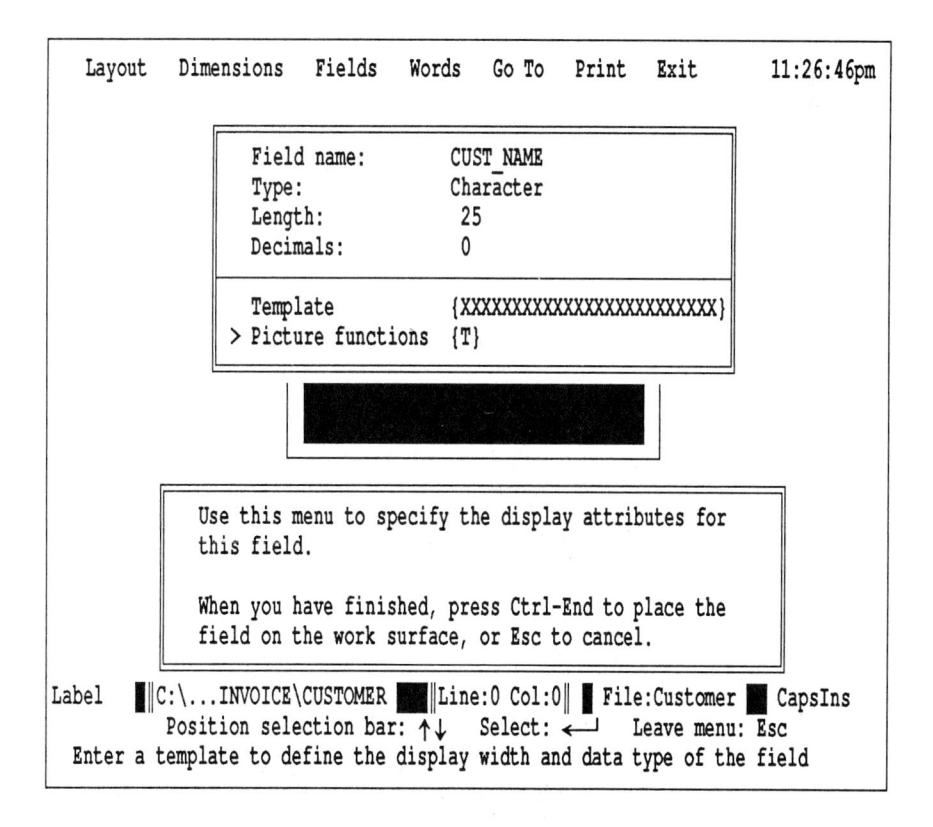

Figure 14.9 Label design screen with the Display Attributes Menu

```
 Layout   Dimensions   Fields   Words   Go To   Print   Exit        11:26:46pm

        ┌──────────────────────────────────────────────────────┐
        │  Field name:       CUST_NAME                         │
        │  Type:             Character                         │
        │  Length:           25                                │
        │  Decimals:         0                                 │
        ├──────────────────────────────────────────────────────┤
        │  Template            {XXXXXXXXXXXXXXXXXXXXXXXXX}     │
        │ > Picture functions  {T}                             │
        └──────────────────────────────────────────────────────┘



        ┌──────────────────────────────────────────────────────┐
        │  Use this menu to specify the display attributes for │
        │  this field.                                         │
        │                                                      │
        │  When you have finished, press Ctrl-End to place the │
        │  field on the work surface, or Esc to cancel.        │
        └──────────────────────────────────────────────────────┘
 Label    ║C:\...INVOICE\CUSTOMER ║Line:0 Col:0║ File:Customer   CapsIns
                    Position selection bar: ↑↓   Select: ↵    Leave menu: Esc
        Enter a template to define the display width and data type of the field
```

Figure 14.10 Label design screen with the Display Attributes Submenu

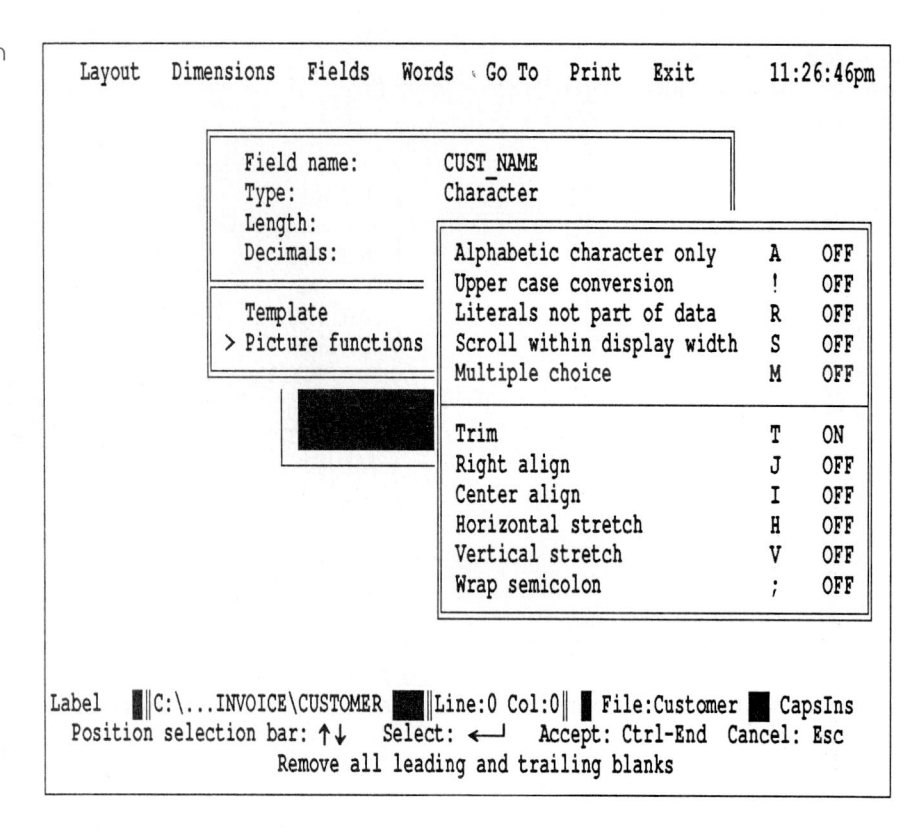

```
 Layout    Dimensions    Fields    Words   Go To    Print     Exit          11:26:46pm

            ┌─────────────────────────┐
            │ Field name:   CUST_NAME │
            │ Type:         Character │
            │ Length:                 │
            │ Decimals:     ┌─────────────────────────────────┬───┬─────┐
            │               │ Alphabetic character only       │ A │ OFF │
            ├───────────────│ Upper case conversion           │ ! │ OFF │
            │ Template      │ Literals not part of data       │ R │ OFF │
            │>Picture functions│ Scroll within display width   │ S │ OFF │
            │               │ Multiple choice                 │ M │ OFF │
            │               ├─────────────────────────────────┼───┼─────┤
            │               │ Trim                            │ T │ ON  │
            │               │ Right align                     │ J │ OFF │
            │               │ Center align                    │ I │ OFF │
            │               │ Horizontal stretch              │ H │ OFF │
            │               │ Vertical stretch                │ V │ OFF │
            │               │ Wrap semicolon                  │ ; │ OFF │
                            └─────────────────────────────────┴───┴─────┘

 Label   ▌C:\...INVOICE\CUSTOMER▐ ▌Line:0 Col:0▐ ▌File:Customer▐ CapsIns
    Position selection bar: ↑↓   Select: ←┘   Accept: Ctrl-End  Cancel: Esc
                     Remove all leading and trailing blanks
```

The first four entries of this submenu are the field name, type, length, and decimals along with their values. These entries are supplied by the system. The fifth option is Template. When this option is highlighted, the message line will read "Enter a template to define the display width and data type of the field." This field is already defined as 25 Xs. Recall that "X" represents any character; and because CUST_NAME is a 25 bytes long character field, this option represents the correct template for this field. So there is no need to change or modify this option. The last option is Picture functions. When it is highlighted, the message line reads "Choose picture function that affects the display or processing of the field." The default value of {T} is already present, which indicates that the TRIM function is ON. In other words, the leading and the trailing blank spaces of the field will be trimmed off.

Note that this option has a ">" symbol before it. Recall that this indicates this option has a submenu. If you highlight this option and select it by pressing the <Return> key, the Picture Functions Submenu as shown in Figure 14.10 will be displayed.

Any number of attributes can be selected from this list of the submenu. Here we need only the TRIM option ON, which is already a default option, so no selection is needed. After defining all the attributes for the CUST_NAME field, press the <Ctrl-End> keys. The system will respond by displaying the screen in Figure 14.9. As indicated in the instructions, press the <Ctrl-End> keys once again to place the CUST_NAME field on the label form, as shown in Figure 14.11.

Follow the method explained previously, and place the CUST_ADDR field on the third row of the label form. Because the first two lines of the label contain single fields, the fields were selected from the Fields

Figure 14.11 Label design screen with the CUST_NAME field placed in it

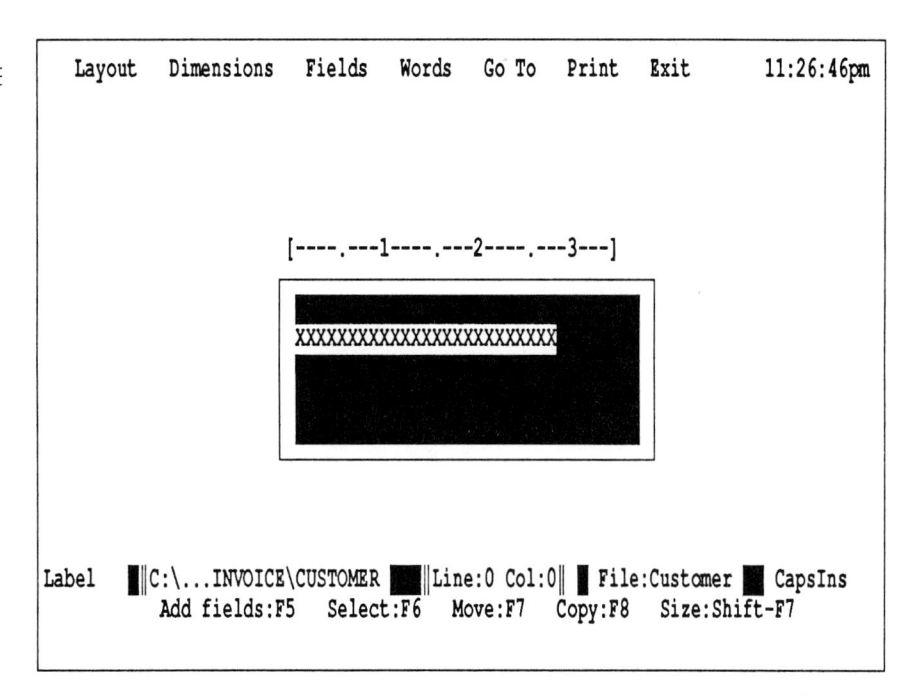

```
 Layout   Dimensions   Fields   Words   Go To   Print   Exit        11:26:46pm




                         [----.---1----.---2----.---3---]

                        ┌─────────────────────────────────┐
                        │                                 │
                        │   XXXXXXXXXXXXXXXXXXXXXXXXXXX   │
                        │                                 │
                        │                                 │
                        └─────────────────────────────────┘




 Label   ║C:\...INVOICE\CUSTOMER║ ║Line:0 Col:0║ ║File:Customer║ CapsIns
              Add fields:F5    Select:F6    Move:F7    Copy:F8    Size:Shift-F7
```

Submenu; and the template was supplied by the system. However, the third line of the label consists of three fields (CUST_CITY, CUST_STATE, and CUST_ZIP), so the process of placing these fields on the label design form will be a little different than with the first two lines.

To place the CUST_CITY, CUST_STATE, and CUST_ZIP fields on the fourth row of the label, move the cursor to the first position of the fourth row, and press the F5 Add Fields function key. The Fields Submenu as shown in Figure 14.8 will be displayed. Now highlight the <create> option of the column named "CALCULATED," and select this option by pressing the <Return> key. The system will respond by displaying the Expression Submenu, as shown in Figure 14.12.

If you highlight the first option, Name, the message line will read "Enter a name for the calculated field." Select this option by pressing the <Return> key. Then following the rules of dBASE to create field names, enter the name for the calculated field here. Because the third line of the label represents the city, state, and zip code fields, let us name this calculated field CS_ZIP. Enter this field name, and press the <Return> key. Now move to the second option, Description. The message line will read "Enter a one-line text description for the calculated field (optional)." Select this option, and enter the appropriate description, if you want to. Then move on to the third option, Expression. The message line will now read "Enter the calculated field expression (can be any valid dBASE expression)." Select this option by pressing the <Return> key, and enter the following expression:

```
TRIM(CUST_CITY) + [, ] + CUST_STATE + [ ] + CUST_ZIP
```

This expression is formed by concatenating (joining) the fields of the CUSTOMER.DBF database file and the literals. The first part of the expression is TRIM(CUST_CITY). The TRIM function will trim off the leading and the trailing blank spaces from the CUST_CITY field. The next

Figure 14.12 Label design screen with the Expression Submenu

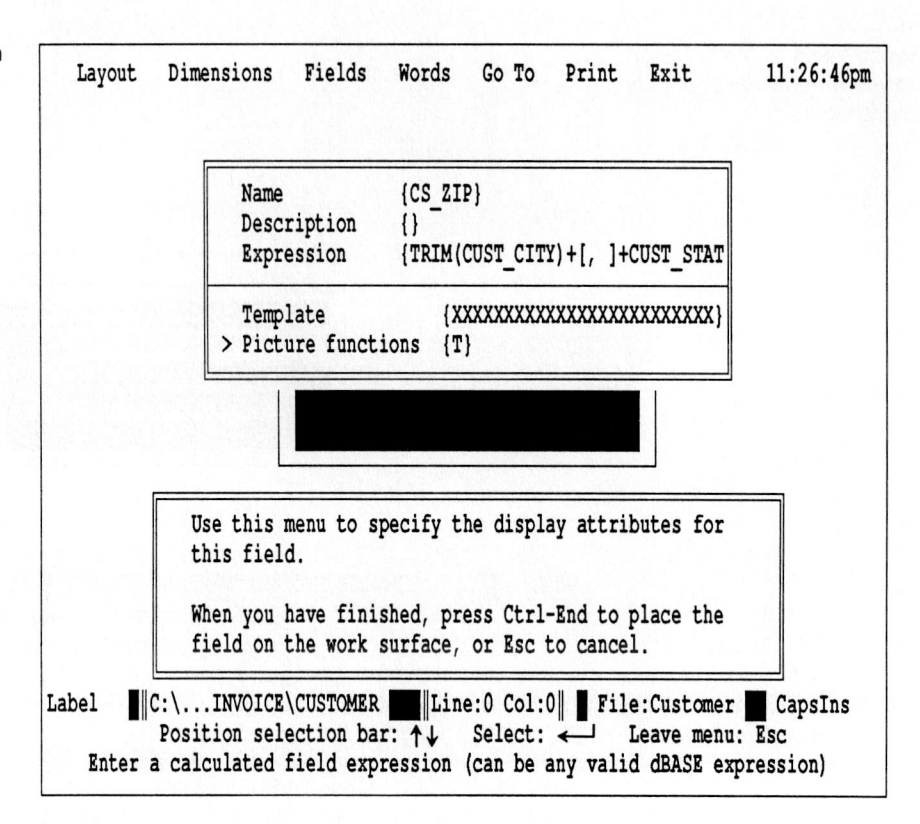

```
  Layout   Dimensions   Fields   Words   Go To   Print   Exit        11:26:46pm


         ┌─────────────────────────────────────────────────┐
         │  Name            {CS_ZIP}                       │
         │  Description     {}                             │
         │  Expression      {TRIM(CUST_CITY)+[, ]+CUST_STAT│
         │                                                 │
         │  Template        {XXXXXXXXXXXXXXXXXXXXXXXX}     │
         │> Picture functions  {T}                         │
         └─────────────────────────────────────────────────┘

              ┌─────────────────────────────────────────────┐
              │ ███████████████████████████████████████████ │
              └─────────────────────────────────────────────┘

         ┌─────────────────────────────────────────────────┐
         │ Use this menu to specify the display attributes for │
         │ this field.                                     │
         │                                                 │
         │ When you have finished, press Ctrl-End to place the │
         │ field on the work surface, or Esc to cancel.    │
         └─────────────────────────────────────────────────┘

  Label    ║C:\...INVOICE\CUSTOMER║ ║Line:0 Col:0║ File:Customer   CapsIns
              Position selection bar: ↑↓    Select: ↵    Leave menu: Esc
         Enter a calculated field expression (can be any valid dBASE expression)
```

part of the expression is [,]. This part will add a "," and a blank space immediately after the city name. The CUST_STATE field value will be added after the blank space. The [ ] will add a blank space after the state name, and the CUST_ZIP value will be added after the blank space. The effect of this concatenated expression will be

  Cincinnati, OH 45241

After entering this expression, press the <Return> key. Now highlight the Template option, and select it by pressing the <Return> key. Modify this template to 30 Xs (20 for the city name + 2 for the comma and a blank space + 2 for the sate + 1 for the blank space + 5 for the zip code). When the modification is complete, press the <Return> key. The next option, Picture functions, already contains the {T} as the default so it needs no change. Now after specifying all the attributes for the calculated expression, press <Ctrl-End> to place the calculated field at the current cursor position.

If you do so, dBASE will respond by displaying the completed label form, as shown in Figure 14.13.

The design process of the label format is now complete. To exit from this format and save it for future use, invoke the Exit Menu by pressing the <Alt-E> keys. Now highlight the Save changes and exit option, and select it by pressing the <Return> keys. dBASE will respond by displaying the dot prompt. The label format will be saved in the CUSTOMER.LBL file.

14.2.2 Producing the Labels

After the design of the label format is complete, the second step of label generation is to produce the labels using it. The dBASE command used for this purpose is the LABEL FORM command.

Figure 14.13 Label design screen with the completed label form

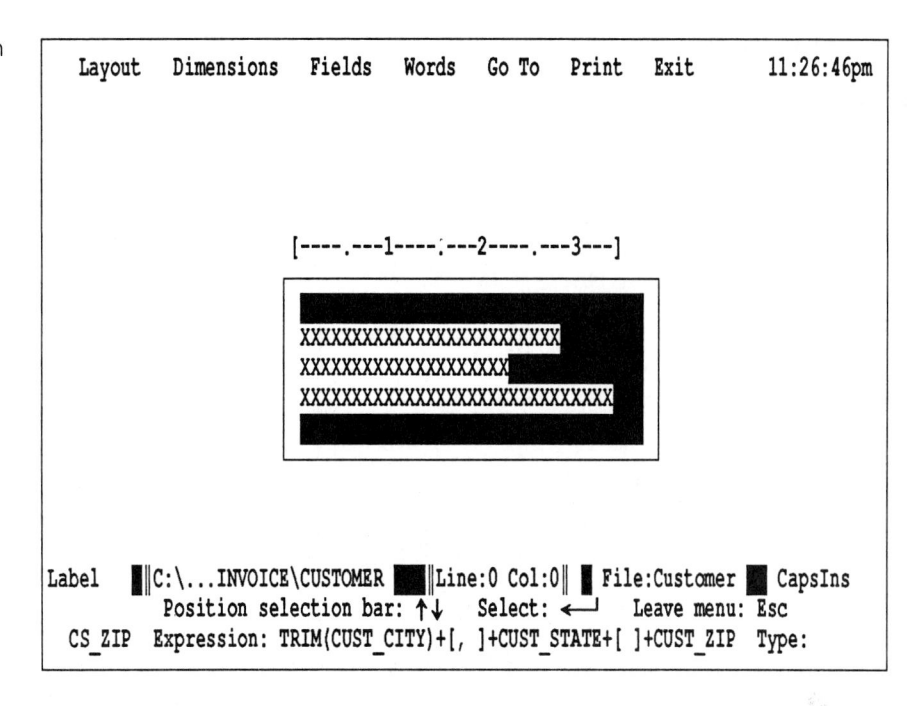

```
 Layout    Dimensions    Fields    Words    Go To    Print    Exit        11:26:46pm




                            [----.---1----.---2----.---3---]

                           ┌──────────────────────────────────┐
                           │                                  │
                           │   XXXXXXXXXXXXXXXXXXXXXXXX       │
                           │   XXXXXXXXXXXXXXXXXXX            │
                           │   XXXXXXXXXXXXXXXXXXXXXXXXXXX    │
                           │                                  │
                           └──────────────────────────────────┘




 Label    ║C:\...INVOICE\CUSTOMER║║Line:0 Col:0║ File:Customer ║ CapsIns
              Position selection bar: ↑↓    Select: ↵    Leave menu: Esc
    CS_ZIP  Expression: TRIM(CUST_CITY)+[, ]+CUST_STATE+[ ]+CUST_ZIP  Type:
```

The LABEL FORM Command

The general format of the LABEL FORM command is

```
LABEL FORM <label format file name> [SAMPLE]
          [<Scope>]
          [FOR <condition>] [WHILE <condition>]
          [TO PRINT/TO FILE <label text file
          name>]
```

where <label format file name> is the name of the label format file, <Scope> is a dBASE Scope option such as REST or NEXT, <condition> is a valid search condition that selects the records from the database file to be displayed or printed, and <label text file name> is the name of the label text file in which the labels will be stored on the disk.

The function of the LABEL FORM command is to print, display, or write the labels on a disk file from the currently active database file using the format specified by the label format file name, which has been created earlier by the CREATE LABEL command.

To display the labels from the CUSTOMER.DBF database file using the CUSTOMER.LBL label format, you'll need the following commands:

```
. USE CUSTOMER                    <Return>
. LABEL FORM CUSTOMER              <Return>
```

If you type these, dBASE will respond by displaying the labels shown in Figure 14.14.

14.2.3 Producing Selective Labels

The general format of the LABEL FORM command discussed in the previous section will produce the labels for all the records present in the CUSTOMER.DBF database file. The LABEL FORM command also allows

Figure 14.14 Labels of the CUSTOMER.DBF database file

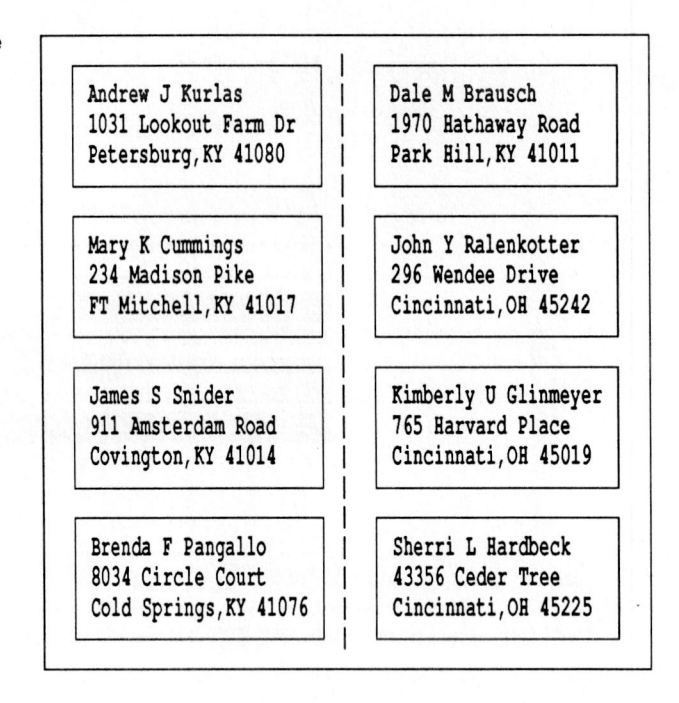

```
Andrew J Kurlas          Dale M Brausch
1031 Lookout Farm Dr     1970 Hathaway Road
Petersburg,KY 41080      Park Hill,KY 41011


Mary K Cummings          John Y Ralenkotter
234 Madison Pike         296 Wendee Drive
FT Mitchell,KY 41017     Cincinnati,OH 45242


James S Snider           Kimberly U Glinmeyer
911 Amsterdam Road       765 Harvard Place
Covington,KY 41014       Cincinnati,OH 45019


Brenda F Pangallo        Sherri L Hardbeck
8034 Circle Court        43356 Ceder Tree
Cold Springs,KY 41076    Cincinnati,OH 45225
```

us to use a predefined label format to display the labels for the selected records of the CUSTOMER.DBF database file. The format for this command is

```
LABEL FORM <label format file name> [FOR
              <condition>]
```

For example, to produce the labels only for the customers of the state of Kentucky, you'll need the following commands:

```
. USE CUSTOMER                                         <Return>
. LABEL FORM CUSTOMER FOR CUST_STATE = 'KY'            <Return>
```

If you type these, dBASE will respond by displaying the labels shown in Figure 14.15.

Figure 14.15 Labels of the CUSTOMER.DBF database file for CUST_STATE = 'KY'

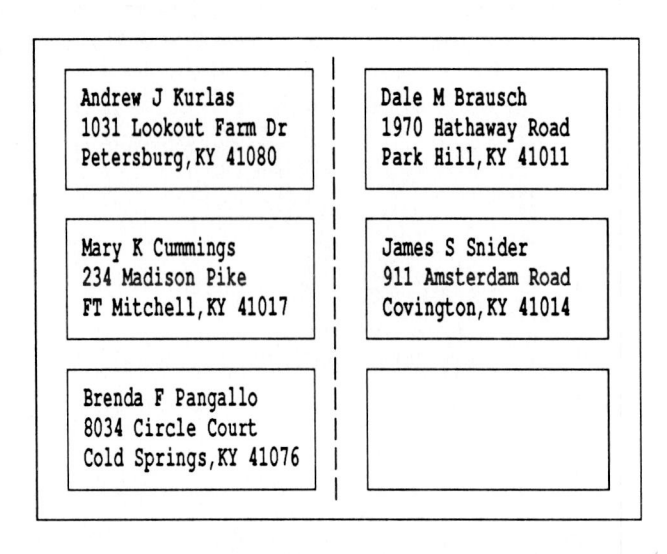

```
Andrew J Kurlas          Dale M Brausch
1031 Lookout Farm Dr     1970 Hathaway Road
Petersburg,KY 41080      Park Hill,KY 41011


Mary K Cummings          James S Snider
234 Madison Pike         911 Amsterdam Road
FT Mitchell,KY 41017     Covington,KY 41014


Brenda F Pangallo
8034 Circle Court
Cold Springs,KY 41076
```

14.2.4 Producing Printed Labels

The two formats of the LABEL FORM commands discussed so far will display the labels on the screen. Labels can also be sent to the printer for printing on self-adhesive label forms by including the TO PRINT option. Three versions of the TO PRINT option of the LABEL FORM command are

```
LABEL FORM <label format file name> TO PRINT
LABEL FORM <label format file name> TO PRINT
           SAMPLE
LABEL FORM <label format file name> TO PRINT FOR
           <condition>
```

The TO PRINT option directs the system to send the labels to the printer as well as to the screen. For example, to direct the labels directly to the printer, you'll need the following commands:

```
. USE CUSTOMER                       <Return>
. LABEL FORM CUSTOMER TO PRINT       <Return>
```

When using the self-adhesive label forms on the printer, you can align them by using the SAMPLE option. The following commands will be needed to achieve this function:

```
. USE CUSTOMER                              <Return>
. LABEL FORM CUSTOMER TO PRINT SAMPLE       <Return>
```

If you type these commands, instead of actually printing the labels, dBASE will print sample dummy labels containing all "*'s," as shown in Figure 14.16. This dummy label helps you adjust the label form alignment by repeating the process of sample labels as often as needed. When the label form is aligned, respond with "N" to the prompt. dBASE will begin printing the actual labels.

The last format of the LABEL FORM command deals with conditional selection of customers from the database and produces labels only for those selected. For example, these commands

```
. USE CUSTOMER    <Return>
. LABEL FORM CUSTOMER TO PRINT FOR CUST_STATE =
  'OH'            <Return>
```

will produce the labels for the customers from the state of Ohio only, as shown in Figure 14.17.

Figure 14.16 Sample labels used for alignment

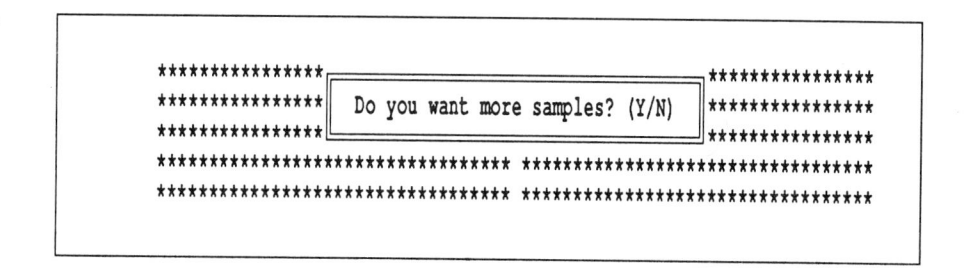

Figure 14.17 Labels of the CUSTOMER.DBF database file for CUST_STATE = 'OH'

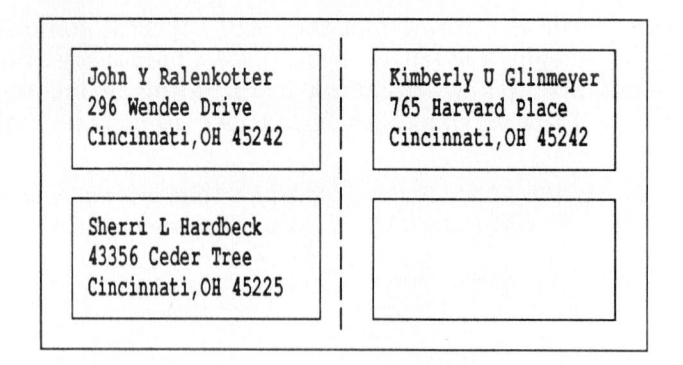

```
John Y Ralenkotter        Kimberly U Glinmeyer
296 Wendee Drive          765 Harvard Place
Cincinnati,OH 45242       Cincinnati,OH 45242


Sherri L Hardbeck
43356 Ceder Tree
Cincinnati,OH 45225
```

14.2.5 Producing Text File for Labels

In addition to being displayed on the screen or printed on the printer, labels can be written as a text file on a disk by adding the TO FILE option to the LABEL FORM command. The format for this option is

```
LABEL FORM <label format file name> TO FILE <label
text file name>
```

To create a label text file and store it on the disk, type the following commands

```
. USE CUSTOMER                                      <Return>
. LABEL FORM CUSTOMER TO FILE CUSTOMER              <Return>
```

dBASE will create a label text file called CUSTOMER.TXT and store it on the disk. This file can be edited later with a word processor, included in other documents, or transported to other computer systems.

The labels from this text file can be printed by the use of the DOS PRINT command or the dBASE TYPE command.

14.3 Summary

The label utility provided by dBASE IV allows you to design the label format, which you can use to print the contents of a database file in a mailing label form. Label generation is a two-step process. In the first step, the label format is designed; in the second step, this format is used to print the contents of the database file in the form of customized mailing labels.

The CREATE LABEL command provides an interactive method of designing the label format. The label format design process consists of defining the label dimensions, placing the data fields to be printed on the labels in the label form, and defining the display attributes for the fields.

The LABEL FORM command can be used to display, print, or write the labels on the disk file from the currently active database file using the earlier created label format.

---

dBASE COMMANDS AND FUNCTIONS

CREATE LABEL command
LABEL FORM command

MODIFY LABEL command
TRIM function

REVIEW QUESTIONS

1. What is the function of the dBASE label utility?
2. Name and explain the two steps of label generation.
3. What dBASE command is used to design the label format?
4. List three functions performed during the design process of the label format.
5. When should the MODIFY LABEL command be used?
6. What is the purpose of the TRIM function?
7. What dBASE command is used to produce the labels?
8. How can the labels for selected records of the database file be produced?
9. How can the labels be printed?
10. What option helps align the labels on the printer?
11. How can the label text file be created?
12. What command(s) can be used to obtain the listing of the label text file?

Chapter 15

Creating Reports

LEARNING OBJECTIVES

Upon successfully completing this chapter, you will be able to:

1. Use the built-in dBASE IV report generator utility.
2. Design the report format using the CREATE REPORT command.
3. Modify the already existing report format using the MODIFY REPORT command.
4. Produce the report using the REPORT FORM command.
5. Produce the report from the conditionally selected records of a database file using the REPORT FORM command.
6. Produce the printed report using the REPORT FORM command.
7. Produce the report text file using the REPORT FORM command.
8. Design the report format for the control break report using the CREATE REPORT command.
9. Produce the control break report using the REPORT FORM command.
10. Design the report format for the summary report using the CREATE REPORT command.
11. Produce the summary report using the REPORT FORM command.

15.1 Overview

This chapter deals with the creation and production of reports using the dBASE IV report generator utility. It starts by introducing the CREATE REPORT command, which is used to design the report format. In the process of designing the report format, the information to be included in its five components, that is, the page headers, report introduction, body, summary, and page footers, are defined. After creating the report format and exiting the design process, you can view the report on the screen as it will look in printed form.

The REPORT FORM command, which is used to produce the report with the help of the report format designed with the CREATE REPORT command, is introduced next. How this command can be used to produce the reports, either for all records or only for the selected records of a database file, is illustrated with examples. Use of this command to print the report and create the report text files is also presented. The method of designing and producing the control break and summary reports using the dBASE IV report generator utility is also explained with illustrative examples.

15.2 Report Generation

The report generator utility, similar to the label generator utility, allows you to design the report format to print the contents of a database file in a report form. dBASE offers three report layouts—column, form, and mailmerge. Discussion in this book is restricted to the column report layout.

The main advantage of the built-in dBASE IV report generator utility over the LIST and DISPLAY commands discussed in Chapter 2 is that it allows you to organize and display database information in an easy-to-read, columnar report by adding page headings, field headings, totals, subtotals, and summary reports. These features provide greater control over the page layout. A sample report is given in Figure 15.1.

Like label generation, report generation is also a two-step process. In the first step, the report format is designed; in the second step, it is used to print the contents of the database file in the form of the columnar report.

15.2.1 Creating a Report Format

The first step of report generation is designing the report format. The dBASE command used for this purpose is the CREATE REPORT command.

The CREATE REPORT Command

The general format of the CREATE REPORT command is

```
CREATE REPORT <report format file name>
```

Figure 15.1 A sample report

```
04/15/89              CREDIT CARD MONTHLY REPORT              13:52:40

DATE        CATEGORY TYPE      STORE NAME & ADDRESS              AMOUNT

03/18/89    Miscellaneous      Eye World #1   Cincinnati    OH     36.95
03/25/89    Restaurant         Chi Chi #245   Cincinnati    OH     25.50
03/28/89    Retail Purchases   Kmart #3507    Sharonville   OH     17.82
03/28/89    Retail Purchases   T J Max 204    Cincinnati    OH      9.78
03/29/89    Auto & Vehicle     Shell Oil Co   Blue Ash      OH     11.65
04/02/89    Restaurant         Ruby Tuesday   Fairfield     OH     32.24
04/02/89    Miscellaneous      NKU Bk Store   Highland Hgts KY     12.37
04/05/89    Auto & Vehicle     Boron #2345    Highland Hgts KY      9.20
04/06/89    Retail Purchases   Makro Inc #2   Cincinnati    OH     45.78
04/06/89    Retail Purchases   Kroger Co #4   Fairfield     OH     23.98
04/06/89    Miscellaneous      I. U. Bursar   Bloomington   IN   1165.00
04/07/89    Auto & Vehicle     Mos Marathon   Blue Ash      OH     15.00
04/08/89    Retail Purchases   Lazarus 2538   Cincinnati    OH     52.78
04/10/89    Retail Purchases   Kids Mart #3   Lima          OH     45.66
04/12/89    Auto & Vehicle     Bigfoot #307   Greensburg    IN      6.00

                                                  Total Due: 1509.71
           Page No.  1
```

where <report format file name> is the name of the file in which the report format is stored on the computer disk.

The CREATE REPORT command provides interactive techniques for designing the report format. It displays a report design screen consisting of a report design form and seven Pull-down menu options, which are used to design the report format using the report design form and the currently active database file. The report format is stored in a disk file with a default extension of .FRM.

When the CREATE REPORT command is issued and if the specified report format file already exists on the disk, dBASE will ask if you want to modify it. In fact, the MODIFY REPORT command, which works similarly to the CREATE REPORT command, should be used to modify the already existing report format.

Consider the CREDIT.DBF database file whose structure is shown in Figure 15.2 to design a report format named CREDIT.FRM. To do this, type the following commands:

```
. USE CREDIT              <Return>
. CREATE REPORT CREDIT    <Return>
```

The first command will open the CREDIT.DBF database file, and the second will start the process of designing the CREDIT.FRM report format. If you type this command, dBASE IV will respond by displaying the report design screen as shown in Figure 15.3.

The report design screen consists of a menu bar at the top with seven Pull-down menu options, which are used to design the report format. The ruler just below the menu bar represents the margins and tabs. In the center of the screen is a report design form consisting of five bands. The

Figure 15.2 Structure of the CREDIT.DBF database file

```
. USE CREDIT
. DISPLAY STRUCTURE
Structure for database : C:\DBASE\INVOICE\CREDIT.DBF
Number of data records :      15
Date of last update    : 04/20/89
Field  Field name  Type       Width  Dec    Index
    1  DATE        Date           8             N
    2  CATEGORY    Character     20             Y
    3  STORE_NAME  Character     32             N
    4  AMOUNT      Numeric        7    2        N
** TOTAL **                      68
```

status bar displaying the current operation, the drive name, the file currently in use, along with other information, and the navigation line providing the special keys used to design the report form are displayed at the bottom of the screen.

Designing the Report Form

Designing the report format involves indicating to dBASE IV what goes into each section of the printed report. There are five parts to a report—the page header, the report introduction, the body of the report (consisting of detail lines), the summary report, and the footer. All reports may not contain all five of these parts. The report design screen, as shown in Figure 15.3, consists of five bands. Each part of the report is defined by using one of these bands.

The Page Header Band The page header band is used for entering the report title and headings. The information defined in this band is printed once at the top of each page of the report. dBASE automatically adds the

Figure 15.3 Report design screen

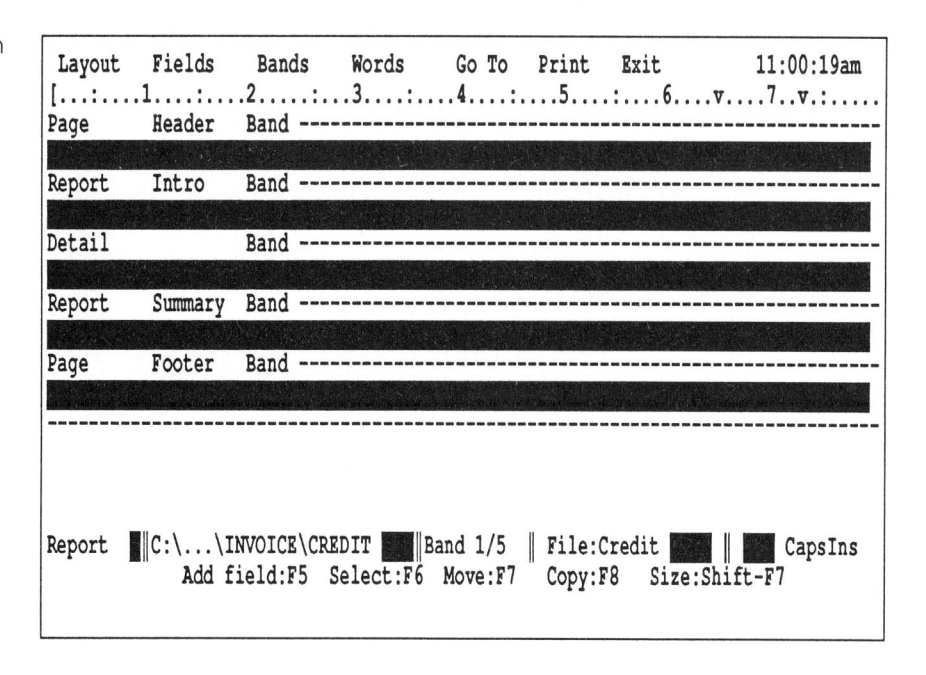

```
 Layout   Fields   Bands   Words    Go To    Print    Exit         11:00:19am
[...:....1....:....2....:....3....:....4....:....5....:....6....v....7..v.:....
Page      Header    Band ----------------------------------------------------

Report    Intro     Band ----------------------------------------------------

Detail              Band ----------------------------------------------------

Report    Summary   Band ----------------------------------------------------

Page      Footer    Band ----------------------------------------------------


Report  ▐C:\...\INVOICE\CREDIT▐Band 1/5 ║ File:Credit  ▐  ▐  CapsIns
              Add field:F5  Select:F6  Move:F7   Copy:F8   Size:Shift-F7
```

predefined fields, such as the page number and the current date, to this band. You can move these fields to different locations, remove them altogether, or add other predefined fields to this area. dBASE also adds the name of the data fields of the currently active database file as column headings to this area. You can change these to the headings of your choice.

The Report Intro Band The report intro band is used for adding the field headings or other information to describe the field names present in the report. The information in this band is printed once at the beginning of the report.

The Detail Band The detail band is used to define the values for the records of the database file. The field values of the records are represented using the field templates. The information in this band is used to print each of the report's detail lines.

The Report Summary Band The report summary band is used to define the column totals or the closing information about the report. The information in this band is printed once at the end of the report.

The Page Footer Band The page footer band is used to define the page footers, such as page numbers or other useful information. The information in this band is printed once at the bottom of each page of the report.

Other Bands In addition to these five bands, other summary bands can also be added to the report form as needed. This option is explained in section 15.3.1.

Now, let us proceed with the design of the CREDIT report format. To do this, we will use one of the three general layouts provided by dBASE IV—a column layout, a form layout, or a mailmerge layout. One of these

Figure 15.4 Report design screen with the submenu of the Layout option of the menu bar

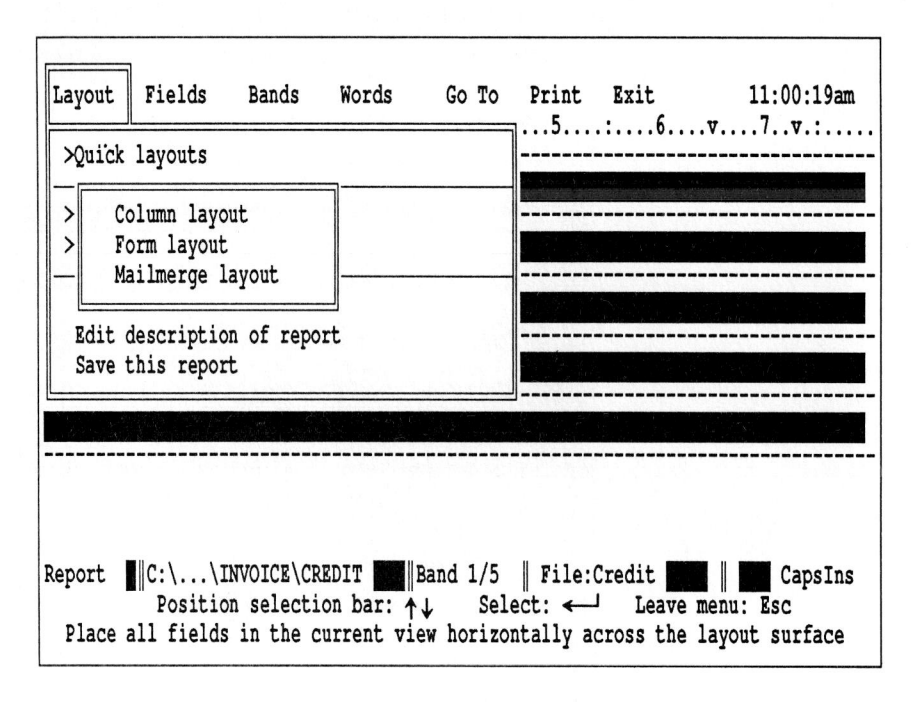

15.2 Report Generation 565

Figure 15.5 Report design screen of the standard columnar report form for the CREDIT.DBF database file

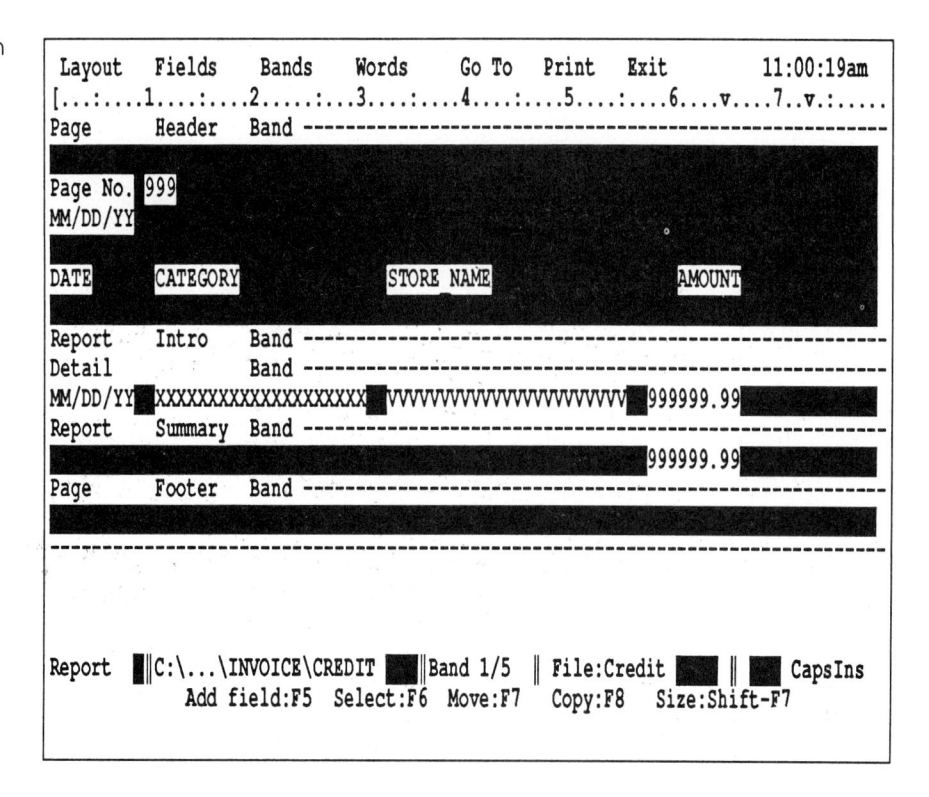

```
Layout    Fields    Bands    Words    Go To    Print    Exit         11:00:19am
[...:....1....:....2....:....3....:....4....:....5....:....6....v....7..v.:....
Page      Header    Band ------------------------------------------------------

Page No. 999
MM/DD/YY

DATE      CATEGORY           STORE NAME               AMOUNT

Report    Intro     Band ------------------------------------------------------
Detail              Band ------------------------------------------------------
MM/DD/YY  XXXXXXXXXXXXXXXXXX VVVVVVVVVVVVVVVVVVVVVVVV 999999.99
Report    Summary   Band ------------------------------------------------------
                                                     999999.99
Page      Footer    Band ------------------------------------------------------


---------------------------------------------------------------------------------
Report    C:\...\INVOICE\CREDIT    Band 1/5    File:Credit         CapsIns
          Add field:F5  Select:F6  Move:F7  Copy:F8  Size:Shift-F7
```

can be used as the starting point for designing your report format, which can be begun by invoking the Layout option of the menu bar.

To select one of the general layouts to design the CREDIT report form, invoke the Layout option of the menu bar by pressing the <Alt-L> keys. dBASE will respond by displaying the Layout Pull-down Menu. Highlight the Quick layout option from this, and select it by pressing the <Return> key. The submenu displaying the three options—Column layout, Form layout, and Mailmerge layout—as shown in Figure 15.4, will be displayed.

Now, select the Column layout option by highlighting it and pressing the <Return> key. At this point, dBASE will respond by displaying the standard columnar report format as shown in Figure 15.5.

The report format is divided into five different sections, each of which is represented by a band. The page header band contains the predefined fields, the page number, and the current date. It also contains the data field names representing the column headings for the report. The detail band contains the template for each data field in the record of the CREDIT.DBF database file. The report summary band contains the template for the amount total field.

After selecting the general columnar layout supplied by dBASE, proceed with the design of the report form to produce the report as shown in Figure 15.1. The page number should be printed at the bottom of the page, not at the top as shown in Figure 15.5. The report title, "CREDIT CARD MONTHLY REPORT," needs to be added, column headings need to be changed, and the system time needs to be included in the page header band. Table 15.1 lists the most commonly used control keys for editing the report or label format.

Table 15.1 Most commonly used control keys for editing the layout form

Key	Function
↑	To move cursor up one row
↓	To move cursor down one row
→	To move cursor one character to the right or to the end of the field template
←	To move cursor one character to the left or to the beginning of the field template
Ins	To switch keyboard between insert and overwrite mode
↵ (Return)	To insert a new line (in insert mode) and move down one row (in overwrite mode)
Tab	To move cursor to the next tab position
Shift-Tab	To move cursor to the previous tab position
Backspace	To move cursor one space back and erase the previous character
Del	To delete a character to the right of the cursor
Ctrl-N	To insert a new blank line
Ctrl-Y	To delete the entire line
Ctrl-T	To delete a word or a field to the right of cursor
PgUp	To move to the top of the form
PgDn	To move to the bottom of the form
Home	To move to the beginning of the line
End	To move to the end of the line

To proceed with these changes, follow these steps:

1. Use the cursor control keys to move the cursor to the letter "P" of the label "Page NO.," and press the <Ctrl-Y> keys. This action will delete the line containing the page number.

2. Now move the cursor to the next line, and position it at the desired location. Type the title "CREDIT CARD MONTHLY REPORT."

3. Move the cursor to column 70 of the same line to make the system time appear on the report. To add the predefined time field, press the F5 Add Field function key. The system will return by displaying the Fields Submenu. Highlight the time field from the predefined fields column, and select it by pressing the <Return> key. The system will respond by displaying "HH:MM:SS" at the location of the cursor.

4. Make the changes in the column headings by moving the cursor to the heading to be changed and typing the changes.

5. Steps 1–4 take care of the changes needed in the page header band. Now move the cursor to the desired location in the report summary band, and type "Total Due:."

6. To make the last change in the page footer band, move the cursor to the center of the band, and type the label "Page No." Now move the cursor two spaces to the right, which is where the page

Figure 15.6 Report design screen after the design of the report form

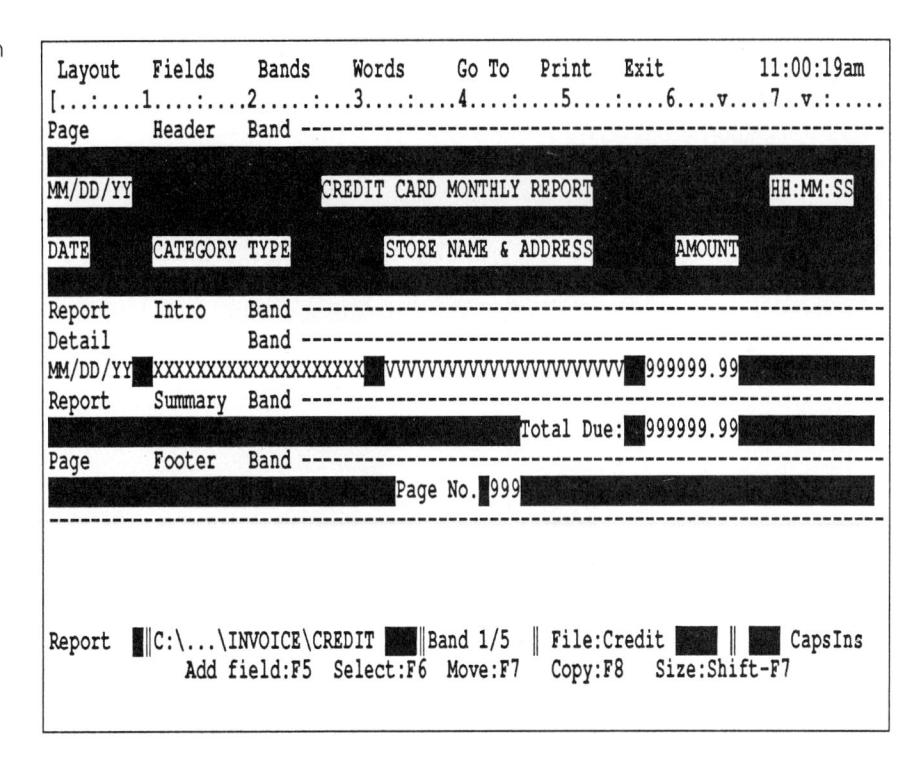

```
Layout   Fields   Bands   Words   Go To   Print   Exit         11:00:19am
[...:....1....:....2....:....3....:....4....:....5....:....6....v....7..v.:.....
Page       Header   Band -------------------------------------------------------

MM/DD/YY                    CREDIT CARD MONTHLY REPORT              HH:MM:SS

DATE       CATEGORY TYPE       STORE NAME & ADDRESS        AMOUNT

Report     Intro    Band -------------------------------------------------------
Detail              Band -------------------------------------------------------
MM/DD/YY  XXXXXXXXXXXXXXXXXX  VVVVVVVVVVVVVVVVVVVVVVVV   999999.99
Report     Summary  Band -------------------------------------------------------
                                                Total Due:  999999.99
Page       Footer   Band -------------------------------------------------------
                                             Page No.  999
--------------------------------------------------------------------------------



Report    C:\...\INVOICE\CREDIT   Band 1/5  | File:Credit    |    CapsIns
          Add field:F5  Select:F6  Move:F7  Copy:F8  Size:Shift-F7
```

number should appear. To add the page number field, press the F5 Add Field function key. The system will return by displaying the Fields Submenu. Highlight the Page No. field from the predefined fields column, and select it by pressing the <Return> key. The system will respond by displaying 999 at the location of the cursor.

The process of making changes needed in the report format is now complete, and the report form will appear as shown in Figure 15.6.

Viewing the Report on the Screen

Before you exit the design process and save the report form for future use, you can view it on the screen as it will appear in printed form. dBASE IV provides this capability so that if any alterations are needed, you can make them before exiting the design process. The view capability is also available for viewing labels on the screen.

To view the report on the screen, invoke the Print option of the menu bar by pressing the <Alt-P> keys. The Print Submenu as shown in Figure 15.7 will be displayed.

Select the View report on screen option from the Pull-down Submenu. dBASE will create a program called CREDIT.FRG to produce the report as shown in Figure 15.1 and store it on the disk. You can modify this program to alter the report format by using the MODIFY COMMAND as it is used with other dBASE programs. dBASE also creates an object code for this program and stores it under CREDIT.FRO on the disk. This code is executed by the system to produce the report. After this, the system will display the report as shown in Figure 15.1 on the screen. To view the rest of the report, follow the instructions given at the bottom of the screen.

Figure 15.7 Report design screen after the design of the report form with the View report on screen option

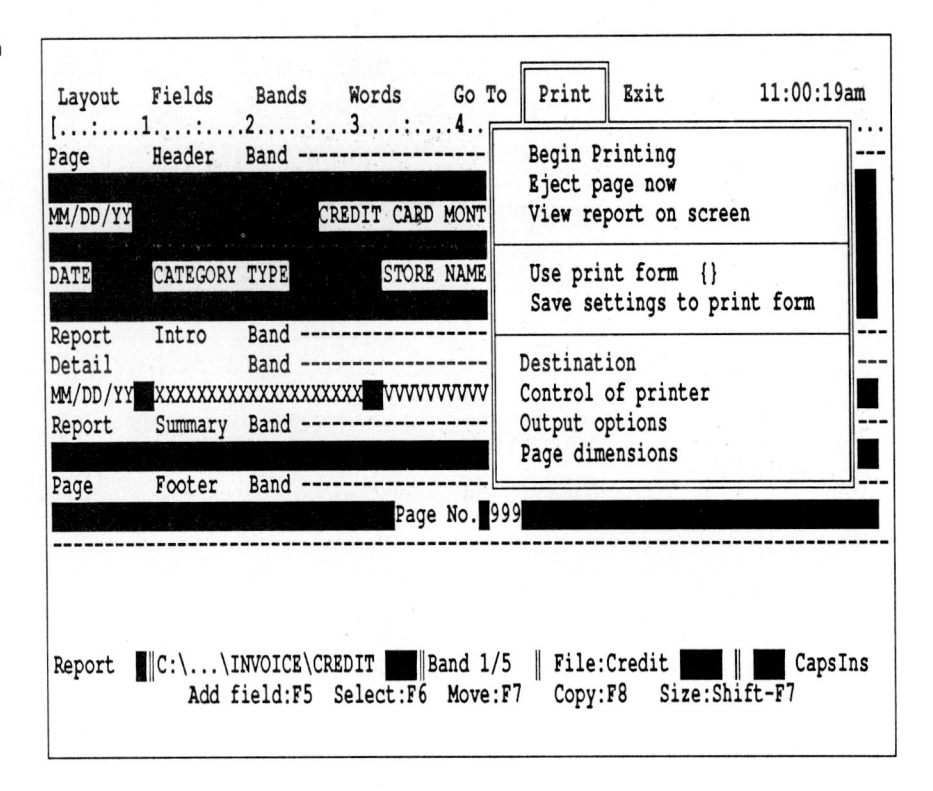

```
 Layout   Fields   Bands   Words   Go To │ Print │ Exit        11:00:19am
[...:.....1.....:.....2.....:.....3.....:...4..├──────────────────────────┤
 Page      Header    Band ─────────────────────│ Begin Printing           │
                                               │ Eject page now           │
 MM/DD/YY                    CREDIT CARD MONT  │ View report on screen    │
                                               ├──────────────────────────┤
 DATE      CATEGORY TYPE     STORE NAME        │ Use print form     {}    │
                                               │ Save settings to print form│
 Report    Intro     Band ─────────────────────├──────────────────────────┤
 Detail              Band ─────────────────────│ Destination              │
 MM/DD/YY  XXXXXXXXXXXXXXXXXX  VVVVVVVVV       │ Control of printer       │
 Report    Summary   Band ─────────────────────│ Output options           │
                                               │ Page dimensions          │
 Page      Footer    Band ─────────────────────└──────────────────────────┘
                                          Page No. 999


 ─────────────────────────────────────────────────────────────────────────

 Report   ║C:\...\INVOICE\CREDIT ║║Band 1/5  ║ File:Credit ║ ║  CapsIns
          Add field:F5  Select:F6  Move:F7   Copy:F8   Size:Shift-F7
```

After displaying the whole report, the system will display the report design screen shown in Figure 15.6.

The design process of the report format is now complete. Save the report format by invoking the Exit option on the menu bar by pressing the <Alt-E> keys. Next, highlight the Save changes and exit option from the Pull-down Submenu, and press the <Return> key to instruct dBASE to save the report format. The report format will be saved under the CREDIT.FRM file name, and the system will respond by displaying the dot prompt.

15.2.2 Producing the Report

The second step of report generation is to produce the report using the format you have designed. The dBASE command used for this purpose is the REPORT FORM command.

The REPORT FORM Command

The general format of the REPORT FORM command is

```
REPORT FORM <report format file name> [SAMPLE]
            [<Scope>] [FOR <condition>]
            [WHILE <condition>]
            [TO PRINT/TO FILE <report text file
            name>]
```

where <report format file name> is the name of the report format file, <Scope> is a dBASE scope option such as REST or NEXT, <condition>

15.2 Report Generation

is a valid search condition that selects the records from the database file to be displayed or printed, and <report text file name> is the name of the text disk file under which the report will be stored.

The function of the REPORT FORM command is to display, print, or write the report on a disk file from the currently active database file. dBASE will use the format specified by the report format file name, which has been created earlier by the CREATE REPORT command.

To display the report for the CREDIT.DBF database file using the CREDIT.FRM report format, you'll need the following commands:

```
. USE CREDIT                <Return>
. REPORT FORM CREDIT        <Return>
```

The first one will open the CREDIT.DBF database file, and the second will display the report using the CREDIT.FRM report format. If you type these commands, dBASE will respond by displaying the report as shown in Figure 15.1.

15.2.3 Producing a Conditional Report

The general format of the REPORT FORM command discussed in the previous section will produce a report containing all the records present in the CREDIT.DBF database file. The REPORT FORM command also allows you to use a predefined report format to display the report containing selected records of the CREDIT.DBF database file. The format of this command is

```
REPORT FORM <label format file name> [FOR
            <condition>]
```

For example, to produce a report containing only the purchases made before April, type the following commands:

```
. USE CREDIT                <Return>
. REPORT FORM CREDIT FOR DATE <
  {04/01/89}                <Return>
```

dBASE will respond by displaying the report shown in Figure 15.8.

Figure 15.8 Report for the CREDIT.DBF database file for March only

```
04/15/89              CREDIT CARD MONTHLY REPORT              13:52:40

DATE        CATEGORY TYPE      STORE NAME & ADDRESS              AMOUNT

03/18/89    Miscellaneous      Eye World #1   Cincinnati    OH     36.95
03/25/89    Restaurant         Chi Chi #245   Cincinnati    OH     25.50
03/28/89    Retail Purchases   Kmart #3507    Sharonville   OH     17.82
03/28/89    Retail Purchases   T J Max 204    Cincinnati    OH      9.78
03/29/89    Auto & Vehicle     Shell Oil Co   Blue Ash      OH     11.65
                                                      Total Due:  101.70
                               Page No.  1
```

15.2.4 Producing a Printed Report

The two formats of the REPORT FORM command discussed so far will display the reports on the screen. They can also be sent to the printer for hard copy output by including the TO PRINT option in the REPORT FORM command. Three versions of the TO PRINT option are

```
REPORT FORM <label format file name> TO PRINT
REPORT FORM <label format file name> TO PRINT
            NOEJECT
REPORT FORM <label format file name> TO PRINT
            PLAIN
```

The TO PRINT option directs the system to send the report to the printer as well as to the screen. For example, to direct the report to the printer, type the following commands:

```
. USE CREDIT                                <Return>
. REPORT FORM CREDIT TO PRINT               <Return>
```

dBASE will print a report on the printer exactly like the one displayed on the screen in Figure 15.1.

Usually dBASE will default to a page eject before it starts printing the report to ensure that the report starts on a new page, unless the NOEJECT option is specified. To achieve this effect, you'll need the following commands:

```
. USE CREDIT                                    <Return>
. REPORT FORM CREDIT TO PRINT NOEJECT           <Return>
```

When a multipage report is printed on the printer, the page number, date, and report heading are printed at the top of every page by default by dBASE. To suppress these items on all pages except the first, include the PLAIN option:

```
. USE CREDIT                                    <Return>
. REPORT FORM CREDIT TO PRINT PLAIN             <Return>
```

15.2.5 Producing a Text File for Reports

In addition to displaying the report on the screen or printing it on the printer, you can direct the report to be written as a report text file on a disk by adding the TO FILE option to the REPORT FORM command. Its format is

```
REPORT FORM <report format file name> TO FILE
            <report text file name>
```

To write the report produced earlier as a report text disk file, type the following commands:

```
. USE CREDIT                                    <Return>
. REPORT FORM CREDIT TO FILE CREDIT             <Return>
```

dBASE will create a report text file called CREDIT.TXT and store it on the disk. This file can be edited later with a word processor, included in other documents, or transported to other computer systems. You can use the

DOS PRINT or the dBASE TYPE commands to obtain the report later from this text file.

15.3 Control Break Reports

One of the most commonly used reports in business applications is the control break report. This contains groups of records listed with a subtotal for that group until all the groups are listed. At the end of the report, the total for the whole file is listed. A control break report is shown in Figure 15.9.

Recall from Section 7.4 that to produce a control break report, you need to have the database file sorted or indexed on the field in which the

Figure 15.9 Control break report

```
04/15/89              CREDIT CARD MONTHLY REPORT           13:52:40

DATE       CATEGORY TYPE      STORE NAME & ADDRESS          AMOUNT

      SUMMARY BY: Auto & Vehicle

03/29/89   Auto & Vehicle     Shell Oil Co  Blue Ash    OH    11.65
04/05/89   Auto & Vehicle     Boron #2345   Highland Hgts KY   9.20
04/07/89   Auto & Vehicle     Mos Marathon  Blue Ash    OH    15.00
04/12/89   Auto & Vehicle     Bigfoot #307  Greensburg  IN     6.00

                                             Subtotal:       41.85

      SUMMARY BY: Miscellaneous

03/18/89   Miscellaneous      Eye World #1  Cincinnati  OH    36.95
04/02/89   Miscellaneous      NKU Bk Store  Highland Hgts KY  12.37
04/06/89   Miscellaneous      I. U. Bursar  Bloomington IN  1165.00

                                             Subtotal:     1214.32

      SUMMARY BY: Restaurant

03/25/89   Restaurant         Chi Chi #245  Cincinnati  OH    25.50
04/02/89   Restaurant         Ruby Tuesday  Fairfield   OH    32.24

                                             Subtotal:       57.74

      SUMMARY BY: Retail Purchases

03/28/89   Retail Purchases   Kmart #3507   Sharonville OH    17.82
03/28/89   Retail Purchases   T J Max 204   Cincinnati  OH     9.78
04/06/89   Retail Purchases   Makro Inc #2  Cincinnati  OH    45.78
04/06/89   Retail Purchases   Kroger Co #4  Fairfield   OH    23.98
04/08/89   Retail Purchases   Lazarus 2538  Cincinnati  OH    52.78
04/10/89   Retail Purchases   Kids Mart #3  Lima        OH    45.66

                                             Subtotal:      195.80

                                          Final Total:     1509.71
                          Page No.  1
```

records in the report should be grouped. In this example, the CREDIT.DBF database file is indexed on the CATEGORY data field (refer to the structure of the database file in Figure 15.2).

15.3.1 Designing the Control Break Report Format

Because the control break report shown in Figure 15.9 is grouped on the category field, the CREDIT.DBF database file should be indexed on this field, and the category index tag should be active when the report is produced. To open the CREDIT.DBF database file and activate the category index tag, type the following commands:

```
. USE CREDIT              <Return>
. SET ORDER TO CATEGORY   <Return>
```

dBASE will respond by displaying the message:

```
Master Index: CATEGORY
```

This message indicates that the category index tag is active, and the records of the CREDIT.DBF database file are available in alphabetic order on the category field. To design the report format named CBREPORT.FRM for the CREDIT.DBF database file, type the following command:

```
. CREATE REPORT CBREPORT    <Return>
```

dBASE will respond by displaying a report design screen similar to the one shown in Figure 15.3. Because the report title, column headings, and data fields arrangement of this report are similar to that of the one used in section 15.2, follow the steps used there to design the report format as shown in Figure 15.6.

We could have saved the time of recreating this format by copying the CREDIT.FRM file to the CBREPORT.FRM file and using the MODIFY REPORT CBREPORT command to continue its modification.

Adding a Summary Band

You can add the group summary band for the records grouped on the CATEGORY field by completing the following steps:

1. Position the cursor at the report intro band, and invoke the Bands option from the menu bar by pressing the <Alt-B> keys.
2. Highlight the Add a group band option, and select this option by pressing the <Return> key. dBASE will respond by displaying the submenu as shown in Figure 15.10.
3. Highlight the Field value option, and select it by pressing <Return>. dBASE will respond by displaying the data fields of the CREDIT.DBF database file, also shown in Figure 15.10.
4. Highlight the category field, and select it by pressing the <Return> key. dBASE will respond by adding two new bands—group 1 intro band and group 1 summary band—as shown in Figure 15.11. The message line will read "Group by Category," indicating that the group summary band for the records grouped on the category field has been added.

Figure 15.10 Report design screen with the Bands option and the Add a Group Band Submenu

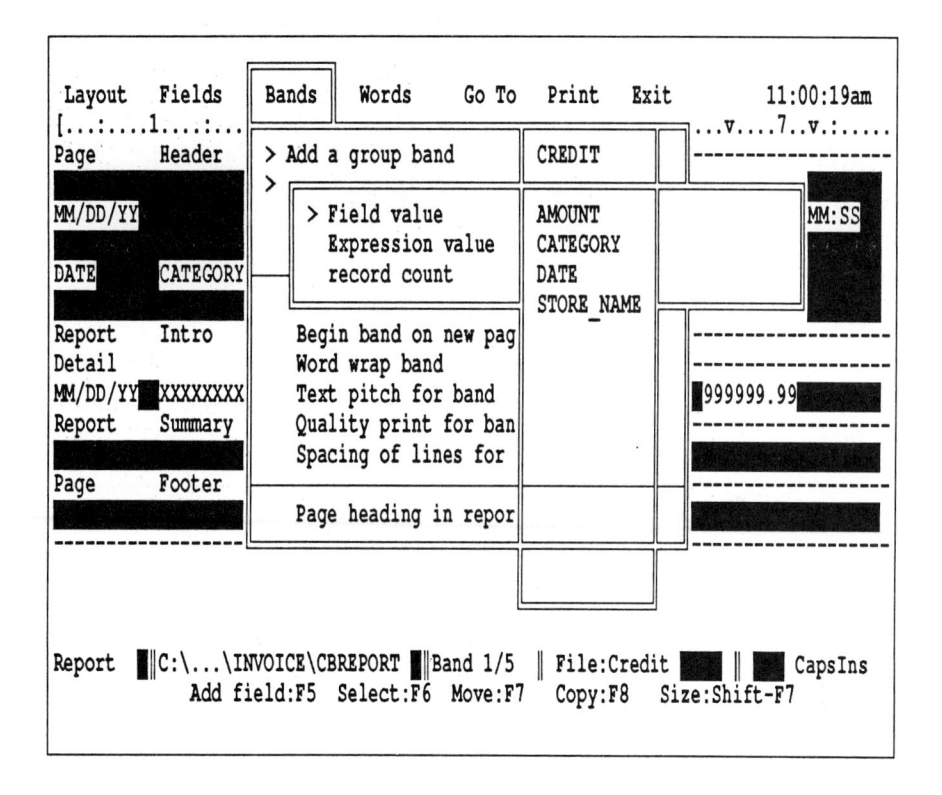

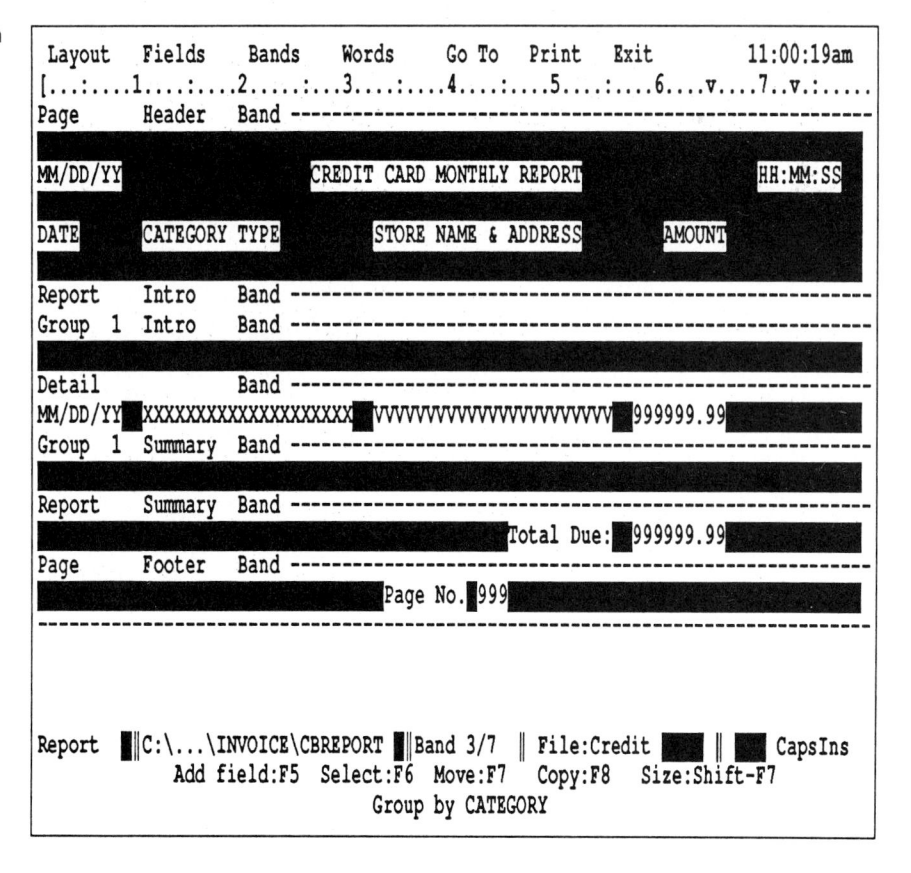

```
Layout    Fields    Bands      Words       Go To    Print    Exit         11:00:19am
[...:....1....:...                                                   ...v....7..v.:.....
Page      Header   > Add a group band        CREDIT           ------------------
                   >
MM/DD/YY             > Field value          AMOUNT                              MM:SS
                       Expression value     CATEGORY
                       record count         DATE
DATE      CATEGORY                          STORE_NAME

Report    Intro      Begin band on new pag              ------------------
Detail               Word wrap band
MM/DD/YY  XXXXXXXX   Text pitch for band                              999999.99
Report    Summary    Quality print for ban
                     Spacing of lines for
Page      Footer
                     Page heading in repor


Report   ‖C:\...\INVOICE\CBREPORT ‖Band 1/5 ‖ File:Credit       ‖   CapsIns
                 Add field:F5 Select:F6 Move:F7  Copy:F8  Size:Shift-F7
```

Figure 15.11 Report design screen after adding the summary band for the category field

```
Layout    Fields    Bands      Words       Go To    Print    Exit         11:00:19am
[...:....1....:....2....:....3....:....4....:....5....:....6....v....7..v.:.....
Page      Header   Band ---------------------------------------------------------

MM/DD/YY            CREDIT CARD MONTHLY REPORT              HH:MM:SS

DATE      CATEGORY TYPE        STORE NAME & ADDRESS         AMOUNT

Report    Intro    Band ---------------------------------------------------------
Group 1   Intro    Band ---------------------------------------------------------

Detail             Band ---------------------------------------------------------
MM/DD/YY  XXXXXXXXXXXXXXXXXXXX VVVVVVVVVVVVVVVVVVVVVVV 999999.99
Group 1   Summary  Band ---------------------------------------------------------

Report    Summary  Band ---------------------------------------------------------
                                                    Total Due: 999999.99
Page      Footer   Band ---------------------------------------------------------
                                            Page No. 999
                   ---------------------------------------------------------


Report   ‖C:\...\INVOICE\CBREPORT ‖Band 3/7 ‖ File:Credit       ‖   CapsIns
                 Add field:F5 Select:F6 Move:F7  Copy:F8  Size:Shift-F7
                                 Group by CATEGORY
```

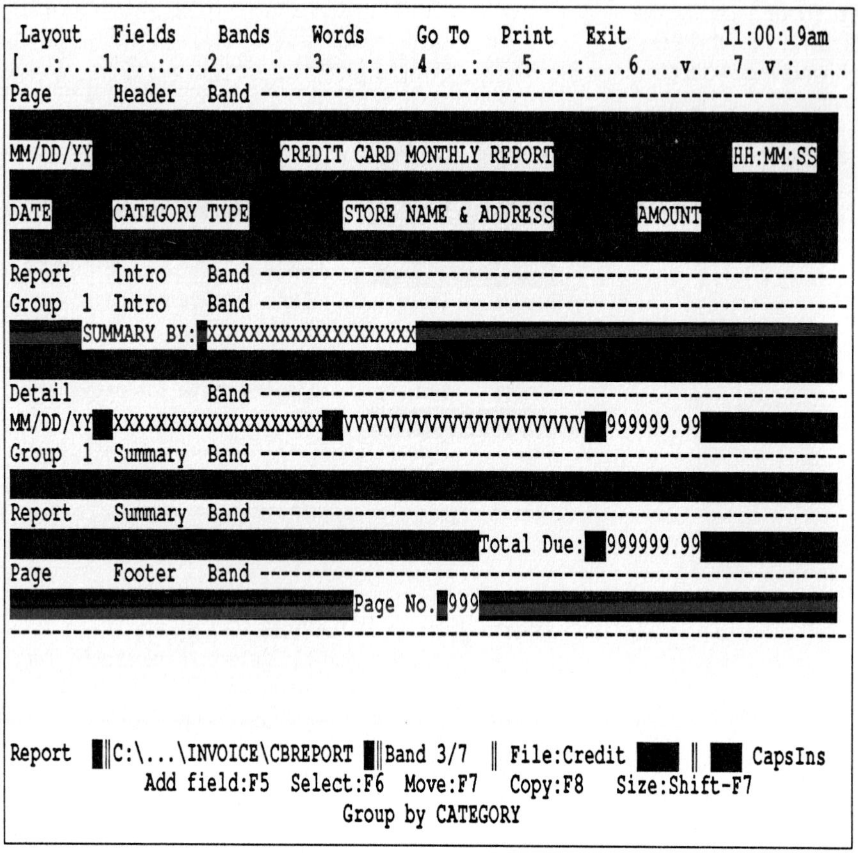

Figure 15.12 Report design screen after adding the summary subheadings for the category field

```
 Layout    Fields   Bands     Words     Go To    Print    Exit        11:00:19am
 [...:.....1.....:.....2.....:.....3.....:.....4.....:.....5.....:.....6....v....7..v.:....
 Page      Header   Band ----------------------------------------------------------

 MM/DD/YY                    CREDIT CARD MONTHLY REPORT                    HH:MM:SS

 DATE            CATEGORY TYPE         STORE NAME & ADDRESS        AMOUNT


 Report    Intro    Band ----------------------------------------------------------
 Group 1   Intro    Band ----------------------------------------------------------
                 SUMMARY BY: XXXXXXXXXXXXXXXXXXXX

 Detail             Band ----------------------------------------------------------
 MM/DD/YY XXXXXXXXXXXXXXXXXXX VVVVVVVVVVVVVVVVVVVVVVVV    999999.99
 Group 1   Summary  Band ----------------------------------------------------------


 Report    Summary  Band ----------------------------------------------------------
                                                       Total Due:  999999.99
 Page      Footer   Band ----------------------------------------------------------
                                               Page No.  999
 -----------------------------------------------------------------------------------



 Report    ||C:\...\INVOICE\CBREPORT ||Band 3/7 || File:Credit  ||   CapsIns
             Add field:F5  Select:F6  Move:F7  Copy:F8  Size:Shift-F7
                                Group by CATEGORY
```

Adding Summary Subheadings

To add the summary subheadings, follow these steps:

1. Position the cursor to the line just below the group 1 intro band, and press the <Ctrl-N> keys. This step will add a blank line.
2. Position the cursor on the line below the group 1 intro band, and type the subheading "SUMMARY BY:." Now move the cursor one position to the right, and invoke the Fields Menu by pressing the F5 Add Field function key. The Fields Submenu similar to the one shown in Figure 14.8 will be displayed.
3. Highlight the category field from the field list, and select it by pressing the <Return> key.
4. Press the <Ctrl-End> keys to choose the default template, and return to the report format screen. The system will respond by adding the category field template, as shown in Figure 15.12.

Adding Summary Subtotal Fields

To add the summary subtotal field for each category, proceed as follows:

1. Position the cursor on the line just below the group 1 summary band, and add a blank line by pressing the <Ctrl-N> keys.

15.3 Control Break Reports

2. Move the cursor to the appropriate position on the second line below the group 1 summary band, and type the subtotal heading "Subtotal:." Now move the cursor one position to the left below the amount field template, and invoke the Fields Menu by pressing the F5 Add Field function key.
3. Highlight the Sum option from the summary column, and select it by pressing the <Return> key. The system will respond by displaying the window showing the attributes for the summary field, as illustrated in Figure 15.13.
4. Specify the display attributes for the summary field by following these steps:
   a. Highlight the Name option, and select it by pressing the <Return> key. Now assign the CS_TOTAL name for the summary total field, and press the <Return> key.
   b. Highlight the Description option, and select it by pressing the <Return> key. Now enter the description for the summary field name as "Category Subtotal," and press the <Return> key.
   c. Highlight the Field to Summarize on option, and select it by pressing the <Return> key. The window showing the fields list of the CREDIT.DBF database file will appear on the screen. Select the AMOUNT field by highlighting it and pressing the <Return> key.

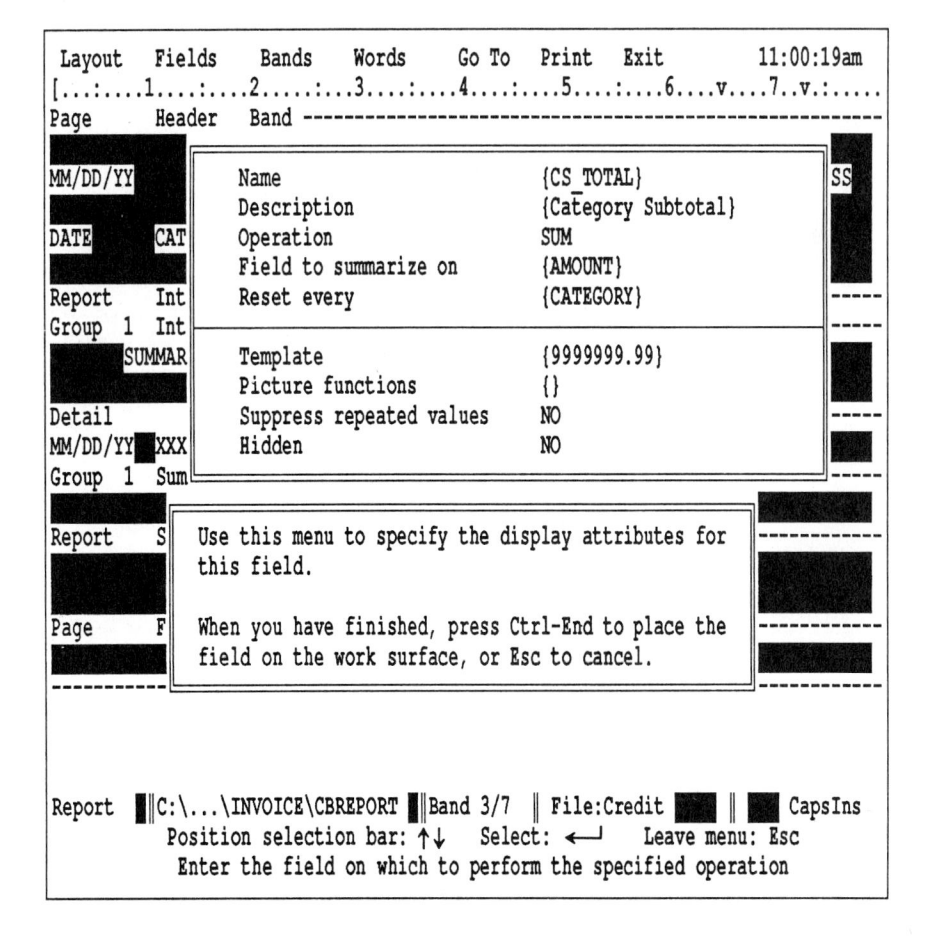

Figure 15.13 Report design screen with a window for defining display attributes for the summary field

```
Layout    Fields    Bands    Words    Go To    Print    Exit         11:00:19am
[...:.....1......:.....2......:......3.......:.....4......:.....5.....:.....6....v....7..v.:.....
Page      Header    Band ----------------------------------------------------------------

MM/DD/YY            Name                        {CS_TOTAL}                          SS
                    Description                 {Category Subtotal}
DATE       CAT      Operation                   SUM
                    Field to summarize on       {AMOUNT}
Report     Int      Reset every                 {CATEGORY}
Group  1   Int
                    Template                    {9999999.99}
           SUMMAR   Picture functions           { }
Detail              Suppress repeated values    NO
MM/DD/YY   XXX      Hidden                      NO
Group  1   Sum

Report     S    | Use this menu to specify the display attributes for |
                | this field.                                          |
                |                                                      |
Page       F    | When you have finished, press Ctrl-End to place the  |
                | field on the work surface, or Esc to cancel.         |

-----------------

Report    ||C:\...\INVOICE\CBREPORT ||Band 3/7 || File:Credit    ||    CapsIns
                  Position selection bar: ↑↓   Select: ←┘   Leave menu: Esc
                  Enter the field on which to perform the specified operation
```

Figure 15.14 Report design screen with a window for defining display attributes for the summary field and Picture Functions Submenu

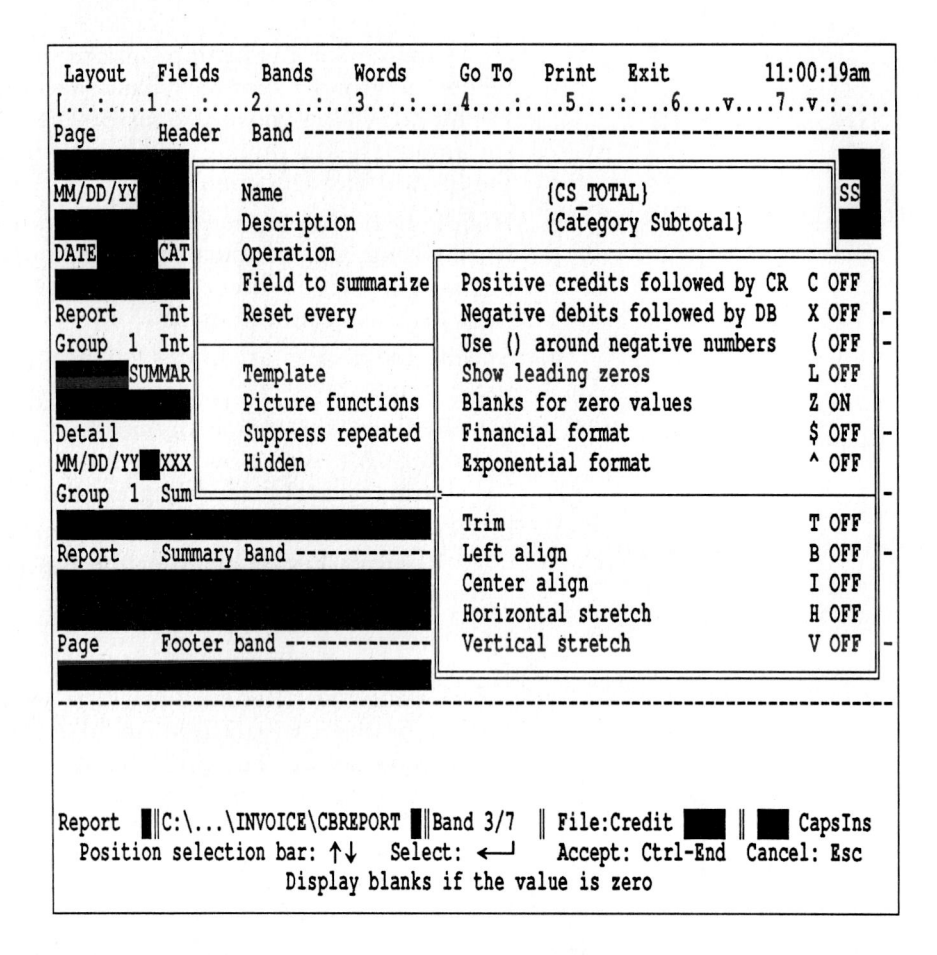

```
Layout    Fields    Bands    Words    Go To    Print    Exit         11:00:19am
[...:....1....:....2....:....3....:....4....:....5....:....6....v....7..v.:.....
Page    Header    Band -----------------------------------------------------

MM/DD/YY            Name                        {CS_TOTAL}                    SS
                    Description                 {Category Subtotal}
DATE        CAT     Operation
                    Field to summarize    Positive credits followed by CR  C OFF
Report      Int     Reset every           Negative debits followed by DB   X OFF
Group 1     Int                           Use () around negative numbers   ( OFF
            SUMMAR  Template              Show leading zeros               L OFF
                    Picture functions     Blanks for zero values           Z ON
Detail              Suppress repeated     Financial format                 $ OFF
MM/DD/YY    XXX     Hidden                Exponential format               ^ OFF
Group 1     Sum
                                          Trim                             T OFF
Report      Summary Band ---------------  Left align                       B OFF
                                          Center align                     I OFF
                                          Horizontal stretch               H OFF
Page        Footer band ----------------  Vertical stretch                 V OFF

--------------------------------------------------------------------------------

Report   ||C:\...\INVOICE\CBREPORT ||Band 3/7 || File:Credit    ||    CapsIns
       Position selection bar: ↑↓    Select: ↵    Accept: Ctrl-End  Cancel: Esc
                          Display blanks if the value is zero
```

d. Highlight the Picture function option, and select it by pressing the <Return> key. A submenu as shown in Figure 15.14 will be displayed. Select the Blanks for zero values option by highlighting it and pressing the <Ctrl-End> keys.

5. Press the <Ctrl-End> keys to save the display attributes, to place the summary field on the work surface, and to return to the report format screen. If you do so, the system will respond by displaying the report format screen with the summary subtotal field, as shown in Figure 15.15.

Modifying the Final Total Headings

Move the cursor to the line just below the report summary band, and add a blank line by pressing the <Ctrl-N> keys. Now move the cursor to the second line below the report summary band, and correct the final total heading to read "Final Total:."

Viewing the Control Break Report on the Screen

Before you exit the design process and save the report form for future use, view the report on the screen as it will appear in the printed form. To do this, invoke the Print option of the menu bar by pressing the <Alt-P> keys.

Figure 15.15 Report design screen with the format for subtotal on the category field

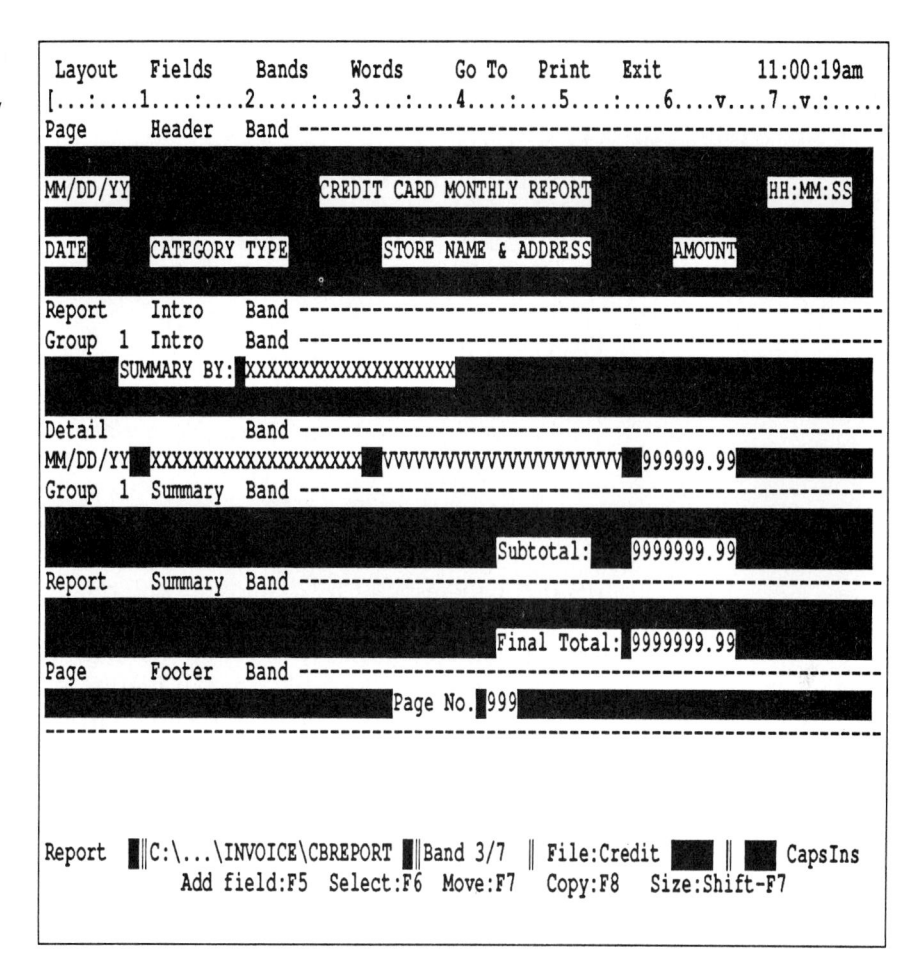

```
 Layout    Fields    Bands    Words    Go To    Print    Exit        11:00:19am
[...:.....1....:....2....:....3....:....4....:....5....:....6....v....7..v.:.....
 Page     Header    Band -------------------------------------------------------

 MM/DD/YY                     CREDIT CARD MONTHLY REPORT              HH:MM:SS

 DATE        CATEGORY TYPE         STORE NAME & ADDRESS         AMOUNT

 Report    Intro     Band -------------------------------------------------------
 Group 1   Intro     Band -------------------------------------------------------
           SUMMARY BY: XXXXXXXXXXXXXXXXXXXX

 Detail              Band -------------------------------------------------------
 MM/DD/YY XXXXXXXXXXXXXXXXXXX VVVVVVVVVVVVVVVVVVVVVVVVV      999999.99
 Group 1   Summary   Band -------------------------------------------------------

                                                 Subtotal:  9999999.99
 Report    Summary   Band -------------------------------------------------------

                                              Final Total: 9999999.99
 Page      Footer    Band -------------------------------------------------------
                                         Page No. 999
 -------------------------------------------------------------------------------



 Report   ║C:\...\INVOICE\CBREPORT║Band 3/7 ║ File:Credit ║       ║ CapsIns
              Add field:F5   Select:F6   Move:F7   Copy:F8   Size:Shift-F7
```

Highlight and then select the View report on screen option from the Pull-down Submenu. dBASE will create a program CBREPORT.FRG and store it on the disk to produce the report as shown in Figure 15.9.

The design process of the report format is now complete. Save the report format by invoking the Exit option on the menu bar, by pressing the <Alt-E> keys. Next, highlight the Save changes and exit option from the Pull-down Submenu, and press the <Return> key. This step will instruct dBASE to save the report format. The report format will be saved under the CBREPORT.FRM file name, and the system will respond by displaying the dot prompt.

The CBREPORT.FRM file can be used to produce a printed report or a text report file with the help of the REPORT FORM command as discussed in section 15.2.

15.4 Summary Reports

Summary reports are modifications of control break reports. The main difference is that they do not contain the detail record lines. Summary reports are usually used by people in higher management.

15.4.1 Designing the Summary Report Format

The summary report format can be designed by simply deleting the detail record line from the control break report format. To design the summary report format SUMMARY.FRM for the CREDIT.DBF database file, copy the control break report format CBREPORT.FRM file to the SUMMARY.FRM file. To do this, use the following command:

```
. COPY FILE CBREPORT.FRM TO
  SUMMARY.FRM      <Return>
```

Deleting the Detail Band

Now modify the summary report format by deleting the detail line from it. To do this, first invoke the SUMMARY.FRM format by using the following command:

```
. MODIFY REPORT SUMMARY     <Return>
```

dBASE will respond by displaying the report format as shown in Figure 15.15. Move the cursor to the detail band format, and press the <Ctrl-Y> keys. This step will delete the detail band as well as its format line, and the report format will look like that in Figure 15.16.

Finally, move the cursor to the main heading in the page header band, and change the heading to read "CREDIT CARD SUMMARY REPORT."

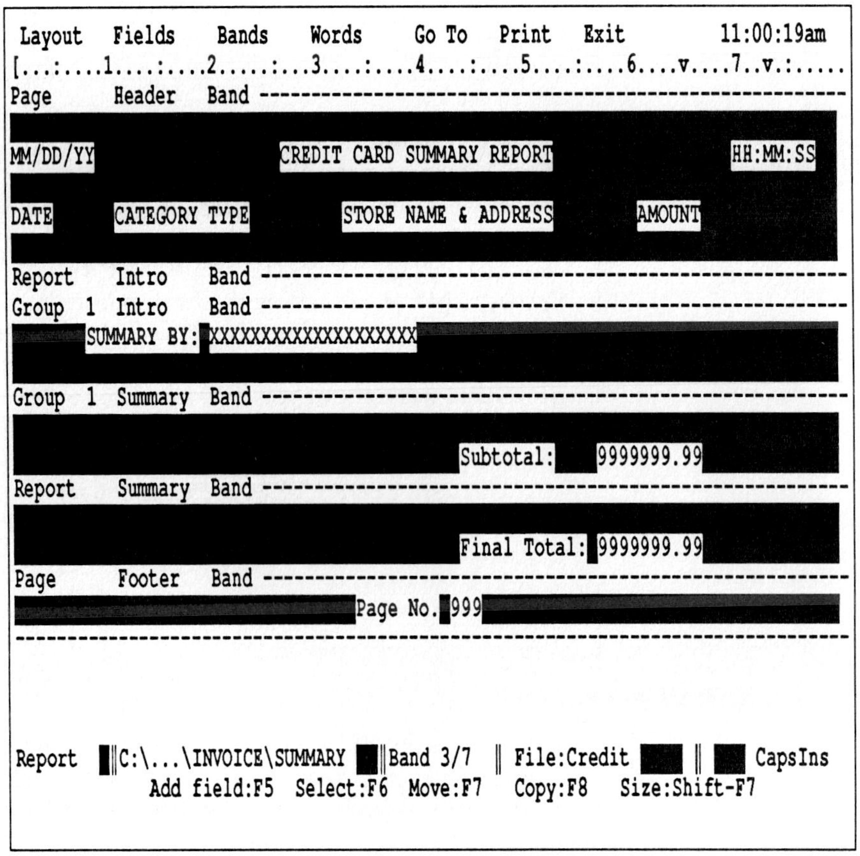

Figure 15.16 Report design screen with the summary report format

```
Layout    Fields    Bands    Words    Go To    Print    Exit         11:00:19am
[....:....1....:....2....:....3....:....4....:....5....:....6....v....7..v.:....
Page      Header    Band -----------------------------------------------------

MM/DD/YY                     CREDIT CARD SUMMARY REPORT              HH:MM:SS

DATE          CATEGORY TYPE         STORE NAME & ADDRESS      AMOUNT

Report    Intro     Band ----------------------------------------------------
Group  1  Intro     Band ----------------------------------------------------
          SUMMARY BY: XXXXXXXXXXXXXXXXXXXX

Group  1  Summary   Band ----------------------------------------------------

                                              Subtotal:   9999999.99
Report    Summary   Band ----------------------------------------------------

                                           Final Total:   9999999.99
Page      Footer    Band ----------------------------------------------------
                              Page No.  999
        ------------------------------------------------------------------



Report    C:\...\INVOICE\SUMMARY   Band 3/7    File:Credit            CapsIns
              Add field:F5  Select:F6  Move:F7  Copy:F8  Size:Shift-F7
```

Figure 15.17 Summary report

```
04/15/89                CREDIT CARD SUMMARY REPORT              13:52:40

DATE         CATEGORY TYPE       STORE NAME & ADDRESS            AMOUNT

    SUMMARY BY: Auto & Vehicle
                                              Subtotal:           41.85
    SUMMARY BY: Miscellaneous
                                              Subtotal:         1214.32
    SUMMARY BY: Restaurant
                                              Subtotal:           57.74
    SUMMARY BY: Retail Purchases
                                              Subtotal:          195.80
                                              Final Total:      1509.71
                            Page No.   1
```

Viewing the Summary Report on the Screen

Before you exit the design process and save the report form for future use, view the report on the screen as it will appear in printed form. To do this, invoke the Print option of the menu bar by pressing the <Alt-P> keys. Highlight and then select the View report on screen option from the Pull-down Submenu. dBASE will create a program called SUMMARY.FRG and store it on the disk to produce the report as shown in Figure 15.17.

This completes the design process of the report format. Now save the report format by invoking the Exit option on the menu bar by pressing the <Alt-E> keys. Next, highlight the Save changes and exit option from the Pull-down Submenu, and press the <Return> key. This step will instruct dBASE to save the report format. It will be saved under the SUMMARY.FRM file name, and the system will respond by displaying the dot prompt.

The SUMMARY.FRM file can be used to produce a printed report or a text report file with the help of REPORT FORM command, as discussed in section 15.2.

15.5 Summary

dBASE provides the report generator utility, which is similar to the label generator utility. The report generator utility allows you to design the report format, which can be used to print the contents of a database file in column, form, or mailmerge report layout. The discussion in this book is restricted to the column report layout. Like label generation, report generation is also a two-step process. In the first step, the report format is designed; in the second step, this format is used to print the contents of the database file in the form of a columnar report.

The CREATE REPORT command provides an interactive method to design the report format. The process of designing the report format involves indicating to dBASE IV what information goes into each section of the printed report. There are five parts to a report—page header, report introduction, body of the report (consisting of detail lines), summary report, and footer. All reports may not contain all five parts. The report design form consists of five bands. Each part of the report is defined by using one of these five bands.

The first band is the page header band, which is used to define the report title and headings. The second is the report intro band, which is used for describing the field headings. The third band is the detail band, which is used to define the data fields present in the record to be printed. The field values of the records are represented using the field templates. The fourth band is the report summary band, which is used to define the column totals. The fifth is the page footer band, which is used to define the information, such as page numbers or other useful information, to be printed at the bottom of each page. In addition to these five bands, other summary bands can also be added to the report form as needed for control break or summary reports.

The report form can be used to display, print, or write the reports to the disk file from the currently active database file using the earlier created report format. One of the most commonly used reports in business applications is the control break report. This contains groups of records listed with a subtotal for each group until all the groups are listed. At the end of the report, the total for the whole file is listed. To produce a control break report, you need to have the database file sorted or indexed on the field in which the records in the report should be grouped.

In the design process of the control break report format, two extra bands—group 1 intro band and group 1 summary band—are added to the report design form. The group 1 intro band is used to add the summary subheading for the group of records. This summary subheading is printed before each group of records. The group 1 summary band is used to add the subtotal for the group of records, which is printed at the end of each group of records.

A special form of the control break report is the summary report. It is similar to the control break report except that it does not contain the detail record lines. The summary report format can be designed by eliminating the detail record line from the control break report format.

dBASE COMMANDS AND FUNCTIONS

CREATE REPORT command
MODIFY REPORT command

REPORT FORM command

REVIEW QUESTIONS

1. What is the function of the dBASE report generator utility?
2. Name and explain the two steps of report generation.
3. What dBASE command is used to design the report format?
4. List five different bands present in the report design form. What is the function of each?
5. What is the purpose of viewing the report on the screen after designing its format?
6. When should the **MODIFY REPORT** command be used?
7. What dBASE command is used to produce the report?
8. How can the report for selected records of the database file be produced?

15.5 Summary

9. How can the report be printed?
10. What is the function of the NOEJECT option in printing the report?
11. What is the function of the PLAIN option in printing the report?
12. How can the report text file be created?
13. What command(s) can be used to obtain the listing of the report text file?
14. What special condition is required for the design and production of the control break report?
15. What is the difference between the control break report and the summary report?

Chapter 16

Foreign Files

LEARNING OBJECTIVES

Upon successfully completing this chapter, you will be able to:

1. Convert the dBASE files to fixed length record ASCII files.
2. Convert the dBASE files to variable length record ASCII files.
3. Append data from the fixed length record ASCII files to the dBASE files.
4. Append data from the variable length record ASCII files to the dBASE files.

16.1 Overview

dBASE IV creates and maintains database files in a special format. As described in section 1.2.5, a database file consists of two components—the database file structure and the database file data. The database file structure describes each field in the database record, indicating its position in the record, the name of the field, the field type, its width in characters, and the number of decimal places (if needed) present in the field. The database file data consists of records of data. The structure is present in the database file as the first record followed by the records of data.

dBASE IV files are not in a format that can be directly used by other software packages such as word processors, spreadsheets, or even programming languages like BASIC and COBOL. But it is possible to convert the database files to ASCII format files that can be accessed by most software packages and programming languages. It is also possible to access ASCII format files and import their data to the database files. Any data file that is *not* a dBASE file is referred to as a **foreign file**. This chapter deals with exporting dBASE file data to foreign files and importing data from foreign files into dBASE files.

16.2 Exporting dBASE File Data to Foreign Files

The COPY command, introduced in Chapter 7, has four optional parameters—FILE, TO, STRUCTURE, and TYPE. Three of them—FILE, TO, and STRUCTURE—have already been discussed in that chapter. The TYPE parameter, when combined with the COPY TO format of the COPY command, is used to convert dBASE IV files to ASCII foreign files. ASCII files do not have a structure; they contain only data records. The two most commonly used formats for ASCII files are the **system data format (SDF) file** and the **delimited format file**.

16.2.1 Converting dBASE Files to SDF Files

The COPY TO ... SDF format of the COPY command is used to convert the active dBASE file to the system data format ASCII file. The general format of this command is

```
COPY [TO <target file name>] [FIELDS <field list>]
     [FOR <condition>] [WHILE <condition>]
     [TYPE SDF]
```

where <target file name> is the name of the target file to which the active database file will be copied, <field list> is a list of the field names separated by commas to be included in the target file, <condition> is a valid search condition that selects records from the database file to be copied, and SDF is the name of the foreign file type.

System data format (SDF) ASCII files are **fixed length record files**. A default extension of .TXT is assigned by dBASE unless otherwise specified.

```
. DISPLAY STRUCTURE
Structure for database : C:\DBASE\INVOICE\FILE16.DBF
Number of data records :      10
Date of last update    : 1/12/89
Field  Field name  Type          Width    Dec      Index
    1  ITEM_NUM    Character         4                N
    2  ITEM_DESC   Character        26                N
    3  UNIT_COST   Numeric           6     2          N
    4  QUANTITY    Numeric           3                N
** TOTAL **                         40
```

Figure 16.1 Structure of the FILE16.DBF database file

Several different forms of the COPY TO ... SDF format are available, depending on the parameters used. A few of these are listed here and discussed on the following pages.

```
COPY [TO <target file name>] [TYPE SDF]
COPY [TO <target file name>] [FOR <condition>] [TYPE
     SDF]
COPY [TO <target file name>] [FIELDS <field list>]
     [TYPE SDF]
```

The COPY TO ... SDF Format

The general format of the COPY TO ... SDF format is

```
COPY [TO <target file name>] [TYPE SDF]
```

This command is used to copy the whole active database file to a fixed length record ASCII foreign file.

Consider the FILE16.DBF database file. Its structure and listing are given in Figures 16.1 and 16.2, respectively. Note that the file contains ten records, each 40 bytes long. Recall that dBASE IV adds one extra byte to mark the record for deletion.

Figure 16.2 Listing of the FILE16.DBF database file

```
. USE FILE16
. LIST
Record#  ITEM_NUM  ITEM_DESC                  UNIT_COST  QUANTITY
      1  1136      Bond Paper, Ream               22.99        38
      2  1910      Ditto Paper, Ream              19.99        35
      3  4012      King Kong Modem 1200          105.99        10
      4  4045      Monochrome Monitor Z-1105      99.99        15
      5  4072      Panasonic Printer KX-P108     269.99         8
      6  3372      Printer Ribbon 10-Box          35.99        19
      7  3375      Typewriter Ribbons 10-Box      23.79        67
      8  1488      Xerographic Paper              19.99        45
      9  4189      Zenith Microcomputer Z-158    829.99         5
     10  2504                                     29.99
```

16.2 Exporting dBASE File Data to Foreign Files

To convert this database file to a fixed length record ASCII foreign file, type the following commands:

```
. USE FILE16                    <Return>
. COPY TO SFILE16 TYPE SDF      <Return>
```

dBASE will respond by displaying the following message:

```
10 records copied
```

indicating that ten records have been copied.

To view the contents of the newly created SFILE16.TXT ASCII foreign file, you will need the following command (ASCII files can be accessed by the DOS or dBASE TYPE command):

```
. TYPE SFILE16.TXT      <Return>
```

If you type this command, dBASE will respond by displaying the listing as shown in Figure 16.3.

The ASCII system data format file SFILE16.TXT in Figure 16.3 consists of ten records as contained in the FILE16.DBF database file. But they are now in fixed length ASCII format, and each record is 39 bytes long.

The COPY TO FOR ... SDF Format

The general format of the COPY TO FOR ... SDF format is

```
COPY [TO <target file name>] [FOR <condition>]
     [TYPE SDF]
```

This command is used to copy only the conditionally selected records from the active database file to a fixed length record ASCII foreign file.

To create a fixed length record ASCII foreign file called SFILE16P.TXT and copy the selected records of the FILE16.DBF database file with UNIT_COST greater than $100, type the following commands:

```
. USE FILE16       <Return>
. COPY TO SFILE16P FOR UNIT_COST > 100 TYPE SDF
   <Return>
```

Figure 16.3 Listing of the SFILE16.TXT file in ASCII system data format

```
. TYPE SFILE16.TXT
1136Bond Paper, Ream              22.99 38
1910Ditto Paper, Ream             19.99 35
4012King Kong Modem 1200         105.99 10
4045Monochrome Monitor Z-1105     99.99 15
4072Panasonic Printer KX-P108    269.99  8
3372Printer Ribbon 10-Box         35.99 19
3375Typewriter Ribbons 10-Box     23.79 67
1488Xerographic Paper             19.99 45
4189Zenith Microcomputer Z-158   829.99  5
2504                              29.99
```

Figure 16.4 Listing of the SFILE16P.TXT file in ASCII system data format

```
. TYPE SFILE16P.TXT
4012King Kong Modem 1200       105.99 10
4072Panasonic Printer KX-P108 269.99  8
4189Zenith Microcomputer Z-158829.99  5
```

dBASE will respond by displaying the following message:

```
3 records copied
```

indicating that three records have been copied.

To view the contents of the SFILE16P.TXT ASCII foreign file, you will need the following command:

```
. TYPE SFILE16P.TXT     <Return>
```

If you type this command, dBASE will respond by displaying the listing as shown in Figure 16.4.

The listing of the SFILE16P.TXT as given in Figure 16.4 is similar to that of Figure 16.3 except that it contains only three selected records of the FILE16.DBF database file whose UNIT_COST field value is greater than $100.

The COPY TO FIELDS ... SDF Format

The general format of the COPY TO FIELDS ... SDF format is

```
COPY [TO <target file name>] [FIELDS <field list>]
    [TYPE SDF]
```

This command is used to copy only the selected fields from the records of the active database file to a fixed length record ASCII foreign file.

To create a fixed length record ASCII foreign file called SFILE16F.TXT containing only the ITEM_DESC and UNIT_COST fields of the FILE16.DBF database file, type the following commands:

```
. USE FILE16      <Return>
. COPY TO SFILE16F FIELDS ITEM_DESC, UNIT_COST
  TYPE SDF        <Return>
```

dBASE will respond by displaying the following message:

```
10 records copied
```

indicating that ten records have been copied.

To view the contents of the SFILE16F.TXT ASCII foreign file, you will need the following command:

```
. TYPE SFILE16F.TXT     <Return>
```

If you type this command, dBASE will respond by displaying the listing as shown in Figure 16.5. The listings of Figure 16.5 reveal that the ASCII

Figure 16.5 Listing of the SFILE16F.TXT file in ASCII system data format containing only the UNIT_DESC and UNIT_COST fields

```
. TYPE SFILE16F.TXT
Bond Paper, Ream             22.99
Ditto Paper, Ream            19.99
King Kong Modem 1200        105.99
Monochrome Monitor Z-1105    99.99
Panasonic Printer KX-P108   269.99
Printer Ribbon 10-Box        35.99
Typewriter Ribbons 10-Box    23.79
Xerographic Paper            19.99
Zenith Microcomputer Z-1588 829.99
                             29.99
```

system data format file SFILE16F.TXT consists of ten records as contained in the FILE16.DBF database file. But they are now in the fixed length ASCII format, and each record contains only the UNIT_DESC and UNIT_COST fields.

16.2.2 Converting dBASE Files to Delimited Files

The COPY TO ... DELIMITED format of the COPY command is used to convert the active database file to the delimited format ASCII file. The general format of this command is

```
COPY [TO <target file name>] [FIELDS <field list>]
     [FOR <condition>] [WHILE <condition>]
     [TYPE DELIMITED]
```

where <target file name> is the name of the target file to which the active database file will be copied, <field list> is a list of the field names, separated by commas, to be included in the target file, <condition> is a valid search condition that selects records from the database file to be copied, and DELIMITED is the name of a foreign file type.

Delimited format ASCII files are **variable length record files**. The fields are also of variable length and are separated by a specific character called a delimiter. A default extension of .TXT is assigned by dBASE unless otherwise specified.

Several different forms of the COPY TO ... DELIMITED format are available, depending on the parameters used. A few of these formats are listed here and discussed on the following pages.

```
COPY [TO <target file name>] [TYPE DELIMITED]
COPY [TO <target file name>] [FOR <condition>] [TYPE
     DELIMITED]
COPY [TO <target file name>] [FIELDS <field list>]
     [TYPE DELIMITED]
```

The COPY TO ... DELIMITED Format

The general format of the COPY TO ... DELIMITED format is

```
COPY [TO <target file name>] [TYPE DELIMITED]
```

This command is used to copy the whole active database file to a variable length record ASCII foreign file.

Once again consider the FILE16.DBF database file. Its structure and its listing are given in Figures 16.1 and 16.2, respectively.

To convert this database file to a variable length record ASCII foreign file, type the following commands:

```
. USE FILE16                              <Return>
. COPY TO DFILE16 TYPE DELIMITED          <Return>
```

dBASE will respond by displaying the following message:

```
10 records copied
```

indicating that ten records have been copied.

To view the contents of the newly created DFILE16.TXT ASCII foreign file, you will need the following command:

```
. TYPE DFILE16.TXT     <Return>
```

If you type this command, dBASE will respond by displaying the listing shown in Figure 16.6.

The listing of the DFILE16.TXT file in Figure 16.6 consists of ten records as contained in the FILE16.DBF database file. All trailing spaces in the character fields have been truncated, and the character fields are enclosed in double quotation marks ("). The fields are separated by commas. Blank character fields are indicated by a pair of double quotation marks (" "), and blank numeric fields are indicated by a zero value.

The simple DELIMITED clause used with the COPY command defaults to double quotation marks as a delimiter. Any other character can be used as a delimiter by using the DELIMITED WITH clause as explained in the next example.

The COPY TO FOR ... DELIMITED Format

The general format of the COPY TO FOR ... DELIMITED format is

```
COPY [TO <target file name>] [FOR <condition>] [TYPE
     DELIMITED]
```

Figure 16.6 Listing of the DFILE16.TXT file in ASCII delimited format

```
. TYPE DFILE16.TXT
"1136","Bond Paper, Ream",22.99,38
"1910","Ditto Paper, Ream",19.99,35
"4012","King Kong Modem 1200",105.99,10
"4045","Monochrome Monitor Z-1105",99.99,15
"4072","Panasonic Printer KX-P108",269.99,8
"3372","Printer Ribbon 10-Box",35.99,19
"3375","Typewriter Ribbons 10-Box",23.79,67
"1488","Xerographic Paper",19.99,45
"4189","Zenith Microcomputer Z-158",829.99,5
"2504"," ",29.99,0
```

Figure 16.7 Listing of the DFILE16P.TXT file in the ASCII delimited format

```
. TYPE DFILE16P.TXT
'4012','King Kong Modem 1200',105.99,10
'4072','Panasonic Printer KX-P108',269.99,8
'4189','Zenith Microcomputer Z-158',829.99,5
```

This command is used to copy only the selected records from the active database file to a variable length record ASCII foreign file.

To create a variable length record ASCII foreign file called DFILE16P.TXT and copy the selected records of the FILE16.DBF database file with UNIT_COST greater than $100, using the single quotation marks (') as a delimiter, type the following commands:

```
. USE FILE16                <Return>
. COPY TO DFILE16P FOR UNIT_COST > 100 TYPE
  DELIMITED WITH '          <Return>
```

dBASE will respond by displaying the following message:

```
3 records copied
```

indicating that three records have been copied.

To view the contents of the DFILE16P.TXT ASCII foreign file, you will need the following command:

```
. TYPE DFILE16P.TXT         <Return>
```

If you type this command, dBASE will respond by displaying the listing shown in Figure 16.7.

The listings of the DFILE16P.TXT file in Figure 16.7 are similar to that of the DFILE16.TXT file in Figure 16.6 except that the character fields are enclosed by single rather than double quotation marks. Also, the file DFILE16P.TXT contains only the selected records of the FILE16 database file whose UNIT_COST field value is greater than $100.

The COPY TO FIELDS ... DELIMITED Format

The general format of the COPY TO FIELDS ... DELIMITED format is

```
COPY [TO <target file name>] [FIELDS <field list>]
     [TYPE DELIMITED]
```

This command is used to copy only the selected fields from the records of the active database file to a variable length record ASCII foreign file.

To create a variable length record ASCII foreign file called DFILE16F.TXT delimited by the slash (/) and containing only the ITEM_DESC and UNIT_COST fields of the FILE16.DBF database file, type the following commands:

```
. USE FILE16                <Return>
. COPY TO DFILE16F FIELDS ITEM_DESC, UNIT_COST
  TYPE DELIMITED WITH /     <Return>
```

Figure 16.8 Listing of the DFILE16F.TXT file in the ASCII delimited format containing only the UNIT_DESC and UNIT_COST fields

```
. TYPE DFILE16F.TXT
/Bond Paper, Ream/,22.99
/Ditto Paper, Ream/,19.99
/King Kong Modem 1200/,105.99
/Monochrome Monitor Z-1105/,99.99
/Panasonic Printer KX-P108/,269.99
/Printer Ribbon 10-Box/,35.99
/Typewriter Ribbons 10-Box/,23.79
/Xerographic Paper/,19.99
/Zenith Microcomputer Z-158/,829.99
/ /,29.99
```

dBASE will respond by displaying the following message:

```
10 records copied
```

indicating that ten records have been copied.

To view the contents of the DFILE16F.TXT ASCII foreign file, you will need the following command:

```
. TYPE DFILE16F.TXT      <Return>
```

If you type this command, dBASE will respond by displaying the listing shown in Figure 16.8.

The listing of the DFILE16F.TXT file in Figure 16.8 is similar to that of Figure 16.6 except that the character fields are enclosed in slash (/) marks and each record contains only the UNIT_DESC and UNIT_COST fields.

16.3 Importing Data from Foreign Files into dBASE Files

The APPEND command works opposite to the COPY TO command, which was introduced in section 7.3.2. It has two optional parameters—FROM and TYPE—available with it. The TYPE parameter, when combined with the APPEND FROM format of the APPEND command, is used to import data from ASCII foreign files into dBASE files.

16.3.1 Importing Data from SDF Files into dBASE Files

The APPEND FROM ... SDF format of the APPEND command is used to import data from the fixed record length ASCII SDF file into the active dBASE file. The general format of this command is

```
APPEND [FROM <file name>] [FOR <condition>]
       [TYPE SDF]
```

where <file name> is the name of the ASCII file from which the data are imported into the active database file, <condition> is a valid search condition that selects records from the ASCII file to be imported, and SDF indicates the type of foreign file from which the data is being imported.

16.3 Importing Data from Foreign Files into dBASE Files

Two forms of the APPEND FROM ... SDF format are listed here and discussed on the following pages.

```
APPEND [FROM <file name>] [TYPE SDF]
APPEND [FROM <file name>] [FOR <condition>] [TYPE
       SDF]
```

The APPEND FROM ... SDF Format

The general format of the APPEND FROM ... SDF format is

```
APPEND [FROM <file name>] [TYPE SDF]
```

This command is used to append (or import) the whole fixed length record ASCII SDF file into the currently active database file.

Consider the FILE16A.DBF database file. Its structure is similar to that shown in Figure 16.1. To open this database file and obtain its listing, type the following commands:

```
. USE FILE16A       <Return>
. LIST              <Return>
```

dBASE will respond by displaying the listing shown in Figure 16.9. It contains seven records, each 40 bytes long. (Refer to the structure of this file in Figure 16.1.)

To append (or import) the data from the fixed length record ASCII SDF file SFILE16P.TXT, whose listing is given in Figure 16.4, to the active FILE16A.DBF database file, type the following command:

```
. APPEND FROM SFILE16P TYPE SDF      <Return>
```

dBASE will respond by displaying the following message:

```
3 records appended
```

indicating that three records have been appended.

You can obtain the listing of the FILE16A.DBF database file either by pressing the F3 List function key or by typing the following command:

```
. LIST      <Return>
```

Figure 16.9 Listing of the FILE16A.DBF database file

```
. USE FILE16A
. LIST
Record#  ITEM_NUM  ITEM_DESC              UNIT_COST  QUANTITY
      1  5818      Calendar Refill             4.99        32
      2  5960      Calendar Stands             5.69        14
      3  3802      Correction Fluid 10-Box     3.39        65
      4  3570      Correction Tape 10-Box      4.29        49
      5  4005      Disks Data Case             5.99        18
      6  4141      Double Sided Disks 10-Pk    8.49        27
      7  2786      Highlighter Pen 10-Box      7.99        86
```

Figure 16.10 Listing of the FILE16A.DBF database file after appending the data from the SFILE16P.TXT foreign ASCII system data format file

```
. LIST
Record#  ITEM_NUM  ITEM_DESC                UNIT_COST  QUANTITY
     1    5818     Calendar Refill              4.99        32
     2    5960     Calendar Stands              5.69        14
     3    3802     Correction Fluid 10-Box      3.39        65
     4    3570     Correction Tape 10-Box       4.29        49
     5    4005     Disks Data Case              5.99        18
     6    4141     Double Sided Disks 10-Pk     8.49        27
     7    2786     Highlighter Pen 10-Box       7.99        86
     8    4012     King Kong Modem 1200       105.99        10
     9    4072     Panasonic Printer KX-P108  269.99         8
    10    4189     Zenith Microcomputer Z-158 829.99         5
```

dBASE will respond by displaying the listing as shown in Figure 16.10. The listing of the FILE16A.DBF database file given in Figure 16.10 now has ten records. Three records of the SFILE16P.TXT ASCII file were converted to the dBASE format and appended to the end of the FILE16A.DBF database file.

The APPEND FROM FOR ... SDF Format

The general format of the APPEND FROM FOR ... SDF format is

```
APPEND [FROM <file name>] [FOR <condition>]
       [TYPE SDF]
```

This command is used to append (or import) only the conditionally selected records from the fixed length record ASCII system data format file to the end of the currently active database file.

To append the conditionally selected records with UNIT_COST less than $25 from the fixed length record ASCII system data format file SFILE16.TXT, whose listing is given in Figure 16.3, to the currently active FILE16A.DBF database file, type the following command:

```
. APPEND FROM SFILE16 FOR UNIT_COST < 25 TYPE
  SDF      <Return>
```

dBASE will return by displaying the following message:

```
4 records appended
```

indicating that four records have been appended.

You can obtain the listing of the FILE16A.DBF database file either by pressing the F3 List function key or by typing the following command:

```
. LIST      <Return>
```

If you do so, dBASE will respond by displaying the listing shown in Figure 16.11. The listing of the FILE16A.DBF database file given in Figure 16.11 now has 14 records. Four selected records of the FILE16.TXT ASCII file whose UNIT_COST field value is less than $25 (after being converted to the dBASE format) have been appended at the end of the FILE16.DBF database file.

Figure 16.11 Listing of the FILE16A.DBF database file after appending the data from the SFILE16P.TXT foreign ASCII system data format file and records from the SFILE16.TXT file with UNIT_COST < $25

```
. LIST
Record#  ITEM_NUM  ITEM_DESC                 UNIT_COST  QUANTITY
     1   5818      Calendar Refill                4.99        32
     2   5960      Calendar Stands                5.69        14
     3   3802      Correction Fluid 10-Box        3.39        65
     4   3570      Correction Tape 10-Box         4.29        49
     5   4005      Disks Data Case                5.99        18
     6   4141      Double Sided Disks 10-Pk       8.49        27
     7   2786      Highlighter Pen 10-Box         7.99        86
     8   4012      King Kong Modem 1200         105.99        10
     9   4072      Panasonic Printer KX-P108    269.99         8
    10   4189      Zenith Microcomputer Z-158   829.99         5
    11   1136      Bond Paper, Ream              22.99        38
    12   1910      Ditto Paper, Ream             19.99        35
    13   3375      Typewriter Ribbons 10-Box     23.79        67
    14   1488      Xerographic Paper             19.99        45
```

16.3.2 Importing Data from the Delimited Files into the dBASE Files

The APPEND FROM ... DELIMITED format of the APPEND command is used to import data from the variable length record ASCII delimited format file into the active dBASE file. The general format of this command is

```
APPEND [FROM <file name>] [FOR <condition>]
       [TYPE DELIMITED]
```

where <file name> is the name of the ASCII delimited format file from which the data are imported into the active database file, <condition> is a valid search condition that selects records from the database file to be imported, and DELIMITED indicates the type of foreign file from which the data are being imported.

Two forms of the APPEND FROM ... DELIMITED format are listed here and discussed on the following pages.

```
APPEND [FROM <file name>] [TYPE DELIMITED]
APPEND [FROM <file name>] [FOR <condition>] [TYPE
       DELIMITED]
```

The APPEND FROM ... DELIMITED Format

The general format of the APPEND FROM ... DELIMITED format is

```
APPEND [FROM <file name>] [TYPE DELIMITED]
```

This command is used to append (or import) the whole variable length record ASCII delimited format file to the end of the currently active database file.

Consider the FILE16B.DBF database file. Its structure is the same as that shown in Figure 16.1. To open this database file and obtain its listing, you will need the following commands:

```
. USE FILE16B    <Return>
. LIST           <Return>
```

Figure 16.12 Listing of the FILE16B.DBF database file

```
. USE FILE11
. LIST
Record#   ITEM_NUM   ITEM_DESC            UNIT_COST   QUANTITY
     1      5130     Letter Opener             1.45         49
     2      1732     Message Pads  10-Pk       2.25         45
     3      1975     Notebook Filler           1.79         65
     4      5890     Paper Puncher             6.99         22
     5      2605     Pencil #2 Box             6.29         54
```

If you type these, dBASE will respond by displaying the listing shown in Figure 16.12. This listing contains five records, each 40 bytes long. (Refer to the structure of this file in Figure 16.1.)

To append (or import) the data from the variable length record ASCII delimited format file DFILE16P.TXT, whose listing is given in Figure 16.7, to the active FILE16B.DBF database file, type the following command:

    . APPEND FROM DFILE16P TYPE DELIMITED   <Return>

dBASE will respond by displaying the following message:

    3 records appended

indicating that three records have been appended.

You can obtain the listing of the FILE16B.DBF database file either by pressing the F3 List function key or by typing the following command:

    . LIST   <Return>

dBASE will respond by displaying the listing as shown in Figure 16.13. The listing of the FILE16B.DBF database file given in Figure 16.13 has eight records. Three records of the DFILE16P.TXT ASCII file (after being converted to the dBASE format) have been appended to the end of the FILE16B.DBF database file.

The APPEND FROM FOR ... DELIMITED Format

The general format of the APPEND FROM FOR ... DELIMITED format is

    APPEND [FROM <file name>] [FOR <condition>] [TYPE
           DELIMITED]

Figure 16.13 Listing of the FILE16B.DBF database file after appending the data from the DFILE16P.TXT foreign ASCII delimited format file

```
. LIST
Record#   ITEM_NUM   ITEM_DESC              UNIT_COST   QUANTITY
     1      5130     Letter Opener               1.45         49
     2      1732     Message Pads  10-Pk         2.25         45
     3      1975     Notebook Filler             1.79         65
     4      5890     Paper Puncher               6.99         22
     5      2605     Pencil #2 Box               6.29         54
     6      4012     King Kong Modem 1200      105.99         10
     7      4072     Panasonic Printer KX-P108 269.99          8
     8      4189     Zenith Microcomputer Z-158 829.99          5
```

Figure 16.14 Listing of the FILE16B.DBF database file after appending the data from the DFILE16P.TXT ASCII delimited format file and records from the DFILE16.TXT with UNIT_COST < $50

```
. LIST
Record#  ITEM_NUM  ITEM_DESC                 UNIT_COST  QUANTITY
     1   5130      Letter Opener                  1.45        49
     2   1732      Message Pads  10-Pk            2.25        45
     3   1975      Notebook Filler                1.79        65
     4   5890      Paper Puncher                  6.99        22
     5   2605      Pencil #2 Box                  6.29        54
     6   2786      Highlighter Pen 10-Box         7.99        86
     7   4012      King Kong Modem 1200         105.99        10
     8   4189      Zenith Microcomputer Z-158   829.99         5
     9   1136      Bond Paper, Ream              22.99        38
    10   1910      Ditto Paper, Ream             19.99        35
    11   3372      Printer Ribbon 10-Box         35.99        19
    12   3375      Typewriter Ribbons 10-Box     23.79        67
    13   1488      Xerographic Paper             19.99        45
    14   2504                                    29.99
```

This command is used to append (or import) only the conditionally selected records from the variable length record ASCII delimited format file at the end of the currently active database file.

To append the conditionally selected record with UNIT_COST less than $50 from the variable length record ASCII delimited format file DFILE16.TXT, whose listing is given in Figure 16.6, to the currently active FILE16B.DBF database file, type the following command:

. APPEND FROM DFILE16 FOR UNIT_COST < 50 TYPE DELIMITED   <Return>

dBASE will return by displaying the following message:

6 records appended

indicating that six records have been appended.

You can obtain the listing of the FILE16B.DBF database file either by pressing the F3 List function key or by typing the following command:

. LIST   <Return>

dBASE will respond by displaying the listing shown in Figure 16.14.

16.4 Summary

dBASE IV creates and maintains database files in a special format. These files can't be used directly by other software packages and programming languages. But dBASE can convert them to non-dBASE data file formats, referred to as foreign files, which can be accessed by most software packages and programming languages.

The two most commonly used formats of the ASCII foreign files are the system data format (SDF) and the delimited format files. System data format ASCII files are fixed length record files, and the delimited format ASCII files are variable length record files.

The COPY TO format of the COPY command is used to convert the dBASE files to ASCII format foreign files. The COPY TO ... SDF format of the COPY command is used to convert the active database file to the SDF ASCII file, and the COPY TO ... DELIMITED format of the COPY command is used to convert the active database file to the delimited format ASCII file.

The APPEND FROM format of the APPEND command is used to append (or import) data from the ASCII format foreign files into dBASE files. The APPEND FROM ... SDF format of the APPEND command is used to append (or import) data from the SDF ASCII file to the currently active dBASE file, and the APPEND FROM ... DELIMITED format of the APPEND command is used to append (or import) data from the delimited format ASCII file to the currently active dBASE file.

KEY CONCEPTS

delimited format file
fixed length record files
foreign file

system data format file
variable length record files

dBASE COMMANDS AND FUNCTIONS

APPEND FROM command

COPY TO command

REVIEW QUESTIONS

1. What is the purpose of converting dBASE files to ASCII files?
2. Explain the following terms:
   a. Foreign files
   b. Fixed length record file
   c. Variable length record file
   d. System data format file
   e. Delimited format file
3. What dBASE command is used to convert dBASE files to fixed length record ASCII files? What options are available with this command? Explain the function of each option.
4. What dBASE command is used to convert dBASE files to variable length record ASCII files? What options are available with this command? Explain the function of each option.
5. What dBASE command is used to append (or import) data from the fixed length record ASCII file to the currently active database file? What options are available with this command? Explain the function of each option.
6. What dBASE command is used to append (or import) data from the variable length record ASCII file to the currently active database file? What options are available with this command? Explain the function of each option.

Appendix A

Introduction to Microcomputers and DOS

A.1 Overview

The purpose of this appendix is twofold: (1) to acquaint you with the different components of a typical microcomputer and (2) to present some specific details of the operating system.

This appendix starts with an introduction to a typical microcomputer, listing its various components, followed by a short description of each. Because of its importance, the keyboard is discussed in great detail. After a brief description of the alphabetic (typewriter) keypad and nonalphabetic keypad, the common control keys of the keyboard are introduced and listed in a table for future reference.

The next section introduces other special keys whose functions vary with the application software program, such as the function keys, the calculator keypad, the cursor control keys, and the group cursor control keys. The section ends with a table containing the most commonly used other special function keys of the keyboard along with their functions.

The third section starts with an introduction to the disk operating system (DOS), listing the various steps needed to boot up (start up) your microcomputer, followed by a brief description of the default drive. The DOS commands are introduced next, starting with the directory command and the various options available with it, such as the paused directory listing, the wide directory listing, and the use of wild card characters.

A few other commonly used commands, such as the CLS, FORMAT, COPY, RENAME, TYPE, PRINT, and DELETE commands, are also introduced. The section ends with a table listing all the DOS commands discussed along with their functions.

A.2 Introduction to Microcomputers

A *microcomputer*, also called a PC, which is an abbreviation for personal computer, is the primary hardware component of the computer system. Its basic parts are the main unit, keyboard, video monitor, and printer. These are shown in Figure A.1.

A.2.1 Main Unit

The *main unit* of a microcomputer consists of the main processing unit, control unit, memory unit, and auxiliary storage unit. The components of the main unit are shown in Figure A.2.

Main Processing Unit

The *main processing unit* of a microcomputer, called a *microprocessor*, provides the computer with its ability to perform arithmetic, comparison, logic, and other functions.

Control Unit

In addition to the microprocessor, the main unit contains special purpose microchips. The collection of these microchips, called the *control unit*, controls all the other components of the microcomputer. The control unit also performs data input, data output, and other computing functions.

A.2 Introduction to Microcomputers 599

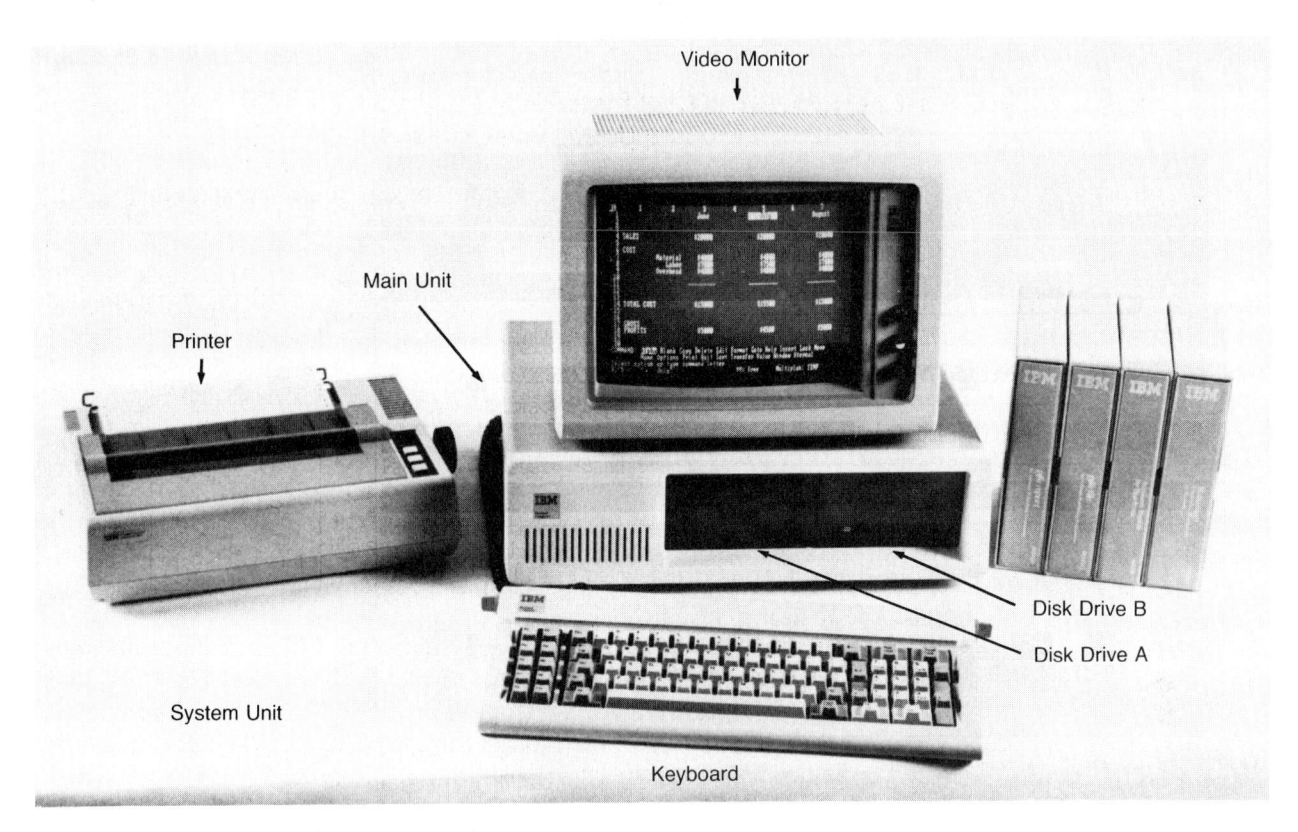

Figure A.1 Microcomputer components

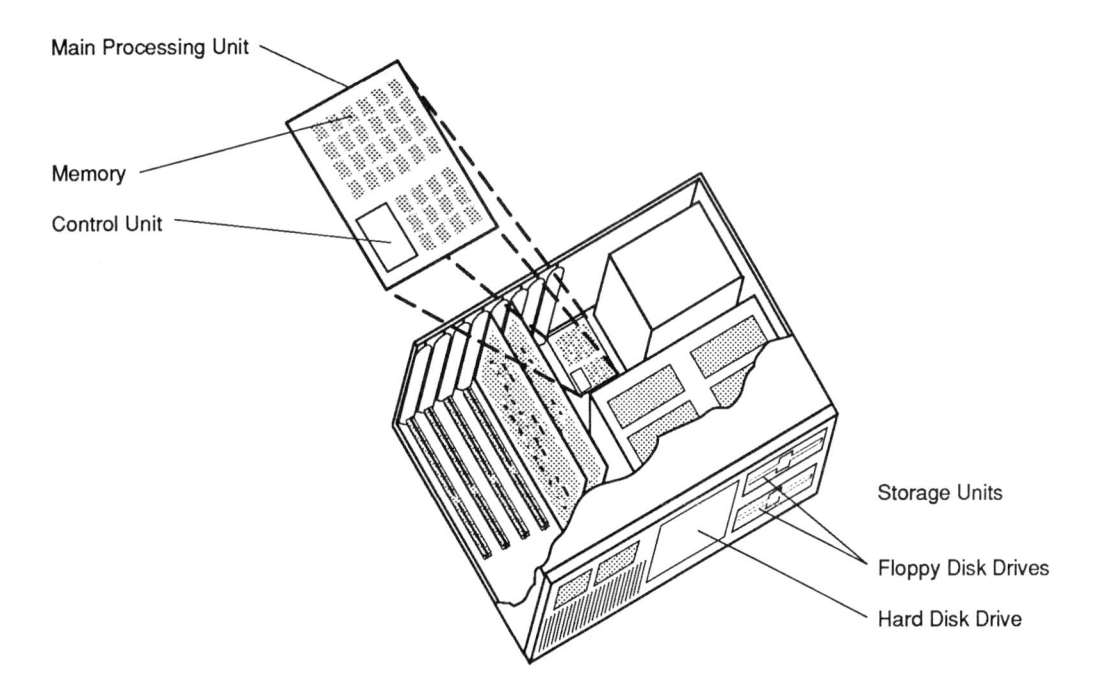

Figure A.2 Main unit components

Memory Unit

The *memory unit* of the microcomputer, also called RAM (random access memory), consists of memory chips, which are also housed in the main unit. The program to be processed and the data to be operated on reside in this unit of the microcomputer. Some typical memory sizes are 256K, 512K, 640K, and 1MB (megabyte).

Auxiliary Storage Unit

The microcomputer's main unit also contains the *auxiliary storage unit*, which is used for long-term storage of programs and data. The two most commonly used auxiliary storage devices are floppy disk drives and hard disk drives. Floppy disks come in two sizes. The $5\frac{1}{4}$-inch floppy disk has 360K and 1.2MB storage capacity; the $3\frac{1}{2}$-inch floppy disk has 720K and 1.44MB storage capacity. The hard disk drive is available in 10MB to 165MB storage capacities and is much faster than the floppy disk drive.

Each disk drive on your computer is identified with a unique alphabetic name called the *drive name*—a single-character name followed by a colon (:). If you have a computer with one floppy disk drive and one hard disk drive, the floppy disk drive is the A: drive, and the hard disk drive is the C: drive. If you have two floppy disk drives and a hard disk drive, the floppy disk drive on the left (or top) is usually the A: drive, and the floppy disk drive on the right (or bottom) is the B: drive. The hard disk drive is still the C: drive. (Note that some microcomputers have drive A: on the bottom and drive B: on the top.)

A.2.2 Keyboard

The *keyboard* is the main input device of the microcomputer. It is used to enter data to be processed and commands, which are instructions for the computer to process data, into the computer's memory. The keyboard is one of the most important components of the microcomputer system.

When you want to converse with the microcomputer, it will be through the keyboard. Because of the keyboard's importance and the amount of time you'll use it, you should spend some time here getting acquainted with the various types of keyboards and the different components of a typical keyboard.

Some of the most commonly used keyboards are shown in Figures A.3, A.4, and A.5.

A typical keyboard is shown in Figure A.6. Short descriptions of its components follow.

Figure A.3 Apple IIe keyboard

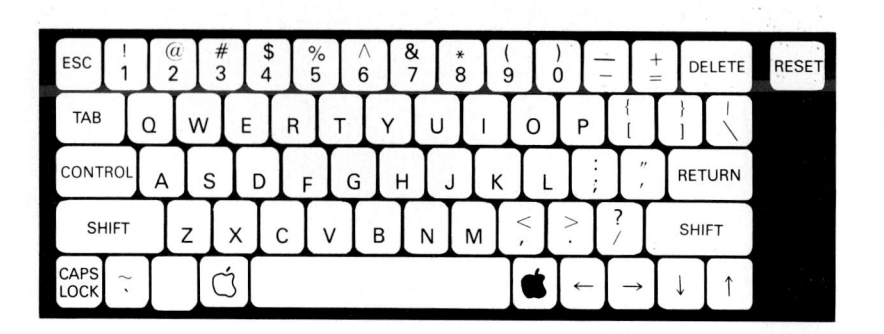

A.2 Introduction to Microcomputers **601**

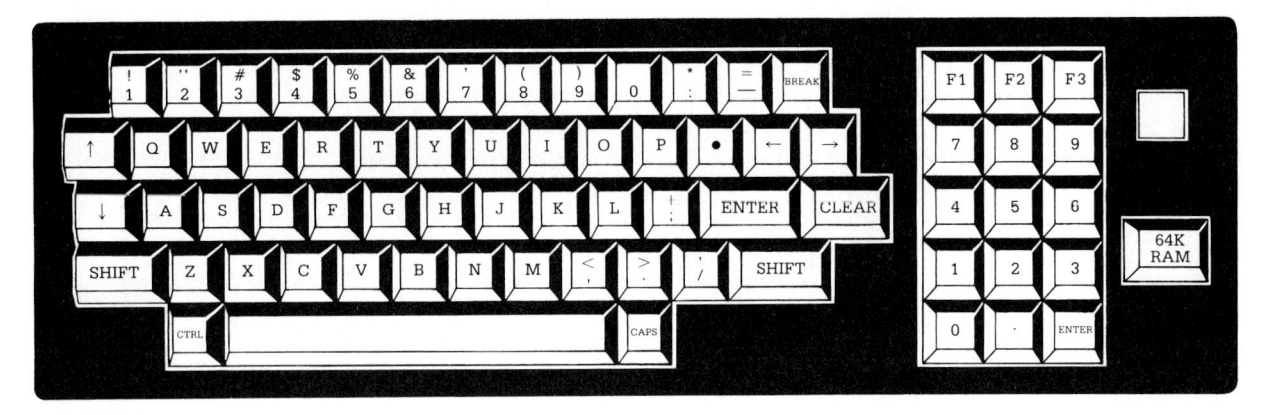

Figure A.4 TRS-80 keyboard

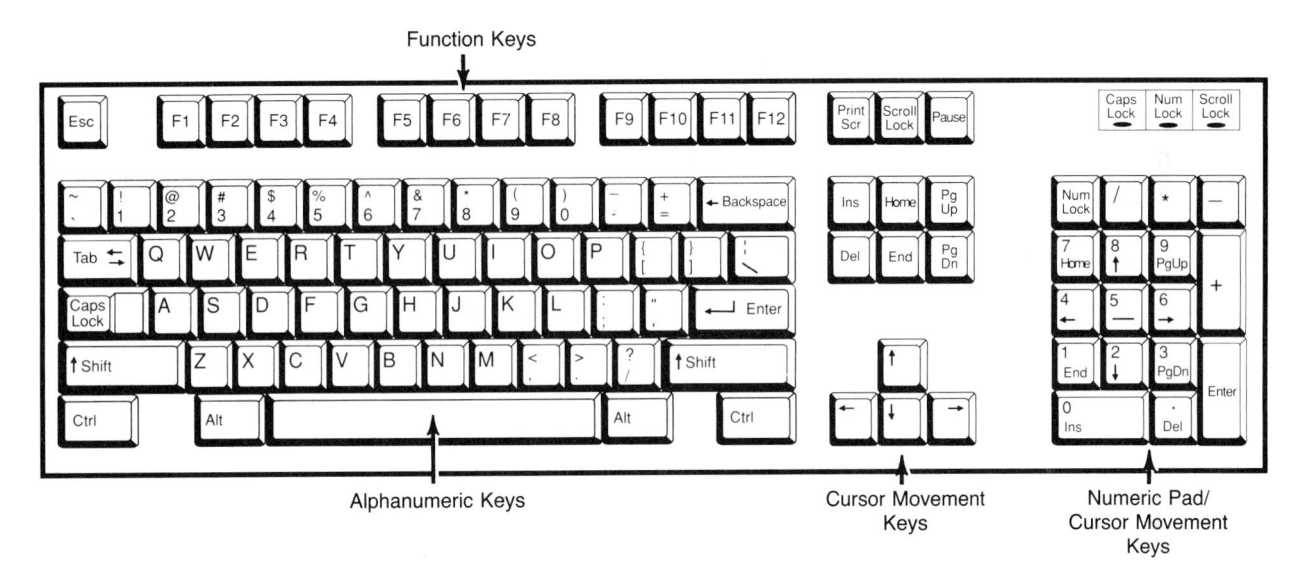

Figure A.5 IBM enhanced keyboard

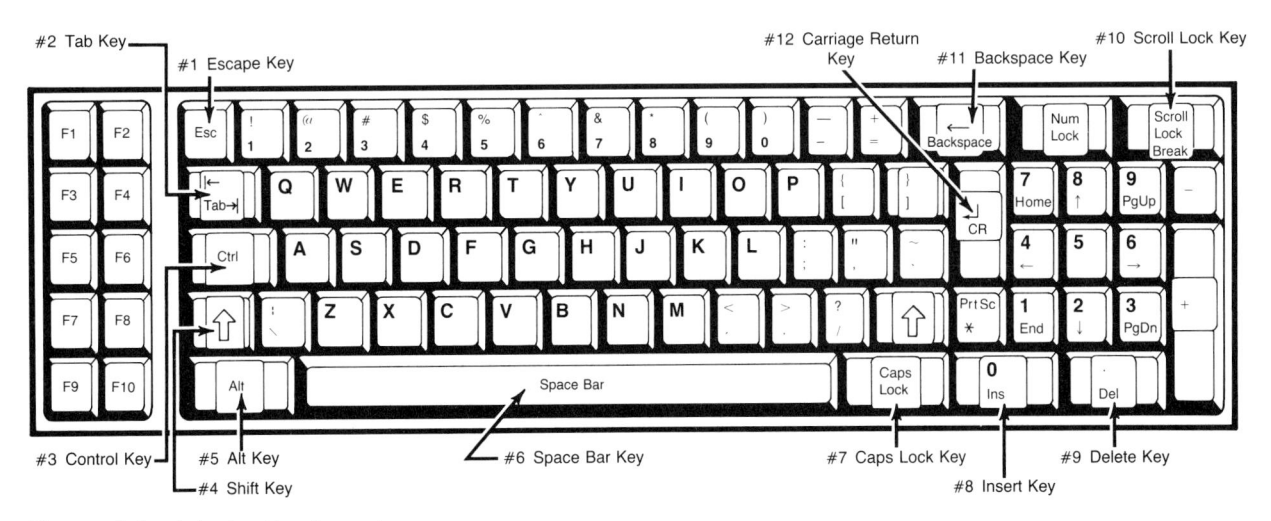

Figure A.6 A typical keyboard

Figure A.7 The alphabetic keypad

Alphabetic (Typewriter) Keypad

The *alphabetic* (*typewriter*) *keypad* component of the microcomputer keyboard, shown in Figure A.7, is similar to a typical typewriter keyboard. It consists of three rows containing the 26 letters of the alphabet arranged as they are on the typewriter. In the regular mode, these keys let you enter the lowercase letters; in the shift mode, which is entered by holding down either shift key, uppercase letters can be entered into the microcomputer. The functions of the other keys in the alphabetic keypad are given in Table A.1.

Nonalphabetic Keypad

The *nonalphabetic keypad* consists of digits 0 through 9, punctuation symbols, arithmetic symbols, and other special characters. It is shown in Figure A.8. The lower symbol on each key can be produced when the keyboard is in regular mode, and the upper symbol is produced when the keyboard is in shift mode. The <Caps Lock> key has no effect on these keys; that is, these keys will be in the regular mode when the shift key is not held down (even when the <Caps Lock> key is on). The nonalphabetic keys will be in the shift mode only when the <Shift> key is held down.

Table A.1 Summary of special keys in the alphabetic keypad

Key	Function
Shift	The <Shift> key appears twice on the keyboard, as indicated by 4 in Figure A.6. It is used to change the keyboard to shift mode (also called the uppercase mode). While in shift mode, pressing the alphabetic key will produce uppercase letters, and the nonalphabetic keys (or the special character keys) will produce the special characters (or symbols) printed on the upper portion of the keys.
Caps Lock	The <Caps Lock> key is indicated by 7 in Figure A.6. It is used to lock the <Shift> key and put the keyboard in the shift mode to produce the uppercase alphabetic characters. The <Caps Lock> key affects only the alphabetic keys. It has no effect on number or special character keys.

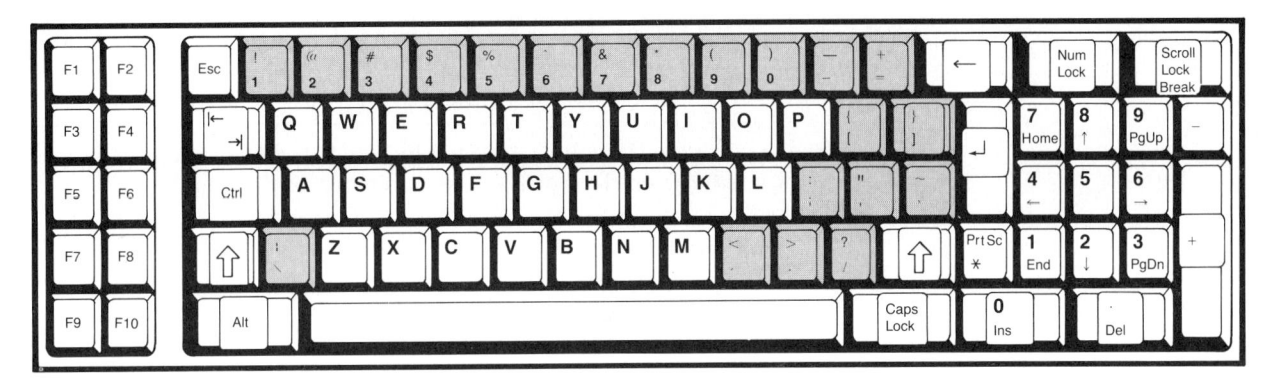

Figure A.8 The nonalphabetic keypad

Common Control Keys

The *common control keys* are shown in Figure A.9. These are the <Space Bar>, <Tab>, <Back Space>, and <Enter> keys. Their functions are summarized in Table A.2.

Special Function Keys

There are several *special function keys* on the keyboard whose functions vary with each application software program.

The Function Keys The 10 *function keys* (marked F1, F2, . . . , F10), shown in Figure A.10, are represented in two columns on the left end of the keyboard. On the IBM enhanced keyboard, there are 12 function keys, marked F1, F2, . . . , F12, located on the top row of the keyboard. Function keys are used to activate the special processing functions within a particular application software package.

The Calculator (Numeric) Keypad The *calculator keypad*, shown in Figure A.11, is located on the right-hand side of the keyboard. The ten numeric keys are arranged in three columns and are normally used when entering large amounts of numeric data. These can be activated for representing numeric data by pressing the <NumLock> key. The top row of the nonalphabetic keypad is used for smaller amounts of numeric data entry.

The Cursor Control Keys The four keys marked ←, ↑, →, and ↓, also known as <Left Arrow>, <Up Arrow>, <Right Arrow>, and <Down

Figure A.9 Common control keys

Table A.2 Summary of common control keys

Key	Function
Space Bar	The <Space Bar> key indicated by 6 in Figure A.6 is used to skip a space between the words of any command or data entry.
Tab	The <Tab> key (⇆) indicated by 2 in Figure A.6 is used to skip multiple spaces across a line.
Backspace	The <Backspace> key (←) is indicated by 11 in Figure A.6. It is used to move the cursor back one position and erase the character present in that position.
Enter	The <Enter> key (↵ or CR, an abbreviation for Carriage Return) is also called the <Return> key. It is indicated by 12 in Figure A.6. Its function is to indicate the end of the command or a line of data to the computer.

Arrow>, are shown in Figure A.12. These are part of the ten numeric keys of the calculator keypad. When in NumLock OFF mode, these keys are used to move the cursor on the screen one position at a time. The functions of the cursor control keys are summarized in Table A.3.

On the IBM enhanced keyboard, there are two sets of cursor control keys. The second set is located between the alphanumeric keypad and the calculator keypad, as shown in Figure A.13.

The Group Cursor Control Keys The four keys <Home>, <End>, <PgDn>, and <PgUp> shown in Figure A.14 are also part of the ten numeric keys of the calculator keypad. When in NumLock OFF mode, these keys are also used to move the cursor on the screen, moving a group of positions at a time. The functions of the group cursor control keys are summarized in Table A.4.

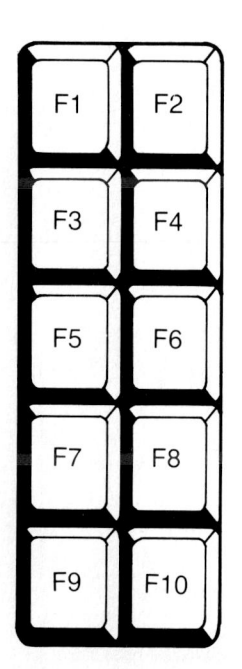

Figure A.10 Function keys

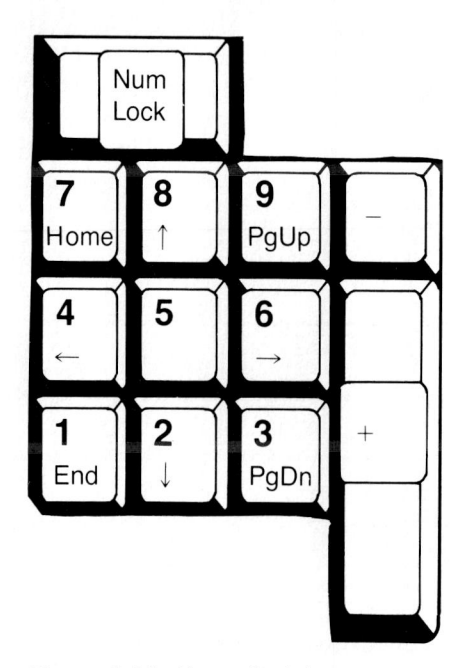

Figure A.11 The calculator (numeric) keypad

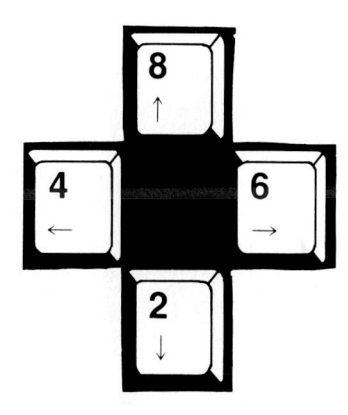

Figure A.12 The cursor control keys

A.2 Introduction to Microcomputers

Table A.3 Summary of cursor control keys

Key	Function
Left Arrow	This key is used to move the cursor to the left one character at a time.
Up Arrow	This key is used to move the cursor up one character at a time.
Right Arrow	This key is used to move the cursor to the right one character at a time.
Down Arrow	This key is used to move the cursor down one character at a time.

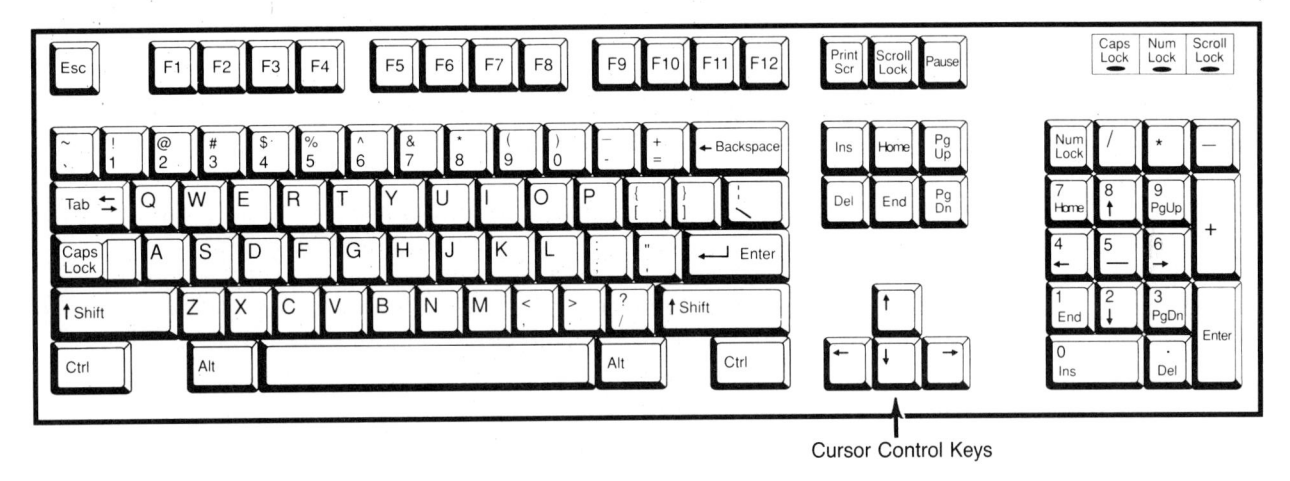

Figure A.13 The cursor control keys (IBM enhanced keyboard)

Figure A.14 Group cursor control keys

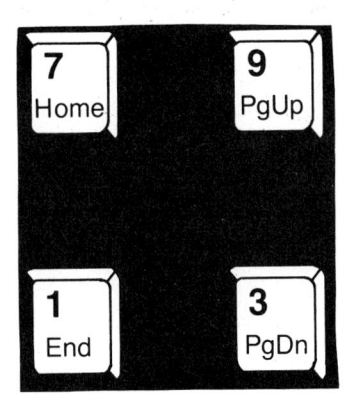

Table A.4 Summary of group cursor control keys

Key	Function
PgUp	This key is used to move the cursor up one page at a time.
PgDn	This key is used to move the cursor down one page at a time.
Home	This key is used to move the cursor to the top left corner of the screen.
End	This key is used to move the cursor to the bottom right corner of the screen.

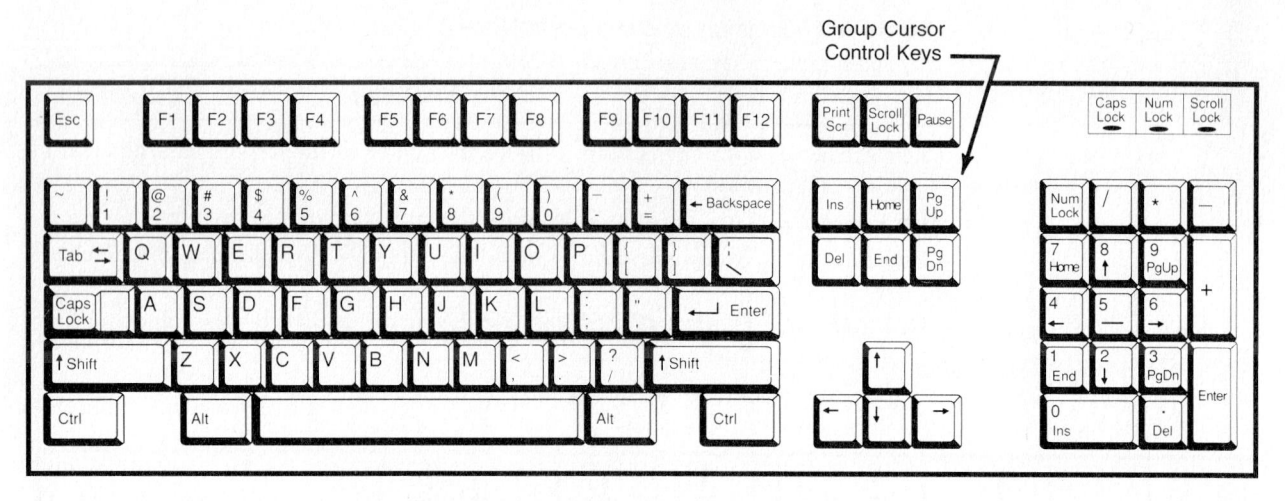

Figure A.15 Group cursor control keys (IBM enhanced keyboard)

Like the cursor control keys, the group control keys are also represented twice on the IBM enhanced keypad and are positioned just above the cursor control keys, as shown in Figure A.15.

Other Special Function Keys There are a few other keys on the keyboard with special functions. These and their functions are given in Table A.5.

Table A.5 Summary of other special keys on the keyboard

Key	Function
Esc	The <Esc> (called Escape) key is indicated by 1 in Figure A.6. It is used to interrupt or abort the operation of the program being executed.
Ctrl	The <Ctrl> (called Control) key is indicated by 3 in Figure A.6. It is always used in combination with other keys of the keyboard. It activates a special function associated with particular application software packages. For example <Ctrl-S> (obtained by holding down the <Ctrl> key and pressing the <S> key) will stop the scrolling of the text on the screen. The scrolling can be continued by pressing any other key of the keyboard.
Alt	The <Alt> (called Alternate) key is indicated by 5 in Figure A.6. It is also used in combination with other keys of the keyboard. It activates special functions associated with particular application software packages.
Ins	The <Ins> (called the Insert) key is indicated by 8 in Figure A.6. It is a toggle key. It is used to covert the keyboard from overwrite mode to insert mode by pressing this key once. To reverse this process, press this key once again.
Del	The <Del> (called the Delete) key is indicated by 9 in Figure A.6. It is used to delete the character above the cursor.
Scroll Lock	The <Scroll Lock> key is indicated by 10 in Figure A.6. It is used in combination with the <Ctrl> key to lock the scrolling of the text on the screen in some application software packages.

A.2.3 Video Monitor

The *video monitor*, also called a *video display terminal* (VDT), is a televisionlike screen plugged into the back of the computer system. It is used as the main output device for the computer system. The output is displayed in a single color on monochrome monitors and in full color on color monitors.

Anything typed on the keyboard is echoed, that is, displayed across a line on the screen. The progress of the keyboard typing can be followed by watching the movement of the *cursor* across the screen. The cursor is usually a blinking underline character showing the current position on the screen where the next character typed on the keyboard will appear. For typical operations, most video monitors display up to 25 lines of text, each containing up to 80 characters.

A.2.4 Printer

The *printer*, also connected to the computer system, is used as an alternate output device to obtain printed output. The most common type of printer is a dot matrix printer, which forms characters through the combination of tiny dots arranged in a rectangular matrix. A single pass of the print head across the page produces draft quality character output, which is supported by all the printers. Some printers also support a near letter quality character output, which is obtained by printing a line of text in two passes across the page, thus filling in the gap between the dots to give a better quality printing effect.

A.3 Introduction to DOS

The software component of the computer system is called the *operating system* or *system software*. The most common operating system for the microcomputer system is MS-DOS. DOS, an abbreviation for disk operating system, is a product of Microsoft Corporation. Many compatible versions of the MS-DOS are available. For example, PC-DOS is the operating system used by IBM for its PCs, and OS2 (Operating System 2) is a newer version of DOS used by IBM. Regardless of the name or its manufacturer, each operating system has the same basic structure; and the available commands are also almost identical for all compatible operating systems.

The main function of the operating system is to link microcomputer components and application software programs and to direct the microcomputer to complete the requested tasks. *Application software* is a collection of programs to perform a specific function. For example, dBASE IV is an application software package to create, update, and manage data effectively.

The following are a few of the other commonly used functions of DOS:

1. Loading data and/or programs from auxiliary storage into the microcomputer's main memory
2. Formatting a disk, that is, preparing a disk so that data and/or programs can be stored on it
3. Displaying on the screen a list of all the files stored in auxiliary storage
4. Copying data and/or program files from one storage area to another

5. Routing input and output data to the appropriate hardware devices
6. Managing data and/or program files stored in auxiliary storage devices

A.3.1 Loading DOS

To provide the link between the microcomputer and the application software, DOS must be loaded into the microcomputer's memory unit, a process known as system "boot up" (also known as start up).

The following steps should be followed to start or boot up the microcomputer system:

1. Turn on all the hardware devices, and then turn on the microcomputer if it is OFF. If the microcomputer is already ON, press and hold down the <Ctrl> and <Alt> keys simultaneously. While holding these two keys down, also press the <Del> key. After pressing the <Del> key, release all three keys.

2. After a few moments, this DOS identification message and a date prompt will be displayed on the screen:

```
MS-DOS version 3.02
Copyright (C) 1985 Zenith Data Systems
Corporation
Current date is Fri 5/10/90
Enter new date:
```

If the date is correct, press the <Return> key. If it is not, enter the current date using the mm/dd/yy format, and then press the <Return> key.

3. At this point, the screen will display:

```
Current time is 13:45:57
Enter new time:
```

If the time is correct, press the <Return> key. If it is not, enter the time using the hh:mm:ss format (in most systems, hours and minutes are sufficient), and then press the <Return> key.

4. DOS will display the system prompt (C>), indicating that you have successfully completed the start-up procedure for a hard disk.

Note: Most AT and many XT machines have clock cards installed on them. These read the date and time automatically or through the AUTOEXEC.BAT file. With these machines, you don't have to enter the date or the time; you simply press the <Return> key at each of the prompts.

Default Drive

The system *default drive* is the drive to which the system goes automatically to read or write information unless another drive name is specified by a command. Initially, the default drive is the drive from which DOS is loaded into the computer's memory when the system is booted. The system default prompt indicates the default drive. In most hard disk systems, the default drive is usually the C: drive. Because the minimum requirement for dBASE IV is a hard disk system (see section B.1), this book assumes you are working with a hard disk system.

The default drive can be changed by entering the drive name (drive letter and a colon) of the desired default drive at the system prompt and pressing the <Return> key. For example, if you have a hard disk system, after loading DOS, the system prompt will be C>, indicating that the current or default drive is C:. If you want to change to drive A:, type A: and press <Return>:

```
C> A:    <Return>
```

The system prompt will change to

```
A>
```

indicating that A: is the current default drive.

Now you can change the default drive back to the C: drive by typing C: at the system prompt A>:

```
A> C:    <Return>
```

The system will respond by displaying the system prompt

```
C>
```

indicating that C: is the current default drive.

A.3.2 DOS Commands

A *command* is an instruction for the computer to perform a particular function. This section covers some of the most commonly used DOS commands. DOS commands may be entered at the system prompt (A> or C>) using the keyboard in either upper- or lowercase and terminating the commands by pressing <Return>. If you make an error while typing a command, use the <Backspace> key to erase the previously typed characters, and retype the correct command.

Each of the following DOS commands must adhere to these rules:

1. The words in capital letters represent valid DOS command names. These must be entered exactly as shown, although uppercase is NOT required.
2. The information contained in the angle brackets is to be supplied by the user. When supplying this information, you do not type the angle brackets.
3. The information contained in the square brackets is optional; but when this information is used, it does not need square brackets around it.
4. An ellipsis (. . .) indicates repetition.
5. All punctuation should be entered as shown in the model format.

The DIR Command

The DIR (directory) command is used to display entries in the current or specified directory. The general format of this command is

```
DIR [<file spec>] [/P] [/W]
```

where <file spec> is the specification of the file(s) whose directory listing is being requested. It consists of the drive name where the file resides, its path, and the file name with its extension. The qualifier /P causes DIR to pause when the page is full, and the /W option causes DIR to display file names and extensions (only without specifying file size, dates, and time) across the page.

The simplest form of this command is

```
DIR
```

This command will display the listing of all the entries (files) of the disk in the default drive.

Typing DIR <CR> causes the list in Figure A.16 to appear on the screen. This is the directory listing (referred to in the future as the *listing*) of the default drive C:. In your case, the listing may be different. The first line indicates that the volume name or the volume label of the disk in drive C: is DUGGAL. The first column in the listing represents the file names of the files residing on the hard disk, and the second column represents their extensions. A *file name* may vary from one to eight characters in length, and the optional extensions can be from one to three characters in length. The third column represents the size of the files in terms of the number of bytes. A byte stores one character of data in computer storage.

Some of the entries in this listing do not have separate entries in the second and third columns, but have a single <DIR> entry. These are *directory entries*, which are discussed in section 1.3. The last two columns give the date and time that these files were created or last accessed. The last line in the listing indicates the total number of files present and the amount of storage available on the disk.

The directory of another drive can be displayed by adding the drive specification to the DIR command. To obtain the listing of the floppy disk

Figure A.16 Directory of the default drive

```
C> DIR
    Volume in drive C: is DUGGAL
    Directory of C:\

    COMMAND   COM     23258   12-18-85  1:11p
    CONFIG    SYS        48    1-27-89  5:42p
    AUTOEXEC  BAT       123    1-24-89  9:08p
    DOS             <DIR>      12-20-85 10:25a
    MMATE           <DIR>      12-20-85 10:26a
    LOTUS           <DIR>      12-20-85 10:27a
    BATCH           <DIR>       2-15-86  2:33p
    SIDEKICK        <DIR>       2-15-86  2:34p
            9 File(s)   8245280 bytes free
```

Figure A.17 Directory of the A: drive

```
C>DIR A:
Volume in drive A: is ABC COMPANY
Directory of A:\

INV     DBF     2560    12-18-88 11:35p
INV1    PRG     3997    12-27-88  7:02p
INV1    BAK     3923    12-24-88  3:38p
 .       .        .        .        .
 .       .        .        .        .
 .       .        .        .        .
INV42   BAK     2367    12-21-88 10:42a
INV42   PRG     2368    12-21-88 10:59a
       51 File(s)    185104 bytes free
```

in drive A:, you need to insert the disk you received with this textbook in drive A: and type the following command at the prompt C>:

C> **DIR A:**   <Return>

The listing shown in Figure A.17 will appear on the screen.

The DIR/P Command

When the simple DIR (or DIR A:) command is used, the listing will be displayed on the screen. But if the listing is large, it is not possible to display it all on one screen. It will scroll off the top of the screen, leaving only the last 25 lines.

To remedy this situation, you can use the *paused directory* command (DIR/P). This will cause the listing to pause when the screen becomes full. Typing the command DIR A:/P at the prompt C> will display a screen similar to that shown in Figure A.18. After viewing the information on the screen, press any key as indicated by the message displayed at the bottom of the screen to continue the listing until the next screen is full or the end of the listing is reached.

The DIR/W Command

This option is an alternate form of the DIR command to be used when the directory listing is also too large and cannot be contained in one screen. It

Figure A.18 Paused directory of the A: drive

```
INV     DBF     2560    12-18-88 11:35p
INV1    PRG     3997    12-27-88  7:02p
INV1    BAK     3923    12-24-88  3:38p
 .       .        .        .        .
 .       .        .        .        .
 .       .        .        .        .
INV23U  BAK     1510    12-20-88  9:24p
INV21   PRG     4057    12-22-88  4:22p
Strike any key when ready . . .
```

Figure A.19 Wide directory of the A: drive

```
C>DIR A:/W

Volume in drive A: is ABC COMPANY
Directory of A:

INV     DBF    INV1    PRG   INV1    BAK   INV23   BAK   INV3    BAK
INV22   BAK    INV13U  PRG   INV21U  PRG   INV11U  PRG   INV     NDX
  .       .      .      .      .      .      .      .     .       .
  .       .      .      .      .      .      .      .     .       .
INV42   &PR    ORDER   DBF   INV4    PRG   INV4    BAK   INV42   BAK
INV42   PRG
     51 File(s)    185104 bytes free
```

is called the *wide directory*. This command will list only file names and their extensions, displaying five files on a line. Typing DIR A:/W at the prompt C> will display a screen similar to that shown in Figure A.19.

The DIR command can also be used to display the listing for any particular file of a disk. For example, if you want to find out whether a particular file is present on a disk, you can simply type the file name and extension after the DIR command:

    C> **DIR A:INV11.PRG**   <Return>

The listing shown in Figure A.20 will be displayed on the screen. This listing indicates that the file is present on the disk. But if the file is not present on the disk, the listing will be as shown in Figure A.21.

Using Wild Card Character Specifications So far we have used the DIR command to display the listing of the contents of the disk or the listing of a particular file on a disk. When the listing for any particular group of files from a disk is needed, the *wild card character specification* is used in place of the file name or file extension. The two valid wild card characters are "*" (asterisk) and "?" (question mark). The * (asterisk) represents multiple characters in a file name. It may be used to represent an entire file name and/or an entire file extension or the remaining characters in either a file name and/or its extension. The ? (question mark) represents only one character in a file name. It may be used in place of any character in the file name and/or the file extension, but its use is position dependent.

```
C>DIR A:INV11.PRG
  Volume in drive A: is ABC COMPANY
  Directory of A:\

  INV11   PRG    3923  12-27-88  7:22p
       1 File(s)    185104 bytes free
```

Figure A.20 Directory of the A: drive with file

```
C>DIR A:INV11.PRG
  Volume in drive A: is ABC COMPANY
  Directory of A:\

  File not found
```

Figure A.21 Directory of the A: drive without file

Figure A.22 Partial directory of the A: drive listing only files with .PRG extension

```
C>DIR A:*.PRG
  Volume in drive A: is ABC COMPANY
  Directory of A:\

    INV1     PRG      3997   12-27-88  7:02p
    INV13U   PRG      1510   11-20-88  5:32p
    INV21U   PRG       310   10-12-88  4:15p
      .        .        .       .        .
      .        .        .       .        .
      .        .        .       .        .
    INV4     PRG      4249   11-08-88  8:35a
    INV42    PRG      2368   12-21-88 10:59a
           21 File(s)    185104 bytes free
```

A few examples of the DIR command using wild card character specifications along with a short description follow:

1. C> **DIR A:*.PRG**   <Return>

   This command will display the listing of the disk in A: drive listing all files with *any* file name and with the .PRG extension, as shown in Figure A.22.

2. C> **DIR A:INV.***   <Return>

   This command will display the directory listing of the disk in A: drive listing all files with the file name INV and with any extension, as shown in Figure A.23.

3. C> **DIR A:*.***   <Return>

   This command will display the listing of the disk in A: drive listing all files with *any* file name and with *any* extension. The effect of this command is the same as that of the DIR A: command. The listing produced as a result of this command is shown in Figure A.24. It is identical to that of Figure A.17.

4. C> **DIR A:INV1?.PRG**   <Return>

   This command will display the listing of the disk in A: drive listing all files with the four characters "INV1" in the first four positions of the file name followed by *any one character in the last position* and with a *.PRG extension*. Its listing is shown in Figure A.25.

Figure A.23 Partial directory of the A: drive listing only files with file name INV and any extension

```
C>DIR A:INV.*
  Volume in drive A: is ABC COMPANY
  Directory of A:\

    INV     DBF     2560   10-15-88 11:35p
    INV     NDX     1024   10-15-88 11:45p
    INV     BAK     4829   10-18-88  2:16p
    INV     PRG     4829   10-18-88  3:59p
           21 File(s)    185104 bytes free
```

Figure A.24 Directory of the A: drive

```
C>DIR A:*.*
Volume in drive A: is ABC COMPANY
Directory of A:\

INV     DBF     2560    12-18-88 11:35p
INV1    PRG     3997    12-27-88  7:02p
INV1    BAK     3923    12-24-88  3:38p
 .       .        .        .        .
 .       .        .        .        .
 .       .        .        .        .
INV42   BAK     2367    12-21-88 10:42a
INV42   PRG     2368    12-21-88 10:59a
       51 File(s)    185104 bytes free
```

Recall that the wild card character ? (question mark) is position dependent, which means it represents only *one character* (in fact, *any one character*) at the position where it is used in the file name or the file extension. In the previous example, the command DIR A:INV1?.PRG represents the listing of the disk in drive A: listing only those files whose extension is .PRG, and whose name contains INV1 as the first four characters, with any character in the fifth place. The use of ? specifies only one character. Having any *one character* in the position where the ? is used is what is meant by *position dependent*. Compare this listing with the use of the wild card character * (asterisk) used in the same position in the following example.

5. C> **DIR A:INV*.PRG**   <Return>

    This command will display the listing of the disk in A: drive containing all files with four characters "INV1" in the first four positions of the file name followed by *any unknown number of positions with any characters in those positions* and with the extension .PRG. Its listing is shown in Figure A.26.

The CLS Command

The CLS (clear screen) command is used to clear the screen and reposition the cursor at the top left corner. When you give the CLS command at the C> prompt, the screen will clear, and the system prompt C> will be displayed at the top left corner.

Figure A.25 Directory of the A: drive using wild card ?

```
C>DIR A:INV1?.PRG
Volume in drive A: is ABC COMPANY
Directory of A:\

INV1    PRG     3997    12-27-88  7:02p
INV11   PRG     4367    11-17-88  1:45p
INV13   PRG     3907    11-20-88  4:23p
INV12   PRG     4415    11-18-88 10:48a
        4 File(s)    185104 bytes free
```

Figure A.26 Directory of the A: drive using wild card *

```
C>DIR A:INV1*.PRG
   Volume in drive A: is ABC COMPANY
   Directory of A:\

   INV1     PRG     3997   12-27-88   7:02p
   INV13U   PRG     1510   11-20-88   5:32p
   INV11U   PRG      270   11-15-88  10:12P
   INV11    PRG     4367   11-17-88   1:45p
   INV13    PRG     3907   11-20-88   4:23p
   INV12    PRG     4415   11-18-88  10:48a
          6 File(s)      185104 bytes free
```

The FORMAT Command

The FORMAT command is used to prepare a new blank disk for receiving information or to erase and reformat old disks for reuse. You cannot use a new disk to store data or programs until it is formatted.

Be very careful when reformatting old disks. Make sure you have inserted the proper floppy disk in the appropriate drive before proceeding with the FORMAT command.

The general format of this command is

```
FORMAT [<d:>] [/V] [/S]
```

where <d:> specifies the drive in which the disk to be formatted is present. The /S qualifier requests the FORMAT command to place the operating system files on the disk after formatting. This file will make the disk bootable; that is, you can boot up your computer system using this disk in the default drive. However, the /V qualifier requests the FORMAT command to pause after formatting the disk and display the prompt to enter a volume label if it is desired. A volume label is an internal label used on the disk for the computer system to identify the disk.

To format a disk, follow these instructions:

1. Boot up the system.
2. At the system prompt C>, type the following command and press the <Return> key:

   ```
   C> FORMAT A:     <Return>
   ```

3. Place the new blank disk in drive A:, and close the latch when the directions on the screen tell you to do so. Then press any key to begin the formatting process.
4. During the formatting process, the system displays the following message:

   ```
   Formatting . . ._
   ```

5. When the formatting process is complete, the following message will be displayed:

   ```
   Formatting . . . Format complete
        362496 bytes total disk space
        362496 bytes available on disk
   Format another (Y/N)?_
   ```

The system is asking you if you want to format another disk. If you do, type "Y," follow the directions on the screen, and insert another disk for formatting. But if you have finished formatting disks, type "N." When the system prompt is displayed, you can remove the newly formatted disk from the A: drive. This disk is now ready for use.

Formatting with Volume Label The /V option used with the FORMAT command allows you to create a volume label for the floppy disk. A *volume label* is an electronic label written on your disk and displayed whenever you get a directory listing of the disk. For example, in Figure A.16, "DUGGAL" is the volume label of the floppy disk that came with this book.

To format a disk and add a volume label, type the following command at the system prompt:

```
C> FORMAT A:/V    <Return>
```

At the completion of the formatting, the system will display the following message:

```
Volume label (11 characters, <Enter> for None)?_
```

The system is requesting you to type a volume label name of up to 11 characters and press the <Return> key. If you opt not to assign a label to the disk, simply press the <Return> key.

Formatting and Copying System Files The /S option used with the FORMAT command allows you to copy the system files onto the newly formatted disk. Three files, namely, IO.SYS (hidden file), MSDOS.SYS or PCDOS.SYS (hidden file), and COMMAND.COM, are copied in the order previously shown. When you get a directory listing of the disk, only the COMMAND.COM file will be displayed. The other two files are not displayed because they are hidden files. On older versions of DOS, the name of the hidden files were IBMBIO.SYS and IBMDOS.SYS.

To format a disk and copy the system files on it, type the following command at the system prompt:

```
C> FORMAT A:/S    <Return>
```

After the formatting process is complete, this disk can be used to boot up any PC.

The COPY Command

The COPY command is used to copy files from one storage area to another. For example, you can copy files from one floppy disk to another, or you can copy files from a floppy disk to a hard disk and vice versa. The COPY command is used to make backup copies of files.

The general format of this command is

```
COPY <file spec1> [<file spec2>]
```

<File spec1> is the specification of the source file to be copied, and <file spec2> is the specification of the target file. Some examples of the COPY command follow.

Place the floppy disk you received with this textbook in drive A:, close the latch on the drive, and type the following command:

```
C> COPY A:CUSTOMER.DBF C:     <Return>
```

This command is telling the system to copy a file named CUSTOMER.DBF from the source disk in drive A: to the target disk in drive C:. Because no file name is given in <file spec2>, the system will use the same name as that of the <file spec1>. This will create a file named CUSTOMER.DBF on drive C:.

In fact, the entry C: is redundant. When no drive is specified, the system goes to the default drive, which in this case is drive C:. So you could have typed the following command and had the same effect:

```
C> COPY A:CUSTOMER.DBF     <Return>
```

The original file CUSTOMER.DBF stored on the floppy disk of drive A: will remain unchanged. The COPY command has no effect on the original file. The COPY command simply makes a duplicate copy of a given file, without changing it, and places the duplicated copy in the requested designation.

If you want to copy the CUSTOMER.DBF file from the floppy disk in drive A: to a file named ADDRESS.DBF (notice that here you are changing only the file name but keeping the same extension) onto the default drive C:, you will need the following command:

```
C> COPY A:CUSTOMER.DBF ADDRESS.DBF     <Return>
```

Note: You need to specify the target file name *only* if it is different from the source file name.

You can use the wild card option to copy a group of files from one location to another. To copy all the files with extension .PRG from the floppy disk in drive A: to the hard disk on the default drive C:, you will need to type the following command:

```
C> COPY A:*.PRG     <Return>
```

The RENAME Command

The general format of the REN (rename) command is

```
REN <file spec1> <file spec2>
```

<File spec1> is the specification of the source file to be renamed, and <file spec2> is the specification of the renamed file.

This command allows you to change the name of a file to a new name. Wild card characters can also be used to change the name of a group of files with one command.

Recall that you have copied a file named ADDRESS.DBF and stored it on the hard disk on drive C:. To change the name of this file to TRY1.PRG, type the following command:

```
C> REN ADDRESS.DBF TRY1.PRG     <Return>
```

You can verify the result by getting a directory listing with the DIR command before and after using the REN command.

The TYPE Command

The general format of this command is

    TYPE <file spec>

<File spec> is the specification of the file to be displayed on the screen.

This command is used to display the contents of a file on the screen. Only standard text files will give you a meaningful display. If you try to display the contents of a nontext file with this command, the screen will be filled with unrecognizable symbols. Try these two examples.

To display the contents of the file named INV.PRG stored on the default drive C:, type the following command:

    C> **TYPE INV.PRG**   <Return>

The file will scroll off the screen. To pause the listing for viewing, press the <Ctrl-S> key (hold down the <Ctrl> key and press the <S> key). <Ctrl-S> will stop the scrolling. To continue, simply press any key.

To display the contents of a nontext file, for example, the COMMAND.COM file stored on the default drive C:, type the following command:

    C> **TYPE COMMAND.COM**   <Return>

Enjoy reading the display listing!

The PRINT Command

The general format of the PRINT command is

    PRINT <file spec> [/]

<File spec> is the specification of the file to be printed on the printer.

The PRINT command is similar to the TYPE command and is used to obtain a printed copy of the contents of a file rather than simply displaying the contents on the screen. To obtain the printed copy of the listing of the file INV.PRG stored on the default drive C:, type the following command:

    C> **PRINT INV.PRG**   <Return>

If during the printing you want to cancel any further printing of the file, simply type:

    C> **PRINT** /P

This command will terminate the printing and return the control to the system prompt C>.

A.3 Introduction to DOS

The DELETE Command

The general format of the DEL (delete) command is

    DEL <file spec>

<File spec> is the specification of the file to be deleted from the disk.

The DEL command is used to remove a file from the disk. The remove the CUSTOMER.DBF file from the default drive C:, type the following command:

    C> **DEL CUSTOMER.DBF**   <Return>

Wild card characters can be used to delete groups of files. Let us remove all the files with extension .PRG from the default drive C:. To do this, type the following command:

    C> **DEL *.PRG**   <Return>

Now all the files with a .PRG extension you copied to the default drive C: have been deleted. You can verify this by getting the directory listing, which should be similar to Figure A.16.

The summary of the commands discussed in this section and their respective functions are given in Table A.6.

Table A.6 Summary of DOS commands

Name	Format	Function
DIR	DIR [<file spec>] [/P] [/W]	To display a directory listing of a file
CLS	CLS	To clear the screen
COPY	COPY<file spec1> [<file spec2>]	To copy one or more files from one memory location to another memory location
FORMAT	FORMAT [<d:>] [/V] [/S]	To prepare a new disk for storing information
REN	REN <file spec1> <file spec2>	To change the name of a file
TYPE	TYPE <file spec>	To display the contents of a file on the screen
PRINT	PRINT <file spec> [/]	To print the contents of a text file
DEL	DEL <file spec>	To delete a file

Appendix B

dBASE IV Installation

B.1 Overview

Before you can use any software on your computer, you must install it. The installation process customizes the application software to your computer's hardware configuration. You need to go through the installation procedure for each software application only once. This appendix discusses general techniques for installing dBASE IV on a single user computer. Please refer to the dBASE IV manual for network installation procedures.

Appendix B starts with listing the minimum requirements needed for running dBASE IV. Before you start installing dBASE IV on your computer system, make sure that your system meets these requirements. The next section presents the step-by-step instructions for installing dBASE IV. The installation process consists of software registration and three phases of the installation of dBASE IV.

At the start of the installation process, the installation program will prompt you to complete a software registration form if dBASE IV is being installed for the first time. The registration form will require you to fill in your name, your company name (if any), and the serial number from the dBASE IV system disk 1 into an onscreen file that dBASE IV presents.

In the first phase of installation, you will need to describe your computer hardware configuration. The first option asks whether you want to install dBASE IV for a single or multiuser system. The next option asks for the display mode (mono or color), which is automatically set by the installation program for your computer. The third option deals with optimizing the color display on your monitor. The last option helps you install the printer(s) to be used for dBASE IV and pick the printer drivers needed for each installed printer.

The second phase of installation is the actual installation (copying) of the system files onto your computer. The installation process will help you select the target drive and create a directory where dBASE IV will be installed (copied). Then the process will proceed to modify the AUTOEXEC.BAT file (if needed) so that dBASE IV can be started automatically from any drive or directory. Finally, it will update the CONFIG.SYS file to meet the minimum requirements for dBASE IV in terms of buffer areas (dBASE IV needs a minimum of 15 buffer areas) and the number of files that can be open at a particular time (dBASE IV requires a minimum of 40 files).

In the third and last phase of the installation, you will install the optional files available with the dBASE IV package. The instructions for installing the sample files and the tutorial files are discussed in this section. This will complete the installation.

After the presentation of the three-part installation procedure follows the procedure for uninstalling dBASE IV from your computer system. Appendix B concludes with instructions for modifying the hardware configuration.

B.2 Hardware and Software Requirements

The following are the requirements for running dBASE IV:

1. An IBM personal computer, PC/XT, PC/AT, or a 100 percent compatible computer; IBM Personal System/2 models 30, 50, 60, or 80; and the Compaq Deskpro 286 or 386
2. IBM personal computer DOS (PC-DOS) or Microsoft DOS (MS-DOS) version 2.0 or higher, Compaq DOS version 3.31 for the DOS version of dBASE IV, or OS/2 for the OS/2 version
3. At least 640k of RAM
4. A hard disk with approximately 3.5MB of available disk space

Before you proceed with the installation, make sure your computer system meets these requirements. You can use the DOS command CHKDSK to find the amount of free disk space on your hard disk drive.

B.2.1 The CHKDSK Command

The CHKDSK command scans the disk in the specified drive (default drive if no drive is mentioned), checks for errors, and finds the amount of free disk space on any drive. For example, if you are logged on to drive C:, to find out the free disk space on the hard disk, type the following command:

```
C> CHKDSK    <Return>
```

Because no drive is specified, it will scan the default drive C: and display an error message, if there are any errors, followed by a status report, as shown in Figure B.1.

The seventh line in Figure B.1 indicates the amount of free disk space available on your hard disk drive. In this case, it is approximately 8.495MB. You need a minimum of 3.5MB of free disk space, but 4MB to 5MB is recommended because you will be storing several database files as well as your own application programs. The last line in Figure B.1 indicates the amount of free RAM storage.

Figure B.1 Status report of drive C:

```
21225472  bytes total disk space
   49152  bytes in 3 hidden files
   98304  bytes in 12 directories
12550144  bytes in 620 users files
   32768  bytes would be recovered in
       4  recovered files
 8495104  bytes available on disk

  655360  bytes total memory
  608128  bytes free
```

B.3 Installing dBASE IV

To install dBASE IV on your system, follow these instructions:

1. Boot up your system. If the system prompt is C>, proceed with step 2. If the prompt is C:\>, skip step 2, and proceed to step 3.
2. Type the following command:

   C> **PROMPT PG**   <Return>

   The system will return with the C:\> prompt.
3. Insert the dBASE IV installation disk in drive A:.
4. Type the command A:, and press <Return>. An A:\> prompt will be displayed, indicating that you have logged on to drive A:.
5. Now type INSTALL, and press <Return>.

In a few seconds, you will see a copyright notice and a prompt to press ↵ to continue. Now press the ↵ key to continue. You will be asked to enter the information discussed in the following sections of this appendix.

B.3.1 Software Registration

The first information you are asked to enter registers your software. Follow the instructions, and fill in your name, your company name, and the serial number from the dBASE IV system disk 1. After completing all the prompts, check the spelling, and make any corrections by using the <Left Arrow> or <Right Arrow> key, if needed. Save this information by pressing <Ctrl-End> (hold down the <Ctrl> key, and press the <End> key).

After the software registration, the instructions given in Figure B.2 will be displayed on the screen.

Figure B.2 Three phases to the installation of dBASE IV

```
There are three phases to the installation of
dBASE IV.  In the first phase, you will
describe your hardware environment.  In the
second phase, you will specify a target drive
and directory and then install dBASE IV.  In
the final phase, you will have the opportunity
to install optional related files.

           Proceed              Exit
```

Figure B.3 Hardware Setup Menu

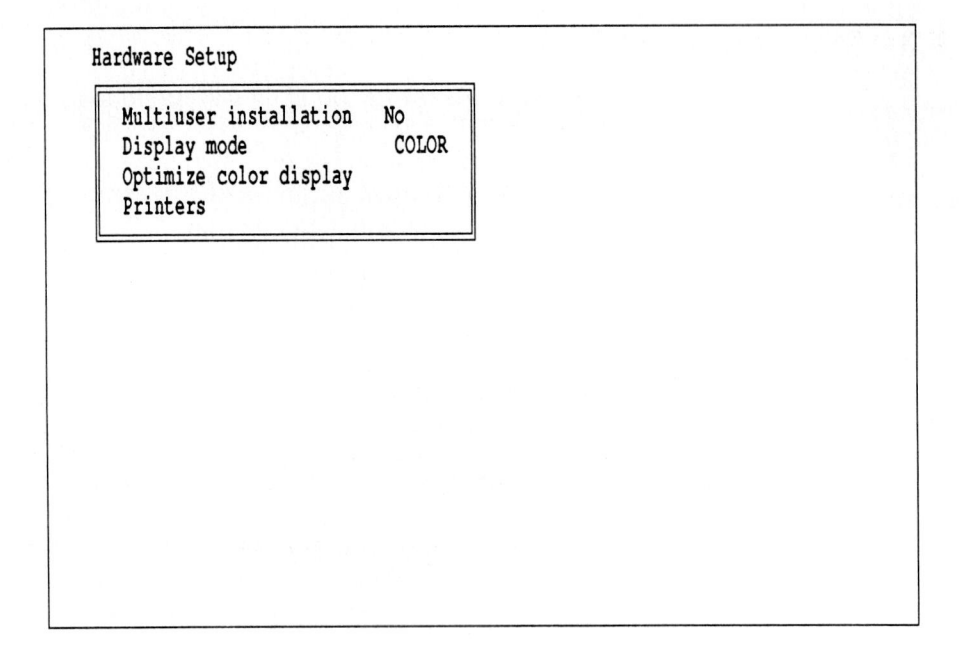

```
Hardware Setup
 ┌─────────────────────────────────────┐
 │ Multiuser installation    No        │
 │ Display mode              COLOR     │
 │ Optimize color display              │
 │ Printers                            │
 └─────────────────────────────────────┘
```

Select the Proceed option using the <Left Arrow> or <Right Arrow> key, press the <Return> to proceed with the installation process, and follow the instructions until you see the menu as shown in Figure B.3.

B.3.2 Hardware Configuration

The first phase of installation of dBASE IV begins with describing your computer's hardware. There are four options in this menu:

1. Because you are installing dBASE IV for a single user system, leave the Multiuser installation option set to no.

2. The Display mode option will be automatically set for your particular computer. To change this default setting, move the highlight to the Display mode option by using the <Left Arrow> or <Right Arrow> key, and press <Return> repeatedly until the appropriate display mode appears next to the prompt.

3. The next option optimizes the use of the color display on your color monitor. To achieve the optimization, move the highlight to the Optimize color display option using the <Up Arrow> or <Down Arrow> key, and press <Return>. Now select Proceed from the options that appear, and press the <Return> key. dBASE IV will ask if you see "snow," that is, interference, on the screen. If you do, type Y. Otherwise, type N. If you do see snow and answered Y, the installation program will try to correct the problem. Finally, press any key to continue when you are prompted.

4. The Printers option lets you specify printers to be used with dBASE. You can install up to four printers for dBASE IV. To continue the process, highlight the Printers option, and press the <Return> key. The information shown in Figure B.4 will be displayed on the screen.

Figure B.4 Printers selection instructions

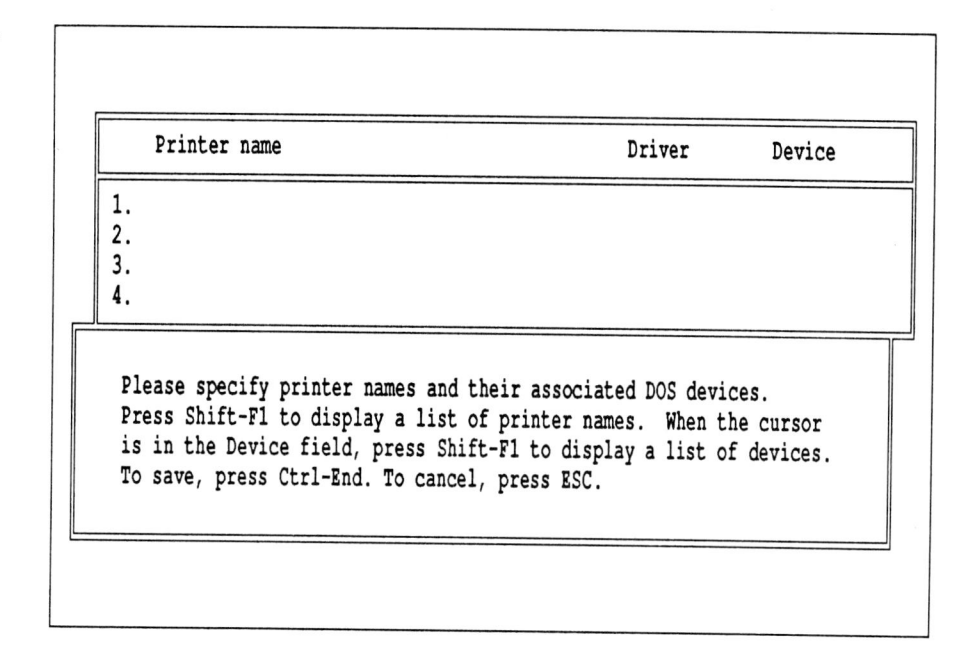

```
      Printer name                    Driver      Device
   ┌─────────────────────────────────────────────────────┐
   │ 1.                                                  │
   │ 2.                                                  │
   │ 3.                                                  │
   │ 4.                                                  │
   └─────────────────────────────────────────────────────┘
   ┌─────────────────────────────────────────────────────┐
   │ Please specify printer names and their associated DOS devices. │
   │ Press Shift-F1 to display a list of printer names.  When the cursor │
   │ is in the Device field, press Shift-F1 to display a list of devices. │
   │ To save, press Ctrl-End. To cancel, press ESC.      │
   └─────────────────────────────────────────────────────┘
```

As indicated in the instructions, press the <Shift-F1> key to display the list of printer names. They will be listed in a window on the left-hand side of the screen, as shown in Figure B.5.

Highlight the name of the company that manufactures your printer. Use the <Down Arrow> key or <Up Arrow> key to scroll through the names of all the listed printers. If you do not see your printer manufacturer listed, highlight generic driver. Now press <Return>. A submenu of specific printer models will be displayed. Highlight the appropriate printer model, and press <Return>. If you selected generic driver, the submenu will not be displayed.

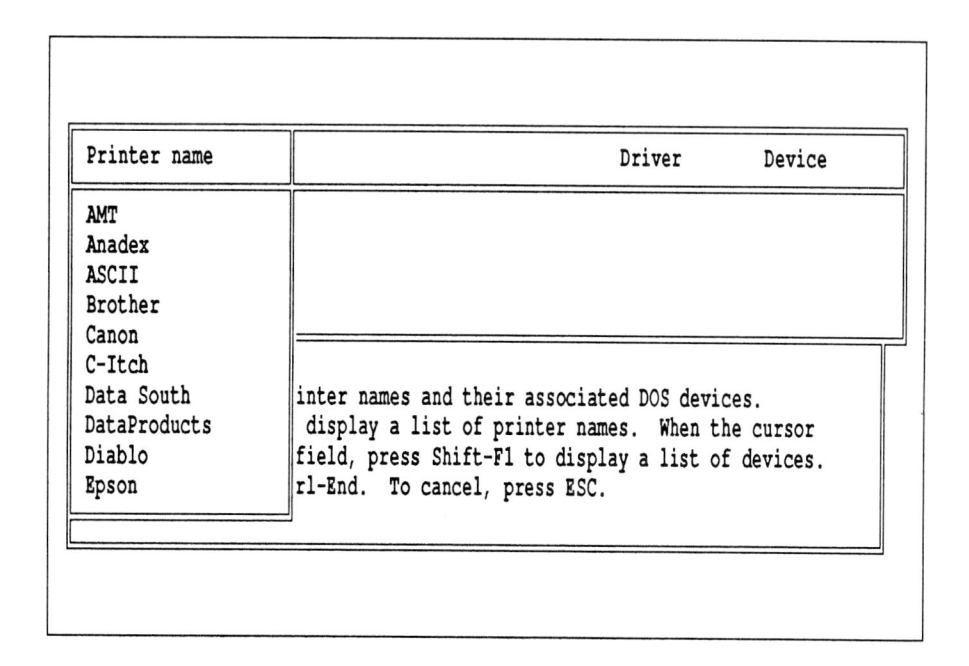

Figure B.5 Printers selection instructions with list of printers

```
      Printer name                    Driver      Device
   ┌──────────────────┬──────────────────────────────────┐
   │ AMT              │                                  │
   │ Anadex           │                                  │
   │ ASCII            │                                  │
   │ Brother          │                                  │
   │ Canon            │                                  │
   │ C-Itch           │                                  │
   │ Data South       │ inter names and their associated DOS devices. │
   │ DataProducts     │  display a list of printer names.  When the cursor │
   │ Diablo           │ field, press Shift-F1 to display a list of devices. │
   │ Epson            │ rl-End. To cancel, press ESC.    │
   └──────────────────┴──────────────────────────────────┘
```

Figure B.6 Printers selection instructions with list of selected printers

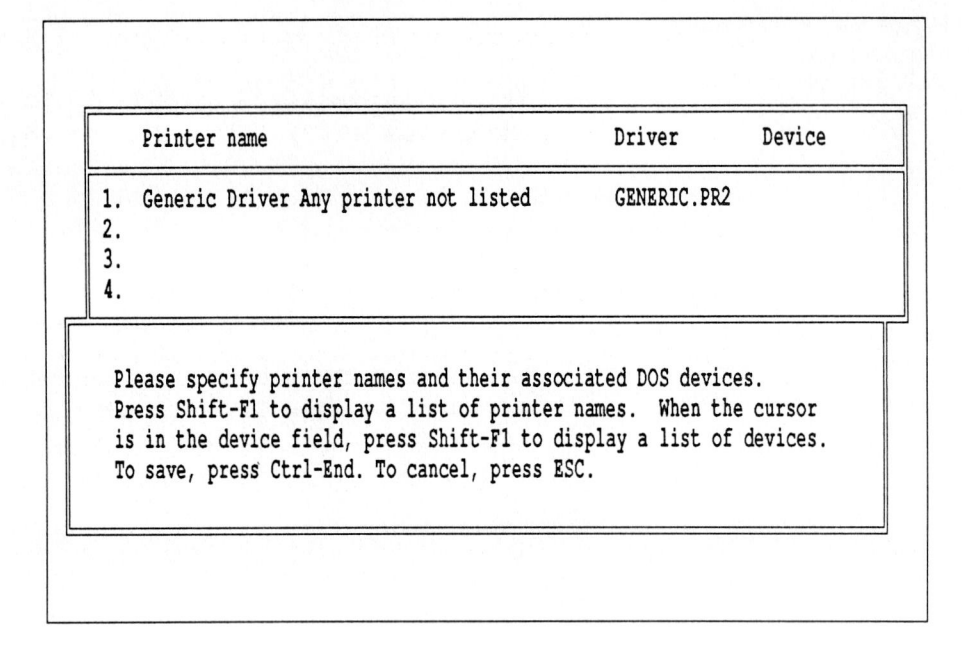

```
        Printer name                          Driver         Device

  1.  Generic Driver Any printer not listed   GENERIC.PR2
  2.
  3.
  4.

  Please specify printer names and their associated DOS devices.
  Press Shift-F1 to display a list of printer names.  When the cursor
  is in the device field, press Shift-F1 to display a list of devices.
  To save, press Ctrl-End. To cancel, press ESC.
```

After you select the printer, the screen will look like Figure B.6. The cursor will be in the device column. As indicated in the instructions, press the <Shift-F1> keys to display a list of devices to which your printer should be connected. Select LPT1 by highlighting and pressing <Return>. At this point, the screen will look like Figure B.7.

These steps complete the selection process for one printer. If your computer supports more than one printer, repeat these steps to select another one. When you have finished the printer selection, press <Ctrl-End> to save the changes. At this point, dBASE will ask you to pick a printer driver from a displayed list. Select one of the drivers listed. If you

Figure B.7 Printers selection instructions with list of selected printers

```
        Printer name                          Driver         Device

  1.  Generic Driver Any printer not listed   GENERIC.PR2    LPT1
  2.
  3.
  4.

  Please specify printer names and their associated DOS devices.
  Press Shift-F1 to display a list of printer names.  When the cursor
  is in the device field, press Shift-F1 to display a list of devices.
  To save, press Ctrl-End. To cancel, press ESC.
```

are not sure which driver to pick, pick the GENERIC.PR2 as a default driver.

To save the printer selections, press <Ctrl-End>. dBASE will display some instructions along with the Proceed, Modify your hardware setup, or Exit options. Select the Proceed option by highlighting it and pressing <Return>. This completes the first phase of installation.

B.3.3 Installing System Files

In this phase, the installation program will request the drive and the directory for dBASE to be installed on and suggest C:\DBASE as the target drive and directory. It is assumed here that the hard disk drive is named C:. Press <Return> to accept the suggested drive and directory, or enter your own drive and directory. If C:\DBASE or the drive and directory you selected do not already exist, dBASE will ask your permission to create one for you. To continue, highlight the Proceed option, and press <Return>.

The remaining prompts appearing on the screen will vary, depending on your version of dBASE IV. Follow these instructions to copy the systems disks of dBASE IV that came with the package. When the installation is complete, the message given in Figure B.8 will be displayed on the screen.

Select the Proceed option by highlighting, and press <Return> to continue. This option will allow you to modify your AUTOEXEC.BAT and CONFIG.SYS files.

Modifying the AUTOEXEC.BAT File

The AUTOEXEC.BAT file stores instructions that DOS reads whenever you first boot your computer. The installation program allows you to change the AUTOEXEC.BAT file so that dBASE IV can be started automatically from any drive or directory. To modify the AUTOEXEC.BAT file, continue by highlighting the Proceed option and pressing <Return>.

Figure B.8 Message for installation completion

```
Single user dBASE IV has been installed successfully.

No errors were encountered in the installation of the
single user dBASE IV system files.  You may now proceed
to modify your Autoexec.bat and Config.sys files, and
to install the sample files and the dBASE IV tutorial.

          Proceed            Exit
```

Modifying the CONFIG.SYS File

The CONFIG.SYS file also stores instructions that DOS reads whenever you first boot your computer to configure itself to software. dBASE IV needs the following minimal settings to run properly on your computer:

```
files = 40
buffers = 15
```

The installation program will ask for your permission to update the CONFIG.SYS file. If you are sure that the CONFIG.SYS file contains these minimum requirements, you can skip this step. If you are not sure, select the Proceed option by highlighting and pressing <Return> to continue. This will complete the second phase of installation, that is, defining the target drive and directory phase.

B.3.4 Copying Other Files

This is the last phase of the installation, in which you install the optional files available with your dBASE IV package.

Copying Sample Files

First, you will be given the option to copy the sample files. The sample files let you explore various aspects of dBASE IV and complement the printed documentation supplied with the software package. To continue, highlight the Proceed option, and press <Return>.

The installation program will request the drive and directory where the sample files will be installed and will suggest C:\DBASE\SAMPLES as the target drive and directory. Press <Return> to accept the suggested drive and directory, or enter your own drive and directory. If the C:\DBASE\SAMPLES or the drive and directory you selected do not already exist, dBASE will ask your permission to create one for you. To continue, highlight the Proceed option, and press <Return>. Now you are ready to copy the sample files. Follow the onscreen instructions, and complete the installation.

Copying Tutorial Files

In this section, you will be given the option of copying the tutorial files. Follow the steps, which are similar to those for copying the sample files, and let the system create for you the directory C:\DBASE\DBTUTOR to store the tutorial files and complete their installation. When all the tutorial files are copied, the installation program will request that you insert the installation disk in the source drive shown on the status bar, which in this case is drive A:. Insert the installation disk in drive A:, and press <Return> to continue. A message screen indicating that the dBASE IV installation was successful will be displayed. The screen will also present the Exit to DOS and Transfer to dBSETUP options. Select Exit to DOS by highlighting and pressing the <Return> key. The control will be returned to DOS, and the A> prompt will be showing on the screen.

Now remove the installation disk from drive A:, and then reboot the computer by pressing the <Ctrl,Alt-Del> key, that is, simultaneously pressing the <Ctrl>, <Alt>, and <Del> keys. (You can also turn OFF your computer and then turn it back ON again.) You have now completed the installation procedure and can run dBASE IV at any time using the instructions presented in Table 2.1 or 2.2.

B.4 Uninstalling dBASE IV

If you are selling your computer or changing to a new one, you will want to remove dBASE IV from your old computer. The process of removing any application software from your computer is called *uninstalling the software*. To uninstall dBASE IV, follow these instructions:

1. Boot up your system. If the system prompt is C>, proceed with step 2. If the prompt is C:\>, skip step 2, and proceed to step 3.
2. Type the following command:

   C> **PROMPT PG**   <Return>

   The system will return with the C:\> prompt.
3. Log on to the DBASE directory, where dBASE is installed (stored), by typing CD\DBASE as shown:

   C:\> **CD \DBASE**   <Return>

   The prompt C:\DBASE> will appear.
4. Type DBSETUP, and press <Return>. You will see a copyright notice and a prompt to press ↵ to continue.
5. Now follow the instructions of the prompt, and press ↵. You will see the DBSETUP Pull-down Menus as shown in Figure B.9.
6. Use the <Down Arrow> key to select the Uninstall dBASE IV option, and press <Return>. The message shown in Figure B.10 will be displayed.

Figure B.9 DBSETUP Pull-down Menu

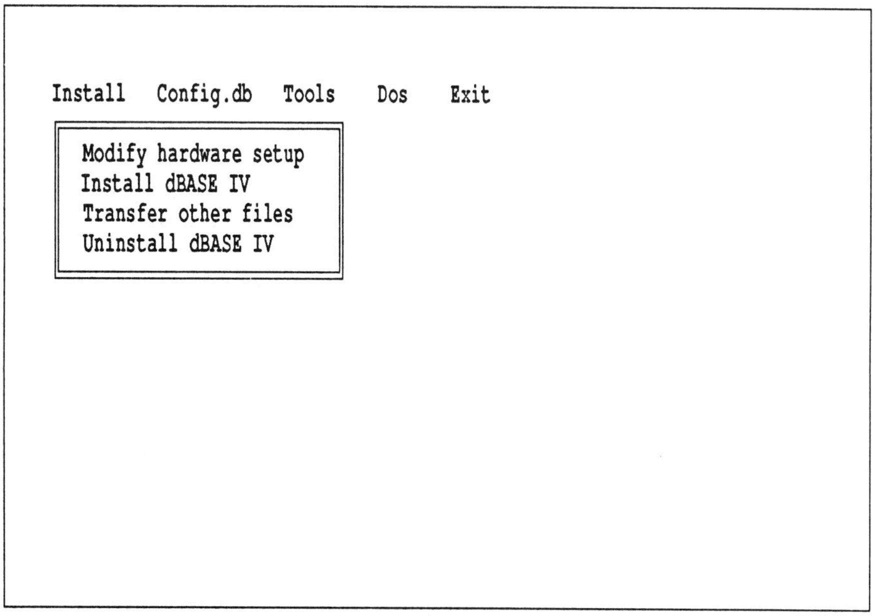

```
Install  Config.db  Tools  Dos  Exit
┌─────────────────────────┐
│ Modify hardware setup   │
│ Install dBASE IV        │
│ Transfer other files    │
│ Uninstall dBASE IV      │
└─────────────────────────┘
```

Figure B.10 Uninstallation drive and directory

```
Please enter the drive and directory from which to
uninstall dBASE IV.

dBASE IV Drive:Directory C:\DBASE
```

7. If dBASE is installed on the suggested drive and directory, press <Return> to continue the uninstall process. Otherwise, type the new drive and directory name from which to uninstall dBASE IV, and press <Return>. When dBASE has been uninstalled, the message shown in Figure B.11 will be displayed on the screen.
8. Press <Return> to return to the Install Menu.
9. Select the Exit option from the top bar menu, and press <Return>. The submenu showing the Exit to DOS option will be displayed. Press <Return> again to exit to DOS.

That completes the uninstallation process for dBASE IV. You can also use the DBSETUP command to select the Modify hardware setup, Install

Figure B.11 dBASE IV successful uninstallation message

```
dBASE IV has been successfully uninstalled.

Only the system files have been removed.  You
may want to delete the remaining dBASE
files.  We recommend you first make backup
copies of any files (such as .dbf files) you
may have created.

Press any key to return to the Install menu.
```

dBASE IV, and Transfer other files options. The procedure for these options is similar to the installation procedure. In addition, you can modify the existing CONFIG.DB file or create a new CONFIG.DB file using this command. Creation of the new CONFIG.DB file is usually automatic when dBASE is installed. Modification of the existing CONFIG.DB file is discussed in detail in section C.2.

B.5 Modifying the Hardware Configuration

The information you provide during installation is used by the installation program to configure dBASE IV to your computer system environment. But if your hardware environment changes (for example, you replace your monochrome monitor with a new color monitor, you change your printer, or you add a new printer to your system), you will need to change the hardware configuration accordingly. These changes can be handled by the DBSETUP program, which is part of dBASE IV and is stored on the same directory (on the DBASE directory on drive C:). For an alternative method, see sections C.3.4 and C.3.12.

Suppose you want to make two changes in your hardware: change your monitor from mono to color and change your printer to a new IBM printer model ProPrinter Low Resolution Graph. To modify these hardware setups, follow these instructions:

1. Boot up your system. If the system prompt is C>, proceed with step 2. If the prompt is C:\>, skip step 2, and proceed to step 3.

2. Type the following command:

   C> **PROMPT PG**   <Return>

   The system will return with the C:\> prompt.

3. At the system prompt, type DBSETUP, and press <Return>. You will see a copyright notice and a prompt to press ↵ to continue.

4. Follow the instructions of the prompt, and press ↵. You will see the DBSETUP Pull-down Menus as shown in Figure B.9.

5. Use the <Up Arrow> or <Down Arrow> key to make a selection. Press <Return> when the Modify hardware setup option is highlighted. The Hardware Setup Menu shown in Figure B.3 will be displayed.

6. a. To make a change for the monitor, highlight the display mode, and press the space bar to change the mono entry to color, as shown in Figure B.12. This will take care of the monitor change from mono to color. If this is the only change needed in the hardware environment, go to step 12. If not, continue with the rest of the instructions.

   b. To make a change in the printer, highlight the Printers option, and press <Return>. The information shown in Figure B.4 will be displayed on the screen.

7. As indicated in the instructions, press <Shift-F1> to display the list of printer names. The list of printer names will be displayed in a window on the left-hand side of the screen, as shown in Figure B.5.

Figure B.12 Hardware Setup Menu with color monitor

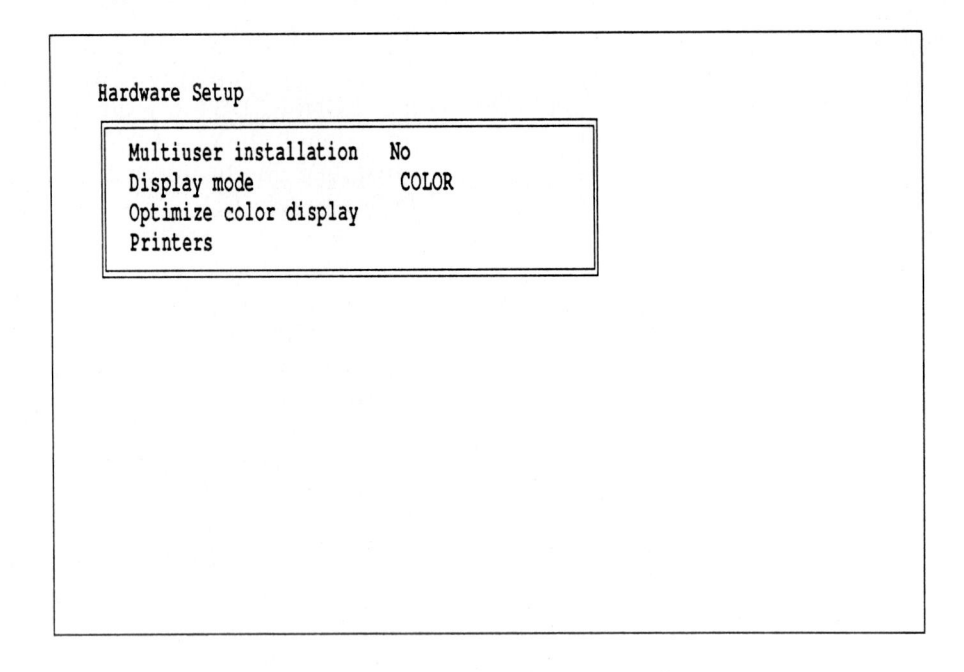

```
Hardware Setup
    Multiuser installation    No
    Display mode              COLOR
    Optimize color display
    Printers
```

8. Highlight IBM selection, and press <Return>. A submenu of specific printer models will be displayed, as shown in Figure B.13.
9. Highlight the ProPrinter low resolution graphs option. You will see the appropriate driver IBMPRO_1.PR2 shown next to the printer model name, as indicated in Figure B.14.
10. Press <Return> to accept this selection. After the selection of the printer, the screen will look like Figure B.15.
11. The cursor will be in the device column. As indicated in the instructions, press <Shift-F1> to display a list of devices to

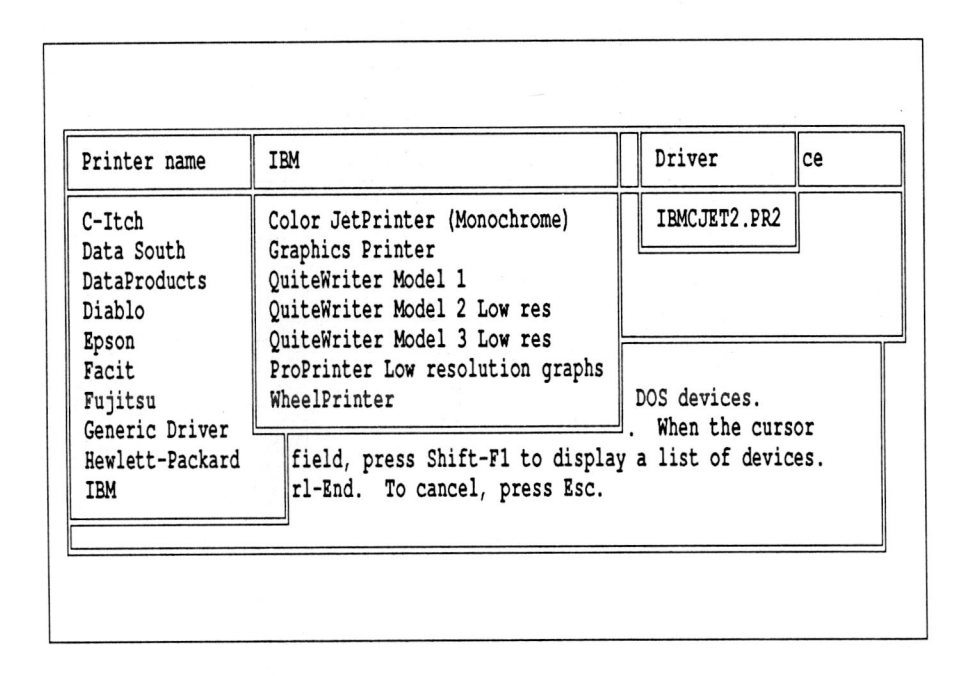

Figure B.13 Printer selection instructions with list of printers and their models

Printer name	IBM	Driver	ce
C-Itch	Color JetPrinter (Monochrome)	IBMCJET2.PR2	
Data South	Graphics Printer		
DataProducts	QuiteWriter Model 1		
Diablo	QuiteWriter Model 2 Low res		
Epson	QuiteWriter Model 3 Low res		
Facit	ProPrinter Low resolution graphs		
Fujitsu	WheelPrinter	DOS devices.	
Generic Driver		When the cursor	
Hewlett-Packard	field, press Shift-F1 to display a list of devices.		
IBM	rl-End. To cancel, press Esc.		

Figure B.14 Printer selection instructions with list of printers with their models and appropriate driver

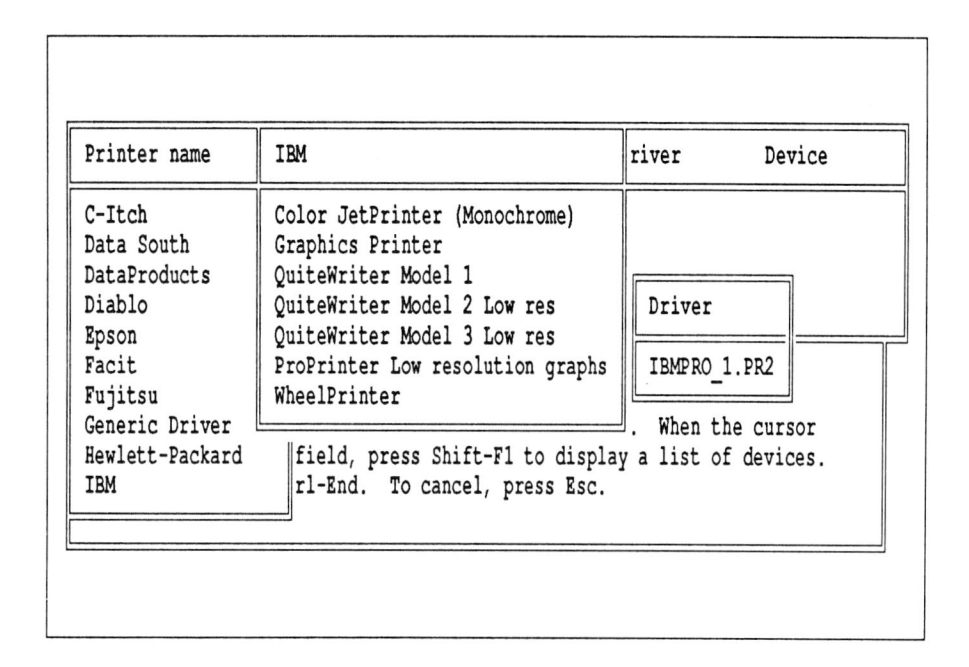

```
Printer name      IBM                                 river       Device

C-Itch            Color JetPrinter (Monochrome)
Data South        Graphics Printer
DataProducts      QuiteWriter Model 1
Diablo            QuiteWriter Model 2 Low res         Driver
Epson             QuiteWriter Model 3 Low res
Facit             ProPrinter Low resolution graphs    IBMPRO_1.PR2
Fujitsu           WheelPrinter
Generic Driver                                      . When the cursor
Hewlett-Packard   field, press Shift-F1 to display a list of devices.
IBM               rl-End.  To cancel, press Esc.
```

which your printer should be connected. Select LPT1 by highlighting and pressing <Return>. At this point, the screen will look like Figure B.16.

12. To save the changes, press <Ctrl-End>. The DBSETUP Pulldown Menu, shown in Figure B.9, will be displayed.

13. Select the Exit option from the top bar menu, and press <Return>. The submenu showing the Exit to DOS option will be displayed. Press <Return> again to exit to DOS.

This completes the modification of the hardware setup.

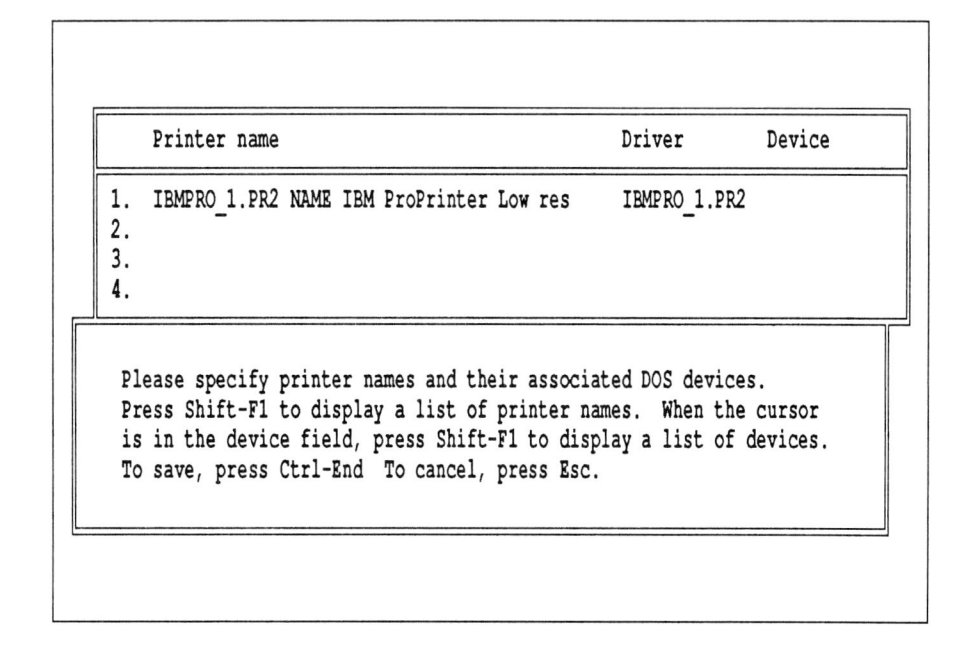

Figure B.15 Printer selection instructions with selected printer

```
    Printer name                             Driver        Device

1.  IBMPRO_1.PR2 NAME IBM ProPrinter Low res  IBMPRO_1.PR2
2.
3.
4.


Please specify printer names and their associated DOS devices.
Press Shift-F1 to display a list of printer names.  When the cursor
is in the device field, press Shift-F1 to display a list of devices.
To save, press Ctrl-End  To cancel, press Esc.
```

Appendix B / dBASE IV Installation

Figure B.16 Printer selection instructions with selected printer and device

```
    Printer name                              Driver       Device

 1. IBMPRO_1.PR2 NAME IBM ProPrinter Low res  IBMPRO_1.PR2 LPT1
 2.
 3.
 4.


   Please specify printer names and their associated DOS devices.
   Press Shift-F1 to display a list of printer names.  When the cursor
   is in the device field, press Shift-F1 to display a list of devices.
   To save, press Ctrl-End  To cancel, press Esc.
```

Appendix C

**Customizing the
dBASE IV Environment**

C.1 Overview

The information you provided during installation as explained in Appendix B was stored by the installation program in the CONFIG.DB file. This file resides in the same directory as dBASE IV, that is, the DBASE directory on drive C:. Every time dBASE IV is loaded, it consults the CONFIG.DB file; and depending on the information contained in this file, it configures itself to your computer system.

After you have gained some experience with dBASE IV, you may wish to configure it to meet your specific needs. You can do this by adding, deleting, and/or changing the existing commands in the CONFIG.DB file. You can use any word processor or the dBASE IV text editor to change the CONFIG.DB file to new settings.

Because all these configuration settings are obtained by changing the contents of the CONFIG.DB file, understanding the commands used in this file will be very helpful. For this reason, Appendix C starts by listing the contents of this file, followed by an explanation of each of the commands used in it. Some of the most commonly used configuration settings customizing dBASE IV are described.

C.2 Explanation of CONFIG.DB File Commands

Load dBASE IV as explained in Table 2.1 and Table 2.2. Now, if you type the following command:

```
. MODIFY COMMAND C:\DBASE\CONFIG.DB      <Return>
```

dBASE IV will display the contents of the CONFIG.DB file, as shown in Figure C.1.

```
*
*     dBASE IV Configuration File

*     Thursday January 5, 1989

*
COLOR OF NORMAL       = W+/B
COLOR OF HIGHLIGHT    = GR+/BG
COLOR OF MESSAGES     = W/N
COLOR OF TITLES       = W/B
COLOR OF BOX          = GR+/BG
COLOR OF INFORMATION  = B/W
COLOR OF FIELDS       = N/BG
COMMAND               = ASSIST
DISPLAY               = COLOR
PDRIVER               = GENERIC.PR2
PRINTER 1             = GENERIC.PR2 NAME "Generic Driver any Printer not Listed"
SQLDATABASE           = SAMPLES
SQLHOME               = C:\DBASE\SQLHOME
STATUS                = ON
```

Figure C.1 Contents of CONFIG.DB file

Initially, the CONFIG.DB file contains 14 commands. The first seven perform color settings of the screen:

COLOR OF NORMAL	= W+/B
COLOR OF HIGHLIGHT	= GR+/BG
COLOR OF MESSAGES	= W/N
COLOR OF TITLES	= W/B
COLOR OF BOX	= GR+/BG
COLOR OF INFORMATION	= B/W
COLOR OF FIELDS	= N/BG

The next command, COMMAND = ASSIST, ensures that every time dBASE IV is loaded, it displays the control center.

The DISPLAY = COLOR command indicates that your computer system has a color monitor. If you change to a monochrome monitor, all you will have to do is change this command to DISPLAY = MONO.

The next two commands are PDRIVER = GENERIC.PR2 and PRINTER 1 = GENERIC.PR2 NAME "Generic Driver any Printer not Listed." The first indicates that the printer driver to be used by your printer is named GENERIC.PR2. The second conveys the name of your printer, which is listed as a generic printer, that is, any other printer not listed in the list provided by the dBASE IV software.

The next two command are SQLDATABASE = SAMPLES and SQLHOME = C:\DBASE\SQLHOME. The first tells the system that SQLDATABASEs that came with the dBASE IV software package are stored in the directory named SAMPLES. The second indicates that the path for the SQLHOME file is C:\DBASE\SQLHOME.

The last command, STATUS = ON, ensures that the status bar is displayed every time dBASE IV is loaded.

C.3 Configuring dBASE IV for Special Needs

The CONFIG.DB file can be used to define a number of settings that will take effect automatically as soon as dBASE IV is loaded, thus avoiding the trouble of typing these commands before the start of each session. A few of the most commonly used settings and the methods of achieving them follow.

C.3.1 Color Setting

You can control the color setting of many aspects of the color screen display. The different aspects of display are the standard display and its background, the enhanced display and its background, and the border. The enhanced display is used for full-screen editing with the GET commands. The general format for this command is

```
COLOR = standard display/background, enhanced
        display/background, border
```

The entry for each category should be separated by a comma and should appear in the same order as given. For example, the following command

```
COLOR = GR+/B,W+/RB,BG+
```

dictates that the color combination on the screen at start-up will be yellow letters (GR+) on a blue (B) background for the standard screen and white letters (W+) on a magenta (RB) background for the enhanced display. The screen border will be light blue (BG+). The plus sign (+) indicates high intensity, and an asterisk (*) causes a blinking effect. The colors used in different color settings of the screen are listed in the Table C.1.

The presence of this command in the CONFIG.DB file will have the same effect as the SET COLOR TO GR+/B,W+/RB,BG+ command entered at the dot prompt.

C.3.2 Loading dBASE IV Directly to the Dot Prompt Mode

dBASE IV comes preset with the feature that every time it is loaded, it displays the control center. To bypass this and go directly to the dot prompt mode, delete the COMMAND = ASSIST command from the CONFIG.DB file.

C.3.3 Automatic Start of a Program

To start a program such as PROG1, enter the DO PROG1 command at the dot prompt. If you want that program to be automatically started when you load dBASE IV, add the COMMAND = DO PROG1 command to the CONFIG.DB file. When dBASE IV is loaded, it will consult this file to configure itself to the hardware configuration. The presence of this command in the file will instruct dBASE IV to execute the DO PROG1 command automatically at the start of dBASE IV and run the PROG1 program every time dBASE IV is loaded.

C.3.4 Changing the Monitor Setting

If you had a monochrome monitor at the time dBASE IV was installed, the installation program created and stored the DISPLAY = MONO command in the CONFIG.DB file. If you later purchase a color monitor, all you have to do is modify this command to DISPLAY = COLOR to configure dBASE IV for the new monitor.

The use of the SET DISPLAY TO COLOR command at the dot prompt will have the same effect. However, the only problem is that this command will have to be entered every time dBASE IV is loaded. Including this command in the CONFIG.DB file will take care of this configuration once and for all.

Table C.1 Different color codes and corresponding color names

Color Code	Color Name	Color Code	Color Name
B	Blue	N	Black
B+	Electric Blue	R	Red
BG	Aqua	R+	Bright Orange
BG+	Light Blue	RB	Magenta
G	Green	RB+	Bright Magenta
G+	Lime Green	W	White (Gray)
GB	Dull Aqua	W+	Bright White
GR	Brown	X	Hidden Display
GR+	Yellow		

C.3.5 Changing the Default Drive

dBASE IV stores and accesses files from the default drive and the directory where dBASE IV is stored. If you want to store all your database files on a floppy disk and later access them from the disk, you will need to change the default drive to A: where the floppy disk will be present. Do this by adding the DEFAULT = A command to the CONFIG.DB file.

Every time a new database is created, it will be stored on the floppy disk on drive A:, and any access command to a file will first direct dBASE IV there. In case it cannot find the file there, dBASE IV will then try to search for it in the other drive and directory mentioned in the SET PATH command.

C.3.6 Removing the Status Bar

dBASE IV comes preset with the feature that every time it is loaded, it displays the status bar. This feature is ensured by the STATUS = ON command present in the CONFIG.DB file. If you remove this command, dBASE IV will not display the status bar.

C.3.7 Changing the Dot Prompt Symbol

dBASE IV comes preset with the dot prompt as a default prompt for the interactive mode. To change the dot prompt to a more appealing prompt, such as dBASE:>, add the PROMPT = dBASE:> command to the CONFIG.DB file. This command will replace the dot prompt with the dBASE:> prompt.

C.3.8 Programming of the Function Keys

The ten function keys have preassigned functions for dBASE IV. These are discussed in section 2.4. To change the function of these keys, use the CONFIG.DB file. For example, to program the F2 key to start execution of the program named INVOICE, add the F2 = DO INVOICE; command to the CONFIG.DB file. The semicolon (;) has the same effect as pressing the <Return> key.

C.3.9 Setting the Path for Directories

Every time dBASE IV wants to access any file, it will first go to the default drive and the directory in which dBASE IV is stored. If your file is stored on a different drive or directory, set the path by informing dBASE IV where to search if the file is not present in the default drive and directory. For example, if your database file is in the subdirectory INVOICES of the DBASE directory on drive C:, set the path for this situation by including the PATH = C:\DBASE\INVOICES command in the CONFIG.DB file. When dBASE IV wants to access this file, it will first search for it in the default drive C:, then in the default directory, the dBASE directory, on drive C:. If it does not find the file there, it will search the subdirectory INVOICES (listed in the path command) of the DBASE directory on drive C:.

C.3.10 Use of the External Text Editor for Program Files

The MODIFY COMMAND command invokes the dBASE IV text editor to create or modify dBASE programs. To use an external text editor, such as MicroSoft Word, to create and modify dBASE programs, add the TEDIT = WORD command to the CONFIG.DB file. With this command present, the MODIFY COMMAND command will not invoke the dBASE IV text editor. Instead, it will invoke the MicroSoft word processor program.

C.3.11 Use of the External Text Editor for Memo Fields

To use an external word processor, such as WordStar, with the memo fields instead of the dBASE IV text editor, add the WP = WS command to the CONFIG.DB file. With this command present, dBASE IV will not invoke the dBASE IV text editor when it is in the append mode and the PgDn key is pressed. Instead, it will invoke the WordStar word processor.

C.3.12 Changing Printer(s) Settings

Suppose you purchase a new IBM ProPrinter with low-resolution graphics and want to use it with your computer system. But you previously had a generic printer. To configure dBase IV to this new printer, you will need to change the following two commands:

```
PDRIVER   = GENERIC.PR2,
PRINTER 1 = GENERIC.PR2 NAME "Generic Driver any
Printer not Listed"
```

to read

```
PDRIVER   = IBMPRO_1.PR2,
PRINTER 1 = ProPrinter Low resolution graphs
```

To do this, you will need to know the name of the printer driver used with your new printer. In the alternate method discussed in section B.5, dBASE IV will help you by providing the printer driver name.

A list of some key words, along with their effects that have not been discussed and that can also be used in the CONFIG.DB file to alter the default settings, is given in Table C.2.

Your CONFIG.DB file will not have any effect until dBASE IV is started from the DOS prompt. If you just modified the CONFIG.DB file using the dBASE IV text editor or an external text editor, you will have to quit dBASE and start it again to see the effect of the changes in the file.

Table C.2 Key words used to change settings in the CONFIG.DB file

Key Word	Effect
GETS	Specifies the number of @, SAY, GETS that may be active at any one time. The default setting is 128.
MVARSIZ	The amount of space allocated for storing memory variables. The default is 6K bytes.

Appendix D

dBASE IV Commands and Functions

D.1 Introduction

The purpose of this appendix is to provide easy reference to all the dBASE commands and functions used in this book. The conventions, the syntax of dBASE commands, the rules for using dBASE commands, and the dBASE commands and functions are summarized.

D.1.1 Conventions in This Book

The examples in this book follow these conventions:

- The word *press* is used for the keys you should press, and the word *type* is used for information you must type in.
- The term *press <Ctrl-W>* means to hold down the Ctrl key, press the W key once, and then release both the keys.
- The term *press <Ctrl,Alt-Del>* means to hold down the Ctrl and Alt keys simultaneously, press the Del key once, and then release all the keys.
- The function keys (F1 . . . F10) are followed with their assigned function (e.g., F1 Help).
- The instructions to be typed appear as shown.
- **DISPLAY STRUCTURE**   <Return>

  You type only the boldface part of the instruction, that is, the **DISPLAY STRUCTURE** command, and press the <Return> key. Don't type the <Return> part with the instruction; it is present in the instruction to indicate that the <Return> key should be pressed after you are done typing the instruction.

D.1.2 Syntax of dBASE IV Commands

dBASE IV dot prompt commands follow a common syntax:

```
VERB [<scope>] [<field/expression list>]
    [FOR <condition>] [WHILE <condition>] [TO
    PRINT/FILE <file name>]
```

The components of a dBASE command are as follows:

Verb represents a dot prompt command (for example, CREATE, USE, DISPLAY, LIST).

Scope is an optional qualifier that specifies what records of the database file the command applies to, depending on the current record order (for example, ALL, RECORD 5, NEXT 6, REST). The absence of the scope in the command defaults to the current record or to all the records of the database file.

Field list is a list of data field names separated by commas (for example, LAST_NAME, FIRST_NAME, AREA_CODE).

Expression list is a list of expressions separated by commas in which an expression is a formula consisting of fields, memory variables, constants, and operators (for example, UNIT_PRICE*MARK_UP, UNIT_PRICE*QUANTITY).

Condition is an expression that limits the records of the database file affected by the command (for example, FOR LAST_NAME =

'SMITH' or WHILE UNIT_COST > 100). More than one condition can be used in a dBASE command. You can also combine conditions with a scope qualifier.

The scope, field list, expression list, and conditions are not required by most dBASE commands. These options are used to refine or restrict their effect.

D.1.3 Rules for Using dBASE Commands

Each dBASE command must follow these rules:

1. The words in all capital letters represent valid dBASE command names. These commands must be entered exactly as shown, except that uppercase is *not* required.
2. The information contained in the angle brackets (<>) is to be supplied by the user. When supplying this information, do not type the angle brackets.
3. The information contained in the square brackets ([]) is optional. When supplying this information, do not type the square brackets.
4. An ellipsis (. . .) indicates repetition.
5. The items separated by a slash (/) are mutually exclusive; that is, only one of the items should be used.
6. All punctuation should be entered as shown in the model format.

D.2 dBASE Commands

The @ ... SAY Command

The general format of the command is

```
@ <row>,<column> SAY [<message>]
```

where <row> is the row number, and <column> is the column number for the screen or printer. The optional <message> can be a character string, memory variable, field, or expression.

The @ ... SAY command consists of two components: @ <row>,<column> and SAY [<message>]. The first positions the cursor or print head to the row and column positions specified by <row> and <column>. You can use a number, memory variable, field, or expression whose evaluated value is an integer for either <row> or <column>. The second component (SAY [<message>]) is optional, and it displays or prints any user-defined expression at the location specified by the first component of this command.

The standard monitor screen is made up of 25 rows and 80 columns. The rows are numbered 0 to 24, the columns, 0 to 79. The address of the upper left corner is 0,0; the address of the bottom right corner is 24,79. Line 0 is normally used to display messages and should be avoided.

This command is mainly used for adding headings to the report produced by dBASE programs.

The @ ... SAY ... GET Command

The general format of this command is

```
@ <row>,<column> SAY [<message>] [GET <variable>]
      [PICTURE <template>] [RANGE <low>,<high>]
      [CLEAR] [TO]
```

where <row> is the row number, and <column> is the column number for the screen or printer. The optional <message> can be a character string, memory variable, field, or expression. The <variable> is the name of a database field or a memory variable. The <template> is a string of valid picture characters and other characters allowed in the template. The <low> and <high> are the values of the range allowed for the variable. These values can be numbers or dates.

The function of the @ ... SAY command is to display or print any user-defined expression at the location specified by the <row>,<column> component of the command. The optional GET component of the command displays the contents of an existing database field or a memory variable in a template matching the size and data type of the database field or the memory variable. The range option specifies the acceptable range for the variable displayed with the GET component. The CLEAR option is used for clearing the portion of the screen, and the TO option is used to draw the lines and/or the boxes.

The @ ... TO Command

The format of the @ ... TO command is

```
@ <row>,<column> TO <row>,<column> [DOUBLE]
```

where <row> is the row number, <column> is the column number for the screen or printer, and DOUBLE is the optional parameter.

This command is used to draw lines and/or boxes. The lines or the boxes drawn using this command are drawn in the default mode of single line drawing. If the optional DOUBLE parameter is used, then the lines or the boxes will be drawn using the double line mode.

The APPEND Command

The simple format of this command is

```
APPEND
```

The APPEND command adds a new blank record to the end of the database currently in use and allows data entry into it. All the active index tags are automatically updated.

The APPEND BLANK Command

The simple format of this command is

```
APPEND BLANK
```

This command is used to add a new blank record to the end of the database currently in use. The newly added record is always the current record. All the active index tags are automatically updated.

The APPEND FROM Command

The general format of this command is

```
APPEND [FROM <file name>] [FOR <condition>]
       [TYPE <file type>]
```

where <file name> is the name of the file from which the data are appended to the active database file, <condition> is a valid search condition that selects records from the file to be appended, and <file type> indicates the type of the foreign file from which the data are being appended (imported).

The APPEND FROM ... SDF Format

The APPEND FROM ... SDF format of the APPEND command is used to import data from the fixed record length ASCII system data format (SDF) file into the active dBASE file. The general format of this command is

```
APPEND [FROM <file name>] [FOR <condition>]
       [TYPE SDF]
```

where <file name> is the name of the ASCII file from which the data are imported into the active database file, <condition> is a valid search condition that selects records from the ASCII file to be imported, and SDF indicates the type of the foreign file from which the data are being imported. There are two forms of the APPEND FROM ... SDF format:

```
APPEND [FROM <file name>] [TYPE SDF]
APPEND [FROM <file name>] [FOR <condition>] [TYPE
       SDF]
```

The first format is used to append (or import) the whole fixed length record ASCII system data format (SDF) file into the currently active database file. The second format is used to append (or import) only the conditionally selected records from the fixed length record ASCII system data format (SDF) file at the end of the currently active database file.

The APPEND FROM ... DELIMITED Format

The general format of this command is

```
APPEND [FROM <file name>] [FOR <condition>]
       [TYPE DELIMITED]
```

where <file name> is the name of the ASCII delimited format file from which the data are imported into the active database file, <condition> is a valid search condition that selects records from the database file to be imported, and DELIMITED indicates the type of the foreign file from which the data are being imported.

Two forms of the APPEND FROM ... DELIMITED format are discussed:

```
APPEND [FROM <file name>] [TYPE DELIMITED]
APPEND [FROM <file name>] [FOR <condition>] [TYPE
       DELIMITED]
```

The first format is used to append (or import) the whole variable length record ASCII delimited format file at the end of the currently active database file. The second format is used to append (or import) only the conditionally selected records from the variable length record ASCII delimited format file at the end of the currently active database file.

The ASSIGNMENT Command

An alternative method to the STORE TO command is the assignment command. Its format is

```
<memory variable name> = <expression>
```

where <expression> and <memory variable name> have the same meaning as in the STORE TO command except that we cannot have a list of memory variable names on the left-hand side of the assignment operator. (See STORE TO command.)

The AVERAGE Command

The AVERAGE command is used to compute the arithmetic mean of a numeric field or fields for all records in the database file or only for selected records that meet a given condition. The general format of the AVERAGE command is

```
AVERAGE [<expression>] [FOR <condition>]
        [WHILE <condition>] [TO <memory variables>]
```

where <expression> is a list of field names or expressions consisting of numeric fields, <condition> is a valid search condition that selects the records from the database file to be averaged, and <memory variables> are the names of the memory variables where the results of this command are to be stored.

The AVERAGE command has several different options available, depending on the parameters used.

The AVERAGE Format

The simplest format of the AVERAGE command is

```
AVERAGE [<expression>]
```

where the <expression> parameter is optional. There are two forms of this command. The first is

```
AVERAGE
```

The simple AVERAGE command without any parameters will compute the arithmetic mean of all the numeric fields present in the data record for all the records of the active database file.

The second form of the AVERAGE command is

```
AVERAGE <expression>
```

This form of the AVERAGE command will compute the arithmetic mean of only the listed fields or expressions of numeric fields for all the records of the active database file. The field names or expressions should be separated by a comma, and you can include up to five of the field names or expressions in the AVERAGE command.

The AVERAGE FOR Format

The format for the AVERAGE FOR command is

```
AVERAGE [<expression>] [FOR <condition>]
```

where the <expression> and the FOR parameters are optional. There are two forms of this format. The first is

```
AVERAGE FOR <condition>
```

This format computes the arithmetic mean of all the numeric fields but only for those records in the active database file for which the given condition is true.

The second form of the AVERAGE FOR command is

```
AVERAGE <expression> FOR <condition>
```

This form of the AVERAGE FOR command computes the arithmetic mean of the listed fields or expressions of numeric fields for all the records of the active database file for which the given condition is true. The field names or expressions should be separated by a comma, and you can include up to five of the field names or expressions in the AVERAGE FOR command.

The AVERAGE FOR TO Format

The format of the AVERAGE FOR TO command is

```
AVERAGE <expression> FOR <condition>
        TO <memory variable>
```

This command computes the arithmetic mean of the listed fields for only those records in the database file for which the condition is true and stores the result to a memory variable or variables. When the TO option of the command is exercised, it should contain a memory variable for each field or expression for which the arithmetic mean (or average) is required. The memory variables should be separated by a comma.

The BROWSE Command

The general format of the BROWSE command is

```
BROWSE [FIELDS <field names>] [FREEZE <field name>]
       [LOCK <numeric expression>]
       [WIDTH <field width>]
```

where <field names> specifies the names of the fields to be displayed on the edit screen, <field name> is the name of the single field on which the editing of the data is allowed, <numeric expression> specifies the number of fields on the left-hand side of the screen that are to be locked, and <field width> is the maximum width allowed for all the fields.

The BROWSE is a full-screen command that allows editing or appending of records in a currently active database file. The BROWSE command displays 17 records at a time with as many fields as will fit across the screen.

Employing the optional FIELDS clause allows you to choose the fields to be included in the edit screen.

The FREEZE clause allows you to specify the name of a single field on which the editing of the data is allowed.

The LOCK clause allows you to specify the number of fields on the left of the screen to be locked. These fields remain locked when you move the cursor to the right of the screen to view the other fields.

The WIDTH clause allows you to specify the maximum width for all the fields or the fields specified in the BROWSE command.

The CALCULATOR Command

dBASE IV provides a useful command called the CALCULATOR command. The format of the command is

```
? <expression>
```

where <expression> may be a field name, an existing memory variable, or an expression. The function of the ? command is to display the result of the expression at the start of a new line. If the ? command is used alone (with no expression), it prints a blank line.

The CLEAR Command

The simple format of the CLEAR command is

```
CLEAR
```

The function of this command is to clear the screen. It is very useful when a report or a menu is to be displayed on the screen.

The CLOSE Command

The general format of the CLOSE command is

```
CLOSE [ALL] [DATABASES] [FORMAT] [INDEX] [PROCEDURE]
```

The CLOSE command is used to close the files that are not needed for processing in the immediate future. The CLOSE command has no effect on memory variables.

A few formats of the CLOSE command and their functions are listed in Table D.1.

Table D.1 Different formats of the CLOSE command

Format	Function
CLOSE ALL	Closes all the open files
CLOSE DATABASES	Closes all the open databases and their associated index (.NDX, .MDX) and format (.FMT) files
CLOSE INDEX	Closes all the open index (.NDX, .MDX) files
CLOSE FORMAT	Closes all the open format (.FMT) files
CLOSE PROCEDURE	Closes all the open procedure files

The COMMENT Command

This command is used for the internal documentation of the program. Comments, description of the program, and other documentation in the program can be added with this command. A simple asterisk "*" symbol at the start of an instruction in the program makes it a comment command. Because the comment lines are ignored by dBASE, they can be placed anywhere in the program.

The CONTINUE Command

The general format of the CONTINUE command is

```
CONTINUE
```

The function of this command is to resume the search started with the LOCATE command to locate the next record in the active database file that meets the condition specified by the most recent LOCATE command.

The CONTINUE command works only with the LOCATE command, not with the FIND or the SEEK commands.

The COPY Command

The general format of the COPY command is

```
COPY [FILE <source file name>] [TO <target file
    name>]
    [FIELDS <field list>] [FOR <condition>]
    [WHILE <condition>] [<scope>] [STRUCTURE]
    [INDEXES <.NDX file names> [TO <.MDX file
    name>]
    [TYPE <file type>]
```

where <source file name> is the name of the source file to be copied, <target file name> is the name of the target file to which the source file will be copied, <field list> is a list of the field names, separated by a comma, to be included in the structure of the target database file, <condition> is a valid search condition that selects records from the database file to be copied, <scope> is a dBASE scope option such as REST or NEXT, and <file type> is the name of a foreign file.

In all the versions of the COPY command, if a file with the target file name already exists, dBASE will overwrite the existing file, provided that SET SAFETY is OFF. Or it will display the error message. But if the file with the target file name already does not exist, dBASE will create a new file with that name and then perform the copy function.

The COPY FILE TO Command

The first version of the COPY command is COPY FILE TO and the general format of this command is

```
COPY FILE <source file name> TO <target file
            name>
```

where <source file name> is the name of the source file to be copied, and <target file name> is the name of the target file to which the source file will be copied.

The function of this command is to copy any file, such as a database file, program file, index file, text file, or any other file that is not active, to a new file. The use of an extension in this command is required in both the source and the target file names. The FOR, WHILE, and FIELDS options are not available with this command.

This command can also be used to copy an entire database file. But if a database file containing a memo field is copied using this command, the memo field will not be copied. It will have to be copied separately.

The COPY TO Command

The second version of the COPY command is COPY TO, and the general format of this command is

```
COPY [TO <target file name>] [FOR <condition>]
     [FIELDS <field list>] [WHILE <condition>]
```

where <target file name> is the name of the target file to which the source file will be copied, <condition> is a valid search condition that selects records from the database file to be copied, and <field list> is a list of the field names, separated by a comma, to be included in the structure of the target database file.

The function of the COPY TO command is to copy an active database file to a new database file including the structure as well as the data records. There are several different formats of this command available, depending on the parameters used. These parameters are

```
COPY TO <target file name>
COPY TO <target file name> FOR <condition>
COPY TO <target file name> FIELDS <field list>
COPY TO <target file name> FIELDS <field list>
        FOR <condition>
```

The COPY TO Format   The general form of the COPY TO format is

```
COPY TO <target file name>
```

where <target file name> is the name of the target file to which the source file will be copied.

This simple format of the COPY TO command is used to copy an entire active database file and its structure as well as its data records to a new database file. The main use of this command is to create backup database files.

If you copy to a file that already exists and SET SAFETY OFF has been issued, the existing file will be overwritten and destroyed without any message to you. In the default condition (SET SAFETY ON), warning messages are given if an existing file is to be overwritten.

When using the COPY command, you should always have SAFETY in the default mode. To be sure, always execute the SET SAFETY ON command before using any COPY command.

The COPY TO FOR Format   The general format of the COPY TO FOR command is

```
COPY TO <target file name> FOR <condition>
```

D.2 dBASE Commands

where <target file name> is the name of the target file to which the source file will be copied, and <condition> is a valid search condition that selects records from the database file to be copied.

This format of the COPY TO command is used to create a new database file by copying the full structure and including only the conditionally selected records of the active database file.

The two formats of the COPY TO command discussed previously dealt with copying an entire structure and then adding to it either all the records or only the conditionally selected records of an active database file. The next two formats of the COPY TO command deal with copying only a portion of the structure and then adding to it either all the records or only the conditionally selected records of the active database file.

The COPY TO FIELDS Format The general format of the COPY TO FIELDS format is:

    COPY [TO <target file name>] [FIELDS <field list>]

where <target file name> is the name of the target file to which the source file will be copied, and <field list> is a list of the field names, each separated by a comma, to be included in the structure of the target database file.

This format of the COPY TO command is used to create a new database file by copying only a portion of the structure and then adding to it all the records of an active database file.

The COPY TO FIELDS FOR Format The general format of the COPY TO FIELDS FOR command is

    COPY [TO <target file name>] [FIELDS <field list>]
        [FOR <condition>]

where <target file name> is the name of the target file to which the source file will be copied, <field list> is a list of the field names, separated by a comma, to be included in the structure of the target database file, and <condition> is a valid search condition that selects records from the database file to be copied.

This format of the COPY TO command is used to create a new database file by copying only a portion of the structure and then adding to it only the conditionally selected records of an active database file.

The COPY INDEXES Command

The third version of the copy command is COPY INDEXES, and the general format of this command is

    COPY INDEXES <.NDX file names> [TO <.MDX file
                name>]

where <.NDX file names> are the names of the individual index files created with dBASE III PLUS to be copied to index tags used in dBASE IV. The list of individual index file names should be separated by commas. <.MDX file name> is the name of the multiple index file in which the index tags will be saved. The TO clause is optional. If it is not specified with the COPY INDEXES command, then the index tags will be saved in the default production multiple index file.

The COPY INDEXES command is used to convert individual index files created with dBASE III PLUS to index tags used in dBASE IV and to save the index tags in the multiple index file.

The COPY STRUCTURE TO Command

The fourth version of the COPY command is COPY STRUCTURE TO, and the general format of this command is

```
COPY STRUCTURE TO <target file name>
                [FIELDS <field list>]
```

where <target file name> is the name of the target file to which the structure of the source file will be copied, and <field list> is a list of the field names, separated by a comma, to be included in the structure of the target database file.

The function of this command is to copy the whole structure or a part of an active database file to a new database file. There are two different formats for this command:

```
COPY STRUCTURE TO <target file name>
COPY STRUCTURE TO <target file name>
                FIELDS <field list>
```

The COPY STRUCTURE TO Format The general format of the COPY STRUCTURE TO command is

```
COPY STRUCTURE TO <target file name>
```

where <target file name> is the name of the target file to which the structure of the source file will be copied.

This format of the COPY STRUCTURE TO command is used to create a new database file by copying only the full structure of the active database file. The resulting database file will be identical to the database file in use but will contain no data.

The COPY STRUCTURE TO FIELDS Format The general format of the COPY STRUCTURE TO FIELDS command is

```
COPY STRUCTURE TO <target file name>
                FIELDS <field list>
```

where <target file name> is the name of the target file to which the structure of the source file will be copied, and <field list> is a list of the field names, separated by a comma, to be included in the structure of the target database file.

This format of the COPY STRUCTURE TO command is used to create a new database file by copying only a portion of the structure of the active database file.

The COUNT Command

The format of the COUNT command is

```
COUNT [<scope>] [FOR <condition>]
      [TO <memory variables>] [WHILE <condition>]
```

where <scope> specifies which parts of the database file are affected by the command, <condition> is a valid search condition that selects the records from the database file to be counted, and <memory variables> are the names of the memory variables to which the results of this command are to be stored.

The COUNT command has several different options available, depending on the parameters used.

The COUNT Format

The simplest form of the COUNT command is

```
COUNT
```

The simple COUNT command without any parameters counts the number of records present in the active database file.

The COUNT FOR Format

The format for the COUNT FOR command is

```
COUNT [FOR <condition>]
```

This command will count the number of records contained in the database file for which the given condition is true.

The COUNT FOR TO Format

The format for the COUNT FOR TO command is

```
COUNT [FOR <condition>] [TO <memory variables>]
```

This command counts the number of records contained in the database file satisfying a given condition and stores the results to a specified memory variable.

The CREATE Command

The CREATE command allows you to define the structure of a new database file. The general form of this command is

```
CREATE <file name>
```

where <file name> is the name of the new database file to be created. Each database file name consists of a primary name and an extension separated by a period. For example:

```
INVNTORY.DBF
CUSTOMER.DBF
```

The user normally assigns only the primary name. You should always try to select primary file names that remind you of the contents of the database. The extension .DBF is automatically added by dBASE IV to the file name. You can also specify your own extension, in which case it will override the one assigned by dBASE.

The primary file name of a database can be any valid DOS file name. The file name can also contain special characters; however, the use of special characters in the file name can cause problems if system utilities are used. Therefore, avoid using special characters in file names.

The new file is created on the currently logged directory (also called the current working directory) unless otherwise specified by the user.

The CREATE LABEL Command

The general format of the CREATE LABEL command is

```
CREATE LABEL <label format file name>
```

where <label format file name> is the name of the file in which the label format is stored on the computer disk for future use.

The CREATE LABEL command provides interactive techniques for designing the label format. It displays a label design screen consisting of a label design form and seven Pull-down menu options. The Pull-down Menus are used to design the label format using the label design form for the currently active database file. The label format is stored in a disk file with a default extension of .LBL.

If the specified label format file already exists on the disk when the CREATE LABEL command is issued, dBASE will ask if you want to modify it. In fact, the MODIFY LABEL command, which works like the CREATE LABEL command, should be used to modify the already existing label format.

The CREATE REPORT Command

The general format of the CREATE REPORT command is

```
CREATE REPORT <report format file name>
```

where <report format file name> is the name of the file in which the report format is stored on the computer disk.

The CREATE REPORT command provides interactive techniques for designing the report format. It displays a report design screen consisting of a report design form and seven Pull-down menu options. The Pull-down Menus are used to design the report format using the report design form and the currently active database file. The report format is stored in a disk file with a default extension of .FRM.

When the CREATE REPORT command is issued and if the specified report format file already exists on the disk, dBASE will ask if you want to modify it. In fact, the MODIFY REPORT command, which works like the CREATE REPORT command, should be used to modify the already existing report format.

The DELETE Command

The general format of the DELETE command is

```
DELETE [<scope>] [FOR <condition>] [WHILE
    <condition>]
```

where <scope> specifies the part of the database file being affected by the DELETE command, and <condition> is a valid search condition that selects the records from the database file to be deleted.

The DELETE command has several different options available, depending on the parameters used. Two of these are discussed.

The DELETE Format

The first format of the DELETE command is

```
DELETE [<scope>]
```

where the <scope> parameter is optional.

Two forms of this command exist. The first is

```
DELETE
```

The simple DELETE command without any parameters will delete the current record from the active database file.

The second form of the DELETE command is

```
DELETE <scope>
```

This form of the DELETE command is used to delete the records from the active database file as specified in the <scope> parameter. The most commonly used value of the <scope> parameter with the DELETE command is RECORD <number>.

The DELETE RECORD <number> Format The DELETE RECORD <number> format of the DELETE command is used to delete a single record from the database file.

The DELETE FOR Format

The format of the DELETE FOR command is

```
DELETE [<scope>] [FOR <condition>]
```

This format of the DELETE command can be used to mark for deletion a group of records that meet a particular condition.

The DELETE FILE Command

The general format of the DELETE FILE command is:

```
DELETE FILE <file name>
```

where <file name> is the name of the file to be deleted.

The DELETE FILE command works identically to the ERASE command. (See ERASE command.)

The DELETE TAG Command

The general format of the DELETE TAG command is

```
DELETE TAG <index tag name> [OF <.MDX file name>]
```

where <index tag name> is the name of the index tag to be deleted, and <.MDX file name> is the name of the multiple index file in which the index tag to be deleted belongs.

The DELETE TAG command is used to delete an existing index tag. If the optional clause OF is not specified with the command, the index tag to be deleted belongs to the default production multiple index file. But if the index tag belongs to a nonproduction multiple index file, the OF clause must be specified. When the optional OF clause is used with the DELETE TAG command, the nonproduction multiple index file, which contains the index tag to be deleted, should be opened by the SET INDEX command *before* the DELETE TAG command is issued.

The DISPLAY Command

The general format of the DISPLAY command is

```
DISPLAY [<scope>] [<field/expression>]
        [WHILE <condition>] [FOR <condition>] [OFF]
        [TO PRINT]
```

where <scope> specifies which parts of the database file are to be affected by the command, <field/expressions> is a list of field names and/or expressions, separated by commas, that restrict the display of fields and expressions that appear in the report, and <condition> is a valid search condition that selects the record from the database file to be displayed.

The DISPLAY command has several different options available, depending on the parameters used. Without any parameters, this command displays the current record in the database file.

DISPLAY OFF

This command will display the current record on the screen without displaying the record number. The OFF option suppresses the display of the record number.

DISPLAY NEXT n

This command displays the current record and the (n − 1) succeeding records; that is, it will display a total of n records starting from the current one. Note that n indicates the total number of records to be displayed.

DISPLAY ALL

The DISPLAY ALL command will display all the records present in the database. It will display 20 records at a time and pause. Pressing any key will display the next 20 records, and this process will continue until the end of the database file is reached.

DISPLAY ALL <field>

This command will display all the records in the database with only the selected fields mentioned after the DISPLAY ALL command.

DISPLAY <field> FOR <condition>

The search condition is used to display a selective set of records from the database file that satisfy the condition.

The DISPLAY HISTORY Command

This command displays the history of the commands entered at the dot prompt. dBASE can store up to 20 commands entered at the dot prompt in the history buffer. To display all the commands of the current session, type the following command:

```
. DISPLAY HISTORY     <Return>
```

dBASE will respond by displaying the list of all the commands issued during that session.

You can restrict the number of dBASE history commands by adding the scope parameter to this command. For example, the DISPLAY HISTORY LAST 10 command will display up to the last ten commands of the current session.

The DISPLAY MEMORY Command

The format of the DISPLAY MEMORY command is

```
DISPLAY MEMORY [TO PRINT]
```

where the TO PRINT option, if used with the command, will direct the output to the printer.

The function of the DISPLAY MEMORY command is to display, print, or send to the specified disk file the names, data types, sizes, contents, and other information about all the currently active memory variables.

The DISPLAY STRUCTURE Command

The general format of this command is

```
DISPLAY STRUCTURE
```

This command displays the structure of the currently selected database file in the currently logged directory.

The DO Command

The format of the DO command is

```
DO <program file name>
```

where <program file name> must be the name of a program file (.PRG).

The DO command executes the program specified in the program file name; that is, it instructs dBASE IV to execute the commands included in the program file and perform the operations specified by them. Because only program files can be specified with the DO command, there is no need to include the .PRG extension with the program file name. But if the program file has an extension other than .PRG, it should be included with the file name.

Unlike dBASE III and its predecessors, dBASE IV has its own compiler. All the previous versions of dBASE used the interpreter. That means that every time a program was executed, each line was checked for syntax errors by the dBASE interpreter and then translated into machine language before execution. Therefore, program execution was not efficient with previous versions of dBASE.

In contrast, dBASE IV has its own built-in compiler. When the program is executed for the first time, dBASE IV compiles the program file (.PRG) into an object file with the same program file name but with the .DBO extension. The compiling process checks each command line for syntax errors and then translates the commands into machine language. Then dBASE IV executes this (.DBO) program to produce the desired results. dBASE does not have to go through the compilation process for every future execution of the program. It simply executes the already compiled program, which accounts for the increased efficiency and speed of dBASE IV.

The DO CASE-ENDCASE Command

The general format of the DO CASE-ENDCASE command is

```
DO CASE
   CASE <condition1>
        <commands set1>
   [CASE <condition2>
        <commands set2>
      .
      .
      .
   .]
   [OTHERWISE
        <commands set>]
ENDCASE
```

where <condition1>, <condition2>, . . . , and <conditionN> are dBASE logical expressions, and <commands set1>, <commands set2>, . . . , and <commands set> are a set of any number of dBASE IV commands. The DO CASE and ENDCASE commands must always be used in pairs. The DO CASE command marks the beginning and the ENDCASE command marks the end of a case control structure. There can be any number of CASE commands between the DO CASE and ENDCASE commands pair. The OTHERWISE command is optional.

The DO CASE-ENDCASE command is normally used with the case control structure. Each of the CASE commands between the DO CASE and ENDCASE commands is evaluated until one is determined to be true. Then dBASE executes all the commands between this CASE command and the next CASE command; that is, the command set associated with the CASE command evaluated to be true is executed. Usually the command sets used in the DO CASE-ENDCASE command are other dBASE programs. After the execution of the command set associated with the CASE command, which was evaluated to be true, dBASE skips all remaining CASE commands up to ENDCASE and transfers control of the program to the first command after the ENDCASE command. This means that the CASE commands in the DO CASE-ENDCASE command are mutually exclusive.

If none of the CASE commands is true, then the command listed between the optional OTHERWISE command and the ENDCASE command is executed. If the optional OTHERWISE command is not present,

D.2 dBASE Commands

then control is transferred to the first command after the ENDCASE command.

The DO WHILE-ENDDO Command

The format of this command is

```
DO WHILE <condition>
    <commands>
ENDDO
```

where <condition> is a logical conditional statement used to determine the condition under which the commands should continue to be repeated, and <commands> are the dBASE valid commands that are repeated.

The DO WHILE-ENDDO commands are used to construct the repetitive process (also called a *loop*) in a program. The loop is initiated by the DO WHILE command. The commands placed between the DO WHILE and ENDDO commands are repeated until the condition specified in the DO WHILE command is false. The ENDDO command is required and marks the end of the repetitive process.

Basically, the DO WHILE-ENDDO command consists of three components:

1. Initialization, which performs the procedures necessary to begin execution of the DO WHILE-ENDDO loop
2. Loop control, which tests a stated condition and controls repeated execution of the DO WHILE-ENDDO loop
3. The body of the loop, which consists of operations to be carried out within the loop (Within the body of the loop must be some element that will change, when appropriate, the test condition so that execution of the loop can be terminated.)

All the instructions contained between the DO WHILE and the ENDDO commands are executed over and over again until the condition of the DO WHILE command is not true.

The EDIT Command

The general format of the EDIT command is

```
EDIT [<scope>] [<record number>] [FIELDS <field
    names>]
    [FOR <condition>] [WHILE <condition>]
```

where <scope> is an optional qualifier specifying the range of the records in the database file (for example, ALL, NEXT, RECORD, and REST), <record number> is the record number to be edited, <field names> specifies the names of the fields to be displayed on the edit screen, and <condition> is any valid condition used with the optional FOR or WHILE clause to limit the records of the database file to be edited.

The EDIT command is a full-screen command that allows data to be edited in the current record of the active database file. The EDIT command displays the default edit screen containing the current record along with all its fields if these fields can fit on one screen. Otherwise, multiple screens will be used. The use of the optional FIELDS clause allows the user to choose the fields to be included in the edit screen.

The default edit screen can be replaced by the customized form. If the customized form is to be used in place of the default edit screen, it should be opened with the SET FORMAT command *before* the EDIT command is issued. In that situation, the EDIT command will invoke the customized form instead of the default edit screen. However, the design and use of the customized screen is beyond the scope of this book.

A few formats of the EDIT command are given below:

The EDIT Format

The simple EDIT command is used to edit the current data record of the active database file.

The EDIT <record number> Format

When working with a very large database file and changing data records that are far apart, you won't find the simple EDIT format discussed previously very useful. In this situation, this format of the EDIT command becomes very handy.

The EDIT FOR Format

Use of the FOR clause and the optional qualifier ALL with the EDIT command allows you to edit the conditionally selected records.

The EDIT FIELDS <field names> Format

This command allows you to edit only the specified fields with the EDIT command. When a list of fields is used, the fields are separated by a comma. When the EDIT command is executed, only the fields specified in it will be displayed and can be edited. Make the required changes, if any, in those fields, and press <PgDn> to proceed to the next record satisfying the search criteria. If no changes are needed, simply press <PgDn> to proceed to the next record. When dBASE finds no more records satisfying the search criteria, the dot prompt is displayed.

The effect of the EDIT function can be cancelled by pressing the <Esc> key or the <Ctrl-Q> keys.

The ERASE Command

The general format of the ERASE command is

```
ERASE <file name>
```

where <file name> is the name of the file to be deleted.

The ERASE command can be used to delete any type of file supported by dBASE IV. Recall that an open file can't be deleted. Therefore, *before* issuing the ERASE command, close the file to be deleted by using the appropriate CLOSE command. Don't forget to add the extension with the file name to be deleted. The dBASE ERASE command does not support wild card characters.

The ERASE command can be used to delete a multiple index file. *But never delete the production multiple index file.* If you do, you will not be able to open the database file.

The FIND Command

The general format of the FIND command is

```
FIND <character string>
```

where <character string> is a string of characters that are part of the index key of the database file. The character string doesn't need to be enclosed in quotes except when the string contains leading blank spaces. If the character string used in the search is a memory variable, the macro symbol "&" should precede the character string.

The FIND command will search for the first record in the indexed database file in use whose index key matches the character string *exactly*. The FIND command will work only if the database file has been indexed and the index tag has been activated by the use of the SET ORDER command.

If the FIND command is not successful, that is, if no match is found, then the FOUND () function is set to .F., the EOF () function is set to .T., and a "Not successful" message is displayed.

The GOTO Command

The general format of the GOTO command is

```
GOTO/GO [[RECORD]<record number>] [TOP/BOTTOM]
```

where GOTO and GO can be used interchangeably. Their use is optional, [RECORD] is optional, and the <record number> is a number or an expression whose result is a number to which the record pointer should move. This command has two different forms. The first is

```
GOTO/GO [[RECORD]<record number>]
```

The function of this command is to move the record pointer to a specified record number in the active database file.

The second form of the GOTO command is

```
GOTO/GO [TOP/BOTTOM]
```

The function of this command is to move the record pointer to the first or last record in the active database file or to the first and last records determined by the current active index file.

The IF-ELSE-ENDIF Command

The general format of the full version of the IF-ELSE-ENDIF command is

```
IF <condition>
   <commands set I>
[ELSE
   <commands set II>]
ENDIF
```

where <condition> is a dBASE logical expression, <commands set I> and <commands set II> are a set of any number of dBASE IV commands, ELSE is an optional part of the command, and ENDIF is the required command to end the IF command structure.

If the <condition> is true, then the <commands set I> is executed. If the <condition> is false, <commands set II> is executed. This process selects one set of commands out of two, depending on whether the <condition> is true or not. In other words, the full version of the IF-ELSE-ENDIF command is used to select one option of the two given.

There are two other possible situations. The first is when there are no commands in the <commands set II>; that is, there are no commands between the ELSE and ENDIF parts of the IF-ELSE-ENDIF command. In this situation, the ELSE part of the command can be omitted, and the command reduces to

```
IF <condition>
   <commands set I>
ENDIF
```

In this situation, the <commands set I> is executed when the <condition> is true, and no action is taken if it is false. This format of the IF-ELSE-ENDIF command is referred to as the IF-ENDIF format. In this case, the optional ELSE component is not present.

The second situation is when there are no commands in the <commands set I>; that is, there are no commands between the IF and ELSE parts of the IF-ELSE-ENDIF command. In this situation, the IF-ELSE-ENDIF command will reduce to

```
IF <condition>
ELSE
   <commands set II>
ENDIF
```

Here the <commands set II> will be executed when the <condition> is false, and no action will be taken if it is true. But this format can be reduced to the IF-ENDIF format by negating the <condition> as

```
IF .NOT. <condition>
   <commands set II>
ENDIF
```

The IF-ENDIF Command

The general format of the IF-ENDIF command is

```
IF <condition>
   <commands set>
ENDIF
```

where <condition> is a dBASE logical expression, <commands set> is a set of any number of dBASE IV commands, and ENDIF is the required command to end the IF command structure.

If the <condition> is true, then the <commands set> is executed; and if the <condition> is false, no action is taken. Therefore, no commands are executed. In other words, you are given only one choice, which can either be accepted or rejected.

The INDEX Command

The general format of the INDEX command is

```
INDEX ON <index key/expression> TO <.NDX file
          name>
          /TAG <index tag name> [OF <.MDX file
          name>]
          [DESCENDING]
```

where <index key/expression> is the name of the index key or the index expression that is a combination of the index fields, <.NDX file name> is the name of the index file, <index tag name> is the name of the index tag, and <.MDX file name> is the name of the multiple index file.

The INDEX command can be used to create either the index file with the .NDX extension if the TO option is specified or the index tag if the TAG option is specified. This discussion is restricted to index tags.

The default option of the indexing order is ascending. The optional **DESCENDING** clause can be added at the end of the INDEX command to change the default order of indexing.

The format of the INDEX command used for creating the single field index tag is

```
INDEX ON <index key> TAG <index tag name>
          [OF <.MDX file name>] [DESCENDING]
```

where <index key> is the name of the index field, which can be any field of the database file except the memo or logical fields. <Index tag name> is the name of the index tag, which can be up to ten characters long consisting of letters, digits, and the underscore (_). When the index tags are created using a single field as the index key, the tag file name should be the same as that of the index field. <.MDX file name> is the name of the multiple index file.

If no multiple index (.MDX) file is specified in the INDEX command, the index tags created are stored in the *production multiple index file* (.MDX) whose name is the same as that of the database file. If the production multiple index (.MDX) file does not exist, it is created; and the index tags are saved in it. But if the multiple index file is specified in the INDEX command, the index tags are stored in the specified .MDX file. If the specified .MDX file does not exist, it is first created; then the index tags are created and stored in it.

A maximum of 47 index tags can be stored in a multiple index file, which is enough for most applications. However, if more than 47 index tags are needed, if you need to group index tags for a database file in more than one category, or if 2 index tags need to be created for the same field in different orders, you can create an additional multiple index file.

Multiple index files other than the production .MDX can be created by using the OF option in the INDEX command to specify the name of the multiple index file.

The format of the INDEX command for creating the multiple field index tags is

```
INDEX ON <index expression> TAG <index tag name>
          [OF <.MDX file name>] [DESCENDING]
```

where <index expression> is the combination of the index fields obtained by joining the index fields with the "+" symbol so that the expression should evaluate to a single data type. Logical and memo field are not allowed in the index expression.

When a database file is indexed on an index expression, the first field in the index expression is considered the *primary index key* and the second, the *secondary index key*. The listing obtained by using the multiple field index tag will be organized in ascending (or alphabetic) order on the primary index key. Within the primary index key, the records will be arranged in ascending (or alphabetic) order on the secondary index key.

When two fields are used in creating the multiple field index tag, they should be of the same data type. If they are of different data types, the data type of one needs to be changed to that of the other. For example, when the date field is used with the character field in the INDEX command to create the multiple field index tag, the date field must be changed to a character string by using the DTOS () function to ensure proper sort.

The LABEL FORM Command

The general format of the LABEL FORM command is

```
LABEL FORM <label format file name> [SAMPLE]
          [<scope>]
          [FOR <condition>] [WHILE <condition>]
          [TO PRINT/TO FILE <label text file
          name>]
```

where <label format file name> is the name of the label format file, <scope> is a dBASE scope option such as REST or NEXT, <condition> is a valid search condition that selects the records from the database file to be displayed or printed, and <label text file name> is the name of the label text file in which the labels will be stored on the disk.

The function of the LABEL FORM command is to print, display, or write the labels on a disk file from the currently active database file using the format specified by the label format file name, which has been created earlier by the CREATE LABEL command.

The LABEL FORM command also allows use of a predefined label format to display the labels for the selected records of a database file. The format for this command is

```
LABEL FORM <label format file name> [FOR
          <condition>]
```

Labels can also be sent to the printer for printing on self-adhesive label forms by including the TO PRINT option. Three versions of the TO PRINT option of the LABEL FORM command are

```
LABEL FORM <label format file name> TO PRINT
LABEL FORM <label format file name> TO PRINT
          SAMPLE
LABEL FORM <label format file name> TO PRINT FOR
          <condition>
```

The TO PRINT option directs the system to send the labels to the printer as well as to the screen.

When using the self-adhesive label forms on the printer, label alignment is achieved by using the SAMPLE option.

The TO FILE option of the LABEL FORM command can be used to write labels to a text file on a disk. This file can be edited later with a word processor, it can be included in other documents, or it can be transported to other computer systems. The labels from this text file can be printed using the DOS PRINT command or the dBASE TYPE command.

The LIST Command

The general format of the LIST command is

```
LIST [<scope>] [<field/expression>]
    [WHILE <condition>] [FOR <condition>] [OFF]
    [TO PRINT]
```

where <scope> specifies which parts of the database file are to be affected by the command, <field/expression> is a list of field names and/or expressions separated by commas that restrict the listing of certain selected fields and expressions appearing in the report, and <condition> is a valid search condition that selects the record from the database file for listing.

The LIST command has several different options available, depending on the parameters used with it.

The LIST command works similarly to the DISPLAY ALL command; that is, it will display all the records in the database, but it will not pause every 20 records. It is a very useful command for a quick check of the contents of the database. To pause the list at any time, simply press <Ctrl-S>; to continue the listing, press any key.

LIST OFF

This command will list the entire database without displaying the record number along with the records.

LIST NEXT n

This command will list the next n number of records, starting from the current record.

LIST <field>

This command will list all the records in the database, but it will display only the fields mentioned after the LIST command. When a list of fields is used, the fields are separated by a comma.

LIST <field> FOR <condition>

This command will list all those records from the database file that meet all the conditions specified in the condition statement.

The LOCATE and the CONTINUE Commands

The general format of the LOCATE and the CONTINUE commands is

```
LOCATE [FOR <condition>] [<scope>] [WHILE
       <condition>]
       <dBASE commands>
CONTINUE
```

where <condition> is a valid search condition that selects the records to be selected, <scope> specifies the part of the database file used for the search by the LOCATE command, and <dBASE commands> are any dBASE commands. The CONTINUE command resumes the search started by the LOCATE command to find the next matching record.

The LOCATE command works similar to the FIND and the SEEK commands except that it does not require an indexed database. The LOCATE command is also not as fast as the FIND and the SEEK commands.

The LOCATE command starts at the first record (or the first indexed record) of the database file and searches through the database file until it finds a record for which the specified condition in the FOR or WHILE part of the command is true. When the match is found, dBASE will respond by displaying the record number of the matched record.

When the dBASE commands mentioned after the LOCATE command have been processed, the CONTINUE command resumes the search started by the LOCATE command to find the next matching record. If another match is found, dBASE will respond by displaying the new record number. The dBASE commands specified after the LOCATE command are once again processed, and the CONTINUE command resumes the search. This process is repeated until there are no more records that satisfy the specified condition. When the LOCATE command fails to find a matching record, the FOUND () function is set to .F., the EOF () function is set to .T., and an "End of LOCATE scope" message is displayed.

The CONTINUE command works only with the LOCATE command. This command is not available with the FIND or the SEEK commands. Thus, the CONTINUE command cannot be used with the FIND or the SEEK commands to resume the search started by these commands to find the next matching record.

The LOCATE command requires quotation marks around the character data and curly brackets around the date data type used in the search condition. The use of the partial key is also allowed as long as it is enclosed in either the quotation marks or the brackets, depending on the data type.

The main difference between the LOCATE and the FIND (or the SEEK) commands, other than that the LOCATE command is used with nonindexed files, is that the search condition does not require an exact match. That is, operators other than the "=" symbol, such as "<" or ">," can also be used in the search condition.

The LOCATE and the CONTINUE commands are used in two particular instances:

1. When you need to find more than the first occurrence of the criteria
2. When you need to find a record that meets a particular criteria, but that criteria is not suitable as an index key

The MODIFY COMMAND Command

The format of the MODIFY COMMAND command is

```
MODIFY COMMAND <program file name>
```

where <program file name> is the name of the program file to be created or edited. The .PRG extension is automatically added to the program by dBASE if the program is created using the dBASE text editor.

The MODIFY COMMAND command is used to invoke the dBASE IV text editor for creating and modifying dBASE programs. When the MODIFY COMMAND command is given to dBASE IV, it searches for the specified file in the current working directory or the directory specified in the path with the program file name. If the file already exists, the dBASE text editor brings it to the screen for editing; but if the file does not exist, the dBASE text editor creates it.

The MODIFY STRUCTURE Command

The general format of this command is

```
MODIFY STRUCTURE
```

This command allows you to change the structure of the existing database file by changing the field name, data type, width, decimal places, and index option on any existing field. You can also add new fields or delete existing fields.

The modified structure of the database file can be saved either by pressing the <Return> key if the cursor is on an empty row past the last defined field or by pressing the <Ctrl-W> keys if the cursor is on a field in the middle of the structure.

The modified database file structure can also be saved by using the menu bar, that is, by pressing <Alt-E> to highlight the Exit option of the menu bar, selecting the Exit option from the Pull-down Menu, and pressing the <Return> key.

To abandon the changes made and retain the original structure of the database file, use the <Ctrl-Q> or the <Esc> keys.

dBASE IV modifies the structure of the database file in three steps:

1. A backup copy of the active database file with a .BAK extension is created.
2. The structure of the database file is modified.
3. The data are restored from the backup file to the modified file.

In the process of modifying the structure of a database file, if you intend to change the field name as well as the width of the same field, do not do this during a single session because the chances are that you will lose some data. To avoid this problem, modify the field name in one session, and immediately save the modified structure. Then start the modify structure process again, change the width field, and save the final modified structure. This procedure will save you hours of labor entering or recovering lost data.

The Nested IF-ELSE-ENDIF Command

The general format of the nested IF-ELSE-ENDIF command is

```
IF <condition 1>
   IF <condition 2>
      Process Step 1
   ELSE
      Process Step 2
   ENDIF
ELSE
   IF <condition 3>
      Process Step 3
```

```
    ELSE
        Process Step 4
    ENDIF
ENDIF
```

<Condition 1>, <condition 2>, and <condition 3> are logical dBASE expressions. Process Step 1, Process Step 2, Process Step 3, and Process Step 4 are a set of any number of dBASE IV commands. ELSE is an optional part of the command. ENDIF is the required command to end the IF command structure.

In business applications, it is common to have a situation in which the first command between the IF and ELSE or ELSE and ENDIF part of the IF-ELSE-ENDIF command is another IF-ELSE-ENDIF command. This situation arises when it is necessary to test a condition only after testing a previous condition regardless of the result of the first testing (either true or false).

The nested IF-ELSE-ENDIF command is also used with the menu program. A menu program provides several different options to the user, the user selects one, and depending on the selection made, the program performs the corresponding function.

The PACK Command

The general format of the PACK command is

```
PACK
```

The function of the PACK command is to physically remove the records marked for deletion from the active database file and then renumber all remaining records.

The process of purging the deleted records using the PACK command physically removes the deleted records from the database file and copies the nondeleted records onto itself. A sudden loss of power while the file is only partially through packing can cause the data to be lost. Therefore, make a *backup copy* of your file *before* using the PACK command.

The main advantage of the PACK command is that it automatically rebuilds all the index tags. The other advantage of the PACK command is that it frees the disk space occupied by the records marked for deletion.

The QUIT Command

The general format of the QUIT command is

```
QUIT
```

The function of this command is to close all open files, terminate the dBASE IV session, and return the control to DOS.

If you loaded dBASE IV from the application directory, the control will return to that directory. To terminate your session with the system, turn it OFF. But if you want to continue your session with the system, change to the root directory, and run the AUTOEXEC.BAT file. The setting of the path from the application subdirectory to the DBASE directory while loading dBASE IV has changed the path defined by the AUTOEXEC.BAT file, when the system was initially booted. Therefore, to reset the initial path, you need to run the AUTOEXEC.BAT file at this point.

The RECALL Command

The general format of the RECALL command is

```
RECALL [<scope>] [FOR <condition>] [WHILE
       <condition>]
```

where <scope> specifies the parts of the database file being affected by the RECALL command, and <condition> is a valid search condition that selects the records from the database file to be recalled.

Because the SET DELETED ON command makes all the deleted records of the database file invisible to all dBASE commands and queries, the RECALL command will not have any effect unless the SET DELETED command is OFF. Therefore, always use the SET DELETED OFF command *before* using the RECALL command.

The RECALL command has several different options available, depending on the parameters used. A few formats of the RECALL command are given below.

The RECALL Format

The first format of the RECALL command is

```
RECALL
```

The simple RECALL command without any parameters will unmark the current record if it is marked for deletion in the active database file. If the current record is not marked for deletion, this command will have no effect on this record.

The RECALL <scope> Format

The second form of the RECALL command is

```
RECALL <scope>
```

This form of the RECALL command is used to unmark the records marked for deletion in the active database file as specified in the <scope> parameter. The RECALL command will not have any effect on those records not marked for deletion. The two most commonly used values of the <scope> parameter used with the RECALL command are RECORD <number> and ALL.

The RECALL RECORD <number> Format The RECALL RECORD <number> format of the RECALL command is used to unmark a single deleted record.

The RECALL ALL Format This format of the RECALL command can be used to unmark all deleted records in a database file.

The RECALL FOR Format

The third format of the RECALL command is

```
RECALL [<scope>] [FOR <condition>]
```

This format of the RECALL command can be used to unmark all the records marked for deletion that meet a particular condition.

The RELEASE Command

The format of the RELEASE command is

```
RELEASE <memory variable list> / ALL
        [LIKE/EXCEPT <skeleton>]
```

where <memory variable list> is the name of the memory variable or the list of the memory variables to be released or deleted. When a list of memory variables is used, the variables are separated by a comma. The ALL option is used to delete all currently active memory variables. As in the SAVE TO command, the <skeleton> refers to the "skeleton" of a variable name used with the ALL LIKE or ALL EXCEPT options to define a group of memory variables.

The function of the RELEASE command is to delete all or a selected group of memory variables from RAM.

The REPLACE Command

The general format of the REPLACE command is

```
REPLACE [<scope>] <field name> WITH <expression>
        [FOR <condition>] [WHILE <condition>]
```

where <scope> specifies which part of the database file is affected by the command, <field name> is the name of the field receiving the new data, <expression> is the new data being placed into the receiving field, and <condition> is a valid query condition.

The REPLACE command is used to replace the contents of a database field with a new value. The new value can be a literal data item, data stored in a memory variable, or the result of an expression. The receiving field and the replacing data must be of the same type. That is, you cannot replace a numeric data field with a character data field.

The REPLACE command is very fast and powerful. It is used to replace the contents of a database field with the value of an expression in all the records of the database file or those of the database file satisfying a specific condition. Its most efficient use is when global replacement is needed, that is, to replace the value of a field by an expression in all the records of the database file.

The REPORT FORM Command

The general format of the REPORT FORM command is

```
REPORT FORM <report format file name> [SAMPLE]
            [<scope>] [FOR <condition>]
            [WHILE <condition>]
            [TO PRINT/TO FILE <report text file
            name>]
```

where <report format file name> is the name of the report format file, <scope> is a dBASE scope option such as REST or NEXT, <condition> is a valid search condition that selects the records from the database file to be displayed or printed, and <report text file name> is the name of the text disk file under which the report will be stored.

The function of the REPORT FORM command is to display, print, or write the report on a disk file from the currently active database file. dBASE will use the format specified by the report format file name, which has been created earlier by the CREATE REPORT command.

The REPORT FORM command also allows you to use a predefined report format to display the report containing selected records of a database file. The format of this command is as follows:

```
REPORT FORM <report format file name> [FOR
             <condition>]
```

The reports can also be sent to the printer for hard copy output by including the TO PRINT option in the REPORT FORM command. The following are three versions of the TO PRINT option:

```
REPORT FORM <report format file name> TO PRINT
REPORT FORM <report format file name> TO PRINT
            NOEJECT
REPORT FORM <report format file name> TO PRINT
            PLAIN
```

The TO PRINT option directs the system to send the report to the printer as well as to the screen.

When a multipage report is printed on the printer, dBASE prints the page number, date, and report heading at the top of every page by default. To suppress these items on all pages except the first, include the PLAIN option in the REPORT FORM command.

The TO FILE option of the REPORT FORM command can be used to send reports to a disk text file. This file can be edited later with a word processor, it can be included in other documents, or it can be transported to other computer systems. The reports from this text file can be printed using the DOS PRINT command or the dBASE TYPE command.

The RESTORE FROM Command

The format of the RESTORE FROM command is

```
RESTORE FROM <memory file name> [ADDITIVE]
```

where <memory file name> is the name of the memory file from which the memory variables are to be retrieved.

The function of the RESTORE FROM command is to retrieve all the memory variables from the specified memory variable file and place them in RAM. If the ADDITIVE option is not specified with the RESTORE FROM command, then all the currently active memory variables are erased from RAM before the new memory variables are retrieved and placed there.

To add new memory variables to the currently active memory variables in RAM, use the ADDITIVE option with the RESTORE FROM command. If the two memory variables, one already in RAM and the other being retrieved, have the same name, the retrieved variable will overwrite the existing variable.

The SAVE TO Command

The format of the SAVE TO command is

```
SAVE TO <memory file name> [ALL LIKE/EXCEPT
        <skeleton>]
```

where <memory file name> is the name of the file in which the memory variables are stored, and <skeleton> refers to the "skeleton" of the memory variable name used with the ALL LIKE or ALL EXCEPT option to specify a group of memory variables.

The function of the SAVE TO command is to store all or part of the currently active memory variables to a disk file. To save part of the currently active memory variables, use the ALL LIKE or ALL EXCEPT options with the SAVE TO command. You can use the ALL EXCEPT option to exclude part of active memory variables from being saved to a memory variable file.

The SEEK Command

The general format of the SEEK command is

```
SEEK <expression>
```

where <expression> is the literal data to be searched. The expression can be the name of the memory variable or a string of characters that are part of the index key of the database file. The character string should be enclosed in quotation marks and the date data value, in curly brackets. But the numeric field should appear without any quotation marks or brackets.

The SEEK command will search for the first record in use in the indexed database file whose index key matches the character string exactly. The SEEK command will work only if the database file has been indexed and the index tag has been activated by use of the SET ORDER TO command.

If the SEEK command is not successful, that is, if no match is found, then the FOUND () function is set to .F., the EOF () function is set to .T., and a "Not successful" message is displayed.

If the SEEK command is unsuccessful in locating a match in the indexed field of the database file, dBASE will indicate this result by displaying the proper message.

The SEEK and the FIND commands work exactly the same way except that the FIND command can be used only with the character field; the SEEK command can be used with the character, numeric, and date fields.

The SELECT Command

The general format of the SELECT command is

```
SELECT <work area/alias>
```

where <work area/alias> can be a number from 1 through 10 inclusively or a letter A through J inclusively. It can also be the name of a database file or an alias defined in the USE command.

The SELECT command allows you to open up to ten work areas numbered 1 through 10 or A through J. It also allows you to select a work area and open a database file there or specify a work area in which a database file is already open.

Multiple database files can be opened at the same time, but only one is active at a given time. The active database file belongs to the currently selected work area, and all the dBASE commands issued are directed to this currently active database file. This limitation can be eliminated by using prefixes or aliases.

The SET Command

dBASE has many default modes of operations that can be changed by using the SET command. Default modes indicate the way dBASE has been set to carry out the operations. Some of the very commonly used SET commands follow.

The SET DELETED ON/OFF Command

The SET DELETED command is OFF by default in dBASE IV. In the off mode, all the deleted records of the database file will be visible to all the dBASE commands and queries. But the SET DELETED ON command makes all the deleted records of the database file invisible to all dBASE commands and queries (except, of course, to the INDEX and REINDEX commands).

The SET DEVELOPMENT ON/OFF Command

The DEVELOPMENT option is ON by default in dBASE IV. In the on mode, when you ask dBASE IV to execute a program file, the dates of the program source file and object file created with an external text editor are compared. If the source file is newer, dBASE IV will recompile the source program file to create a matching object file before executing it.

So whenever you are using an external editor, use SET DEVELOPMENT ON, by either including this command in your CONFIG.DB file or entering this command at the start of the session.

The SET HEADING ON/OFF Command

The HEADING option is ON by default in dBASE IV. In the on mode, it displays the field names as column titles for each displayed field, memory variable, or expression with the DISPLAY, LIST, SUM, and AVERAGE commands. The SET HEADING OFF command is used to suppress display of the column titles. Once the command is issued, it will remain in effect until you exit dBASE IV or reset it by using the SET HEADING ON command.

The SET INDEX TO Command

The general format of the SET INDEX TO command is

```
SET INDEX TO <.MDX file names>
```

where <.MDX file names> is the names of the nonproduction multiple index files of a database file.

When a database file is opened, all the index tags of the productive multiple index file are also automatically opened, but those of the nonproduction multiple index file are not. The SET INDEX TO command is used to open the index tags of the nonproduction multiple index file of the database file and are added to the list of already open index tags of the production multiple index file. Also, the SET INDEX TO command (without any file name) deactivates the currently active index tag and sets the database file in the natural order.

If a database file has more than one multiple index file, the nonproduction multiple index file should be opened using the SET INDEX TO command before any updating is done to the records of the database file. Otherwise, the index tags present in the nonproduction multiple index file will not be automatically adjusted.

The SET ORDER TO Command

The general format of the SET ORDER TO command is

```
SET ORDER TO <index tag name> [OF <.MDX file
            name>]
```

where <index tag name> is the name of the index tag that designates the controlling index, OF is an optional clause that indicates the multiple index file in which the index tag resides, and <.MDX file name> is the name of the multiple index file.

The SET ORDER TO command is used to designate or activate the index tag of the specified multiple index file. The designated index tag controls the sort order of the records of the database file and is called the *controlling index tag*. This is used to obtain the listing of the database file arranged in a particular order. The designated index tag also determines the field that will be used to search using the FIND or SEEK commands.

The SET ORDER TO command is used only after opening the database file. If the optional clause OF is not specified with the command, the default production multiple index file is assumed. If no index tag file name is specified with the SET ORDER TO command, the natural sort order will be set; that is, no index tag will be in control. In other words, the database file records will be available in the natural order (the physical order in which they are stored in the database file). The controlling index can be changed by issuing another SET ORDER TO command.

The SET PRINT ON/OFF Command

The SET PRINT command is OFF by default in dBASE IV. In the off mode, the LIST command displays on the screen the data specified in the LIST command. If the SET PRINT ON command is used before the LIST command, the data will be displayed on the screen as well as printed on the printer.

The SET RELATION TO Command

The general format of the SET RELATION TO command is

```
SET RELATION TO <key field name>
            INTO <file name/alias>
```

where <key field name> is the name of the key field common to both files, and <file name/alias> is the name, or the alias name, of the database file being linked.

The SET RELATION TO command is used to define the relationship between two database files using the common field between them. Both database files should be open to define the relationship. The link should be defined from the active database file to the database file in the unselected work area. The database file in the unselected work area should be indexed on the common field, and the index must be active.

The SET SAFETY Command

The general format of the SET SAFETY command is

```
SET SAFETY [ON] [OFF]
```

where ON is the default option.

The function of the SET SAFETY command is to protect against overwriting or destroying a database file. The SET SAFETY is ON by default, and the system will display the warning message before overwriting or deleting an existing database file.

The SET SAFETY OFF command is used to bypass this safety feature in the programming mode. Once this command is issued, it will remain in effect until you exit dBASE or reset it by using the SET SAFETY ON command.

The SET STATUS ON/OFF Command

The STATUS option is ON by default in dBASE IV. In the on mode, dBASE displays the current working environment by displaying the status bar on row 22 of the screen.

The ON option is very helpful when you are working in the dot prompt mode because it keeps you informed about the current working environment, such as the current command, drive name, current database in use, current record number, keyboard case mode, insert/overwrite mode, and NumLock status. But the presence of the status bar in the output report is unattractive. The SET STATUS OFF command can be used to suppress its appearance in the output reports. Use the SET STATUS OFF command at the start of each program file to eliminate the presence of the status bar from the output reports displayed on the screen. Use SET STATUS ON before the end of the program to provide information feedback during the dot prompt mode.

When the status bar is off, the toggle key indicators (also called *scoreboard information*) appear on row 0 at the top of the screen.

The SET TALK ON/OFF Command

The TALK option is ON by default in dBASE IV. In the on mode, it displays all the interactive messages on the screen during processing of the commands from the dot prompt. It keeps you informed about the results of commands and calculations.

The ON option is very helpful in the dot prompt mode because it keeps you informed about the status of dBASE IV at the end of the execution of each command. But the interactive messages displayed by the ON option are not only distracting during program file execution; they also clutter the screen with unwanted information. The SET TALK OFF command can be used to suppress these interactive messages. Use the SET TALK OFF command to eliminate the distraction and cluttering of the screen at the start of each program file, and set it back ON before the end of the program to provide information feedback during the dot prompt mode.

Because the ON option displays the results of commands and calculations during program execution, it can be used for debugging the program. Afterwards it can be set back to the OFF option.

The SKIP Command

The general format of the SKIP command is

```
SKIP [<number>]
```

The optional parameter <number> refers to the number of records the record pointer should move. It can be a positive or a negative number or an expression whose calculated value is a numeric value.

The SKIP command moves the record pointer forward or backward in a database file by a specified number of records from its current location. If no number is specified, it moves the cursor to the next record.

The SKIP command can also be used to move the record pointer forward by more than one position by specifying the optional <number> parameter along with it.

The SKIP command can also be used to move the record pointer backward by specifying the optional <number> parameter with a negative value.

In an indexed database file, the simple SKIP command skips the record pointer to the next record defined by the index file.

The SORT Command

The general format of the SORT command is

```
SORT TO <sorted file name> ON <field1>[/A][/D]
     [,<field2>[/A][/D] ...] [<scope>]
     [FOR <condition>] [WHILE <condition>]
```

where <sorted file name> is the name of the database file where the sorted records will be stored, <field1> is the name of the required primary sort field, <field2> . . . are the optional secondary fields on which the records are sorted, <scope> is a dBASE scope option such as REST or NEXT, and <condition> is a valid search condition that selects records from the database file to be sorted. The /A and /D are sorting order options that can be used with each field name to specify the order in which the data should be sorted. If no sorting order option is specified with the field, the default option of ascending order is assumed by dBASE.

The SORT command is used to arrange the records of a database file, either in full or containing only the selected records from the database file, in ascending or descending order, depending on the contents of a specified data field or fields. The data field or fields on which the database file is sorted are called the *sort key*, and the individual fields used in the sort are called *sort field(s)*.

The SORT command sorts the data by physically rearranging the record order of the database file and storing the sorted records in a new database file. The newly created database file is called the target file. The *target database file* should be unopened. The extension .DBF is automatically added by dBASE to the target file name unless you specify your own. You cannot sort a database file to itself, and a logical or memo field cannot be used as a sort key.

Several formats of the SORT commands are discussed in the following pages.

Single Field SORT

The format of the SORT command with one sort field is

```
SORT TO <sorted file name> ON <field>[/A][/D]
```

where <field> is the name of the required sort field, and /A or /D are the sorting order options that can be used with the sort field to indicate the sorting order.

This format of the SORT command is used to arrange the records of the database file in ascending or descending order on a single specified field of the data record. In this case, this single field is called the sort key field.

To obtain the listing of the sorted file, open the sorted database file before issuing the LIST command. This step is very important. Whenever a database file is sorted, open it before performing any function with it.

Multiple Fields SORT

The format of the SORT command with multiple sort fields is

```
SORT TO <sorted file name> ON <field1>[/A][/D]
       [,<field2>[/A][/D] ...]
```

where <field1> is the name of the required primary sort field, <field2> . . . are the optional secondary fields on which the records are sorted, and /A or /D are the sorting order options that can be used with each sort field to indicate the sorting order.

This format of the SORT command is used to arrange the records of the database file on multiple fields of the data record. When you use multiple fields, separate them by a comma. You can include up to ten sort fields in the SORT command. The order of the sort fields should be according to their importance.

When using multiple sort fields with the SORT command, keep the following rules in mind:

1. The primary field should be mentioned first in the list of sort fields.
2. Each sort field should have its own sort ordering option attached to it. The /A option can be omitted because it is the default option.
3. In a single SORT command, different sort fields can have different sort options.

Conditional SORT

The general format of the conditional SORT command is

```
SORT TO <sorted file name> ON <field1>[/A][/D]
       [,<field2>[/A][/D] ...] [FOR <condition>]
```

where <condition> is a valid search condition that selects from the database file the records to be sorted.

The conditional SORT command is used to arrange only the selected records from the database file in ascending or descending order, depending on the contents of a specified data field or fields.

The most useful feature of the SORT command is its ability to create a sorted database of records that satisfies a given condition.

When using the SORT command, keep the following rules in mind:

1. When all the records of a database file are sorted, dBASE creates a target database file equal in size to the original database file to store the sorted records.
2. You cannot sort a database file to itself.
3. The target database file should be unopened.
4. You cannot sort a database file on a logical or memo field.
5. After the SORT command, always use the USE <sorted file name> command. Otherwise you won't see the effect of the sorting on the data stored in the sorted file.

Sorting can be very useful in certain instances, for example, when you want to permanently change the order of the records in a database file that consists of a relatively small number of records. But there are also a few disadvantages to sorting:

1. Sorting very large files is time-consuming because the sorted records are physically rearranged into a new database file.
2. Because sorting an entire database file creates another sorted database file of equal size, the disk storage requirements may be a problem for large files.
3. When new records are added to a sorted database file, they are not automatically sorted. The database must be sorted again every time new records are added.

These drawbacks of sorting can be overcome by indexing the database files. (See INDEX command.)

The STORE TO Command

The format of the STORE TO command is

```
STORE <expression> TO <memory variable list>
```

where <expression> is a literal, a variable name, a field name, or an expression; and <memory variable list> is the list of memory variable(s) to be created and/or initialized.

The function of the STORE TO command is to create and initialize by assigning the value of the expression to one or more memory variables or to simply initialize the existing memory variable by assigning the value of the expression.

To store a character string to a memory variable, you must enclose the string in double quotes (" "), single quotes (' '), or square brackets ([ ]).

The STORE command can be used to create and/or assign a date value to the memory variable. To do this, enclose the date in curly brackets called braces ({ }).

The STORE command can also be used to create and/or assign a logical value to the memory variable. To do this, enclose the logical value in periods (.T. or .F.).

The STORE command can also be used to assign a single value to several memory variables using a single command. This procedure is very useful when several variables need to be initialized by the same value.

The SUM Command

The SUM command computes the totals of the numeric field or fields for all the records in the database file or for selected records in it that meet the given conditions. The general format of the SUM command is

```
SUM [<expression>] [FOR <condition>]
    [WHILE <condition>] [TO <memory variables>]
```

where <expression> is a list of field names or expressions consisting of numeric fields, <condition> is a valid search condition that selects the records from the database file to be summed, and <memory variables> are the names of the memory variables to which the results of this command are to be stored.

The SUM command has several different options available, depending on the parameters used.

The SUM Format

The first format of the SUM command is

```
SUM
```

The simple SUM command without any parameters will total all the numeric fields present in the data record for all the records of the active database file.

The SUM <expression> Format

The second format of the SUM command is

```
SUM <expression>
```

This format of the SUM command will total only the listed fields or expressions of numeric fields for all the records of the active database file. The field names or expressions should be separated by a comma, and you can include up to five names or expressions in the SUM command.

The SUM FOR Format

The third format for the SUM command is

```
SUM [<expression>] [FOR <condition>]
```

where the <expression> and FOR parameters are optional.

There are two forms of this format. The first is

```
SUM FOR <condition>
```

This format totals all numeric fields, but only for those records in the active database file for which the given condition is true.

The second form of the SUM FOR command is

```
SUM <expression> FOR <condition>
```

This form of the SUM FOR command will total only the listed fields or expressions of numeric fields for all the records of the active database file for which the given condition is true. The field names or expressions should be separated by a comma, and you can include up to five of the fields or expressions in the SUM FOR command.

The SUM FOR TO Format

The format of the SUM FOR TO command is

```
SUM <expression> FOR <condition> TO <memory
    variables>
```

This command totals the listed fields for only those records in the database file for which the condition is true and stores the result to a memory variable or variables. When the TO option of the command is used, there should be a memory variable present in it for each field or expression for which the total (or sum) is required. The memory variables should be separated by commas.

The TYPE Command

The general format of the command is

```
TYPE <program file name>
    [TO PRINT/TO FILE <text file name>]
```

where <program file name> is the name of the program file whose contents are to be displayed, **TO PRINT** and **TO FILE** are optional parameters to be used to print or send the contents of the program file to a disk text file, and <text file name> is the name of the target text file.

The TYPE command is used to display, print, or send the contents of an ASCII text or program file to disk text file. When this command is used, the extension should be provided with the program or text file name.

The USE Command

The simple format of the USE command is

```
USE [<file name>]
```

where <file name> is the name of an existing database file. Because only a database (.DBF) file can be accessed with the USE command, you do not need to specify the extension with the file name.

The USE <file name> form of the command is used to open an existing database file whose name is mentioned in the command. For example, to open the database file FILE1.DBF, you need to type the following:

```
. USE FILE1     <Return>
```

After the command has been executed, the contents of the database file FILE1 are copied to the computer's internal memory (RAM) and are available for access. The database file FILE1 is said to be *active* or *open* now.

When the USE command is used to open a database file, it will close any previously open database file.

Recall that items enclosed in square brackets ([]) are optional. So if we use the USE command without the file name, it will not open any database file because none is mentioned with it. However, it will close any previously open database file.

D.3 dBASE Functions

The DATE () Function

The format of the DATE () function is

```
DATE ()
```

The DATE () function returns the current system date in the default format of mm/dd/yy.

The DELETED () Function

The format of the DELETED () function is

```
DELETED ([<alias of the database file>])
```

where the parameter [<alias of the database file>] is optional.

The simple form of the DELETED () function is used to test if the current record of the active database file has been deleted or not. If it has, dBASE will return a logical true (.T.) value; otherwise it will return a logical false (.F.) value.

The DELETED () function can also be used as a condition for including or excluding those deleted records from the listing of the database file. This function can be chosen by including the DELETED () function or .NOT. DELETED () function, respectively, as a condition in the DISPLAY or LIST command.

The DTOS () Function

The general format of the DTOS () function is

```
DTOS (<date expression>)
```

where <date expression> is the date in the MM/DD/YY form.

The EOF () Function

The DTOS () function, called "date to string," converts the date field of MM/DD/YY form to the character string of YYYYMMDD form. To ensure proper sort order for the date field, always convert it to character string by using the DTOS () function before using as an index key.

The format of the EOF () function is

```
EOF ( )
```

where EOF stands for end of file.

The EOF () is a dBASE function used as a logical condition to control the repetition of the loop in a DO WHILE command to process every record in the database file. When the record pointer points to the end of file marker, the function returns the logical true (.T.) value; otherwise it returns the logical false (.F.) value.

The INT () Function

The most commonly used mathematical function in business applications is the INT () (called integer) function. Its general format is

```
INT <expression>
```

where <expression> may be a number, numeric variable, or numeric expression. The INT () function converts a numeric value to an integer by truncating its decimal portion, for example:

.? INT (6.327)   will yield 6
.? INT (−3.25)   will yield −3

The main use of the INT () function is for rounding dollar amounts. To round an expression to two decimal places, use the following formula:

INT (expression * 100 + 0.5) / 100

The TIME () Function

The format of the TIME () function is

```
TIME ( )
```

The TIME () function returns the current system time in the default format of hh:mm:ss.

INDEX

@ ... SAY command, 112, 155, 643
@ ... TO command, 157, 644
@ ... SAY ... GET command, 162, 644

A

active database file, 503
active data record, 506
aliases, 505
alphabetic keypad, 602
analysis phase, 125, 129
APPEND, 65, 86, 644
APPEND FROM command, 590, 645
APPEND BLANK command, 458, 644
ASSIGNMENT command, 176, 646
ASSIST command, 86
attribute, 9
AUTOEXEC.BAT file, 117, 627
auxiliary storage unit, 600
AVERAGE command, 187, 646

B

batch processing method, 6
batch programs, 127
BROWSE command, 65, 68, 468, 647
bug, 126
business application system, 346

C

CALCULATOR command, 172, 648
calculator keypad, 603
case control structure, 327
character data type, 8, 58
CLEAR command, 103, 155, 648
CLOSE ALL command, 443, 648
coding conventions, 147
coding phase, 126, 147
cohesion, 138
command file, 96
comment (*), 104, 649
common control keys, 603
common coupling, 141
conditional editing, 475
CONFIG.DB file, 119, 628, 636
CONTINUE command, 483, 649
control break, 287
control break report, 571
control center mode, 35, 40
control coupling, 141
control field, 287

control unit, 598
controlling index tag, 436
COPY command, 275, 649
COPY FILE TO command, 275, 649
COPY INDEXES command, 443, 651
COPY STRUCTURE TO command, 284, 652
COPY TO command, 276, 583, 587, 650
COUNT command, 182, 653
coupling, 140
CREATE command, 49, 653
CREATE LABEL command, 547, 654
CREATE REPORT command, 561, 572, 654
CREATE STRUCTURE command, 427
current record, 74
current working directory, 15
cursor control keys, 603

D

database, 4
data coupling, 141
database design form, 55, 57
database design screen, 49
database file, 5
database file data, 6, 9, 46
database file structure, 6, 7, 46, 62
database management system (DBMS), 5
date data type, 8, 58
DATE () function, 156, 681
dBASE command, 39
dBASE IV, 6
dBASE program file, 96
dBASE text editor, 97
debugging, 126
decimal places, 9, 60
default drive, 608
DELETE command, 394, 654
DELETE FILE command, 445, 655
DELETE TAGS command, 444, 655
DELETED () function, 397, 681
deleted records, 396
delimited format file, 583
design phase, 126, 134
designing report form, 563
detailed design phase, 126, 143
DIR command, 86, 101
directory, 12
DISPLAY command, 74, 75, 76, 77, 86, 656
DISPLAY HISTORY command, 78, 657
DISPLAY MEMORY command, 177, 255, 657

DISPLAY STATUS command, 86
DISPLAY STRUCTURE command, 64, 82, 86
DO command, 100, 657
DO CASE-ENDCASE command, 328, 658
DO WHILE-ENDDO command, 105, 158, 659
DOS, 607
DOS commands, 609
    CD command, 15
    CHKDSK command, 622
    CLS command, 614
    COPY command, 616
    DELETE command, 619
    DIR command, 14, 610, 611
    FORMAT command, 615
    MD command, 14
    PRINT command, 618
    PROMPT command, 15
    RD command, 22
    RENAME command, 617
    TYPE command, 618
dot prompt mode, 35, 39
DTOS () function, 441, 681

E
EDIT command, 86, 230, 467, 476, 479, 659
editing, 230, 467
EOF () function, 106, 682
ERASE command, 444, 660
error message box, 49
external text editor, 117

F
field, 5
field name, 7, 57
field number, 7
field type, 7, 8
field width, 7, 8, 59
file extension, 9
FIND command, 445, 661
fixed length record files, 583
flagged records, 393
flat directory structure, 12
float data type, 8, 58
foreign file, 583

G
global editing, 480
GOTO command, 228, 661
group cursor control keys, 604

H
HELP command, 86
hierarchical directory structure, 12

I
IF-ELSE-ENDIF command, 114, 318, 320, 661
IF-ENDIF command, 160, 319, 662
INDEX command, 432, 663
index file, 429
index key, 425
index tag, 425, 435
indexing, 265, 424
    single field indexing, 427
    multiple field indexing, 440
initiate processing, 137, 139, 332, 334, 409, 411
install dBASE IV, 27, 623
INTEGER function, 173, 682
interactive processing method, 6
interactive programs, 127
iteration control structure, 136

K
key field, 266
keyboard, 600

L
LABEL FORM command, 555, 664
label dimensions, 548
label generation, 546
label printing, 557
label text file, 558
LIST command, 79, 80, 81, 86, 665
loading dBASE IV, 35, 47, 48
loading DOS, 608
LOCATE command, 448, 476, 479, 483, 665
logical control structure, 135
logical data type, 8, 58
logical errors, 126
loop, 136

M
main processing, 137, 139, 332, 334, 409, 411
main processing unit, 598
main unit, 598
memo data type, 8, 58
memory unit, 600
memory variable, 174
menu bar, 51
menu program, 127, 325
message line, 57
microcomputer, 598
MODIFY COMMAND command, 97, 636, 666
MODIFY LABEL command, 547
MODIFY REPORT command, 562
MODIFY STRUCTURE command, 233, 429, 667
multilevel directories, 13

N
navigation key, 54
navigation line, 57
nested IF-ELSE-ENDIF command, 323, 667
nonalphabetic keyboard, 602
nonproduction multiple index file, 435
numeric data type, 8, 58

P
PACK command, 402, 668
path, 20
physical system, 346
picture function, 208
prefixes, 504
primary field, 270
primary file name, 9
primary index key, 440
private variable, 177
procedure, 211
PROCEDURE command, 211
procedure file, 211
production multiple index file, 428
program development process, 125
program documentation, 104
programming language mode, 6, 39
pseudocode, 143
public variable, 177
pull-down menu, 52
purging deleted records, 402

Q
QUIT command, 42, 668

R
RECALL command, 399, 669
recalling deleted records, 399
record, 5
    adding, 411
    deleting, 411
    updating, 411
records marked for deletion, 399
relation, 9
relational database management system, 6
RELEASE command, 179, 255, 670
REPLACE command, 481, 670
REPORT FORM command, 568, 670
report generation, 561
report printing, 570
report text file, 570
RESTORE FROM command, 181, 256, 671

S
SAVE TO command, 178, 672
scoreboard, 109

secondary field, 270
secondary index key, 440
SEEK command, 446, 672
SELECT command, 501, 672
selection control structure, 135
sequence control structure, 135
SET command, 153, 673
SET CARRY ON command, 71
SET DELETED command, 397, 673
SET DEVELOPMENT command, 117, 673
SET HEADING command, 109, 673
SET HISTORY TO command, 79
SET INDEX TO command, 437, 673
SET ORDER TO command, 436, 674
SET PRINT ON command, 82, 674
SET PROCEDURE TO command, 212
SET RELATION TO command, 507, 674
SET SAFETY command, 272, 675
SET STATUS command, 109, 675
SET TALK command, 108, 675
SKIP command, 106, 161, 226, 676
SORT TO command, 266, 676
sorting, 265
    single field sort, 266, 677
    conditional sort, 271, 678
    multiple field sort, 268, 677
span of control, 141
special function keys, 603
status bar, 47, 55
STORE TO command, 174, 678
structure chart, 138
structured approach to system development, 347
structured system analysis phase, 347
structured system design phase, 347
structured system implementation phase, 347
stub program, 354, 362
subdirectory, 12
subsystem, 346
SUM command, 184, 679
summary report, 577, 579
suprasystem, 346
syntactical errors, 126
system, 346
system data format file, 583

T
table, 9
terminate processing, 138, 139, 333, 334, 410, 411
testing and debugging phase, 126, 163
TIME () function, 156, 682
TO PRINT command, 81

tree directory structure, 12
TRIM function, 553
TYPE command, 116, 680
tuple, 9

U
uninstalling dBASE IV, 629
USE command, 72, 74, 158, 680

V
variable length record files, 587
video monitor, 607

W
wild card, 612
work area, 501